American Manufactured Furniture

★ AMERICAN ★ MANUFACTURED ★ FURNITURE ★

A complete guide to
furniture produced
in the 1920s.
Includes a
Guide to
Today's Prices

Schiffer Publishing Ltd

77 Lower Valley Road, Atglen, PA 19310

Copyright © 1988 by Don Fredgant
Library of Congress Catalog Number: 87-63482

Printed in the United States of America
ISBN: 0-88740-770-6

We are interested in hearing from authors
with book ideas on related topics.

Published by Schiffer Publishing Ltd.
77 Lower Valley Road
Atglen, PA 19310
Please write for a free catalog.
This book may be purchased from the publisher.
Please include $2.95 postage.
Try your bookstore first.

Table of Contents

Zone 3 Book 7a

Alphabetical List 9a
    of concerns who sell their products to furniture dealers

Geographical List 18a
    of concerns who sell their products to furniture dealers

Classified Index of Products 30a

Trade Names Index 51a

Woods and Finishes, 1928-1929 1

Price Guide 408

ZONE 3 BOOK

This book does not contain pages numbered as follows:

393 (Z1)	403 (Z1)	413 (Z1)	423 (Z1)	393 (Z2)
394 (Z1)	404 (Z1)	414 (Z1)	424 (Z1)	394 (Z2)
395 (Z1)	405 (Z1)	415 (Z1)	425 (Z1)	395 (Z2)
396 (Z1)	406 (Z1)	416 (Z1)	426 (Z1)	396 (Z2)
397 (Z1)	407 (Z1)	417 (Z1)	427 (Z1)	397 (Z2)
398 (Z1)	408 (Z1)	418 (Z1)	428 (Z1)	
399 (Z1)	409 (Z1)	419 (Z1)	429 (Z1)	
400 (Z1)	410 (Z1)	420 (Z1)	430 (Z1)	
401 (Z1)	411 (Z1)	421 (Z1)	431 (Z1)	
402 (Z1)	412 (Z1)	422 (Z1)		

The above list represents the catalog page numbers of manufacturers who have ordered their catalogs distributed to dealers within the territory covered by Zones 1 or 2.

While the above page numbers appear in the indexes of all books, the pages themselves appear only in books going to the States within Zones 1 or 2.

All pages numbered 393 (Z3) to 407 (Z3) are included in this Zone 3 Book, but are not included in books distributed to Zones 1, 2 or 4.

Zone 1 includes:	Zone 2 includes:	Zone 3 includes:	Zone 4 includes:
Maine	North Carolina	Ohio	Idaho
New Hampshire	South Carolina	Illinois	Wyoming
Vermont	Georgia	Indiana	Colorado
Massachusetts	Florida	Michigan	New Mexico
Rhode Island	Tennessee	Wisconsin	Arizona
Connecticut	Kentucky	Minnesota	Utah
New York	Alabama	Montana	Nevada
New Jersey	Mississippi	Iowa	Washington
Pennsylvania	Oklahoma	North Dakota	Oregon
Delaware	Texas	South Dakota	California
Maryland	Arkansas	Nebraska	
Virginia	Louisiana	Kansas	
West Virginia		Missouri	
District of Columbia			

ALPHABETICAL LIST
OF CONCERNS WHO SELL THEIR PRODUCTS TO FURNITURE DEALERS

A

A & J Mfg. Co., Gadsden, Ala.
A. B. Stove Co., Battle Creek, Mich.
Abbott & Co., Theo. A., Philadelphia, Pa.
Abbott Estate, John G., Antrim, N. H.
Abendroth Bros., Port Chester, N. Y.
Abernathy Furn. Co., Kansas City, Mo.
Abramson, Ginsberg & Co., New York, N. Y.
Acme Chair Co., Reading, Mich.
Acme Furniture Co., Jamestown, N. Y.
Acme Furniture Co., High Point, N. C.
Acme Furniture Mfg. Co., Los Angeles, Cal.
Acme Lamp Shade Co., Chicago, Ill.
Acme Upholstering Co., Hartford, Conn.
Active Furniture Co., Jamestown, N. Y.
Adler Veneer Seat Co., Long Island City, N. Y.
Advance Furniture Co., Jamestown, N. Y.
Advance Spring & Wire Co., Chicago, Ill.
Advance Stove Works, Evansville, Ind.
Aeroshade Company, Waukesha, Wis.
Aimone Furniture Co., Jersey City, N. J.
Aimone Manufacturing Co., New York, N. Y.
Akerson-Ringstrom & Co., Keokuk, Iowa
Alaska Refrigerator Co., Muskegon, Mich.
Akron Mattress Mfg. Co., Akron, Ohio
Albano Company, New York, N. Y.
Albert Furniture Co., Shelbyville, Ind.
ALBERT CO., L. R., PHILADELPHIA, PA.
See Statton Furniture Mfg. Co. 418 (Z1)
Albert, Phillip, New York, N. Y.
Algoma Wood Products Co., Algoma, Wis.
All Steel Equipment Co., Aurora, Ill.
Allegan Furniture Shops, Adrian, Mich.
Allen Chair Company, Concord Junction, Mass.
Allen Furniture Mfg. Co., Spencerville, O.
ALLEN MANUFACTURING COMPANY, NASHVILLE, TENN.
Catalog 136
Home Furnishing and Decoration Section 10
Alliance Furniture Co., Jamestown, N. Y.
Allied Furniture Co., Jamestown, N. Y.
Alma Furniture Co., High Point, N. C.
Alonzi Furniture Co., Chicago, Ill.
AMERICAN ART BUREAU, CHICAGO, ILL. .. 378-379
American Beauty Mattress Co., Lynchburg, Va.
American Bed Company, St. Louis, Mo.
American Cabinet Company, Holland, Mich.
American Carriage & Wicker Works, Minneapolis, Minn.
American Chair Company, Sheboygan, Wis.
American Chair Mfg. Co., Hallstead, Pa.
American Emblem Co., New Hartford, N. Y.
American Furniture Co., Batesville, Ind.
American Furniture Co., Martinsville, Va.
American Furniture Novelty Co., Chicago, Ill.
American Glass & Beveling Co., Cincinnati, O.
American Lamp & Shade Co., Chicago, Ill.
American Linoleum Mfg. Co., Linoleumville, N. Y.
American Mfg. Concern, Jamestown, N. Y.
American Mattress Co., Boston, Mass.
American Metal Bed Company, Newark, N. J.
American Moulding Co., Boston, Mass.
American National Co., Toledo, O.
AMERICAN PARLOR FURNITURE COMPANY, CHICAGO, ILL. 91
American Pile Fabric Co., Phila., Pa.
American Reed & Fibre Co., Boston, Mass.
American Rug & Carpet Co., Chicago, Ill.
American Seating Co., Chicago, Ill.
American Specialty Co., Indianapolis, Ind.
American Stove Company, Lorain, O.
American Toy & Novelty Works, York, Pa.
American Uph. & Mfg. Co., Detroit, Mich.
AMERICAN WALNUT MANUFACTURERS' ASSOCIATION, CHICAGO, ILL. 380-381
American Wood Products Corp., Minneapolis, Minn.
Ames Body Corp., Owensboro, Ky.
Anchor Furniture Co., Jamestown, N. Y.
ANCHOR SPRING & BEDDING COMPANY, NASHVILLE, TENNESSEE 393 (Z2)
Anchor Stove & Range Co., New Albany, Ind.
Anderson Furn. Co., Inc., Clinton, Iowa
Anderson & Co., Geo. H., Chicago, Ill.
Angel Novelty Co., Fitchburg, Mass.
Angert Brothers, Cincinnati, O.
Appleton Chair Company, Appleton, Wis.
Arcadia Furn. Co., Arcadia, Mich.
Ariel Cabinet Co., Peru, Ind.
Arlington Refrigerator Co., Arlington, Vt.
ARMSTRONG CORK COMPANY, LINOLEUM DIVISION, LANCASTER, PA.
Catalog 81
Home Furnishing and Decoration Section 9
Armstrong Stove & Mfg. Co., Perryville, Md.
Arnold, Constable & Co., New York, N. Y.
ARONSON, A. A., ST. PAUL, MINN.
See Chicago Mirror and Art Glass Co. 395 (Z3)
Arrow Metal Bed Corp., New York, N. Y.
Arrow Upholstery Co., New York, N. Y.
Art Bilt Furniture Co., Milwaukee, Wis.
Art Craft Uph. Co., Boston, Mass.
Art Craft Uph. Co., Inc., Jamaica, N. Y.
Art Embroidery Co., Louisville, Ky.
Art Furniture Co., Sheboygan, Wis.
Art Lamp Shade Mfg. Co., Chicago, Ill.
Art Loom Rug Mills, Philadelphia, Pa.
Art Stove Company, Detroit, Mich.
Art Upholstery Co., Pittsburgh, Pa.
Artistic Furniture Co. Inc., St. Louis, Mo.
Ashland Mfg. Co. Inc., Ashland, Mass.
Ashley Furniture Co. Inc., New York, N. Y.
ASSOCIATIONS:
AMERICAN ART BUREAU 378-379
AMERICAN WALNUT MANUFACTURERS ASSOCIATION 380-381
EVANSVILLE FURNITURE MANUFACTURERS ASSOCIATION 382-383
HARDWOOD MANUFACTURERS INSTITUTE 384-386
Oak Service Bureau 384-385
Gumwood Service Bureau 386
JAMESTOWN FURNITURE MARKET ASSOCIATION 387
New York Furniture Exchange Association
NORTHERN HEMLOCK & HARDWOOD MANUFACTURERS ASSOCIATION 388-391
Hard Maple 388-389
Birch 390-391
Athens Furniture Co., Athens, Pa.
ATHENS TABLE & MANUFACTURING CO., ATHENS, TENN 190
Atherton-Craig Furn. Co., Louisville, Ky.
Athol Table Mfg. Co., Athol, Mass.
Atlanta Mirror & Beveling Co., Atlanta, Ga.
Atlanta Stove Works, Atlanta, Ga.
Atlanta Table Company, Atlanta, Ga.
Atlantic Chair Co., Gardner, Mass.
Atlantic Excelsior Mfg. Co., New York, N. Y.
Atlantic Reed & Rattan Furn. Co., Boston, Mass.
ATLAS FURNITURE COMPANY, JAMESTOWN, N. Y. 241
Atlas Glass & Mirror Co., Chicago, Ill.
Atlas Parlor Suite Mfg. Co., Waltham, Mass.
Atlas Upholstering Co., Chicago, Ill.
Atlin Company, C. B., Knoxville, Tenn.
Auburndale Furn. Mfg. Co., Auburndale, Fla.
Auglaize Furniture Co., New Bremen, O.
Augusta Bedding Company, Augusta, Ga.
AULSBROOK & JONES FURNITURE COMPANY, STURGIS, MICH 242
Aulsbrook Co., Detroit, Mich.
Austell Cabinet Co., Austell, Ga.
Austell Furn. Co., Austell, Ga.
Automatic Cradle Co., Stevens Point, Wis.
Automatic File & Index Co., Green Bay, Wis.
AUTOMATIC SHADE COMPANY, SAUK RAPIDS, MINN.
Catalog 189
Home Furnishing and Decoration Section 9

B

Bache, Semon & Co., New York, N. Y.
Bacon Brothers, Toledo, O.
Bacon Co., Francis H., Boston, Mass.
Badger Furn. Co., Sheboygan, Wis.
Bailey & Co., James C., Chicago, Ill.
Bailey-Schmitz Co., Los Angeles, Cal.
Bailey Table Co., Jamestown, N. Y.
Bailie Basket Co., Somerville, Mass.
Baker & Co., Adrian, Mich.
Baker & Co., A. T., Philadelphia, Pa.
BAKER FURNITURE FACTORIES, INC., ALLEGAN, MICH. 243
Baker Stove Works, Belleville, Ill.
Bald Knob Furn. Co., Rockymount, Va.
Baldwin Mfg. Co. Inc., Philadelphia, Pa.
Baldwin Refrigerator Co., Burlington, Vt.
Ballman Cabinet Co., Covington, Ky.
Baltimore Spring Bed Co., Baltimore, Md.
Banderob-Chase Mfg. Co., Oshkosh, Wis.
Banta Furniture Co., Goshen, Ind.
Barber & Co., J. W., Philadelphia, Pa.
BARCALO MANUFACTURING COMPANY, BUFFALO, N. Y. 393 (Z1)
Bardes Range & Foundry Co., E. H., Cincinnati, O.
Barker Brothers, Los Angeles, Cal.
Barnard & Simonds Co., Rochester, N. Y.
Barrelmeyer, Theo., St. Louis, Mo.
Barrile & Co., S., Boston, Mass.
Barstow Stove Co., Providence, R. I.
Bartlett, Waldo W., Leominster, Mass.
BASIC FURNITURE COMPANY, WAYNESBORO, VA. 244
Bassett Furniture Co., Bassett, Va.
Bassett Mfg. Co., Bassett, Va.
Bassett-McNabb Company, Philadelphia, Pa.
Bassett Mirror Co., Bassett, Va.
Bauman & Co., Henry L., Newark, N. J.
Bay State Uph. Co., Boston, Mass.
BAY VIEW FURNITURE COMPANY, HOLLAND, MICH. 393 (Z3)
Beachley Furn. Co., Hagerstown, Md.
Beals Furn. Co., Thos. P., Portland, Me.
Bear Furn. Co. G. H., Allentown, Pa.
BEATTIE MANUFACTURING COMPANY, NEW YORK, N. Y. 82
Beaver Refrigerator Co., New Brighton, Pa.
Beaver State Furn. Mfg. Co., Portland, Ore.
Bechtold Bros. Uph. Co., Grand Rapids, Mich.
Beck & Company, Lititz, Pa.
Becker & Company, D., Philadelphia, Pa.
Beckwith Company, Dowagiac, Mich.
Bedell Furniture Co., Milford, Ind.
Bedell Mfg. Corp., Marion, Ind.
Bedford Chair Co., Brooklyn, N. Y.
Beebe & Runyan Furn. Co., Omaha, Neb.
Beecher Falls Co., Beecher Falls, Vt.
Behnke-Fink Mfg. Co., Chicago, Ill.
Behr, Henry, Brooklyn, N. Y.
Behrend, Jacob, Philadelphia, Pa.
Beifield & Co., Chas. H., Phila., Pa.
Belding-Hall Company, Belding, Mich.
Bell Furniture & Mattress Co., Wichita Falls, Tex.
Bellaire Stove Co., Bellaire, O.
Belleville Stove & Range Co., Belleville, Ill.
Bemis-Riddell Co., Sheboygan, Wis.
Benner Mfg. Co., Lancaster, Pa.
Bennett Company, J. F., Toledo, O.
Benson Furn. Co., Sioux City, Iowa.
Bent & Bros., S., Gardner, Mass.
Benziger Bros., New York, N. Y.
Berkeley Wicker Works, Berkeley, Cal.
BERKEY & GAY FURNITURE COMPANY, GRAND RAPIDS, MICH.
Berkey and Gay Furniture Company 248-251
Grand Rapids Upholstering Company 252-253
Berkey Furn. Co., Wm. A., Grand Rapids, Mich.
Berks Furn. Co., Harrisburg, Pa.
Berkshire Uph. Co. Inc., Springfield, Mass.
Berne Furn. Co. Inc., Berne, Ind.
Bernhard's, Inc., San Francisco, Cal.
Bernhardt Chair Co., Lenoir, N. C.
Berry, Ostlere & Shepherd, Inc., New York, N. Y.
Bethlehem Furn. Co., Bethlehem, Pa.
Better Bedding Alliance of America, Chicago, Ill.
Betts St. Furniture Co., Cincinnati, O.
Beutser Spring Bed Co., Beaumont, Tex.
Bibb Stove Co., B. C., Baltimore, Md.
Bien, Albert H., Philadelphia, Pa.
Bierfield Co., Louis, Chicago, Ill.
Biernacki Furn. Co. Inc., F., St. Louis, Mo.
Big Rapids Furn. Mfg. Co., Big Rapids, Mich.
Bigelow-Hartford Carpet Co., New York, N. Y.
Bilt-Rite Chair Co., New York, N. Y.
Biltrite Furniture Co., Elkin, N. C.
Biltrite Furn. Corp., New York, N. Y.
Biltrite Mfg. Co., Chicago, Ill.
Biltwell Chair & Furn. Co., Thomasville, N. C.
Binswanger Company, Richmond, Va.
Binks Spray Equipment Co., Chicago, Ill.
Bintliff Mfg. Co., Minneapolis, Minn.
BIRCH MANUFACTURERS AND THE ROTARY BIRCH CLUB, OSHKOSH, WIS. .. 390-391
Bird & Son, Walpole, Mass.
Birmingham Buggy Co., Birmingham, Ala.
Birmingham Stove & Range Co., Birmingham, Ala.
Bison Upholstery Co., Buffalo, N. Y.
Bissell Carpet Sweeper Co., Grand Rapids, Mich.
Blabon Co., Geo. W., Philadelphia, Pa.
BLACKHAWK FURNITURE COMPANY, ROCKFORD, ILL. 245-247
Blackmore Mfg. Co., St. Louis, Mo.
Blanchard & Son, Acton, Mass.
Blanchard-Hamilton Furn. Co., Shelbyville, Ind.
Blank, Mayer, Chester, Pa.
Bloch Go-Cart Co., Egg Harbor City, N. J.
Bloch Go-Cart Co., Philadelphia, Pa.
Block-Portelier Co., Chicago, Ill.
Bloom & Godley Co., Trenton, N. J.
Bloom, Charles, New York, N. Y.
Bloom Co., Jacob, Philadelphia, Pa.
Blumenthal & Co., Sidney, New York, N. Y.
Boatwright Furn. Co., Danville, Va.
Bobbett Electric Mfg. Co., Chicago, Ill.
Bockstege Furn. Co., Evansville, Ind.
Bodenstein & Kuemmerle, Philadelphia, Pa.
Bogardus-McDanell Co., Warsaw, Ky.
Boher & Hosfeld Co., Shippensburg, Pa.
Bohn Refrigerator Co., St. Paul, Minn.
Bombayreed Willow Furn. Co., Phila, Pa.
Bonhard Art Furn. Co., Cleveland, O.
Bonner Furn. Mfg. Co., Nashville, Tenn.
Booth Furn. Mfg. Co., Indianapolis, Ind.
Borgwardt & Ernst, Inc., Chicago, Ill.
Borin Mfg. Co., Chicago, Ill.
Boring & Bros., H. E., York, Pa.
Bostick Stove Co., Lapeer, Mich.
Boston Mirror Co., Boston, Mass.
Boston Parlor Frame Co., Boston, Mass.
Boston Stove Foundry Co., Reading, Pa.
Bott Furn. Co., C. M., Buffalo, N. Y.
Boxall, James, Los Angeles, Cal.
Bozart Rug Co., Springfield, Mass.
Bradley & Hubbard Mfg. Co., Meriden, Conn.
Brandt Cabinet Works, Hagerstown, Md.
Brandt Upholstery Co., A. H., Fort Worth, Tex.
BRANDTS FURNITURE CO., CELINA, OHIO 394 (Z3)
Brandwein & Co., A., Chicago, Ill.
Brayman Furniture Co., Wilkes Barre, Pa.
Breslin Bros. Co., Gloucester, N. J.
Breslin Textile Mills, Philadelphia, Pa.
Brewer-Titchener Corp., Cortland, N. Y.
Brickwede Bros. Co., Marietta, O.
Bridge & Beach Mfg. Co., St. Louis, Mo.
Bridgeport Bed Spring Mfg. Co., Bridgeport, Conn.
Bridgeport Chair Co., Bridgeport, Conn.
Briggs Mfg. Co., High Point, N. C.
Brighton Furn. Co., Island Point, Vt.
Brighton Mills, Inc., New York, N. Y.
Broadway Rattan Shoppe, Los Angeles, Cal.
Brockman Co., Chicago, Ill.
Brocton Furniture Co., Brocton, N. Y.
Brodsky-Klein Furn. Co., Chicago, Ill.
BROMLEY ADVERTISING AGENCY, MINNEAPOLIS, MINN.
See Automatic Shade Company 189
Bronx Mfg. Co., Brooklyn, N. Y.
Brooklyn Chair Co., New York, N. Y.
Brooklyn Dining Room Chair Co., Brooklyn, N. Y.
Brooklyn Wire Chair Co., Brooklyn, N. Y.
Brooks Bros. & Co., Philadelphia, Pa.
Brooks Parlor Furn. Co., Minneapolis, Minn.
Brookville Furn. Co., Brookville, Ind.
Broude Co., W. S., Chicago, Ill.
Brower Furn. Co., Grand Rapids, Mich.
Brown Bed Mfg. Co., Kansas City, Mo.
Brown Bros. Co., Gardner, Mass.
Brown Carriage Co., Cincinnati, O.
Brown-Irion Furn. Co., Frankfort, Ky.
Brown-Morse Co., Muskegon, Mich.
Brown Products Corp., Jermyn, Pa.
Brumby Chair Co., Marietta, Ga.
Bruner, Inc., Francis A., Phila, Pa.
Brunswick-Kroeschell Co., New Brunswick, N. J.
Bub Company, Jos., Milwaukee, Wis.
Buchman Co., L., Brooklyn, N. Y.
Buck, T. & E. R., West Sterling, Mass.
Buck's Stove & Range Co., St. Louis, Mo.
Buckeye Chair Co., Ravenna, O.
Buckeye Mfg. Co., Springfield, O.

Buckley & Company, Troy, N. Y.
Buckstaff Mfg. Co., Oshkosh, Wis.
Buckwalter Stove Co., Royersford, Pa.
Buehner Chair Co., Evansville, Ind.
Buffalo Davenport Bed Co., Buffalo, N. Y.
Buffalo Furniture Mfg. Co., Buffalo, N. Y.
BUFFALO LOUNGE COMPANY, BUFFALO, N. Y.
Catalog 394 (Z1)
Home Furnishing and Decoration Section 10
Buffelen, Hubbert & Loonam, Tacoma, Wash.
Buhain Mfg. Co., Chicago, Ill.
Bunday Bedding Co., Lansing, Mich.
Burch Company, A. F., Grand Rapids, Mich.
Burdett, Smith & Co., Troy, N. Y.
BUREAU OF ENGRAVING, MINNEAPOLIS, MINN.
See Retailers' Service Bureau 413 (Z1)
Burdick Cabinet Co., Milton, Wis.
Burkhardt Furn. Co., Miamisburg, O.
Burlington Blanket Co., Burlington, Iowa.
Burns Bros. Mfg. Co., New York, N. Y.
BURNS-LEVEE CO., CHICAGO, ILL.
See Statesville Furniture Co. Catalog 346
Burrowes Co., E. T., Portland, Me.
BURROWS BROS. COMPANY, PICTURE ROCKS, PA. 395-397 (Z1)
Burrows Co., The E. T., Portland, Ore.
Burt Brothers, Inc., Philadelphia, Pa.
Burton-Dixie Corp., Chicago, Ill.
Burton Range Co., Cincinnati, O.
Bush & Diamond, Philadelphia, Pa.
Butler Mfg. Co., Syracuse, N. Y.

C

Cabinet Makers' Union, Inc., Indianapolis, Ind.
Cabinet Shops, Inc., Grand Rapids, Mich.
CALDWELL FURNITURE COMPANY, LENOIR, N. C. 398 (Z1)
Cambria Carpet Co., Philadelphia, Pa.
Cambridge Furn. Co., Cambridge, Md.
Campbell Smith & Ritchie Co., Lebanon, Ind.
CANFIELD, H. C., BATESVILLE, IND.
See Period Cabinet Mfg. Co. 307
CANTERBURY DECORATIVE FABRICS (Marshall Field & Co., Wholesale), CHICAGO, ILL. 87
Capital City Chair Co., Atlanta, Ga.
Carbon Stove Co., Belleville, Ill.
Carbone, Inc., Boston, Mass.
Cardarelli & Co., G., New York, N. Y.
Cardinal Cabinet Company, Wabash, Ind.
Carey Chair Mfg. Co., Keene, N. H.
Carlson Mfg. Co., Rockford, Ill.
Carman Mfg. Co., Seattle, Wash.
Carman Mfg. Co., Tacoma, Wash.
Carolina Parlor Furn. Co., Statesville, N. C.
Carolina Wood Products Co., Asheville, N. C.
Carrollton Furn. Mfg. Co., Carrollton, Ky.
Carrom Co., Ludington, Mich.
Carson & Son, Robert, Philadelphia, Pa.
Carter & Campbell, Inc., Winchendon, Mass.
Carthage Superior Spring Bed Mfg. Co., Carthage, Mo.
Casper-Stehle Bedding Co., St. Louis, Mo.
Cass Company, N. D., Athol, Mass.
Cass Company of Vermont, Manchester, Vt.
Caswell-Runyan Co., Huntington, Ind.
Catawba Furn. Co., Marion, N. C.
Caton & Goodman, Concord, N. C.
Cecil Mfg. Co., High Point, N. C.
Cedar Craft Co., Cedar Rapids, Iowa.
Celina Maid Furn. Co., Celina, O.
CENTRAL FURNITURE COMPANY, ROCKFORD, ILL. 254-257
Central Furn. Co., St. Louis, Mo.
Central Glass Co., Louisville, Ky.
Central Glass Co., Bristol, Va.
Central States Gen. Elec. Sup. Co., Chicago, Ill.
CENTURY FURNITURE COMPANY, GRAND RAPIDS, MICH. 92
Century Stove & Mfg. Co., Johnstown, Pa.
Certainteed Products Co., Trenton, N. J.
Chair & Furn. Industry, Fort Madison, Iowa.
Chair City Uph. Co., Gardner, Mass.
Challenge Refrigerator Co., Grand Haven, Mich.
Chambers Mfg. Co., Shelbyville, Ind.
Champion Spring Co., Cleveland, O.
Channon-Emery Stove Co., Quincy, Ill.
Character Furn. Co., Medina, N. Y.
Charak Furn. Co., Boston, Mass.
Charlotte Chair Co., Cadillac, Mich.
CHARLOTTE FURNITURE CO., CHARLOTTE, MICH.
Catalog 258
Home Furnishing and Decoration Section 11
Charlotte Mills, New York, N. Y.
Chase & Co., L. C., Boston, Mass.
Chase Furn. Co., H. W., Grand Rapids, Mich.
Chatham Uph. Corp., New York, N. Y.
Chatham Chair Mfg. Co., Siler City, N. C.
Chattahoochie Furn. Co., Flowery Branch, Ga.
CHATTANOOGA FURNITURE COMPANY, CHATTANOOGA, TENN. 259
Chautauqua Cabinet Co. Inc., Mayville, N. Y.
Cheese Co., John P., San Francisco, Cal.
Chelsea Fibre Mills, Brooklyn, N. Y.
Cherkezian Bros., New York, N. Y.
Cherman Furn. Mfg. Co., Los Angeles, Cal.
Chesapeake Mfg. Co., Baltimore, Md.
Chesterfield Furn. Co., Long Island City, N. Y.
Chesterton Furn. Co., New York, N. Y.
Chicago Asbestos Table Mat Co., Chicago, Ill.
Chicago Cast Spring Co., Chicago, Ill.
Chicago Furn. Frame Co., Chicago, Ill.
Chicago Handle Bar Co., Shelby, Ohio.
Chicago Hardware Foundry Co., N. Chicago, Ill.
CHICAGO MIRROR & ART GLASS CO., CHICAGO, ILL. 395 (Z3)
Chicago Society of Art Needlework, Chicago, Ill.
Chicago Uph. Furn. Co., Chicago, Ill.
Children's Furn. & Toy Co., Los Angeles, Cal.
Children's Vehicle Corp., E. Templeton, Mass.
Chillicothe Furn. Co., Chillicothe, Mo.
CHITTENDEN & EASTMAN COMPANY, BURLINGTON, IOWA. 377
Cincinnati Wrought Iron Co., Cincinnati, O.
City Refrigerator Co., Los Angeles, Cal.
Clare Mfg. Co., Philadelphia, Pa.
Cleeland's Sons, Robert, Philadelphia, Pa.
Cleveland Chair Co., Cleveland, Tenn.
Cleveland Co-operative Stove Co., Cleveland, O.
Cleveland Folding Bed Co., Cleveland, O.
Cleveland Furn. Mfg. Co., Cleveland, O.
Cleveland Metal Products Co., Cleveland, O.
Cleveland Wire Spring Co., Cleveland, O.
Climax Crib Co., Newark, N. J.
Clinton Carpet Co., Chicago, Ill.
Clock Mfrs. Ass'n of America, Phila, Pa.
Clore & Hawkins, Brightwood, Va.
Clune Co., M., Indianapolis, Ind.
Cocheo Brothers, Long Island City, N. Y.
Cochran Chair Co., Aurora, Ind.
Cochrane Co., Chas. P., Philadelphia, Pa.
Coffin Chair Company, Gardner, Mass.
Cohen, Louis, New York, N. Y.
Cold Blast Feather Co., Philadelphia, Pa.
Cold Storage Ref. Co., Eau Claire, Wis.
Cole Manufacturing Co., Chicago, Ill.
Coleman-Vaughan Furn. Co., Pulaski, Va.
Collier-Keyworth Co., Gardner, Mass.
Collins & Aikman Co., New York, N. Y.
COLONIAL DESK COMPANY, ROCKFORD, ILL. 138-141
COLONIAL DRAPERY FABRICS (Marshall Field & Co., Wholesale), CHICAGO, ILL.
Catalog 84
Home Furnishing and Decoration Section 30-32
Colonial Furniture Co., Grand Rapids, Mich.
Colonial Furniture Co., Boston, Mass.
COLONIAL FURNITURE COMPANY, HIGH POINT, N. C. 93-95
Colonial Lamp & Fixture Works, Chicago, Ill.
Colonial Lamp & Shade Corp., Chicago, Ill.
Colonial Mantel & Ref. Co., Brooklyn, N. Y.
COLONIAL MANUFACTURING COMPANY, ZEELAND, MICH. 142-143
Colonial Show Case Co., Brooklyn, N. Y.
Colonial Upholstery Co., Anoka, Minn.
Colorado Bedding Co., Denver, Colo.
Colorado Mattress Mfg. Co., Denver, Colo.
Columbia & Meyers Co., Boston, Mass.
Columbia Carpet Mills, Philadelphia, Pa.
Columbia Feather Co., Chicago, Ill.
Columbia Furn. & Mfg. Co., Newton, N. J.
Columbia Mills, New York, N. Y.
Columbia Parlor Furn. Mfg. Co., Chicago, Ill.
Columbia Wood Turning Co., Chicago, Ill.
Columbus Bed Spring Co., Columbus, O.
Comey Company, R. H., Camden, N. J.
Commercial Furn. Co., Chicago, Ill.
Commercial Parlor Frame Company, Chicago, Ill.
Commercial Reed & Rattan Co., Boston, Mass.
Commonwealth Uph. Co., Boston, Mass.
Community Rug Mills, Inc., Slatington, Pa.
Comstock-Castle Stove Co., Quincy, Ill.
CONANT-BALL COMPANY, BOSTON, MASS.
Catalog 191
Home Furnishing and Decoration Section 11
Conant Brothers Company, Somerville, Mass.
CONANT'S SONS, INC., F. H., CAMDEN, N. Y.
Catalog 192
Home Furnishing and Decoration Section 12
Concord Colonial Chair Co., Ashland, Mass.
Conewango Company, Warren, Pa.
Conewango Furn. Co., Hanover, Pa.
Congoleum Nairn, Philadelphia, Pa.
Conner Furniture Co., New Albany, Ind.
Connersville Furn. Co., Connersville, Ind.
Conrades Mfg. Co., St. Louis, Mo.
Consolidated Lamp & Shade Co., Chicago, Ill.
Conroy-Prugh Company, Pittsburgh, Pa.
Consolidated Trimming Co., New York, N. Y.
CONTINENTAL FURNITURE CO., HIGH POINT, N. C. 260-261
Continental Mfg. Co., Chicago, Ill.
Continental Desk Co., Rockford, Ill.
Converse & Son Co., Morton E., Winchendon, Mass.
Cook, Inc., Arthur Lee, New York, N. Y.
Cook & Company, Medina, N. Y.
Cook & Company, C. A., Cambridge, Mass.
Cook Co., C. Lawrence, Pittsburgh, Pa.
Cooper Mfg. Co., Waco, Tex.
Co-operative Foundry Co., Rochester, N. Y.
Co-operative Furn. Co., Rockford, Ill.
Co-operative Furn. Mfg. Co., Los Angeles, Cal.
Coopersmith Bed Company, St. Louis, Mo.
Copper Clad Malleable Range Co., St. Louis, Mo.
Coppes Bros. & Zook, Inc., Nappanee, Ind.
Coral Mfg. Co., Norristown, Pa.
Corn Mattress Co., Tulsa, Okla.
Corry Case Goods Co., Corry, Pa.
Corry Chair Co., Corry, Pa.
Corry Fibre Furn. Co., Corry, Pa.
Costikyan & Co., New York, N. Y.
Cott-A-Lap Company, Somerville, N. J.
Cotton Belt Mfg. Co., Rocky Mount, N. C.
Covington Furn. Mfg. Co., Covington, Ky.
Craig Mfg. Co., N. B., Washington C. H. O.
Crandall-Bennett-Porter Co., Montoursville, Pa.
Cranford Industries, Ashboro, N. C.
Crashaw Carpet Co., Newburgh, N. Y.
Cravens-Green Co., Huntington, W. Va.
Crescent Bed Co., New Orleans, La.
Crescent Furn. & Mattress Co., New Orleans, La.
Crescent Furn. Co., Evansville, Ind.
Crescent Show Case Co., Brooklyn, N. Y.
Crescent Stove Works, Evansville, Ind.
Crest Company, Chicago, Ill.
Crex Carpet Company, New York, N. Y.
CROCKER CHAIR COMPANY, SHEBOYGAN, WIS.
Catalog 137
Home Furnishing and Decoration Section 12
Cron Company, Piqua, Ohio.
Cron-Kills Company, Piqua, Ohio.
Crown City Mfg. Co., Pasadena, Cal.
Crown Stove Works, Chicago, Ill.
Crystal Refrigerator Co., Fremont, Neb.
Culler Furniture Co., Williamsport, Pa.
Culter & Proctor Stove Co., Peoria, Ill.
Culver Art & Frame Co., Westerville, O.
Currahee Furn. Co., Toccoa, Ga.
Curtis Chair Co., Ashburnham, Mass.
CURTISS & SON, WM. P., RICHLAND, N. Y. 399 (Z1)
Cushman Mfg. Co., H. T., Bennington, Vt.
CUTTING, C. M., RICHMOND, VA.
See Caldwell Furniture Co 398 (Z1)
Cuyahoga Picture Frame Co., Cleveland, O.

D

D & S Fibre Co., Brooklyn, N. Y.
Daemicke Company, Paul, Chicago, Ill.
Dahlin Brothers, Minneapolis, Minn.
Dallastown Furn. Co., Dallastown, Pa.
Daltex Spring Bed Co., Dallas, Tex.
Dalton Furn. Co., High Point, N. C.
Dame Furn. Co., Harriman, Tenn.
Dan River Furn. Corp., Leaksville, N. C.
Danville Stove Mfg. Co., Danville, Pa.
Danziger Furniture Co., Shelbyville, Ind.
DAVIS-BIRELY TABLE COMPANY, SHELBYVILLE, IND. 193
DAVIS FURNITURE CORPORATION, JAMESTOWN, N. Y. 262
Davis, Horwich & Steinman, Inc., Chicago, Ill.
Davis Mfg. Co., Minneapolis, Minn.
Davis Mfg. Co., Racine, Wis.
Davis Uph. & Furn. Co., Los Angeles, Cal.
Day Sons & Co., H. L., Bangor, Me.
Dayton Mattress Mfg. Co., Dayton, O.
Dearborn Company, Chicago, Ill.
DE BOER MANUFACTURING CO., SYRACUSE, N. Y. 133
Debski, F., New York, N. Y.
DECKER, INC., ISAAC C., MONTGOMERY, PA.
Catalog 96
Home Furnishing and Decoration Section 13
Decorative Lamp & Shade Co., Philadelphia, Pa.
Decorators Furn. Co., New York, N. Y.
Deemer Furn. Co., A. D., Brookville, Pa.
De France Lamp & Shade Co., Los Angeles, Cal.
De Frehn & Sons, W., Johnstown, Pa.
Delaware Chair Co., Delaware, O.
Delaware Mfg. Co., Philadelphia, Pa.
DELKER BROS. MFG. CO., HENDERSON, KY. 97
Deltox Grass Rug Co., Oshkosh, Wis.
De Luxe Carpet Co., Chicago, Ill.
De Luxe Fibre Furn. Co., Los Angeles, Cal.
De Luxe Furn Co., Chicago, Ill.
Dennis Company, Knightstown, Ind.
Denton Mfg. Co., Denton, N. C.
Dependable Furn. Mfg. Co., San Francisco, Cal.
Derby & Company, P., Gardner, Mass.
Derry Made Products Co., Derry, N. H.
Detroit Bedding Co., Detroit, Mich.
Detroit Cabinet Co., Detroit, Mich.
Detroit Chair Mfg. Co., Detroit, Mich.
Detroit Lamp Mfg. Co., Detroit, Mich.
Detroit Rack Company, Detroit, Mich.
Detroit Stove Works, Detroit, Mich.
Detroit Vapor Stove Co., Detroit, Mich.
Deutsch & Co., J. M., Hornell, N. Y.
Develon Sons, Thos., Philadelphia, Pa.
Dewitt-Seitz Co., Duluth, Minn.
Diamond Furniture Co., Jamestown, N. Y.
Dickerman & Company, Gardner, Mass.
Dickman & Sons, Joseph A., Sedalia, Mo.
Dieringer Bros. Furn. Mfg. Co., San Francisco, Cal.
Dillingham Mfg. Co., Sheboygan, Wis.
Disbrow & Kofahl, Inc., New York, N. Y.
Dixie Bedding Co., Monroe, La.
DIXIE FURNITURE COMPANY, LEXINGTON, N. C. 263
Dixie Mattress Co., Richmond, Va.
Dobson, John & James, New York, N. Y.
Dodge-Dickinson Co., Bloomington, Ill.
Dodge Furn. Co., C., Manchester, Mass.
Doehler Die Casting Co., New York, N. Y.
Doernbecher Mfg. Co., Portland, Ore.
DOETSCH & BAUER COMPANY, CHICAGO, ILL. 375
DOMES OF SILENCE, INC., NEW YORK, N. Y. 134
Donchian & Company, New York, N. Y.
Donchian Rug. Co., Samuel, Hartford, Conn.
Donnelly-Kelly Glass Co., Holland, Mich.
DORAN CO., LOUIS J., NEW YORK, N. Y.
See Dixie Furniture Co 263
DORSON CO., LOUIS J., NEW YORK, N. Y.
See Statesville Furniture Co. 346
Dornan Carpet & Rug Mills, Philadelphia, Pa.
Dorothy Lamp Shade Co., New York, N. Y.
Doup Company, L. G., Omaha, Neb.
Downing, George H., Tidioute, Pa.
Drake Company, Chicago, Ill.
Drake, Inc., Louis Stoughton, Boston, Mass.
Draper Shade Company, L. C., Spiceland, Ind.
Dresser & Son, Inc., C. H., Hartford, Conn.
Drexel Furn. Co., Drexel, N. C.
Drusch & Co., Cape Girardeau, Mo.
Duane Chair Co., Inc., Dalton, Ga.
Dubs, John A., Philadelphia, Pa.
Dubuque Mattress Factory, Dubuque, Iowa.
Duffy-Trowbridge Stove Mfg. Co., Hannibal, Mo.
Du-Lux Living Room Furn. Co., Buffalo, N. Y.
DUNBAR FURNITURE MANUFACTURING CO., BERNE, IND 98
Dunkirk Uph. Co., Dunkirk, N. Y.
Dunn Company, John A., Gardner, Mass.
Dura-Bilt Uph. Furn. Co., Philadelphia, Pa.
Dwelle-Kiser Co., Buffalo, N. Y.
Dworkin & Company, Inc., B., Hartford, Conn.

E

EAGLE-OTTAWA LEATHER CO., GRAND HAVEN, MICH.
Catalog 83
Home Furnishing and Decoration Section 13
Eagle Upholstery Co., Brooklyn, N. Y.
Eagle-Wabash Corp., Chicago, Ill.
Early Foundry Co., Dickson City, Pa.
East Tennessee Wood Working Co., Morristown, Tenn.
Eastern Hardware & Supply Co., Baltimore, Md.
Eastern Lounge Co., New Milford, Conn.
Eastern Rug & Trading Co., New York, N. Y.
EASTON FURNITURE MFG. CO., EASTON, MD. 400 (Z1)
Eastman Mfg. Co., Union City, Pa.
Eaton Chair Company, Chicago, Ill.
Ebbecke Furn. Co., Hoboken, N. J.

Eberhardt & Co., H., Chicago, Ill.
EBERT FURNITURE CO., RED LION, PA.
Catalog distributed to all States 264
Catalog distributed to Zone 1 .... 402-403 (Z1)
Ecker, Fred, High Point, N. C.
Eckerson Bedding Co., Mechanicsville, N. Y.
Eckstein Co., N., New York, N. Y.
Eddy & Sons Company, D., Boston, Mass.
Edwards Chair Co., Galax, Va.
Electair Company, Chicago, Ill.
Elgin Stove & Oven Co., Elgin, Ill.
ELITE FURNITURE COMPANY, JAMESTOWN, N. Y. 146
Elk Furniture Co., Jamestown, N. Y.
Elk Furniture Co., Lexington, N. C.
Elk River Mfg. Co., Butler, Tenn.
Elkin Furniture Co., Elkin, N. C.
Elins Ref. & Fix. Co., Elkins, W. Va.
Ellis Mfg. Co., Evansville, Ind.
Emerson Glass Corp., Jamestown, N. Y.
Emmerich & Co., Charles, Chicago, Ill.
Empire Carpet Co., New York, N. Y.
EMPIRE CASE GOODS COMPANY, JAMESTOWN, N. Y.
Catalog 266-267
Home Furnishing and Decoration Section 14
EMPIRE CHAIR COMPANY, JOHNSON CITY, TENN 194-196
Empire Couch Company, Medina, N. Y.
EMPIRE FURNITURE CO., HUNTINGTON, W. VA. 268
Empire Furn. Mfg. Co., Texas, Md.
Empire Manufacturing Co., Rockford, Ill.
Empire Mattress Co., Chicago, Ill.
Empire Uph. Co., Boston, Mass.
Emrich, C., Columbus O.
Emrich Furn. Co., Indianapolis, Ind.
Englander Spring Bed Co., Brooklyn, N. Y.
Englishtown Carpet Co., Englishtown, N. J.
Engstrom & Johnson Furn. Co., Grand Rapids, Mich.
Enterprise Bed Co., Hammond, Ind.
Enterprise Metal Bed Co., Brooklyn, N. Y.
Enterprise Parlor Furn. Co., Chicago, Ill.
Erie Stove & Mfg. Co., Erie, Pa.
Erskine-Danforth Corp., New York, N. Y.
Ervin Mfg. Co., Canton, O.
Espey Uph. Corp. Jamestown, N. Y.
ESTEY MANUFACTURING COMPANY, OWOSSO, MICH.
Catalog 265
Home Furnishing and Decoration Section 15
Evansville Desk Co., Evansville, Ind.
Evansville Furn. Co., Evansville, Ind.
EVANSVILLE FURN. MFRS.' ASS'N, EVANSVILLE, IND. 382-383
Evansville Mattress & Couch Co., Evansville, Ind.
Evansville Metal Bed Co., Evansville, Ind.
Evart Fibre Furn. Co., Evart, Mich.
EVERS, J. A., MINNEAPOLIS, MINN.
See Automatic Shade Company 189
Excel Mfg. Co., Rockford, Ill.
Excelsior Art Iron Works, New York, N. Y.
Excelsior Company, Columbus, O.
Excelsior Stove & Mfg. Co., Quincy, Ill.
Excelsior Wrapper Co., Grand Rapids, Mich.
Expert Wood Turning Corp., Chicago, Ill.
Exum Furniture Co., Johnson City, Tenn.

F

FAIR FOUNDRY COMPANY, INC., KNOXVILLE, TENN. 394 (Z2)
Fairfield Chair Co., Lenoir, N. C.
Falcon Mfg. Co., Big Rapids, Mich.
Falconer Plate Glass Corp., Jamestown, N. Y.
FANCHER FURNITURE CO., SALAMANCA, N. Y. 270
Farley & Loetscher Mfg. Co., Dubuque, Iowa.
Farrell, Edward P., Toledo, O.
Faucett-Umphrey Chair Co., Morganton, Ind.
Faultless Caster Co., Evansville, Ind.
Favorite Stove & Range Co., Piqua, O.
Federal Equipment Co., Carlisle, Pa.
Federal Furn. Factories, Hoboken, N. J.
Federal-Montauk Corp., Hoboken, N. J.
Federal Parlor Furn. Co., Chicago, Ill.
Federal Parlor Suite Co., Brooklyn, N. Y.
Feldman Co., Manuel, New York, N. Y.
Feldstein, Joseph, Brooklyn, N. Y.
Feltite Chair Corp., New York, N. Y.
FENSKE BROS., CHICAGO, ILL. 99
Ferguson Bros. Mfg. Co., Hoboken, N. J.
Ferguson Carpet Co., Philadelphia, Pa.
Fetterolf Co., H. G., Philadelphia, Pa.
Fibercraft Chair Co., Columbia, S. C.
Fibre Craft Chair Co., Frankfort, Ky.
Fibrecraft Chair Co, Jefferson City, Mo.
Ficks Reed Company, Cincinnati, O.
FIELD & COMPANY, WHOLESALE, MARSHALL, CHICAGO, ILL.
Home Furnishing and Decoration Section 30-32
Colonial Drapery Fabrics Catalog 84
Zion Lace Curtains and Nets Catalog 85
Home Crest Floor Coverings Catalog 86
Canterbury Decorative Fabrics Catalog 87
Home Crest Upholstered Furniture Catalog 100-101
Fireside Industries, Adrian, Mich.
Firth Carpet Co., New York, N. Y.
Fischer Furn. Co., Chicago, Ill.
Fischer, John, Pittsburgh, Pa.
Fischer Leaf Co., Louisville, Ky.
Fisher Furniture Co., Buffalo, N. Y.
Fishman, Wm., Albany, N. Y.
Fiske Iron Works, J. W., New York, N. Y.
Fitts-Crabtree Mfg. Co., Sanford, N. C.
Flood Chair Co., C. E., Cleveland, O.
Florence Stove Co., Gardner, Mass.
FLORENCE TABLE AND MANUFACTURING CO., MEMPHIS, TENN.
Catalog 271
Home Furnishing and Decoration Section 15
Florida Spring Bed Mfg. Co., Jacksonville, Fla.
Florida Wicker Works, South Palm Beach, Fla.
Fogle Furn. Co., Winston-Salem, N. C.
Folding Furn. Works, Inc., Stevens Point, Wis.
Fond du Lac Table Mfg. Co., Fond du Lac, Wis.
Forbes Mfg. Co., Hopkinsville, Ky.
Forest Furn. Co., N. Wilkesboro, N. C.
Forest Furn. Co., Youngsville, Pa.
Forman, Ford & Co., Minneapolis, Minn.
FORSYTH FURNITURE LINES, INC., WINSTON-SALEM, N. C.
Catalog 272
Home Furnishing and Decoration Section 16
Fort Pitt Bedding Co., Pittsburgh, Pa.
Fort Scott Mattress Co., Fort Scott, Kan.
Fort Smith Furn. Mfrs. Co., Fort Smith, Ark.
Fort Smith Metal Prod. Co., Fort Smith, Ark.
FOSTER BROS. MFG. CO., UTICA, N. Y. 69
Foster Stove Co., Ironton, O.
Fox Furnace Co., Elyria, O.
Fox Mfg. Co., Atlanta, Ga.
Foy Lumber & Mfg. Co., Mt. Airy, N. C.
Frank & Son, New York, N. Y.
Frankfort Chair Co., Frankfort, Ky.
Franklin & Co., S., Chicago, Ill.
FRANKLIN FURNITURE CO., COLUMBIANA, O.
Catalog 102
Home Furnishing and Decoration Section 17
Freeman Bros. Inc., Long Island City, N. Y.
Freese & Sons Co., J. D., Chicago, Ill.
French & Heald Co., Boston, Mass.
French-American Mfg. Co., New York, N. Y.
French Furn. Co., Wm. A., Minneapolis, Minn.
Frewsburg Furn. Co. Inc., Frewsburg, N. Y.
FRIEDMAN, JOSEPH, NEW YORK, N. Y.
See Statton Furniture Mfg. Co. 418 (Z1)
Friedrichs, H., San Francisco, Cal.
Frischman & Son F., Brooklyn, N. Y.
Fritts & Co., D. H., Chicago, Ill.
Fritz & La Rue Company, New York, N. Y.
Frost Sons Co., J. C., Towanda, Pa.
Fuldner & Sons, Henry, New York, N. Y.
Fuller-Warren Co., Milwaukee, Wis.
FULLERTON FURNITURE FACTORIES, FULLERTON, PA. 103
Fulton Furniture Corp., New York, N. Y.
Fulton Metal Bed Mfg. Co., Atlanta, Ga.
Furnas Office Furn. Co., Indianapolis, Ind.
FURNITURE CITY UPHOLSTERY CO., GRAND RAPIDS, MICH. 104
Furniture Exchange, San Francisco, Cal.
Furniture Sales Co., Minneapolis, Minn.
FURNITURE SALES CO., MINNEAPOLIS, MINN.
See Mersman Bros. Corporation 216-221
FURNITURE SHOPS, GRAND RAPIDS, MICH.
(Division of the Luce Furniture Shops)
Catalog 160-161
Home Furnishing and Decoration Section 16
Furniture Studios, Inc., Grand Rapids, Mich.
FURST BROS. & COMPANY, BALTIMORE, MD. 78
Fusfield, J., Brooklyn, N. Y.
Fynetone Mfg. Co., Lansdale, Pa.

G

G & W Refrigerator Co., Cloquet, Minn.
Gallup-Ruffing Co., Norwalk, O.
Gangelhaff Bros., Minneapolis, Minn.
Gardner Chair Co., Gardner, Mass.
Gardner Reed & Rattan Co., Gardner, Mass.
Gardner Table Mfg. Co., Gardner, Mass.
Gardner Uph. Furn Co., Gardner, Mass.
Garfield Felt Corp., Chicago, Ill.
Garland Chair Co., Garland, Pa.
Garland Uph. Co., Chicago, Ill.
Garrett Go-Cart & Car Co., Chicago, Ill.
Garrison Co. Inc., Fort Smith, Ark.
Garton Toy Co., Sheboygan, Wis.
Garver Furn. Co., Tippecanoe City, O.
Gay's Sons, John, Philadelphia, Pa
Gebert & Son, Chris, Philadelphia, Pa.
Geffner, H., Providence, R. I.
Geisel Mfg. Co., A., St. Louis, Mo.
Gem City Stove Mfg. Co., Quincy, Ill.
Gem Crib & Cradle Co., Gardner, Mass.
Gem Hammock & Fly Net Co., Milwaukee, Wis.
Gem Mfg. Co., Bascom, O.
Gendron Wheel Co., Toledo, O.
General Fireproofing Co., Chicago, Ill.
General Furn. Co., Seattle, Wash.
General Reed Furn. Co., St. Louis, Mo.
General Wood Turning Co., Chicago, Ill.
Gennet, Jacob, Newark, N. J.
Georgia Chair Co., Gainesville, Ga.
Gerner Stove Co., Erie, Pa.
Gessinger, Gerhard B., Baltimore, Md.
Gettysburg Furn. Co., Gettysburg, Pa.
Geyler Furn. Mfg. Co., Hillsboro, O.
Gholstin Spring & Mattress Co., Atlanta, Ga.
Giant Furn. Co., High Point, N. C.
Gibson Co., Wm. D., Chicago, Ill.
Gibson Refrigerator Co., Greenville, Mich.
Gilbert Clock Co., Wm. L., Winsted, Conn.
Gillis Co., Jas. W., Rochester, N. Y.
Gilson Mfg. Co., Port Washington, Wis.
Ginsberg, Jos. W., New York, N. Y.
Giordano & Co., P., W. Hoboken, N. J.
Glaenzer Trading Corp. New York, N. Y.
Glanton Furn. Co., J. A., Columbus, Ind.
Glascock Stove & Mfg. Co., Greensboro, N. C.
Glass Novelty Co., Chicago, Ill.
Glenwood Range Co., Taunton, Mass.
GLOBE-BOSSE-WORLD FURNITURE CO., EVANSVILLE, IND.
Catalog 273
Home Furnishing and Decoration Section 17
Globe Chair Co., Hillsboro, O.
Globe Company, Sheboygan, Wis.
GLOBE MANUFACTURING CO., HIGH POINT, N. C. 106-107
GLOBE PARLOR FURNITURE CO., HIGH POINT, N. C. 106-107
Globe Stove & Range Co., Kokomo, Ind.
Globe-Wernicke Co., Cincinnati, O.
Gobelin Textile Corp., New York, N. Y.
Gohmann Bros. & Kahler Co., New Albany, Ind.
Gold Furn. Co., Chicago, Ill.
Gold Medal Camp Furn. Mfg. Co., Racine, Wis.
Gold Metal Furn. Mfg. Co., Richmond, Va.
Goldberg Bros., Chicago, Ill.
Goldstein Chair Co., Jos., New York, N. Y.
Goldstrom Bros., Baltimore, Md.
Good Furn. Magazine, Grand Rapids, Mich.
Gordon-Chapman Co., Detroit, Mich.
Gordon-Joseph Furn. Co., Chicago, Ill.
Gorrell & Co., A. D., Chicago, Ill.
Goshen Novelty & Lamp Co., Goshen, Ind.
Gottlieb & Son, J., Chicago, Ill.
Gould Mfg. Co., Oshkosh, Wis.
Graham & Son, John M., Columbia, S. C.
Graham & Sons, Thos., Madison, Ind.
Graham Mfg. Co., Jas., San Francisco, Cal.
Grand, John R., Baton Rouge, La.
Grand Central Wicker Shop, New York, N. Y.
Grand Ledge Chair Co., Grand Ledge, Mich.
Grand Rapids Bedding Co., Grand Rapids, Mich.
Grand Rapids Book Case & Chair Co., Hastings, Mich.
Grand Rapids Chair Co., Grand Rapids, Mich.
GRAND RAPIDS DESK CO., GRAND RAPIDS, MICHIGAN
See Stow-Davis Furniture Co. 76-77
Grand Rapids Fancy Furn. Co., Grand Rapids, Mich.
Grand Rapids Furn. Co., Grand Rapids, Mich.
Grand Rapids Market Ass'n, Grand Rapids, Mich.
Grand Rapids Ref. Co., Grand Rapids, Mich.
GRAND RAPIDS UPHOLSTERING COMPANY, GRAND RAPIDS, MICH 252-253
Grand Uph. Furn. Co., Philadelphia, Pa.
Grassyfork Fisheries, Inc., Indianapolis, Ind.
Grau-Curtis Company, Minneapolis, Minn.
Graulich & Co., C., Evansville, Ind.
Graveley Nov. Co., Martinsville, Va.
Gray & Dudley Co., Nashville, Tenn.
Grayson Mfg. Co., J. H., Athens, O.
Great Northern Chair Co., Chicago, Ill.
Great Western Stove Co., Leavenworth, Kan.
Greater New York Bedding Co., New York, N. Y.
GREEN MANUFACTURING CO., CHICAGO, ILL. 376
Greene Mfg. Co., Greene, N. Y.
Greenpoint Metallic Bed Co., Brooklyn, N. Y.
Greenpoint Parlor Suite Co., Brooklyn, N. Y.
Greensburg Swing Co., Greensburg, Pa.
Greenspan, Wolf & Son, Brooklyn, N. Y.
Greenstein & Sons, Sam., New York, N. Y.
Greenwood Associates, Gardner, Mass.
Gregory Furn. Mfg. Co., Tacoma, Wash.
Greilick Mfg. Co., Traverse City, Mich.
GRIFFITH FURN. WORKS, MUNCIE, IND. 147
Grinberg Bros., New York, N. Y.
Griswold-Guest Co., Big Rapids, Mich.
Grobhiser-Cabinet Makers Co., Sturgis, Mich.
Groff-Bent Corp., New York, N. Y.
Gross & Co., H. E., Pittsburgh, Pa.
Gross Co., Ed., New York, N. Y.
Grossfeld, Inc., Albert, New York, N. Y.
Grow & Cuttle, Inc., Chicago, Ill.
Gudeman & Company, New York, N. Y.
Guerney Ref. Co., Fond du Lac, Wis.
Guilford Parlor Furn. Co., High Point, N. C.
Gulbenkian, Gullabi & Co., New York, N. Y.
GUMWOOD SERVICE BUREAU.
Hardwood Manufacturers' Institute 386
GUNLOCKE CHAIR CO., W. H. WAYLAND, N. Y. 401 (Z1)
GUNN FURNITURE COMPANY, GRAND RAPIDS, MICH.
Catalog 396 (Z3)
Home Furnishing and Decoration Section 19
Gustafson, Carl. J., Albert City, Iowa.
GUTTER, S. J., NEW YORK, N. Y.
See Caldwell Furniture Co. 398 (Z1)

H

Haas, Joseph, Brooklyn, N. Y.
Haberbritz, Phillip, New York, N. Y.
Haberkorn Co., C. H., Detroit, Mich.
Hacker, David, New York, N. Y.
Hageman Glass Co., Cincinnati, O.
Hagerstown Furn. Co., Hagerstown, Md.
Hagerstown Table Works, Hagerstown, Md.
Haggard & Marcusson Co., Chicago, Ill.
Hagmaier Uph. Co., Philadelphia, Pa.
Hagmaier Uph. Co., Pittsburgh, Pa.
Hale Mfg. Co., F. E., Herkimer, N. Y.
Hall & Lyon Furn. Co., Waverly, N. Y.
Hall & Sons, Frank A, New York, N. Y.
Hall, Charles, New York, N. Y.
Hallagan-Thompson Co., Newark, N. Y.
Hallen & Weiner, New York, N. Y.
HALLENSTEIN, A., CHICAGO, ILL.
See Mersman Bros. Corporation 216-221
Halpern & Son, M., Philadelphia, Pa.
Halstrick, Wm. F., Cincinnati, O.
Hamblin & Russell Mfg. Co., Worcester, Mass.
Hamilton Ross Factories, Chicago, Ill.
Hanauer Furn. Co., Chicago, Ill.
HANNAHS MANUFACTURING COMPANY, KENOSHA, WIS. 197
Hannon, John A., Jersey City, N. J.
Hanpeter Furn. Co., F. W., St. Louis, Mo.
Hansen Furn. Co., Ed., Chicago, Ill.
HANSON CLOCK COMPANY, INC., ROCKFORD, ILL. 148-149
Hanson Furn. Co., Janesville, Wis.
Hanson Co., Louis, Chicago, Ill.
Harahorn, Inc., C. H., Gardner, Mass.
Harberer Furn. Co., J. E., Lowville, N. Y.
HARD MANUFACTURING CO., BUFFALO, N. Y. 404 (Z1)
HARDEN COMPANY, FRANK S., McCONNELLSVILLE, N. Y.
Catalog 108-109
Home Furnishing and Decoration Section 18
Harder, Frank H., San Francisco, Cal.
Harder Mfg. Co., Cobleskill, N. Y.
Hardwick & Magee Co., Philadelphia, Pa.
HARDWOOD MANUFACTURERS' INSTITUTE, MEMPHIS, TENN.
Oak Service Bureau 384-385
Gumwood Service Bureau 386
Hardwood Milling Co., Estherville, Iowa.
Hargrave Cedar Chest Co., Chatham, Va.
Harmon & Co., F. W., Tacoma, Wash.
Harper Furn. Co., Lenoir, N. C.
Harris, Edelstein, Perth Amboy, N. J.
Harris, John D., New York, N. Y.

Harrison Co., H., Philadelphia, Pa.
Hartmeier & Sons Co., Paterson, N. J.
Hartwig & Kemper, Baltimore, Md.
Harrison Son Co. Inc., B. J., Winsted, Conn.
Hart Mirror Plate Co., Grand Rapids, Mich.
HARTEVELD, N., CINCINNATI, OHIO
See Chicago Mirror and Art Glass Co.........395 (Z3)
Hartfelder, John E., Rochester, N. Y.
Hartford Spring Bed Co., Hartford, Conn.
Hartmann-Malcolm Co., Chicago, Ill.
Harvard Co., Canton, Ohio.
Harvey Fibre Carpet Co., Phila., Pa.
Harvey, Murray M., New York, N. Y.
Hasselbarth, C. O., Albany, N. Y.
HASTINGS TABLE CO., HASTINGS, MICH. 150-151
Hausske & Co., August, Chicago, Ill.
Hawthorne Furn. Shops, Los Angeles, Cal.
Hax-Smith Furn. Co. Inc., St. Joseph, Mo.
Hayden Co., New York, N. Y.
Hayim, Rashti & Co., New York, N. Y.
Haynes Chair & Table Co., Mocksville, N. C.
Haynes Mattress Factory, Sealy, Tex.
Haywood Furn. Mfg. Co., Waynesville, N. C.
HEBENSTREIT'S, INC., MILWAUKEE, WIS. 397 (Z3)
Hedstrom-Union Company, Gardner, Mass.
Heermans Mfg. Co., Dallas, Tex.
Heilman & Co., A. H., Williamsport, Pa.
Heinz & Munschauer, Inc., Buffalo, N. Y.
Heinz Stove Co., C., St. Louis, Mo.
HEKMAN FURNITURE COMPANY, GRAND RAPIDS, MICH. 398 (Z3)
HELLAM FURNITURE CO., INC., HELLAM, PA. 406-407 (Z1)
Helmers Mfg. Co., Kansas City, Mo.
HEMSING MANUFACTURING CO., SOUDERTON, PA. 405 (Z1)
Henderson & Co., Wm., Philadelphia, Pa.
Herhold Chair Co., Chicago, Ill.
HERMAN MILLER CLOCK CO.
See Miller Clock Co., Herman
HERMAN MILLER FURNITURE CO.
See Miller Furniture Co., Herman
Herrick Mfg. Co., Jamestown, N. Y.
Herrick Ref. & Cold Stor. Co., Waterloo, Iowa.
Herrmann Furn. Co., H., New York, N. Y.
Hester Furn. Co., Tampa, Fla.
Hexter & Co., S. M., Cleveland, O.
Heyer & Son, Henry, Milwaukee, Wis.
Heywood-Wakefield Co. Boston, Mass.
Hibriten Furn. Co., Lenoir, N. C.
Hickory Furn. Co., Hickory, N. C.
Hickory Furn. Co., Hickory, Va.
Hickory Handle Mfg. Co., Conover, N. C.
Hickory Table & Nov. Co., Hickory, N. Y.
High Point Bending & Chair Co., Siler City, N. C.
High Point Buggy Co., High Point, N. C.
High Point Furn. Co., High Point, N. C.
High Point Mirror Co., High Point, N. C.
High Point Ref. Co., High Point, N. C.
High Point Uph. Co., High Point, N. C.
HIGHTSTOWN RUG CO., HIGHTSTOWN, N. J. 88
Hilleman, Geo., Altamont, Ill.
Hincher Mfg. Co., Washington, Ind.
Hind & Harrison Plush Co., Clark Mills, N. Y.
Hirschman Co., J. C., Indianapolis, Ind.
Hirst-Rogers Co., Philadelphia, Pa.
Hix Furn. Co., Fort Plain, N. Y.
Hodell Furn. Co., Shelbyville, Ind.
Hodges Carpet Co., Indian Orchard, Mass.
Hoeffeld Co., Harry, Cincinnati, O.
Hoel Mfg. Co., South Bend, Ind.
Hoenigsberger, A., Chicago, Ill.
Hoey & Co. John, San Francisco, Cal.
Holland Chair Co., Holland, Mich.
Holland Furniture Co., Holland, Mich.
Hollatz Bros. Co., Chicago, Ill.
Holmes & Son, Archibald, Phila., Pa.
Holmes Sons Co., Henry, Phila., Pa.
Holtgrewe-Vornbrock Furn. Co., St. Louis, Mo.
HOME-CREST FLOOR COVERINGS (Marshall Field & Co., Wholesale), CHICAGO, ILL. 86
HOME-CREST UPHOLSTERED FURNITURE (Marshall Field & Co., Wholesale), CHICAGO, ILL. 100-101
HOME FURNITURE COMPANY, YORK, PA. 408-409 (Z1)
Home Made Chair Co., Statesville, N. C.
Home Products Corp., Jackson, Mich.
Home Stove & Foundry Co., Chicago, Ill.
Homes Chair Co., N. Wilkesboro, N. C.
Hood Chair Co., Loudon, Tenn.
Hooker-Bassett Furn. Co., Martinsville, Va.
Hoosier Desk Co., Jasper, Ind.
HOOSIER MANUFACTURING CO., NEW CASTLE, IND.
Catalog 72
Home Furnishing and Decoration Section........ 19
Hoosier Stove Co., Marion, Ind.
Hoover Chair Co., Lexington, N. C.
Hoover Co., Chicago, Ill.
Hopkins Mfg. Co., L., N. Girard, Pa.
Hopper Furn. Co., C. T., Sioux City, Iowa.
HORN & COMPANY, J. P., LANCASTER, PA. 410 (Z1)
Horn Bros. Co., New York, N. Y.
Horn Bros. Mfg. Co., Chicago, Ill.
Horton Mfg. Co., Fort Wayne, Ind.
Hotel Mattress Mills, Elgin, Ill.
Hough Shade Co., Janesville, Wis.
Howard Stove & Furn. Co., Ralston, Neb.
Howe-Spaulding Co., Gardner, Mass.
Howell Co., W. H., Geneva, Ill.
Howes Co., S. M., Boston, Mass.
Hoy, Raymond, & Co., Huntington, W. Va.
Hub Furn. Co., Fort Worth, Tex.
Hubbard Chair Co., Martinsville, Ind.
Hubbard, Eldredge & Miller, Rochester, N. Y.
Huenefeld Co., Cincinnati, O.
Hughes Furn. Mfg. Co., Baltimore, Md.
Hughesville Furn. Co., Hughesville, Pa.
Hulse Co., E. M., Columbus, O.
Hunt Spring Bed Co., Chattanooga, Tenn.
Huntingburg Furn. Co., Huntingburg, Ind.
Huntington Spring Bed Co., Huntington, W. Va.
HUNTLEY FURNITURE CO., B. F., WINSTON-SALEM, N. C.
Catalog 274
Home Furnishing and Decoration Section........ 20

I

Idaho Mattress Co., Boise City, Idaho.
Ideal Art Metal Co., Chicago, Ill.
Ideal Chair Co., Brooklyn, N. Y.
Ideal Furn. Co., Athens, Ga.
Illinois Cabinet Co., Rockford, Ill.
Illinois Felt Co., Chicago, Ill.
Illinois Lamp & Novelty Co., Chicago, Ill.
Illinois Moulding Co., Chicago, Ill.
Illinois Ref. Co., Madison, Ill.
Ils & Co., John G., San Francisco, Cal.
Imperial Desk Co., Evansville, Ind.
IMPERIAL FURNITURE COMPANY, GRAND RAPIDS, MICH.
Catalog 198-205
Home Furnishing and Decoration Section........ 21- 22
Imperial Furn. Mfg. Co., Statesville, N. C.
Imperial Steel Range Co., Cleveland, O.
Imperial Uph. Co., Lowell, Mass.
Independent Furn. Co., Los Angeles, Cal.
Independent Stove Co., Owosso, Mich.
Indiana Furn. Co., Evansville, Ind.
Indiana Furn. Mfg. Co., Shelbyville, Ind.
Indiana Stove Works, Evansville, Ind.
INDIANAPOLIS CHAIR & FURNITURE CO., AURORA, IND.
Catalog 152
Home Furnishing and Decoration Section........ 20
Inglewood Mfg. Co., Inglewood, Cal.
Ingraham Co., E., Bristol, Conn.
Inland Furn. Co., Sheboygan, Wis.
Inman Company, Louisville, Ky.
Innis, Pearce & Co., Rushville, Ind.
INTERIOR DECORATING SERVICE BUREAU, CHICAGO, ILL.
See Western Shade Cloth Company..........405 (Z3)
International Furn. Co., Chicago, Ill.
Ionic Mills, Philadelphia, Pa.
Iowa Furn. & Mfg. Co., Clinton, Iowa.
Iredell Uph. Furn. Co., Statesville, N. C.
IRWIN COMPANY, ROBERT W., GRAND RAPIDS, MICH. 275
Island Furn. Co., Minneapolis, Minn.
I. X. L. Mfg. Co., Goshen, Ind.

J

Jackes-Evans Mfg. Co., St. Louis, Mo.
Jackson Glass Works, Jackson, Mich.
Jacksonville Furn. Mfg. Co., Jacksonville, Fla.
Jaeger Geo. A., New York, N. Y.
James River Furn. Co., Richmond, Va.
Jamestown Case Goods Co., Jamestown, N. Y.
JAMESTOWN CHAIR COMPANY, JAMESTOWN, N. Y. 206
JAMESTOWN FURNITURE MARKET ASSOCIATION, JAMESTOWN, N. Y......... 387
JAMESTOWN LOUNGE COMPANY, JAMESTOWN, N. Y. 105
JAMESTOWN TABLE COMPANY, JAMESTOWN, N. Y. 276
JAMESTOWN UPHOLSTERY COMPANY, INC., JAMESTOWN, N. Y.
Catalog 110
Home Furnishing and Decoration Section........ 21
Japanese Fan Co., New York, N. Y.
Jarnow & Co., New York, N. Y.
Jasper Chair Co., Jasper, Ind.
Jasper Desk Co., Jasper, Ind.
Jasper Novelty Works, Jasper, Ind.
Jasper Office Furn. Co., Jasper, Ind.
Jeffersonville Mfg. Co., Jeffersonville, Ind.
Jennings Furn. Co., Lenoir, N. C.
Jersey City Go-Cart Co., Jersey City, N. J.
Jessen & Roseberg Co., Chicago, Ill.
Jewett & Company, Buffalo, N. Y.
Joering & Pelchmann, St. Louis, Mo.
JOERNS BROTHERS FURNITURE CO., STEVENS POINT, WIS.
Catalog 277
Home Furnishing and Decoration Section........ 23
Joesting & Schilling Co., St. Paul, Minn.
John Henry Stores, Newark, N. J.
JOHNSON & SONS FURNITURE CO., A. J., CHICAGO, ILL. 278-279
Johnson, P., Chicago, Ill.
Johnson Chair Co., Chicago, Ill.
Johnson Furn. Mfg. Co., J. B., Antwerp, O.
Johnson, Handley & Johnson, Grand Rapids, Mich.
Johnson-Randall Co., Traverse City, Mich.
Johnston & Klare Mfg. Co., Lawrenceburg, Ind.
Johnstown National Bedding Co., Johnstown, Pa.
Jonas & Sons, Jacob H., Los Angeles, Cal.
Jordan Parlor Furn. Co., Allentown, Pa.
Jorgensen Furn. Co., C. E., Chicago, Ill.
Josten, Peter, Philadelphia, Pa.
Judd Co., H. L., New York, N. Y.
Junger Stove & Range Co., Grafton, Wis.
Justh Mfg. Co., Cleveland, O.

K

K & L Furn. Co., High Point, N. C.
K & S Mfg. Co., Chicago, Ill.
Kaipers Sons Co., Chas., Covington, Ky.
Kalamazoo Stove Co., Kalamazoo, Mich.
Kalter Bros., New York, N. Y.
Kansas City Furn. Mfg. Co., Kansas City, Mo.
Kapital Lamp Mfg. Co., Chicago, Ill.
Kaplan Furn. Co., Cambridge, Mass.
Kaplan, Inc., Chicago, Ill.
Kappler-Fox Foundry Co., Phila., Pa.
Karagheusian, A. & M., New York, N. Y.
KARGES FURNITURE COMPANY, EVANSVILLE, IND. 280
KARPEN & BROS., S., CHICAGO, ILL.
Catalog 112-119
Home Furnishing and Decoration Section...... 25- 29
Karr Range Co., Adam, Belleville, Ill.
Kass Bros. & Co., Brooklyn, N. Y.
Katz & Co., M. A., San Francisco, Cal.
Katz Bros. Co., Chicago, Ill.
Kauffman Mfg. Co., Ashland, O.
Kaufman Plush Co., Philadelphia, Pa.
Kawner Company, Niles, Mich.
Kay Mfg. Co., Brooklyn, N. Y.
Kearns Furn. Co., High Point, N. C.
Keeley Stove Co., Columbia, Pa.
Keene Chair Co., Keene, N. H.
Keep Bros., Philadelphia, Pa.
Keiser Mfg. Co., Jacob, St. Louis, Mo.
KELLER, J. C., EVANSVILLE, IND.
See Evansville Furniture Mfrs. Association.....382-383
Keller Mfg. Co., Minneapolis, Minn.
Kellman Abraham, Chicago, Ill.
Kelly Bros., Inc., Gardner, Mass.
Kelly Mfg. Co., Clinton, Iowa.
Kelton-Aurand Mfg. Co., Bay City, Mich.
Kemper Bros. Inc., Richmond, Ind.
Kemper Furn. Co., Cincinnati, O.
Kennedy-McCandless Corp., Rochester, N. Y.
Kenney Furn. Co., Frankfort, Ky.
Ke-No Company, Sheboygan, Wis.
Kensington Mfg. Co., New York, N. Y.
Kent-Coffey Mfg. Co., Lenoir, N. C.
KENT-COSTIKYAN, NEW YORK, N. Y.
Catalog 89
Home Furnishing and Decoration Section........ 23
Kentucky Stove Company, Louisville, Ky.
Keppel & Co., Chester, Pa.
Kernersville Furn. Mfg. Co., Kernersville, N. C.
Kerney Mfg. Co., Chicago, Ill.
Ketcham & Rothschild Co., Chicago, Ill.
Key City Uph. Co., N. Wilkesboro, N. C.
Keystone Cabinet Co., High Point, N. C.
Keystone Cabinet Co., Littlestown, Pa.
Keystone Furn. Co., Williamsport, Pa.
KEYSTONE TABLE COMPANY, MT. WOLF, PA. 411 (Z1)
KIEL FURNITURE COMPANY, MILWAUKEE, WIS 208-215
Kimlark Rug Co., Neenah, Wis.
Kindel Bedding Co., Denver, Colo.
KINDEL FURNITURE COMPANY, GRAND RAPIDS, MICH.
Poster and Windsor Beds Catalog..............282-283
Day Beds Catalog..............................372-373
Home Furnishing and Decoration Section........ 24
King-Fisher Mattress Co., Portland, Ore.
King Furn. Co., Warren, O.
King-Haase Furn. Co., Memphis, Tenn.
King Stove & Range Co., Sheffield, Ala.
Kingsley Furn. Co., Inc., Chicago, Ill.
Kirsch Mfg. Co., Sturgis, Mich.
Kitchen Craft Co., West Bend, Wis.
Kitchen Made Equipment, New York, N. Y.
Kittelberger Bros., Rochester, N. Y.
Kittinger Company, Buffalo, N. Y.
Klaine & Co., F. A., Cincinnati, O.
KLAMER FURNITURE CORPORATION, EVANSVILLE, IND.
Catalog 288-289
Home Furnishing and Decoration Section...... 33
Klearfax Linen Looms, Duluth, Minn.
Klein Bros. Co., Long Island City, N. Y.
Klemp Furn. Co., H. W., Leavenworth, Kan.
Klerner Furn. Co., Peter, New Albany, Ind.
Kling Factories, Mayville, N. Y.
Kling Mfg. Co., Los Angeles, Cal.
Klinker Co., B., Cincinnati, O.
Klise Mfg. Co., Grand Rapids, Mich.
Klopstock Bros., San Francisco, Cal.
Kloud, Joseph, Chicago, Ill.
Knapp & Tubbs, Chicago, Ill.
Knell, W. W. & W. H., Philadelphia, Pa.
Knott & Carmichael, Atlanta, Ga.
KNOX STOVE WORKS, KNOXVILLE, TENN. 395 (Z2)
Knox Uph. Co., High Point, N. C.
Knoxville Furn. Co., Knoxville, Tenn.
Knoxville Table & Chair Co., Knoxville, Tenn.
Knoxville Uph. Furn. Co., Knoxville, Tenn.
Koch & Co., Isse, New York, N. Y.
Kohn, Jacob & Joseph & Mundus, New York, N. Y.
Kompass & Stoll Co., Niles, Mich.
Kopp Company, Wm., Louisville, Ky.
Kopriwa Co., E., Chicago, Ill.
K. P. L. Furn. Co., Corry, Pa.
Kraan Furn. Co., Henry, Phila., Pa.
Kramer & Sons, M., Philadelphia, Pa.
Kramer Mfg. Co., Indianapolis, Ind.
Kraus-Winograd Co., Cleveland, O.
Krebs, Stengel & Co., New York, N. Y.
Kreiss Co., Wm. F., Philadelphia, Pa.
Krieg-Mellem Furn. Co., Indianapolis, Ind.
Kroder, John, & Henry Reubel Co., New York, N. Y.
Kroehler Mfg. Co., Naperville, Ill.
Kronheim Furn. Mfg. Co., Cleveland, O.
Krueger Mfg. Co., Atlanta, Ga.
Kruissink Brothers, Chicago, Ill.
Krupka Company, Inc., S. C., Bridgeport, Conn.
Kuchins Furn. Mfg. Co., St. Louis, Mo.
Kumfy-Kab Co., La Porte, Ind.
Kurtz Case Goods Co., Corry, Pa.
Kwong Yuen & Company, New York, N. Y.

L

Lack, L., Brooklyn, N. Y.
Lack Manufacturing Co., Paducah, Ky.
La France Art Co., Philadelphia, Pa.
La France Textile Mills, Phila., Pa.
LAHL & KIDNEY, MILWAUKEE, WIS.
See Mersman Bros. Corpn..................216-221
Laird, Marshall, Los Angeles, Cal.
Lakeland Mfg. Co., Lakeland, Fla.
Lakeside Craft Co., Sheboygan, Wis.
Lakeside Uph. Co., Chicago, Ill.
Lamp & Company, Nashville, Tenn.
Lamb Bros. & Greene, Inc., Nappanee, Ind.
Lamb, George L., Nappanee, Ind.
LAMB, GEO. N., CHICAGO, ILL.
See American Walnut Mfrs. Assn.............380-381
Lambert & Latimer, Leominster, Mass.
Lambeth Furn. Co., Thomasville, N. C.
Lammert Furn. Co., St. Louis, Mo.

La Mond & Robertson Co., Paterson, N. J.
Landau Mfg. Co., St. Louis, Mo.
Land-Dilks Co., Richmond, Ind.
LANDSTROM FURNITURE CORPORATION, ROCKFORD, ILL. 290-301
See also Central Furniture Co. Catalog 254-257
Lane Chair Factory, Swanzey, N. H.
Lane Company
LANE COMPANY, INC., ALTA VISTA, VA.
Catalog 153
Home Furnishing and Decoration Section 34
Lang Mfg. Co., Buffalo, N. Y.
Larson & Sons, Peter, Chicago, Ill.
Larson, Gustave E., Kewanee, Ill.
Lash-Handler Uph. Co., Brooklyn, N. Y.
LASSAHN FURNITURE COMPANY, CHICAGO, ILL. 154
Lassen & Woren, New York, N. Y.
Lauter Company, H., Indianapolis, Ind.
Lauzon-Morse Furn. Co., Grand Rapids, Mich.
Lavick Bedding Co., Duluth, Minn.
Lawsonia Mfg. Co., Philadelphia, Pa.
Lears & Sons, C. H., Baltimore, Md.
Lebanon Valley Furn. Co., Lebanon, Pa.
Leedom Co., Thos. L., Bristol, Pa.
Lee-Marion Company, Chicago, Ill.
Lefkaw-King Company, Chicago, Ill.
Leggett & Platt Spring Bed Mfg. Co., Carthage, Mo.
Lehigh Star Bedding Co., Allentown, Pa.
Lehigh Uph. Co., Allentown, Pa.
Lehman, J. A., New York, N. Y.
Lehman Co. of America, Cannelton, Ind.
Leibe Refrigerator Mfg. Co., Wm., New Orleans, La.
Leiber Co., H., Indianapolis, Ind.
Lenoir Furn. Corp., Lenoir, N. C.
Lenoir Mirror Co., Lenoir, N. C.
Lentz Table Co., Nashville, Tenn.
Leonard & Baker Stove Co., Taunton, Mass.
Leopold Desk Co., Burlington, Iowa.
Leroi Furn. Mfg. Co., St. Louis, Mo.
LESCH, RUDOLPH, NEW YORK, N. Y. 79
Lesher, Whitman & Co., New York, N. Y.
Leubrie & Elkus, New York, N. Y.
Level Furn. Co., Jamestown, N. Y.
Levenson & Zenitz, Baltimore, Md.
LEVIN BROTHERS, INC., MINNEAPOLIS, MINN.
Catalog 111
Home Furnishing and Decoration Section 34
Levinson Mfg. Co., Jersey City, N. J.
Levy & Sons, M. E., Seattle, Wash.
Levy, Ralph M., New York, N. Y.
Lewis Bros. Co., Milwaukee, Wis.
Lewis, Co., Robert, Philadelphia, Pa.
Lewis-Geer Mfg. Co., Ypsilanti, Mich.
Lewis-Waller Mfg. Co., Utica, N. Y.
Lewisburg Chair Corp., Lewisburg, Pa.
Lexington Chair Co., Lexington, N. C.
Liberty Lamp & Shade Co., New York, N. Y.
Lieberman Bed Spring Co., Chicago, Ill.
Liffman, Julius, Los Angeles, Cal.
Lima Quality Cushion Co., Lima, O.
LIMBERT COMPANY, CHARLES P., HOLLAND, MICH.
Catalog 281
Home Furnishing and Decoration Section 39
Lincoln Company, Inc., Marion, Va.
Lincoln Furn. Co., Philadelphia, Pa.
Lincoln Furn. Mfg. Co., Cleveland, O.
LINCOLN FURNITURE MANUFACTURING CO., MARION, VA. 362-363
Lindemann & Hoverson Co., A. J., Milwaukee, Wis.
Linn Furn. Co., Cleveland, O.
Little-Jones Co., New York, N. Y.
Little Rock Furn. Mfg. Co., Little Rock, Ark.
Livermore Chair Co., Livermore, Ky.
Lloyd Mfg. Co., Menominee, Mich.
Lloyd Textiles, Inc., Chicago, Ill.
Lobdel & Emery Mfg. Co., Onaway, Mich.
Lock Haven Chair Corp., Lock Haven, Pa.
Loeblein & Dietzel, Inc., Cincinnati, O.
Logan Company, Louisville, Ky.
Logan Furn. Co., Gallipolis, O.
Logan Furniture Co., Logan, O.
Lomax Carpet Mills, Jos., Phila., Pa.
Lombard, F. W., Ashburnham, Mass.
Long Furn. Co., Hanover, Pa.
Long Valley Rug Mills, Mertztown, Pa.
Longbeach Sash & Door Co., Longbeach, Cal.
Lorberbaum & Co., Israel, Brooklyn, N. Y.
Lord Lumber Co., La Grange, Ill.
Los Angeles Period Furn. Mfg. Co., Los Angeles, Cal.
Los Angeles Uph. Co., Los Angeles, Cal.
Loth Stove Co., W. J., Waynesboro, Va.
Louck & Hill Co. Inc., Richmond, Ind.
Louisville Bedding Co., Louisville, Ky.
LOUISVILLE CHAIR AND FURNITURE CO., LOUISVILLE, KY 396 (Z2)
Lubke Sons Co., Fred, Cincinnati, O.
LUCE FURNITURE SHOPS, GRAND RAPIDS, MICH.
Furniture Shops Catalog 160-161
Furniture Shops Home Furnishing and Decoration Section 16
Luce Furniture Company Catalog 156-159
Michigan Chair Company Catalog 162-163
Ludlow & Minor, New York, N. Y.
Ludwig, A., New York, N. Y.
Ludwig, H., Buffalo, N. Y.
LUGER FURNITURE COMPANY, MINNEAPOLIS, MINN.
Catalog 399 (Z3)
Home Furnishing and Decoration Section 35
Luminier Company, New York, N. Y.
Lussky, White & Coolidge Co., Chicago, Ill.
Lutz Mfg. Co., John J., Loudon, Tenn.
Luxury Furn. Co., Grand Rapids, Mich.
Lycoming Furn. Co., Hughesville, Pa.
Lycoming Uph. Co., Montgomery, Pa.
Lynch Sales Co., Cleveland, O.
Lynch Sales Co., Jos. P., Grand Rapids, Mich.
Lyon Carpet Co., Lowell, Mass.
Lyon Metallic Mfg. Co., Aurora, Ill.

M

McCain J. H., Alexandria, La.
McClellan Mfg. Co., Los Angeles, Cal.
McCANN-PLEAS CO., SAN FRANCISCO, CALIF.
See Period Cabinet Mfg. Co 307
McCONNELL, T. F., HOLLYWOOD, CALIF.
See Period Cabinet Mfg. Co 307
McCoy Couch Furn. Mfg. Co., Benton, Ark.
McCracken, George M., Danville, Ill.
McDaniell Furn. Mfg. Co., Warsaw, Ky.
McDonald Co., C. E., Tacoma, Wash.
McDonald Moulding Co., Chicago, Ill.
McDougal Company, Frankfort, Ind.
McDowell, David, Philadelphia, Pa.
McDowell Furn. Co., Marion, N. C.
McEntire Brothers, Topeka, Kansas.
McKee Refrigerator Co., Brooklyn, N. Y.
McKim & Cochran Furn. Co., Madison, Ind.
McLelland Buck & Wise Co., La Porte, Ind.
McLeod & Smith, Minneapolis, Minn.
McLeod Furn. Co., Laurel, Miss.
McMahen Co., Wm., H., Philadelphia, Pa.
McMurtry Mfg. Co., Denver, Colo.
McNeill Chair Co., Sheboygan, Wis.
Macco, Inc., New York, N. Y.
Macc & Co., L. H., New York, N. Y.
Macey Company, Grand Rapids, Mich.
Macon Lumber & Mfg. Co., Macon, Ga.
MADDEN MFG. CO., JOHN J., INDIANAPOLIS, IND. 120
Maddox Table Co., Jamestown, N. Y.
Made Well Chair Co., Sheboygan, Wis.
MAGES COMPANY, GEORGE C., CHICAGO, ILL. 80
Magee Carpet Co., Broomburg, Pa.
Magic City Furn. & Mfg. Co. Inc., Birmingham, Ala.
Magner Furniture Co., Brooklyn, N. Y.
Mahogany Association, New York, N. Y.
Mahon Company, New York, N. Y.
Mahoney Chair Company, Gardner, Mass.
Maibrunn Company, New York, N. Y.
Maiden Chair Company, Maiden, N. C.
Maihlin-Walters Co., Milwaukee, Wis.
Maine Mfg. Co., Nashua, N. H.
Majestic Baby Carriage Co., New York, N. Y.
Majestic Chair Co., Brooklyn, N. Y.
Majestic Steel Cabinet Co., Chicago, Ill.
Majestic Stove Co., St. Louis, Mo.
MALLEABLE IRON RANGE COMPANY, BEAVER DAM, WIS.
Catalog 73
Home Furnishing and Decoration Section 35
Malleable Steel Range Mfg. Co., South Bend, Ind.
MALLEN & COMPANY, H. Z., CHICAGO, ILL. 121
Mallen, E., Los Angeles, Cal.
Malley-Long Furn. Mfg. Co., San Francisco, Cal.
Mallin Brothers, New York, N. Y.
Mallinson Imp. Co., Geo. E., New York, N. Y.
Manchester Furn. Co., Manchester, O.
Manhattan Bed Co., Brooklyn, N. Y.
Manhattan Mantel Co., Brooklyn, N. Y.
Manhattan Rubber Mfg. Co., New York, N. Y.
Manhattan Spring Bed Co., New York, N. Y.
Manhattan Uph. Co., New York, N. Y.
Manistee Mfg. Co., Manistee, Mich.
Mann, Adam, Brooklyn, N. Y.
Manne Uph. Co., L., St. Louis, Mo.
Manthey Bros., Stockton, Calif.
Manufacturers' Agency, Inc., St. Louis, Mo.
MAPLE
See Northern Hard Maple Manufacturers 388-389
Marble & Shattuck Chair Co., Cleveland, O.
Marble Chair Co., B. L., Bedford, O.
Marer & Co., Arthur A., Chicago, Ill.
Marion Stove Co., Marion, Ind.
Markle Mfg. Co., Markle, Ind.
Marietta Chair Co., Marietta, O.
Marsh Furniture Co., High Point, N. C.
MARSHALL FIELD & COMPANY, WHOLESALE. See Field & Company, Wholesale, Marshall.
MARSTALL FURNITURE CO., INC., HENDERSON, KY 397 (Z2)
MARTIN, H. D., HIGH POINT, N. C., AND GREENSBORO, N. C.
See Mersman Bros. Corporation 216-221
MARTIN, JESS L., DETROIT, MICHIGAN
See Chicago Mirror and Art Glass Co 395 (Z3)
Martin's Merc. Co., Chicago, Ill.
Martinsville Chair & Mfg. Co., Martinsville, Va.
Marvel Furn. Co., Jamestown, N. Y.
Marvel Uph. Co. Inc., Brooklyn, N. Y.
Mascot Stove Mfg. Co., Chattanooga, Tenn.
Masland & Sons, C. H., Philadelphia, Pa.
Mason Art, Inc., New York, N. Y.
Mason Mfg. Co., Paris, Maine.
Mason Mfg. Co., Paris, Ky.
Mastercraft Reed Corp., New York, N. Y.
Master Parlor Furn. Co., Chicago, Ill.
Matot, Duff A., Chicago, Ill.
Maurer & Sons Co., F. W., Phila., Pa.
Maxwell Company, E. A., Chicago, Ill.
Maxwell-Ray Company, Milwaukee, Wis.
Mayhew Company, Milwaukee, Wis.
Mayhew Shops, Inc., Milwaukee, Wis.
Mebane Bedding Co., Mebane, N. C.
Mebane Iron Bed Co., Mebane, N. C.
MECHANICS FURNITURE CO., ROCKFORD, ILL.
Desks, Cabinets and Highboys 155
Dining Room Furniture 302
Mecky Company, A., Philadelphia, Pa.
Meibach Chair Co., Brooklyn, N. Y.
Meier & Pohlmann Co., St. Louis, Mo.
Meilahn Brothers, Chicago, Ill.
Meinecke Mfg. Co., Milwaukee, Wis.
Meloy Mfg. Co., Shelbyville, Ind.
MEMPHIS FURNITURE MANUFACTURING CO., MEMPHIS, TENN.
Catalog 303
Home Furnishing and Decoration Section 36
Mentrup Co., C. J., New York, N. Y.
Mentzer-Read Co., Grand Rapids, Mich.
Merriam, Hall & Co., Leominster, Mass.
Mersereau Metal Bed Co., Jersey City, N. J.
MERSMAN BROTHERS CORPORATION, CELINA, OHIO
Catalog 216-221
Home Furnishing and Decoration Section 39-41
Metal Furn. Co., Evansville, Ind.
Metal Kitchen Cabinet & Table Co., Kalamazoo, Mich.
Metal Office Furn. Co., Grand Rapids, Mich.
Metal Stamping Corp., Streator, Ill.
Metropolitan Chair Co., Hartford, Conn.
Metropolitan Furn. Mfg. Co., San Francisco, Cal.
Metropolitan Picture Frame Co., Chicago, Ill.
Metz Furn. Co., J. L., Chicago, Ill.
Metzger Mattress Co., Atlanta, Ga.
Miami Cabinet Co., Middletown, O.
Michaelson Furn. Co., Geo. J., Rochester, N. Y.
Michigan Cedarcraft Co., Greenbush, Mich.
MICHIGAN CHAIR COMPANY, GRAND RAPIDS, MICH.
(Division of the Luce Furniture Shops) 162-163
Michigan Seating Co., Jackson, Mich.
Michigan Stove Co., Detroit, Mich.
Mid-City Uph. Furn. Co., Chicago, Ill.
Midland Wood Products Co., Chicago, Ill.
Midwest Fibre Co., Sheboygan, Wis.
Midwest Furn. & Chair Co., St. Joseph, Mo.
Midwest Glass Co., Cincinnati, O.
Milan Furn. Mfg. Co., Milan, Ind.
Milch, D., New York, N. Y.
Miller & Co., Ed., Meriden, Conn.
Miller & Company, John, New York, N. Y.
Miller & Goldberg Co., Boston, Mass.
Miller Cabinet Co., Rochester, N. Y.
Miller Cabinet Shops, Chicago, Ill.
MILLER CLOCK COMPANY, HERMAN, ZEELAND, MICH. 144
MILLER FURNITURE CO., HERMAN, ZEELAND, MICH.
Catalog 145
Home Furnishing and Decoration Section 36
Miller, Jacob D., Brooklyn, N. Y.
MILLER, M. I., NEW YORK, N. Y.
See Mersman Bros. Corporation 216-221
Mills & Gibb Corp., New York, N. Y.
MILNE CHAIR COMPANY, CHATTANOOGA, TENN. 207
Milwaukee Bedding Co., Milwaukee, Wis.
Milwaukee Woven Wire Works, Milwaukee, Wis.
Minerva Uph. Co., Inc., New York, N. Y.
Minneapolis Deck Mfg. Co., Minneapolis, Minn.
Minneapolis Furn. Co., Minneapolis, Minn.
Minneapolis Supply Co., Minneapolis, Minn.
MINTURN BROS., KANSAS CITY, MO.
See Mersman Bros. Corpn 216-221
Mission Foundry & Stove Works, San Francisco, Cal.
Mississippi Valley Furn. Co., Memphis, Tenn.
Mississippi Valley Furn. Mfg. Co., Greenwood, Miss.
Missouri Furn. Co., St. Louis, Mo.
Mitnick Uph. Co., Newark, N. J.
Model Mills Co., Philadelphia, Pa.
Model Uph. Co., New York, N. Y.
Modern Parlor Furn. Co., Chicago, Ill.
Modern Reed & Willow Furn. Co., Boston, Mass.
Modern Uph. Co., Newark, N. J.
Moe-Bridges Co., Milwaukee, Wis.
Moffitt Furn. & Uph. Co., Lexington, N. C.
Mogul Wagon Mfg. Co., Hopkinsville, Ky.
Mohawk Carpet Mills, Amsterdam, N. Y.
Mohlhenrich Furn. Co., Baltimore, Md.
Monarch Furn. Co., Jamestown, N. Y.
Mondshun, Louis, New Orleans, La.
MONITOR FURNITURE CO., EVANSVILLE, IND. 288-289
Monitor Furn. Co., Jamestown, N. Y.
Montag Stove Works, Portland, Ore.
Montauk Rug Mills, Inc., Brooklyn, N. Y.
Montgomery Lounge Co., Montgomery, Pa.
Montgomery Mfg. Co., H. J., Silver Creek, N. Y.
Montgomery Table & Desk Works, Montgomery, Pa.
Montour Furn. Co., Montoursville, Pa.
Moore Brothers Co., Joliet, Ill.
MOORE CO., J. H., TULSA, OKLAHOMA
See Chicago Mirror and Art Glass Co 395 (Z3)
Moore Company, Muncie, Ind.
Mooresville Furn. Co., Mooresville, Ind.
Mooresville Furn. Co., Mooresville, N. C.
Morgan Furn. Mfg. Co., Dayton, Tenn.
MORGANTON FURNITURE COMPANY, MORGANTON, N. C. 304
Morimura Bros. Inc., New York, N. Y.
Morrell Mills, Philadelphia, Pa.
Morrell's Reed & Rattan Co., Newfield, N. J.
Morris & Bendien, New York, N. Y.
Morris & Sons, L., Athol, Mass.
Morris, Edward S., Los Angeles, Cal.
MORRIS, R. C., KERNERSVILLE, N. C.
See Caldwell Furniture Co 398 (Z1)
Morristown Chair Co., Morristown, Tenn.
Morton Furn. Mfg. Co., Berkeley, Cal.
Mosaic Shade Co., Chicago, Ill.
Moser-Royster Furn. Co., Lynchburg, Va.
Moss Rose Mfg. Co., Philadelphia, Pa.
Mothguard Laboratories, New York, N. Y.
Mott Mfg. Co., Adrian, Mich.
Mottville Chair Works, Mottville, N. Y.
Moulton Co., C. W. H., Somerville, Mass.
Mount Airy Chair Co., Mount Airy, N. C.
Mount Airy Furn. Co., Mount Airy, N. C.
Mount Airy Mantel & Table Co., Mount Airy, N. C.
Mount Airy Mirror Mfg. Co., Mount Airy, N. C.
Mt. Wolf Furn. Co., Mt. Wolf, Pa.
MOUNTVILLE WOOD PRODUCTS CO., INC., MOUNTVILLE, PA 412 (Z1)
Mouw, Inc., Andy, Grand Rapids, Mich.
Muecke & Sons Co., Macon, Ga.
Mueller Bros. Art & Mfg. Co., Chicago, Ill.
Mueller Furn. Co., Grand Rapids, Mich.
Muller Furn. Mfg. Co., New Orleans, La.
Munago Company, Chicago, Ill.
Muncy Furn. Co., Muncy, Pa.
Murdock & Wilcek, Los Angeles, Cal.
Murphy Chair Co., Owensboro, Ky.
Murphy Door Bed of Chicago, Chicago, Ill.
Murphy Mfg. Co., Tacoma, Wash.
Muscoda Mfg. Co., Muscoda, Wis.
MUTSCHLER BROTHERS COMPANY, NAPPANEE, IND. 74
Mutual Furn. Co., Miamisburg, O.
Mutual Lamp Mfg. Co., New York, N. Y.
Myers-Spalti Mfg. Co., Houston, Tex.
MYERS & SCHWARTZ, SAN FRANCISCO AND LOS ANGELES, CALIF.
See Mersman Bros. Corporation 216-221
Myrtle Desk Co., High Point, N. C.

N

Nachman Company, Chicago, Ill.
Nachtegel Mfg. Co., Grand Rapids, Mich.

Nashville Chair Co., Nashville, Tenn.
Nathan & Co., P., New York, N. Y.
National Cabinet & Furn. Mfg. Co., Los Angeles, Cal.
National Chair Co., Inc., Rockford, Ill.
National Chair Co., St. Louis, Mo.
National Chair Co., Brooklyn, N. Y.
National Feather & Pillow Co., Nashville, Tenn.
National Fibre Reed Co., Aurora, Ind.
National Fumigation Sales Co., Chicago, Ill.
National Furn. & Bedding Co., Leavenworth, Kan.
National Furn. Co., Jamestown, N. Y.
NATIONAL FURNITURE COMPANY, MOUNT AIRY, N. C. 124
National Furn. Mfg. Co., Evansville, Ind.
National Mattress Co., Huntington, W. Va.
National Mattress Co., Lynchburg, Va.
National Mirror Co., Buffalo, N. Y.
National Mirror Works, Rockford, Ill.
National Parlor Suite Co., Brooklyn, N. Y.
National Screen & Mfg. Co., Cincinnati, O.
National Spring & Wire Co., Grand Rapids, Mich.
National Tapestry Co., Philadelphia, Pa.
National Uph. Furn. Co., Philadelphia, Pa.
National Uph. Co., Oakland, Cal.
National Uph. Co., High Point, N. C.
Neidhoefer Company, Milwaukee, Wis.
Neuer Glass Co., H., Cincinnati, O.
New England Bedding Co., Boston, Mass.
New England Cabinet Co., Somerville, Mass.
New England Reed Co., Boston, Mass.
New Farson Mfg. Co., Chester, Pa.
New Hampshire Bedding Co., Manchester, N. H.
New Haven Clock Co., New Haven, Conn.
New Orleans Chair Co., New Orleans, La.
New Orleans Furn. Mfg. Co., New Orleans, La.
New Waterford Furn. Co., New Waterford, O.
New Way Ref. Co., Greenville, O.
New York Bed Spring Mfg. Co., Detroit, Mich.
New York Chair Co., New York, N. Y.
New York Furn. & Bedding Mfg. Co., San Francisco, Cal.
New York Furn. Ex. Ass'n., New York, N. Y.
New York Lamp Shade Co., New York, N. Y.
New York Mattress Co., Boston, Mass.
Newark Ohio Furn. Co., Newark, O.
Newberry Bros. & Covell, Dunn, N. C.
Newcomb Mfg. Co., F. J., New York, N. Y.
Newcombe & Son, E. A., Greenfield, Mass.
Newman & Sons, David, Philadelphia, Pa.
Newton Furn. Co., Newton, N. C.
Newton Lumber Co., Pueblo, Colo.
Niagara Reed Craft Furn. Co., Niagara Falls, N. Y.
Nichols, Geo. & Co., New York, N. Y.
Nichols & Cox Lumber Co., Grand Rapids, Mich.
Nichols & Stone Co., Gardner, Mass.
Nicholson Furn. Co., K., Chase City, Va.
NICHOLSON-KENDLE FURNITURE CO., HUNTINGTON, W. VA. 269
NEILSON SALES CO., A. T., PHILADELPHIA, PA.
See Caldwell Furniture Co. 398 (Z1)
Niemann & Company, H. C., Chicago, Ill.
Niemann Table Co., Chicago, Ill.
Nonnast & Sons Co., Louis F., Chicago, Ill.
Nonnenbacher & Co., New York, N. Y.
Nordwald Co., H., El Paso, Tex.
Norfolk Mattress Co., Norfolk, Va.
NORQUIST CO., A. C., JAMESTOWN, N. Y. 305
North Dighton Stove Co., Taunton, Mass.
North Star Furn. Co., Evansville, Ind.
North State Furn. Mfg. Co., Statesville, N. C.
North Vernon Lumber Mills, North Vernon, Ind.
Northern Chair Co., Cadillac, Mich.
Northern Furn. Co., Sheboygan, Wis.
NORTHERN HARD MAPLE MANUFACTURERS, OSHKOSH, WIS. 388-389
Northern Mfg. Co., Chicago, Ill.
Northern Picture Frame Co., Chicago, Ill.
NORTHFIELD COMPANY, SHEBOYGAN, WIS.
Catalog 122-123
Home Furnishing and Decoration Section 37
Northwestern Art Shade Co., Chicago, Ill.
Northwestern Cabinet Co. Inc., Burlington, Iowa
Northwestern Chair Co., Tacoma, Wash.
Northwestern Reed & Fibre Co., Minneapolis, Minn.
Northwestern Uph. Co., Minneapolis, Minn.
NORTON SALES SERVICE, C. S., CHICAGO, ILL. 374
Norwalk Uph. Co., Norwalk, O.
Norwood, Calef & Co., Keene, N. H.
Novelty Wood Works, Inc., Union City, Pa.
Nurre Glass Co., Memphis, Tenn.
Nurre, Henry, Cincinnati, O.
Nurre Mirror Plate Co., Bloomington, Ind.
Nutting, Wallace, Inc., Ashland, Mass.
Nypenn Furn. Co., Warren, Pa.

O

O'Brien Furn. Mfg. Co., Los Angeles, Cal.
O'Hearn Mfg. Co., Gardner, Mass.
O'Keefe & Merrit Co., Los Angeles, Cal.
O'Leary, Thos. J., Oakland, Cal.
O'Mara Parlor Frame Co., Chicago, Ill.
O'Neil & Graves Co., San Francisco, Cal.
Oak City Chair Co., Seymour, Tenn.
Oak City Furn. Co., Tuscaloosa, Ala.
Oak Furn. Co., N. Wilkesboro, N. C.
OAK SERVICE BUREAU,
Hardwood Manufacturers Institute, MEMPHIS, TENN. 384-385
Occidental Furn. Mfg. Co., San Francisco, Cal.
Odin Stove Mfg. Co., Erie, Pa.
Ohio Art Company, Bryan, O.
Ohio Chair Co., Williamsburg, O.
Ohio Mattress Co., Cleveland, O.
Ohio State Stove Mfg. Co., Columbus, O.
Ohio Stove Co., Portsmouth, O.
O. K. Stove & Range Company, Louisville, Ky.
Oklahoma Furn. Mfg. Co., Oklahoma City, Okla.
Oklahoma Mattress Mfg. Co., Oklahoma City, Okla.
Oklahoma Spring Bed Mfg. Co., Oklahoma City, Okla.
Olbrich & Golbeck Co., Chicago, Ill.
Old Colony Chair Co., Rockford, Ill.
Old Colony Furn. Co., Boston, Mass.
Old Dominion Table Works, Portsmouth, Va.
Old Hickory Furn. Co., Martinsville, Ind.
Olive & Myers Mfg. Co., Dallas, Tex.
Olive Stove Works, Rochester, Pa.
Oliver Furn. Co., Adrian, Mich.
Oneidacraft, Inc., Oneida, N. Y.
Onondaga Bed Mfg. Co., Syracuse, N. Y.
Orchard & Wilhelm Furn. Factory, Ralston, Neb.
Orchard & Wilhelm Mattress Co., Omaha, Neb.
Orinoco Furn. Co., Columbus, Ind.
Orleans Cabinet Co., Orleans, Ind.
Orpin Desk Co., Boston, Mass.
Orrville Bedding Co., Orrville, O.
Orsenigo Co., Long Island City, N. Y.
Osiason, J., Fall River, Mass.
OSTERMAN, LOUIS, BROOKLYN, N. Y.
See Chicago Mirror and Art Glass Co 395 (Z3)
Ottawa Furn. Co., Holland, Mich.
Owen Mfg. Co., Logan, Ohio.
Owen Shops Co., Cleveland, O.
Oxford Buggy Co., Oxford, N. C.

P

PAALMAN FURNITURE COMPANY, GRAND RAPIDS, MICH. 400 (Z3)
P. & E. Furn. Co., Montoursville, Pa.
Pacific Chair Co., Seattle, Wash.
Pacific Fibre Furn. Co., Seattle, Wash.
Pacific Furn. Mfg. Co., Tacoma, Wash.
Pacific States Bedding & Furn. Co., Los Angeles, Cal.
Pahl & Co., A. F., Milwaukee, Wis.
Paiget-Donnelly Co., Grand Rapids, Mich.
Palmer & Embury Mfg. Co., New York, N. Y.
Palmer & Hardin, Louisville, Ky.
Palmer & Son, A. E., Adrian, Mich.
Palmer Bros. Co., New London, Conn.
Palmer Co., I. E., Middletown, Conn.
Pan-American Furn. Factory, New Orleans, La.
Paoli Furn. Co., Paoli, Ind.
Paramount Uph. Co., Brooklyn, N. Y.
Paris Mfg. Co., Paris, Me.
Park Furn. Co., Rushville, Ind.
Parker Co., Chas., Meriden, Conn.
Parker-Young Co., Boston, Mass.
Parks Ball Bearing Mch. Co., Cincinnati, O.
Parlor Furn. & Mattress Co., Fremont, Neb.
Parlor Furn. Mfg. Co., Cedar Rapids, Iowa
Patching & Co., John F., New York, N. Y.
Patchogue-Plymouth Mills Corp., New York, N. Y.
Patoka Furn. Mfg. Co., Huntingburg, Ind.
Patterson Carpet Mills, Philadelphia, Pa.
PATTON-MC CRAY COMPANY, BLUFFTON, IND. 306
Paul, Otto, Milwaukee, Wis.
Peabody Sons, Henry W., New York, N. Y.
Peacock Parlor Furn. Works, Chicago, Ill.
Pearce & Co., J. E., New York, N. Y.
Pearce & Son, S. K., Gardner, Mass.
Pearce Furn. Mfg. Co., Boston, Mass.
Pearson & Co., Fred, Philadelphia, Pa.
PECK & HILLS FURNITURE COMPANY, CHICAGO, ILL.
Catalog 392
Home Furnishing and Decoration Section 45
Peckham Furn. Co., Lowell, Mich.
Pee Dee Furn. Co., Hartsville, S. C.
Peerless Furn. Co., Shippensburg, Pa.
Peerless Mfg. Co., Louisville, Ky.
Peerless Mattress Co., Lexington, N. C.
Peerless Spring Co., Chicago, Ill.
Peerless Uph. Co., Boston, Mass.
Peninsula Stove Co., Detroit, Mich.
Penn. Furn. Co., Conneautville, Pa.
Penn Furn. Mfg. Co., Montgomery, Pa.
PENN TABLE COMPANY, HUNTINGTON, W. VA. 268
Penna. Axminster Carpet Corp., Philadelphia, Pa.
Penning Reed Co., Bridgeport, Conn.
Pennsylvania Furn. Co., York, Pa.
Pennsylvania Textile Mills, New York, N. Y.
Pensacola Mattress Co., Pensacola, Fla.
Peoria Lounge & Mattress Co., Peoria, Ill.
Perfection Bed Spring Co., Mansfield, O.
Perfection Mfg. Co., St. Louis, Mo.
Perfection Mattress & Spring Co., Birmingham, Ala.
Perfection Parlor Furn. Co., Chicago, Ill.
Perfection Rest-Easy Mattress Co., Kalamazoo, Mich.
Perfection Stove Co., Cleveland, O.
PERIOD CABINET MANUFACTURING CO., NEW ALBANY, IND.
Catalog 307
Home Furnishing and Decoration Section 38
Periodical Publishing Co., Grand Rapids, Mich.
Perrin, Chas. O., Pasadena, Cal.
Persian Rug Mfg. Co., New York, N. Y.
Peters Furn. Co., Jos., St. Louis, Mo.
Peters Furn. Co., Juneau, Wis.
PETERSON ART FURNITURE CO., FARIBAULT, MINN. 164
Petersen Woodcraft Co., St. Paul, Minn.
Pettit Feather & Bedding Co., Portland, Ore.
Pharaoh Drapery Co., New York, N. Y.
Phenix Co., Leroy C., Los Angeles, Cal.
Phenix Furn. Co., Warren, Pa.
Philadelphia Carpet Co., Phila., Pa.
Philadelphia Excelsior Co., Phila., Pa.
Philadelphia Pile Fabric Co., Phila., Pa.
Philadelphia Table Co., Phila., Pa.
Philadelphia Tapestry Mills, Phila., Pa.
Phillips & Butteroff Mfg. Co., Nashville, Tenn.
PHOENIX CHAIR COMPANY, SHEBOYGAN, WIS.
Catalog 222-235
Home Furnishing and Decoration Section 42-44
Phoenix Company, Chicago, Ill.
Phoenix Furn. Co., Grand Rapids, Mich.
Phoenix Furn. Corp., Cambria, Va.
Phoenix Trimming Co., Chicago, Ill.
Pick, Richard, Mfg. Co., Chicago, Ill.
Pico Bedding Co., Los Angeles, Cal.
Pierce & Son, S. K., Brooklyn, N. Y.
Pimes & Co., M., Baltimore, Md.
Pioneer Appliance Co., Chicago, Ill.
Pittsburgh Iron Folding Bed Co., Pittsburgh, Pa.
Pittsburgh Plate Glass Co., Pittsburgh, Pa.
Plail Bros. Co., Wayland, N. Y.
Platt & Co., M., Philadelphia, Pa.
Plymouth Foundry Co., Plymouth, Mass.
Plymouth Furn. Co., Plymouth, Wis.
Poeltl John, Davenport, Iowa
Pokorny & Co., St. Louis, Mo.
Pollock-Huston Co., Philadelphia, Pa.
Pooley Furn. Co., Philadelphia, Pa.
Porter Mattress Co., Tulsa, Okla.
Porter Mirror & Glass Co., Fort Smith, Ark.
Portland Furn. Mfg. Co., Portland, Ore.
Portland Stove Foundry Co., Portland, Me.
Portsmouth Stove & Range Co., Portsmouth, O.
POSTON MANUFACTURING CO., B. C., CHILLICOTHE, O. 401 (Z3)
Poulson Co., Chas. W., New York, N. Y.
Powell, Wm. M., Rochester, N. Y.
Prasser Furn. Co., Milwaukee, Wis.
Pratt Mfg. Co., Coldwater, Mich.
Premier Bed & Spring Co., San Francisco, Cal.
Premier Cabinet Corp., Jamestown, N. Y.
Premier Carpet Co., Los Angeles, Cal.
Premier Furn. Co., Rockford, Ill.
Premier Furn. Mfg. Co., High Point, N. C.
Premier Stove Co., Belleville, Ill.
Premier Uph. Co. Inc., Boston, Mass.
Prime Uph. Co., Boston, Mass.
Primrose Tapestry Co., Philadelphia, Pa.
Pritchett-Powers Co., Grand Rapids, Mich.
Progress Bedding Co., Detroit, Mich.
Progress Furn. Mfg. Co., Los Angeles, Cal.
Progress Stove & Range Co., Louisville, Ky.
Progressive Furn. Co., Toledo, O.
Progressive Table Mfg. Co., Brooklyn, N. Y.
Prufrock-Litton Furn. Co., St. Louis, Mo.
Pulaski Furn. Co., Pulaski, Va.
Pulaski Mirror Co., Pulaski, Va.
PULLMAN COUCH COMPANY, INC., CHICAGO, ILL.
Catalog 128-129
Home Furnishing and Decoration Section 46
Pullman Metal Specialties Co., Philadelphia, Pa.
Puritan Parlor Frame Co., Boston, Mass.
Pyramid Furn. Mfg. Co., Los Angeles, Cal.

Q

Quad Stove Mfg. Co., Columbus, O.
Quakertown Stove Works, Quakertown, Pa.
Quality Furn. Co., Evansville, Ind.
Quality Lamp & Shade Co., Chicago, Ill.
Quality Mattress Co., Rochester, Pa.
Quality Metal Bed Co., Chicago, Ill.
Quality Stove & Range Co., Belleville, Ill.
Queen City Furn. Co., Gadsden, Ala.
Quincy Stove Mfg. Co., Quincy, Ill.

R

Raedlein Basket Co., Chicago, Ill.
RAGAN, CHARLES E., HIGH POINT, N. C.
See Statesville Furniture Co. 346
Rainer Furn. Mfg. Co., Seattle, Wash.
Ramsdell & Co., L. B., Gardner, Mass.
Ramseur Furn. Co., Ramseur, N. C.
Ramsey Furn. Co., Bassett, Va.
Randall Co., A. L., Chicago, Ill.
Randall Mattress Co., Cleveland, O.
Randleman Mfg. Co., Randleman, N. C.
Randolph Furn. Works, Randolph, N. Y.
Ranney Refrigerator Co., Grand Rapids, Mich.
Rastetter & Sons, Louis, Fort Wayne, Ind.
Rattan Furn. Mfg. Co., Seattle, Wash.
Rattan Mfg. Co., New Haven, Conn.
Read & Son, E. C., Philadelphia, Pa.
Reading Stove Works, Reading, Pa.
Readsboro Chair Co., Readsboro, Vt.
Reale Mfg. Co., A., New York, N. Y.
Red Lion Furn. Co., Red Lion, Pa.
Red Wing Furn. Co., Red Wing, Minn.
Red Wing Mfg. Co., Red Wing, Minn.
Reddinger Mfg. Co., P. H., Evansville, Ind.
Reece-Handley Co., J. W., Shelbyville Ind.
Reed, Guy A., New York, N. Y.
Reed Mfg. Co., Springfield, O.
Reedcraft Co., Los Angeles, Cal.
Regent Shops, New York, N. Y.
Regent Stove Co., Wyandotte, Mich.
Regina Corp., Rahway, N. J.
Reifsnieder & Son, John J., Philadelphia, Pa.
Reinthal & Newman, New York, N. Y.
Reischmann Chair Co., New York, N. Y.
Reischmann Co., New York, N. Y.
Reliable Furn. Mfg. Co., Chicago, Ill.
Reliable Metal Bed Co., Brooklyn, N. Y.
Reliable Stove Co., Cleveland, O.
Reliable Table Co., Brooklyn, N. Y.
Rembrandt Lamp Corp., Chicago, Ill.
Republic Stove & Mfg. Co., Cleveland, O.
RETAILERS' SERVICE BUREAU, MINNEAPOLIS, MINN. 413 (Z1)
Reuter, William, New York, N. Y.
Revene Clock Co., Cincinnati, O.
Rex Furn. Co., Chicago, Ill.
Rhinelander Refrigerator Co., Rhinelander, Wis.
Richards & Co., Benj., Winsted, Conn.
Richardson & Boynton Co., Chicago, Ill.
Richardson Bros., Inc., Sheboygan Fall, Wis.
Richmond Cabinet Co., Richmond, Ind.
Richmond Chair Factory, Richmond, Ind.
Richmond Furn. Mfg. Co., Los Angeles, Cal.
Richmond Mfg. Co., Wm. C., Peru, Ind.
Richmond Stove Co., Richmond, Va.
Richmond Wood Working Co., Richmond, Va.
Richter Furn. Co., New York, N. Y.
Ricker Bros., Delphis, O.
Riddell Furn. Co., Louisville, Ky.
Rieber & Co., L., Philadelphia, Pa.
Rilling Co., J. E., Milwaukee, Wis.
Rindsberger Mfg. Corp., Chicago, Ill.
Rinkenberger, Wm., Washington, Ill.
Ritchie & Co., Robert J., Phila., Pa.
Ritter & Bros. Inc., Wm., Phila., Pa.
Riverside Mfg. Co., Moultrie, Ga.
Roaring River Furn. Co., Roaring River, N. C.
Robbins Table Co., Owosso, Mich.

Roberti Bros., Los Angeles, Cal.
Roberts-Cohen Co., Huntington Park, Cal.
Roberts, John H., Los Angeles, Cal.
Roberts Mattress Co., Muskogee, Okla.
Robertson Co., H. P., Jamestown, N. Y.
Robertson Table Co., Topeka, Kansas.
Robinson-Clay Prod. Co., Akron, O.
Robinson's Furn. Mfg. Co., Los Angeles, Cal.
Rock Island Stove Co., Rock Island, Ill.
Rockford Cabinet Co., Rockford, Ill.
ROCKFORD CEDAR FURN. CO., ROCKFORD, ILL. 165
ROCKFORD CHAIR & FURNITURE CO., ROCKFORD, ILL. 308-313
ROCKFORD DESK CO., ROCKFORD, ILL.
See Rockford Furniture Co 314-321
ROCKFORD EAGLE FURNITURE CO., ROCKFORD, ILL. 166-167
ROCKFORD FURNITURE COMPANY, ROCKFORD, ILL.
Catalog 314-321
Home Furnishing and Decoration Section 48-49
Rockford Metal Specialty Co., Rockford, Ill.
ROCKFORD NATIONAL FURNITURE COMPANY, ROCKFORD, ILL 324-326
ROCKFORD PALACE FURNITURE COMPANY, ROCKFORD, ILL 322-323
ROCKFORD PEERLESS FURNITURE COMPANY, ROCKFORD, ILL 168-171
Rockford Republic Furn. Co., Rockford, Ill.
ROCKFORD STANDARD FURNITURE CO., ROCKFORD, ILL.
Catalog 327-331
Home Furnishing and Decoration Section 47
Rockford Superior Furn. Co., Rockford, Ill.
Rockford Wood Turning Co., Rockford, Ill.
Rockford World Furn. Co., Rockford, Ill.
Rockwood Stove Works, Rockwood, Tenn.
Rodgers-Wade Furn. Co., Paris, Tex.
Roesch Enamel Range Co., Belleville, Ill.
Rogers Co., Chas. P., New York, N. Y.
ROGERS, INC., M. H., NEW YORK, N. Y.
Catalog 90
Home Furnishing and Decoration Section 45
Rohmann Sons & Co., C. F., Brooklyn, N. Y.
Rood Furn. Co., V. J., Honeoye Falls, N. Y.
Roman Furn. Mfg. Co., Miami, Fla.
ROME COMPANY, INC., THE, CHICAGO, ILL. 70-71
Rome Furn. Co., Rome, Ga.
Rome Stove & Range Co., Rome, Ga.
Rominger Furn. Co., WinstonSalem, N. C.
Roos Mfg. Co., Chicago, Ill.
Roos Co. of Forest Park, Ed., Forest Park, Ill.
Rose Spring & Mattress Co., Memphis, Tenn.
Rose Co., Geo., New York, N. Y.
Roseberg Mfg. Co., J. H., Chicago, Ill.
Rothman, J., New York, N. Y.
Rowe Glass Co., James, St. Paul, Minn.
Roxbury Carpet Co., Boston, Mass.
Roxbury Carpet Co., New York, N. Y.
Royal Art Glass Co., New York, N. Y.
Royal Bedding Co., St. Louis, Mo.
Royal Blue Bed Spring Co., Cincinnati, O.
Royal Easy Chair Co., Sturgis, Mich.
Royal Furn. Mfg. Co., Goldsboro, N. C.
ROYAL MANTEL & FURNITURE CO., ROCKFORD, ILL. 332-334
Royal Metal Mfg. Co., Chicago, Ill.
Royal Parlor Furn. Co., Chicago, Ill.
Royal Uph. Furn. Co., Philadelphia, Pa.
Royal Uph. Co., Jamestown, N. Y.
Royall & Borden Mfg. Co., Goldsboro, N. C.
Royersford Spring Bed Co., Royersford, Pa.
Royle & Co., Geo., Philadelphia, Pa.
Royle & Pilkington Co., Mt. Holly, N. J.
Rublemann, G. A., St. Louis, Mo.
Rubloff Mfg. Co., Chicago, Ill.
Rule Co., Inc., Knoxville, Tenn.
Rumpf's Sons, Frederick, So. Langhone, Pa.
Runyan Mfg. Co., J. D., Jersey City, N. J.
Rushville Furn. Co., Rushville, Ind.
Rusk Mfg. Co., Hawkins, Wis.
RUSSELL, PIERRE L., INC., DALLAS, TEXAS
See Chicago Mirror and Art Glass Co 395 (Z3)
Russell & Sons, C. L., Keene, N. H.
Russian Antique Co., New York, N. Y.
RUSTIC HICKORY FURNITURE CO., LA PORTE, IND. 68
Rutland Mfg. Co., Rutland, Vt.
Ryan & McGahan, Brooklyn, N. Y.

S

S & E Mfg. Co., Gardner, Mass.
Sabel & Phillips, Brooklyn, N. Y.
Saco-Lowell Shops, Lowell, Mass.
Safran & Gluckman, New York, N. Y.
Sage-Fifield Lumber Co. Inc., Delavan, Wis.
Sager, W. D., Chicago, Ill.
Saginaw Furn. Shops, Inc., Saginaw, Mich.
Saginaw Mirror Works, Saginaw, Mich.
St. Charles Net & Hammock Co., St. Charles, Ill.
ST. JOHNS TABLE COMPANY, CADILLAC, MICH. 236
St. Louis Furn. Workers' Ass'n, St. Louis, Mo.
St. Paul Glass Co., St. Paul, Minn.
Salamanca Furn. Works, Salamanca, N. Y.
Salem Feltex Co., New York, N. Y.
Salisbury & Satterlee Co., Minneapolis, Minn.
Salisbury Bros. Furn. Co., Randolph, Vt.
Salt Lake Mattress & Mfg. Co., Salt Lake City, Utah
Salter Mfg. Co., Chicago, Ill.
Salterini, John B., New York, N. Y.
San Hygiene Uph. Co., Akron, O.
San Francisco Stove Works, San Francisco, Cal.
Sanford & Sons, Inc., Stephen, New York, N. Y.
Sani-Bedding Co., New Orleans, La.
Sanitary Bedding Co., Delray, Fla.
Sanitary Mattress Co., Minneapolis, Minn.
Sanitary Mattress Co., Youngstown, O.
Sanitary Ref. Co., Denver, Colo.
Sanitary Ref. Co., Fond du Lac, Wis.
Sargent's Sons, N. W., Booneville, N. Y.
Saroff, Moses, San Francisco, Cal.
SAUER, CHARLES P., NEW YORK, N. Y.
See Tillotson Furniture Corp 358
Sauer Co., Theo., New York, N. Y.
Saxe Co., S., Philadelphia, Pa.
Schaaf & Schnaus Mfg. Co., Jasper, Ind.
Schadt & Mathewson, Detroit, Mich.
Schantz Co., Wm. D., Allentown, Pa.
SCHEIBE, R. R., SOMERVILLE, MASS.
Catalog 414 (Z1)
Home Furnishing and Decoration Section 44
Scheid Sons Co., Jos., Cincinnati, O.
Schenck & Co., E. J., Allentown, Pa.
Schiefer Furn. Mfg. Co., National City, Cal.
Schilling Bros. Furn. Co., Kingston, N. Y.
Schiller Bros. Mfg. Co., South Bend, Ind.
Schilling Bros. Table Co., Kingston, N. Y.
Schilling Furn. Co., New York, N. Y.
Schimmel & Co., Faribault, Minn.
Schirmer Furn. Co., Cincinnati, O.
SCHLITTEN MICHAELS CO., NEW YORK, N. Y.
See Hellam Furniture Co 406-407 (Z1)
Schmidt Mfg. Co., H., Chicago, Ill.
Schmieg, Hungate & Kotzian, New York, N. Y.
Schmit Furn. Co., Cincinnati, O.
Schmitt & Henry Mfg. Co., Des Moines, Ia.
Schmoe Furn. Co., C. F., Shelbyville, Ind.
Schneider & Sons Co., Peter, New York, N. Y.
Schober, Charles, Philadelphia, Pa.
SCHOECK MFG. CO., INC., SYRACUSE, N. Y.
Catalog 415 (Z1)
Home Furnishing and Decoration Section 50
Schoonbeck Co., H., Grand Rapids, Mich.
Schottland, Benj., New York, N. Y.
Schultheis, Henry, New York, N. Y.
Schultz & Hirsch Co., Chicago, Ill.
Schulze & Van Stee Mfg. Co., Jamestown, N. Y.
Schumacher & Co., F., New York, N. Y.
Schutte Furn. Co., Geo. W., Cincinnati, O.
Schwabe, Ed. J., New York, N. Y.
Schwartz, C. E., Philadelphia, Pa.
Scranton Bedding Co., Scranton, Pa.
Scranton Stove Works, Scranton, Pa.
Scroll Art Studios, Bridgeport, Conn.
SEABURG MANUFACTURING COMPANY, JAMESTOWN, N. Y. 416 (Z1)
Sealy Mattress Co., St. Paul, Minn.
Sealy Mattress Co., Los Angeles, Cal.
Seeger Refrigerator Co., St. Paul, Minn.
Seely Mattress Co., Sugarland, Tex.
Segal Bros. Furn. Co., New York, N. Y.
Segal Co. Inc., Morris S., New York, N. Y.
Segal Mfg. Co., Long Island City, N. Y.
Seldner Co., Geo. L., Baltimore, Md.
Sellers & Sons Co., G. I., Elwood, Ind.
Seneca Furn. Corp., Randolph, N. Y.
Seng Co., Chicago, Ill.
Sextro Mfg. Co., Cincinnati, O.
Shanahan Furn. Co., Grand Rapids, Mich.
Shannon Ref. & But. Sup. Co., Atlanta, Ga.
Shannon Spring Bed Mfg. Co., Louisville, Ky.
Shapiro Bros. Uph. Co., Brooklyn, N. Y.
Shaw, I. M. & N., Newark, N. J.
Shaw Co., H. E., Grand Rapids, Mich.
Shaw Furn. Co., Cambridge, Mass.
Shaw-Walker Co., Muskegon, Mich.
Shear-Maddox Furn. Co., Grand Rapids, Mich.
Shearman Bros. Co., Jamestown, N. Y.
Sheboygan Chair Co., Sheboygan, Wis.
Sheboygan Fibre Furn. Co., Sheboygan, Wis.
Sheboygan Mattress Co., Sheboygan, Wis.
Sheboygan Novelty Co., Sheboygan, Wis.
Sheets Mfg. Co., Wapakoneta, O.
Sheffield Furn. Co., Sheffield, Pa.
Shelbyville Wardrobe Mfg. Co., Shelbyville, Ind.
Shelton Basket Co., Shelton, Conn.
Sherrill-Green Furn. Co., Statesville, N. C.
Shippensburg Cabinet Co., Shippensburg, Pa.
Shott Mfg. Co., Cincinnati, O.
SHOWERS BROTHERS COMPANY, BLOOMINGTON, IND.
Kitchen Cabinets Catalog 75
Radio Furniture Catalog 188
Bedroom and Dining Room Furniture Catalog ... 336-341
Showers Bros., Burlington, Iowa
SHREVE CHAIR COMPANY, INC., UNION CITY, PA 237
Shreveport Mattress Co., Shreveport, La.
Shucknell Co., Chicago, Ill.
Shuff, Samuel, Brooklyn, N. Y.
Shull Furn. Mfg. Co., Philadelphia, Pa.
Shull, Samuel, Philadelphia, Pa.
Sidway-Topliff Co., Washington, Pa.
Siebert Co., O. W., Gardner, Mass.
Sieghardt, Inc., F. J., New York, N. Y.
Sieling Furniture Co., Railroad, Pa.
Sigmon Furn. Mfg. Co., Oklahoma City, Okla.
SIKES CHAIR COMPANY, BUFFALO, N. Y. ... 238
Silver Creek Case Goods Co., Silver Creek, N. Y.
Silverman & Co., J. K., New York, N. Y.
Silvers Cabinet Co., Waterloo, Iowa
Simmons Co., New York, N. Y.
Simon & Co., J. R., New York, N. Y.
Simon Mattress Mfg. Co., San Francisco, Cal.
Simonds Co., Elgin A., Syracuse, N. Y.
Simplex Mfg. Co., Nashville, Tenn.
SIMPSON, WARREN T., BOSTON, MASS.
See Mersman Bros. Corporation 216-221
Sinclair-Allen Mfg. Corp., Mottville, N. Y.
Singer & Sons, M., New York, N. Y.
Singer, Inc., Boston, Mass.
Siskin, Harry, Los Angeles, Cal.
Slack, Bassnick & Co., New York, N. Y.
SKANDIA FURNITURE COMPANY, ROCKFORD, ILL.
Desks and Bookcases Catalog 172-185
Dining Room Furniture Catalog 342-345
SLIGH FURNITURE COMPANY, GRAND RAPIDS, MICH. 335
Sloane, W. & J., New York, N. Y.
Small & Scheloskey Co., Evansville, Ind.
Smith & Davis Mfg. Co., St. Louis, Mo.
Smith & Son, Wm. T., Philadelphia, Pa.
Smith & Sons Carpet Co., Alexander, New York, N. Y.
Smith & Sons Co., Oscar, Philadelphia, Pa.
Smith, B. J., Scranton, Pa.
SMITH, C. DEWEY, MONTCLAIR, N. J.
See Schoeck Manufacturing Co., Inc 415 (Z1)
SMITH, ROYAL B., JR., NEW YORK, N. Y.
See Schoeck Manufacturing Co., Inc 415 (Z1)
See also Period Cabinet Mfg. Co 307
Smith-Day Co., Baldwinsville, Mass.
Smith Mfg. Co., Fred O., New Vineyard, Me.
Smith Mfg. Co., Geo., Chicago, Ill.
Smokador Mfg. Co. Inc., New York, N. Y.
Snell Co., Charles W., Chicago, Ill.
Snidow-McWane Furn. Co., Lynchburg, Va.
Snyder Uph. Co., Berl C., Winston-Salem, N. C.
Sobel-Marx Furn. Co., Louisville, Ky.
Somersworth Foundry Co., Salmon Falls, N. H.
Somerville Stove Works, Somerville, N. J.
Sons-Cunningham Reed & Rattan Co., New York, N. Y
Soronow's Furn. Mfg. Co., Los Angeles, Cal.
Southard-Robertson Co., New York, N. Y.
Southern Chair Co., High Point, N. C.
Southern Couch Mfg. Co., Baltimore, Md.
Southern Desk & Table Co., Atlanta, Ga.
Southern Furn. Co., Burlington, N. C.
Southern Furn. Co., Texarkana, Tex.
Southern Furn. Market Ass'n, High Point, N. C.
Southern Mattress Co., Little Rock, Ark.
Southern Mirror Co., High Point, N. C.
Southern Stove Works, Evansville, Ind.
Southern Stove Works, Richmond, Va.
Southwestern Furn. Co., Tell City, Ind.
Souto Co., B., New York, N. Y.
Spach Wagon Works, J. C., Winston-Salem, N. C.
Spaulding & Sons Co., J., Rochester, N. Y.
Spear & Co., Pittsburgh, Pa.
Specialty Furn. Co., Evansville, Ind.
Specialty Mattress Co., Huntington, W. Va.
Spence-Baggs Stove Co., Martins Ferry, O.
Spencer-Cardinal Corp., Marion, Ind.
SPENCER-DUFFY COMPANY, INC., GRAND RAPIDS, MICH 125-127
Spiegel Furn. Co., Shelbyville, Ind.
Spiegel Furn. Mfg. Co., M. W., Chicago, Ill.
Spindler Co., Geo., Baltimore, Md.
Sprague & Carleton, Keene, N. H.
Sprague-Hathaway Studios, Inc., Somerville, Mass.
Spratt Chair Company, Atlanta, Ga.
Springfield Furn. Co., Springfield, Mo.
Springfield Mattress Co., Springfield, Ill.
Springfield Mattress Co., Springfield, Mass.
Stakmore Co., Inc., New York, N. Y.
Stamford Gas Stove Co., Stamford, Conn.
Standard Bedding Co., Milwaukee, Wis.
Standard Chair Co., Thomasville, N. C.
STANDARD CHAIR COMPANY, UNION CITY, PA. 239
Standard Furn. Co., Chicago, Ill.
Standard Furn. Co., Nashville, Tenn.
Standard Furn. Mfg. Co., Los Angeles, Cal.
Standard Furn. Mfg. Co., Baltimore, Md.
Standard Furn. Mfg. Co., St. Louis, Mo.
Standard Gas Equip. Corp., New York, N. Y.
Standard Lamp & Nov. Co., Chicago, Ill.
Standard Mfg. Co., Cambridge City, Ind.
Standard Mat. & Furn. Co., San Diego, Cal.
Standard Novelty Works, New York, N. Y.
Standard Parlor Frame Co. Inc., Boston, Mass.
Standard Ref. Co., Philadelphia, Pa.
Standard Screen Co., Chicago, Ill.
Standard Textile Prod. Co., New York, N. Y.
Standard Uph. Furn. Co., Detroit, Mich.
Standard Uph. Furn. Co., Philadelphia, Pa.
Standard Uph. Co., Los Angeles, Cal.
Standard Uph. Co., Boston, Mass.
Standardized Furn. Co., Grand Rapids, Mich.
Stanley Furn. Co., Bassett, Va.
Staples & Hanford Co., Newburgh, N. Y.
Star Bedding Co., St. Louis, Mo.
Star Foundry Co., Covington, Ky.
Star Furn. Co., Jamestown, N. Y.
Star Furn. Co., Lenoir, N. C.
Star Wood Turning Co., Chicago, Ill.
Starr Mattress Co., Oakland, Cal.
Starr Piano Co., Richmond, Ind.
STATESVILLE CHAIR COMPANY, STATESVILLE, N. C. 417 (Z1)
STATESVILLE FURNITURE COMPANY, STATESVILLE, N. C. 346
STATTON FURNITURE MFG. CO., HAGERSTOWN, MD. 418 (Z1)
STAUNTON, H. A., PHILADELPHIA, PA.
See Chicago Mirror and Art Glass Co 395 (Z3)
Stead & Miller Co., Philadelphia, Pa.
Steel Fixture Mfg. Co., Topeka, Kan.
Stearns & Foster Co., Lockland, O.
Steiger & Kerr Stove & Foundry Co., San Francisco, Cal.
Steil Shops, Grand Rapids, Mich.
Steinman & Meyer Furn. Co., Cincinnati, O.
Sterchi Bros. Mfg. Co., Knoxville, Tenn.
Sterling Furn. Co., Grand Rapids, Mich.
STERLING FURNITURE COMPANY, SALAMANCA, N. Y. 347
Sterling Furn. Co., Greensboro, N. C.
Sterling Range & Furn. Corp., Rochester, N. Y.
STEUL & SONS, INC., HENRY C., BUFFALO, N. Y.
Catalog 348
Home Furnishing and Decoration Section 49
Stevens Co. Inc., B. A., Toledo, O.
Stewart Co., G. S., Norwalk, O.
Stewartstown Cab. Co., Stewartstown, Pa.
STEWARTSTOWN FURNITURE COMPANY, STEWARTSTOWN, PA.
Catalog 350-351
Home Furnishing and Decoration Section 51
Stickley Bros. Co., Grand Rapids, Mich.
STICKLEY, INC., L. & J. G., FAYETTEVILLE, N. Y., and STICKLEY MFG. CO., INC., SYRACUSE, N. Y.
Catalog 352-353
Home Furnishing and Decoration Section 52
Stiles Furn. Co., Boston, Mass.
Stille & Duhlmeier & Co., Cincinnati, O.
Stockwell Co., O. W., Los Angeles, Cal.
Stomps-Burkhardt Co., Columbus, O.
Stones, Inc., Geo. L., Grand Rapids, Mich.
Stoneville Cabinet Co., Stoneville, N. C.
Stout Furn. Co., Brazil, Ind.
Stove & Range Co. of Pittsburgh, Pittsburgh, Pa.
STOW-DAVIS FURNITURE COMPANY, GRAND RAPIDS, MICH.
Catalog 76-77
Home Furnishing and Decoration Section 53
Strand Uph. Furn. Co., New York, N. Y.
Strassel Co., J. L., Louisville, Ky.
Stratton & Terstegge Co., Louisville, Ky.

STREIT MFG. COMPANY, C. F., CINCINNATI, O.
Catalog 130-131
Home Furnishing and Decoration Section 54
Stroud, D. H., Philadelphia, Pa.
Stuart Furn. Co., Grand Rapids, Mich.
Sturgis Mfg. Co., Sturgis, Mich.
Style-Bilt Furn. Co., Harrisburg, Pa.
Success Furn. Corp., St. Louis, Mo.
Success Mfg. Co., Gloucester, Mass.
Sueme Furn. Co., Chas., St. Louis, Mo.
Suitt Bros. Mfg. Co., Cambridge, O.
Sulo, Sylvester P., Rahway, N. J.
SULTAN & COMPANY, WILLIAM, CHICAGO, ILL.
Catalog 132
Home Furnishing and Decoration Section 51
Sultan Mfg. Co., Ernest J., San Francisco, Cal.
Sumergrade & Sons, N., New York, N. Y.
Summit Foundry Co., Geneva, N. Y.
Sunray Stove Co., Delaware, O.
Sunset Feather Co., San Francisco, Cal.
Superior Cabinet Co., Muskegon, Mich.
Superior Felt & Bedding Co., Chicago, Ill.
Superior Furn. Co., Chicago, Ill.
Superior Furn. Co., Grand Rapids, Mich.
Superior Furn. Co., Toledo, O.
Superior Lamp & Shade Co., Chicago, Ill.
Superior Metal Bed Co., Chicago, Ill.
Superior Uph. Co., Brooklyn, N. Y.
Supplee-Biddle Hardware Co., Philadelphia, Pa.
Supreme Furn. Mfg. Co., Jamestown, N. Y.
Sussman, H., New York, N. Y.
Sutton Carpet Lining Co., E. W., Brooklyn, N. Y.
Sweat-Cummings Co., Richford, Vt.
Swinton & Co., Port Jervis, N. Y.
Sykes Co., Philadelphia, Pa.

T

Ta-Bed Corp., Chicago, Ill.
Taber-Prang Art Co., Springfield, Mass.
Table Rock Furn. Co., Morganton, N. C.
Tablescope Co., Jamestown, N. Y.
Tampa Chair & Table Co., Tampa, Fla.
Tampa Wicker Furn. Co., Tampa, Fla.
Taplin-Rice-Clerkin Co., Akron, O.
Tappan Stove Co., Mansfield, O.
TATE FURNITURE CO., HIGH POINT, N. C. 354-357
TAUBER PARLOR FURNITURE CO., CHICAGO, ILL. 402 (Z3)
Tavshajian, H. S., New York, N. Y.
Taylor Bedding Mfg. Co., Taylor, Tex.
Taylor Chair Co., Bedford, O.
Taylor Mattress Co., Salisbury, N. C.
Taylor, Samuel L., Mount Sterling, Ky.
Teague Furn. Co., Lexington, N. C.
TEEPE-WHITNEY CORPORATION, LONG ISLAND CITY, N. Y.
See Whitney Company, Inc., W. F. 240
TELL CITY CHAIR COMPANY, TELL CITY, IND. 403 (Z3)
Tell City Furn. Co., Tell City, Ind.
Temple-Stuart Co., Baldwinsville, Mass.
Tenafly Lumber & Supply Co., Tenafly, N. J.
Tennessee Chair & Table Co., Sevierville, Tenn.
Tennessee Furn. Corp., Chattanooga, Tenn.
Tennessee Red Cedar & Nov. Co., Chattanooga, Tenn.
Tennessee Table Co., Knoxville, Tenn.
Thauwald Co., C. F., Cincinnati, O.
Thayer Co., E. N., Erie, Pa.
Theise Mfg. Co., Fred, Boston, Mass.
Thomas Co., Oscar G., Taunton, Mass.
Thomas Uph. Furn. Co., Muncie, Ind.
THOMASVILLE CHAIR COMPANY, THOMASVILLE, N. C. 349
Thomasville Furn. Co., Thomasville, N. C.
Thompson Chair Corp., E. L., Baldwinsville, Mass.
Thompson Mfg. Co., Holland, Mich.
Thonet Bros., New York, N. Y.
Thornhill & Sons, Albert, Xenia, O.
Thornton, L. M., St. Louis, Mo.
Three "C" Davenport Cor., Oshkosh, Wis.
TILLOTSON FURNITURE CORPORATION, JAMESTOWN, N. Y. 358
Tindall-Wagner Mfg. Co., Shelbyville, Ind.
Tinnerman Stove & Range Co., Cleveland, O.
Tipp Bldg. & Mfg. Co., Tippecanoe City, O.
Tipton Furn. Co., Tipton, Ind.
Toccoa Furn. Co., Toccoa, Ga.
Todd Carpet Mfg. Co., Carlisle, Pa.
Toledo Nat'l Bed. Co., Toledo, O.
TOLEDO PARLOR FURNITURE CO., TOLEDO, O. 404 (Z3)
Toledo Stove & Range Co., Toledo, O.
Tollner Sons Co., Chas. Pulaski, N. Y.
Tomlinson Chair Co., High Point, N. C.
Tonsing Bros., Portland, Ore.
Toy Co. of America, Appleton, Wis.
Travers Co., Geo. W., Hoboken, N. J.
Treaty Co., Greenville, O.
Trenkamp Stove & Mfg. Co., Cleveland, O.
Trenton Spring Mattress Co., Trenton, N. J.
Trimble Mfg. Co., E. M., Rochester, N. Y.
Trogdon Furn. Co., Inc., Toccoa, Ga.
Troy Chair Co., Troy, Ind.
Troy Sunshade Co., Toledo, O.
Tucker Duck & Rubber Co., Fort Smith, Ark.
Tulsa Furn. Mfg. Co., Tulsa, Okla.
Turner Mfg. Co., Chicago, Ill.
Twin City Uph. Co., Minneapolis, Minn.
Tyre Bros. Glass Co., Los Angeles, Cal.
Tyson & Jones Buggy Co., Carthage, N. C.

U

Udell & Predock Mfg. Co., St. Louis, Mo.
UDELL WORKS, INC., INDIANAPOLIS, IND. 419 (Z1)
Umphrey Mfg. Co., Crawfordsville, Ind.
Unagusta Mfg. Co., Hazelwood, N. C.
Uneeda Chair Co., New York, N. Y.
Union Bed & Spring Co., Chicago, Ill.
UNION BROTHERS, BALTIMORE, MD. 420 (Z1)
Union City Chair Co., Union City, Pa.
Union Frame Co., High Point, N. C.
Union Furn. & Nov. Co., Warren, Pa.
UNION FURNITURE COMPANY, BATESVILLE, IND.
Catalog 421 (Z1)
Home Furnishing and Decoration Section 55
UNION FURNITURE COMPANY, ROCKFORD, ILL.
Library Furniture Catalog 186-187
Dining Room Furniture Catalog 360-361
Union Furn. Co., High Point, N. C.
Union Furn. Co., Jamestown, N. Y.
Union Mirror Co., Lenoir, N. C.
Union Parlor Furn. Co., Boston, Mass.
Union Parlor Suite Co., Brooklyn, N. Y.
Union Table & Spring Co., Glendale, N. Y.
Union Uph. Furn. Co., Philadelphia, Pa.
Union Uph. Co., Jefferson, Wis.
Unique Furn. Co. Inc., Cambridge, Mass.
Unique Furn. Co., Winston-Salem, N. C.
United Cabinet Mfg. Co., Chicago, Ill.
UNITED FURNITURE COMPANY, LEXINGTON, N. C. 359
UNITED FURNITURE MFG. CO., BALTIMORE, MD.
See Union Bros. 420 (Z1)
United Mfg. Co., Portland, Ore.
United Mattress Mchry. Co., Boston, Mass.
United Spring Bed Co., Brooklyn, N. Y.
U. S. Bedding Co., St. Paul, Minn.
United States Bedding Co., Memphis, Tenn.
United States Furn. Co., Evansville, Ind.
United States Mat. Co., Harrisburg, Pa.
United States Rattan Co., Hoboken, N. J.
United States Spring Bed Co., Springfield, Mass.
United States Willow Furn. Co., Hoboken, N. J.
United Tapestry Mills, Inc., Philadelphia, Pa.
United Uph. Co., Wilkes-Barre, Pa.
Universal Cabinet Co., Chicago, Ill.
Universal Metal Bed Co., Brooklyn, N. Y.
Universal Uph. Co., Brooklyn, N. Y.
UNIVERSAL WILLOW & REED WARE CO., INC., BROOKLYN, N. Y. 422 (Z1)
Unterman, Louis, New York, N. Y.
Upham Mfg. Co., Marshfield, Wis.
Upholstered Construction Co., Buffalo, N. Y.
Urbana Furn. Mfg. Co., Urbana, O.

V

Valentine-Seaver Co., Chicago, Ill.
Valley City Desk Co., Grand Rapids, Mich.
Valley Furn. Co. Inc., St. Louis, Mo.
Valley Furn. Co., Sheboygan, Wis.
Van Vorst, Inc., C. B., Los Angeles, Cal.
Vander Ley Brothers, Grand Rapids, Mich.
Van Dorn Iron Works Co., Cleveland, O.
Vaughan-Bassett Furn. Co., Galax, Va.
Vaughan Furn. Co., Galax, Va.
Veal & Son, R., Albany, Ore.
Veith & Sons, Chas. H., New York, N. Y.
Venetian Art Lamp Co., Chicago, Ill.
Venezian Art Screen Co., New York, N. Y.
Vermont Shade Roller Co., Burlington, Vt.
Victor Stove Co., Salem, O.
Vilas-Harsha Mfg. Co., Chicago, Ill.
Vincennes Furn. Mfg. Co., Vincennes, Ind.
Vincent-McCall Co., Kenosha, Wis.
Violante & Onorado, New York, N. Y.
Virginia Furn. Co., Martinsville, Va.
VIRGINIA-LINCOLN FACTORIES, MARION, VA. 362-363
Virginia Mirror Co., Martinsville, Va.
VIRGINIA TABLE CO., MARION, VA 362-363
Vogeley & Lackman, Brooklyn, N. Y.
Vogt Mfg. Co., Louisville, Ky.
Volker Co., Wm., Kansas City, Mo.
Volkman & Co., Chicago, Ill.
Volckmann Furn. & Cab. Co., Clinton, Iowa
VOSS, L. C., LOUISVILLE, KENTUCKY
See Period Cabinet Mfg. Co. 307

W

Wagemaker Co., Grand Rapids, Mich.
Wagner Furn. Co., Herkimer, N. Y.
Wait Furn. Co., Portsmouth, O.
Waite Carpet Co., Oshkosh, Wis.
Walker & Pratt Mfg. Co., Boston, Mass.
Walkertown Chair Co., Walkertown, N. C.
Wallace Furn. Co., Grand Rapids, Mich.
Walmer Furn. Mfg. Co., Chicago, Ill.
WALNUT
See American Walnut Manufacturers Assn. 380-381
Walrus Mfg. Co., Decatur, Ill.
WARD FURNITURE MANUFACTURING CO., FORT SMITH, ARK. 364
Warner Shade & Novelty Co., Brooklyn, N. Y.
Warren Chair Works, Warren, Pa.
Warren Furn. Co., Warren, Pa.
Washington Furn. Mfg. Co., Seattle, Wash.
Washington Mfg. Co., Martha, Chicago, Ill.
Washington Parlor Furn. Co., Chicago, Ill.
Washington Parlor Furn. Co., Tacoma, Wash.
Wasmuth-Endicott Co., Andrews, Ind.
Waterbury Mattress Co., Waterbury, Conn.
Watsontown Table & Furn. Co., Watsontown, Pa.
Wausau Novelty Co., Wausau, Wis.
Wawasee Cedar Chest Co., Syracuse, Ind.
Waxman & Co., A., Philadelphia, Pa.
Way Sagless Spring Co., Minneapolis, Minn.
Wayne Furn. Mfg. Co., Goldsboro, N. C.
Waynesville Furn. Co., Hazelwood, N. C.
Webster Furn. Co., Rochester, N. Y.
Webster Mfg. Co., Superior, Wis.
Weigell & Son, August, Milwaukee, Wis.
Weigle-Mitchell Co., Chicago, Ill.
Weiman Co., Chicago, Ill.
Weiner & Sons, L., Philadelphia, Pa.
Weir Stove Co., Taunton, Mass.
Weis Mfg. Co., Monroe, Mich.
Welch Furn. Co., High Point, N. C.
Weller-Foard Co., Morristown, Tenn.
Wellington-Stone Co., Chicago, Ill.
Wells Co., Floyd, Royersford, Pa.
WELLSVILLE UPHOLSTERING COMPANY, WELLSVILLE, N. Y. 423 (Z1)
Welsh-Coffey Mirror & Beveling Co., St. Louis, Mo.
Wemyss Furn. Co., Evansville, Ind.
WEST BRANCH NOVELTY CO., MILTON, PA.
Catalog 424-428 (Z1)
Home Furnishing and Decoration Section 56
West Coast Chair Co., Tacoma, Wash.
West End Furniture Co., Rockford, Ill.
WEST MICHIGAN FURNITURE COMPANY, HOLLAND, MICH.
Colonial Bedroom Furniture Catalog 284-285
Bedroom Furniture Catalog 286-287
Home Furnishing and Decoration Section 57
Western Cab. & Fix. Mfg. Co., Kansas City, Mo.
Western Fibre Furn. Co., Tacoma, Wash.
Western Furn. Co., Batesville, Ind.
Western Furn. Co., Indianapolis, Ind.
Western Furn. Co., Sheboygan, Wis.
Western Furn. Mfg. Co., Los Angeles, Cal.
Western Furn. Uph. Co., San Francisco, Cal.
Western Mirror Plate Co., Sheboygan, Wis.
Western Reserve Furn. Co., Warren, O.
WESTERN SHADE CLOTH COMPANY, CHICAGO, ILL.
Catalog 405 (Z3)
Home Furnishing and Decoration Section 59
Western Uph. Co., Los Angeles, Cal.
Western Wicker Works, Los Angeles, Cal.
Western Wire Prod. Co., St. Louis, Mo.
Westfield Mfg. Co., Westfield, Mass.
Westgate Mfg. Co., Ann Arbor, Mich.
Wetter Mfg. Co., H., Memphis, Tenn.
Wetterhold Mattress Co., Geo., Wichita, Kan.
Wheeler-Okell Co., Nashville, Tenn.
Whitcombe-McGeachin, New York, N. Y.
White Chair Co., Baldwinsville, Mass.
White Co., H. C., Bennington, Vt.
WHITE FURNITURE COMPANY, MEBANE, N. C.
Catalog 365
Home Furnishing and Decoration Section 55
White, J. H., Williamsburg, O.
White Mfg. Co., Ashburnham, Mass.
White Oak Chair Mfg. Co., Culpeper, Va.
White River Chair Co., Brattleboro, Vt.
White-Seideman Co., Baltimore, Md.
White-Smith Mfg. Co., Los Angeles, Cal.
White-Warner Co., Taunton, Mass.
Whitely & Collier, Philadelphia, Pa.
Whitlock Co., J. W., Rising Sun, Ind.
Whitman & Co., Wm., New York, N. Y.
WHITNEY COMPANY, INC., W. F., SOUTH ASHBURNHAM, MASS.
Catalog 240
Home Furnishing and Decoration Section 58
Whitney Carriage Co., F. A., Leominster, Mass.
Whitney Co., Alfred H., Ashburnham, Mass.
Whitney Reed Corp., Leominster, Mass.
Whittall Associates, M. J., Worcester, Mass.
Wichita Mattress Co., Wichita, Kansas
Wichita Wholesale Furn. Co., Wichita, Kan.
Wickercraft Co., Pasadena, Cal.
Wicker-Kraft Corp., Newburgh, N. Y.
WIDDICOMB CO., JOHN, GRAND RAPIDS, MICH.
Catalog 366
Home Furnishing and Decoration Section 58
WIDDICOMB FURNITURE CO., GRAND RAPIDS, MICH.
Catalog 367
Home Furnishing and Decoration Section 59
WIENER COMPANY, E., MILWAUKEE, WIS.
Catalog 406 (Z3)
Home Furnishing and Decoration Section 60
Wild & Co., Jos., New York, N. Y.
Wilder Mfg. Co., Inc., Brooklyn, N. Y.
Wilhelm Furn. Co., Sturgis, Mich.
Wilkinson Mfg. Co., Binghampton, N. Y.
Williams Co., A. C., Ravenna, O.
WILLIAMS, JOSEPH G., MINNEAPOLIS, MINN.
See Schoeck Mfg. Co., Inc. 415 (Z1)
Williams Furn. Co., Richmond, Ind.
Williams-Kimp Furn. Co., Grand Rapids, Mich.
Williams Mfg. Co., Temple, Ga.
Williamsburg Furn. Co., Williamsburg, O.
WILLIAMSPORT FURNITURE COMPANY, WILLIAMSPORT, PA. 429 (Z1)
Wilmort Mfg. Co., Chicago, Ill.
Wilson & Glickson Uph. Co., Boston, Mass.
Wilson & Jansen, San Francisco, Cal.
WILSON FURN. CO., LOUISVILLE, KY.
Zone 1 Catalog 430 (Z1)
Zone 3 Catalog 407 (Z3)
Wilson Stove & Mfg. Co., Metropolis, Ill.
WILSON, W. E., COLUMBUS, O.
See Schoeck Manufacturing Co., Inc. 415 (Z1)
Wilt, W. M., Syracuse, Ind.
Winchendon Chair Co., Winchendon, Mass.
Wincroft Stove Works, Middletown, Pa.
Windsor Furn. Co., Chicago, Ill.
Windsor Furn. Co., Grand Rapids, Mich.
Winn Bros., Harrisville, N. H.
WINNEBAGO MANUFACTURING CO., ROCKFORD, ILL. 368-371
Winnebago Furn. Mfg. Co., Fond du Lac, Wis.
Winstian, Louis, Hudson, N. Y.
Winston-Salem Chair Co., Winston-Salem, N. C.
Winter, John I., Fort Worth, Tex.
Wire Goods Co., Worcester, Mass.
Wisconsin Furn. Co., Milwaukee, Wis.
Wisconsin Mfg. Co., Jefferson, Wis.
Wise-Bundock Co., Rochester, N. Y.
WITZ FURNITURE CORPORATION, J. L., STAUNTON, VA. 244
Wolf & Kraemer Furn. Co., St. Louis, Mo.
Wolfe Bros. & Co., Piney Flats, Tenn.
Wolverine Uph. Co., Grand Rapids, Mich.
Wood & Bishop Co., Bangor, Me.
Wood Batik Shops, Inc., Grand Rapids, Mich.
Wood Mfg. Co., Inc., Marshall C., Truxton, N. Y.
Wood Products Co., Watsontown, Pa.
Woodcraft Furn. Co., Newark, N. J.
Woodcraft Mfg. Co., Schenectady, N. Y.
Woods & Sons Co., Jos. W., New York, N. Y.
Woods-Evertz Stove Co., Springfield, Mo.
Woodward Furn. Co., Owosso, Mich.
Worrick & Co., F. C., Athol, Mass.
Wrenn-Columbia Furn. Co., High Point, N. C.
Wrought Iron Range Co., St. Louis, Mo.

Y

Yadkin Valley Furn. Co., Ronda, N. C.
Yawman & Erbe Mfg. Co., Chicago, Ill.
YEAGER FURNITURE COMPANY,
    ALLENTOWN, PA. 431 (Z1)
Yeager Mfg. Co., Hickory, N. C.
Yeaple, B. J., Brooklyn, N. Y.
Yelson, John, Philadelphia, Pa.
Yoder, Levi M., Belleville, Pa.
York County Chair Co., Red Lion, Pa.

York Furn. Mfg. Co. Inc., York, Pa.
YOUNGBLOOD, C. M., ATLANTA, GEORGIA
    See Chicago Mirror and Art Glass Co........395 (Z3)
Young & Sons, J. M., Camden, N. Y.
Young Bros. Co., Worcester, Mass.
Youngsville Mfg. Co., Youngsville, Pa.
YPSILANTI REED FURNITURE CO.,
    IONIA, MICH.
    Catalog 135
    Home Furnishing and Decoration Section.........60

Z

Zahn & Bowly Co., New York, N. Y.
Zaldin Sons & Co., Brooklyn, N. Y.
Zenith Mills, Philadelphia, Pa.
Zimmer Furn. Co., St. Paul, Minn.
Zimmermann & Co., Hermann, New York, N. Y.
Zucchi Furn. Co., New York, N. Y.
Zimmerman & Sons, John, Philadelphia, Pa.
ZION LACE CURTAINS AND NETS
    (Marshall Field & Co., Wholesale),
    CHICAGO, ILL..........................85

GEOGRAPHICAL LIST
OF CONCERNS WHO SELL THEIR PRODUCTS
TO FURNITURE DEALERS

ALABAMA

BIRMINGHAM
Birmingham Buggy Company
Birmingham Stove & Range Company
Magic City Furn. & Mfg. Co. Inc.
PECK & HILLS FURNITURE COMPANY
  Catalog 392
  Home Furnishing & Decoration Sec............ 45
Perfection Mattress & Spring Company
GADSDEN
A & J Mfg. Company
Queen City Furniture Company
SHEFFIELD
King Stove & Range Company
TUSCALOOSA
Oak City Furniture Company

ARIZONA

PHOENIX
ROME COMPANY, INC.......................70-71

ARKANSAS

BENTON
McCoy Couch Furniture Mfg. Co.
FORT SMITH
Fort Smith Furn. Mfrs. Company
Fort Smith Metal Products Co. Inc.
Garrison Company, Inc.
Porter Mirror & Glass Company
Tucker Duck & Rubber Company
WARD FURNITURE MFG. COMPANY........ 364
LITTLE ROCK
Little Rock Furniture Mfg. Co.
Southern Mattress Company

CALIFORNIA

BERKELEY
Berkeley Wicker Works
Morton Furniture Mfg. Co.
FRESNO
PECK & HILLS FURNITURE COMPANY
  Catalog 392
  Home Furnishing & Decoration Sec............ 45
HOLLYWOOD
McCONNELL, T. F.
  See Period Cabinet Mfg. Co............ 307
HUNTINGTON PARK
Roberts-Cohen Company
INGLEWOOD
Inglewood Manufacturing Company
LONGBEACH
Longbeach Sash & Door Company
LOS ANGELES
Acme Furniture Manufacturing Co.
Bailey-Schmitz Company
Barker Brothers
Boxall, James
Broadway Rattan Shoppe
Cherman Furniture Mfg. Co.
Children's Furniture & Toy Co.
City Refrigerator Company
Co-operative Furniture Mfg. Co.
Davis Upholstery & Furniture Co.
De Luxe Fibre Furniture Company
De France Lamp & Shade Company
GUNN FURNITURE CO.
  Catalog 396 (Z3)
  Home Furnishing & Decoration Section.......... 19
Hawthorne Furniture Shops
Independent Furniture .Company
Jonas & Sons, Jacob H.
KARPEN & BROS., S.
  Catalog 112-119
  Home Furnishing & Decoration Sec............25-29
KENT-COSTIKYAN
  Catalog 89
  Home Furnishing & Decoration Section.......... 23
Kling Manufacturing Company
Laird, Marshall
Liffman, Julius
Los Angeles Period Furn. Mfg. Co.
Los Angeles Upholstering Company
McClellan Manufacturing Company
Mallen, E.
Morris, Edward S.
Murdock & Wilcek
MYERS & SCHWARTZ
  See Mersman Bros. Corpn.....................216-221
National Cabinet & Furn. Mfg. Co.
O'Keefe & Merrit Company, Inc.
O'Brien Furniture Mfg. Co.
Pacific States Bedding & Furn. Co.
PECK & HILLS FURNITURE COMPANY
  Catalog 392
  Home Furnishing & Decoration Sec............ 45
Phenix Company, Leroy C.
Pico Bedding Company
Premier Carpet Company
Progress Furn. Mfg. Co.
Pyramid Furniture Manufacturing Co.
Reedcraft Company
Richmond Furniture Manufacturing Co.

Roberti Brothers
Roberts, John H.
Robinson's Furn. Mfg. Company
ROGERS, INC., M. H......................... 90
ROME COMPANY, INC........................70-71
Sealy Mattress Co. of Pacific Coast
Siskin, Harry
Soronow's Furniture Mfg. Co.
Standard Furniture Mfg. Co.
Standard Upholstering Company
Stockwell Company, L. W.
Tyre Bros. Glass Company
Van Vorst, Inc., C. B.
Western Furniture Mfg. Co.
Western Upholstering Company
Western Wicker Works
White Smith Mfg. Company
NATIONAL CITY
Schiefer Furn. Mfg. Company
O'Leary, Thomas J.
OAKLAND
National Upholstering Company
PECK & HILLS FURNITURE COMPANY
  Catalog 392
  Home Furnishing & Decoration Sec............ 45
Star Mattress Company
PASADENA
Crown City Manufacturing Co.
Perrin, Charles O.
Wickercraft Company, The
SACRAMENTO
PECK & HILLS FURNITURE COMPANY
  Catalog 392
  Home Furnishing & Decoration Sec............ 45
SAN DIEGO
PECK & HILLS FURNITURE COMPANY
  Catalog 392
  Home Furnishing & Decoration Sec............ 45
Standard Mattress & Furn. Co.
SAN FRANCISCO
ALLEN MANUFACTURING COMPANY
  Catalog 136
  Home Furnishing & Decoration Section.......... 10
ARMSTRONG CORK COMPANY
  Catalog 81
  Home Furnishing & Decoration Section.......... 9
BASIC FURNITURE CO...................... 244
Bernhard's, Inc.
Cleese Company, John P.
Dependable Furniture Mfg. Co.
Dieringer Bros. Furn. Mfg. Co.
EAGLE OTTAWA LEATHER COMPANY
  Catalog 83
  Home Furnishing & Decoration Section.......... 13
EBERT FURNITURE COMPANY
  Catalog distributed to all States................ 264
  Zone 1 Catalog.......................402-403 (Z1)
Friedrichs, H.
Furniture Exchange
Graham Manufacturing Co., Jas.
GUNN FURNITURE COMPANY
  Catalog 396 (Z3)
  Home Furnishing & Decoration Section.......... 19
Harder, Frank H.
Hoey & Company, John
HOOSIER MANUFACTURING COMPANY
  Catalog 72
  Home Furnishing & Decoration Section.......... 19
Ils & Company, John G.
KARPEN & BROS., S.
  Catalog 112-119
  Home Furnishing & Decoration Sec............25-29
Katz & Company, M. A.
KENT-COSTIKYAN
  Catalog 89
  Home Furnishing & Decoration Section.......... 23
KLAMER FURNITURE CORPORATION
  Catalog 288-289
  Home Furnishing & Decoration Section.......... 33
Klopstock Brothers
LANE COMPANY, INC.
  Catalog 153
  Home Furnishing & Decoration Section.......... 34
McCANN-PLEAS CO.
  See Period Cabinet Mfg. Co............ 307
Malley-Long Furniture Mfg. Co.
MERSMAN BROS. CORPORATION
  Catalog 216-221
  Home Furnishing & Decoration Section.........39-41
Metropolitan Furniture Mfg. Co.
Misson Foundry & Stove Works
MONITOR FURNITURE COMPANY
  Catalog 288-289
  Home Furnishing & Decoration Section.......... 33
MORGANTON FURNITURE CO.............. 304
MYERS & SCHWARTZ
  See Mersman Bros. Corpn.....................216-221
New York Furniture & Bedding Mfg. Co.
NORQUIST COMPANY, A. C.............. 305
Occidental Furniture Mfg. Co.
O'Neil & Graves Company
PECK & HILLS FURNITURE COMPANY
  Catalog 392
  Home Furnishing & Decoration Sec............ 45
Premier Bed & Spring Company
ROGERS, INC., M. H.
  Catalog 90
  Home Furnishing & Decoration Section.......... 45
ROME COMPANY, INC.......................70-71
San Francisco Stove Works
Saroff, Moses
Simon Mattress Manufacturing Co.
Steiger & Kerr Stove & Foundry Co.
Sultan Manufacturing Co., Ernest J.
Sunset Feather Company
UNION FURNITURE COMPANY (Batesville, Ind.)
  Catalog 421 (Z1)
  Home Furnishing & Decoration Section.......... 55

UNION FURNITURE COMPANY (Rockford, Ill.)
  Desks and Bookcases Catalog...................186-187
  Dining Room Furniture Catalog...............360-361
Western Furniture Upholstering Co.
Wilson & Jansen
WITZ FURNITURE CORPN., J. L.............. 244
STOCKTON
Manthey Bros.

COLORADO

DENVER
ARMSTRONG CORK COMPANY
  Catalog 81
  Home Furnishing & Decoration Section.......... 9
Colorado Bedding Company
Colorado Mattress Mfg. Co.
FURNITURE CITY UPHOLSTERY CO......... 104
Kindel Bedding Company
McMurtry Manufacturing Company
PECK & HILLS FURNITURE COMPANY
  Catalog 392
  Home Furnishing & Decoration Sec............ 45
ROME COMPANY, INC.......................70-71
Sanitary Refrigerator Company
PUEBLO
Newton Lumber Company

CONNECTICUT

BRIDGEPORT
Bridgeport Bed Spring Mfg. Co.
Bridgeport Chair Company
Krupka Company, Inc., S. C.
Penning Reed Company
Scroll Art Studios
BRISTOL
Ingraham Company, E.
HARTFORD
Acme Upholstering Company
Donchian Rug Company, Samuel
Dresser & Son, Inc., C. H.
Dworkin & Company, Inc., B.
Hartford Spring Bed Company
Metropolitan Chair Company
MERIDEN
Bradley & Hubbard Mfg. Co., The
Miller & Co. Inc., Edw.
Parker Company, Chas.
MIDDLETOWN
Palmer Company, I. E.
NEW HAVEN
New Haven Clock Company
Rattan Manufacturing Company
ROME COMPANY, INC.......................70-71
SHELTON
Shelton Basket Company, The
STAMFORD
Stamford Foundry Company
Stamford Gas Stove Company
NEW LONDON
Palmer Brothers Company
NEW MILFORD
Eastern Lounge Company
WATERBURY
Waterbury Mattress Company
WINSTED
Gilbert Clock Company, William L.
Harrison Son Co. Inc., B. J.
Richards & Company, Benjamin

FLORIDA

AUBURNDALE
Auburndale Furniture Mfg. Company
DELRAY
Sanitary Bedding Company
JACKSONVILLE
Florida Spring Bed Manufacturing Co.
Jacksonville Furniture Mfg. Co.
ROME COMPANY, INC.......................70-71
LAKELAND
Lakeland Manufacturing Company
MIAMI
Roman Furniture Manufacturing Company
PENSACOLA
Pensacola Mattress Company
SOUTH PALM BEACH
Florida Wicker Works
TAMPA
Hester Furniture Company
Tampa Chair & Table Company
Tampa Wicker Furniture Co.

GEORGIA

ATHENS
Ideal Furniture Company
ATLANTA
ARMSTRONG CORK COMPANY
  Catalog 81
  Home Furnishing & Decoration Section.......... 9

Atlanta Mirror & Beveling Company
Atlanta Stove Works
Atlanta Table Company
Capital City Chair Company
CHICAGO MIRROR & ART GLASS COMPANY 395 (Z3)
Fox Manufacturing Company
Fulton Metal Bed Mfg. Co.
Gholstin Spring & Mattress Company
Knott & Carmichael
Krueger Manufacturing Company
Metzger Mattress Company
ROME COMPANY, INC 70-71
Shannon Ref. & Butcher Supply Co.
Southern Desk & Table Company
Spratt Chair Company
WESTERN SHADE CLOTH COMPANY
Catalog 405 (Z3)
Home Furnishing & Decoration Section 59
YOUNGBLOOD, C. M.
See Chicago Mirror & Art Glass Co 395 (Z3)

AUGUSTA
Augusta Bedding Company
ROME COMPANY, INC 70-71

AUSTELL
Austell Cabinet Company
Austell Furniture Company

DALTON
Duane Chair Company, Inc.

FLOWERY BRANCH
Chattahoochie Furniture Company

GAINESVILLE
Georgia Chair Company

MACON
Macon Lumber & Manufacturing Co.
Muecke & Sons Company

MARIETTA
Brumby Chair Company

MOULTRIE
Riverside Manufacturing Company

ROME
Rome Furniture Company
Rome Stove & Range Company

TEMPLE
Williams Manufacturing Company

TOCCOA
Currahee Furniture Company
Toccoa Furniture Company
Trogdon Furniture Company, Inc.

IDAHO

BOISE CITY
Idaho Mattress Company

ILLINOIS

ALTAMONT
Hillemann, George

AURORA
All Steel Equipment Company
Lyon Metallic Manufacturing Co.

BELLEVILLE
Baker Stove Works
Belleville Stove & Range Company
Karr Range Company, Adam
Orbon Stove Company
Premier Stove Company
Quality Stove & Range Company
Roesch Enamel Range Company

BLOOMINGTON
Dodge-Dickinson Company

CHICAGO
Acme Lamp Shade Company
Advance Spring & Wire Company
Alonzi Furniture Company
AMERICAN ART BUREAU 378-379
American Furniture Novelty Co.
American Lamp & Shade Company
AMERICAN PARLOR FURNITURE COMPANY 91
American Rug & Carpet Company
American Seating Company
AMERICAN WALNUT MANUFACTURERS' ASSOCIATION 380-381
Anderson & Company, Geo. H.
ARMSTRONG CORK COMPANY
Catalog 81
Home Furnishing & Decoration Section 9
Art Lamp Manufacturing Company
ATHENS TABLE & MANUFACTURING COMPANY 190
Atlas Glass & Mirror Company
Atlas Upholstering Company
Bailey & Company, Jas. C.
BASIC FURNITURE COMPANY 244
BEATTIE MANUFACTURING CO 82
Behnke-Fink Manufacturing Company
Better Bedding Alliance of America
Bierfield Company, Louis
Biltrite Manufacturing Company
Binks Spray Equipment Company
BLACKHAWK FURN. CO 245-247
Block-Portelier Company
Bobbett Electric Mfg. Co.
Borgwardt & Ernst, Inc.
Borin Manufacturing Company
Brandwein & Company, A.
Brockman Company
Brodsky-Klein Furniture Co.
Broude Company, W. S.
Buhai Manufacturing Company
BURNS-LEVEE CO.
See Statesville Furniture Co 346
Burton-Dixie Corporation
CALDWELL FURNITURE COMPANY 398 (Z1)
CANTERBURY DECORATIVE FABRICS (Marshall Field and Company, Wholesale) 87
CENTRAL FURNITURE CO 254-257
Central States General Elec. Sup. Co.
CHATTANOOGA FURNITURE CO 259
Chicago Asbestos Table Mat Company
Chicago Cast Spring Company
Chicago Furniture Frame Company
Chicago Hardware Foundry Company
CHICAGO MIRROR & ART GLASS COMPANY 395 (Z3)
Chicago Society of Art Needlework
Chicago Upholstered Furniture Co.
CHITTENDEN & EASTMAN CO 377
Clinton Carpet Company
Cole Manufacturing Company
COLONIAL DRAPERY FABRICS (Marshall Field & Co., Wholesale)
Catalog 84
Home Furnishing & Decoration Section 30-32
Colonial Lamp & Fixture Works
Colonial Lamp & Shade Corporation
Columbia Feather Company
Columbia Parlor Furn. Mfg. Co.
Columbia Wood Turning Company
Commercial Furniture Company
Commercial Parlor Furniture Company
Consolidated Lamp & Shade Company
CONTINENTAL FURNITURE CO 260-261
Continental Manufacturing Company
Crest Company, The
CROCKER CHAIR COMPANY
Catalog 137
Home Furnishing & Decoration Section 12
Crown Stove Works
Daemicke Company, Paul
Davis Horwich & Steinman, Inc.
Dearborn Company
De Luxe Carpet Company
De Luxe Furniture Company
DIXIE FURNITURE CO 263
DOETSCH & BAUER COMPANY 375
Drake Company, The
DUNBAR FURNITURE MANUFACTURING CO. 98
EAGLE-OTTAWA LEATHER COMPANY
Catalog 83
Home Furnishing & Decoration Section 13
Eagle-Wabash Corporation
Eaton Chair Company
Eberhardt & Company, H.
EBERT FURNITURE COMPANY
Catalog distributed to all States 264
Catalog distributed to Zone 1 .... 402-403 (Z1)
Electair Company, The
Emmerich & Company, Chas.
EMPIRE CASE GOODS COMPANY
Catalog 266-267
Home Furnishing & Decoration Section 14
EMPIRE CHAIR COMPANY 194-196
EMPIRE FURNITURE CO 268
Empire Mattress Company
Enterprise Parlor Furniture Co.
Expert Wood Turning Corporation
Federal Parlor Furniture Co.
FENSKE BROTHERS 99
FIELD & COMPANY, WHOLESALE, MARSHALL
Home Furnishing & Decoration Section 30-32
Colonial Drapery Fabrics Catalog 84
Zion Lace Curtains and Nets Catalog 85
Home-Crest Floor Coverings Catalog 86
Canterbury Decorative Fabrics Catalog 87
Home-Crest Upholstered Furniture Catalog 100-101
Fischer Furniture Company
FLORENCE TABLE & MFG. CO.
Catalog 271
Home Furnishing & Decoration Section 15
FORSYTH FURNITURE LINES, INC.
Catalog 272
Home Furnishing & Decoration Section 16
Franklin & Company, S.
Freese & Sons, Co., J. D.
Fritts & Company, D. H.
FURST BROS. & COMPANY 78
Garfield Felt Corporation
Garland Upholstering Company
Garrett Go Cart & Car Company
General Fireproofing Co. of Ill.
General Wood Turning Company
Gibson Company, Wm. D.
Glass Novelty Company
GLOBE-BOSSE-WORLD FURNITURE COMPANY
Catalog 273
Home Furnishing & Decoration Section 17
GLOBE PARLOR FURNITURE CO 106-107
Gold Furniture Co. Inc.
Goldberg Brothers
Gordon-Joseph Furniture Co.
Gorrell & Company, A. D.
Gottlieb & Son, J.
Great Northern Chair Company
GREEN MANUFACTURING CO 376
GRIFFITH FURNITURE WORKS 147
Grow & Cuttle, Inc.
Haggard & Marcusson Company
HALLENSTEIN, A.
See Mersman Bros. Corpn 216-221
Hamilton Ross Factories
Hanauer Furniture Company
HANNAHS MANUFACTURING COMPANY 197
Hansen Furniture Co. Inc., Ed.
HANSON CLOCK COMPANY 148-149
Hanson Company, Louis
HARDEN COMPANY, FRANK S.
Catalog 108-109
Home Furnishing & Decoration Section 18
Hartmann Malcom Company
Hausske & Company, August
Herhold Chair Company
Hoenigsberger, A.
Hollatz Brothers Co.
HOME-CREST FLOOR COVERINGS (Marshall Field and Company, Wholesale) 86
HOME-CREST UPHOLSTERED FURNITURE (Marshall Field and Company, Wholesale) 100-101
Home Stove & Foundry Company
HOOSIER MANUFACTURING COMPANY
Catalog 72
Home Furnishing & Decoration Section 19
Hoover Company, The
Horn Brothers Mfg. Co.
Ideal Art Metal Company
Illinois Felt Company
Illinois Lamp & Novelty Company
Illinois Moulding Company
INDIANAPOLIS CHAIR AND FURNITURE CO.
Catalog 152
Home Furnishing & Decoration Section 20
INTERIOR DECORATING SERVICE BUREAU
See Western Shade Cloth Co 405 (Z3)
International Furniture Company
Jessen & Roseburg Company
Johnson, P.
JOHNSON & SONS FURN. CO., A. J. 278-279
Johnson Chair Company
Jorgenson Furniture Co., C. E.
K. & S. Manufacturing Company
Kapitol Lamp Manufacturing Co.
Kaplan, Inc.
KARGES FURNITURE COMPANY 280
KARPEN & BROS, S.
Catalog 112-119
Home Furnishing and Decoration Section 25-29
Katz Bros. Co.
Kellman, Abraham
KENT-COSTIKYAN
Catalog 89
Home Furnishing and Decoration Section 23
Kerney Manufacturing Co.
Ketcham & Rothschild Company
Kingsley Furniture Co. Inc.
KLAMER FURNITURE CORPORATION
Catalog 288-289
Home Furnishing & Decoration Section 33
Kloud, Joseph
Knapp & Tubbs
KOCH, ISSE & CO.
See Stewartston Furniture Co 350-351
Kopriwa Company, E.
Kruissink Brothers
Lakeside Upholstering Company
LAMB, GEORGE N.
See American Walnut Mfrs. Assn 380-381
LANDSTROM FURNITURE CORPORATION
Bedroom Furniture, Bookcases and Desks
Catalog 290-301
See also Central Furniture Co. Catalog 254-257
LANE COMPANY
Catalog 153
Home Furnishing & Decoration Section 34
Larson & Sons, Peter
LASSAHN FURNITURE COMPANY 154
Lee-Marion Company
Lefkow-King Company
Lieberman Bed Spring Company
LINCOLN FURNITURE MFG. CO 362-363
Lloyd Textile, Inc.
LUGER FURNITURE COMPANY
Catalog 399 (Z3)
Home Furnishing & Decoration Section 35
Lussky, White & Coolidge Company
McDonald Moulding Company
MADDEN MANUFACTURING COMPANY, JOHN J. 120
MAGES COMPANY, GEO. C. 80
Majestic Steel Cabinet Company
MALLEN & COMPANY, H. Z 121
Marer & Company, Arthur A.
MARSHALL FIELD & COMPANY, WHOLESALE
See Field and Company, Wholesale, Marshall
Martin's Mercantile Company
Master Parlor Furniture Company
Matot, Duff A.
Maxwell Company, S. A.
Meilahn Brothers
MEMPHIS FURNITURE MANUFACTURING CO.
Catalog 303
Home Furnishing & Decoration Section 36
MERSMAN BROS. CORPORATION
Catalog 216-221
Home Furnishing & Decoration Section 39-41
Metropolitan Picture Frame Company
Metz Furniture Company, J. L.
Mid City Upholstered Furn. Co.
Midland Wood Products Company
Miller Cabinet Shops
MILNE CHAIR COMPANY 207
Modern Parlor Furniture Company
MONITOR FURNITURE COMPANY
Catalog 288-289
Home Furnishing & Decoration Section 33
MORGANTON FURNITURE CO 304
Mosaic Shade Company, The
Mueller Bros. Art & Mfg. Co.
Munago Company
Murphy Door Bed of Chicago
MUTSCHLER BROTHERS CO. 74
Nachman Company
National Fumigation Sales Company
Niemann Table Company
Niemann & Company, H. C.
Nonnast & Sons Co., Louis F.
NORQUIST COMPANY, A. C. 305
Northern Manufacturing Company
Northern Picture Frame Company
NORTHFIELD COMPANY
Catalog 122-123
Home Furnishing & Decoration Section 37
Northwestern Art Shade Company
NORTON SALES SERVICE, C. S. 374
Olbrich & Golbeck Company
O'Mara Parlor Frame Company
PATTON-McCRAY COMPANY 306
Peacock Parlor Furniture Works
PECK & HILLS FURNITURE COMPANY
Catalog 392
Home Furnishing & Decoration Section 45
Peerless Spring Company
PENN TABLE CO 268
Perfection Parlor Furniture Co.
PETERSON ART FURNITURE CO 164
PHOENIX CHAIR COMPANY
Catalog 222-235
Home Furnishing & Decoration Section 42-44
Phoenix Company, The
Phoenix Trimming Company
Pick, Richard, Manufacturing Co.
Pioneer Appliance Company
PULLMAN COUCH COMPANY
Catalog 128-129
Home Furnishing and Decoration Section 46
Quality Lamp & Shade Company
Quality Metal Bed Company
Raedlein Basket Company
Randall Company, A. L.
Reliable Furniture Mfg. Co.

Rembrandt Lamp Corp., The
Rex Furniture Company,
Richardson & Boynton Company
Rindsberger Mfg. Corporation
ROCKFORD DESK CO.
See Rockford Furniture Co. 314-321
ROCKFORD EAGLE FURNITURE
  COMPANY 166-167
ROCKFORD FURNITURE CO. 314-321
ROCKFORD STANDARD FURNITURE CO.
  Catalog 327-331
  Home Furnishing and Decoration Section........ 47
ROGERS, INC., M. H.
  Catalog 90
  Home Furnishing & Decoration Section......... 45
ROME COMPANY, THE 70-71
Roos Manufacturing Company
Rosberg Manufacturing Co., J. H.
Royal Metal Manufacturing Co.
Royal Parlor Furniture Company
Rubloff Manufacturing Co.
Sager, W. D.
ST. JOHNS TABLE CO. 236
Saginaw Furniture Shops, Inc.
Salter Manufacturing Co. Inc.
Schmidt Manufacturing Company, H.
Schuckmell Company, The
Schultz & Hirsch Company
Seng Company, The
SHOWERS BROTHERS COMPANY
  Kitchen Cabinets Equipment Catalog............ 75
  Radio Furniture Catalog...................... 188
  Bedroom and Dining Room Furniture Catalog..336-341
SHREVE CHAIR COMPANY, INC. 237
Smith Manufacturing Company, Geo.
Snell Company, Chas. W.
Spiegel Furn. Mfg. Co., M. W.
STANDARD CHAIR COMPANY 239
Standard Furniture Company
Standard Lamp & Novelty Company
Standard Screen Company
Star Wood Turning Company
STATESVILLE FURNITURE COMPANY...... 346
STEWARTSTOWN FURNITURE CO. 350-351
STREIT MANUFACTURING CO., C. F. 349
  Catalog 130-131
  Home Furnishing and Decoration Section....... 54
SULTAN & COMPANY, WILLIAM
  Catalog 132
  Home Furnishing and Decoration Section........ 51
Superior Felt & Bedding Company
Superior Furniture Company
Superior Lamp & Shade Company
Superior Metal Bed Company
Ta-Bed Corporation
TATE FURNITURE CO. 354-357
TAUBER PARLOR FURNITURE
  COMPANY 402 (Z3)
TELL CITY CHAIR COMPANY...........403 (Z3)
THOMASVILLE CHAIR COMPANY 349
Turner Manufacturing Company
UDELL WORKS, INC. 419 (Z1)
Union Bed & Spring Company
UNION FURNITURE COMPANY, (Batesville, Ind.)
  Catalog 421 (Z1)
  Home Furnishing & Decoration Section......... 55
UNION FURNITURE COMPANY, (Rockford, Ill.)
  Desks and Bookcases Catalog.................186-187
  Dining Room Furniture Catalog...............360-361
United Cabinet Manufacturing Co.
UNITED FURNITURE COMPANY 359
Universal Cabinet Company
Valentine-Seaver Company
Venetian Art Lamp Company
Vilas-Harsha Manufacturing Co.
VIRGINIA-LINCOLN FACTORIES 362-363
VIRGINIA TABLE CO. 362-363
Volkman & Company
Walmer Furniture Manufacturing Co.
Walrus Mfg. Company, Martha
Washington Parlor Furniture Co.
Weigle Mitchell Company
Weiman Company, The
Wellington Stone Company
WESTERN SHADE CLOTH COMPANY
  Catalog 405 (Z3)
  Home Furnishing & Decoration Section......... 59
WHITNEY COMPANY, INC., W. F.
  Catalog 240
  Home Furnishing & Decoration Section......... 58
Wilmort Manufacturing Company
Windsor Furniture Company
WINNEBAGO MANUFACTURING CO. 368-371
WITZ FURNITURE CORP., J. L. 244
Yawman & Erbe Manufacturing Co.
YPSILANTI REED FURNITURE COMPANY
  Catalog 135
  Home Furnishing & Decoration Section......... 60
Zangerle & Peterson Company
ZION LACE CURTAINS AND NETS
  (Marshall Field and Company, Wholesale)...... 85

CICERO
Exello Products Corporation
DANVILLE
McCracken, Geo. M.
DECATUR
Walrus Manufacturing Co.
ELGIN
Elgin Stove & Oven Company
Hotel Mattress Mills
FOREST PARK
Roos Company of Forest Park, Ed.
GALVA
Best & Sons, John H.
GENEVA
Howell Company, W. H.
JOLIET
Moore Bros. Company
KEWANEE
Larson, Gustave E.
LA GRANGE
Lord Lumber Company
METROPOLIS
Wilson Stove & Manufacturing Co.
MORRISON
Illinois Refrigerator Company

NAPERVILLE
Kroehler Manufacturing Company
NORTH CHICAGO
Chicago Hardware Foundry Company
PEORIA
Culter & Proctor Stove Company
Peoria Lounge & Mattress Company
QUINCY
Channon-Emery Stove Company
Comstock-Castle Stove Company
Excelsior Stove & Manufacturing Co.
Gem City Stove Manufacturing Co.
Quincy Stove Manufacturing Co.
ROCKFORD
BLACKHAWK FURNITURE COMPANY....245-247
Carlson Manufacturing Co., A. J.
CENTRAL FURNITURE COMPANY........254-257
COLONIAL DESK COMPANY 138-141
Continental Desk Company
Co-operative Furniture Company
Empire Manufacturing Company
Excel Manufacturing Company
HANSON CLOCK COMPANY, INC........148-149
Illinois Cabinet Company
LANDSTROM FURNITURE CORPORA-
TION
  Bedroom Furniture, Bookcases and Desks
    Catalog 290-301
  See also Central Furniture Co., Catalog.......254-257
MECHANICS FURNITURE COMPANY
  Desks, Cabinets and Highboys Catalog.......... 155
  Dining Room Furniture Catalog................. 302
National Chair Company, Inc.
National Mirror Company
Old Colony Chair Company
Premier Furniture Company
Rockford Cabinet Company
ROCKFORD CEDAR FURNITURE COMPANY 165
ROCKFORD CHAIR & FURNITURE
  COMPANY 308-313
ROCKFORD DESK CO.
  See Rockford Furniture Co. 314-321
ROCKFORD EAGLE FURNITURE
  COMPANY 166-167
ROCKFORD FURNITURE COMPANY
  Catalog 314-321
  Home Furnishing & Decoration Section.........48-49
Rockford Metal Specialty Company
ROCKFORD NATIONAL FURNITURE
  COMPANY 324-326
ROCKFORD PALACE FURNITURE
  COMPANY 322-323
ROCKFORD PEERLESS FURNITURE
  COMPANY 168-171
Rockford Republic Furniture Company
ROCKFORD STANDARD FURNITURE
  COMPANY
  Catalog 327-331
  Home Furnishing & Decoration Section......... 47
Rockford Superior Furniture Company
Rockford World Turning Company
Rockford World Furniture Company
ROYAL MANTEL & FURNITURE
  COMPANY 332-334
SKANDIA FURNITURE COMPANY
  Desks & Bookcases Catalog....................172-185
  Dining Room Furniture Catalog...............342-345
UNION FURNITURE COMPANY
  Desks & Bookcases Catalog....................186-187
  Dining Room Furniture Catalog...............360-361
West End Furniture Company
WINNEBAGO MANUFACTURING
  COMPANY 368-371
ROCK ISLAND
Rock Island Stove Company
ST. CHARLES
St. Charles Net & Hammock Company
SPRINGFIELD
Springfield Mattress Company
STREATOR
Metal Stamping Corporation
WASHINGTON
Rinkenberger, William

INDIANA

ANDREWS
Wasmuth-Endicott Company
AURORA
Cochran Chair Company
INDIANAPOLIS CHAIR AND FURNITURE CO.
  Catalog 152
  Home Furnishing and Decoration Section........ 20
National Fibre Reed Company
BATESVILLE
American Furniture Company
CANFIELD, H. C.
  See Period Cabinet Mfg. Co. 307
UNION FURNITURE COMPANY
  Catalog 421 (Z1)
  Home Furnishing and Decoration Section........ 55
Western Furniture Company
BERNE
Berne Furniture Company, Inc.
DUNBAR FURNITURE MANUFACTURING
  COMPANY 98
BLOOMFIELD
SHOWERS BROS. COMPANY
  Kitchen Cabinets Catalog..................... 75
  Radio Furniture Catalog..................... 188
  Bedroom and Dining Room Furniture.........336-341
BLOOMINGTON
Nurre Mirror Plate Company
SHOWERS BROS. COMPANY
  Kitchen Cabinets Catalog..................... 75
  Radio Furniture Catalog..................... 188
  Bedroom and Dining Room Catalog...........336-341
BLUFFTON
PATTON-McCRAY COMPANY 306
BRAZIL
Stout Furniture Company
BROOKVILLE
Brookville Furniture Company

CAMBRIDGE CITY
Standard Manufacturing Company
CANNELTON
Lehman Company of America
COLUMBUS
Glanton Furniture Company, J. A.
Orinoco Furniture Company
CONNERSVILLE
Connersville Furniture Company
CRAWFORDSVILLE
Umphrey Manufacturing Company
ELWOOD
Sellers & Sons Company, G. I.
EVANSVILLE
Advance Stove Works
Bockstege Furniture Company
Buehner Chair Company
Crescent Furniture Company
Crescent Stove Works
Ellis Manufacturing Company
Evansville Desk Company
EVANSVILLE FURNITURE MANU-
  FACTURERS' ASSOCIATION 382-383
Evansville Furniture Company
Evansville Mattress & Couch Company
Evansville Metal Bed Company
Evansville Period Mfg. Co.
Faultless Caster Company
GLOBE-BOSSE-WORLD FURNITURE
  COMPANY
  Catalog 273
  Home Furnishing & Decoration Section......... 17
Graulich & Company, C.
Hoosier Lamp Works
Imperial Desk Company
Indiana Furniture Company
Indiana Stove Works
KARGES FURNITURE COMPANY 280
KELLER, J. C.
  See Evansville Furniture Mfrs. Assn. 382-383
KLAMER FURNITURE CORPORATION
  Catalog 288-289
  Home Furnishing & Decoration Section......... 33
Metal Manufacturing Company
MONITOR FURNITURE COMPANY
  Catalog 288-289
  Home Furnishing & Decoration Section......... 33
National Furniture Manufacturing Co.
North Star Furniture Company
Quality Furniture Company
Reddinger Manufacturing Co., P. H.
Small & Scheloskey Company
Southern Stove Works
Specialty Furniture Company
United States Furniture Company
Wemyss Furniture Company
Wilson Manufacturing Company
FORT WAYNE
Horton Manufacturing Company
Rastetter & Sons, Louis
FRANKFORT
McDougal Company
GOSHEN
Banta Furniture Company
Goshen Novelty & Lamp Company
I. X. L. Manufacturing Company
HAMMOND
Enterprise Bed Company
HUNTINGBURG
Huntingburg Furniture Company
Patoka Furniture Mfg. Co.
HUNTINGTON
Caswell-Runyan Company
INDIANAPOLIS
American Specialty Company
Booth Furniture Mfg. Co.
Cabinet Makers' Union, Inc., The
Clune Company, M.
Emrich Furniture Company
Furnas Office Furniture Company
Grassyfork Fisheries, Inc.
Hirschman Company, J. C.
Kramer Manufacturing Company
Krieg-Mellem Furniture Company
Lauter Company, H.
Leiber Company, The H.
MADDEN MANUFACTURING COMPANY,
  JOHN J. 120
ROME COMPANY, INC. 70-71
UDELL WORKS, INC. 419 (Z1)
Western Furniture Company
WESTERN SHADE CLOTH COMPANY
  Catalog 405 (Z3)
  Home Furnishing & Decoration Section......... 59
JASPER
Hoosier Desk Company
Jasper Chair Company
Jasper Desk Company
Jasper Novelty Works
Jasper Office Furniture Company
Schaaf & Schnaus Mfg. Co.
JEFFERSONVILLE
Jeffersonville Manufacturing Co.
KNIGHTSTOWN
Dennis Company, The
KOKOMO
Globe Stove & Range Company
LA PORTE
Kumfy-Kab Company
McLelland Buck & Wise Company
RUSTIC HICKORY FURNITURE COMPANY.. 68
LAWRENCEBURG
Johnston & Klare Mfg. Co.
LEBANON
Campbell Smith & Ritchie Company
MADISON
Graham & Sons, Thos.
McKim & Cochran Furniture Company
MARION
Bedell Manufacturing Corporation
Hoosier Stove Company
Marion Stove Company
Spencer Cardinal Corporation
MARKLE
Markle Manufacturing Company

MARTINSVILLE
Hubbard Chair Company
Old Hickory Furniture Company
MICHIGAN CITY
KARPEN & BROS., S.
  Catalog 112-119
  Home Furnishing & Decoration Sec. 25-29
MILAN
Milan Furniture Mfg. Company
MILFORD
Bedell Furniture Company
MOORESVILLE
Morresville Furniture Company
MORGANTON
Faucett-Umphrey Chair Company
MUNCIE
GRIFFITH FURNITURE WORKS 147
Moore Company, The
Thomas Upholstered Furniture Co.
NAPPANEE
Coppes Bros. & Zook, Inc.
Lamb Bros. & Greene, Inc.
Lamb, George L.
MUTSCHLER BROTHERS COMPANY. 74
NEW CASTLE
HOOSIER MANUFACTURING COMPANY
  Catalog 72
  Home Furnishing & Decoration Section. 19
NEW ALBANY
Anchor Stove & Range Company
Conner Furniture Company
Gohmann Bros. & Kahler Company
Klerner Furniture Company, Peter
PERIOD CABINET MANUFACTURING
COMPANY
  Catalog 307
  Home Furnishing & Decoration Section. 38
NO. MANCHESTER
Syracuse Cabinet Company
NORTH VERNON
North Vernon Lumber Mills
ORLEANS
Orleans Cabinet Company
PAOLI
Paoli Furniture Company
PEORIA
ROME COMPANY, INC. 70-71
PERU
Ariel Cabinet Company
Redmond Manufacturing Co., Wm. C.
RICHMOND
Kemper Bros., Inc.
Land-Dilks Company
Louck & Hill Co. Inc.
Richmond Cabinet Company, The
Richmond Chair Factory
Starr Piano Company
Williams Furniture Company
RISING SUN
Whitlock Company, J. W.
RUSHVILLE
Innis Pearce & Company
Park Furniture Company
Rushville Furniture Company
SHELBYVILLE
Albert Furniture Company
Blanchard-Hamilton Furniture Co.
Chambers Manufacturing Company
Danziger Furniture Company
DAVIS-BIRELY TABLE COMPANY. 193
Hodell Furniture Company
Indiana Furniture Mfg. Co.
Meloy Manufacturing Company
Reece Handley Company
Schmoe Furniture Co., C. F.
Shelbyville Wardrobe Mfg. Co.
Speigel Furniture Company
Tindall Wagner Mfg. Co.
SOUTH BEND
Hoel Manufacturing Company
Malleable Steel Range Mfg. Co.
Shiller Bros. Mfg. Co.
SPICELAND
L. O. Draper Shade Company
SYRACUSE
Wawasee Cedar Chest Company
Wilt, W. M.
TELL CITY
Southwestern Furniture Company
TELL CITY CHAIR COMPANY. 403 (Z3)
Tell City Furniture Company
TIPTON
Tipton Furniture Company
TROY
Troy Chair Company
VINCENNES
Vincennes Furniture Mfg. Co.
WABASH
Cardinal Cabinet Company
WASHINGTON
Hincher Manufacturing Company

IOWA

ALBERT CITY
Gustafson, Carl J.
BURLINGTON
CHITTENDEN & EASTMAN COMPANY. 377
Leopold Desk Company
North Western Cabinet Company, Inc.
SHOWERS BROTHERS COMPANY
  Kitchen Cabinets Equipment Catalog. 75
  Radio Furniture Catalog. 188
  Bedroom and Dining Room Furniture Catalog. . . .336-341
CEDAR RAPIDS
Cedar Craft Company
Parlor Furniture Mfg. Co.
CLINTON
Andersen Furniture Co. Inc.
Kelly Manufacturing Company

Iowa Furniture & Mfg. Co.
Volckmann Furn. & Cabinet Co.
DAVENPORT
Poeltl, John
DES MOINES
ALLEN MANUFACTURING COMPANY
  Catalog 136
  Home Furnishing & Decoration Section. 10
ROME COMPANY, INC. 70-71
Schmitt & Henry Mfg. Co.
DUBUQUE
Dubuque Mattress Factory
Farley & Loetscher Mfg. Co.
ESTHERVILLE
Hardwood Milling Company
FORT MADISON
Chair & Furniture Industry
KEOKUK
Akerson Ringstrom & Company
SIOUX CITY
Benson Furniture Company
Hopper Furniture Company, C. T.
ROME COMPANY, INC. 70-71
WATERLOO
Herrick Refrigerator & Cold Stor. Co.
Silvers Cabinet Company

KANSAS

FORT SCOTT
Fort Scott Mattress Company
LEAVENWORTH
Great Western Stove Company
Klemp Furniture Company, H. W.
National Furniture & Bedding Co.
TOPEKA
McEntire Brothers
Robertson Table Company
Steel Fixture Mfg. Co.
WICHITA
Wetterhold Mattress Co., Geo.
Wichita Mattress Company
Wichita Wholesale Furn. Co.

KENTUCKY

CARROLLTON
Carrollton Furniture Mfg. Co.
COVINGTON
Ballman Cabinet Company
Covington Furn. Mfg. Co.
Kaipers Sons Co., Chas.
Star Foundry Company
FRANKFORT
Brown-Irion Furniture Co.
Fibre Craft Chair Company
Frankfort Chair Company
Kenney Furniture Company
HENDERSON
DELKER BROTHERS MANUFACTURING
COMPANY 97
MARSTALL FURNITURE COMPANY, INC. 397 (Z2)
HOPKINSVILLE
Forbes Manufacturing Company
Mogul Wagon Manufacturing Company
LIVERMORE
Livermore Chair Company
LOUISVILLE
Art Embroidery Company
Atherton-Craig Furniture Co.
Central Glass Company
Fischer Leaf Company
Inman Company
Kentucky Stove Company
Kopp Company, Wm.
Logan Company, The
Louisville Bedding Company
LOUISVILLE CHAIR AND FURNITURE
COMPANY 396 (Z2)
O. K. Stove & Range Company
Palmer & Hardin
Peerless Manufacturing Co.
Progress Stove & Range Company
Riddell Furniture Company
ROME COMPANY, INC. 70-71
Shannon Spring Bed Mfg. Co.
Sobel-Marx Furniture Co.
Strassel Company, The J. L.
Stratton & Terstegge Company
Vogt Manufacturing Company
VOSS, L. C.
  See Period Cabinet Mfg. Co. 307
WILSON FURNITURE COMPANY, INC.
  Zone 1 Catalog. 430 (Z1)
  Zone 3 Catalog. 407 (Z3)
Taylor, Samuel L.
MOUNT STERLING
Ames Body Corporation
Murphy Chair Company
OWENSBORO
Mason Manufacturing Company
PARIS
Lack Manufacturing Company
PADUCAH
Bogardus-McDanell Company
McDanell Furniture Mfg. Co.
WARSAW

LOUISIANA

ALEXANDRIA
McCain, J. H.
BATON ROUGE
Grand, John R.
MONROE
Dixie Bedding Company

NEW ORLEANS
ARMSTRONG CORK COMPANY
  Catalog 81
  Home Furnishing & Dec. Sec. 9
Crescent Bed Company
Crescent Furniture & Mattress Co.
Leibe Refrigerator Mfg. Co., Wm.
Mondshun, Louis
Muller Furniture Mfg. Co.
New Orleans Chair Company
New Orleans Furniture Mfg. Co.
Pan-American Furniture Factory
ROME COMPANY, INC. 70-71
Sani-Bedding Company
SHREVEPORT
Shreveport Mattress Company

MAINE

BANGOR
Day Sons & Company, H. L.
ROME COMPANY, INC. 70-71
Wood & Bishop Company
NEW VINEYARD
Smith Manufacturing Co., Fred O.
PARIS
Paris Manufacturing Company
Mason Manufacturing Company
PORTLAND
Beals Furniture Co., Thos. P.
Burrowes Company, E. T.
Portland Stove Foundry Company

MARYLAND

BALTIMORE
Baltimore Spring Bed Company
Bibb Stove Company, B. C.
Chesapeake Manufacturing Company
Eastern Hardware & Supply Co.
FORSYTH FURNITURE LINES, INC.
  Catalog 272
  Home Furnishing & Dec. Sec. 16
FURST BROTHERS & COMPANY. 78
Gassinger, Gerhard B.
Goldstrom Brothers
Hartwig & Kemper
Hughes Furniture Mfg. Co.
International Bedding Company
Lears & Sons, C. H.
Levenson & Zenitz
Mohlhenrich Furniture Company
Pimes & Company, M.
ROME COMPANY, INC. 70-71
Seldner Company, George L.
Southern Couch Mfg. Co.
Spindler Company, Geo.
Standard Furniture Mfg. Co.
UNION BROTHERS. 420 (Z1)
UNITED FURNITURE MFG. CO. 420 (Z1)
White-Seidenman Company
CAMBRIDGE
Cambridge Furniture Company
EASTON
EASTON FURNITURE MANUFACTURING
COMPANY 400 (Z1)
HAGERSTOWN
Beachley Furniture Company
Brandt Cabinet Works
Hagerstown Furniture Company
Hagerstown Table Works
STATTON FURNITURE MANUFACTURING
COMPANY 418 (Z1)
PERRYVILLE
Armstrong Stove & Manufacturing Company
TEXAS
Empire Furniture Manufacturing Company

MASSACHUSETTS

ACTON
Blanchard & Son
ASHBURNHAM
Curtis Chair Company
Lombard, F. W.
White Manufacturing Company
Whitney Company, Alfred H.
(SOUTH ASHBURNHAM)
WHITNEY COMPANY, INC., W. F.
  Catalog 240
  Home Furnishing & Dec. Sec. 58
ASHLAND
Ashland Manufacturing Co. Inc.
Concord Colonial Chair Company
Wallace Nutting, Inc.
ATHOL
Athol Table Mfg. Co.
Cass Company, N. D.
Morris & Sons, L.
Worrick & Company, F. C.
BALDWINSVILLE
Smith-Day Company
Temple-Stuart Company
Thompson Chair Corp., E. L.
Waite Chair Company
BOSTON
ALLEN MFG. CO.
  Catalog 136
  Home Furnishing & Decoration Section. 10
American Mattress Company
American Moulding Company
American Reed & Fibre Company
Art Craft Upholstering Company
Atlantic Reed & Rattan Furn. Co.
Bacon Company, Francis H.
BARCALO MANUFACTURING CO. 393 (Z1)
Barrile & Company, S.
Bay State Upholstering Co.

Boston Mirror Company
Boston Parlor Frame Company
CANTERBURY DECORATIVE FABRICS
  (Marshall Field & Co., Wholesale).............. 87
Carbone, Inc.
Charak Furniture Company
Chase & Company, L. C.
Colonial Furniture Mfg. Co.
Columbia & Meyers Company
Commercial Reed & Rattan Co.
Commonwealth Upholstering Co.
CONANT-BALL COMPANY
  Catalog 191
  Home Furnishing & Dec. Sec............... 11
EASTON FURNITURE MFG. CO.............400 (Z1)
EBERT FURNITURE COMPANY
  Catalog distributed to all States............... 264
  Zone 1 Catalog....................402-403 (Z1)
Eddy & Sons Company, D.
Empire Upholstering Company
French & Heald Company
Heywood-Wakefield Company
Howes Company, S. M.
KENT-COSTIKYAN
  Catalog 89
  Home Furnishing & Decoration Section.......... 23
MERSMAN BROS. CORPORATION
  Catalog 216-221
  Home Furnishing & Decoration Section.........39-41
Miller & Goldberg Company
Modern Reed & Willow Furn. Co.
MORGANTON FURNITURE CO.............. 304
New England Bedding Company
New England Reed Company
New York Mattress Company
Old Colony Furniture Company
Orpin Desk Company
Parker-Young Company, The
Pearce Furniture Manufacturing Co.
PECK & HILLS FURNITURE COMPANY
  Catalog 392
  Home Furnishing & Decoration Sec............ 45
Peerless Upholstery Company
Premier Upholstery Co. Inc.
Prime Upholstery Company
PULLMAN COUCH COMPANY, INC.
  Catalog 128-129
  Home Furnishing & Dec. Sec.................. 46
Puritan Parlor Frame Company
ROGERS, INC., M. H.
  Catalog 90
  Home Furnishing & Decoration Sec............ 45
ROME COMPANY, INC......................70-71
Roxbury Carpet Company
SIMPSON, WARREN T.
  See Mersman Bros. Corp...................216-221
Singer, Inc.
ST. JOHNS TABLE CO...................... 236
Standard Parlor Frame Co. Inc.
Standard Upholstering Co.
Stiles Furniture Company
Stoughton Drake, Inc., Louis
Theise Manufacturing Co., Fred
Union Parlor Furniture Company
United Mattress Machinery Co.
Walker & Pratt Mfg. Company
Wilson & Glickson Uph. Co.

BRIGHTON
CAMBRIDGE
Cook & Company, C. A.
Kaplan Furniture Company
Shaw Furniture Company
Unique Furniture Co. Inc.
CONCORD JUNCTION
Allen Chair Company
E. TEMPLETON
Children's Vehicle Corp.
FALL RIVER
Osiason, J.
FITCHBURG
Angel Novelty Company
GARDNER
Atlantic Chair Company
Bent & Bros., S.
Brown Bros. Company
Chair City Upholstery Company
Coffin Chair Company
Collier-Keyworth Company
CONANT-BALL COMPANY
  Catalog 191
  Home Furnishing & Decoration Section.......... 11
Derby & Company, P.
Dickerman & Company
Dunn Company, John A.
Florence Stove Company
Gardner Chair Company
Gardner Reed & Rattan Company
Gardner Table Mfg. Co. Inc.
Gardner Upholstered Furn. Co.
Gem Crib & Cradle Company
Greenwood Associates
Harshorn, Inc., C. H.
Hedstrom-Union Company
Howe Spaulding Company
Kelly Bros., Inc.
Mahoney Chair Company
Nichols & Stone Company
O'Hearn Manufacturing Company
Pearce & Son, S. K.
Ramsdell & Co. L. B.
S. & E. Manufacturing Company
Siebert Company, O. W.
GLOUCESTER
Success Manufacturing Company
GREENFIELD
Newcombe & Son, E. A.
INDIAN ORCHARD
Hodges Carpet Company
LEOMINSTER
Bartlett, Waldo W.
Lambert & Latimer
Merriam, Hall & Company
Whitney Carriage Company, F. A.
Whitney Reed Corporation
LOWELL
Imperial Upholstery Company
Lyon Carpet Company
Saco-Lowell Shops

MANCHESTER
Dodge Furniture Company, C.
PLYMOUTH
Plymouth Foundry Company
READING
Boston Stove Foundry Company
SOMERVILLE
Bailie Basket Company
Conant Brothers Company
Moulton Company, C. W. H.
New England Cabinet Company
SCHEIBE, R. R.
  Catalog 414 (Z1)
  Home Furnishing & Decoration Section.......... 44
Sprague Hathaway Studios, Inc.
SPRINGFIELD
Berkshire Uph. Co. Inc.
Bozart Rug Company
ROME COMPANY, INC......................70-71
Springfield Mattress Company
Taber-Prang Art Company
United States Spring Bed Company
TAUNTON
Glenwood Range Company
Leonard & Baker Stove Company
North Dighton Stove Company
Thomas Company, Oscar G.
Weir Stove Company
White-Warner Company
WALPOLE
Bird & Son
WALTHAM
Atlas Parlor Suite Mfg. Co.
WESTFIELD
Westfield Manufacturing Co.
WEST STERLING
T. & E. R. Buck
WINCHENDON
Carter & Campbell, Inc.
Converse & Son Company, Morton E.
Winchendon Chair Company
WORCESTER
Hamblin & Russell Mfg. Co.
ROME COMPANY, INC......................70-71
Whittall Associates, M. J.
Wire Goods Company
Young Brothers Company

MICHIGAN

ADRIAN
Fireside Industries
Mott Manufacturing Company
Palmer & Son, A. E.
ALLEGAN
Allegan Furniture Shops
BAKER FURNITURE FACTORIES, INC...... 243
Oliver Furniture Company
ANN ARBOR
Westgate Manufacturing Company
ARCADIA
Arcadia Furniture Company
BATTLE CREEK
A. B. Stove Company
BAY CITY
Kelton-Aurand Manufacturing Co.
BELDING
Belding-Hall Company
BIG RAPIDS
Big Rapids Furn. Mfg. Co.
Falcon Mfg. Company
Griswold Guest Company
CADILLAC
Northern Chair Company
ST. JOHNS TABLE COMPANY................ 236
CHARLOTTE
Charlotte Chair Company
CHARLOTTE FURNITURE COMPANY
  Catalog 258
  Home Furnishing & Dec. Sec.................... 11
COLDWATER
Pratt Manufacturing Company
DETROIT
American Uph. & Mfg. Co.
Art Stove Company
Aulsbrook Company, The
BARCALO MANUFACTURING COMPANY.393 (Z1)
CHICAGO MIRROR & ART GLASS CO.....395 (Z3)
Detroit Bedding Company
Detroit Cabinet Company
Detroit Chair Mfg. Co.
Detroit Lamp Mfg. Co.
Detroit Rack Company
Detroit Stove Works
Detroit Vapor Stove Company
FORSYTH FURNITURE LINES, INC.
  Catalog 272
  Home Furnishing & Decoration Sec............ 16
Gordon-Chapman Company
Haberkorn Company, C. H.
MARTIN, JESS L.
  See Chicago Mirror & Art Glass Co.........395 (Z3)
Michigan Stove Company
New York Bed Spring Mfg. Co.
Peninsular Stove Company
Progress Bedding Company
ROME COMPANY, INC......................70-71
Schadt & Mathewson
Standard Uph. Furniture Co.
WESTERN SHADE CLOTH COMPANY
  Catalog 405 (Z3)
  Home Furnishing & Decoration Sec............ 59
DOWAGIAC
Beckwith Company, The
EVART
Evart Fibre Furniture Company
GRAND HAVEN
Challenge Refrigerator Company
EAGLE-OTTAWA LEATHER COMPANY
  Catalog 83
  Home Furnishing & Decoration Sec.......... 13

GRAND LEDGE
Grand Ledge Chair Company
GRAND RAPIDS
ALLEN MANUFACTURING COMPANY
  Catalog 136
  Home Furnishing & Decoration Sec.... 10
AULSBROOK & JONES FURNITURE CO... 242
BAKER FURNITURE FACTORIES, INC..... 243
BAY VIEW FURNITURE COMPANY......393 (Z3)
Bechtold Brothers Uph. Co.
Berkey Furniture Company, Wm. A.
BERKEY & GAY FURNITURE COMPANY
  Berkey and Gay Furniture Co.........248-251
  Grand Rapids Upholstery Co...........252-253
Bissell Carpet Sweeper Company
Brower Furniture Company
BUFFALO LOUNGE COMPANY
  Catalog 394 (Z1)
  Home Furnishing & Dec. Section......... 10
CENTURY FURNITURE COMPANY.......... 92
CHARLOTTE FURNITURE COMPANY
  Catalog 258
  Home Furnishing & Decoration Sec............ 11
Chase Furniture Company, H. W.
CHATTANOOGA FURNITURE CO....... 259
COLONIAL DESK COMPANY............138-141
Colonial Furniture Company
COLONIAL MFG. CO.
  Catalog 142-143
CONANT-BALL COMPANY
  Catalog 191
  Home Furnishing & Decoration Section.......... 11
CONANT'S SONS, INC., F. H.
  Catalog 192
  Home Furnishing & Decoration Section.......... 12
DAVIS-BIRELY TABLE COMPANY.......... 193
EMPIRE FURNITURE COMPANY.......... 268
Engstrom & Johnson Furniture Co.
Excelsior Wrapper Company
Kindel Furniture Company
FURNITURE CITY UPHOLSTERY
  COMPANY 104
FURNITURE SHOPS
  (Division of the Luce Furniture Shops)
  Catalog 160-161
  Home Furnishing & Decoration Section.......... 16
Furniture Studios, Inc.
Good Furniture Magazine
Grand Rapids Bedding Company
Grand Rapids Chair Company
GRAND RAPIDS DESK CO.
  See Stow-Davis Furniture Co...............76-77
Grand Rapids Fancy Furniture Company
Grand Rapids Furniture Company
Grand Rapids Market Association
Grand Rapids Refrigerator Company
GRAND RAPIDS UPHOLSTERING
  COMPANY 252-253
GUNN FURNITURE COMPANY
  Catalog 396 (Z3)
  Home Furnishing & Decoration Section......... 19
HARDEN COMPANY, FRANK S.
  Catalog 108-109
  Home Furnishing & Decoration Section.......... 18
Hart Mirror Plate Company
HASTINGS TABLE COMPANY............150-151
HEKMAN FURNITURE COMPANY......398 (Z3)
IMPERIAL FURNITURE COMPANY
  Catalog 198-205
  Home Furnishing & Dec. Sec............21-22
IRWIN COMPANY, ROBERT W............. 275
JAMESTOWN TABLE COMPANY.......... 276
JAMESTOWN UPHOLSTERY COMPANY, INC.
  Catalog 110
  Home Furnishing & Decoration Section.......... 21
Johnson Handley & Johnson
KINDEL FURNITURE COMPANY
  Poster and Windsor Beds...........282-283
  Day Beds 372-373
  Home Furnishing & Decoration Sec............ 24
Klise Manufacturing Company
Lauzon-Morse Furniture Company
LIMBERT COMPANY, CHARLES P.
  Catalog 281
  Home Furnishing & Decoration Section......... 39
LUCE FURNITURE CO...................156-159
  (Division of the Luce Furniture Shops)
LUCE FURNITURE SHOPS
  Furniture Shops, Home Furnishing and
    Decoration Section 16
  Furniture Shops, Catalog 160-161
  Luce Furniture Co., Catalog.........156-159
  Michigan Chair Company, Catalog.....162-163
Luxury Furniture Company
Lynch Sales Company, Jos. P.
Macey Company
Mentzer Read Company
Metal Office Furniture Company
MICHIGAN CHAIR COMPANY...........162-163
  (Division of the Luce Furniture Shops)
MILLER, HERMAN CLOCK CO........ 144
MILLER FURNITURE CO., HERMAN
  Catalog 145
  Home Furnishing & Decoration Section......... 36
Mouw, Inc., Andy
Mueller Furniture Company
Nachtegel Manufacturing Company
NATIONAL FURNITURE CO.
  Catalog 124
National Spring & Wire Company
Nichols & Cox Lumber Company
PAALMAN FURNITURE COMPANY.......400 (Z3)
Paiget Donnelly Company
PENN TABLE COMPANY.................... 268
PERIOD CABINET MANUFACTURING CO.
  Catalog 307
  Home Furnishing & Decoration Section......... 38
Periodical Publishing Company
Phoenix Furniture Company
Pritchett-Powers Company
ROCKFORD CHAIR & FURNITURE CO.....308-313
ROCKFORD PALACE FURNITURE CO......322-323
SCHOECK MANUFACTURING CO. INC.
  Catalog 415 (Z1)
  Home Furnishing & Decoration Sec.......... 50
Schoonbeck Company, H.
Shanahan Furniture Company
Shaw Company, H. E.
Shear-Maddox Furniture Company
SIKES CHAIR COMPANY.................... 238

SKANDIA FURNITURE COMPANY
  Desks and Bookcases Catalog..................172-185
  Dining Room Furniture Catalog................342-345
SLIGH FURNITURE COMPANY.............. 335
SPENCER-DUFFY COMPANY, INC.........125-127
  Standardized Furniture Company
Steil Shops
Sterling Furniture Company
STEUL & SONS, INC., HENRY C.
  Catalog 348
  Home Furnishing & Decoration Section.......... 49
Stickley Brothers Company
STICKLEY, INC., L. & J. G. AND STICKLEY
  MANUFACTURING CO. INC.
  Catalog 352-353
  Home Furnishing & Decoration Sec............ 52
Stone, Inc., Geo. L.
STOW-DAVIS FURNITURE COMPANY
  Catalog 76-77
  Home Furnishing & Decoration Section.......... 53
Stuart Furniture Company
Superior Furniture Company
TILLOTSON FURNITURE CORP.............. 358
UNION FURNITURE COMPANY, (Rockford, Ill.)
  Desks and Bookcases Catalog..................186-187
  Dining Room Furniture Catalog................360-361
Valley City Desk Company
Vander Ley Brothers
Wallace Furniture Company
WEST MICHIGAN FURNITURE CO.
  Colonial Bedroom Furniture Catalog...........284-285
  Bedroom Furniture Catalog...................286-287
  Home Furnishing & Decoration Section.......... 57
WHITE FURNITURE CO..................... 365
WIDDICOMB COMPANY, JOHN
  Catalog 366
  Home Furnishing & Dec. Sec............ 58
WIDDICOMB FURNITURE COMPANY
  Catalog 367
  Home Furnishing & Decoration Section.......... 59
WIENER COMPANY, E.
  Catalog 406 (Z3)
  Home Furnishing & Decoration Section.......... 60
Williams Kimp Furniture Company
Windsor Furniture Company
Wolverine Upholstery Company
Wood Batik Shops, Inc.
Wagemaker Company
YPSILANTI REED FURNITURE COMPANY
  Catalog 135
  Home Furnishing & Decoration Section.......... 60
GREENBUSH
Michigan Cedarcraft Company
GREENVILLE
Gibson Refrigerator Company
Ranney Refrigerator Company
HASTINGS
Grand Rapids Book Case & Chair Co.
HASTINGS TABLE COMPANY...............150-151
HOLLAND
American Cabinet Company
BAY VIEW FURNITURE COMPANY......393 (Z3)
Donnelly Kelley Glass Company
Holland Chair Company
Holland Furniture Company
LIMBERT COMPANY, CHAS. P.
  Catalog 281
  Home Furnishing & Decoration Section.......... 39
Ottawa Furniture Company
Thompson Manufacturing Company
WEST MICHIGAN FURNITURE COMPANY
  Colonial Bedroom Furniture Catalog...........284-285
  Bedroom Furniture Catalog...................286-287
  Home Furnishing & Dec. Sec................... 57
IONIA
YPSILANTI REED FURNITURE COMPANY
  Catalog 135
  Home Furnishing & Decoration Section.......... 60
JACKSON
Home Products Corporation
Jackson Glass Works
Michigan Seating Company
KALAMAZOO
Kalamazoo Stove Company
Metal Kitchen Cabinet & Table Co.
Perfection Rest-Easy Mattress Co.
LANSING
Bunday Bedding Company
LAPEER
Bostick Stove Company
LOWELL
Peckham Furniture Company
LUDINGTON
Carrom Company, The
MANISTEE
Manistee Manufacturing Company
MENOMINEE
Lloyd Manufacturing Company
MONROE
Weis Manufacturing Company
MUSKEGON
Alaska Refrigerator Company
Browne-Morse Company
Shaw-Walker Company
Superior Cabinet Company
NASHVILLE
Lentz Table Company
NILES
Kawner Company
Kompass & Stoll Company
ONAWAY
Lobdel & Emery Manufacturing Co.
OWOSSO
ESTEY MANUFACTURING COMPANY
  Catalog 265
  Home Furnishing & Decoration Section.......... 15
Independent Stove Company
Robbins Table Company
Woodard Furniture Company
READING
Acme Chair Company
SAGINAW
Saginaw Furniture Shops
Saginaw Mirror Works

STURGIS
AULSBROOK & JONES FURNITURE
  COMPANY 242
Grobhiser-Cabinet Makers Co. Inc.
Kirsch Manufacturing Company
Royal Easy Chair Company
Sturgis Manufacturing Company
Wilhelm Furniture Company
TRAVERSE CITY
Greilick Manufacturing Company
Johnson-Randall Company
WYANDOTTE
Regent Stove Company
YPSILANTI
Lewis-Geer Manufacturing Co.
ZEELAND
COLONIAL MANUFACTURING COMPANY..142-143
MILLER CLOCK CO., HERMAN.... 144
MILLER FURNITURE COMPANY, HERMAN
  Catalog 145
  Home Furnishing & Decoration Section.......... 36

MINNESOTA

ANOKA
Colonial Upholstery Company
CLOQUET
G. & W. Refrigerator Company
DULUTH
Dewitt-Seitz Company
Klearfax Linen Looms
Lavick Bedding Company
FARIBAULT
PETERSON ART FURNITURE COMPANY.... 164
Schimmel & Company
MINNEAPOLIS
ALLEN MANUFACTURING COMPANY
  Catalog 136
  Home Furnishing & Decoration Section.......... 10
American Carriage & Wicker Works
American Wood Products Corporation
ARMSTRONG CORK COMPANY
  Catalog 81
  Home Furnishing & Decoration Section.......... 9
AUTOMATIC SHADE COMPANY
  Catalog 189
  Home Furnishing & Decoration Section.......... 9
Bintliff Manufacturing Company
BROMLEY ADVERTISING AGENCY
  See Automatic Shade Co..................... 189
Brooks Parlor Furniture Company
BUREAU OF ENGRAVING
  See Retailers Service Bureau..............413 (Z1)
Cleveland Co., H. S.
Dahlin Bros.
Davis Manufacturing Company
EVERS, J. A.
  See Automatic Shade Co..................... 189
Forman Ford & Company
French Furniture Company, Wm. A.
FURNITURE SALES CO.
  See Mersman Bros. Corpn.....................216-221
Gangelhoff Brothers
Grau-Curtis Company
Island Furniture Company
Keller Manufacturing Company
LEVIN BROTHERS, INC.
  Catalog 111
  Home Furnishing & Decoration Section.......... 34
LUGER FURNITURE COMPANY
  Catalog 399 (Z3)
  Home Furnishing & Decoration Section.......... 35
McLeod & Smith
MERSMAN BROS. CORPORATION
  Catalog 216-221
  Home Furnishing & Decoration Section.......39-41
Minneapolis Desk Manufacturing Co.
Minneapolis Furniture Company
Minneapolis Supply Company
Northwestern Reed & Fibre Company
Northwestern Upholstery Company
RETAILERS' SERVICE BUREAU..........413 (Z1)
ROME COMPANY, INC.....................70-71
Salisbury & Satterlee Company
Sanitary Mattress Company
SCHOECK MFG. CO., INC.................415 (Z1)
Twin City Upholstery Company
Way Sagless Spring Company
WILLIAMS, JOSEPH G.
  See Schoeck Mfg. Co., Inc.................415 (Z1)
RED WING
Red Wing Furniture Company
Red Wing Manufacturing Company
ST. PAUL
ARONSON, A. A.
  See Chicago Mirror and Art Glass Co.........395 (Z3)
Bohn Refrigerator Company
CHICAGO MIRROR & ART GLASS
  COMPANY 395 (Z3)
CHITTENDEN & EASTMAN CO............. 377
Joesting & Schilling Company
Rowe Glass Company, Jas.
St. Paul Glass Company
Sealy Mattress Company of Minn.
Seeger Refrigerator Company
U. S. Bedding Company
Zimmer Furniture Company
SAUK RAPIDS
AUTOMATIC SHADE COMPANY
  Catalog 189
  Home Furnishing & Decoration Section.......... 9
WATERVILLE
Petersen Woodcraft Company

MISSISSIPPI

LAUREL
McLeod Furniture Company
GREENWOOD
Mississippi Valley Furn. Mfg. Co.

MISSOURI

CAPE GIRARDEAU
Drusch & Company, E.
CARTHAGE
Carthage Superior Spring Bed Mfg. Co.
Leggett & Platt Spring Bed Mfg. Co.
CHILLICOTHE
Chillicothe Furniture Company
HANNIBAL
Duffy Trowbridge Stove Mfg. Co.
JEFFERSON CITY
Fibercraft Chair Company
KANSAS CITY
Abernathy Furniture Company
ARMSTRONG CORK COMPANY
  Catalog 81
  Home Furnishing & Decoration Section.......... 9
Brown Bed Manufacturing Co.
Comstock Castle Stove Company
Helmers Manufacturing Company
K. C. Furniture Manufacturing Co.
MINTURN BROS.
  See Mersman Bros. Corpn.....................216-221
ROME COMPANY, INC.....................70-71
Volker Company, Wm.
Western Cabinet & Fixture Mfg. Co.
ST. JOSEPH
ALLEN MANUFACTURING COMPANY
  Catalog 136
  Home Furnishing & Decoration Section.......... 10
Biernacki Furniture Co. Inc., Frank
Hax-Smith Furniture Co. Inc.
Midwest Furniture & Chair Company
ST. LOUIS
American Bed Company
ARMSTRONG CORK COMPANY
  Catalog 81
  Home Furnishing & Decoration Section.......... 9
Artistic Furniture Co. Inc.
Barrelmeyer, Theo.
Blackmore Manufacturing Company
Bridge & Beach Manufacturing Company
Brownie Woodcraft Shops
Buck's Stove & Range Company
Casper Stehle Bedding Company
Central Furniture Company
Conrades Manufacturing Company
Coopersmith Bed Company
Copper Clad Malleable Range Co.
FOSTER BROS. MFG. CO................... 69
Geisel Manufacturing Co., A.
General Reed Furniture Company
Hanpeter Furniture Company, F. W.
Heinz Stove Company, C.
Holtgrewe-Vornbrock Furniture Co. Inc.
Jackes-Evans Manufacturing Company
Joering & Pelchmann
Kaiser Manufacturing Company, Jacob
Kuchins Furniture Mfg. Co.
Lammert Furniture Company
Landau Manufacturing Company
Leroi Furniture Mfg. Co.
Majestic Stove Company
Manne Upholstery Company, L.
Manufacturers' Agency, Inc.
Meier & Pohlmann Company
Missouri Furniture Company
National Chair Company
Perfection Manufacturing Company
Peters Furniture Company, Jos.
Pokorny & Company
Prufrock-Litton Furniture Co.
ROME COMPANY, INC.....................70-71
Royal Bedding Company
Ruhlmann, C. A.
St. Louis Furniture Works' Ass'n
Smith & Davis Manufacturing Co.
Standard Furniture Manufacturing Co.
Star Bedding Company
Success Furniture Corporation
Sueme Furniture Company, Chas.
Thornton, L. M.
Udell & Predock Manufacturing Co.
Valley Furniture Co. Inc.
Welsh-Coffey Mirror & Beveling Co.
WESTERN SHADE CLOTH COMPANY
  Catalog 405 (Z3)
  Home Furnishing & Decoration Section.......... 59
Western Wire Products Company
Wolf & Kraemer Furniture Company
Wrought Iron Range Company
SEDALIA
Dickman & Sons, Joseph A.
SPRINGFIELD
Springfield Furniture Company
Woods-Evertz Stove Company

MONTANA

BUTTE
ROME COMPANY, INC.....................70-71
MISSOULA
ALLEN MANUFACTURING COMPANY
  Catalog 136
  Home Furnishing & Decoration Section.......... 10

NEBRASKA

FREMONT
Crystal Refrigerator Company
Parlor Furniture & Mattress Company
OMAHA
Beebe & Runyan Furniture Company
Doup Company, L. G.
Orchard & Wilhelm Mattress Company
ROME COMPANY, INC.....................70-71
RALSTON
Howard Stove & Furniture Company
Orchard & Wihelm Furniture Factory

NEW HAMPSHIRE

ANTRIM
Abbott Estate, John G.
DERRY
Derry Made Products Company, Inc.
HARRISVILLE
Winn Brothers
KEENE
Carey Chair Manufacturing Company
Keene Chair Company
Norwood Calef & Company
Russell & Sons, C. L.
Sprague & Carleton
MANCHESTER
New Hampshire Bedding Company
MILFORD
French & Heald
NASHUA
Maine Manufacturing Company
ROCHESTER
Spaulding & Sons Company, J.
SALMON FALLS
Somersworth Foundry Company
SWANZEY
Lane Chair Factory

NEW JERSEY

CAMDEN
Comey Company, R. H.
EGG HARBOR CITY
Bloch Go-Cart Company
ENGLISHTOWN
Englishtown Carpet Company
GLOUCESTER
Breslin Brothers Company
HIGHTSTOWN
HIGHTSTOWN RUG COMPANY.............. 88
HOBOKEN
Ebbecke Furniture Company
Federal Furniture Factories
Federal-Montauk Corporation
Ferguson Bros. Mfg. Company
Travers Company, Geo. W.
United States Rattan Company
United States Willow Furniture Co.
JERSEY CITY
Aimone Furniture Company
Hannon, John A.
Jersey City Go-Cart Company
Levinson Manufacturing Company
Mersereau Metal Bed Company
PECK & HILLS FURNITURE COMPANY
  Catalog 392
  Home Furnishing & Dec. Sec. 45
Runyan Manufacturing Co., J. D.
LITTLE FALLS
BEATTIE MANUFACTURING COMPANY.... 82
MONTCLAIR
SCHOECK MANUFACTURING COMPANY, INC.
  Catalog 415 (Z1)
  Home Furnishing & Decoration Section.......... 50
SMITH, C. DEWEY
  See Schoeck Manufacturing Co., Inc.....415 (Z1)
MT. HOLLY
Royle & Pilkington Company
NEWARK
American Metal Bed Company
Bauman & Company, Henry L.
Climax Crib Company
CURTISS & SON, WM. P.................399 (Z1)
Gennet, Jacob
John Henry Stores
Mitnick Upholstery Company
Modern Upholstery Company
ROME COMPANY, INC.....................70-71
Shaw, I. M. & N.
Woodcraft Furniture Company
NEW BRUNSWICK
Brunswick-Kroescheck Company
NEWFIELD
Morrell's Reed & Rattan Company
NEWTON
Columbia Furniture & Mfg. Co.
PATERSON
Hartmeier & Sons Company
LaMond & Robertson Company
PERTH AMBOY
Harris Edelstein
RAHWAY
Regina Corporation, The
Sulo, Sylvester P.
SOMERVILLE
Cott-A-Lap Company
Somerville Stove Works
TENAFLY
Tenafly Lumber & Supply Company
TRENTON
Bloom & Godley Company
Trenton Spring Mattress Company
WEST HOBOKEN
Giordano & Company, P.

NEW YORK

ALBANY
Fishman, Wm.
Hasselbarth, C. O.
ROME COMPANY, INC........................70-71
AMSTERDAM
Mohawk Carpet Mills
BINGHAMTON
Wilkinson Manufacturing Co. Inc.

BOONEVILLE
Sargent's Sons, N. W.
Union Loom Works, Inc.
BROCTON
Brocton Furniture Company
BROOKLYN
Bedford Chair Company
Behr, Henry
Bronx Manufacturing Company
Brooklyn Dining Room Chair Co.
Brooklyn Wire Chair Company
Buchman Company, L.
Chelsea Fibre Mills
CHICAGO MIRROR & ART GLASS
  COMPANY 395 (Z3)
Crescent Show Case Company
Colonial Show Case Company
Colonial Mantel & Refrigerator Co.
D & S Fibre Company
Eagle Upholstery Company
Englander Spring Bed Company
Enterprise Metal Bed Company
Federal Montauk Corporation
Federal Parlor Suite Company
Feldstein, Joseph
FORSYTH FURNITURE LINES, INC.
  272
  Home Furnishing & Decoration Section.......... 16
Frischman & Son, F.
Fusfield, J.
Greenpoint Metallic Bed Company
Greenpoint Parlor Suite Company
Greenspan Wolf & Son
Haas, Joseph
Herz-Englander Co.
Ideal Chair Company
Kass Brothers & Company
Kay Manufacturing Co. Inc.
Lack, L.
Lash-Handler Upholstery Co. Inc.
Lorberbaum & Company, Israel
McKee Refrigerator Company
Magner Furniture Company
Majestic Chair Company
Manhattan Bed Company
Manhattan Mantel Company
Mann, Adam
Marvel Upholstery Co. Inc.
Meibach Chair Company, Inc.
Miller, Jacob D.
Montauk Rug Mills, Inc.
National Chair Company
National Parlor Suite Company
OSTERMAN, LOUIS
  See Chicago Mirror & Art Glass Co..........395 (Z3)
Paramount Upholstery Company
Pierce & Son, S. K.
Progressive Table Mfg. Company
Reliable Metal Bed Company
Reliable Table Company
Rohmann Sons & Company, C. F.
Ryan & McGahan
Sabel & Phillips
Shapiro Bros. Upholstery Co.
Shuff, Samuel
Stein & Ehrlick
Superior Upholstery Company
Sutton Carpet Lining Co., E. W.
Union Parlor Suite Company
United Spring Bed Company
Universal Metal Bed Company
Universal Upholstery Company
UNIVERSAL WILLOW & REED WARE
  COMPANY, INC. 422 (Z1)
Vogeley & Lackman
Warner Shade & Novelty Company
Wilder Manufacturing Co. Inc.
Yeaple, B. J.
Zaldin Sons & Company
BUFFALO
BARCALO MANUFACTURING
  COMPANY 393 (Z1)
Bison Upholstery Company
Bott Furniture Company, C. M.
Buffalo Davenport Bed Company
Buffalo Furniture Mfg. Co.
BUFFALO LOUNGE COMPANY
  Catalog 394 (Z1)
  Home Furnishing & Decorating Section.......... 10
Du-Lux Living Room Furniture Co.
Dwelle-Kiser Company
Fisher Furniture Company
HARD MANUFACTURING COMPANY.....404 (Z1)
Heinz & Munschauer, Inc.
Jewett & Company
Kittinger Company
Lang Manufacturing Company
Ludwig, H.
National Mirror Company
ROME COMPANY, INC.....................70-71
SIKES CHAIR COMPANY....................238
STEUL & SONS, INC., H. C.
  Catalog 348
  Home Furnishing & Decoration Section.......... 49
Upholstered Construction Company
WESTERN SHADE CLOTH COMPANY
  Catalog 405 (Z3)
  Home Furnishing & Decoration Section.......... 59
CAMDEN
CONANTS' SONS INC., F. H.
  Catalog 192
  Home Furnishing & Decoration Section.......... 12
HARDEN COMPANY, FRANK S.
  Catalog 108-109
  Home Furnishing & Decoration Section.......... 18
Young & Sons, J. M.
CLARK MILLS
Hind & Harrison Plush Company
COBLESKILL
Harder Manufacturing Company
CORTLAND
Brewer-Titchener Corp.
DUNKIRK
Dunkirk Upholstery Company
FORT PLAIN
Hix Furniture Company
FREWSBURG
Frewsburg Furniture Company, Inc.

FAYETTEVILLE
STICKLEY, INC., L. & J. G.
  Catalog 352-353
  Home Furnishing & Decoration Section.......... 52
GENEVA
Andes Range & Furnace Corp.
Summit Foundry Company
GLENDALE
Union Table & Spring Company
GREENE
Greene Mfg. Company
HERKIMER
Hale Manufacturing Co., F. E.
Wagner Furniture Company
HICKORY
Hickory Table & Novelty Company
HONEOYE FALLS
Rood Furniture Company, V. J.
HORNELL
Deutsch & Company, J. M.
HUDSON
Winstian, Louis
JAMAICA
Art-Craft Upholstery Co. Inc.
JAMESTOWN
Acme Furniture Company
Active Furniture Company
Advance Furniture Company
Alliance Furniture Company
Allied Furniture Company
American Manufacturing Concern
Anchor Furniture Company
ATLAS FURNITURE COMPANY.............. 241
Bailey Table Company
BUFFALO LOUNGE COMPANY
  Catalog 394 (Z1)
  Home Furnishing & Decoration Section.......... 10
DAVIS FURNITURE CORPORATION........ 262
Diamond Furniture Company
ELITE FURNITURE COMPANY.............. 146
Elk Furniture Company
Emerson Glass Corporation
EMPIRE CASE GOODS COMPANY
  Catalog 266-267
  Home Furnishing & Decoration Section.......... 14
Espey Furniture Corporation
Falconer Plate Glass Corp.
Herrick Manufacturing Company
Jamestown Case Goods Company
JAMESTOWN CHAIR COMPANY............. 206
JAMESTOWN FURNITURE MARKET
  ASSOCIATION 387
JAMESTOWN LOUNGE COMPANY........... 105
JAMESTOWN TABLE COMPANY............. 276
JAMESTOWN UPHOLSTERY COMPANY INC.
  Catalog 110
  Home Furnishing & Decoration Section.......... 21
Level Furniture Company
Maddox Table Company
Marvel Furniture Company
Monarch Furniture Company
Monitor Furniture Company
National Furniture Company
NORQUIST COMPANY, A. C. 305
Premier Cabinet Corporation
Robertson Company, H. P.
Royal Upholstery Company
Schulze & Van Stee Manufacturing Co.
SEABURG MANUFACTURING COMPANY.416 (Z1)
Shearman Brothers Company
Star Furniture Company
Supreme Furniture Mfg. Co.
Tablescope Company, The
TILLOTSON FURNITURE
  CORPORATION 358
Union Furniture Company
KINGSTON
Shilling Bros. Furniture Co.
Shilling Bros. Table Company
LINOLEUMVILLE
American Linoleum Manufacturing Co.
LONG ISLAND CITY
Adler Veneer Seat Company
Chesterfield Furniture Company
Cocheo Brothers
Freeman Bros., Inc.
KARPEN & BROS., S.
  Catalog 112-119
  Home Furnishing & Decoration Section..........25-29
Klein Brothers Company
Orsenigo Company
PULLMAN COUCH COMPANY
  Catalog 128-129
  Home Furnishing & Decoration Section.......... 46
ROME COMPANY, INC.....................70-71
Segal Manufacturing Company
TEEPE-WHITNEY CORPORATION
  See W. F. Whitney Co., Inc. 240
LOWVILLE
Haberer Furniture Company, J. E.
McCONNELLSVILLE
HARDEN COMPANY, FRANK S.
  Catalog 108-109
  Home Furnishing & Decoration Section.......... 18
MAYVILLE
Chautauque Cabinet Company, Inc.
Kling Factories
MECHANICSVILLE
Eckerson Bedding Company
MEDINA
Cook & Company, S. A.
Empire Couch Company
Character Furniture Company
MOTTVILLE
Mottville Chair Works, Inc.
Sinclair-Allen Mfg. Corp.
NEWARK
Hallagan Mfg. Company, Inc.
NEWBURGH
Crawshaw Carpet Company
Staples & Hanford Company
Wicker-Kraft Corporation
NEW HARTFORD
American Emblem Company

NEW YORK

Abramson, Ginsburg & Company
Aimone Manufacturing Company
Albano Company, The
Albert, Phillip
American Pile Fabric Company
ARMSTRONG CORK COMPANY
Catalog 81
Home Furnishing & Decoration Section.......... 9
Arnold, Constable & Company
Arrow Metal Bed Corporation
Arrow Upholstery Company, The
Ashley Furniture Company, Inc.
Atlantic Excelsior Manufacturing Co.
Bache Semon & Company
Baker & Company, A. T.
Barry, Ostlere & Shepherd, Inc.
BASIC FURNITURE COMPANY.............. 244
BEATTIE MANUFACTURING COMPANY...... 82
Benziger Brothers
Bigelow-Hartfort Carpet Company
Bilt-Rite Chair Company
Biltrite Furniture Corporation
Bloom, Charles
Blumenthal & Company, Sidney
Brighton Mills, Inc.
Brooklyn Chair Company
Burns Bros. Manufacturing Co.
BURROWS BROTHERS COMPANY....395-397 (Z1)
CALDWELL FURNITURE CO...............398 (Z1)
CANTERBURY DECORATIVE FABRICS
(Marshall Field and Company, Wholesale)........ 87
Cardarelli & Company, G.
CHARLOTTE FURNITURE COMPANY
Catalog 258
Home Furnishing & Decoration Section.......... 11
Charlotte Mills
Chatham Upholstery Corporation
Cherkezian Brothers
Chesterton Furniture Company
Cohen, Louis
Collins & Aikman Company
COLONIAL DRAPERY FABRICS
(Marshall Field and Company, Wholesale) Catalog 84
Home Furnishing and Decoration Section..........30-32
Columbia Mills
Consolidated Trimming Company
Cook, Inc., Arthur Lee
Cook's Linoleum Co.
Costikyan & Company
Crex Carpet Company
Decorators Furniture Company
Debski, F.
Disbrow & Kofahl, Inc.
Dobson, John & James
Doehler Die Cast Co.
DOMES OF SILENCE, INC.................... 134
Donchian & Company
DORAN CO., LOUIS J.
See Dixie Furniture Co......................... 263
DORSON CO., LOUIS J.
See Statesville Furniture Co.................... 346
Dorothy Lamp Shade Company
EAGLE-OTTAWA LEATHER COMPANY
Catalog 83
Home Furnishing & Decoration Section.......... 13
Eastern Rug & Trading Company
EASTON FURNITURE MFG. CO...........400 (Z1)
EBERT FURNITURE COMPANY
Catalog distributed to all States............... 264
Catalog distributed to Zone 1............402-403 (Z1)
Eckstein Company, N.
Empire Carpet Company
EMPIRE CASE GOODS COMPANY
Catalog 266-267
Home Furnishing & Decoration Section.......... 14
EMPIRE FURNITURE CO...................... 268
Erskine-Danforth Corporation
Excelsior Art Ironworks
Feldman Company, Manuel
Firth Carpet Company
Fiske Iron Works, J. W.
FIELD & CO., WHOLESALE, MARSHALL
Home Furnishing & Decoration Section..........30-32
Colonial Drapery Fabrics Catalog............... 84
Zion Lace Curtains and Nets Catalog........... 85
Home-Crest Floor Coverings Catalog........... 86
Canterbury Decorative Fabrics Catalog......... 87
Home-Crest Upholstered Furniture Catalog......100-101
Feltite Chair Corporation
FORSYTH FURNITURE LINES, INC.
Catalog 272
Home Furnishing & Decoration Section.......... 16
Frank & Son
French American Manufacturing Co.
FRIEDMAN, JOSEPH
See Statton Furniture Mfg. Co..............418 (Z1)
Fritz & La Rue Company
Fuldner & Sons, Henry
Fulton Furniture Corporation
FURST BROS. & COMPANY.................. 78
Ginsberg, Jos. W.
Glaenzer Trading Corporation
GLOBE-BOSSE-WORLD FURNITURE COMPANY
Catalog 273
Home Furnishing & Decoration Section.......... 17
GLOBE PARLOR FURNITURE CO...........106-107
Gobelin Textile Corporation
Goldstein Chair Company, Joseph
Grand Central Wicker Shop
Greater New York Bedding Company
Greenstein & Sons, Samuel
GRIFFITH FURNITURE WORKS............ 147
Grinberg Brothers
Groff-Bent Corporation
Gross Company, Edward
Grossfeld, Inc., Albert
Gudeman & Company
Gulbenkian Gullabi & Company
GUNN FURNITURE COMPANY
Catalog 396 (Z3)
Home Furnishing & Decoration Section.......... 19
GUTTER, S. J.
See Caldwell Furniture Co..................398 (Z1)
Haberbritz, Phillip
Hacker, David
Hall & Sons, Frank A.
Hall, Charles
HANSON CLOCK COMPANY, INC..........148-149
Harris, John D.
Harvey, Murray M.
Hayim Rashti & Company
Hallen & Weiner
HARDEN COMPANY, FRANK S.
Catalog 108-109
Home Furnishing & Decoration Section.......... 18
Hayden Company
HELLAM FURNITURE CO. INC.......406-407 (Z1)
Herrmann Furniture Co., H.
HIGHTSTOWN RUG COMPANY.............. 88
HOME-CREST FLOOR COVERINGS
(Marshall Field and Company, Wholesale)........ 86
HOME FURNITURE COMPANY........408-409 (Z1)
Horn Brothers Company
Jaeger, Geo. A.
Japanese Fan Company
Jarnow & Company
Judd Company, H. L.
Kalter Brothers
Karagheusian, A. & M.
KARGES FURNITURE COMPANY............ 280
KARPEN & BROS., S.
Catalog 112-119
Home Furnishing & Decoration Sec..............25-29
Kensington Manufacturing Company
KENT-COSTIKYAN
Catalog 89
Home Furnishing & Decoration Section.......... 23
Kitchen Made Equipment
KLAMER FURNITURE CORPORATION
Catalog 288-289
Home Furnishing & Decoration Section.......... 33
KOCH, ISSE & CO.
See Stewartstown Furniture Co................350-351
Kohn, Jacob & Joseph & Mundus
Krebs, Stengel & Company
Kroder, John, & Henry Reubel Company
Kwong Yuen & Company
LANE COMPANY, INC.
Catalog 153
Home Furnishing & Decoration Section.......... 34
LESCH, RUDOLPH 79
Lesher Whitman & Company
Leubrie & Elkus
LINCOLN FURNITURE MFG. CO...........362-363
Lassen & Woron
Lehman, J. A.
Levy, Ralph M.
Liberty Lamp & Shade Company
Little-Jones Company, The
Ludlow & Minor
Ludwig, A.
Luminier Company
Macco, Inc.
Mace & Company, L. H.
Mahogany Association
Maibrunn Company, The
Majestic Baby Carriage Company
Mallin Brothers
Mallinson Imp. Co., Geo. E.
Manhattan Rubber Mfg. Co.
Manhattan Spring Bed Company
Manhattan Upholstering Co.
Mason Art, Inc.
Mastercraft Reed Corporation
Mentrup Company, C. J.
MERSMAN BROS. CORPORATION
Catalog 216-221
Home Furnishing & Decoration Section..........39-41
Milch, D.
MILLER, M. I.
See Mersman Bros. Corp......................216-221
Mills & Gibb Corporation
Minerva Upholstery Co. Inc.
Model Upholstery Company
MORGANTON FURNITURE CO............... 304
MONITOR FURNITURE COMPANY
Catalog 288-289
Home Furnishing & Decoration Section.......... 33
Morimura Bros., Inc.
Morris & Bendien
Mothguard Laboratories
Mutual Lamp Manufacturing Co.
Nahon Company
Nathan & Company, P.
Newcomb Manufacturing Co., F. J.
New York Chair Company, Inc.
New York Furniture Exchange Ass'n, Inc.
New York Lamp Shade Company
Nichols & Co., George
Nonnenbacher & Company
Palmer & Embury Manufacturing Co.
Patching & Company, John F.
Patchogue-Plymouth Mills Corp.
Peabody Sons, Henry W.
Pearce & Company, J. E.
PECK & HILLS FURNITURE COMPANY
Catalog 392
Home Furnishing & Decoration Sec.............. 45
Pennsylvania Textile Mills
Persian Rug Manufactory
Pharaoh Drapery Company
Poulson Company, Chas. W.
PULLMAN COUCH COMPANY INC.
Catalog 128-129
Home Furnishing & Decoration Section.......... 46
Regent Shops
Reale Manufacturing Co., A.
Reed, Guy A.
Reinthal & Newman
Reischmann Chair Company
Reischmann Company, The
Reuter, William
Richter Furniture Company
ROCKFORD PALACE FURNITURE CO......322-323
ROCKFORD STANDARD FURNITURE CO.
Catalog 327-331
Home Furnishing & Decoration Section.......... 47
Rogers Company, Chas. P.
ROGERS, INC., M. H.
Catalog 90
Home Furnishing & Decoration Section.......... 45
Ross Company, Geo.
Rothman, J.
Roxbury Carpet Company
Royal Art Glass Company
Russian Antique Company
ST. JOHNS TABLE CO....................... 236
Safran & Gluckman
Salem Feltex Company
Salterini, John B.
Sanford & Sons, Inc., Stephen
SAUER, CHARLES P.
See Tillotson Furniture Corpn.................. 358
Sauer Company, Theo.
Schilling Furniture Company
SCHLITTEN, MICHAELS CO.
See Hellam Furniture Co., Inc............406-407 (Z1)
Schmieg Hungate & Kotzian
Schneider & Sons Company, Peter
SCHOECK MANUFACTURING COMPANY, INC.
Catalog 415 (Z1)
Home Furnishing & Decoration Section.......... 50
Schottland, Benjamin
Schultheis, Henry
Schumacher & Company, F.
Schwabe, Edwin J.
SEABURG MANUFACTURING COMPANY 416 (Z1)
Segal Bros., Furniture Company
Segal Company, Inc., Morris S.
SHOWERS BROTHERS COMPANY
Kitchen Cabinets Catalog...................... 75
Radio Furniture Catalog...................... 188
Bedroom and Dining Room Furniture Catalog..336-341
Sieghardt, Inc., F. J.
SIKES CHAIR COMPANY..................... 238
SKANDIA FURNITURE COMPANY
Desks and Bookcases Catalog.................172-185
Dining Room Furniture Catalog................342-345
Silverman & Company, J. K.
Simmons Company
Simon & Company, J. R.
Singer & Sons, M.
Slack Rassnick & Company
Sloane, W. & J.
Smith & Sons Carpet Company, Alexander
SMITH, JR., ROYAL B.
See Schoeck Manufacturing Company, Inc....415 (Z1)
SMITH, ROYAL B.
See Period Cabinet Mfg. Co.................... 307
Smokador Manufacturing Co., Inc.
Sons-Cunningham Reed & Rattan Company
Southard-Robertson Company
Souto Company, B.
Stakmore Company, Inc.
Standard Gas Equipment Corporation
Standard Novelty Works
Standard Textile Products Company
STATESVILLE FURNITURE COMPANY.... 346
STATTON FURNITURE MANUFACTURING CO. 418 (Z1)
STEWARTSTOWN FURNITURE COMPANY.350-351
Strand Upholstery Furn. Co.
STREIT MANUFACTURING CO., C. F.
Catalog 130-131
Home Furnishing & Decoration Section.......... 54
Sumergrade & Sons, N.
Sussman, H.
TATE FURNITURE CO.......................354-357
Tavshanjian, H. S.
THOMASVILLE CHAIR COMPANY.......... 349
Thonet Brothers
TILLOTSON FURNITURE CORPORATION... 358
UDELL WORKS, INC. 419 (Z1)
Uneeda Chair Company
UNION FURNITURE COMPANY, (Batesville, Ind.)
Catalog 421 (Z1)
Home Furnishing & Decoration Section.......... 55
UNION FURNITURE COMPANY, (Rockford, Ill.)
Desks and Bookcases Catalog.................186-187
Dining Room Furniture Catalog................360-361
UNITED FURNITURE COMPANY.............. 359
UNIVERSAL WILLOW & REED WARE CO. INC. 422 (Z1)
Unterman, Louis
Veith & Sons, Chas. H.
Venezian Art Screen Company
Violante & Onorado
VIRGINIA-LINCOLN FACTORIES...........362-363
VIRGINIA TABLE CO......................362-363
WEST BRANCH NOVELTY COMPANY
Catalog 424-428 (Z1)
Home Furnishing & Decoration Section.......... 56
WESTERN SHADE CLOTH COMPANY
Catalog 405 (Z3)
Home Furnishing & Decoration Section.......... 59
Wild & Company, Joseph
Witcombe-McGeachin
WITZ FURNITURE CORPORATION, J. L..... 244
Woods & Sons Company, Jos. W.
YPSILANTI REED FURNITURE COMPANY
Catalog 135
Home Furnishing & Decoration Section.......... 60
Zahn & Bowly Company
Zimmermann & Company, Hermann
ZION LACE CURTAINS AND NETS
(Marshall Field and Company, Wholesale)...... 85
Zucchi Furniture Company

NIAGARA FALLS

Niagara Reed Craft Furniture Co.

PORT CHESTER

Abendroth Bros.

PORT JERVIS

Swinton & Company

ONEIDA

Oneidacraft, Inc.

PULASKI

Tollner Sons Company, Chas.

RANDOLPH

Randolph Furniture Works
Seneca Furniture Corporation

RICHLAND

CURTISS & SON, WM. P..................399 (Z1)

ROCHESTER

Barnard & Simonds Company
Co-operative Foundry Company
Gillis Company, Jas. W.
Hartfelder, John E.
Hubbard, Eldredge & Miller
Kennedy-McCandless Corporation
Kittelberger Brothers
Michaelson Furniture Co., Geo. J.
Miller Cabinet Company
Powell, Wm. M.
Quality Mattress Company
Sterling Range & Furniture Corp.
Trimble Manufacturing Co., E. M.
Webster Furniture Company
Wise-Bundock Company

ROME
ROME COMPANY, INC. 70-71
SALAMANCA
FANCHER FURNITURE COMPANY 270
Salamanca Furniture Works
STERLING FURNITURE COMPANY 347
SCHENECTADY
Woodcraft Manufacturing Company
SILVER CREEK
Montgomery Manufacturing Co., H. J.
Silver Creek Case Goods Company
SYRACUSE
ALLEN MANUFACTURING COMPANY
  Catalog 136
  Home Furnishing & Decoration Section 10
Butler Manufacturing Company
DE BOER MANUFACTURING COMPANY 133
Onondaga Bed Manufacturing Co.
SCHOECK MANUFACTURING COMPANY, INC.
  Catalog 415 (Z1)
  Home Furnishing & Decoration Section 50
Simonds Company, Elgin A.
STICKLEY MANUFACTURING COM-
PANY, INC.
  Catalog 352-353
  Home Furnishing & Decoration Section 52
TROY
Buckley & Company
Burdett Smith & Company
TRUXTON
Wood Manufacturing Co. Inc., Marshall C.
UTICA
FOSTER BROTHERS MANUFACTURING
COMPANY 69
Lewis-Weller Manufacturing Co.
WAVERLY
Hall & Lyon Furniture Company
WAYLAND
GUNLOCKE CHAIR COMPANY, W. H. 401 (Z1)
Plail Brothers Company
WELLSVILLE
WELLSVILLE UPHOLSTERING
COMPANY 423 (Z1)

NORTH CAROLINA

ASHBORO
Cranford Industries
ASHEVILLE
Carolina Wood Products Company
BURLINGTON
Southern Furniture Company
CARTHAGE
Tyson & Jones Buggy Company
CONCORD
Caton & Goodman
CONOVER
Hickory Handle Manufacturing Co.
DENTON
Denton Manufacturing Company
DREXEL
Drexel Furniture Company
DUNN
Newberry Bros. & Cowell
ELKIN
Biltrite Furniture Company
Elkin Furniture Company
GOLDSBORO
Royal Furniture Manufacturing Co.
Royall & Borden Manufacturing Co.
Wayne Furniture Manufacturing Co.
GREENSBORO
Glascock Stove & Manufacturing Co.
MARTIN, H. D.
  See Mersman Bros. Corpn. 216-221
Sterling Furniture Company
HAZELWOOD
Unagusta Manufacturing Company
Waynesville Furniture Company
HICKORY
Hickory Furniture Company
Yeager Manufacturing Company
HIGH POINT
Acme Furniture Company
Alma Furniture Company
Briggs Manufacturing Company
CALDWELL FURNITURE CO. 398 (Z1)
Cecil Manufacturing Company
COLONIAL FURNITURE COMPANY 93-95
Colonial Manufacturing Company
CONTINENTAL FURNITURE COMPANY ... 260-261
Dalton Furniture Company
DIXIE FURNITURE CO. 263
EBERT FURNITURE COMPANY
  Catalog distributed to all States 264
  Catalog distributed to Zone 1 .... 402-403 (Z1)
Ecker, Ferd.
FORSYTH FURNITURE LINES, INC.
  Catalog 272
  Home Furnishing & Decoration Section 16
FURST BROS. & COMPANY 78
Giant Furniture Company
GLOBE MANUFACTURING CO. 106-107
GLOBE PARLOR FURNITURE COMPANY .. 106-107
GRIFFITH FURNITURE WORKS 147
Guilford Parlor Furniture Company
High Point Buggy Company
High Point Furniture Company
High Point Mirror Company
High Point Refrigerator Company
High Point Upholstery Company
K. & L. Furniture Company
Kearns Furniture Company
Keystone Cabinet Company
Knox Upholstery Company
Marsh Furniture Company
MARTIN, H. D.
  See Mersman Bros. Corpn. 216-221
MERSMAN BROS. CORPORATION
  Catalog 216-221
  Home Furnishing & Decoration Section 39-41

Myrtle Desk Company
National Upholstery Company
Premier Furniture Manufacturing Company
RAGAN, CHARLES E.
  See Statesville Furniture Company 346
ROME COMPANY, INC. 70-71
Southern Chair Company
Southern Furniture Market Ass'n
Southern Mirror Company
STATESVILLE FURNITURE COMPANY 346
TATE FURNITURE COMPANY 354-357
THOMASVILLE CHAIR COMPANY 349
Tomlinson Chair Company
Union Frame Company
Union Furniture Company
UNITED FURNITURE COMPANY 359
Welch Furniture Company
WHITE FURNITURE COMPANY
  Catalog 365
  Home Furnishing & Decoration Section 55
Wrenn-Columbia Furniture Co.
KERNERSVILLE
Kernersville Furniture Mfg. Co.
MORRIS, R. C.
  See Caldwell Furniture Co. 398 (Z1)
LEAKSVILLE
Dan River Furniture Corp. Inc.
LENOIR
Bernhardt Chair Company
CALDWELL FURNITURE COMPANY 398 (Z1)
Fairfield Chair Company
Harper Furniture Company
Hibriten Furniture Company
Jennings Furniture Company
Kent-Coffey Manufacturing Company
Lenoir Furniture Corporation
Lenoir Mirror Company
Star Furniture Company
Union Mirror Company
LEXINGTON
DIXIE FURNITURE COMPANY 263
Elk Furniture Company
Hoover Chair Company
Lexington Chair Company
Moffitt Furniture & Uph. Co.
Peerless Mattress Company
UNITED FURNITURE COMPANY 359
MAIDEN
Maiden Chair Company
MARION
Catawba Furniture Company
McDowell Furniture Company
Teague Furniture Company
MEBANE
Mebane Bedding Company
Mebane Iron Bed Company
WHITE FURNITURE COMPANY
  Catalog 365
  Home Furnishing & Decoration Section 55
MOCKSVILLE
Haynes Chair & Table Company
MOORESVILLE
Mooresville Furniture Company
MORGANTON
MORGANTON FURNITURE COMPANY 304
Table Rock Furniture Company
MOUNT AIRY
Foy Lumber & Manufacturing Company
Mount Airy Chair Company
Mount Airy Furniture Company
Mount Airy Mantel & Table Company
Mount Airy Mirror Manufacturing Co.
NATIONAL FURNITURE COMPANY 124
NEWTON
Newton Furniture Company
NORTH WILKESBORO
Forest Furniture Company
Homes Chair Company
Key City Upholstery Company
Oak Furniture Company
OXFORD
Oxford Buggy Company
RAMSEUR
Ramseur Furniture Company
RANDLEMAN
Randleman Manufacturing Company
ROARING RIVER
Roaring River Furniture Company
ROCKY MOUNT
Cotton Belt Manufacturing Company
RONDA
Yadkin Valley Furniture Co. Inc.
SANFORD
Fitts-Crabtree Manufacturing Co.
SALISBURY
Taylor Mattress Company
SILER CITY
Chatham Chair Manufacturing Co.
High Point Bending & Chair Co.
STATESVILLE
Carolina Parlor Furniture Company
Home Made Chair Company
Imperial Furniture Manufacturing Co.
Iredell Upholstered Furniture Co.
North State Furniture Mfg. Co.
Sherrill Green Furniture Company
STATESVILLE CHAIR COMPANY 417 (Z1)
STATESVILLE FURNITURE COMPANY 346
STONEVILLE
Stoneville Cabinet Company
THOMASVILLE
Biltwell Chair & Furniture Co.
Lambeth Furniture Company
Standard Chair Company
THOMASVILLE CHAIR COMPANY 349
Thomasville Furniture Company
WALKERTOWN
Walkertown Chair Company
WAYNESVILLE
Haywood Furniture Mfg. Co.
WINSTON-SALEM
Fogle Furniture Company

FORSYTH FURNITURE LINES
  Catalog 272
  Home Furnishing & Decoration Section 16
HUNTLEY FURNITURE COMPANY, B. F.
  Catalog 274
  Home Furnishing & Decoration Section 20
Rominger Furniture Company
Snyder Upholstery Co., Berl C.
Spach Wagon Works, J. C.
Unique Furniture Company
Winston-Salem Chair Company

OHIO

AKRON
Akron Mattress Manufacturing Co.
Robinson-Clay Products Company
San Hygene Upholstery Company
Taplin-Rice-Clerkin Company
ANTWERP
Johnson Furniture Mfg. Co., J. B.
ASHLAND
Kauffman Manufacturing Company
ATHENS
Grayson Manufacturing Co., J. H.
BASCOM
Gem Manufacturing Company
BEDFORD
Marble Chair Company, B. L.
Taylor Chair Company
BELLAIRE
Bellaire Stove Company
BRYAN
Ohio Art Company
CAMBRIDGE
Suitt Brothers Manufacturing Co.
CANTON
Ervin Manufacturing Company
Harvard Company, The
CELINA
BRANDTS FURNITURE COMPANY 394 (Z3)
Celina Maid Furniture Company
MERSMAN BROTHERS CORPORATION
  Catalog 216-221
  Home Furnishing & Decoration Section 39-41
CHILLICOTHE
POSTON MANUFACTURING
COMPANY, B. C. 401 (Z3)
CINCINNATI
American Glass & Beveling Company
Angert Brothers
ARMSTRONG CORK COMPANY
  Catalog 81
  Home Furnishing & Decoration Section 9
Bardes Range & Foundry Co., E. H.
Betts St. Furniture Company
Brown Carriage Company
Burton Range Company
CHICAGO MIRROR & ART GLASS
COMPANY 395 (Z3)
Cincinnati Wrought Iron Company
Ficks Reed Company
Globe-Wernicke Company
Hageman Glass Company
Halstrick, Wm. F.
HARTEVELD, N.,
  See Chicago Mirror & Art Glass Co. 395 (Z3)
Hoeffeld Company, Harry
Huenefeld Company, The
Kemper Furniture Company
Klaine & Company, F. A.
Klinker Company, The B.
Lubke Sons Company, Fred
Midwest Glass Company
National Screen & Manufacturing Co.
Neuer Glass Company, H.
Nurre, Henry
Parks Bell Bearing Machine Co.
Revere Clock Company
ROME COMPANY, INC. 70-71
Royal Blue Bed Spring Company
Stille & Duhlmeier Company
Scheid Sons Company, Jos.
Schirmer Furniture Company
Schmit Furniture Company, Henry
Schutte Furniture Company, Geo. W.
Sextro Manufacturing Company
Shott Manufacturing Company
Steinman & Meyer Furniture Co.
STREIT MANUFACTURING COMPANY, C. F.
  Catalog 130-131
  Home Furnishing & Decoration Section 54
Thauwald Company, C. F.
CLEVELAND
ARMSTRONG CORK COMPANY
  Catalog 81
  Home Furnishing & Decoration Section 9
BARCALO MANUFACTURING COMPANY 393 (Z1)
Bonhard Art Furniture Company
Champion Spring Company
Cleveland Co-op. Stove Company
Cleveland Folding Bed Company
Cleveland Furniture Mfg. Co.
Cleveland Metal Products Company
Cleveland Wire Spring Company
Cuyahoga Picture Frame Company
Flood Chair Company, C. E.
Imperial Steel Range Company
Justh Manufacturing Company
Kraus-Winograd Company
Kronheim Furniture Mfg. Co.
Hexter & Company, S. M.
Lincoln Furniture Mfg. Co.
Linn Furniture Company
Loeblein & Dietzel, Inc.
Marble & Shattuck Chair Company
Ohio Mattress Company
Owen Shops Company
Perfection Stove Company
Randall Mattress Company
Reliable Stove Company
Republic Stove & Manufacturing Co.
Lynch Sales Company
Tinnerman Stove & Range Company
Trenkamp Stove & Mfg. Co.
Van Dorn Iron Works Company

COLUMBIANA
FRANKLIN FURNITURE COMPANY
  Catalog 102
  Home Furnishing & Decoration Section.......... 17
COLUMBUS
ALLEN MANUFACTURING COMPANY
  Catalog 136
  Home Furnishing & Decoration Section.......... 10
Columbus Bed Spring Co.
Emrich, C.
Excelsior Company, The
Hulse Company, E. M.
Ohio State Stove Mfg. Co.
Quad Stove Manufacturing Co.
ROME COMPANY, INC....................70-71
SCHOECK MANUFACTURING COMPANY, INC.
  Catalog 415 (Z1)
  Home Furnishing & Decoration Section.......... 50
WESTERN SHADE CLOTH COMPANY
  Catalog 405 (Z3)
  Home Furnishing & Decoration Section.......... 59
WILSON, W. E.
  See Schoeck Manufacturing Co., Inc.........415 (Z1)
DAYTON
Dayton Mattress Mfg. Co.
Stomps-Burkhardt Company
DELAWARE
Delaware Chair Company
Sunray Stove Company
DELPHOS
Ricker Brothers
ELYRIA
Fox Furnace Company
GALLIPOLIS
Logan Furniture Company
GREENVILLE
New Way Refrigerator Company
Treaty Company, The
HILLSBORO
Geyler Furniture Mfg. Co.
Globe Chair Company
IRONTON
Foster Stove Company
LIMA
Lima Quality Cushion Company
LORAIN
American Stove Company
LOCKLAND
Stearns & Foster Company
LOGAN
Logan Furniture Company
Owen Manufacturing Company
MANCHESTER
Manchester Furniture Company
MANSFIELD
Perfection Bed Spring Company
Tappan Stove Company
MARIETTA
Brickwede Brothers Company
Marietta Chair Company
MARTINS FERRY
Spence-Baggs Stove Company
MIAMISBURG
Burkhardt Furniture Company, The
Mutual Furniture Company
MIDDLETOWN
Miami Cabinet Company
NEWARK
Newark Ohio Furniture Company
NEW BREMEN
Auglaize Furniture Company
NEW WATERFORD
New Waterford Furniture Co.
NORWALK
Gallup-Ruffing Company
Norwalk Upholstery Company
Stewart Company, G. S.
ORRVILLE
Orrville Bedding Company
PIQUA
Cron Company, The
Cron-Kills Company
Favorite Stove & Range Co.
PORTSMOUTH
Ohio Stove Company
Portsmouth Stove & Range Co.
Wait Furniture Company, The
RAVENNA
Buckeye Chair Company
Williams Company, A. C.
SALEM
Victor Stove Company
SHELBY
Chicago Handle Bar Company
SPENCERVILLE
Allen Furniture Manufacturing Co.
SPRINGFIELD
Buckeye Manufacturing Company
Reed Manufacturing Company
TIPPECANOE CITY
Garver Furniture Company
Tipp Bldg. & Mfg. Co.
TOLEDO
American National Company
Bacon Brothers, The
Bennett Company, J. F.
Farrell, Edward P.
Gendron Wheel Company
Progressive Furniture Company
ROME COMPANY, INC....................70-71
Stevens Company, Inc., B. A.
Superior Furniture Company
Toledo National Bedding Co.
TOLEDO PARLOR FURNITURE
COMPANY 404 (Z3)
Toledo Stove & Range Company
Troy Sunshade Company
URBANA
Urbana Furniture Mfg. Co.
WAPAKONETA
Sheets Manufacturing Company

WARREN
King Furniture Company
Western Reserve Furniture Co.
WASHINGTON C. H.
Craig Manufacturing Co., N. B.
WESTERVILLE
Culver Art & Frame Company
WILLIAMSBURG
Ohio Chair Company
White, J. H.
Williamsburg Furniture Co.
XENIA
Thornhill & Sons, Albert
YOUNGSTOWN
Sanitary Mattress Company

OKLAHOMA

MUSKOGEE
Roberts Mattress Company
OKLAHOMA CITY
Oklahoma Furniture Mfg. Co.
Oklahoma Mattress Mfg. Co.
Oklahoma Spring Bed Mfg. Co.
ROME COMPANY, INC.....................70-71
Sigmon Furniture Mfg. Co.
TULSA
CHICAGO MIRROR & ART GLASS
COMPANY 395 (Z3)
Corn Mattress Company
MOORE CO., J. H.
  See Chicago Mirror & Art Glass Co.........395 (Z3)
Porter Mattress Company
Tulsa Furniture Mfg. Co.

OREGON

ALBANY
Veal & Son, R.
PORTLAND
ALLEN MANUFACTURING COMPANY
  Catalog 136
  Home Furnishing & Decoration Section.......... 10
Beaver State Furn. Mfg. Co.
Burrows Company, The E. T.
Montag Stove Works
King-Fisher Mattress Company
Doernbecher Mfg. Co.
Pettit Feather & Bedding Company
Portland Furniture Mfg. Co.
ROME COMPANY, INC.....................70-71
Tonsing Brothers
United Manufacturing Company
PECK & HILLS FURNITURE COMPANY
  Catalog 392
  Home Furnishing & Decoration Sec............. 45

PENNSYLVANIA

ALLENTOWN
Bear Furniture Company, G. H.
Lehigh Star Bedding Company
Lehigh Upholstery Company
Jordan Parlor Furniture Company
Schantz Company, Wm. D.
Schenck & Company, E. J.
YEAGER FURNITURE COMPANY........431 (Z1)
ATHENS
Flynn Furniture Company
BELLEVILLE
Yoder, Levi M.
BETHLEHEM
Bethlehem Furniture Company
BLOOMSBURG
Magee Carpet Company
BRISTOL
Leedom Company, Thos. L.
BROOKVILLE
Deemer Furniture Company, A. D.
CARLISLE
Federal Equipment Company
Todd Carpet Manufacturing Company
CHESTER
Blank Mayer
Keppel & Company
New Farson Manufacturing Co.
COLUMBIA
Keeley Stove Company
CONNEAUTVILLE
Penn. Furniture Company
CORRY
Corry Case Goods Company
Corry Chair Company
Corry Fibre Furniture Company
K. P. L. Furniture Company
Kurtz Case Goods Company
DALLASTOWN
Dallastown Furniture Company
DANVILLE
Danville Stove Mfg. Company
DICKSON CITY
Early Foundry Company
ERIE
Erie Stove & Mfg. Co.
Germer Stove Company
Odin Stove Manufacturing Co.
Thayer Company, E. N.
FULLERTON
FULLERTON FURNITURE FACTORIES........103
GARLAND
Garland Chair Company
GETTYSBURG
Gettysburg Furniture Company
GREENSBURG
Greensburg Swing Company

HALLSTEAD
American Chair Mfg. Co.
HANOVER
Conewango Furniture Company
Long Furniture Company
HARRISBURG
ALLEN MANUFACTURING COMPANY
  Catalog 136
  Home Furnishing & Decoration Section.......... 10
Berks Furniture Company
Style-Bilt Furniture Company
United States Mattress Company
HELLAM
HELLAM FURNITURE COMPANY,
INC. 406-407 (Z1)
HUGHESVILLE
Hughesville Furniture Company
Lycoming Furniture Company
JERMYN
Brown Products Corporation
JOHNSTOWN
Century Stove & Mfg. Company
De Frehn & Sons, W.
Johnstown National Bedding Co.
LANCASTER
ARMSTRONG CORK COMPANY
  Catalog 81
  Home Furnishing & Decoration Section.......... 9
Benner Manufacturing Company
HORN & COMPANY, J. P.................410 (Z1)
LANSDALE
Fynetone Manufacturing Company
LEBANON
Lebanon Valley Furniture Company
LEWISBURG
Lewisburg Chair Corporation
LITITZ
Beck & Company
LITTLESTOWN
Keystone Cabinet Company
LOCK HAVEN
Lock Haven Chair Corporation
MERTZTOWN
Long Valley Rug Mills
MIDDLETOWN
Wincroft Stove Works
MILTON
WEST BRANCH NOVELTY COMPANY
  Catalog 424-428 (Z1)
  Home Furnishing & Decoration Section.......... 56
MONTGOMERY
DECKER, INC., ISAAC C.
  Catalog 96
  Home Furnishing & Decoration Section.......... 13
Lycoming Upholstering Company
Montgomery Lounge Company
Montgomery Table & Desk Works
Penn Furniture Manufacturing Co.
MONTOURSVILLE
Crandall-Bennett-Porter Company
Montour Furniture Company
P. & E. Furniture Company
MOUNTVILLE
MOUNTVILLE WOOD PRODUCTS
CO. INC.....................................412 (Z1)
MT. WOLF
KEYSTONE TABLE COMPANY...........411 (Z1)
Mt. Wolf Furniture Company
MUNCY
Muncy Furniture Company
NEW BRIGHTON
Beaver Refrigerator Company
NORRISTOWN
Coral Manufacturing Company
NORTH GIRARD
Hopkins Manufacturing Co., L.
PHILADELPHIA
Abbott & Company, Theo. A.
ALBERT, L. R.
  See Statton Furn. Mfg. Co.................418 (Z1)
American Pile Fabric Company
Art Loom Rug Mills
Baker & Company, A. T.
Baldwin Manufacturing Co. Inc.
Barber & Company, J. W.
Bassett McNab Company
Becker & Sons, D.
Behrend, Jacob
Beifield & Company, Chas. H.
Bien, Albert H.
Blabon Company, Geo. W.
Bloch Go-Cart Company
Bloom Company, Jacob
Bodenstein & Kuemmerle
Bombayreed Willow Furniture Co.
Breslin Textile Mills
Brooks Brothers & Company
Bruner, Inc., Francis A.
Burt Brothers, Inc.
Bush & Diamond
CANTERBURY DECORATIVE FABRICS
  (Marshall Field & Co., Wholesale)............. 87
Cambria Carpet Company
Carson & Son, Robert
CHICAGO MIRROR & ART GLASS
COMPANY 395 (Z3)
Clare Manufacturing Co.
Cleeland's Sons, Robert
Clock Manufacturers' Ass'n of America
Cochrane Company, Chas. P.
Cold Blast Feather Company
Columbia Carpet Mills
Congoleum Nairn
Decorative Lamp & Shade Co.
Delaware Manufacturing Co.
Develon Sons, Thos.
Dornan Carpet & Rug Mills
Dubs, John A.
Dura-Bilt Upholstered Furn. Co.
EBERT FURNITURE COMPANY
  Catalog distributed to all States................. 264
  Catalog distributed to Zone 1............402-403 (Z1)
Ferguson Carpet Company
Fetterolf Company, H. G.

FURST BROS. & COMPANY.................. 78
Gay's Sons, John
Gebert & Son, Chris
Grand Upholstered Furniture Co.
Hagmaier Upholstery Company
Halpern & Son, M.
Hardwick & Magee Company
Harrison Company, H.
Harvey Fibre Carpet Company
Henderson & Company, Wm.
Hirst Rogers Company
Holmes & Son, Archibald
Holmes Son Company, Henry
Ionic Mills
Josten, Peter
Kappler-Fox Foundry Company
Kaufman Plush Company
Keep Brothers
KENT-COSTIKYAN
   Catalog 89
   Home Furnishing & Decoration Section.......... 23
Knell, W. W. & W. H.
Kraan Furniture Company, Henry
Kramer & Sons, M.
Kreiss Company, Wm. F.
La France Art Company
La France Textile Company
Lawsonia Manufacturing Company
Lewis Company, Robert
Lincoln Furniture Company
Lomax Carpet Mills, Jos.
McDowell, David
McMahen Company, Wm. H.
Masland & Sons, C. H.
Maurer & Sons Company, F. W.
Mecky Company, A.
Model Mills Company
Morrell Mills
Moss Rose Manufacturing Co.
National Tapestry Company
National Upholstered Furn. Co.
Newman & Sons, David
NEILSON, A. T. SALES CO.
   See Caldwell Furniture Co..................398 (Z1)
Patterson Carpet Mills
Pearson & Company, Fred
PECK & HILLS FURNITURE COMPANY
   Catalog 392
   Home Furnishing & Decoration Sec............. 45
Penna Axminster Carpet Corp.
Philadelphia Carpet Company
Philadelphia Excelsior Company
Philadelphia Cable Company
Philadelphia Pile Fabric Mills
Philadelphia Tapestry Company
Platt & Company, M.
Pollock-Huston Company
Pooley Furniture Company
Primrose Tapestry Company
Pullman Metal Specialties Company
Read & Son, Edw. C.
Reifsnieder & Son, John J.
Rieber & Company, L.
Ritchie & Company, Robert J.
Ritter & Bros., Inc., Wm.
ROME COMPANY, INC......................70-71
Royal Upholstered Furniture Co.
Royle & Company, George
Saxe Company, S.
Schober, Charles
Schwartz, C. E.
Shull Furniture Mfg. Co.
Shull, Samuel
SIKES CHAIR COMPANY.................... 238
Smith & Sons Company, Oscar
Smith & Son, Wm. T.
Standard Refrigerator Company
Standard Upholstered Furn. Co.
STATTON FURNITURE MANUFAC-
   TURING COMPANY...................418 (Z1)
STAUNTON, H. A.
   See Chicago Mirror & Art Glass Co..........395 (Z3)
Stead Miller & Company
Stroud, D. H.
Supplee-Biddle Hardware Company
Sykes Company, The
Union Upholstered Furniture Co.
United Tapestry Mills, Inc.
Waxman & Company, A.
Weiner & Sons, L.
Whiteley & Collier
Yelson, John
Zenith Mills
Zimmerman & Sons, John

PICTURE ROCKS
BURROWS BROTHERS COMPANY....395-397 (Z1)

PITTSBURGH
Art Upholstery Company
Conroy-Prugh Company
Cook Company, C. Lawrence
Fischer, John
Fort Pitt Bedding Company
Gross & Company, H. E.
Hagmaier Upholstery Company
Pittsburgh Iron Folding Bed Co.
Pittsburgh Plate Glass Company
ROME COMPANY, INC......................70-71
Spear & Company
Stove & Range Co. of Pittsburgh

QUAKERTOWN
Quakertown Stove Works

RAILROAD
Sieling Furniture Company

READING
Reading Stove Works

RED LION
EBERT FURNITURE COMPANY
   Catalog distributed to all States................ 264
   Zone 1 Catalog......................402-403 (Z1)
Red Lion Furniture Company
York County Chair Company

ROCHESTER
Olive Stove Works

ROYERSFORD
Buckwalter Stove Company
Royersford Spring Bed Company
Wells Company, Floyd

SCRANTON
Scranton Bedding Company
Scranton Stove Works
Smith, B. J.

SHEFFIELD
Sheffield Furniture Company

SHIPPENSBURG
Boher & Hosfeld Company
Peerless Furniture Company
Shippensburg Cabinet Company

SHREWSBURY
Shrewsbury Furniture Company

SLATINGTON
Community Rug Mills, Inc.

SOUDERTON
HEMSING FURNITURE MANUFAC-
   TURING COMPANY.....................405 (Z1)

SOUTH LANGHORNE
Rumpf's Sons, Frederick

STEWARTSTOWN
Stewartstown Cabinet Company
STEWARTSTOWN FURNITURE COMPANY
   Catalog 350-351
   Home Furnishing & Decorating Section.......... 51

TIDIOUTE
Downing, Geo. H.

TOWANDA
Frost Sons Company, J. O.

UNION CITY
Eastman Manufacturing Company
Novelty Wood Works, Inc.
SHREVE CHAIR COMPANY.................. 237
STANDARD CHAIR COMPANY.............. 239
Union City Chair Company

WARREN
Conewango Company
Nypenn Furniture Company
Phenix Furniture Company
Union Furniture & Novelty Co.
Warren Chair Works
Warren Furniture Company

WASHINGTON
Sidway-Topliff Company

WATSONTOWN
Watsontown Table & Furniture Co.
Wood Products Company

WILKES-BARRE
Brayman Furniture Company
ROME COMPANY, INC......................70-71
United Upholstery Company

WILLIAMSPORT
Culler Furniture Company
Heilman & Company, A. H.
Keystone Furniture Company
WILLIAMSPORT FURNITURE COMPANY.429 (Z1)

YORK
American Toy & Novelty Works
Boring & Bros., H. E.
HOME FURNITURE COMPANY........408-409 (Z1)
Pennsylvania Furniture Company
York Furniture Mfg. Co. Inc.

YOUNGSVILLE
Forest Furniture Company
Youngsville Manufacturing Co.

RHODE ISLAND

PROVIDENCE
Barstow Stove Company
Geffner, H.
ROME COMPANY, INC......................70-71

SOUTH CAROLINA

COLUMBIA
Fibercraft Chair Company
Graham & Son, John M.

HARTSVILLE
Pee Dee Furniture Company

TENNESSEE

ATHENS
Athens Stove Company
ATHENS TABLE & MANUFACTURING
   COMPANY 190

BUTLER
Elk River Manufacturing Co.

CHATTANOOGA
CHATTANOOGA FURNITURE COMPANY..... 259
Hunt Spring Bed Company
Mascot Stove Manufacturing Co.
MILNE CHAIR COMPANY.................... 207
Tennessee Furniture Corporation
Tennessee Red Cedar & Novelty Company
Wade & Brown

CLEVELAND
Cleveland Chair Company

DAYTON
Morgan Furniture Mfg. Co.

ELIZABETHTON
EMPIRE CHAIR COMPANY 194-196

HARRIMAN
Dame Furniture Company

JOHNSON CITY
EMPIRE CHAIR COMPANY 194-196
Exum Furniture Company

KNOXVILLE
Atkin Company, C. B.
FAIR FOUNDRY COMPANY INC.........394 (Z2)
KNOX STOVE WORKS 395 (Z2)
Knoxville Furniture Company
Knoxville Table & Chair Co.
Knoxville Upholstered Furniture Co.

Rule Company, Inc.
Sterchi Bros. Manufacturing Co.
Tennessee Table Company

LOUDON
Hood Chair Company
Lutz Manufacturing Co., John J.

MEMPHIS
ARMSTRONG CORK COMPANY
   Catalog 81
   Home Furnishing & Decoration Section.......... 9
Binswanger & Co. of Tennessee
FLORENCE TABLE AND MANUFAC-
   TURING COMPANY
   Catalog 271
   Home Furnishing & Decoration Section.......... 15
GUMWOOD SERVICE BUREAU,
   Hardwood Manufacturers' Institute............ 386
King-Haase Furniture Company
HARDWOOD MANUFACTURERS'
   INSTITUTE........................384-386
   Oak Service Bureau...................384-385
   Gumwood Service Bureau.................. 386
MEMPHIS FURNITURE MANUFAC-
   TURING COMPANY
   Catalog 303
   Home Furnishing & Decoration Section.......... 36
Mississippi Valley Furniture Company
Nurre Glass Company
OAK SERVICE BUREAU
   Hardwood Manufacturers' Institute............384-385
ROME COMPANY, INC......................70-71
Rose Spring & Mattress Company
United States Bedding Company
Wetter Manufacturing Co., H.

MORRISTOWN
East Tennessee Wood Working Co.
Morristown Chair Company
Weller-Foard Company

NASHVILLE
ALLEN MANUFACTURING COMPANY
   Catalog 136
   Home Furnishing & Decoration Section.......... 10
ANCHOR SPRING & BEDDING CO.....393 (Z2)
Bonner Furniture Mfg. Co.
Gray & Dudley Company
Lamb & Company
National Feather & Pillow Co.
Phillips & Buttorff Mfg. Co.
Simplex Manufacturing Company
Nashville Chair Company
Standard Furniture Company
Wheeler-Okell Company

PINEY FLATS
Wolfe Brothers & Company

ROCKWOOD
Rockwood Stove Works

SEVIERVILLE
Tennessee Chair & Table Company

SEYMOUR
Oak City Chair Company

TEXAS

BEAUMONT
Beutser Furniture Company, B.

DALLAS
ALLEN MANUFACTURING COMPANY
   Catalog 136
   Home Furnishing & Decoration Section.......... 10
ARMSTRONG CORK COMPANY
   Catalog 81
   Home Furnishing & Decoration Section.......... 9
CHICAGO MIRROR & ART GLASS
   COMPANY 395 (Z3)
Daltex Spring Bed Company
FORSYTH FURNITURE LINES, INC.
   Catalog 272
   Home Furnishing & Decoration Section.......... 16
Heermans Manufacturing Co.
Olive & Myers Manufacturing Co.
PECK & HILLS FURNITURE COMPANY
   Catalog 392
   Home Furnishing & Decoration Sec............. 45
PULLMAN COUCH COMPANY
   Catalog 128-129
   Home Furnishing & Decoration Section.......... 46
ROME COMPANY, INC......................70-71
RUSSELL, PIERRE L.
   See Chicago Mirror & Art Glass Co..........395 (Z3)
Nordwald Company, H.

EL PASO
ROME COMPANY, INC......................70-71

FORT WORTH
Brandt Upholstery Co., A. H.
Hub Furniture Company
Winter, John I.

HOUSTON
Myers Spalti Mfg. Co.
ROME COMPANY, INC......................70-71

PARIS
Rodgers-Wade Furniture Co.

SEALY
Haynes Mattress Factory

SUGARLAND
Seely Mattress Company

TAYLOR
Taylor Bedding Mfg. Co.

TEXARKANA
Southern Furniture Company

WACO
Cooper Manufacturing Company

WICHITA FALLS
Bell Furniture & Mattress Company

UTAH

SALT LAKE CITY
ROME COMPANY, INC......................70-71
Salt Lake Mattress & Mfg. Co.

VERMONT

ARLINGTON
Arlington Refrigerator Company
BEECHER FALLS
Beecher Falls Company
BENNINGTON
Cushman Manufacturing Co., H. T.
White Company, H. C.
BRATTLEBORO
White River Chair Company
BURLINGTON
Baldwin Refrigerator Company
Vermont Shade Roller Company
ISLAND POND
Brighton Furniture Company
MANCHESTER
Cass Company of Vermont, N. D.
RANDOLPH
Salisbury Bros. Furniture Co.
READSBORO
Readsboro Chair Company
RICHFORD
Sweat-Cummings Company
RUTLAND
Rutland Manufacturing Co.
WATERBURY
Demeritt-Fisher Company

VIRGINIA

ALTA VISTA
LANE COMPANY, INC.
  Catalog 153
  Home Furnishing & Decoration Section........... 34
BASSETT
Bassett Furniture Company
Bassett Mfg. Company, J. D.
Bassett Mirror Company
Ramsey Furniture Company
Stanley Furniture Company
BRIGHTWOOD
Clore & Hawkins
BRISTOL
Central Glass Co. of Virginia
CAMBRIA
Phoenix Furniture Corporation
CHASE CITY
Nicholson Furniture Co., K.
CHATHAM
Hargrave Cedar Chest Company
CULPEPER
White Oak Chair Mfg. Company
DANVILLE
Boatwright Furniture Company
GALAX
Edwards Chair Company
Vaughan-Bassett Furniture Co.
Vaughan Furniture Company
HICKORY
Hickory Furniture Company
LYNCHBURG
American Beauty Mattress Co.
Moser-Royster Furniture Co.
National Mattress Company
Snidow McWane Furniture Co.
MARION
Lincoln Company, Inc., The
LINCOLN FURNITURE MANUFACTURING
  COMPANY 362-363
VIRGINIA-LINCOLN FACTORIES 362-363
VIRGINIA TABLE COMPANY..............362-363
MARTINSVILLE
American Furniture Company
Graveley Novelty Company
Hooker-Bassett Furniture Co.
Martinsville Chair & Mfg. Co.
Virginia Furniture Company
Virginia Mirror Company
NORFOLK
Norfolk Mattress Company
PORTSMOUTH
Old Dominion Table Works
PULASKI
Coleman-Vaughan Furniture Co.
Pulaski Furniture Company
Pulaski Mirror Company
RICHMOND
Binswanger Company
CUTTING, C. M.
  See Caldwell Furniture Co..................398 (Z1)
Dixie Mattress Company
Gold Metal Furniture Mfg. Co.
James River Furniture Company
Richmond Stove Company
Richmond Wood Working Company
ROME COMPANY, INC.......................70-71
Southern Stove Works
ROCKYMOUNT
Bald Knob Furniture Co.
STAUNTON
WITZ FURNITURE CORPORATION, J. L..... 244

WAYNESBORO
BASIC FURNITURE COMPANY............... 244
Loth Stove Company, W. J.
WINCHESTER
Acorn Manufacturing Concern

WASHINGTON

SEATTLE
ALLEN MANUFACTURING COMPANY
  Catalog 136
  Home Furnishing & Decoration Section.......... 10
ARMSTRONG CORK COMPANY
  Catalog 81
  Home Furnishing & Decoration Section.......... 9
Carman Manufacturing Co.
General Furniture Company
Levy & Sons, M. E.
Pacific Chair Company
Pacific Fibre Furniture Co.
PECK & HILLS FURNITURE COMPANY
  Catalog 392
  Home Furnishing & Decoration Section.......... 45
Rainer Furniture Mfg. Co.
Rattan Furniture Mfg. Co.
ROGERS, INC., M. H.
  Catalog 90
  Home Furnishing & Decoration Section.......... 45
Washington Furniture Mfg. Co.
SPOKANE
ALLEN MANUFACTURING COMPANY
  Catalog 136
  Home Furnishing & Decoration Section.......... 10
Buffelen Hubbert & Loonam
PECK & HILLS FURNITURE COMPANY
  Catalog 392
  Home Furnishing & Decoration Sec.......... 45
ROME COMPANY, INC.......................70-71
TACOMA
Carman Manufacturing Co.
Gregory Furniture Mfg. Co.
Harmon & Company, F. W.
McDonald Company, C. E.
Murphy Manufacturing Company
Northwestern Chair Company
Pacific Furniture Mfg. Co.
PECK & HILLS FURNITURE COMPANY
  Catalog 392
  Home Furnishing & Decoration Sec.......... 45
Washington Parlor Furn. Co.
West Coast Chair Company
Western Fibre Furniture Co.

WEST VIRGINIA

ELKINS
Elkins Refrigerator & Fix. Co.
HUNTINGTON
Cravens-Green Company
EMPIRE FURNITURE COMPANY............ 268
Hoy Raymond & Company
Huntington Spring Bed Company
National Mattress Company
NICHOLSON-KENDLE FURNITURE COM-
  PANY 269
PENN TABLE COMPANY..................... 268
Specialty Mattress Company

WISCONSIN

ALGOMA
Algoma Wood Products Company
APPLETON
Appleton Chair Company
Toy Company of America
BEAVER DAM
MALLEABLE IRON RANGE COMPANY
  Catalog 73
  Home Furnishing & Decoration Section.......... 35
BURLINGTON
Burlington Blanket Company
DELAVAN
Sage-Fifield Lumber Co. Inc.
Cold Storage Refrigerator Co.
EAU CLAIRE
Fond du Lac Table Mfg. Co.
FOND DU LAC
Guerney Refrigerator Company
Sanitary Refrigerator Company
Winnebago Furniture Mfg. Co.
GRAFTON
Junger Stove & Range Company
GREEN BAY
Automatic File & Index Company
HAWKINS
Rusk Manufacturing Company
JANESVILLE
Hanson Furniture Company
Hough Shade Company
JEFFERSON
Union Upholstering Company
Wisconsin Manufacturing Company
JUNEAU
Peters Furniture Company

KENOSHA
HANNAHS MANUFACTURING COMPANY.... 197
Vincent-McCall Company
MARSHFIELD
Upham Manufacturing Company
MILTON
Burdick Cabinet Company
MILWAUKEE
ALLEN MANUFACTURING COMPANY
  Catalog 136
  Home Furnishing & Decoration Section.......... 10
Art Bilt Furniture Company
Bub Company, Jos.
Fuller Warren Company
Gen Hammock & Fly Net Company
HEBENSTREIT'S, INC. 397 (Z3)
Heyer & Son, Henry
KIEL FURNITURE COMPANY............ 208-215
LAHL & KIDNEY
  See Mersman Bros. Corpn...................216-221
Lane Company
Lewis Bros. Company
Lindemann & Hoverson Company, A. J.
Maihlin Walters Company
Maxwell Ray Company
Mayhew Company
Mayhew Shops, Inc.
Meinecke Manufacturing Company
Milwaukee Bedding Company
Milwaukee Woven Wire Works
Moe-Bridges Company
Neidhoefer Company
Pahl & Company, A. F.
Paul, Otto
Prasser Furniture Company
Rilling Company, J. E.
ROME COMPANY, INC.....................70-71
Standard Bedding Company
Weigell & Son, August
WIENER COMPANY, E.
  Catalog 406 (Z3)
  Home Furnishing & Decoration Section.......... 60
Wisconsin Furniture Company
MUSCODA
Muscoda Manufacturing Company
NEENAH
Kimlark Rug Company
OSHKOSH
Banderob-Chase Mfg. Company
BIRCH MANUFACTURERS AND THE ROTARY
  BIRCH CLUB 390-391
Buckstaff Manufacturing Company
Deltox Grass Rug Company
Gould Manufacturing Company
NORTHERN HARD MAPLE MANUFAC-
  TURERS 388-389
Three "C" Davenport Company
Waite Carpet Company
PLYMOUTH
Plymouth Furniture Company
PORT WASHINGTON
Gilson Manufacturing Company
RACINE
Davis Manufacturing Company
Gold Medal Camp Furn. Mfg. Co.
RHINELANDER
Rhinelander Refrigerator Co.
SHEBOYGAN
American Chair Company
Art Furniture Company
Badger Furniture Company
Bemis Riddell Company
CROCKER CHAIR COMPANY
  Catalog 137
  Home Furnishing & Decoration Section.......... 12
Dillingham Manufacturing Co.
Garton Toy Company
Globe Company, The
Inland Furniture Company
Ke-No Company
Lakeside Craft Company
McNeill Chair Company
Made Well Chair Company
Midwest Fibre Company
Northern Furniture Company
NORTHFIELD COMPANY
  Catalog 122-123
  Home Furnishing & Decoration Section.......... 37
PHOENIX CHAIR COMPANY
  Catalog 222-235
  Home Furnishing & Decoration Section.......... 42-44
Sheboygan Chair Company
Sheboygan Fibre Furniture Co.
Sheboygan Mattress Company
Sheboygan Novelty Company
Valley Furniture Company
Western Furniture Company
Western Mirror Plate Company
SHEBOYGAN FALLS
Richardson Bros. Co. Inc.
STEVENS POINT
Automatic Cradle Company
Folding Furn. Works, Inc.
JOERNS BROS. FURNITURE COMPANY
  Catalog 277
  Home Furnishing & Decoration Section.......... 23
SUPERIOR
Webster Manufacturing Company
WAUKESHA
Aeroshade Company, The
WAUSAU
Wausau Novelty Company
WEST BEND
Kitchen Craft Company, The

Classified Index of Products

A

Adam
——**Chairs**
See **Chairs,** Adam
——**Mirrors**
See **Mirrors,** Adam
Adjustable Chairs
——**Florentine**
See **Chairs, Adjustable,** Florentine
——**Heppelwhite**
See **Chairs, Adjustable,** Heppelwhite
——**Queen Anne**
See **Chairs, Adjustable,** Queen Anne
——**Tudor**
See **Chairs, Adjustable,** Tudor
Advertising Services, Direct Mail
See **Direct Mail Advertising Services**
American Empire
——**Buffets, Dining Room**
See **Dining Room Buffets,** American Empire
——**Suites, Complete, Dining Room**
See **Dining Room Suites, Complete,** American Empire
Andirons
See **Dog Irons**
Antique Fereghan Carpets and Rugs
See **Carpets and Rugs,** Antique Fereghan
Apartment Size
——**Buffets, Dining Room**
See **Dining Room Buffets,** Apartment Size
——**China Cabinets and Closets, Dining Room**
See **Dining Room China Cabinets and Closets,** Apartment Size
——**Cupboards, Dining Room**
See **Dining Room Cupboards,** Apartment Size
——**Suites, Complete, Dining Room**
See **Dining Room Suites, Complete,** Apartment Size
——**Tables, Dining Room**
See **Dining Room Tables,** Apartment Size
Aquariums, Reed and Fibre
See **Reed and Fibre Aquariums**
Arm Chairs
——**Reed and Fibre**
See **Reed and Fibre Arm Chairs**
——**Tablet**
See **Tablet Arm Chairs**
——**Upholstered**
Illustrated or Described
American Parlor Furniture Company 91
Berkey & Gay Furniture Company 248–251
Brandts Furniture Company 394 (Z3)
Conant Ball Company 191
Conant's Sons, Inc., F. H. 192
Decker, Inc., Isaac C. 96
Delker Bros. Mfg. Co. 97
Dunbar Furniture Mfg. Co. 98
Empire Chair Company 194–196
Fenske Bros. 99
Field & Company, Marshall (Wholesale) 100–101
Franklin Furniture Co. 102
Fullerton Furniture Factories 103
Furniture City Upholstery Co. 104
Globe Parlor Furniture Co. 106–107
Harden Company, Frank S. 108–109
Hastings Table Company 150–151
Hebenstreit's, Inc. 397 (Z3)
Horn & Company, J. P. 410 (Z1)
Indianapolis Chair & Furniture Co. 152
Jamestown Lounge Company 105
Jamestown Upholstery Co., Inc. 110
Karpen & Bros., S. 112–119
Louisville Chair & Furn. Co. 396 (Z2)
Levin Bros., Inc. 111
Madden Mfg. Co., John J. 120
Michigan Chair Company 162–163
Northfield Company 122–123
Phoenix Chair Company 222–235
Poston Mfg. Co., B. C. 401 (Z3)
Sikes Chair Company 238
Spencer Duffy Company, Inc. 125–127
Statesville Chair Company 417 (Z1)
Sultan & Company, William 132
Tauber Parlor Furniture Co. 402 (Z3)
Toledo Parlor Furniture Co. 404 (Z3)
Whitney Company, Inc., W. F. 240
Wiener Company, E. 406
Charles II 112–119
Chippendale 112–119; 125–127
Colonial (Early American) 132
Cromwellian 112–119
French Provincial 112–119
Georgian 162–163
Heppelwhite 162–163
High Back 112–119; 120; 410 (Z1)
High Back (Italian) 162–163; 394 (Z3)
Italian 112–119
Lawson 100–101
Louis XIV 112–119
Louis XVI 112–119; 132
Modern 112–119; 222–235
Normandy 112–119
Queen Anne 162; 238
Venetian 112–119

Mentioned Only
Century Furniture Company 92
Chittenden & Eastman Company 377
Crocker Chair Company 137
Gunlocke Chair Company, W. H. 401 (Z1)
Memphis Furniture Mfg. Co. 303
Steul & Son, Henry C. 348
Union Brothers 420 (Z1)
Yeager Furniture Company 431 (Z1)

——**Wood**
Illustrated or Described
Colonial Furniture Company 93–95
Empire Chair Company 194–196
Phoenix Chair Company 222–235

Arm Chairs
——**Upholstered, Wood** *(continued)*
Mentioned Only
Century Furniture Company 92
Conant Ball Company 191
Fenske Bros. 99
Gunlocke Chair Co., W. H. 401 (Z1)
Hastings Table Company 150–151
Indianapolis Chair & Furn. Co. 152
Memphis Furniture Mfg. Co. 303
Standard Chair Company 239
Sultan & Company, William 132
Tell City Chair Company 403 (Z3)

Arm Tables
Mentioned Only
Davis-Birely Table Company 193

Art Moderne
See **Modern**

Ash Trays
Mentioned Only
Furst Bros. & Company 78

Assembly Hall Chairs
Mentioned Only
Conant Ball Company 191

Associations
American Art Bureau 378–379
American Walnut Mfrs'. Ass'n 380–381
Evansville Furniture Mfrs. Ass'n. 382–383
Hardwood Manufacturers' Institute 384–386
Oak Service Bureau 384–385
Gumwood Service Bureau 386
Jamestown Furniture Market Ass'n. 387
Northern Hemlock & Hardwood Mfrs. Ass'n. 388–391
Hard Maple 388–389
Birch 390–391

Aubusson
——**Carpets and Rugs**
See **Carpets and Rugs,** Aubusson
——**Tapestries**
See **Drapery and Upholstery Fabrics,** Tapestries, Aubusson

Auto Spring Seat Rockers
See **Rockers, Auto Spring Seat**

Awnings, Hammock
See **Hammock Awnings**

Axminster
——**Oval Rugs**
See **Carpets and Rugs,** Axminster, Oval
——**Seamless Carpets and Rugs**
See **Carpets and Rugs,** Axminster, Seamless

B

Babies'
——**Furniture**
See **Infants Furniture.** (*See* Also **Nursery Furniture**)
——**High Chairs**
See **Children's High Chairs**

Baby Carriages, Go-Carts, and Sulkies
Mentioned Only
Chittenden & Eastman Company 377

Banjo Clocks
See **Clocks, Banjo**

Bank and Office
——**Chairs** (*See* Also **Metal Office Chairs**)
Illustrated or Described
Imperial Furniture Company 198–205
Stow-Davis Furniture Company 76–77
Swivel 76–77

Mentioned Only
Chittenden & Eastman Company 377
Crocker Chair Company 137
Empire Chair Company 194–195
Gunlocke Chair Co., W. H. 401 (Z1)
Horn & Company, J. P. 410 (Z1)
Mallen & Company, H. Z. 121
Shreve Chair Co., Inc. 237
Sikes Chair Company 238
Standard Chair Company 239
Tauber Parlor Furniture Co. 402 (Z3)
Tell City Chair Company 403 (Z3)

Swivel 239; 403 (Z3)
Typewriter Desk 137; 194–196; 377

——**Davenports**
Mentioned Only
Mallen & Company, H. Z. 121
Sikes Chair Company 238
Stow-Davis Furniture Co. 76–77
Tauber Parlor Furniture Co. 402 (Z3)

——**Desks** (*See* Also **Metal Office Desks**)
Illustrated or Described
Gunn Furniture Company 396 (Z3)
Imperial Furniture Company 198–205
Stow-Davis Furniture Co. 76–77
Composition Top 396 (Z3)

Mentioned Only
Century Furniture Company 92
Chittenden & Eastman Company 377
Curtiss & Son, Wm. P. 399 (Z1)
Empire Chair Company 194–196

Typewriter 76–77; 194–196; 396 (Z3); 399 (Z1)

——**Filing Cabinets**
Mentioned Only
Stow-Davis Furniture Co. 76–77

——**Furniture**
Mentioned Only
Buffalo Lounge Company 394 (Z1)
Imperial Furniture Company 198–205
Jamestown Lounge Co. 105

Bank and Office
——**Settees**
Mentioned Only
Crocker Chair Company 137

——**Stools**
Mentioned Only
Chittenden & Eastman Company 377
Crocker Chair Company 137
Standard Chair Company 239

——**Tables**
Illustrated or Described
Stow-Davis Furniture Company 76–77
Directors 76–77

Mentioned Only
Century Furniture Company 92
Chittenden & Eastman Company 377
Curtiss & Son, Wm. P. 399 (Z1)
Gunn Furniture Co. 396 (Z3)
Hastings Table Co. 150–151
Kiel Furniture Company 208–215
Luger Furniture Co. 399 (Z3)
Mutschler Bros. Co. 74
St. Johns Table Co. 236

Directors 74; 92; 150–151; 208–215; 377; 399 (Z3)
Typewriter 76–77; 236; 396 (Z3); 399 (Z1)

——**Telephone Stands**
Illustrated or Described
Imperial Furniture Company 198–205
Stow-Davis Furniture Company 76–77

——**Wardrobes**
Mentioned Only
Stow-Davis Furniture Company 76–77

——**Waste Baskets**
Illustrated or Described
Stow-Davis Furniture Company 76–77

Banquet Table Tops
Mentioned Only
Luger Furniture Company 399

Banquet Tables, Folding
Illustrated or Described
Luger Furniture Company 399 (Z3)

Bases, Kitchen Cabinet
See **Kitchen Cabinet Bases**

Baskets
——**And Carriers, Magazine**
See **Magazine Baskets and Carriers**
——**And Carriers, Magazine, Canterbury Type**
See **Magazine Baskets and Carriers,** Canterbury
——**Fuel, Fireside, Reed and Fibre**
See **Reed and Fibre Fuel Baskets, Fireside**
——**Grate**
See **Grate Baskets**
——**Sewing, Reed and Fibre**
See **Reed and Fibre Sewing Baskets**
——**Waste**
See **Waste Baskets**
——**Waste, Reed and Fibre**
See **Reed and Fibre Waste Baskets**

Bassinettes
Mentioned Only
Chittenden & Eastman Company 377

Bathroom
——**Cabinet Mirrors**
Mentioned Only
Chicago Mirror & Art Glass Co. 395 (Z3)

——**Chairs**
Mentioned Only
Crocker Chair Company 137
Whitney Co., Inc., W. F. 240

——**Medicine Cabinets**
Mentioned Only
Chittenden & Eastman Company 377
Furst Bros. & Company 78
Peterson Art Furniture Co. 164

——**Mirrors**
Mentioned Only
Chittenden & Eastman Company 377
Furst Bros. & Company 78

——**Stools**
Mentioned Only
Crocker Chair Company 137
Standard Chair Company 239
Thomasville Chair Company 349

Bed
——**Constructions, Davenport**
See **Davenport Bed Constructions**
——**Davenports, Cane**
See **Cane Davenport Beds**
——**Fixtures, Davenport**
See **Davenport Bed Fixtures**
——**Short Rails for Displaying Beds**
Mentioned Only
De Boer Manufacturing Company 133

——**Springs, Box and Coil**
Illustrated or Described
Anchor Spring & Bedding Company 393 (Z2)
Barcalo Manufacturing Company 393 (Z1)
Foster Bros. Mfg. Co. 69
Rome Company, Inc. 70–71

Mentioned Only
Chittenden & Eastman Company 377
Hard Mfg. Co. 404 (Z1)

——**Stays**
Illustrated or Described
De Boer Manufacturing Co. 133

Bed
——Suites, Davenport
See **Davenport Bed Suites**
Bedroom
——Beds
See Separate Classification—**Beds** *following* **Bedroom Wardrobes**
——Benches
Illustrated or Described
Atlas Furniture Company 241
Aulsbrook & Jones Furniture Co 242
Blackhawk Furniture Co 245–247
Continental Furniture Co 260–261
Empire Case Goods Company 266–267
Johnson & Sons Furn. Co., A. J 278–279
Landstrom Furn. Corp 290–301
Luce Furniture Company 156–159
Miller Furn. Co., Herman 145
Rockford Peerless Furniture Company 168–171
Tate Furniture Co 354–357
Union Furniture Company 421 (Z1)
West Michigan Furniture Co 286–287
White Furniture Company 365
Widdicomb Furniture Company 367
Wilson Furniture Co., Inc .... 407 (Z3) and 430 (Z1)
Winnebago Mfg. Co 368–371
COLONIAL (Early American) 278–279
DUNCAN PHYFE 368–371
FIBRE SEAT 260–261
FRENCH 368–371
FRENCH COLONIAL 278–279
HEPPELWHITE 368–371
LOUIS XV 278–279
MODERN 145; 156–159
Mentioned Only
Blackhawk Furniture Co 245–247
Charlotte Furniture Company 258
Chittenden & Eastman Company 377
Conant Ball Company 191
Davis Furniture Corporation 262
Dixie Furniture Co 263
Empire Chair Company 194–196
Estey Mfg. Co 265
Globe-Bosse-World Furniture Co 273
Globe Parlor Furniture Co 106–107
Horn & Company, J. P 410 (Z1)
Huntley Furniture Company, B. F 274
Indianapolis Chair & Furn. Co 152
Joerns Bros. Furniture Co 277
Karges Furniture Company 280
Lincoln Furniture Mfg. Co 362–363
Louisville Chair & Furn. Co 396 (Z2)
Memphis Furn. Mfg. Co 303
Nicholson-Kendle Furniture Co 269
Norquist Company, A. C 305
Showers Brothers Company 336–341
Sikes Chair Company 238
Standard Chair Company 239
Statesville Chair Company 417 (Z1)
Statesville Furniture Company 346
Statton Furniture Mfg. Co 418 (Z1)
Stewartstown Furniture Co 350–351
Tauber Parlor Furniture Co 402 (Z3)
Tillotson Furniture Corp 358
Union Brothers 420 (Z1)
Ward Manufacturing Co 364
Wellsville Upholstering Co 423 (Z1)
Whitney Co., Inc., W. F 240
Wiener Company, E 406 (Z3)
Williamsport Furniture Co 429 (Z1)
DRESSING TABLE TYPE 152; 260–261; 280; 305; 346
TOILET TABLE TYPE
...... 152; 194–196; 239; 265; 280; 305; 429 (Z1)
——Chair Sets
Illustrated or Described
Landstrom Furn. Corp 290–301
Mentioned Only
Blackhawk Furniture Co 245–247
Century Furniture Company 92
Chittenden & Eastman Company 377
Conant Ball Company 191
Continental Furniture Co 260–261
Empire Chair Company 194–196
Huntley Furniture Company, B. F 274
Indianapolis Chair & Furn. Co 152
Karges Furniture Company 280
Memphis Furn. Mfg. Co 303
Michigan Chair Company 162–163
Milne Chair Company 207
National Furniture Co 124
Norquist Company, A. C 305
Statesville Chair Company 417 (Z1)
Statesville Furniture Company 346
Stewartstown Furniture Company 350–351
Tate Furniture Company 354–357
Thomasville Chair Company 349
Union Furniture Company 421 (Z1)
United Furniture Company 359
Ward Mfg. Co 364
White Furniture Company 365
Whitney Company, Inc., W. F 240
Widdicomb Company, John 366
Widdicomb Furniture Company 367
Winnebago Manufacturing Company 368–371
——Chairs
Illustrated or Described
Aulsbrook & Jones Furn. Co 242
Blackhawk Furniture Co 245–247
Continental Furniture Co 260–261
Empire Case Goods Company 266–267
Empire Chair Company 194–195
Johnson & Sons Furn. Co., A. J 278–279
Luce Furniture Company 156–159
Michigan Chair Company 162–163
Miller Furn. Co., Herman 145
Phoenix Chair Company 222–235
Statton Furniture Mfg. Co 418 (Z1)
Sterling Furniture Company 347
Tate Furniture Company 354–357
Union Furniture Company 421 (Z1)
West Michigan Furniture Company 286–287
White Furniture Company 365
Widdicomb Furniture Company 367
Wilson Furniture Co., Inc .... 407 (Z3) and 430 (Z1)
Winnebago Manufacturing Co 368–371
COLONIAL (Early American) 278–279
DUNCAN PHYFE 368–371
FRENCH 368–371
FRENCH COLONIAL 278–279
HEPPELWHITE 368–371

Bedrooom
——Chairs *(continued)*
LOUIS XV 278–279
LOUIS XVI 286–287
MODERN 145; 156–159
SLIPPER TYPE 92; 194–195
Mentioned Only
Baker Furniture Factories, Inc 243
Century Furniture Company 92
Charlotte Furniture Co 258
Chittenden & Eastman Company 377
Conant Ball Company 191
Crocker Chair Company 137
Davis Furniture Corp 262
Dixie Furniture Co 263
Gunlocke Chair Company, W. H 401 (Z1)
Harden Company, Frank S 108–109
Horn & Company, J. P 410 (Z1)
Huntley Furniture Co., B. F 274
Hebenstreit's, Inc 397 (Z3)
Globe Parlor Furniture Co 106
Jamestown Chair Company 206
Jamestown Lounge Company 105
Jamestown Upholstery Co., Inc 110
Joerns Bros. Furn. Co 277
Karges Furniture Co 280
Levin Bros., Inc 111
Lincoln Furniture Mfg. Co 362–363
Louisville Chair & Furn. Co 396 (Z2)
Luger Furniture Company 399 (Z3)
Mallen & Company, H. Z 121
Memphis Furniture Mfg. Co 303
Norquist Company, A. C 305
Showers Bros. Company 336–341
Sikes Chair Company 238
Standard Chair Company 239
Statesville Chair Company 417 (Z1)
Statesville Furniture Co 346
Stewartstown Furniture Co 350–351
Sultan & Company, William 132
Tauber Parlor Furn. Co 402 (Z3)
Thomasville Chair Company 349
Tillotson Furniture Corp 358
Union Brothers 420 (Z1)
Union Furniture Co 421 (Z1)
Wellsville Upholstering Co 423 (Z1)
Whitney Company, Inc., W. F 240
Williamsport Furniture Co 429 (Z1)
Yeager Furniture Company 431 (Z1)
SLIPPER TYPE 110; 132; 222–235
——Chest Toilets
Mentioned Only
Charlotte Furniture Company 258
——Chests of Drawers
Illustrated or Described
Blackhawk Furniture Co 245–247
Conant Ball Company 191
Continental Furniture Company 260–261
Empire Case Goods Company 266–267
Jamestown Table Company 276
Landstrom Furn. Corp 290–301
Lincoln Furn. Mfg. Co 362–363
Luce Furniture Company 156–159
Memphis Furn. Mfg. Co. 303
National Furn. Co. 124
Norquist Company, A. C. 305
Schoeck Mfg. Co., Inc 415 (Z1)
Showers Brothers Company 336–341
Sterling Furniture Company 347
Stewartstown Furn. Co 350–351
Tate Furniture Co 354–357
Union Furniture Co 421 (Z1)
United Furniture Co 359
Ward Manufacturing Co 364
West Michigan Furniture Co 286–287
Winnebago Manufacturing Co 368–371
COLONIAL (Early American) 124; 286–287; 305
DUNCAN PHYFE 368–371
FRENCH 368–371
HEPPELWHITE 368–371
MODERN 156–159
Mentioned Only
Caldwell Furniture Company 398 (Z1)
Dixie Furniture Co 263
Globe-Bosse-World Furniture Co 273
Huntley Furniture Co., B. F 274
Joerns Bros. Furn. Co 277
Karges Furniture Co 280
Luger Furniture Co 399 (Z3)
White Furniture Co 365
Widdicomb Company, John 366
Widdicomb Furniture Co 367
——Chiffoniers
Illustrated or Described
Atlas Furniture Company 241
Estey Manufacturing Company 265
Nicholson-Kendle Furn. Co 269
West Michigan Furniture Co 286–287
White Furniture Company 365
Mentioned Only
Caldwell Furniture Company 398 (Z1)
Chittenden & Eastman Company 377
Continental Furniture Co 260–261
Estey Manufacturing Co 265
Globe-Bosse-World Furn. Co 273
Huntley Furniture Co., B. F 274
Indianapolis Chair & Furn. Co 152
Karges Furniture Company 280
Luger Furniture Co 399 (Z3)
Norquist Company, A. C 305
Statesville Furniture Co 346
Stewartstown Furn. Co 350–351
Tate Furniture Co 354–357
Tillotson Furniture Corp 358
Union Furniture Co 421 (Z1)
Widdicomb Company, John 366
Widdicomb Furniture Co 367
——Chifforettes
Illustrated or Described
Aulsbrook & Jones Furniture Co 242
Johnson & Sons Furn. Co., A. J 278–279
COLONIAL (Early American) 278–279
FRENCH COLONIAL 278–279
LOUIS XV 278–279
Mentioned Only
Chittenden & Eastman Company 377
Continental Furniture Co 260–261
Indianapolis Chair & Furn. Co 152

Bedroom
——Chifforettes
Mentioned Only
Joerns Bros. Furn. Co 277
Karges Furniture Co 280
Luger Furniture Co 399 (Z3)
Memphis Furn. Mfg. Co 303
Nicholson-Kendle Furniture Co 269
Norquist Company, A. C 305
Statesville Furniture Co 346
Stewartstown Furn. Co 350–351
Tate Furniture Co 354–357
Union Furniture Co 421 (Z1)
White Furniture Co 365
——Chifforobes
Illustrated or Described
Landstrom Furn. Corp 290–301
Lincoln Furn. Mfg. Co 362–363
Marstall Furn. Co., Inc 397 (Z2)
Showers Brothers Company 336–341
Tate Furniture Co 354–357
Williamsport Furniture Co 429 (Z1)
Wilson Furniture Co., Inc .... 407 (Z3) and 430 (Z1)
Mentioned Only
Caldwell Furniture Company 398 (Z1)
Chittenden & Eastman Company 377
Continental Furniture Co 260–261
Dixie Furniture Co 263
Empire Case Goods Co 266–267
Globe-Bosse-World Furn. Co 273
Huntley Furn. Co., B. F 274
Indianapolis Chair & Furn. Co 152
Joerns Bros. Furn. Co 277
Karges Furniture Co 280
Memphis Furn. Mfg. Co 303
Morganton Furniture Company 304
Nicholson-Kendle Furniture Co 269
Statesville Furn. Co 346
Stewartstown Furn. Co 350–351
Tillotson Furn. Corp 358
Union Furniture Co 421 (Z1)
United Furniture Co 359
White Furniture Co 365
Widdicomb Company, John 366
Widdicomb Furniture Co 367
——Desks
Illustrated or Described
Aulsbrook & Jones Furn. Co 242
Continental Furniture Co 260–261
White Furniture Co 365
Widdicomb Furniture Co 367
Mentioned Only
Century Furniture Co 92
Chittenden & Eastman Company 377
Empire Case Goods Co 266–267
Estey Manufacturing Co 265
Huntley Furn. Co., B. F 274
Indianapolis Chair & Furn. Co 152
Karges Furniture Co 280
Luger Furniture Co 399 (Z3)
Peterson Art Furniture Co 164
Steul & Sons, Henry C 348
Tate Furniture Co 354–357
Tillotson Furniture Corp 358
White Furniture Co 365
Widdicomb Company, John 366
——Dresserobes
Illustrated or Described
Marstall Furniture Co., Inc 397 (Z2)
Mentioned Only
Continental Furniture Co 260–261
Globe-Bosse-World Furn. Co 273
Karges Furniture Co 280
Memphis Furn. Mfg. Co 303
Statesville Furniture Co 346
White Furniture Co 365
——Dressers
Illustrated or Described
Atlas Furniture Co 241
Aulsbrook & Jones Furn. Co 242
Blackhawk Furniture Co 245–247
Charlotte Furniture Co 258
Continental Furniture Co 260–261
Davis Furniture Corp 262
Dixie Furniture Co 263
Empire Case Goods Co 266–267
Estey Manufacturing Co 265
Forsyth Furniture Lines, Inc 272
Hemsing Manufacturing Co 405 (Z1)
Huntley Furn. Co., B. F 274
Jamestown Table Company 276
Joerns Bros. Furn. Co 277
Johnson & Sons Furn. Co., A. J 278–279
Klamer Furniture Corp 288–289
Lincoln Furn. Mfg. Co 362–363
Luce Furniture Company 156–159
Luger Furniture Company 399 (Z3)
Memphis Furn. Mfg. Co 303
Miller Furn. Co., Herman 145
Monitor Furniture Co 288–289
National Furniture Co 124
Nicholson-Kendle Furniture Co 269
Norquist Company, A. C. 305
Showers Brothers Company 336–341
Statesville Furniture Co 346
Statton Furn. Mfg. Co 418 (Z1)
Sterling Furn. Co 347
Stewartstown Furn. Co 350–351
Tate Furniture Co 354–357
Union Furniture Co 421 (Z1)
West Michigan Furn. Co 286–287
White Furniture Co 365
Widdicomb Company, John 366
Widdicomb Furn. Co 367
Williamsport Furniture Co 429 (Z1)
Wilson Furn. Co., Inc .... 407 (Z3) and 430 (Z1)
Winnebago Manufacturing Co 368–371
COLONIAL (Early American)
.... 124; 278–279; 286–287; 305; 366
DUNCAN PHYFE 368–371
FRENCH 368–371
FRENCH COLONIAL 278–279
HEPPELWHITE 368–371
LOUIS XV 278–279
MODERN 145; 156–159

Bedroom
——Dressers *(continued)*
Mentioned Only
Caldwell Furniture Company 398 (Z1)
Charlotte Furniture Co. 258
Chittenden & Eastman Company 377
Globe-Bosse-World Furn. Co. 273
Indianapolis Chair & Furn. Co. 152
Karges Furniture Co. 280
Morganton Furniture Company 304
Stickley, L. & J. G. & Stickley Mfg. Co. 352–353
Tillotson Furniture Corp. 358
United Furniture Company 359
PRINCESS TYPE 358

——Dressing Tables
Illustrated or Described
Aulsbrook & Jones Furniture Co. 242
Estey Manufacturing Company 265
Luce Furniture Company 156–159
Johnson & Sons Furn. Co., A. J. 278–279
Miller Furniture Co., Herman 145
Norquist Company, A. C. 305
West Michigan Furniture Co. 286–287
COLONIAL (Early American) 286–287; 278–279; 305
LOUIS XV 278–279
MODERN 145; 156–159
Mentioned Only
Baker Furniture Factories, Inc. 243
Century Furniture Company 92
Continental Furniture Co. 260–261
Empire Case Goods Co. 266–267
Globe-Bosse-World Furn. Co. 273
Huntley Furniture Co., B. F. 274
Indianapolis Chair & Furn. Co. 152
Karges Furniture Co. 280
Luger Furniture Company 399 (Z3)
Nicholson-Kendle Furniture Co. 269
Statesville Furniture Co. 346
Tillotson Furniture Corp. 358
Union Furniture Co. 421 (Z1)
White Furniture Company 365
Widdicomb Company, John 366
Williamsport Furniture Co. 429 (Z1)
Winnebago Manufacturing Company 368–371
DROP LEAF TYPE 152

——Make-Up and Powder Cases and Tables
Illustrated or Described
Schoeck Mfg. Co., Inc. 415 (Z1)
Furniture Shops 160–161
COLONIAL (Early American) 160–161
Mentioned Only
Baker Furniture Factories, Inc. 243
Century Furniture Company 92
Charlotte Furniture Company 258
Huntley Furniture Company, B. F. 274

——Mansrobes
Illustrated or Described
Memphis Furniture Mfg. Co. 303

——Mirrors
Illustrated or Described
Charlotte Furniture Company 258
Chicago Mirror & Art Glass Co. 395 (Z3)
Johnson & Sons, Furn. Co., A. J. 278–279
Landstrom Furn. Corp. 290–301
Miller Furniture Co., Herman 145
Norquist Company, A. C. 305
Widdicomb Company, John 366
COLONIAL (Early American) 278–279; 286–287; 305; 366
FRENCH COLONIAL 278–279
LOUIS XV 278–279
Mentioned Only
Chittenden & Eastman Company 377
Furst Bros. & Company 78
Luce Furniture Company 156–159
Tillotson Furniture Corp. 358
Union Furniture Company 421 (Z1)

——Night Tables
Illustrated or Described
Athens Table & Mfg. Co. 190
Aulsbrook & Jones Furn. Co. 242
Blackhawk Furniture Co. 245–247
Charlotte Furniture Co. 258
Conant Ball Company 191
Continental Furniture Co. 260–261
Empire Case Goods Company 266–267
Estey Mfg. Co. 265
Johnson & Sons Furn. Co., A. J. 278–279
Keystone Table Company 411 (Z1)
Landstrom Furn. Corp. 290–301
Lincoln Furn. Mfg. Co. 362–363
Luce Furniture Company 156–159
Miller Furniture Co., Herman 145
Norquist Company, A. C. 305
Showers Brothers Company 336–341
Statton Furniture Mfg. Co. 418 (Z1)
Sterling Furniture Co. 347
Tate Furniture Company 354–357
Union Furniture Company 421 (Z1)
West Michigan Furniture Co. 286–287
White Furniture Co. 365
Widdicomb Furniture Co. 367
Williamsport Furniture Co. 429 (Z1)
Wilson Furn. Co. Inc. 407 (Z3) and 430 (Z1)
Winnebago Mfg. Co. 368–371
COLONIAL (Early American) 278–279; 286–287; 305
DUNCAN PHYFE 368–371
FRENCH 368–371
FRENCH COLONIAL 278–279
HEPPELWHITE 368–371
LOUIS XV 278–279
MODERN 156–159
Mentioned Only
Chittenden & Eastman Company 377
Conant-Ball Company 191
Curtiss & Son, Wm. P. 399 (Z1)
Davis-Birely Table Company 193
Davis Furniture Corp. 262
Dixie Furniture Co. 263
Elite Furniture Company 146
Hannahs Mfg. Co. 197
Huntley Furniture Co., B. F. 274
Indianapolis Chair & Furn. Co. 152
Joerns Bros. Furn. Co. 277
Karges Furniture Company 280
Luger Furniture Company 399 (Z3)
Memphis Furn. Mfg. Co. 303
Morganton Furniture Company 304

Bedroom
——Night Tables *(continued*
Mentioned Only
National Furniture Co. 124
Nicholson-Kendle Furniture Co. 269
Norquist Company, A. C. 305
Peterson Art Furn. Co. 164
Schoeck Mfg. Co., Inc. 415 (Z1)
Seaburg Mfg. Co. 416 (Z1)
Statesville Furn. Co. 346
Stewartstown Furn. Co. 350–351
Tillotson Furn. Corp. 358
United Furniture Co. 359
COLONIAL (Early American) 124

——Rockers
Illustrated or Described
Continental Furniture Co. 260–261
Empire Case Goods Co. 266–267
Phoenix Chair Company 222–235
Tate Furniture Company 354–357
White Furniture Company 365
Mentioned Only
Chittenden & Eastman Company 377
Davis Furniture Corp. 262
Dixie Furniture Company 263
Empire Chair Company 194–196
Harden Company, Frank S. 108–109
Hebenstreit's, Inc. 397 (Z3)
Huntley Furniture Co., B. F. 274
Indianapolis Chair & Furn. Co. 152
Karges Furniture Company 280
Levin Bros., Inc. 111
Lincoln Furn. Mfg. Co. 362–363
Louisville Chair & Furn. Co. 396 (Z2)
Luger Furniture Company 399 (Z3)
Memphis Furn. Mfg. Co. 303
Nicholson-Kendle Furniture Co. 269
Norquist Company, A. C. 305
Showers Bros. Company 336–341
Sikes Chair Company 238
Standard Chair Company 239
Statesville Chair Company 417 (Z1)
Statesville Furniture Co. 346
Statton Furn. Mfg. Co. 418 (Z1)
Stewartstown Furn. Co. 350–351
Union Furniture Company 421 (Z1)
Wellsville Upholstering Co. 423 (Z1)
Whitney Co., Inc., W. F. 240
Williamsport Furniture Co. 429 (Z1)

——Suites, Complete (Including Bench, Chair, Rocker and Night Table)
Illustrated or Described
Atlas Furniture Company 241
Aulsbrook & Jones Furn. Co. 242
Berkey & Gay Furniture Company 248–251
Blackhawk Furniture Co. 245–247
Continental Furniture Co. 260–261
Dixie Furniture Co. 263
Empire Case Goods Company 266–267
Estey Manufacturing Co. 265
Forsyth Furn. Lines, Inc. 272
Jamestown Table Company 276
Joerns Bros. Furn. Co. 277
Johnson & Sons Furn. Co., A. J. 278–279
Klamer Furniture Corp. 288–289
Landstrom Furn. Corp. 290–301
Lincoln Furn. Mfg. Co. 362–363
Luce Furniture Company 156–159
Miller Furniture Co., Herman 145
Monitor Furniture Co. 288–289
Nicholson Kendle Furniture Co. 269
National Furniture Company 124
Norquist Company, A. C. 305
Showers Brothers Company 336–341
Statesville Furniture Co. 346
Statton Furniture Mfg. Co. 418 (Z1)
Sterling Furniture Co. 347
Stewartstown Furn. Co. 350–351
Tate Furniture Co. 354–357
Union Furniture Co. 421 (Z1)
West Michigan Furniture Co. 386–387
White Furniture Co. 365
Widdicomb Company, John 366
Widdicomb Furniture Co. 367
Williamsport Furniture Co. 429 (Z1)
Wilson Furniture Co., Inc. 407 (Z3) and 430 (Z1)
Winnebago Mfg. Co. 368–371
CHIPPENDALE 421 (Z1)
COLONIAL (Early American) 248–251; 260–261; 278–279; 286–287; 305; 366; 421 (Z1)
DUNCAN PHYFE 368–371
FRENCH 368–371
FRENCH COLONIAL 278–279
HEPPELWHITE 368–371
LOUIS XV 378–379
MODERN 145; 156–159
WILLIAM AND MARY 269
Mentioned Only
Chittenden & Eastman Company 377
Davis Furniture Corp. 262
Huntley Furn. Co., B. F. 274
Indianapolis Chair & Furn. Co. 152
Irwin Company, Robert W. 275
Karges Furniture Co. 280
Luger Furniture Co. 399 (Z3)
Memphis Furn. Mfg. Co. 303
Morganton Furniture Company 304
Sligh Furn. Co. 335
Statesville Furniture Co. 346
Thomasville Chair Co. 349
Tillotson Furniture Corp. 358
United Furniture Co. 359
Ward Mfg. Co. 364
COLONIAL (Early American) 359
EARLY ENGLISH 359
JACOBEAN 359
WILLIAM AND MARY 359

——Suites, Four Pieces only
Illustrated or Described
Blackhawk Furniture Co. 245–247
Davis Furniture Corp. 262
Dixie Furniture Company 263
National Furniture Company 124
Nicholson-Kendle Furniture Co. 269
COLONIAL (Early American) 124
Mentioned Only
Caldwell Furniture Co. 398 (Z1)
Empire Case Goods Co. 266–267
Estey Manufacturing Co. 265

Bedroom
——Suites, Four Pieces only
Mentioned Only
Karges Furniture Company 280
Memphis Furn. Mfg. Co. 303
Statesville Furn. Co. 346
Tate Furniture Company 354–357
Tillotson Furniture Corp. 358
Ward Mfg. Co. 364
White Furniture Co. 365

——Suites, Three Pieces Only
Illustrated or Described
Ward Manufacturing Company 364

——Toilet Tables
Mentioned Only
Charlotte Furniture Company 258
Empire Case Goods Company 266–267
Landstrom Furniture Corporation 290–301
Luger Furniture Company 399 (Z3)
Statesville Furniture Co. 346
Union Furniture Company 421 (Z1)

——Vanities
Illustrated or Described
Atlas Furniture Company 241
Blackhawk Furniture Co. 245–247
Continental Furniture Co. 260–261
Davis Furniture Corp. 262
Dixie Furniture Company 263
Empire Case Goods Co. 266–267
Forsyth Furniture Lines, Inc. 272
Jamestown Table Company 276
Joerns Bros. Furn. Co. 277
Johnson & Sons Furn. Co., A. J. 278–279
Klamer Furniture Corp. 288–289
Landstrom Furn. Corp. 290–301
Lincoln Furn. Mfg. Co. 362–363
Luce Furniture Company 156–159
Memphis Furn. Mfg. Co. 303
Monitor Furniture Co. 288–289
National Furniture Company 124
Showers Brothers Company 336–341
Statton Furn. Mfg. Co. 418 (Z1)
Sterling Furn. Co. 347
Stewartstown Furn. Co. 350–351
Tate Furniture Co. 354–357
Union Furniture Co. 421 (Z1)
United Furniture Co. 359
Ward Mfg. Co. 364
White Furniture Co. 365
Widdicomb Furn. Co. 367
Wilson Furn. Co., Inc. 407 (Z3) and 430 (Z1)
Winnebago Mfg. Co. 368–371
COLONIAL (Early American) 124
DUNCAN PHYFE 368–371
FRENCH 368–371
FRENCH COLONIAL 278–279
HEPPELWHITE 368–371
MODERN 156–159
Mentioned Only
Estey Manufacturing Co. 265
Globe-Bosse-World Furn. Co. 273
Huntley Furn. Co., B. F. 274
Karges Furniture Co. 280
Luger Furniture Co. 399 (Z3)
Nicholson-Kendle Furn. Co. 269
Widdicomb Company, John 366

——Vanities, Semi
Illustrated or Described
Landstrom Furn. Corp. 290–301
Tate Furniture Company 354–357
Mentioned Only
Indianapolis Chair & Furn. Co. 152
Karges Furniture Company 280
Luger Furniture Company 399 (Z3)
Memphis Furn. Mfg. Co. 303
Union Furniture Co. 421 (Z1)
Widdicomb Company, John 366
Winnebago Mfg. Co. 368–371

——Vanity Dressers
Illustrated or Described
Williamsport Furniture Co. 429 (Z1)
Mentioned Only
Century Furniture Co. 92
Dixie Furniture Co. 263
Estey Manufacturing Co. 265
Huntley Furn. Co., B. F. 274
Joerns Bros. Furn. Co. 277
Karges Furn. Co. 280
Luger Furniture Co. 399 (Z3)
Morganton Furniture Company 304
Norquist Company, A. C. 305
Statesville Furniture Co. 346
Tate Furniture Co. 354–357
Tillotson Furn. Corp. 358
Union Furniture Co. 421 (Z1)

——Vanity Tables
Mentioned Only
Century Furniture Company 92
Statesville Furniture Co. 346

——Wardrobes
Illustrated or Described
Landstrom Furn. Corp. 290–301
Stewartstown Furniture Co. 350–351
Mentioned Only
Chittenden & Eastman Company 377
Continental Furniture Co. 260–261
Estey Manufacturing Co. 265
Globe-Bosse-World Furniture Co. 273
Huntley Furniture Co., B. F. 274
Karges Furniture Company 280
Marstall Furn. Co., Inc. 397 (Z2)
Memphis Furn. Mfg. Co. 303
Morganton Furniture Company 304
Norquist Company, A. C. 305
Statesville Furniture Co. 346
Statton Furniture Mfg. Co. 418 (Z1)
Tillotson Furniture Corp. 358
Union Furniture Company 421 (Z1)
White Furniture Company 365
Williamsport Furniture Co. 429 (Z1)
DRESSER COMBINATION TYPE 260–261; 280
CHEST TYPE 274
CHIFFONIER TYPE 274; 304

Beds
Illustrated or Described
Atlas Furniture Company 241

Beds (*continued*)
Aulsbrook & Jones Furniture Co 242
Blackhawk Furn. Company 245–247
Charlotte Furniture Company 258
Conant-Ball Company 191
Continental Furniture Co 260–261
Davis Furniture Corp 262
Dixie Furniture Company 263
Empire Case Goods Company 266–267
Estey Manufacturing Company 265
Hemsing Manufacturing Co 405 (Z1)
Johnson & Sons Furn. Co., A. J 278–279
Karges Furniture Company 280
Keystone Table Company 411 (Z1)
Kindel Furniture Company 282–283
Klamer Furniture Corp 288–289
Landstrom Furn. Corp 290–301
Luce Furniture Shops 156–159
Memphis Furn. Mfg. Co 303
Miller Furniture Company, Herman 145
Monitor Furniture Company 288–289
National Furniture Company 124
Nicholson-Kendle Furniture Co 269
Norquist Company, A. C 305
Patton-McCray Company 306
Statesville Furniture Co 346
Statton Furn. Mfg. Co 418 (Z1)
Sterling Furniture Co 347
Stewartstown Furn. Co 350–351
Showers Brothers Company 336–341
Tate Furniture Company 354–357
Union Furniture Company 421 (Z1)
Ward Manufacturing Company 364
West Michigan Furniture Co 286–287
Widdicomb Furniture Co 367
Williamsport Furniture Co 429 (Z1)
White Furniture Co 365
Winnebago Manufacturing Co 368–371
Wilson Furniture Co., Inc .... 407 (Z3) and 430 (Z1)
Colonial (Early American) ... 278–279; 282–283; 305
Duncan Phyfe 368–371
French 368–371
French Colonial 278–279
Hepplewhite 368–371
Ladder Back 191
Louis XV 278–279; 288–289
Modern 156–159

Mentioned Only
Baker Furniture Factories, Inc 243
Caldwell Furniture Company 398 (Z1)
Indianapolis Chair & Furn. Co 152
Morganton Furniture Company 304
Stickley, L. & J. G. and Stickley Mfg. Co 352–353

——Bow End
Illustrated or Described
Williamsport Furniture Co 429 (Z1)
Mentioned Only
Blackhawk Furniture Company 245–247
Caldwell Furniture Company 398 (Z1)
Chittenden & Eastman Company 377
Continental Furniture Company 260–261
Dixie Furniture Company 263
Globe-Bosse-World Furn. Co 273
Huntley Furn. Co., B. F 274
Indianapolis Chair & Furn. Co 152
Karges Furniture Co 280
Landstrom Furniture Corporation 290–301
Memphis Furn. Mfg. Co 303
Morganton Furniture Company 304
Nicholson-Kendle Furn. Co 269
Norquist Co., A. C 305
Showers Bros. Co 336–341
Statesville Furn. Co 346
Stewartstown Furniture Co 350–351
Union Furniture Co 421 (Z1)
United Furniture Co 359
Ward Manufacturing Co 364
White Furniture Company 365
Widdicomb Company, John 366
Widdicomb Furniture Co 367
Winnebago Manufacturing Co 368–371

——Children's
See **Children's Beds**
——Davenette, Reed and Fibre
See **Reed and Fibre Davenette Beds**
——Davenport
See **Davenport Beds**
——Day, Wood
See **Day Beds**
——Day, Metal
See **Metal Day Beds**
——Day, Reed and Fibre
See **Reed and Fibre Day Beds**

——Four Poster (Colonial)
Illustrated or Described
Berkey & Gay Furniture Company 248–251
Davis Furniture Corp 262
Charlotte Furniture Co 258
Conant-Ball Company 191
Continental Furniture Co 260–261
Dixie Furniture Company 263
Empire Case Goods Company 266–267
Estey Manufacturing Company 265
Hemsing Manufacturing Co 405 (Z1)
Keystone Table Company 411 (Z1)
Kindel Furniture Co 282–283
Landstrom Furn. Corp 290–301
National Furniture Co 124
Norquist Company, A. C 305
Patton-McCray Company 306
Mentioned Only
Blackhawk Furniture Company 245–247
Globe-Bosse-World Furn. Co 273
Indianapolis Chair & Furniture Co 152
Joerns Bros. Furn. Co 277
Memphis Furn. Mfg. Co 303
Nicholson-Kendle Furniture Co 269
Showers Bros. Co 336–341
Statesville Furn. Co 346
Tillotson Furn. Corp 358
United Furniture Company 359
Ward Manufacturing Company 364
White Furniture Company 365
Widdicomb Company, John 366
Winnebago Manufacturing Co 368–371
Yeager Furniture Company 431 (Z1)

——Hospital, Metal
See **Metal Hospital Beds**
——Lawn and Porch
See **Lawn and Porch Beds**

Beds
——Metal
See **Metal Beds**
——Odd
Mentioned Only
Nicholson-Kendle Furniture Co 269
Norquist Company, A. C 305
Union Furniture Company 421 (Z1)
——Porch, Metal
See **Metal Porch Beds**
——Spool
Illustrated or Described
Patton-McCray Company 306
——Straight End
Illustrated or Described
Atlas Furniture Company 241
Continental Furniture Company 260–261
Empire Case Goods Company 266–267
Landstrom Furn. Corp 290–301
Memphis Furniture Mfg. Co 303
Miller Furniture Co., Herman 145
National Furniture Company 124
Showers Bros. Company 336–341
Statesville Furniture Co 346
Statton Furn. Mfg. Co 418 (Z1)
Sterling Furniture Co 347
Stewartstown Furn. Co 350–351
Tate Furniture Company 354–357
Winnebago Manufacturing Co 368–371
Mentioned Only
Chittenden & Eastman Company 377
Estey Manufacturing Company 265
Globe-Bosse-World Furn. Co 273
Indianapolis Chair & Furn. Co 152
Karges Furniture Company 280
Memphis Furn. Mfg. Co 303
Nicholson-Kendle Furn. Co 269
Norquist Company, A. C 305
Stewartstown Furniture Co 350–351
United Furniture Co 359
Ward Manufacturing Company 364
Widdicomb Company, John 366
White Furniture Company 365
Widdicomb Furniture Company 367
Winnebago Manufacturing Co 368–371
——Toy
See **Toy Beds**
——Twin
Illustrated or Described
Aulsbrook & Jones Furniture Co 242
Continental Furniture Company 260–261
Dixie Furniture Company 263
Kindel Furniture Company 282–283
Luce Furniture Company 156–159
Patton-McCray Company 306
West Michigan Furniture Co 286–287
White Furniture Company 365
Widdicomb Furniture Company 367
Mentioned Only
Chittenden & Eastman Company 377
Davis Furniture Corp 262
Estey Manufacturing Co 265
Huntley Furniture Co., B. F 274
Indianapolis Chair & Furn. Co 152
Karges Furniture Company 280
Morganton Furniture Company 304
Norquist Company, A. C 305
Statesville Furniture Company 346
Stewartstown Furniture Co 350–351
Tate Furniture Co 354–357
Widdicomb Company, John 366
Winnebago Manufacturing Co 368–371
Union Furniture Company 421 (Z1)
——Windsor
Illustrated or Described
Kindel Furniture Company 282–283

Bedside Tables, Invalids'
See **Invalids' Bedside Tables**
Benches
——Bedroom
See **Bedroom Benches**
——Breakfast Room
See **Breakfast Room Benches**
——Cane Seat
See **Cane Seat Benches**
——Desk
See **Desk Benches**
——Dining Room
See **Dining Room Benches**
——Dressing Table
See **Bedroom Benches,** Dressing Table Type
——Fireside
See **Fireside Benches**
——Golf
See **Golf Benches**
——Living Room
See **Living Room Benches**
——Piano and Organ
See **Piano and Organ Benches**
——Radio
See **Radio Benches**
——Reed and Fibre
See **Reed and Fibre Benches**
——Toilet Table
See **Bedroom Benches,** Toilet Table Type
——Water
See **Water Benches**
Bentwood Chairs
Mentioned Only
Crocker Chair Company 137
Birch
Illustrated or Described
Birch Manufacturers and The Rotary Birch Club 390–391
Bird Cages
See **Reed and Fibre Bird Cages**
Boards, Ironing
See **Ironing Boards**
Boilers, Kettles and Cooking Utensils, Cast Iron
See **Kettles, Boilers, and Cooking Utensils, Cast Iron**
Book Ends
Mentioned Only
Chittenden & Eastman Company 377
Davis-Birely Table Company 193
Furst Bros. & Company 78
Peterson Art Furniture Co 164
Scheibe, R. R 414 (Z1)

Book, Magazine and Newspaper Racks and Stands
See Also **Reed and Fibre Book, Magazine and Newspaper Racks and Stands**
Illustrated or Described
Crocker Chair Company 137
Furniture Shops 160–161
Griffith Furniture Works 147
Hannahs Manufacturing Co 197
Imperial Furniture Company 198–205
Karpen & Bros., S 112–119
Keystone Table Company 411 (Z1)
Lassahn Furniture Company 154
Schoeck Manufacturing Co., Inc 415 (Z1)
Modern 112–119
Sheraton 160–161
Mentioned Only
Aulsbrook & Jones Furn. Co 242
Century Furniture Company 92
Chittenden & Eastman Company 377
Conant-Ball Company 191
Curtiss & Son, Wm. P 399 (Z1)
Davis-Birely Table Company 193
Elite Furniture Company 146
Hastings Table Company 150–151
Indianapolis Chair & Furn. Co 152
Klamer Furniture Corp 288–289
Memphis Furn. Mfg. Co 303
Monitor Furniture Co 288–289
Paalman Furniture Co 400 (Z3)
Peterson Art Furniture Co 164
St. Johns Table Company 236
Scheibe, R. R 414 (Z1)
Yeager Furniture Company 431 (Z1)
Book Racks and Davenport Tables Combined
See **Davenport Tables,** Book Rack Combination
Bookcases
See Also **Desks, Home, Bookcase Combination**
Illustrated or Described
Colonial Desk Company 138–141
Furniture Shops 160–161
Gunn Furniture Company 396 (Z3)
Hemsing Mfg. Co 405 (Z1)
Peterson Art Furniture Co 164
Rockford Chair & Furn. Co 308–313
Rockford National Furn. Co 324–326
Rockford Standard Furn. Co 327–331
Skandia Furniture Company 172–185
Udell Works, Inc 419 (Z1)
Union Furniture Company 186–187
Mentioned Only
Bay View Furniture Co 393 (Z3)
Century Furniture Company 92
Imperial Furniture Company 198–205
Memphis Furn. Mfg. Co 303
Irwin Company, Robert W 275
——Fireside
See **Fireside Bookcases**
——Glassed In
Illustrated or Described
Colonial Desk Company 138–141
Hemsing Manufacturing Company 405 (Z1)
Peterson Art Furn. Co 164
Rockford Chair & Furn. Co 308–313
Rockford National Furn. Co 324–326
Skandia Furniture Company 172–185
Udell Works, Inc 419 (Z1)
Chippendale 405 (Z1)
Mentioned Only
Bay View Furniture Co 393 (Z3)
Century Furniture Company 92
——Open Shelf
Illustrated or Described
Furniture Shops 160–161
Rockford Chair & Furn. Co 308–313
Rockford Standard Furn. Co 327–331
Skandia Furniture Company 172–185
Union Furniture Company 186–187
Sheraton 160–161
Mentioned Only
Bay View Furniture Co 393 (Z3)
Century Furniture Company 92
Colonial Desk Company 138–141
Gunn Furniture Co 396 (Z3)
Memphis Furn. Mfg. Co 303
Peterson Art Furniture Co 164
——Pier Type
See **Pier Bookcases**
——Reed and Fibre
See **Reed and Fibre Bookcases**
——Sectional
Illustrated or Described
Gunn Furniture Company 396 (Z3)
Skandia Furniture Company 172–185
Udell Works, Inc 419 (Z1)
Mentioned Only
Chittenden & Eastman Company 377
Bookshelves, Hanging
Mentioned Only
Conant-Ball Company 191
Hannahs Manufacturing Co 197
Irwin Company, Robert W 275
Michigan Chair Company 162–163
Book Troughs
Mentioned Only
Davis-Birely Table Company 193
Elite Furniture Company 146
Griffith Furniture Works 147
Hannahs Mfg. Co 197
Indianapolis Chair & Furn. Co 152
Lassahn Furniture Company 154
Luger Furniture Company 399 (Z3)
St. Johns Table Company 236
Seaburg Mfg. Co 416 (Z1)
Book Troughs and End Tables Combined
Illustrated or Described
Griffith Furniture Works 147
Imperial Furniture Company 198–205
Kiel Furniture Company 208–215
Paalman Furniture Company 400 (Z3)
Schoeck Mfg. Co., Inc 415 (Z1)

Bow Back Chairs
Mentioned Only
Crocker Chair Company 137
Curtiss & Son, Wm. P. 399 (Z1)
Standard Chair Company 239
Tell City Chair Company 403 (Z3)

Bow End Beds
See **Beds, Bow End**
Box
——**And Coil Bed Springs**
See **Bed Springs, Box and Coil**
——**Chairs, Theatre**
See **Theatre Box Chairs**
Brass Trimmed Cedar Chests
See **Cedar Chests,** Brass Trimmed
Breakfast Room
——**Benches**
Mentioned Only
Steul & Sons, Henry C. 348

——**Buffets**
Illustrated or Described
Curtiss & Son, Wm. P. 399 (Z1)
Mentioned Only
Century Furniture Company 92
Conant-Ball Company 191
Florence Table & Mfg. Co. 271
Hastings Table Company 150–151
Hoosier Manufacturing Co. 72
Luger Furniture Company 399 (Z3)
Memphis Furn. Mfg. Co. 303
Steul & Sons, Henry C. 348

——**Chairs**
Illustrated or Described
Curtiss & Son, Wm. P. 399 (Z1)
Hoosier Mfg. Co. 72
Mutschler Bros. Company 74
Phoenix Chair Company 222–235
Shreve Chair Company, Inc. 237
Standard Chair Company 239
Tell City Chair Company 403 (Z3)
Thomasville Chair Company 349
In-The-White 239; 403 (Z3)
Windsor 222–235
Mentioned Only
Century Furniture Company 92
Chittenden & Eastman Company 377
Conant-Ball Company 191
Florence Table & Mfg. Co. 271
Hastings Table Company 150–151
Indianapolis Chair & Furn. Co. 152
Luger Furniture Company 399 (Z3)
Memphis Furniture Mfg. Co. 303
St. Johns Table Company 236
Sikes Chair Company 238
Standard Chair Company 239
Steul & Sons, Henry C. 348
Whitney Co., Inc., W. F. 240
In-The-White 74; 92; 191; 239; 399 (Z3)

——**China Cabinets and Closets**
Illustrated or Described
Curtiss & Son, Wm. P. 399 (Z1)
Mentioned Only
Century Furniture Company 92
Indianapolis Chair & Furn. Co. 152
Steul & Sons, Henry C. 348

——**Dutch Cabinets**
Illustrated or Described
Thomasville Chair Company 349

——**Servers and Serving Tables**
Illustrated or Described
Curtiss & Son, Wm. P. 399 (Z1)
Mentioned Only
Century Furniture Company 92
Conant-Ball Company 191
Hoosier Manufacturing Co. 72
Indianapolis Chair & Furn. Co. 152
Memphis Furn. Mfg. Co. 303
St. Johns Table Company 236

——**Serving Tables and Cabinets Combined**
Mentioned Only
Conant-Ball Company 191
Indianapolis Chair & Furn. Co. 152
Luger Furniture Company 399 (Z3)
St. Johns Table Company 236
Steul & Sons, Henry C. 348

——**Sets** (Tables and Chairs)
Illustrated or Described
Hoosier Manufacturing Co. 72
Mutschler Bros. Company 74
Phoenix Chair Company 222–235
Shreve Chair Company, Inc. 237
Mentioned Only
Florence Table & Mfg. Co. 271
Hastings Table Company 150–151
Indianapolis Chair & Furn. Co. 152
Luger Furniture Company 399 (Z3)
Memphis Furn. Mfg. Co. 303
St. Johns Table Company 236
Steul & Sons, Henry C. 348
Whitney Co., Inc., W. F. 240
Yeager Furniture Co. 431 (Z1)
In-The-White 303

——**Suites**
Illustrated or Described
Curtiss & Son, Wm. P. 399 (Z1)
Phoenix Chair Company 222–235
Thomasville Chair Company 349
Mentioned Only
Century Furniture Company 92
Chittenden & Eastman Company 377
Conant-Ball Company 191
Florence Table & Mfg. Co. 271
Forsyth Furn. Lines, Inc. 272
Furniture Shops 160–161
Hastings Table Company 150–151
Indianapolis Chair & Furn. Co. 152

Breakfast Room
——**Suites** (*continued*)
Mentioned Only
Klamer Furniture Corp. 288–289
Luger Furniture Company 399 (Z3)
Memphis Furn. Mfg. Co. 303
Michigan Chair Company 162–163
Monitor Furniture Co. 288–289
St. Johns Table Company 236
Steul & Sons, Inc., Henry C. 348

——**Tables**
See Also **Reed and Fibre Breakfast Room Tables**
Illustrated or Described
Curtiss & Son, Wm. P. 399 (Z1)
Hoosier Mfg. Co. 72
Mutschler Bros. Company 74
Phoenix Chair Company 222–235
Shreve Chair Co., Inc. 237
Thomasville Chair Company 349
Drop Leaf 222–235; 399 (Z1)
Extension 237
Mentioned Only
Athens Table & Mfg. Co. 190
Baker Furniture Factories, Inc. 243
Century Furniture Company 92
Chittenden & Eastman Company 377
Conant-Ball Company 191
Florence Table & Mfg. Co. 271
Hastings Table Company 150–151
Indianapolis Chair & Furn. Co. 152
Luger Furniture Company 399 (Z3)
Memphis Furn. Mfg. Co. 303
Peterson Art Furniture Company 164
St. Johns Table Company 236
Steul & Sons, Inc., Henry C. 348
Whitney Co., Inc., W. F. 240
Extension 92; 150–151; 191; 236; 348; 399 (Z3)
In-The-White 74; 236; 399 (Z3)

——**Welsh Dressers**
Illustrated or Described
Phoenix Chair Company 222–235
Mentioned Only
Hoosier Mfg. Co. 72

Brocade
See **Drapery and Upholstery Fabrics, Brocade**

Brocatelle
See **Drapery and Upholstery Fabrics, Brocatelle**

Buffets
——**Breakfast Room**
See **Breakfast Room Buffets**
——**Dining Room**
See **Dining Room Buffets**
——**Dinette**
See **Dinette Buffets**
Buildings, Exhibition
See **Exhibition Spaces**
Butterfly Tables
See Also **Drop Leaf Tables**
Illustrated or Described
Athens Table & Mfg. Co. 190
Furniture Shops 160–161
Hastings Table Company 150–151
Whitney Co., Inc., W. F. 240
Colonial (Early American) 160–161
Spanish 150–151
Mentioned Only
Baker Furniture Factories, Inc. 243
Conant-Ball Company 191
Crocker Chair Company 137
Davis-Birely Table Company 193
Hannahs Mfg. Co. 197
Imperial Furniture Co. 198–205
St. Johns Table Company 236
Steul & Sons, Henry C. 348
Yeager Furniture Company 431 (Z1)

C

Cabinet
——**Bases, Kitchen**
See **Kitchen Cabinet Bases**
——**Desks**
Illustrated or Described
Colonial Desk Company 138–141
Mechanics Furniture Co. 155
Skandia Furniture Company 172–185
Mentioned Only
Century Furniture Company 92
Chittenden & Eastman Company 377
Indianapolis Chair & Furn. Co. 152
Lassahn Furniture Company 154
Rockford Standard Furniture Co. 327–331

——**Mirrors, Bathroom**
See **Bathroom Cabinet Mirrors**
Cabinets
——**And Chests, Linen**
See **Linen Cabinets and Chests**
——**And China Closets, Breakfast Room**
See **Breakfast Room China Cabinets and Closets**
——**And China Closets, Dining Room**
See **Dining Room China Cabinets and Closets**
——**And China Cupboards, Dinette**
See **Dinette China Cabinets and Cupboards**
——**And Corner Closets**
See **Corner Cabinets and Closets**
——**And Radio Tables**
See **Radio Cabinets and Tables**
——**And Serving Tables Combined, Breakfast Room**
See **Breakfast Room Serving Tables and Cabinets Combined**
——**And Sewing Stands**
See **Sewing Cabinets and Stands**
——**And Sewing Stands, Reed and Fibre**
See **Reed and Fibre Sewing Cabinets and Stands**
——**And Smokers' Stands**
See **Smokers' Cabinets and Stands**
——**And Telephone Stands, Reed and Fibre**
See **Reed and Fibre Telephone Cabinets and Stands**
——**Console**
See **Console Cabinets**

Cabinets
——**Corner, Dining Room**
See **Dining Room Corner Cabinets**
——**Curio**
See **Curio Cabinets**
——**Dutch, Breakfast Room**
See **Breakfast Room Dutch Cabinets**
——**Elizabethan**
Mentioned Only
Rockford Peerless Furniture Company 168–171

——**English**
Mentioned Only
Rockford Peerless Furniture Company 168–171

——**Filing, Bank and Office**
See **Bank and Office Filing Cabinets**
——**For Bottles, Decanters, Glasses, Etc.**
See **Cellarets**
——**Gothic**
Mentioned Only
Rockford Peerless Furniture Company 168–171

——**Hutch**
See **Hutch Cabinets**

——**Italian**
Illustrated or Described
Hastings Table Company 150–151

——**Jacobean**
Mentioned Only
Rockford Peerless Furniture Company 168–171

——**Kitchen**
See **Kitchen Cabinets**
——**Living Room**
See **Living Room Cabinets**

——**Louis XIV**
Mentioned Only
Rockford Peerless Furniture Company 168–171

——**Medicine, Bathroom**
See **Bathroom Medicine Cabinets**
——**Music**
See **Music Cabinets**
——**Pier Type**
See **Pier Cabinets**
——**Secretary**
See **Secretary Cabinets**
——**Silver, Dining Room**
See **Dining Room Silver Cabinets**

——**Spanish**
Illustrated or Described
Rockford Peerless Furn. Co. 168–171

——**Stands, and Sets, Telephone**
See **Telephone Cabinets, Stands and Sets**

——**Wall**
See **Wall Cabinets**

Cafe, Lunchroom and Restaurant
——**Chairs**
See **Restaurant Chairs**
——**Tables**
See **Restaurant Tables**

Cages and Fernery Combination Cages for Birds
See **Reed and Fibre Bird Cages and Reed and Fibre Bird Cages,** Fernery Combination

Candle Sticks and Stands
Mentioned Only
Scheibe, R. R. 414 (Z1)
Stickley, L. & J. G. and Stickley Mfg. Co. 352–353

Cane
——**Back Chairs and Rockers**
Illustrated or Described
Century Furniture Company 92
Spencer-Duffy Company, Inc. 125–127
Statesville Chair Company 417 (Z1)
Mentioned Only
Chittenden & Eastman Company 377
Conant-Ball Company 191
Empire Chair Company 194–196
Fenske Bros. 99
Fullerton Furniture Factories 103
Globe-Parlor Furniture Co. 106–107
Indianapolis Chair & Furn. Co. 152
Jamestown Lounge Company 105
Delker Bros. Mfg. Co. 97

——**Back and Seat Chairs and Rockers**
Mentioned Only
Chittenden & Eastman Company 377
Empire Chair Company 194–196
Fullerton Furniture Factories 103
Indianapolis Chair & Furn. Co. 152
Mallen & Company, H. Z. 121
Tell City Chair Company 403 (Z3)

——**Back Rockers with Loose Cushions**
Mentioned Only
Chittenden & Eastman Company 377
Delker Bros. Mfg. Co. 97
Empire Chair Company 194–196
Fenske Bros. 99
Indianapolis Chair & Furn. Co. 152

——**Davenports**
Mentioned Only
Delker Bros. Mfg. Co. 97
Globe Parlor Furn. Co. 106–107

——**Davenport Beds**
Mentioned Only
Fullerton Furniture Factories 103
Memphis Furniture Mfg. Co. 303
Globe Parlor Furn. Co. 106–107

——**Living Room Suites**
Mentioned Only
Delker Bros. Mfg. Co. 97
Fenske Bros. 99
Globe Parlor Furn. Co. 106–107
Gunlocke Chair Co., W. H. 401 (Z1)

Cane
——Seat Benches
Illustrated or Described
Estey Manufacturing Company 265
Mentioned Only
Century Furniture Company 92
Chittenden & Eastman Company 377
Empire Chair Company 194–196
Indianapolis Chair & Furn. Co. 152
Sikes Chair Company 238
Statesville Chair Company 417 (Z1)
Widdicomb Company, John 366

——Seat Chairs and Rockers
Illustrated or Described
Estey Manufacturing Company 265
Colonial Furniture Company 93–95
Mentioned Only
Century Furniture Company 92
Conant-Ball Company 191
Crocker Chair Company 137
Huntley Furniture Co., B. F. 274
Indianapolis Chair & Furn. Co. 152
Norquist Company, A. C. 305
Statesville Chair Company 417 (Z1)
Tell City Chair Company 403 (Z3)
Tillotson Furniture Corporation 358
Union Furniture Company 421 (Z1)
Widdicomb Company, John 366
Williamsport Furniture Company 429 (Z1)

——Seat Rockers with Loose Cushions
Mentioned Only
Chittenden & Eastman Company 377
Indianapolis Chair & Furn. Co. 152

——Wing Chairs
Mentioned Only
Chittenden & Eastman Company 377
Fullerton Furniture Factories 103
Gunlocke Chair Co., W. H. 401 (Z1)
Indianapolis Chair & Furn. Co. 152

Canterbury Magazine Baskets and Carriers
See **Magazine Baskets and Carriers,** CANTERBURY

Card Tables
Illustrated or Described
Keystone Table Company 411 (Z1)
Hastings Table Company 150–151
COLONIAL 150–151
Mentioned Only
Century Furniture Company 92
Chittenden & Eastman Company 377
Schoeck Mfg. Company 415 (Z1)

Carriers and Baskets, Magazine
See **Magazine Baskets and Carriers**

Carvings, Decorative, and Tassel Pulls for Window Shades
See **Window Shades,** TASSEL PULLS AND DECORATIVE CARVINGS FOR

Cases and Tables, Bedroom, Powder and Make-Up
See **Bedroom Make-Up and Powder Cases and Tables**

Casters, Glides, Slides and Felt Feet
Illustrated or Described
Domes of Silence, Inc. 134

Carpets and Rugs
Illustrated or Described
Armstrong Cork Company 81
Beattie Manufacturing Co. 82
Highstown Rug Company 88
Home Crest Floor Coverings 86
Kent-Costikyan 89
ANTIQUE FEREGHAN 89
AXMINSTER, SEAMLESS 88
BORDERED PLAIN CARPETS 89
BROADLOOM 82
FELT BASE RUGS 81
KENTSHAH PLAIN CARPET 89
LINOLEUM 81
SPECIAL TO ORDER 89
Mentioned Only
Chittenden & Eastman Company 377
AUBUSSON 89
AXMINSTER 86; 377
AXMINSTER OVAL 88
AXMINSTER SEAMLESS 86
CHENILLE RUGS 89
CHENILLE SEAMLESS CARPETS 89
CHINESE RUGS 89
COLONIAL RAG RUGS 89
EMBLEM RUGS 89
EUROPEAN HAND TUFT RUGS 89
HOOKED RUGS 89
IMPORTED RUGS 89
LINOLEUM 86
ORIENTAL 86
SAVONNERIE RUGS 89
SPANISH RUGS 89
WILTON SEAMLESS CARPETS 86; 89

——Linoleum, Cement and Paste
Mentioned Only
Armstrong Cork Company 81

Casement Cloth
See **Drapery and Upholstery Fabrics, Casements, Silk, Cotton, Rayon and Mohair**

Cedar Chests
Illustrated or Described
Karpen & Bros., S. 112–119
Lane Company, Inc. 153
Mountville Wood Products Co., Inc. 412 (Z1)
Rockford Cedar Furniture Co. 165
Rockford Eagle Furniture Co. 166–167
Seaburg Mfg. Co. 416 (Z1)
West Branch Novelty Company 424–428 (Z1)
BOX COUCH TYPE 112–119
BRASS TRIMMED 424–428 (Z1)
COLONIAL LOWBOY 424–428 (Z1)
CONSOLE 165; 166–167; 424–428 (Z1)
ITALIAN RENAISSANCE 165; 166–167
JACOBEAN 165; 166–167
LOUIS XVI 424–428 (Z1)
QUEEN ANNE 165; 166–167; 424–428 (Z1)
SOLID 166–167

Cedar Chests *(continued)*
SPANISH 165; 166–167; 424–428 (Z1)
STORAGE (Large Size) 424–428 (Z1)
WINDOW SEAT TYPE 165; 166–167; 424–428 (Z1)
Mentioned Only
Chittenden & Eastman Company 377
CHIPPENDALE 412 (Z1)
QUEEN ANNE 412 (Z1)
SPANISH 377; 412 (Z1)

Cedar Lined
——Console Cabinets
See **Console Cabinets,** CEDAR LINED

——Mahogany and Walnut Chests
Illustrated or Described
Lane Company, Inc. 153
Mountville Wood Products Co., Inc. 412 (Z1)
Rockford Cedar Furniture Co. 165
Rockford Eagle Furniture Co. 166–167
Seaburg Manufacturing Co. 416 (Z1)
West Branch Novelty Company 424–428 (Z1)

Cellarets
Mentioned Only
Elite Furniture Company 146
Furniture Shops 160–161
Imperial Furniture Company 198–205

Celluloid Tacks
See **Tacks, Celluloid**

Cement and Paste for Linoleum
See **Carpets and Rugs, Linoleum, Cement and Paste**

Center Tables
Mentioned Only
Aulsbrook & Jones Furniture Co. 242
Chittenden & Eastman Company 377
Conant-Ball Company 191
Davis-Birely Table Company 193
Elite Furniture Company 146
Hannahs Manufacturing Co. 197
Hastings Table Company 150–151
Kiel Furniture Company 208–215
Luger Furniture Co. 399 (Z3)
Memphis Furn. Mfg. Co. 303
St. Johns Table Company 236
Seaburg Mfg. Co. 416 (Z1)

Chair
——And Rocker Sets
Illustrated or Described
Empire Chair Company 194–196
——Seats Upholstered
Mentioned Only
Chittenden & Eastman Company 377
Indianapolis Chair & Furn. Co. 152

——Sets for Bedrooms
See **Bedroom Chair Sets**

Chairs
Illustrated or Described
Colonial Furniture Company 93–95
Hastings Table Company 150–151
Empire Chair Company 194–196
Karpen & Bros., S. 112–119
Rockford Peerless Furniture Company 168–171
Sikes Chair Company 238
Tauber Parlor Furniture Co. 402 (Z3)
COLONIAL 93–95
ITALIAN 150–151
NORMANDY 112–119
LOUIS XV 112–119; 402 (Z3)
LOUIS XVI 112–119; 168–171
QUEEN ANNE 112–119
SPANISH RENAISSANCE 194–196
SPANISH 168–171; 238
Mentioned Only
Conants', Sons, Inc., F. H. 192
Crocker Chair Company 137
Curtiss & Son, W. T. 399 (Z1)
Empire Chair Company 194–196
Globe Parlor Furniture Co. 106
Hastings Table Company 150–151
Indianapolis Chair & Furn. Co. 152
Jamestown Chair Company 206
Klamer Furniture Corp. 288–289
Michigan Chair Company 162–163
Milne Chair Company 207
Monitor Furniture Co. 288–289
Peterson Art Furn. Co. 164
Shreve Chair Company 237
Spencer-Duffy Co., Inc. 125–127
Statesville Chair Co. 417 (Z1)
Stickley, L. & J. G. & Stickley Mfg. Co. 352–353
Streit Mfg. Co., C. F. 130–131
Tell City Chair Company 403 (Z3)
Wellsville Uph. Co. 423 (Z1)
Yeager Furniture Co. 431 (Z1)
ADAM 168–171
CHIPPENDALE 207
COLONIAL (Early American) 162–163; 207
EARLY ENGLISH 192
EMPIRE 192
FIDDLE BACK 399 (Z1)
GOTHIC 168–171
HEPPELWHITE 192; 207
ITALIAN RENAISSANCE 192; 207
LOUIS XVI 207
QUEEN ANNE 192; 207
ROMAN 150–151; 125–127
SPANISH RENAISSANCE 207
SPECIAL TO ORDER 137; 152; 417 (Z1)
SPOT 106

——Adjustable
Illustrated or Described
Streit Mfg. Co., C. F. 130–131
Wellsville Upholstering Co. 423 (Z1)
FLORENTINE 130–131
HEPPELWHITE 130–131
QUEEN ANNE 130–131
TUDOR 130–131
Mentioned Only
Chittenden & Eastman Company 377

——And Rockers, Cane Back
See **Cane Back Chairs and Rockers**
——And Rockers, Cane Back and Seat
See **Cane Back and Seat Chairs and Rockers**

Chairs
——And Rockers, Cane Seat
See **Cane Seat Chairs and Rockers**
——And Rockers, Fibre Seat
See **Fibre Seat Chairs and Rockers**
——And Rockers, Porch, Reed and Fibre
See **Reed and Fibre Porch Chairs and Rockers**
——And Rockers, Sewing
See **Sewing Chairs and Rockers**
——And Table Sets, Breakfast Room
See **Breakfast Room Sets (Tables and Chairs)**
——Arm, Reed and Fibre
See **Reed and Fibre Arm Chairs**
——Arm, Upholstered
See **Arm Chairs, Upholstered**
——Arm, Wood
See **Arm Chairs, Wood**
——Assembly Hall
See **Assembly Hall Chairs**
——Bank and Office
See **Bank and Office Chairs**
——Bathroom
See **Bathroom Chairs**
——Bedroom
See **Bedroom Chairs**
——Bentwood
See **Bentwood Chairs**
——Bow Back
See **Bow Back Chairs**
——Breakfast Room
See **Breakfast Room Chairs**
——Cafe
See **Restaurant Chairs**
——Children's
See **Children's Chairs**
——Club
See **Club Chairs for the Home**
——Coxwell
See **Coxwell Chairs**
——Desk, Home
See **Desk Chairs, Home**
——Desk, Home, Reed and Fibre
See **Reed and Fibre Desk Chairs**
——Dinette
See **Dinette Chairs**
——Dining Room
See **Dining Room Chairs**
——Easy Lounging Chairs
See **Easy Lounging Chairs**
——Fireside
See **Fireside Chairs**
——Folding
See **Folding Chairs**
——Hall, Home
See **Hall Chairs, Home**
——High, Children's
See **Children's High Chairs**
——High Back
See **High Back Chairs**
——High Back, Reed and Fibre
See **Reed and Fibre High Back Chairs**
——Hotel and Club
See **Hotel and Club Chairs**
——Howlett
See **Howlett Chairs**
——John Bunny
See **John Bunny Chairs**
——Kitchen
See **Kitchen Chairs**
——Knock-Down
See **Knock-Down Chairs**
——Ladderback
See **Ladder Back Chairs**
——Lawn and Porch
See **Lawn and Porch Chairs**
——Leather, Upholstered
See **Leather Upholstered Chairs**
——Library
See **Library Chairs**
——Low Back
See **Low Back Chairs**
——Lunchroom
See **Restaurant Chairs**
——Mission
See **Mission Chairs**
——Nests of
See **Nests of Chairs**
——Pull-Up
See **Pull-Up Chairs**
——Reading
See **Reading Chairs**
——Reed and Fibre
See **Reed and Fibre Chairs**
——Restaurant
See **Restaurant Chairs**
——Rush Seat
See **Rush Seat Chairs**
——Side
See **Side Chairs**
——Sleepy Hollow
See **Sleepy Hollow Chairs**
——Slip Seat
See **Slip Seat Chairs**
——Slip Seat, Leather
See **Leather Slip Seat Chairs**
——Spinet
See **Spinet Chairs**
——Splint
See **Splint Chairs**
——Tablet Arm
See **Tablet Arm Chairs**
——Theatre Box
See **Theatre Box Chairs**
——Theatre Box, Reed and Fibre
See **Reed and Fibre Theatre Box Chairs**
——Throne
See **Throne Chairs**
——Tub
See **Tub Chairs**
——Swivel
See **Bank and Office Chairs, Swivel**
——Typewriter Desk
See **Bank and Office Chairs, Typewriter Desk**
——Windsor
See **Windsor Chairs**
——Wing
See **Wing Chairs**
——Wing, Cane
See **Cane Wing Chairs**
——With Upholstered Seats
Mentioned Only
Fenske Bros. 99

Chairs
——**Wood Seat**
   Mentioned Only
   Conant-Ball Company...........................191
   Hastings Table Company..................150–151
   Shreve Chair Company, Inc....................237
   Tell City Chair Company..................403 (Z3)

Chaise Lounges
  See Also **Lawn and Porch Chaise Lounges and
    Reed and Fibre Chaise Lounges**
   Illustrated or Described
   Field & Company, Marshall.............100–101
   Horn & Company, J. P.....................410 (Z1)
   Karpen & Bros., S.......................112–119
   Levin Bros., Inc..............................111
   Louis XVI..............................112–119
   MODERN................................112–119
   Mentioned Only
   American Parlor Furniture Co.................91
   Century Furniture Company....................92
   Irwin Company, Robert W....................275
   Jamestown Lounge Company..................105
   Mallen & Company, H. Z....................121
   Memphis Furniture Mfg. Co..................303
   Michigan Chair Company................162–163
   Spencer-Duffy Company, Inc.............125–127
   Sultan & Company, William..................132
   Tauber Parlor Furniture Co.............402 (Z3)
   Wiener Company, E.....................406 (Z3)

Charles II Day Beds
  See **Day Beds**, CHARLES II

Chenille
——**Rugs**
  See **Carpets and Rugs**, CHENILLE RUGS
——**Seamless Carpet**
  See **Carpets and Rugs**, CHENILLE SEAMLESS CARPET

Chest
——**Toilets, Bedroom**
  See **Bedroom Chest Toilets**
——**Wardrobes, Bedroom**
  See **Bedroom Wardrobes**, CHEST TYPE

Chests
  See Also **Linen Cabinets and Chests; Cedar Chests;
    Console Chests; and Cedar Lined Mahogany
    and Walnut Chests**
   Illustrated or Described
   Charlotte Furniture Company.................258
   Colonial Desk Company..................138–141
   LUXOR-MAHOGANY....................138–141
   DESK COMBINATION........................258
   Mentioned Only
   Baker Furniture Factories, Inc..............243
   Century Furniture Company....................92
   Furniture Shops.......................160–161
   Stickley, L. & J. G. and Stickley Mfg. Co.....352–353

Chests of Drawers
  See Also **Bedroom Chests of Drawers**
   Illustrated or Described
   Hemsing Manufacturing Company..........405 (Z1)
   Rockford Peerless Furn. Co...............168–171
   Skandia Furniture Company..............172–185
   CHIPPENDALE.........................405 (Z1)
   Mentioned Only
   Century Furniture Company....................92
   Chittenden & Eastman Company...............377
   Furniture Shops.......................160–161
   Imperial Furniture Company............198–205
   Indianapolis Chair & Furn. Co..............152
   Morganton Furniture Company...............304
   Rockford Peerless Furniture Company....168–171
   Rockford Standard Furn. Co...........327–331
   Steul & Sons, Henry C......................348

Cheval Mirrors
  See **Mirrors, Cheval**

Chiffonier Wardrobes
  See **Bedroom Wardrobes**, CHIFFONIER TYPE

Chiffoniers
  See **Bedroom Chiffoniers**

Chifforettes
  See **Bedroom Chifforettes**

Chifforobes
  See **Bedroom Chifforobes**

Children's
——**Beds**
  See Also **Metal Cribs**
   Mentioned Only
   Chittenden & Eastman Company...............377
——**Chairs**
   Mentioned Only
   Century Furniture Company....................92
   Chittenden & Eastman Company...............377
   Conant-Ball Company........................191
   Crocker Chair Company......................137
   Memphis Furniture Mfg. Co..................303
   Phoenix Chair Company................222–235
   Shreve Chair Company, Inc....................237
   Standard Chair Company.....................239
   Tell City Chair Company..................403 (Z3)
   Whitney Co., Inc., W. F.....................240
   WINDSOR.............................222–235
——**Desks**
   Mentioned Only
   Gunn Furniture Company..................396 (Z3)
——**High Chairs**
   Illustrated or Described
   Phoenix Chair Company..................222–235
   Mentioned Only
   Crocker Chair Company......................137
   Memphis Furniture Mfg. Co..................303
   Standard Chair Company.....................239
   Tell City Chair Company..................403 (Z3)
——**Rockers**
   Illustrated or Described
   Phoenix Chair Company..................222–235
   WINDSOR.............................222–235
   Mentioned Only
   Thomasville Chair Company..................349

Chime Clocks
  See **Clocks, Chime**

China Cabinets
——**And Closets, Breakfast Room**
  See **Breakfast Room China Cabinets and Closets**
——**And Closets, Dining Room**
  See **Dining Room China Cabinets and Closets**
——**And Cupboards, Dinette**
  See **Dinette China Cabinets and Cupboards**

Chinese
——**And Japanese Furniture**
  See **Japanese and Chinese Furniture**
——**Rugs**
  See **Carpets and Rugs**, CHINESE RUGS

Chippendale
——**Bookcases, Glassed In**
  See **Bookcases, Glassed In**, CHIPPENDALE
——**Buffets, Dining Room**
  See **Dining Room Buffets**, CHIPPENDALE
——**Cedar Chests**
  See **Cedar Chests**, CHIPPENDALE
——**Chairs**
  See **Chairs**, CHIPPENDALE
——**Chairs, Arm, Upholstered**
  See **Arm Chairs, Upholstered**, CHIPPENDALE
——**Chairs, Dining Room**
  See **Dining Room Chairs**, CHIPPENDALE
——**Chests of Drawers**
  See **Chests of Drawers**, CHIPPENDALE
——**China Cabinets and Closets, Dining Room**
  See **Dining Room China Cabinets and Closets,**
    CHIPPENDALE
——**Day Beds**
  See **Day Beds**, CHIPPENDALE
——**Desks, Home**
  See **Desks, Home**, CHIPPENDALE
——**High Boys**
  See **Highboys**, CHIPPENDALE
——**Mirrors**
  See **Mirrors**, CHIPPENDALE
——**Servers and Serving Tables, Dining Room**
  See **Dining Room Servers and Serving Tables,**
    CHIPPENDALE
——**Suites, Complete, Bedroom**
  See **Bedroom Suites, Complete (Including Bench,
    Chair, Rocker and Night Table)**, CHIPPENDALE
——**Suites, Complete, Dining Room**
  See **Dining Room Suites, Complete**, CHIPPENDALE
——**Tables, Dining Room**
  See **Dining Room Tables**, CHIPPENDALE

Church Furniture
   Mentioned Only
   Colonial Furniture Company...............93–95
   Conant-Ball Company........................191
   Curtiss & Son, Wm. P....................399 (Z1)

Clocks
   Illustrated or Described
   Colonial Manufacturing Company.........142–143
   Furst Bros. & Company........................78
   Hanson Clock Company, Inc..............148–149
   Miller Clock Company, Herman..............144
——**Banjo**
   Illustrated or Described
   Furst Bros. & Company........................78
   Miller Clock Company, Herman..............144
——**Chime**
   Illustrated or Described
   Colonial Manufacturing Company.........142–143
   Hanson Clock Company, Inc..............148–149
   Miller Clock Company, Herman..............144
   Mentioned Only
   Furst Bros. & Company.......................78
——**Electric**
   Illustrated or Described
   Miller Clock Company, Herman..............144
——**Hall**
   Illustrated or Described
   Colonial Manufacturing Company.........142–143
   Hanson Clock Company, Inc..............148–149
——**Kitchen**
   Mentioned Only
   Furst Bros. & Company.......................78
——**Mantel**
   Illustrated or Described
   Miller Clock Company, Herman..............144
   Mentioned Only
   Furst Bros. & Company.......................78

Closet Racks, Clothes
  See **Racks, Clothes Closet**

Closets
——**And China Cabinets, Breakfast Room**
  See **Breakfast Room China Cabinets and Closets**
——**And China Cabinets, Dining Room**
  See **Dining Room China Cabinets and Closets**
——**And Corner Cabinets**
  See **Corner Cabinets and Closets**
——**Kitchen**
  See **Kitchen Closets**

Clothes
——**Closet Racks**
  See **Racks, Clothes Closet**
——**Drying Racks**
  See **Racks, Clothes Drying**

Club
——**And Hotel Chairs**
  See **Hotel and Club Chairs**
——**And Hotel Furniture**
  See **Hotel and Club Furniture**
——**And Hotel Furniture, Reed and Fibre**
  See **Reed and Fibre Hotel and Club Furniture**
——**And Hotel Tables**
  See **Hotel and Club Tables**
——**Chairs**
   Illustrated or Described
   Brandts Furniture Company.............394 (Z3)
   Conants' Sons, Inc., F. H....................192
   Globe Parlor Furniture Company........106–107
   Karpen & Bros., S.......................112–119
   Poston Mfg. Co., B. C...................401 (Z3)
   ENGLISH........................112–119; 192

Coffee Tables
   Illustrated or Described
   Davis-Birely Table Company.................193
   Furniture Shops........................160–161
   Imperial Furniture Company.............198–205
   Rockford Peerless Furniture Company....168–171
   Whitney Co., Inc., W. F.....................240
   DUNCAN PHYFE......................160–161
   ITALIAN RENAISSANCE.................160–161
   LOUIS XIV..........................168–171
   QUEEN ANNE........................160–161
   Mentioned Only
   Aulsbrook & Jones Furniture Co.............242
   Century Furniture Company....................92
   Chittenden & Eastman Company...............377
   Colonial Desk Company................138–141
   Conant-Ball Company........................191
   Crocker Chair Company......................137
   Elite Furniture Company....................146
   Hastings Table Company................150–151
   Indianapolis Chair & Furn. Co..............152
   Kiel Furniture Company................208–215
   Klamer Furniture Corp.................288–289
   Mersman Bros. Corp...................216–221
   Michigan Chair Company................162–163
   Monitor Furniture Company............288–289
   St. Johns Table Company....................236
   MARBLE TOP.....................208–215; 377

Coil and Box Bed Springs
  See **Bed Springs, Coil and Box**

Colonial (Early American)
——**Beds**
  See **Beds**, COLONIAL
——**Benches, Bedroom**
  See **Bedroom Benches**, COLONIAL
——**Buffets, Dining Room**
  See **Dining Room Buffets**, COLONIAL
——**Chairs**
  See **Chairs**, COLONIAL
——**Chairs, Arm, Upholstered**
  See **Arm Chairs, Upholstered**, COLONIAL
——**Chairs, Bedroom**
  See **Bedroom Chairs**, COLONIAL
——**Chairs, Dining Room**
  See **Dining Room Chairs**, COLONIAL
——**Chairs, Easy Lounging**
  See **Easy Lounging Chairs**, COLONIAL
——**Chairs, Side**
  See **Side Chairs**, COLONIAL
——**Chests of Drawers, Bedroom**
  See **Bedroom Chests of Drawers**, COLONIAL
——**Chifforettes, Bedroom**
  See **Bedroom Chifforettes**, COLONIAL
——**China Cabinets and Closets, Dining Room**
  See **Dining Room China Cabinets and Closets,**
    COLONIAL
——**Cupboards, Dining Room**
  See **Dining Room Cupboards**, COLONIAL
——**Davenports and Sofas**
  See **Davenports and Sofas**, COLONIAL
——**Day Beds**
  See **Day Beds**, COLONIAL
——**Dressers, Bedroom**
  See **Bedroom Dressers**, COLONIAL
——**Dressing Tables, Bedroom**
  See **Bedroom Dressing Tables**, COLONIAL
——**Highboys**
  See **Highboys**, COLONIAL
——**Lowboy Cedar Chests**
  See **Cedar Chests**, COLONIAL LOWBOY
——**Lowboys**
  See **Lowboys**, COLONIAL
——**Make-Up and Powder Cases and Tables, Bedroom**
  See **Bedroom Make-Up and Powder Cases and
    Tables**, COLONIAL
——**Mirrors, Bedroom**
  See **Bedroom Mirrors**, COLONIAL
——**Mirrors, Convex**
  See **Mirrors, Convex** COLONIAL
——**Night Tables, Bedroom**
  See **Bedroom Night Tables**, COLONIAL
——**Rag Rugs**
  See **Carpets and Rugs**, COLONIAL RAG RUGS
——**Rockers**
  See **Rockers**, COLONIAL
——**Servers and Serving Tables, Dining Room**
  See **Dining Room Servers and Serving Tables,**
    COLONIAL
——**Sewing Cabinets and Stands**
  See **Sewing Cabinets and Stands**, COLONIAL
——**Suites, Bedroom, Complete**
  See **Bedroom Suites, Complete (Including Bench,
    Chair, Rocker and Night Table)**, COLONIAL
——**Suites, Dining Room, Complete**
  See **Dining Room Suites, Complete**, COLONIAL
——**Suites, Living Room**
  See **Living Room Suites**, COLONIAL
——**Tables**
  See **Tables**, COLONIAL
——**Tables, Butterfly**
  See **Butterfly Tables**, COLONIAL
——**Tables, Card**
  See **Card Tables**, COLONIAL
——**Tables, Console**
  See **Console Tables**, COLONIAL
——**Tables, Dining Room**
  See **Dining Room Tables**, COLONIAL
——**Tables, Gateleg**
  See **Gateleg Tables**, COLONIAL

Color Prints
  See **Pictures and Picture Frames**, COLOR PRINTS

Combination
——**Bird Cages and Ferneries, Reed and Fibre**
  See **Reed and Fibre Bird Cages**, FERNERY COMBI-
    NATION
——**Book Racks and Davenport Tables**
  See **Davenport Tables**, BOOK RACK COMBINATION
——**Book Troughs and End Tables**
  See **Book Troughs and End Tables, Combined**
——**Dining Room and Living Room Tables**
  See **Tables, Combination Living Room and Dining
    Room**
——**Dressers and Wardrobes**
  See **Bedroom Wardrobes**, DRESSER COMBINATION
    TYPE
——**Home Desks and Bookcases**
  See **Desks, Home, Book Case Combination**

Commodes
Illustrated or Described
Irwin Company, Robert W.................... 275
Colonial Desk Company....................138–141
WILLIAM AND MARY........................138–141
Mentioned Only
Century Furniture Company.................... 92

Complete Suites
——Bedroom
See **Bedroom Suites, Complete (Including Bench, Chair, Rocker and Night Table)**
——Dining Room
See **Dining Room Suites, Complete**

Composition Top
——Desks
See **Bank and Office Desks,** COMPOSITION TOP
——Tables
See **Tables,** COMPOSITION TOP
——Tables, Cafe, Lunchroom, and Restaurant
See **Restaurant Tables,** COMPOSITION TOP

Console
——Cabinets
Illustrated or Described
Furniture Shops............................160–161
Lane Company, Inc............................ 153
CEDAR LINED.................................. 153
SHERATON...................................160–161
Mentioned Only
Century Furniture Company.................... 92
Easton Furniture Mfg. Co.................400 (Z1)
Hastings Table Company...................150–151
Peterson Art Furniture Co.................... 164
Yeager Furniture Company..................431 (Z1)
——Cedar Chests
See **Cedar Chests,** CONSOLE
——Chests
Illustrated or Described
Mountville Wood Products Co., Inc..........412 (Z1)
Mentioned Only
Chittenden & Eastman Company................ 377
Seaburg Mfg. Co..........................416 (Z1)
Union Furniture Company..................421 (Z1)
——Mirrors
Illustrated or Described
Chicago Mirror & Art Glass Co..............395 (Z3)
Grand Rapids Upholstering Co...............252–253
Mentioned Only
Century Furniture Company.................... 92
Chittenden & Eastman Company................ 377
Conant-Ball Company......................... 191
Crocker Chair Company....................... 137
Elite Furniture Company..................... 146
Furst Bros. & Company........................ 78
Hekman Furniture Company.................398 (Z3)
Peterson Art Furn. Co........................ 164
Williamsport Furn. Co....................429 (Z1)
Yeager Furniture Co......................431 (Z1)
——Tables
Illustrated or Described
Baker Furniture Factories, Inc................ 243
Elite Furniture Company....................... 146
Furniture Shops............................160–161
Grand Rapids Upholstering Co...............252–253
Hastings Table Company....................150–151
Hekman Furniture Co.......................398 (Z3)
Imperial Furniture Co......................198–205
Keystone Table Company....................411 (Z1)
Kiel Furniture Company.....................208–215
Mersman Bros. Corp.........................216–221
Michigan Chair Company.....................162–163
Rockford Peerless Furn. Co.................168–171
COLONIAL...................................150–151
DUNCAN PHYFE...............................198–205
FOLDING.........................146; 198–205; 243
QUEEN ANNE.................................160–161
Mentioned Only
Athens Table & Mfg. Co....................... 190
Aulsbrook & Jones Furn. Co................... 242
Century Furniture Company.................... 92
Colonial Desk Company....................138–141
Conant-Ball Company.......................... 191
Crocker Chair Company........................ 137
Florence Table & Mfg. Co..................... 271
Hannahs Mfg. Co.............................. 197
Indianapolis Chair & Furn. Co................ 152
Irwin Company, Robert W...................... 275
Klamer Furniture Corp....................288–289
Lassahn Furniture Co......................... 154
Luger Furniture Company..................399 (Z3)
Memphis Furn. Mfg. Co........................ 303
Monitor Furniture Company................288–289
St. Johns Table Company...................... 236
Seaburg Mfg. Co..........................416 (Z1)
Sultan & Company, William.................... 132
Union Furniture Co.......................421 (Z1)
Yeager Furniture Co......................431 (Z1)
WROUGHT IRON.......................193; 208–215
——Tables with Mirrors
Illustrated or Described
Charlotte Furniture Co........................ 258
Grand Rapids Upholstering Co...............252–253
Imperial Furniture Co......................198–205
Mersman Bros. Corp.........................216–221
Michigan Chair Company.....................162–163
Rockford Peerless Furn. Co.................168–171
Mentioned Only
Chittenden & Eastman Company................ 377
Crocker Chair Company........................ 137
Davis-Birely Table Co........................ 193
Furniture Shops..........................160–161
Luger Furniture Company..................399 (Z3)
Mallen & Company, H. Z....................... 121
Memphis Furn. Mfg. Co........................ 303
Michigan Chair Company....................162–163
Union Furniture Co.......................421 (Z1)
Yeager Furniture Co......................431 (Z1)

Constructions, Davenport Bed
See **Davenport Bed** CONSTRUCTIONS

Convex Mirrors, Colonial
See **Mirrors, Convex,** COLONIAL

Cooking Utensils, Cast Iron
See **Kettles, Boilers, and Cooking Utensils, Cast Iron**

Corner
——Cabinets and Closets
Illustrated or Described
Colonial Desk Company......................138–141
Rockford Peerless Furn. Co.................168–171
Skandia Furniture Company..................172–185
Mentioned Only
Century Furniture Company.................... 92
Mechanics Furn. Co........................... 155
——Cabinets, Dining Room
See **Dining Room Corner Cabinets**
——Wall Shelves
Mentioned Only
Conant-Ball Company......................... 191

Costumers
——Metal
See **Metal Costumers**
——Wood
Illustrated or Described
Seaburg Mfg. Co...........................416 (Z1)
Stow-Davis Furn. Co..........................76–77
Mentioned Only
Continental Furniture Co..................260–261
Crocker Chair Company........................ 137
Imperial Furniture Co.....................198–205
Luger Furniture Co.......................399 (Z3)
Peterson Art Furn. Co........................ 164
Tillotson Furn. Corp......................... 358
White Furniture Co........................... 365

Cots, Folding, Metal
See **Metal Folding Cots**

Couch Hammocks
Illustrated or Described
Anchor Spring & Bedding Co................393 (Z2)
Barcalo Mfg. Co...........................393 (Z1)
Hard Mfg. Co..............................404 (Z1)
Rome Company, Inc............................70–71
Mentioned Only
Chittenden & Eastman Company................ 377

Couches (*See Also* **Metal Couches**)
Mentioned Only
Century Furniture Company.................... 92
Decker, Inc., Isaac C......................... 96
Dunbar Furn. Mfg. Co.......................... 98
Fenske Bros................................... 99
Field & Company, Marshall................100–101
Hebenstreit's, Inc.......................397 (Z3)
Poston Mfg. Co., B. C....................401 (Z3)
Sikes Chair Company.......................... 238
Toledo Parlor Furniture Co...............404 (Z3)
Wellsville Uph. Co.......................423 (Z1)

Coxwell Chairs
Illustrated or Described
Buffalo Lounge Company....................394 (Z1)
Conants' Sons, Inc., F. H..................... 192
Decker, Inc., Isaac C.......................... 96
Empire Chair Company.......................194–196
Fenske Bros.................................... 99
Field & Company, Marshall..................100–101
Franklin Furn. Co............................. 102
Fullerton Furniture Factories................. 103
Harden Company, Frank S....................108–109
Hebenstreit's, Inc........................397 (Z3)
Karpen & Bros., S..........................112–119
Levin Bros., Inc.............................. 111
Louisville Chair & Furn. Co...............396 (Z2)
Northfield Company.........................122–123
Phoenix Chair Company......................222–235
Poston Mfg. Co., B. C.....................401 (Z3)
Streit Mfg. Co., C. F......................130–131
Tauber Parlor Furn. Co....................402 (Z3)
Wellsville Upholstering Co................423 (Z1)
Mentioned Only
American Parlor Furn. Co...................... 91
Chittenden & Eastman Company................ 377
Crocker Chair Company........................ 137
Delker Bros. Mfg. Co.......................... 97
Dunbar Furn. Mfg. Co.......................... 98
Furniture City Uph. Co....................... 104
Globe Parlor Furniture Co.................106–107
Gunlocke Chair Co., W. H.................401 (Z1)
Indianapolis Chair & Furn. Co................ 152
Jamestown Lounge Company..................... 105
Jamestown Upholstery Co., Inc................ 110
Madden Mfg. Co., John J...................... 120
Memphis Furniture Mfg. Co.................... 303
Michigan Chair Company....................162–163
Sikes Chair Company.......................... 238
Sultan & Company, William.................... 132
Toledo Parlor Furniture Co...............404 (Z3)
Union Brothers...........................420 (Z1)
Wiener Company, E........................406 (Z3)
Yeager Furniture Co......................431 (Z1)

Cribs, Metal
See **Metal Cribs**

Cupboards
——And China Cabinets, Dinette
See **Dinette China Cabinets and Cupboards**
——Dining Room
See **Dining Room Cupboards**
——Kitchen
See **Kitchen Cupboards**

Curio Cabinets
Mentioned Only
Century Furniture Company.................... 92
Indianapolis Chair & Furn. Co................ 152

Curtain Materials (*See Also* **Drapery and Upholstery Fabrics**)
Illustrated or Described
Zion Lace Curtains and Nets.................... 85
Mentioned Only
Rogers, Inc., M. H............................ 90

Curtains, Lace, Net, and Novelty
Illustrated or Described
Zion Lace Curtains and Nets.................... 85

Cushions
——Kapok
Mentioned Only
Fullerton Furniture Factories................ 103
——Special to Order
Mentioned Only
Spencer-Duffy Company, Inc................125–127

Cuts (or Engravings), Drawings, Store Literature and Advertising Plans
See **Direct Mail Advertising Services**

D

Damask
See **Drapery and Upholstery Fabrics, Damask**

Davenette
——Beds, Reed and Fibre
See **Reed and Fibre Davenette Beds**
——Suites
Mentioned Only
Globe Parlor Furniture Co.................106–107
Klamer Furn. Corp.........................288–289
Monitor Furn. Co..........................288–289
Poston Mfg. Co., B. C....................401 (Z3)

Davenettes
Mentioned Only
American Parlor Furniture Co.................. 91
Chittenden & Eastman Company................ 377
Memphis Furn. Mfg. Co........................ 303
Poston Mfg. Co., B. C....................401 (Z3)
SETTEE STYLE................................... 91

Davenport
——Bed Constructions
Mentioned Only
Fullerton Furniture Factories................ 103
Harden Company, Frank S..................108–109
Tauber Parlor Furn. Co...................402 (Z3)
Union Brothers...........................420 (Z1)
——Bed Fixtures
Mentioned Only
Foster Bros. Mfg. Co.......................... 69
——Bed Suites (*See Also* **Reed and Fibre Davenport Bed Suites**)
Illustrated or Described
Delker Bros. Mfg. Co........................... 97
Northfield Company.........................122–123
Pullman Couch Company.....................128–129
Mentioned Only
American Parlor Furniture Co.................. 91
Chittenden & Eastman Company................ 377
Decker, Inc., Isaac C......................... 96
Fenske Bros................................... 99
Globe Parlor Furniture Co.................106–107
Harden Company, Frank S..................108–109
Madden Manufacturing Co., John J............. 120
Memphis Furn. Mfg. Co........................ 303
Tauber Parlor Furn. Co...................402 (Z3)
Union Brothers...........................420 (Z1)
Wellsville Upholstering Co...............423 (Z1)
——Beds (*See Also* **Cane Davenport Beds**)
Illustrated or Described
Delker Bros. Mfg. Co........................... 97
Northfield Company.........................122–123
Pullman Couch Company.....................128–129
Stickley, L. & J. G. & Stickley Mfg. Co....352–353
Mentioned Only
American Parlor Furniture Co.................. 91
Chittenden & Eastman Company................ 377
Fenske Bros................................... 99
Fullerton Furniture Factories................ 103
Furniture City Upholstery Co................. 104
Harden Company, Frank S..................108–109
Hebenstreit's, Inc.......................397 (Z3)
Levin Bros., Inc.............................. 111
Memphis Furn. Mfg. Co........................ 303
Northfield Company........................122–123
Streit Mfg. Co............................130–131
Tauber Parlor Furn. Co...................402 (Z3)
Toledo Parlor Furn. Co...................404 (Z3)
Union Brothers...........................420 (Z1)
Wellsville Upholstering Co...............423 (Z1)
——Tables (*See Also* **Reed and Fibre Davenport Tables**)
Illustrated or Described
Athens Table & Mfg. Co........................ 190
Crocker Chair Company......................... 137
Hastings Table Company.....................150–151
Keystone Table Company....................411 (Z1)
Kiel Furniture Co..........................208–215
Mersman Bros. Corp.........................216–221
St. Johns Table Company....................... 236
Seaburg Mfg. Co...........................416 (Z1)
ELIZABETHAN................................150–151
EXTENSION..........411 (Z1); 416 (Z1); 236; 208–215
BOOK RACK COMBINATION......................... 190
Mentioned Only
Century Furniture Company.................... 92
Chittenden & Eastman Company................ 377
Davis-Birely Table Co........................ 193
Elite Furniture Co........................... 146
Florence Table & Mfg. Co..................... 271
Hannahs Mfg. Co.............................. 197
Hastings Table Company...................150–151
Indianapolis Chair & Furn. Co................ 152
Klamer Furniture Corp....................288–289
Luger Furniture Co.......................399 (Z3)
Memphis Furn. Mfg. Co........................ 303
Monitor Furn. Company....................288–289
Yeager Furn. Co..........................431 (Z1)
EXTENSION...................193; 152; 399 (Z3); 303

Davenports
——And Sofas
Illustrated or Described
American Parlor Furn. Co....................... 91
Brandts Furniture Co......................394 (Z3)
Buffalo Lounge Company....................394 (Z1)

Davenports
——And Sofas (*continued*)
Decker, Inc., Isaac C. 96
Delker Bros. Mfg. Co. 97
Dunbar Furn. Mfg. Co. 98
Fenske Bros. 99
Field & Company, Marshall 100–101
Franklin Furniture Company 102
Fullerton Furniture Factories 103
Furniture City Upholstery Co. 104
Globe Parlor Furn. Co. 106–107
Grand Rapids Upholstering Co. 252–253
Harden Company, Frank S. 108–109
Hebenstreit's, Inc. 397 (Z3)
Horn & Company, J. P. 410 (Z1)
Jamestown Lounge Company 105
Jamestown Upholstery Co., Inc. 110
Karpen & Bros., S. 112–119
Levin Bros., Inc. 111
Madden Mfg. Co., John J. 120
Mallen & Co., H. Z. 121
Northfield Company 122–123
Poston Mfg. Co., B. C. 401 (Z3)
Pullman Couch Company 128–129
Phoenix Chair Company 222–235
Spencer-Duffy Company, Inc. 125–127
Sultan & Company, William 132
Tauber Parlor Furn. Co. 402 (Z3)
Toledo Parlor Furn. Co. 404 (Z3)
Wiener Company, E. 406 (Z3)
Yeager Furniture Co. 431 (Z1)
DUNCAN PHYFE 106–107; 112–119
CHIPPENDALE 112–119; 252–253
COLONIAL (Early American) 132
CROMWELLIAN 112–119
FRENCH PROVINCIAL 112–119
GEORGIAN 121
ITALIAN 112–119
LAWSON TYPE 100–101
LOUIS XV 402 (Z3)
LOUIS XVI 132
MODERN 112–119; 222–235
QUEEN ANNE 112–119; 121
TUXEDO TYPE 410 (Z1)
VENETIAN 112–119

Mentioned Only
Century Furniture Company 92
Chittenden & Eastman Company 377
Irwin Company, Robert W. 275
Jamestown Lounge Company 105
Memphis Furniture Mfg. Co. 303
Rockford Chair & Furn. Co. 308–313
Showers Brothers Company 336–341
Union Brothers 420 (Z1)
Wellsville Upholstering Co. 423 (Z1)
LAWSON TYPE 106–107
MODERN 106–107
SPANISH 106–107

——And Sofas, Reed and Fibre
See **Reed and Fibre Davenports and Sofas**
——Bank and Office
See **Bank and Office Davenports**
——Cane
See **Cane Davenports**
——Gliding, Metal
See **Metal Gliding Davenports**
——Leather, Upholstered
See **Leather Upholstered Davenports**

Day Beds (*See Also* **Metal Day Beds; Reed and Fibre Day Beds**)
Illustrated or Described
Barcalo Manufacturing Co. 393 (Z1)
Fenske Bros. 99
Foster Bros. Mfg. Co. 69
Karpen & Bros., S. 112–119
Kindel Furniture Company 372–373
Pullman Couch Company, Inc. 128–129
CHARLES II 372–373
CHIPPENDALE 372–373
COLONIAL (Early American) 112–119; 372–373
DOUBLE 372–373
ENGLISH COLONIAL 372–373
EQUIPPED WITH BED FIXTURES 99
FRENCH PROVINCIAL 372–373
LADDERBACK 372–373
LOUIS XVI 372–373
VENETIAN 372–373
WITH BACKS 372–373

Mentioned Only
American Parlor Furniture Co. 91
Chittenden & Eastman Company 377
Hard Mfg. Co. 404 (Z1)
Jamestown Lounge Company 105
Klamer Furn. Corp. 288–289
Mallen & Company, H. Z. 121
Memphis Furn. Mfg. Co. 303
Monitor Furniture Co. 288–289
Stickley, L. & J. G. & Stickley Mfg. Co. 352–353
Widdicomb Company, John 366
Yeager Furniture Company 431 (Z1)

Desk
——Benches
Mentioned Only
Lassahn Furniture Company 154
Peterson Art Furniture Co. 164
St. Johns Table Company 236
Skandia Furniture Company 172–185
——Cabinets
See **Cabinet Desks**
——Chairs (Home)
Illustrated or Described
Phoenix Chair Company 222–235
Rockford Peerless Furn. Co. 168–171
Mentioned Only
Century Furniture Company 92
Colonial Desk Company 138–141
Conant-Ball Company 191
Crocker Chair Company 137
Davis-Birely Table Company 193
Empire Chair Company 194–196
Gunlocke Chair Company 401 (Z1)
Hastings Table Company 150–151
Indianapolis Chair & Furn. Co. 152
Peterson Art Furn. Co. 164
Sikes Chair Company 238
Standard Chair Company 239
Steul & Sons, Henry C. 348
Sultan & Company, William 132
Whitney Co., Inc., W. F. 240
Yeager Furniture Company 431 (Z1)

Desk
——Chairs, Home, Reed and Fibre
See **Reed and Fibre Desk Chairs**
——Chests, Combination
See **Chests,** DESK COMBINATION

Desks
——Bank and Office
See **Bank and Office Desks**
——Bedroom
See **Bedroom Desks**
——Bookcase Combination
Illustrated or Described
Peterson Art Furniture Company 164
Rockford Chair & Furniture Co. 308–313
Rockford Furniture Co. 314–321
Rockford Peerless Furn. Co. 168–171
Udell Works, Inc. 419 (Z1)
ADAM 168–171
Mentioned Only
Century Furniture Company 92
Gunn Furniture Co. 396 (Z3)
Indianapolis Chair & Furn. Co. 152
Mechanics Furniture Co. 155
——Children's
See **Children's Desks**
——Glass Tops for
See **Glass Tops for Desks**
——Governor Winthrop
See **Governor Winthrop Desks**
——Home
Illustrated or Described
Hekman Furniture Co. 398 (Z3)
Hemsing Manufacturing Co. 405 (Z1)
Mechanics Furniture Co. 155
Rockford Chair & Furn. Co. 308–313
Rockford Furniture Company 314–321
Rockford Standard Furniture Co. 327–331
Union Furniture Company 186–187
CHIPPENDALE 405 (Z1)
DROP LID 398 (Z3)
SHERATON 314–321
Mentioned Only
Baker Furniture Factories, Inc. 243
Charlotte Furniture Co. 258
Furniture Shops 160–161
Irwin Company, Robert W. 275
Stickley, L. & J. G. & Stickley Mfg. Co. 352–353
——Kidney Shaped
See **Kidney Shaped Desks**
——Ladies'
See **Ladies' Desks**
——Library
See **Library Desks**
——Reed and Fibre
See **Reed and Fibre Desks**
——Roll Top
See **Roll Top Desks**
——Secretary
See **Secretary Desks**
——Spinet
See **Spinet Desks**
——Table
See **Table Desks**
——Tambour
See **Tambour Desks**
——Typewriter
See **Bank and Office Desks,** TYPEWRITER
——Wall
See **Wall Desks**
——Writing
See **Writing Desks**

Dinette
——Buffets
Illustrated or Described
Phoenix Chair Company 222–235
Rockford Peerless Furniture Company 168–171
St. Johns Table Company 236
Mentioned Only
Colonial Desk Company 138–141
——Chairs
Mentioned Only
Colonial Desk Company 138–141
——China Cabinets and Cupboards
Illustrated or Described
Phoenix Chair Company 222–235
Rockford Peerless Furniture Company 168–171
Mentioned Only
Colonial Desk Company 138–141
——Suites (*See Also* **Dining Room Suites, Complete, Apartment Size**)
Illustrated or Described
Phoenix Chair Company 222–235
Rockford Peerless Furniture Company 168–171
St. Johns Table Company 236
DUNCAN PHYFE 168–171
Mentioned Only
Colonial Desk Company 138–141
Fancher Furniture Co. 270
Klamer Furniture Corp. 288–289
Monitor Furniture Co. 288–289
Rockford National Furn. Co. 324–326
Thomasville Chair Company 349
Virginia Table Company 362–363
——Tables
Illustrated or Described
Phoenix Chair Company 222–235
Rockford Peerless Furniture Company 168–171
St. Johns Table Company 236
Mentioned Only
Colonial Desk Company 138–141
EXTENSION TYPE 222–235

Dining Room
——And Living Room Tables Combined
See **Tables,** COMBINATION LIVING ROOM AND DINING ROOM
——Benches
Mentioned Only
Hastings Table Company 150–151
Steul & Sons, Henry C. 348

Dining Room
——Buffets (*See Also* **Dining Room Sideboards**)
Illustrated or Described
Basic Furniture Company 244
Burrows Bros. Company 395–397 (Z1)
Central Furniture Company 254–257
Chattanooga Furniture Company 259
Crocker Chair Company 137
Easton Furniture Mfg. Co. 400 (Z1)
Ebert Furniture Company 264; 402–403 (Z1)
Empire Chair Company 194–195
Fancher Furniture Company 270
Florence Table & Mfg. Co. 271
Forsyth Furn. Lines, Inc. 272
Globe-Bosse-World Furn. Co. 273
Hemsing Mfg. Co. 405 (Z1)
Hellam Furniture Company 406–407 (Z1)
Home Furniture Company 408–409 (Z1)
Huntley Furniture Company 274
Imperial Furniture Company 198–205
Johnson & Sons Furn. Co., A. J. 278–279
Klamer Furniture Corp. 288–289
Luce Furniture Company 156–159
Mechanics Furniture Co. 302
Monitor Furniture Company 288–289
Period Cabinet Mfg. Co. 307
Peterson Art Furn. Co. 164
Phoenix Chair Company 222–235
Rockford Chair & Furn. Co. 308–313
Rockford Furniture Company 314–321
Rockford National Furn. Co. 324–326
Rockford Palace Furn. Co. 322–323
Rockford Standard Furn. Co. 327–331
Royal Mantel & Furn. Co. 332–334
St. Johns Table Company 236
Showers Brothers Company 336–341
Skandia Furniture Company 342–345
Statesville Furniture Co. 346
Steul & Sons, Henry C. 348
Thomasville Chair Co. 349
Union Furniture Co. 360–361
Virginia Table Co. 362–363
White Furniture Co. 365
Wilson Furn. Co., Inc. 407 (Z3) and 430 (Z1)
Witz Furn. Corp., J. L. 244
AMERICAN EMPIRE 405 (Z1)
APARTMENT SIZE 198–305; 222–235; 236
CHIPPENDALE 322–323
COLONIAL (Early American) 395–397 (Z1); 222–235; 342–345; 254–257; 308–313; 314–321
EARLY ENGLISH 408–409 (Z1)
ELIZABETHAN 314–321
ELIZABETHAN AND RENAISSANCE COMBINED 314–321
ENGLISH 314–321
FRENCH 322–323
HEPPELWHITE 278–279; 322–323; 342–345
JACOBEAN 406–407 (Z1); 278–279
LOUIS XVI 314–321
MODERN 156–159; 314–321
SHERATON 314–321; 408–409 (Z1); 342–345
SPANISH RENAISSANCE 348
Mentioned Only
Century Furniture Company 92
Conant-Ball Company 191
Davis Furniture Corp. 262
Huntley Furniture Co., B. F. 274
Landstrom Furniture Corp. 290–301
Luger Furniture Co. 399 (Z3)
Memphis Furn. Mfg. Co. 303
Statesville Furniture Co. 346
COLONIAL (Early American) 92; 191; 324–326

——Chairs
Illustrated or Described
Basic Furniture Co. 244
Berkey & Gay Furniture Company 248–251
Burrows Brothers Company 395–397 (Z1)
Central Furniture Co. 254–257
Chattanooga Furniture Co. 259
Colonial Furniture Co. 93–95
Easton Furn. Mfg. Co. 400 (Z1)
Ebert Furniture Co. 264; 402–403 (Z1)
Empire Chair Company 194–195
Fancher Furniture Co. 270
Florence Table & Mfg. Co. 271
Globe-Bosse-World Furn. Co. 273
Grand Rapids Upholstering Co. 252–253
Imperial Furniture Co. 198–205
Klamer Furniture Corp. 288–289
Hellam Furniture Co. 406–407 (Z1)
Home Furniture Co. 408–409 (Z1)
Johnson & Sons Furn. Co., A. J. 278–279
Limbert Company, Charles P. 281
Luce Furniture Company 156–159
Mechanics Furniture Co. 302
Milne Chair Company 207
Monitor Furniture Co. 288–289
Period Cabinet Mfg. Co. 307
Peterson Art Furniture Co. 164
Phoenix Chair Company 222–235
Rockford Chair & Furn. Co. 308–313
Rockford Furniture Co. 314–321
Rockford National Furn. Co. 324–326
Rockford Palace Furn. Co. 322–323
Rockford Standard Furn. Co. 327–331
Royal Mantel & Furn. Co. 332–334
St. Johns Table Company 236
Showers Brothers Company 336–341
Skandia Furniture Company 342–345
Stickley, L. & J. G. & Stickley Mfg. Co. 342–345
Union Furniture Company 360–361
White Furniture Company 365
Wilson Furniture Co., Inc. 407 (Z3) and 430 (Z1)
Witz Furn. Corp., J. L. 244
Steul & Sons, Henry C. 348
CHIPPENDALE 322–323
COLONIAL (Early American) 222–235; 308–313; 314–321; 342–345; 352–353; 395–397 (Z1)
DUNCAN PHYFE 222–235
EARLY ENGLISH 408–409 (Z1)
ELIZABETHAN 314–321
ELIZABETHAN AND RENAISSANCE COMBINED 314–321
ENGLISH 314–321
FRENCH PEASANT 222–235
FRENCH 322–323
HEPPELWHITE 278–279; 322–323; 342–345
JACOBEAN 278–279; 406–407 (Z1)
LOUIS XVI 314–321
MODERN 156–159; 314–321
SHERATON 254–257; 314–321; 342–345; 408–409 (Z1)
SPANISH RENAISSANCE 254–257; 348

Dining Room

——Chairs *(continued)*

Mentioned Only

Baker Furniture Factories, Inc. 243
Century Furniture Company 92
Chittenden & Eastman Company 377
Colonial Desk Company 138–141
Davis Furniture Corp 262
Hastings Table Co 150–151
Huntley Furniture Co., B. F. 274
Indianapolis Chair & Furn. Co. 152
Jamestown Chair Company 206
Landstrom Furniture Corp. 290–301
Louisville Chair & Furn. Co. 396 (Z2)
Luger Furniture Company 399 (Z3)
Memphis Furniture Mfg. Co. 303
Michigan Chair Company 162–163
Morganton Furniture Company 304
Statesville Chair Co. 417 (Z1)
Statesville Furniture Co. 346
Tell City Chair Company 403 (Z3)
Thomasville Chair Company 349
Virginia Table Company 362–363
Whitney Co., Inc., W. F. 240
Special to Order 281

——China Cabinets and Closets

Illustrated or Described

Basic Furniture Company 244
Burrows Bros. Co. 395–397 (Z1)
Central Furniture Company 254–257
Colonial Desk Company 138–141
Crocker Chair Company 137
Easton Furniture Mfg. Co. 400 (Z1)
Ebert Furniture Co. 264; 402–403 (Z1)
Empire Chair Company 194–195
Fancher Furniture Co. 270
Florence Table & Mfg. Co. 271
Globe-Bosse-World Furn. Co. 273
Hellam Furniture Co. 406–407 (Z1)
Home Furniture Company 408–409 (Z1)
Imperial Furniture Co. 198–205
Johnson & Sons Furn. Co., A. J. 278–279
Klamer Furniture Corp. 288–289
Limbert Co., Charles P. 281
Luce Furniture Company 156–159
Mechanics Furniture Company 302
Monitor Furniture Co. 288–289
Morganton Furniture Company 304
Period Cabinet Mfg. Co. 307
Peterson Art Furn. Co. 164
Phoenix Chair Company 222–235
Rockford Chair & Furn. Co. 308–313
Rockford Furniture Co. 314–321
Rockford National Furn. Co. 324–326
Rockford Palace Furn. Co. 322–323
Rockford Standard Furn. Co. 327–331
Royal Mantel & Furn. Co. 332–334
Showers Brothers Company 336–341
Skandia Furniture Company 342–345
Stickley, L. & J. G. & Stickley Mfg. Co. 352–353
Union Furniture Company 360–361
Virginia Table Company 362–363
White Furniture Company 365
Wilson Furn. Co., Inc. 407 (Z3) and 430 (Z1)
Witz Furniture Corp., J. L. 244
Apartment Size 198–205
Chippendale 322–323
Colonial (Early American) 222–235; 308–313; 314–321; 342–345; 352–353; 395–397 (Z1)
Early English 408–409 (Z1)
Elizabethan 314–321
Elizabethan and Renaissance Combined 314–321
English 314–321
French 322–323
Heppelwhite 278–279; 322–323; 342–345
Jacobean 278–279; 406–407 (Z1)
Louis XVI 314–321
Modern 156–159; 314–321
Sheraton 254–257; 314–321; 342–345; 408–409 (Z1)
Spanish 222–235; 254–257

Mentioned Only

Century Furniture Co. 92
Chattanooga Furniture Co. 259
Chittenden & Eastman Company 377
Conant-Ball Company 191
Hastings Table Company 150–151
Huntley Furn. Co., B. F. 274
Landstrom Furniture Corp. 290–301
Memphis Furn. Mfg. Co. 303
Statesville Furniture Co. 346
Steul & Sons, Henry C. 348

——Corner Cabinets

Illustrated or Described

Baker Furniture Factories, Inc. 243
Skandia Furniture Company 172–185

Mentioned Only

Steul & Sons, Henry C. 348

——Cupboards

Illustrated or Described

Phoenix Chair Company 222–235
Stickley, L. & J. G. & Stickley Mfg. Co. 352–353
Apartment Size 222–235
Duncan Phyfe 222–235
Colonial (Early American) 352–353
French Peasant 222–235

——Dutch Cabinets

Illustrated or Described

Skandia Furniture Company 172–185

——Mirrors

Illustrated or Described

Chicago Mirror & Art Glass Co. 395 (Z3)

Mentioned Only

Furst Bros. & Company 78

——Servers and Serving Tables

Illustrated or Described

Basic Furniture Company 244
Burrows Bros. Company 395–397 (Z1)
Central Furniture Co. 254–257
Chattanooga Furniture Co. 259
Easton Furn. Mfg. Co. 400 (Z1)
Ebert Furniture Co. 402–403 (Z1)
Empire Chair Company 194–195
Fancher Furniture Company 270
Globe-Bosse-World Furn. Co. 273
Hellam Furniture Co. 406–407 (Z1)
Home Furniture Co. 408–409 (Z1)

Dining Room

——Servers and Serving Tables *(continued)*

Johnson & Sons Furn. Co., A. J. 278–279
Luce Furniture Co. 156–159
Mechanics Furniture Co. 302
Morganton Furniture Company 304
Rockford Chair & Furn. Co. 308–313
Rockford Furniture Company 314–321
Rockford National Furn. Co. 324–326
Rockford Palace Furn. Co. 322–323
Rockford Standard Furn. Co. 327–331
Royal Mantel & Furn. Co. 332–334
Showers Brothers Company 336–341
Skandia Furniture Company 342–345
Steul & Sons, Henry C. 348
Union Furniture Company 360–361
White Furniture Company 365
Wilson Furn. Co., Inc. 407 (Z3) and 430 (Z1)
Witz Furn. Corp., J. L. 244
Chippendale 322–323
Colonial (Early American) 308–313; 314–321; 342–345
Early English 408–409 (Z1)
Elizabethan 314–321
Elizabethan and Renaissance Combined 314–321
English 314–321
French 322–323
Heppelwhite 278–279; 322–323; 342–345
Jacobean 278–279; 406–407 (Z1)
Louis XVI 314–321
Modern 156–159; 314–321
Sheraton 254–257; 314–321; 342–345; 408–409 (Z1)
Spanish 254–257; 348

Mentioned Only

Century Furniture Co. 92
Chittenden & Eastman Company 377
Conant-Ball Company 191
Davis Furniture Corp. 262
Florence Table & Mfg. Co. 271
Huntley Furniture Co., B. F. 274
Imperial Furniture Co. 198–205
Indianapolis, Chair and Furniture Co. 152
Landstrom Furniture Corporation 290–301
Limbert Company, Charles P. 281
Luger Furniture Co. 399 (Z3)
Memphis Furniture Mfg. Co. 303
Period Cabinet Mfg. Co. 307
Statesville Furn. Co. 346
Virginia Table Company 362–363
Colonial (Early American) 395–397 (Z1)
Hutch Type 395–397 (Z1)

——Sideboards *(See Also* **Dining Room Buffets)**

Illustrated or Described

Limbert Company, Charles P. 281

Mentioned Only

Century Furniture Co. 92
Luger Furniture Company 399 (Z3)

——Silver Cabinets

Illustrated or Described

Berkey & Gay Furniture Company 248–251
Century Furniture Company 92
Luce Furniture Company 156–159
Mechanics Furniture Co. 155
Rockford Peerless Furn. Co. 168–171
Steul & Sons, Henry C. 348
English 168–171
Modern 156–159
Spanish Renaissance 348

Mentioned Only

Chittenden & Eastman Company 377
Colonial Desk Company 138–141
Yeager Furniture Co. 431 (Z1)

——Suites, Complete

Illustrated or Described

Basic Furniture Company 244
Burrows Bros. Company 395–397 (Z1)
Central Furniture Co. 254–257
Chattanooga Furniture Co. 259
Easton Furn. Mfg. Co. 400 (Z1)
Ebert Furniture Co. 264; 402–403 (Z1)
Empire Chair Company 194–195
Fancher Furniture Company 270
Florence Table & Mfg. Co. 271
Forsyth Furn. Lines, Inc. 272
Globe-Bosse-World Furn. Co. 273
Hellam Furn. Co., Inc. 406–407 (Z1)
Home Furniture Co. 408–409 (Z1)
Imperial Furniture Company 198–205
Johnson & Sons Furn. Co., A. J. 278–279
Klamer Furniture Corp. 288–289
Limbert Company, Charles P. 281
Luce Furniture Company 156–159
Mechanics Furniture Co. 302
Monitor Furniture Co. 288–289
Morganton Furniture Company 304
Period Cabinet Mfg. Co. 307
Peterson Art Furniture Co. 164
Phoenix Chair Company 222–235
Rockford Chair & Furn. Co. 308–313
Rockford Furniture Company 314–321
Rockford National Furn. Co. 324–326
Rockford Palace Furniture Co. 322–323
Rockford Standard Furniture Co. 327–331
Royal Mantel & Furn. Co. 332–334
St. Johns Table Company 236
Showers Brothers Company 336–341
Skandia Furniture Co. 342–345
Statesville Furniture Co. 346
Steul & Sons, Henry C. 348
Thomasville Chair Company 349
Union Furniture Company 360–361
Virginia Table Company 362–363
White Furniture Company 365
Wilson Furniture Co., Inc. 407 (Z3) and 430 (Z1)
Witz Furn. Corp., J. L. 244
Apartment Size 198–205; 222–235; 236; 254–257
Chippendale 322–323
Colonial (Early American) 222–235; 308–313; 314–321; 342–345; 395–397 (Z1)
Duncan Phyfe 222–235; 327–331
Early English 327–331; 408–409 (Z1)
Elizabethan 314–321
Elizabethan and Renaissance Combined 314–321
English 314–321
French 322–323; 327–331
French Peasant 222–235
Heppelwhite 278–279; 322–323; 342–345
Jacobean 194–195; 278–279; 281; 307; 406–407 (Z1)
Louis XVI 314–321
Modern 156–159; 314–321
Sheraton 254–257; 307; 314–321; 342–345; 408–409 (Z1)

Dining Room

——Suites Complete *(continued)*

Spanish Renaissance 254–257; 348
Tudor 194–195

Mentioned Only

Berkey & Gay Furniture Company 248–251
Century Furniture Company 92
Chittenden & Eastman Company 377
Conant-Ball Company 191
Davis Furniture Corp 262
Hastings Table Company 150–151
Hemsing Mfg. Co. 405 (Z1)
Huntley Furn. Co., B. F. 274
Indianapolis Chair & Furn. Co. 152
Irwin Company, Robert W. 275
Landstrom Furniture Corp. 290–301
Mechanics Furniture Co. 302
Memphis Furn. Mfg. Co. 303
Michigan Chair Co. 162–163
Period Cabinet Mfg. Co. 307
Sligh Furn. Co. 335
Ward Mfg. Co. 364
American Empire 405 (Z1)
Apartment Size 162–163; 191; 302; 307; 364
Colonial (Early American) 281
Duncan Phyfe 270
Early English 244; 270
Elizabethan 281; 395–397 (Z1)
English Colonial 281
French Renaissance 406–407 (Z1)
French 281
Heppelwhite 406–407 (Z1)
Italian Renaissance 395–397 (Z1); 406–407 (Z1)
Modern 281
Queen Anne 244
Sheraton 406–407 (Z1)
Spanish Renaissance 395–397 (Z1); 406–407 (Z1)

——Tables

Illustrated or Described

Athens Table & Mfg. Co. 190
Basic Furniture Co. 244
Burrows Bros. Co. 395–397 (Z1)
Central Furniture Company 254–257
Century Furniture Company 92
Chattanooga Furniture Co. 259
Crocker Chair Company 137
Easton Furn. Mfg. Co. 400 (Z1)
Ebert Furniture Company 264; 402–403 (Z1)
Empire Chair Company 194–195
Fancher Furniture Co. 270
Florence Table & Mfg. Co. 271
Globe Bosse World Furn. Co. 273
Hellam Furniture Co. 406–407 (Z1)
Home Furniture Co. 408–409 (Z1)
Imperial Furniture Co. 198–205
Johnson & Sons Furn. Co., A. J. 278–279
Limbert Company, Chas. P. 281
Luce Furniture Company 156–159
Mechanics Furniture Company 302
Morganton Furniture Company 304
Period Cabinet Mfg. Co. 307
Peterson Art Furniture Co. 164
Phoenix Chair Company 222–235
Rockford Chair & Furn. Co. 308–313
Rockford Furniture Co. 314–321
Rockford National Furn. Co. 324–326
Rockford Palace Furn. Co. 322–323
Rockford Standard Furn. Co. 327–331
Royal Mantel & Furn. Co. 332–334
St. Johns Table Company 236
Showers Brothers Company 336–341
Skandia Furniture Company 342–345
Statesville Furniture Co. 346
Steul & Sons, Henry C. 348
Stickley, L. & J. G. & Stickley Mfg. Co. 352–353
Union Furniture Company 360–361
Virginia Table Company 362–363
White Furniture Company 365
Wilson Furn. Co., Inc. 407 (Z3) and 430 (Z1)
Witz Furn. Corp., J. L. 244
Apartment Size 190; 222–235; 254–257; 236
Chippendale 322–323; 308–313
Colonial (Early American) 395–397 (Z1); 222–235; 342–345; 314–321
Draw Top 352–353
Drop Leaf 222–235; 362–363
Duncan Phyfe 222–235; 342–345; 408–409 (Z1)
Early English 408–409 (Z1)
Elizabethan 314–321
Elizabethan and Renaissance Combined 314–321
English 314–321
Extension 190; 198–205; 222–235; 281; 302; 307; 314–321; 324–326; 327–331; 332–334; 336–341; 348; 362–363; 400 (Z1); 402–403 (Z1)
French 322–323
French Peasant 222–235
Heppelwhite 278–279; 322–323
Jacobean 278–279; 406–407 (Z1)
Louis XVI 314–321
Modern 156–159; 314–321
Sheraton 254–257; 314–321; 342–345
Spanish 222–235; 254–257
Spanish Renaissance 348

Mentioned Only

Chittenden & Eastman Company 377
Conant-Ball Company 191
Davis Furniture Co. 262
Hastings Table Company 150–151
Huntley Furn. Co., B. F. 274
Landstrom Furniture Corp. 290–301
Luger Furniture Co. 399 (Z3)
Memphis Furn. Mfg. Co. 303
Statesville Furn. Co. 346
Drop Leaf Type 92; 346
Extension Type 191; 262; 346

——Welsh Dressers

Mentioned Only

Century Furniture Company 92
Conant-Ball Company 191
Imperial Furniture Co. 198–205
Steul & Sons, Henry C. 348

Direct Mail Advertising Services
(Including Preparation and Printing of Store Literature, Drawings, Cuts and Consulting Service on Advertising Plans)

Retailer's Service Bureau 413 (Z1)

Directors' Tables, Bank and Office
See **Bank and Office Tables, Directors'**

Display

——Mirrors, Window
See **Window Display Mirrors**

Display
——Rails, Short, for Displaying Beds
    See Bed Short Rails for Displaying Beds
——Tables

    Mentioned Only
    Mutschler Bros. Company..................... 74

Divans, Metal
    See Metal Divans

Dog Irons
    Mentioned Only
    Fair Foundry Company....................394 (Z2)
    Knox Stove Works........................395 (Z2)

Double Day Beds
    See Day Beds, Double

Drapery and Upholstery Fabrics. *See Also* Curtain Materials; Curtains, Lace, Net and Novelty
——Brocade
    Mentioned Only
    Canterbury Decorative Fabrics............... 87
    Chittenden & Eastman Company.............. 377
    Rogers, Inc., M. H....................... 90
——Brocatelle
    Mentioned Only
    Canterbury Decorative Fabrics............... 87
    Chittenden & Eastman Company.............. 377
——Chintz
    Mentioned Only
    Canterbury Decorative Fabrics............... 87
    Colonial Drapery Fabrics................... 84
——Crash
    Mentioned Only
    Colonial Drapery Fabrics................... 84
——Cretonne
    Illustrated or Described
    Colonial Drapery Fabrics................... 84
    Mentioned Only
    Canterbury Decorative Fabrics............... 87
——Damask
    Illustrated or Described
    Colonial Drapery Fabrics................... 84
    Mentioned Only
    Canterbury Decorative Fabrics............... 87
    Chittenden & Eastman Company.............. 377
    Rogers, Inc., M. H....................... 90
——Embroidered Decorative Fabrics
    Mentioned Only
    Canterbury Decorative Fabrics............... 87
——Frieze, Linen
    Mentioned Only
    Canterbury Decorative Fabrics............... 87
    Rogers, Inc., M. H....................... 90
——Frieze, Silk
    Mentioned Only
    Canterbury Decorative Fabrics............... 87
    Rogers, Inc., M. H....................... 90
——Frieze, Wool
    Mentioned Only
    Canterbury Decorative Fabrics............... 87
——Gauzes
    Mentioned Only
    Canterbury Decorative Fabrics............... 87
——India Prints
    Mentioned Only
    Canterbury Decorative Fabrics............... 87
——Moires
    Mentioned Only
    Canterbury Decorative Fabrics............... 87
——Mohair
    Mentioned Only
    Chittenden & Eastman Company.............. 377
——Moquettes
    Mentioned Only
    Canterbury Decorative Fabrics............... 87
——Needlepoint
    Mentioned Only
    Rogers, Inc., M. H....................... 90
    GENUINE.............................. 90
    HAND LOOM........................... 90
——Piano Scarfs
    Mentioned Only
    Canterbury Decorative Fabrics............... 87
——Plush
    Mentioned Only
    Canterbury Decorative Fabrics............... 87
——Printed Linens
    Mentioned Only
    Canterbury Decorative Fabrics............... 87
——Reps and Poplins
    Mentioned Only
    Canterbury Decorative Fabrics............... 87
——Slip Cover Fabrics
    Mentioned Only
    Canterbury Decorative Fabrics............... 87
——Satins and Sateens
    Mentioned Only
    Canterbury Decorative Fabrics............... 87
——Silks
    Mentioned Only
    Canterbury Decorative Fabrics............... 87

Drapery and Upholstery Fabrics (*continued*)
——Table Runners
    Mentioned Only
    Canterbury Decorative Fabrics............... 87
——Taffetas
    Mentioned Only
    Canterbury Decorative Fabrics............... 87
    Rogers, Inc., M. H....................... 90
——Taffetas, Plain and Figured
    Mentioned Only
    Canterbury Decorative Fabrics............... 87
——Tapestries
    Mentioned Only
    Canterbury Decorative Fabrics............... 87
    Chittenden & Eastman Company.............. 377
    Rogers, Inc., M. H....................... 90
    AUBUSSON............................ 90
    COTTON AND WOOL.................... 87
    FLEMISH............................. 90
——Tapestry Panels
    Mentioned Only
    Canterbury Decorative Fabrics............... 87
——Velours
    Mentioned Only
    Canterbury Decorative Fabrics............... 87
    Rogers, Inc., M. H....................... 90
    DE GENE............................. 90
    LINEN............................... 377
    PLAIN AND FANCY WEAVES.............. 87
——Velvets
    Mentioned Only
    Canterbury Decorative Fabrics............... 87
    Chittenden & Eastman Company.............. 377
    PLAIN AND FANCY WEAVES.............. 87
    RAMIE.............................87, 377

Draw Top
——Tables
    See Refectory Tables
——Tables, Dining Room
    See Dining Room Tables, DRAW TOP

Drawings, Cuts (Engravings), Store Literature and Advertising Plans and Services
    See Direct Mail Advertising Services

Dresser Wardrobes
    See Bedroom Wardrobes, DRESSER COMBINATION TYPE

Dresserobes, Bedroom
    See Bedroom Dresserobes

Dressers
——Bedroom
    See Bedroom Dressers
——Bedroom, Vanity
    See Bedroom Vanity Dressers
——Breakfast Room, Welsh
    See Breakfast Room Welsh Dressers
——Dining Room, Welsh
    See Dining Room Welsh Dressers
——Lawn and Porch
    See Lawn and Porch Dressers

Dressing
——Table Benches
    See Bedroom Benches, DRESSING TABLE TYPE
——Tables, Bedroom
    See Bedroom Dressing Tables

Drop Leaf
——Tables (*See Also* Butterfly Tables)
    Illustrated or Described
    Crocker Chair Company.................... 137
    Kiel Furniture Company................208–215
    Mentioned Only
    Aulsbrook & Jones Furn. Co............... 242
    Conant-Ball Company..................... 191
    Davis-Birely Table Co................... 193
    Elite Furniture Company................. 146
    Florence Table & Mfg. Co................ 271
    Hastings Table Company.............150–151
    Imperial Furniture Co................198–205
    Luger Furniture Co....................399 (Z3)
    Mallen & Company, H. Z................. 121
    Memphis Furniture Mfg. Co............... 303
    St. Johns Table Company................ 236
    Schoeck Mfg. Co., Inc................415 (Z1)
    Steul & Sons, Henry C................. 348
    Yeager Furniture Company............431 (Z1)
——Tables, Breakfast Room
    See Breakfast Room Tables, DROP LEAF
——Tables, Dining Room
    See Dining Room Tables, DROP LEAF
——Tables, Dressing, Bedroom
    See Bedroom Dressing Tables, DROP LEAF

Drop Lid Desks, Home
    See Desks, Home, Drop Lid

Drum Tables
    Illustrated or Described
    Furniture Shops.......................160–161

Drying Racks, Clothes
    See Racks, Clothes Drying

Duncan Phyfe
——Beds
    See Beds, Duncan Phyfe
——Benches, Bedroom
    See Bedroom Benches, DUNCAN PHYFE
——Chairs, Bedroom
    See Bedroom Chairs, DUNCAN PHYFE
——Chairs, Dining Room
    See Dining Room Chairs, DUNCAN PHYFE
——Chests of Drawers, Bedroom
    See Bedroom Chests of Drawers, DUNCAN PHYFE
——Cupboards, Dining Room
    See Dining Room Cupboards, DUNCAN PHYFE
——Davenports and Sofas
    See Davenports and Sofas, DUNCAN PHYFE
——Dinette Suites
    See Dinette Suites, DUNCAN PHYFE
——Dressers, Bedroom
    See Bedroom Dressers, DUNCAN PHYFE

——Night Tables, Bedroom
    See Bedroom Night Tables, DUNCAN PHYFE
——Vanities, Bedroom
    See Bedroom Vanities, DUNCAN PHYFE
——Suites, Complete, Bedroom
    See Bedroom Suites, Complete, Including Bench, Chair, Rocker and Night Table, DUNCAN PHYFE
——Suites, Complete, Dining Room
    See Dining Room Suites, Complete, DUNCAN PHYFE
——Tables, Coffee
    See Coffee Tables, DUNCAN PHYFE
——Tables, Console
    See Console Tables, DUNCAN PHYFE
——Tables, Dining Room
    See Dining Room Tables, DUNCAN PHYFE
——Tables, Odd and Occasional
    See Odd and Occasional Tables, DUNCAN PHYFE
——Tables, Pembroke
    See Pembroke Tables, DUNCAN PHYFE
——Tables, Swing Top
    See Swing Top Tables, DUNCAN PHYFE

Dutch Cabinets
——Breakfast Room
    See Breakfast Room Dutch Cabinets
——Dining Room
    See Dining Room Dutch Cabinets

E

Early American
    See Colonial

Early English
——Buffets, Dining Room
    See Dining Room Buffets, EARLY ENGLISH
——Chairs
    See Chairs, EARLY ENGLISH
——Chairs, Dining Room
    See Dining Room Chairs, EARLY ENGLISH
——China Cabinets and Closets, Dining Room
    See Dining Room China Cabinets and Closets, EARLY ENGLISH
——Servers and Serving Tables, Dining Room
    See Dining Room Servers and Serving Tables, EARLY ENGLISH
——Suites, Complete, Bedroom
    See Bedroom Suites, Complete (Including Bench, Chair, Rocker and Night Table), EARLY ENGLISH
——Suites, Complete, Dining Room
    See Dining Room Suites, Complete, EARLY ENGLISH
——Tables
    See Tables, EARLY ENGLISH
——Tables, Dining Room
    See Dining Room Tables, EARLY ENGLISH

Easy Lounging Chairs
    Illustrated or Described
    Field & Company, Marshall.............100–101
    Furniture City Upholstery Co............ 104
    Harden Company, Frank S.............108–109
    Hebenstreit's, Inc....................397 (Z3)
    Indianapolis Chair & Furn. Co........... 152
    Karpen & Bros., S...................112–119
    Levin Bros., Inc...................... 111
    Louisville Chair & Furn. Co...........396 (Z2)
    Mallen & Company, H. Z............... 121
    Michigan Chair Company..............162–163
    Poston Mfg. Co., B. C...............401 (Z3)
    Pullman Couch Company..............128–129
    Sikes Chair Company................. 238
    Spencer-Duffy Co., Inc..............125–127
    Streit Mfg. Co., C. F...............130–131
    Wellsville Upholstering Co...........423 (Z1)
    Wiener Company, E.................406 (Z3)
    COLONIAL............................ 238
    ENGLISH STYLE....................... 111
    QUEEN ANNE......................162–163
    Mentioned Only
    American Parlor Furn. Co............... 91
    Chittenden & Eastman Company.......... 377
    Conant-Ball Company................. 191
    Empire Chair Company..............194–195
    Fenske Bros......................... 99
    Globe-Parlor Furniture Co...........106–107
    Horn & Company, J. P...............410 (Z1)
    Jamestown Lounge Company........... 105
    Jamestown Upholstery Co., Inc......... 110
    Memphis Furn. Mfg. Co............... 303
    Sultan & Company, William........... 132
    Tauber Parlor Furn. Co.............402 (Z3)

Egyptian Mahogany Chests
    See Chests, LUXOR-MAHOGANY

Elizabethan
——Cabinets
    See Cabinets, Elizabethan
——Davenport Tables
    See Davenport Tables, ELIZABETHAN
——Suites, Complete, Dining Room
    See Dining Room Suites, Complete, ELIZABETHAN

Electric Clocks
    See Clocks, Electric

Emblem Rugs
    See Carpets and Rugs, EMBLEM RUGS

Embroidered Decorative Fabrics
    See Drapery and Upholstery Fabrics, Embroidered Decorative Fabrics

Empire Chairs
    See Chairs, EMPIRE

English
——Cabinets
    See Cabinets, English
——Club Chairs
    See Club Chairs, for Home Use, ENGLISH
——Colonial Day Beds
    See Day Beds, ENGLISH COLONIAL
——Colonial Suites, Complete, Dining Room
    See Dining Room Suites, Complete, ENGLISH COLONIAL
——Easy Lounging Chairs
    See Easy Lounging Chairs, ENGLISH STYLE

End Tables (*See Also* Book Troughs and End Tables Combined; *and* Reed and Fibre End Tables)
    Illustrated or Described
    Bay View Furniture Co................393 (Z3)
    Furniture Shops.....................160–161

End Tables (continued)

Hannahs Mfg. Co.	197
Hastings Table Company	150–151
Imperial Furniture Co.	198–205
Keystone Table Company	411 (Z1)
Kiel Furniture Company	208–215
Lassahn Furniture Co.	154
Mersman Bros. Corp.	216–221
Paalman Furniture Co.	400 (Z3)
Rockford Peerless Furniture Company	168–171
Schoeck Mfg. Co., Inc.	415 (Z1)
Drop Leaf	208–215
French	168–171
Sheraton	160–161
Spanish	150–151

Mentioned Only

American Parlor Furniture Co.	91
Athens Table & Mfg. Co.	190
Aulsbrook & Jones Furn. Co.	242
Century Furniture Company	92
Chittenden & Eastman Company	377
Conant-Ball Company	191
Crocker Chair Company	137
Elite Furniture Company	146
Florence Table & Mfg. Co.	271
Furniture Shops	160–161
Griffith Furniture Works	147
Hastings Table Company	150–151
Hekman Furniture Co.	398 (Z3)
Indianapolis Chair & Furn. Co.	152
Kiel Furniture Co.	208–215
Klamer Furniture Corp.	288–289
Luger Furniture Co.	399 (Z3)
Memphis Mfg. Co.	303
Michigan Chair Company	162–163
Monitor Furniture Co.	288–289
Peterson Art Furn. Co.	164
Seaburg Mfg. Co.	416 (Z1)
St. John's Table Co.	236
Yeager Furniture Co.	431 (Z1)
Wrought Iron	208–215

European Hand Tuft Rugs
See Carpets and Rugs, European Hand Tuft

Exhibition Spaces

Illustrated or Described

Evansville Furniture Manufacturers Assn.	382–383
Jamestown Furniture Market Assn.	387
Peck and Hills Furn. Co.	392

Extension
—Slides, Table
  See Slides for Extension Tables
—Tables, Breakfast Room
  See Breakfast Room Tables, Extension
—Tables, Davenport
  See Davenport Tables, Extension
—Tables, Dining Room
  See Dining Room Tables, Extension Type
—Tables, Gateleg
  See Gateleg Tables, Extension

F

Fabrics, Drapery and Upholstery
See Drapery and Upholstery Fabrics

Felt
—Base Rugs
  See Carpets and Rugs, Felt Base Rugs
—Feet, Casters, Glides, and Slides
  See Casters, Glides, Slides and Felt Feet

Fereghan Carpets and Rugs
See Carpets and Rugs, Antique Fereghan

Fences and Gates: Lawn and Garden

Mentioned Only

Rustic Hickory Furniture Co.	68

Ferneries

Mentioned Only

Lassahn Furniture Co.	154
Memphis Mfg. Co.	303
Shreve Chair Company	237
Yeager Furniture Co.	431 (Z1)

Fibre
—And Reed
  See Reed and Fibre
—Seat Benches, Bedroom
  See Bedroom Benches, Fibre Seat

—Seat Chairs and Rockers

Illustrated or Described

Phoenix Chair Company	222–235
Empire Chair Company	194–195
Milne Chair Company	207

—Seat Rockers, Windsor
  See Windsor Rockers, Fibre Seat

Fiddle Back Chairs
See Chairs, Fiddle Back

Fireplace
—Andirons
  See Dog Irons
—Grate Baskets
  See Grate Baskets

—Screens

Mentioned Only

Century Furniture Company	92
Furst Bros. & Company	78
St. Johns Table Company	236

Fireside
—Baskets for Fuel, Reed and Fibre
  See Reed and Fibre Fuel Baskets, Fireside
—Benches

Illustrated or Described

Conants' Sons, Inc., F. H.	192

Mentioned Only

Decker, Inc., Isaac C.	96
Delker Bros. Mfg. Co.	97
Empire Chair Company	194–195
Fenske Bros.	99

Jamestown Lounge Company	105
Kiel Furniture Company	208–215
Levin Bros., Inc.	111
Sikes Chair Company	238
Sultan & Company, William	132
Tauber Parlor Furn. Co.	402 (Z3)

—Bookcases

Mentioned Only

Udell Works, Inc.	419 (Z1)

—Chairs

Illustrated or Described

Buffalo Lounge Company	394 (Z1)
Conants' Sons, Inc., F. H.	192
Delker Bros. Mfg. Co.	97
Dunbar Furniture Mfg. Co.	98
Furniture City Uph. Co.	104
Gunlocke Chair Co., W. H.	401 (Z1)
Harden Company, Frank S.	108–109
Indianapolis Chair & Furn. Co.	152
Phoenix Chair Company	222–235
Poston Mfg. Co., B. C.	401 (Z3)

Mentioned Only

Chittenden & Eastman Company	377
Conant-Ball Company	191
Empire Chair Company	194–195
Fenske Bros.	99
Fullerton Furniture Factories	103
Jamestown Lounge Company	105
Levin Bros., Inc.	111
Sikes Chair Company	238
Spencer Duffy Company	125–127
Sultan & Company, William	132
Tauber Parlor Furn. Co.	402 (Z3)
Wellsville Upholstering Co.	423 (Z1)
Yeager Furniture Co.	431 (Z1)

—Rockers

Mentioned Only

American Parlor Furniture Co.	91
Wellsville Upholstering Co.	431 (Z1)
Fenske Bros.	99

Fixtures
—Davenport Bed
  See Davenport Bed Fixtures
—Lighting
  See Lighting Fixtures

Flag Seat Rockers
See Rockers, Flag Seat

Flip Top Tables

Mentioned Only

Conant-Ball Company	191
Davis-Birely Table Company	193
Indianapolis Chair & Furn. Co.	152
Kiel Furniture Co.	208–215
St. Johns Table Company	236

Florentine Chairs, Adjustable
See Chairs, Adjustable, Florentine

Floor Coverings
See Carpets and Rugs

Folding Chairs

Mentioned Only

Chittenden & Eastman Company	377
Crocker Chair Company	137

—Cots, Metal
  See Metal Folding Cots
—Tables, Banquet
  See Banquet Tables, Folding
—Tables, Console
  See Console Tables, Folding
—Trays and Stands
  See Trays and Stands, Folding

Footstools and Uttomans
See Also Reed and Fibre Footstools and Ottomans

Illustrated or Described

Decker, Inc., Isaac C.	96
Empire Chair Company	194–195
Field & Company, Marshall	100–101
Harden Company, Frank S.	108–109
Karpen & Bros., S.	112–119
Phoenix Chair Company	222–235
Poston Mfg. Co., B. C.	401 (Z3)
Streit Mfg. Co., C. F.	130–131
Tauber Parlor Furn. Co.	402 (Z3)
Wellsville Upholstering Co.	423 (Z1)
Modern	112–119

Mentioned Only

Conant-Ball Company	191
Conants' Sons, Inc., F. H.	192
Crocker Chair Company	137
Delker Bros. Mfg. Co.	97
Dunbar Furn. Mfg. Co.	98
Fenske Bros.	99
Franklin Furniture Co.	102
Furniture City Upholstery Co.	104
Globe Parlor Furn. Co.	106–107
Hebenstreit's, Inc.	397 (Z3)
Horn & Company, J. P.	410 (Z1)
Irwin Company, Robert W.	275
Jamestown Lounge Company	105
Jamestown Upholstery Co.	110
Levin Bros., Inc.	111
Madden Mfg. Co., John J.	120
Mallen & Company, H. Z.	121
Memphis Furn. Mfg. Co.	303
Michigan Chair Company	162–163
Sikes Chair Company	238
Spencer Duffy Company, Inc.	125–127
Statesville Chair Company	417 (Z1)
Sultan & Company, William	132
Toledo Parlor Furn. Co.	404 (Z1)
Union Brothers	420 (Z1)
Wiener Company, E.	406 (Z3)
Yeager Furniture Company	431 (Z1)

Four
—Piece Bedroom Suites
  See Bedroom Suites, Four Pieces Only
—Poster Beds
  See Beds, Four Poster; See Also Beds, Colonial

Framed and Unframed Tapestries
See Tapestries, Framed and Unframed

End Tables (continued)
—Frames
—For Upholstered Furniture

Illustrated or Described

Doetsch & Bauer Company	375
Green Mfg. Company	376

Mentioned Only

Conant-Ball Company	191
Fullerton Furniture Factories	103
Union Brothers	420 (Z1)

—Photograph
  See Photograph Frames
—Picture
  See Picture Frames

French
—Beds
  See Beds, French
—Benches, Bedroom
  See Bedroom Benches, French
—Buffets, Dining Room
  See Dining Room Buffets, French
—Chairs, Bedroom
  See Bedroom Chairs, French
—Chairs, Dining Room
  See Dining Room Chairs, French
—Chairs, Odd and Occasional
  See Odd and Occasional Chairs, French Type
—Chests of Drawers, Bedroom
  See Bedroom Chests of Drawers, French
—China Cabinets and Closets, Dining Room
  See Dining Room China Cabinets and Closets, French
—Dressers, Bedroom
  See Bedroom Dressers, French
—End Tables
  See End Tables, French
—Night Tables, Bedroom
  See Bedroom Night Tables, French
—Servers and Serving Tables, Dining Room
  See Dining Room Servers and Serving Tables, French
—Suites, Complete, Bedroom
  See Bedroom Suites, Complete (Including Bench, Chair, Rocker and Night Table), French
—Suites, Complete, Dining Room
  See Dining Room Suites, Complete, French
—Tables, Dining Room
  See Dining Room Tables, French
—Vanities, Bedroom
  See Bedroom Vanities, French

French Colonial
—Beds
  See Beds, French Colonial
—Benches, Bedroom
  See Bedroom Benches, French Colonial
—Chairs, Bedroom
  See Bedroom Chairs, French Colonial
—Chifforettes, Bedroom
  See Bedroom Chifforettes, French Colonial
—Dressers, Bedroom
  See Bedroom Dressers, French Colonial
—Mirrors, Bedroom
  See Bedroom Mirrors, French Colonial
—Night Tables, Bedroom
  See Bedroom Night Tables, French Colonial
—Suites, Complete, Bedroom
  See Bedroom Suites, Complete (Including Bench, Chair, Rocker and Night Table), French Colonial
—Vanities, Bedroom
  See Bedroom Vanities, French Colonial

French Peasant
—Chairs, Dining Room
  See Dining Room Chairs, French Peasant
—Cupboards, Dining Room
  See Dining Room Cupboards, French Peasant
—Suites, Complete, Dining Room
  See Dining Room Suites, Complete, French Peasant
—Tables, Dining Room
  See Dining Room Tables, French Peasant

French Provincial Day Beds
See Day Beds, French Provincial

French Renaissance Dining Room Suites, Complete
See Dining Room Suites, Complete, French Renaissance

Frieze, Linen, Silk and Wool
See Drapery and Upholstery Fabrics, Frieze, Linen, Frieze, Silk, and Frieze, Wool

Fuel Baskets
—Fireplace or Grate
  See Grate Baskets
—Fireside, for Fuel, Reed and Fibre
  See Reed and Fibre Fuel Baskets, Fireside

Furnaces, Parlor
See Parlor Furnaces

Furniture
—And Picture Mouldings
  See Mouldings, Furniture and Picture
—Casters, Glides, Slides and Felt Feet
  See Casters, Glides, Slides and Felt Feet

—Forwarding Service

Illustrated or Described

Jamestown Furniture Market Assn.	387

—Frames
  See Frames for Upholstered Furniture

—Legs

Mentioned Only

Luger Furniture Company	399 (Z3)

G

Garden and Lawn Fences and Gates
See Fences and Gates, Lawn and Garden

Gas Ranges
See Kitchen Ranges

Gateleg Tables

Illustrated or Described

Crocker Chair Company	137
Elite Furniture Company	146
Furniture Shops	160–161
Hannahs Mfg. Co.	197
Imperial Furniture Company	198–205
Keystone Table Company	411 (Z1)

Gateleg Tables (*continued*)
Rockford Peerless Furniture Company........168–171
Seaburg Mfg. Co...........................416 (Z1)
COLONIAL (Early American)................160–161
EXTENSION...........................146; 198–205

Mentioned Only
Aulsbrook & Jones Furniture Co............... 242
Baker Furniture Factories, Inc................. 243
Bay View Furniture Company...............393 (Z3)
Chittenden & Eastman Company................ 377
Conant-Ball Company........................ 191
Curtiss & Son, Wm. P.....................399 (Z1)
Davis-Birely Table Co........................ 193
Hastings Table Company...................150–151
Lassahn Furniture Company.................. 154
Luger Furniture Company..................399 (Z3)
Mersman Bros. Corp.......................216–221
St. Johns Table Company..................... 236
Steul & Sons, Henry C....................... 348
Virginia Table Company...................362–363

EXTENSION 150–151; 154; 168–171; 191; 197; 236; 242; 348; 377; 399 (Z3); 431 (1)

Gates and Fences, Lawn and Garden
See **Fences and Gates, Lawn and Garden**

Gauzes
See **Drapery and Upholstery Fabrics, Gauzes**

Genuine Needlepoint
See **Drapery and Upholstery Fabrics, Needlepoint,** GENUINE

Georgian
——**Arm Chairs, Upholstered**
See **Arm Chairs, Upholstered,** GEORGIAN
——**Davenports and Sofas**
See **Davenports and Sofas,** GEORGIAN

Glass
——**Top Tables**
See **Tables,** GLASS TOP
——**Tops for Desks**

Mentioned Only
Stow-Davis Furniture Co......................76–77

Glassed In Bookcases
See **Bookcases, Glassed In**

Glides, Casters, Slides and Felt Feet
See **Casters, Glides, Slides and Felt Feet**

Gliding Davenports, Metal
See **Metal Gliding Davenports**

Go-Carts, Baby Carriages and Sulkies
See **Baby Carriages, Go-Carts, and Sulkies**

Golf Benches

Mentioned Only
Rustic Hickory Furn. Co...................... 68

Gothic
——**Cabinets**
See **Cabinets, Gothic**
——**Chairs**
See **Chairs, Gothic**

Governor Winthrop Desks
Illustrated or Described
Hemsing Manufacturing Company..........405 (Z1)
Landstrom Furniture Corporation...........290–301
Rockford Chair & Furn. Co................308–313
Rockford Standard Furn. Co................327–331
Skandia Furniture Company.................172–185
Union Furniture Company..................186–187

Mentioned Only
Chittenden & Eastman Company................ 377
Yeager Furniture Company.................431 (Z1)

Grate Baskets

Mentioned Only
Fair Foundry Company....................394 (Z2)

Grates
Illustrated or Described
Fair Foundry Company....................394 (Z2)

Mentioned Only
Knox Stove Works.........................395 (Z2)

Gumwood
Illustrated or Described
Hardwood Manufacturers Institute—Gumwood Service Bureau.......................... 386

H

Hall
——**Chairs, Assembly**
See **Assembly Hall Chairs**
——**Chairs, Home**
Illustrated or Described
Phoenix Chair Company...................222–235

Mentioned Only
Century Furniture Company.................... 92
Chittenden & Eastman Company............... 377
Conant-Ball Company......................... 191
Crocker Chair Company....................... 137
Empire Chair Company.....................194–195
Fenske Bros.................................. 99
Franklin Furniture Co........................ 102
Globe Parlor Furniture Co..................106–107
Gunlocke Chair Co., W. H..................401 (Z1)
Harden Company, Frank S..................108–109
Indianapolis Chair & Furn. Co................ 152
Jamestown Lounge Company................... 105
Mallen & Company, H. Z...................... 121
Sikes Chair Company......................... 238
Union Brothers...........................420 (Z1)
Wellsville Upholstering Co..................423 (Z1)

——**Clocks**
See **Clocks, Hall**

Hall
——**Mirrors**
Illustrated or Described
Chicago Mirror & Art Glass Company.......395 (Z3)

Mentioned Only
Chittenden & Eastman Company............... 377
Conant-Ball Company......................... 191
Furst Bros. & Company........................ 78
Yeager Furniture Company.................431 (Z1)

——**Tables**

Mentioned Only
Conant-Ball Company......................... 191
Crocker Chair Company....................... 137
Davis-Birely Table Company.................. 193
Seaburg Mfg. Co..........................416 (Z1)

Hammock
——**Awnings**

Mentioned Only
Rome Company, Inc..........................70–71

——**Stands, Metal**
See **Metal Hammock Stands**

Hammocks, Couch
See **Couch Hammocks**

Hand
——**And Shaving Mirrors**
See **Mirrors, Hand and Shaving**
——**Loom Needlepoint**
See **Drapery and Upholstery Fabrics, Needlepoint, Hand Loom**

Hanging Bookshelves
See **Bookshelves, Hanging**

Heaters
Illustrated or Described
Fair Foundry Company...................394 (Z2)
Knox Stove Works........................395 (Z2)

Mentioned Only
Malleable Iron Range Co...................... 73

Heppelwhite
——**Beds**
See **Beds,** HEPPELWHITE
——**Benches, Bedroom**
See **Bedroom Benches,** HEPPELWHITE
——**Buffets, Dining Room**
See **Dining Room Buffets,** HEPPELWHITE
——**Chairs**
See **Chairs,** HEPPELWHITE
——**Chairs, Adjustable**
See **Chairs, Adjustable,** HEPPELWHITE
——**Chairs, Arm, Upholstered**
See **Arm Chairs, Upholstered,** HEPPELWHITE
——**Chairs, Bedroom**
See **Bedroom Chairs,** HEPPELWHITE
——**Chairs, Dining Room**
See **Dining Room Chairs,** HEPPELWHITE
——**Chests of Drawers, Bedroom**
See **Bedroom Chests of Drawers,** HEPPELWHITE
——**China Cabinets and Closets, Dining Room**
See **Dining Room China Cabinets and Closets,** HEPPELWHITE
——**Dressers, Bedroom**
See **Bedroom Dressers,** HEPPELWHITE
——**Night Tables, Bedroom**
See **Bedroom Night Tables,** HEPPELWHITE
——**Servers and Serving Tables, Dining Room**
See **Dining Room Servers and Serving Tables,** HEPPELWHITE
——**Suites, Complete, Bedroom, Including Bench, Chair, Rocker and Night Table**
See **Bedroom Suites, Complete (Including Bench, Chair, Rocker and Night Table),** HEPPELWHITE
——**Suites, Complete, Dining Room**
See **Dining Room Suites, Complete,** HEPPELWHITE
——**Tables, Dining Room**
See **Dining Room Tables,** HEPPELWHITE
——**Vanities, Bedroom**
See **Bedroom Vanities,** HEPPELWHITE

High Chairs, Children's
See **Children's High Chairs**

High Back Chairs (*See Also* **Arm Chairs, Upholstered,** HIGH BACK, **Reed and Fibre High Back Chairs, Windsor Chairs,** HIGH BACK)
Illustrated or Described
Brandts Furniture Co.....................394 (Z3)
Century Furniture Company.................. 92
Michigan Chair Company..................162–163
ITALIAN...................................162–163

Mentioned Only
American Parlor Furniture Co................. 91
Dunbar Furniture Mfg. Co.................... 98
Fullerton Furniture Factories................. 103
Globe Parlor Furniture Co..................106–107

Highboys
Illustrated or Described
Berkey & Gay Furniture Company...........248–251
Colonial Desk Company....................138–141
Continental Furniture Co..................260–261
Davis Furn. Corp............................ 262
Hemsing Manufacturing Co................405 (Z1)
Mechanics Furniture Co...................... 155
Skandia Furniture Company................172–185
Statton Furn. Mfg. Co.....................418 (Z1)
West Michigan Furniture Company..........284–285
Wilson Furn. Co., Inc.........407 (Z3) and 430 (Z1)
CHIPPENDALE..............................405 (Z1)
COLONIAL................138–141; 172–185; 286–287

Mentioned Only
Baker Furniture Factories, Inc................ 243
Charlotte Furniture Co....................... 258
Chittenden & Eastman Company............... 377
Huntley Furn. Co., B. F...................... 274
Karges Furniture Company................... 280
Memphis Furn. Mfg. Co...................... 303
Morganton Furniture Company................ 304
Nicholson-Kendle Furniture Co............... 269
Norquist Co., A. C........................... 305
Statesville Furniture Co...................... 346
Steul & Sons, Henry C........................ 348
Stickley, L. & J. G. & Stickley Mfg. Co.......352–353
Tillotson Furniture Corp...................... 358
Udell Works, Inc..........................419 (Z1)
Union Furniture Co........................421 (Z1)
White Furniture Co........................... 365
Williamsport Furniture Co..................429 (Z1)

Home
——**Desk Chairs**
See **Desk Chairs, Home**
——**Desks**
See **Desks, Home**
——**Seats**
See **Seats, Upholstered, Home**

Hooked Rugs
See **Carpets and Rugs,** HOOKED RUGS

Hospital
——**And Institution Furniture**

Mentioned Only
Chittenden & Eastman Company............... 377
Conant-Ball Company......................... 191
Crocker Chair Company....................... 137
Hard Mfg. Co.............................404 (Z1)
Mutschler Bros. Co........................... 74
Rome Company, Inc..........................70–71

——**Beds, Metal**
See **Metal Hospital Beds**

Hot Plates

Mentioned Only
Malleable Iron Range Co...................... 73

ELECTRIC...................................... 73
GAS... 73

Hotel and Club
——**Chairs**
Illustrated or Described
Phoenix Chair Company...................222–235
Spencer-Duffy Co., Inc....................125–127

Mentioned Only
Century Furniture Company................... 92
Colonial Furniture Co.......................93–95
Conant, Ball Company........................ 191
Empire Chair Company....................194–195
Harden Company, Frank S.................108–109
Horn & Company, J. P.....................410 (Z1)
Indianapolis Chair & Furn. Co................ 152
Levin Bros., Inc.............................. 111
Sikes Chair Company......................... 238
Tauber Parlor Furn. Co....................402 (Z3)
Whitney Co., Inc., W. F...................... 240

——**Desks**

Mentioned Only
St. Johns Table Co........................... 236

——**Furniture**
Illustrated or Described
Spencer-Duffy Company, Inc...............125–127

Mentioned Only
Buffalo Lounge Company...................394 (Z1)
Chittenden & Eastman Company............... 377
Colonial Furniture Company.................93–95
Conant, Ball Company........................ 191
Continental Furniture Co..................260–261
Crocker Chair Company....................... 137
Davis-Birely Table Co........................ 193
Dunbar Furniture Mfg. Co..................... 98
Furniture City Uph. Co....................... 104
Gunlocke Chair Co., W. H..................401 (Z1)
Hastings Table Co.........................150–151
Jamestown Lounge Company................... 105
Jamestown Upholstery Co., Inc................ 110
Levin Bros., Inc.............................. 111
Limbert Co., Charles P....................... 281
Luger Furniture Co........................399 (Z3)
Statesville Furn. Co.......................... 346
Sultan & Company, William................... 132
Wellsville Upholstering Co..................423 (Z1)
White Furniture Co........................... 365
Wiener Company, E........................406 (Z3)

——**Furniture, Reed and Fibre**
See **Reed and Fibre Hotel and Club Furniture**
——**Tables** (*See Also* **Banquet Table Tops** *and* **Banquet Tables, Folding**)

Mentioned Only
Chittenden & Eastman Company............... 377
Davis-Birely Table Co........................ 193
Phoenix Chair Co..........................222–235
St. Johns Table Co........................... 236

Houses, Summer
See **Summer Houses**

Howlett Chairs
Illustrated or Described
Spencer-Duffy Company, Inc...............125–127

Humidors (*See Also* **Smokers' Cabinets and Stands**)
Illustrated or Described
Griffith Furniture Works...................... 147
Lassahn Furniture Company................... 154

Mentioned Only
Chittenden & Eastman Company............... 377
Furniture Shops............................160–161
Imperial Furniture Co......................198–205

Hutch Cabinets
Illustrated or Described
Rockford Peerless Furn. Co.................168–171
ENGLISH..................................168–171
SHERATON.................................168–171

Hutch Type Servers and Serving Tables, Dining Room
See **Dining Room Servers and Serving Tables,** HUTCH TYPE

I

Ice Boxes
See **Refrigerators**

Imported Rugs
See **Carpets and Rugs,** IMPORTED RUGS

India Prints
See **Drapery and Upholstery Fabrics, India Prints**

Infants' Furniture (*See Also* Nursery Furniture)
  Mentioned Only
    Conant, Ball Company........................ 191
    Memphis Furniture Mfg. Co.................. 303
——High Chairs
    See Children's High Chairs
Institution and Hospital Furniture
    See Hospital and Institution Furniture
In-the-White
——Chairs, Breakfast Room
    See Breakfast Room Chairs, In-the-White
——Chairs, Ladder Back
    See Ladder Back Chairs, In-the-White
——Chairs, Rush Seat
    See Rush Seat Chairs, In-the-White
——Chairs, Windsor
    See Windsor Chairs, In-the-White
——Sets, Breakfast Room
    See Breakfast Room Sets, In-the-White
——Tables, Breakfast Room
    See Breakfast Room Tables, In-the-White
Invalids' Bedside Tables
  Mentioned Only
    Chittenden & Eastman Company................ 377
    Tillotson Furniture Corp.................... 358
——Trays and Stands
    See Trays and Stands, Invalids'
Iron Console Tables
    See Console Tables, Wrought Iron
Ironing Boards
  Mentioned Only
    Chittenden & Eastman Company................ 377
    Curtiss & Son, Wm. P...................399 (Z1)
Italian
——Chairs
    See Chairs, Italian
——Chairs, High Back
    See High Back Chairs, Italian
——Chairs, High Back, Arm, Upholstered
    See Arm Chairs, Upholstered, High Back Italian
——Cabinets
    See Cabinets, Italian
Italian Renaissance
——Chairs
    See Chairs, Italian Renaissance
——Cedar Chests
    See Cedar Chests, Italian Renaissance
——Suites, Complete, Dining Room
    See Dining Room Suites, Complete, Italian Renais-
      sance
——Tables
    See Tables, Italian Renaissance
——Tables, Coffee
    See Coffee Tables, Italian Renaissance

J

Jacobean
——Buffets, Dining Room
    See Dining Room Buffets, Jacobean
——Cabinets
    See Cabinets, Jacobean
——Cedar Chests
    See Cedar Chests, Jacobean
——Chairs, Dining Room
    See Dining Room Chairs, Jacobean
——China Cabinets and Closets, Dining Room
    See Dining Room China Cabinets and Closets, Jacobean
——Servers and Serving Tables, Dining Room
    See Dining Room Servers and Serving Tables, Jacobean
——Suites, Complete, Bedroom, Including Bench, Chair, Rocker and Night Table
    See Bedroom Suites, Complete (Including Bench, Chair, Rocker and Night Table), Jacobean
——Suites, Complete, Dining Room
    See Dining Room Suites, Complete, Jacobean
——Table Desks
    See Table Desks, Jacobean
——Tables, Dining Room
    See Dining Room Tables, Jacobean
——Tables, Nests of
    See Nests of Tables, Jacobean
Japanese and Chinese Furniture
  Mentioned Only
    Yeager Furniture Co....................431 (Z1)
Jardineres and Jardinere Stands (*See Also* Reed and Fibre Jardineres and Jardinere Stands)
  Mentioned Only
    Chittenden & Eastman Company................ 377
    Luger Furniture Co.....................399 (Z3)
    Seaburg Manufacturing Company...........416 (21)
John Bunny Chairs
  Illustrated or Described
    Jamestown Upholstery Co., Inc............... 110
  Mentioned Only
    Decker, Inc., Isaac C....................... 96
John Hancock Desks
    See Governor Winthrop Desks
Junior or Small Size
——Buffets, Dining Room
    See Dining Room Buffets, Apartment Size
——China Cabinets and Closets, Dining Room
    See Dining Room China Cabinets and Closets, Apartment Size
——Cupboards, Dining Room
    See Dining Room Cupboards, Apartment Size
——Suites, Complete, Dining Room
    See Dining Room Suites, Complete, Apartment Size
——Tables, Dining Room
    See Dining Room Tables, Apartment Size

K

Kapok Cushions
    See Cushions, Kapok

Kentshah Plain Carpet
    See Carpets and Rugs, Kentshah Plain Carpets
Kettles, Boilers and Cooking Utensils: Cast Iron
  Mentioned Only
    Knox Stove Works.......................395 (Z2)
Kidney Shaped Desks
  Mentioned Only
    Century Furniture Company.................. 92
    Chittenden & Eastman Company............... 377
    Davis-Birely Table Co...................... 193
    Imperial Furniture Co..................198–205
Kindergarten and School Furniture
  Mentioned Only
    Curtiss & Son, Wm. P...................399 (Z1)
    Davis-Birely Table Co...................... 193
    Luger Furniture Co.....................399 (Z3)
    Mutschler Bros. Co......................... 74
    St. Johns Table Company.................... 236
Kitchen
——Cabinet Bases
  Illustrated or Described
    Mutschler Bros. Company.................... 74
——Cabinets
  Illustrated or Described
    Hoosier Mfg. Co............................ 72
    Mutschler Bros. Co......................... 74
    Showers Brothers Co........................ 75
  Mentioned Only
    Chittenden & Eastman Company............... 377
    Globe-Bosse-World Furn. Co................. 273
    Memphis Furn. Mfg. Co...................... 303
——Chairs
  Illustrated or Described
    Phoenix Chair Company.................222–235
  Mentioned Only
    Chittenden & Eastman Company............... 377
    Crocker Chair Company...................... 137
    Luger Furniture Co.....................399 (Z3)
    Memphis Furn. Mfg. Co...................... 303
    Mutschler Bros. Co......................... 74
    Standard Chair Company..................... 239
    Tell City Chair Company................403 (Z3)
    Thomasville Chair Co....................... 349
    Whitney Co., Inc., W. F.................... 240
——Clocks
    See Clocks, Kitchen
——Closets
  Illustrated or Described
    Hoosier Mfg. Co............................ 72
    Mutschler Bros. Co......................... 74
  Mentioned Only
    Globe-Bosse-World Furniture Co............. 273
——Cupboards
  Illustrated or Described
    Mutschler Bros. Company.................... 74
  Mentioned Only
    Globe-Bosse-World Furniture Co............. 273
    Memphis Furn. Mfg. Co...................... 303
——Racks for Utensils
  Illustrated or Described
    Domes of Silence, Inc...................... 134
——Ranges
  Illustrated or Described
    Fair Foundry Company...................394 (Z2)
    Knox Stove Works.......................395 (Z2)
    Malleable Iron Range Co.................... 73
    Coal-Wood.........................73; 394 (Z2); 395 (Z2)
    Combination Coal, Wood and Gas 73; 394 (Z2); 395 (Z2)
    Electric 73
——Safes
  Mentioned Only
    Chittenden & Eastman Company............... 377
    Globe-Bosse-World Furniture Co............. 273
    Memphis Furn. Mfg. Co...................... 303
——Stools and Stepladders
  Mentioned Only
    Chittenden & Eastman Company............... 377
    Crocker Chair Company...................... 137
    Hoosier Mfg. Co............................ 72
    Standard Chair Company..................... 239
    Tell City Chair Company................403 (Z3)
    Thomasville Chair Co....................... 349
——Tables
  Illustrated or Described
    Curtiss & Son, Wm. P...................399 (Z1)
    Mutschler Bros. Co......................... 74
  Mentioned Only
    Crocker Chair Company...................... 137
    Luger Furniture Co.....................399 (Z3)
    Memphis Furniture Mfg. Co.................. 303
Knock-Down Chairs
  Mentioned Only
    Standard Chair Company..................... 239

L

Lace, Net, and Novelty Curtains
    See Curtains, Lace, Net, and Novelty
Ladder Back
——Beds
    See Beds, Ladder Back
——Chairs
  Illustrated or Described
    Colonial Furniture Co...................93–95
    Conant-Ball Company........................ 191

Empire Chair Company...................194–195
Karpen & Bros., S......................112–119
Milne Chair Company........................ 207
Phoenix Chair Company..................222–235
Tell City Chair Company................403 (Z3)
Whitney Co., Inc., W. F.................... 240
In-the-White...........................403 (Z3)
  Mentioned Only
    Crocker Chair Company...................... 137
——Day Beds
    See Day Beds, Ladder Back
——Rockers
  Illustrated or Described
    Phoenix Chair Company..................222–235
Ladies' Desks
  Illustrated or Described
    Colonial Desk Company..................138–141
    Rockford Chair & Furn. Co..............308–313
    Rockford Peerless Furn. Co.............168–171
    Rockford Standard Furn. Co.............327–331
    Skandia Furniture Company..............172–185
  Mentioned Only
    Chittenden & Eastman Company............... 377
    Davis-Birely Table Co...................... 193
    Hastings Table Company.................150–151
    Indianapolis Chair & Furn. Co.............. 152
    Landstrom Furniture Corporation........290–301
    Lassahn Furniture Company.................. 154
    Mechanics Furn. Co......................... 155
    Seaburg Mfg. Co........................416 (Z1)
    Steul & Sons, Henry C...................... 348
    Union Furniture Co.....................186–187
    Yeager Furniture Co....................431 (Z1)
Lamp Shades and Stands
  Mentioned Only
    Huntley Furniture Co., B. F................ 274
    Rockford Peerless Furn. Co.............168–171
    Stewartstown Furn. Co..................350–351
    Ypsilanti Reed Furn. Co.................... 135
Lamps (*See Also* Reed and Fibre Lamps)
  Illustrated or Described
    Rockford Peerless Furniture Company.....168–171
  Mentioned Only
    Chittenden & Eastman Company............... 377a
Lawn and Garden Fences and Gates
    See Fences and Gates, Lawn and Garden
Lawn and Porch (*See Also* Reed and Fibre Lawn Furniture)
——Beds
  Mentioned Only
    Rustic Hickory Furn. Co.................... 68
——Chairs
  Illustrated or Described
    Rustic Hickory Furniture Co................ 68
  Mentioned Only
    Chittenden & Eastman Company............... 377
    Tell City Chair Company................403 (Z3)
——Chaise Lounges
  Illustrated or Described
    Rustic Hickory Furniture Co................ 68
——Dressers
  Mentioned Only
    Rustic Hickory Furn. Co.................... 68
——Rockers
  Illustrated or Described
    Rustic Hickory Furniture Co................ 68
  Mentioned Only
    Tell City Chair Company................403 (Z3)
——Settees
  Illustrated or Described
    Rustic Hickory Furniture Co................ 68
——Swings (*See Also* Reed and Fibre Lawn and Porch Swings)
  Illustrated or Described
    Anchor Spring & Bedding Co.............393 (Z2)
    Rustic Hickory Furniture Co................ 68
  Mentioned Only
    Hard Mfg. Co...........................404 (Z1)
——Tables
  Illustrated or Described
    Rustic Hickory Furniture Co................ 68
  Mentioned Only
    Chittenden & Eastman Company............... 377
    Yeager Furniture Co....................431 (Z1)
Lawson
——Arm Chairs, Upholstered
    See Arm Chairs, Upholstered, Lawson
——Davenports and Sofas
    See Davenports and Sofas, Lawson Type
——Living Room Suites
    See Living Room Suites, Lawson Type
——Love Seats
    See Love Seats, Lawson Type
Leather
——Slip Seat Chairs
  Mentioned Only
    Empire Chair Company..................194–195
    Indianapolis Chair & Furn. Co............. 152
    Louisville Chair & Furn. Co............396 (Z2)
    Statesville Chair Company..............417 (Z1)
——Upholstered Chairs
  Illustrated or Described
    Berkey & Gay Furniture Company.........248–251
    Horn & Company, J. P...................410 (Z1)
    Karpen & Bros., S......................112–119
    Sikes Chair Company........................ 238
    Spencer-Duffy Co., Inc.................125–127
  Mentioned Only
    American Parlor Furniture Co............... 91
    Chittenden & Eastman Company............... 377
    Crocker Chair Company...................... 137

Leather
——Upholstered Chairs *(continued)*
Mentioned Only
Decker, Inc., Isaac C. 96
Empire Chair Company 194–195
Fenske Bros 99
Furniture City Upholstery Co 104
Jamestown Lounge Company 105
Jamestown Upholstery Co., Inc 110
Levin Bros., Inc 111
Sikes Chair Company 238
Sultan & Co., William 132
Tauber Parlor Furniture Co 402 (Z3)
Toledo Parlor Furn. Co 404 (Z3)
Wellsville Upholstering Co 423 (Z1)
Wiener Company, E 406 (Z3)

——Upholstered Davenports
Illustrated or Described
Karpen & Bros., S. 112–119
Spencer-Duffy Company, Inc 125–127

——Upholsterers'
Illustrated or Described
Eagle-Ottawa Leather Company 83

Legs, Furniture
See **Furniture Legs**

Library
——Chairs
Mentioned Only
Conant, Ball Company 191
Fenske Bros 99
Gunlocke Chair Co., W. H 401 (Z1)
Harden Company, Frank S 108–109
Jamestown Lounge Company 105
Sikes Chair Company 238
Yeager Furniture Company 431 (Z1)

——Desks (*See Also* **Table Desks**)
Mentioned Only
Century Furniture Company 92
Chittenden & Eastman Company 377
Gunn Furniture Co 396 (Z3)
Hastings Table Company 150–151
Lassahn Furniture Company 154
Luger Furniture Co 399 (Z3)
Peterson Art Furn. Co 164
Rockford Standard Furn. Co 327–331
Steul & Sons, Henry C 348
Tillotson Furn. Corp 358

——Tables (*See Also* **Reed and Fibre Library Tables**)
Illustrated or Described
Hemsing Mfg. Co 405 (Z1)
Keystone Table Co 411 (Z1)
Chippendale 405 (Z1)
Mentioned Only
Athens Table & Mfg. Co 190
Crocker Chair Company 137
Davis-Birely Table Co 193
Elite Furniture Co 146
Florence Table & Mfg. Co 271
Hannahs Mfg. Co 197
Hastings Table Company 150–151
Indianapolis Chair & Furn. Co 152
Kiel Furniture Co 208–215
Lassahn Furniture Company 154
Mallen & Co., H. Z 121
Luger Furniture Co 399 (Z3)
Memphis Furn. Mfg. Co 303
Mersman Bros. Corp 216–221
Peterson Art Furn. Co 164
Seaburg Mfg. Co 416 (Z1)
St. Johns Table Company 236
Extension 152; 190; 236; 399 (Z3); 416 (Z1)

Lighting Fixtures
Mentioned Only
Chicago Mirror & Art Glass Co 395 (Z3)

Linen
——Cabinets and Chests
Mentioned Only
Charlotte Furniture Co 258
Colonial Desk Company 138–141
——Frieze
See **Drapery and Upholstery Fabrics, Frieze, Linen**
——Velour
See **Drapery and Upholstery Fabrics, Velour, Linen**

Linoleum
See **Carpets and Rugs,** Linoleum
——Cement and Paste
See **Carpets and Rugs, Linoleum Cement and Paste**

Living Room
——And Dining Room Tables Combined
See **Tables,** Combination Living Room and Dining Room
——Benches
Illustrated or Described
Conant-Ball Company 191
Decker, Inc., Isaac C. 96
Harden Company, Frank S. 108–109
Imperial Furniture Co 198–205
Indianapolis Chair & Furn. Co 152
Michigan Chair Company 162–163
Spencer-Duffy Company, Inc 125–127
William and Mary 162–163
Mentioned Only
American Parlor Furniture Co 91
Chittenden & Eastman Company 377
Delker Bros. Mfg. Co 97
Dunbar Furn. Mfg. Co 98
Fenske Bros 99
Field & Company, Marshall 100–101
Franklin Furniture Co 102
Fullerton Furniture Factories 103
Furniture City Upholstery Co 104
Globe Parlor Furniture Co 106–107
Horn & Company, J. P 410 (Z1)
Indianapolis Chair & Furn. Co 152
Irwin Company, Robert W 275
Jamestown Lounge Company 105
Levin Bros., Inc 111
Mallen & Company, H. Z 121
Memphis Furn. Mfg. Co 303
Michigan Chair Company 162–163
Sikes Chair Company 238
Stickley, L. & J. G. & Stickley Mfg. Co 352–353

Living Room
——Benches *(continued)*
Mentioned Only
Sultan & Company, William 132
Tauber Parlor Furn. Co 402 (Z3)
Toledo Parlor Furn. Co 404 (Z3)
Union Brothers 420 (Z1)
Wellsville Upholstering Co 423 (Z1)
——Cabinets
Illustrated or Described
Berkey & Gay Furniture Company 248–251
Century Furniture Company 92
Imperial Furniture Company 198–205
Rockford Peerless Furn. Co 168–171
Hutch Type 168–171
Mentioned Only
Furniture Shops 160–161
Hastings Table Co 150–151
Indianapolis Chair & Furn. Co 152
Irwin Company, Robert W 275
Lassahn Furniture Company 154
Memphis Furn. Mfg. Co 303
Yeager Furniture Co 431 (Z1)
——Suites (*See Also* **Cane Living Room Suites**)
Illustrated or Described
Brandts Furniture Co 394 (Z3)
Decker, Inc., Isaac C. 96
Dunbar Furniture Mfg. Co 98
Fenske Bros 99
Field & Company, Marshall 100–101
Fullerton Furniture Factories 103
Furniture City Uph. Co 104
Globe Parlor Furniture Co 106–107
Horn & Company, J. P 410 (Z1)
Jamestown Lounge Company 105
Jamestown Upholstery Co., Inc 110
Karpen & Bros., S 112–119
Levin Bros., Inc 111
Madden Mfg. Co., John J 120
Northfield Company 122–123
Phoenix Chair Company 222–235
Poston Mfg. Co., B. C 401 (Z3)
Spencer-Duffy Company, Inc 125–127
Sultan & Company, William 132
Tauber Parlor Furniture Co 402 (Z3)
Toledo Parlor Furn. Co 404 (Z3)
Chippendale 112–119
Colonial (Early American) 132
Cromwellian 112–119
French Provincial 112–119
Italian 112–119
Lawson Type 100–101
Louis XV 402 (Z3)
Louis XVI 132
Modern 112–119; 222–235
Venetian 112–119
Virginia Type 106–107
Mentioned Only
American Parlor Furniture Co 91
Buffalo Lounge Company 394 (Z1)
Franklin Furn. Co 102
Michigan Chair Company 162–163
Pullman Couch Company 128–129
Showers Brothers Company 336–341
Union Brothers 420 (Z1)
——Tables (*See Also* **Reed and Fibre Living Room Tables**)
Illustrated or Described
Hannahs Mfg. Co 197
Imperial Furniture Co 198–205
Mentioned Only
Irwin Company, Robert W 275
Memphis Furn. Mfg. Co 303

Lodge Furniture
Illustrated or Described
Spencer-Duffy Company, Inc 125–127
Mentioned Only
Dunbar Furn. Mfg. Co 98
Furniture City Uph. Co 104
Jamestown Lounge Company 105
Levin Bros., Inc 111
Wiener Company, E 406 (Z3)

Louis XIV Cabinets
See **Cabinets, Louis XIV**

Louis XV
——Beds
See **Beds,** Louis XV
——Benches, Bedroom
See **Bedroom Benches,** Louis XV
——Chairs
See **Chairs,** Louis XV
——Chairs, Bedroom
See **Bedroom Chairs,** Louis XV
——Chiffonettes, Bedroom
See **Bedroom Chiffonettes,** Louis XV
——Dressers, Bedroom
See **Bedroom Dressers,** Louis XV
——Dressing Tables, Bedroom
See **Bedroom Dressing Tables,** Louis XV
——Love Seats
See **Love Seats,** Louis XV
——Mirrors, Bedroom
See **Bedroom Mirrors,** Louis XV
——Night Tables, Bedroom
See **Bedroom Night Tables,** Louis XV
——Suites, Complete, Bedroom, Including Bench, Chair Rocker and Night Table
See **Bedroom Suites Complete (Including Bench, Chair, Rocker, and Night Table)** Louis XV
——Suites, Living Room
See **Living Room Suites,** Louis XV

Louis XVI
——Cedar Chests
See **Cedar Chests,** Louis XVI
——Chairs
See **Chairs,** Louis XVI
——Chairs, Arm, Upholstered
See **Arm Chairs, Upholstered,** Louis XVI
——Chairs, Bedroom
See **Bedroom Chairs,** Louis XVI
——Davenports and Sofas
See **Davenports and Sofas,** Louis XVI
——Day Beds
See **Day Beds,** Louis XVI
——Living Room Suites
See **Living Room Suites,** Louis XVI

Lounges
——Chaise
See **Chaise Lounges**
——Chaise, Reed and Fibre
See **Reed and Fibre Chaise Lounges**

Lounging Chairs, Easy
See **Easy Lounging Chairs**

Love Seats
Illustrated or Described
Buffalo Lounge Company 394 (Z1)
Fullerton Furniture Factories 103
Globe Parlor Furniture Co 106–107
Harden Company, Frank S 108–109
Horn & Company, J. P 410 (Z1)
Karpen & Bros., S 112–119
Mallen & Company, H. Z 121
Sultan & Company, William 132
Lawson 410 (Z1)
Louis XV 132
Modern 112–119
Queen Anne 112–119
Mentioned Only
American Parlor Furn. Co 91
Century Furniture Company 92
Conants' Sons, Inc., F. H 192
Dunbar Furniture Mfg. Co 98
Fenske Bros 99
Field & Company, Marshall 100–101
Franklin Furniture Co 102
Hebenstreit's, Inc 397 (Z3)
Irwin Company, Robert W 275
Jamestown Lounge Company 105
Levin Bros., Inc 111
Michigan Chair Company 162–163
Spencer-Duffy Company, Inc 125–127
Tauber Parlor Furniture Co 402 (Z3)
Toledo Parlor Furn. Co 404 (Z3)
Wiener Company, E 406 (Z3)
Wellsville Upholstering Co 423 (Z1)
Yeager Furniture Co 431 (Z1)

Low Back Chairs
Mentioned Only
Globe Parlor Furniture Co 106–107

Lowboys
Illustrated or Described
Colonial Desk Company 138–141
West Michigan Furn. Co 286–287
Colonial 138–141; 286–287
Mentioned Only
Joerns Bros. Furn. Co 277
Karges Furniture Company 280
Nicholson-Kendle Furniture Co 269
Statesville Furniture Co 346
Statton Furn. Mfg. Co 418 (Z1)
Stewartstown Furn. Co 350–351
Stickley, L. & J. G. & Stickley Mfg. Co 352–353
Tillotson Furniture Corp 358
Union Furniture Co 421 (Z1)
Widdicomb Company, John 366

Lowboy Cedar Chests, Colonial
See **Cedar Chests,** Colonial Lowboy

Luggage Racks and Stands
Mentioned Only
Chittenden & Eastman Company 377
Crocker Chair Company 137
Davis-Birely Table Co 193
Huntley Furniture Co., B. F 274
Luger Furniture Co 399 (Z3)
Statesville Chair Co 417 (Z1)
White Furniture Co 365

Luncheon, Cafe, and Restaurant
——Chairs
See **Restaurant Chairs**
——Tables
See **Restaurant Tables**

Luxor-Mahogany Chests
See **Chests, Luxor-Mahogany**

M

Magazine Baskets and Carriers
Illustrated or Described
Crocker Chair Company 137
Furniture Shops 160–161
Hannahs Mfg. Co 197
Scheibe, R. R 414 (Z1)
Paalman Furniture Company 400 (Z3)
Canterbury 160–161

Magazine, Newspaper and Book Racks and Stands
See **Book, Magazine, and Newspaper Racks and Stands.** (*See Also* **Reed and Fibre Book, Magazine, and Newspaper Racks and Stands**)

Mahogany
——And Walnut Chests, Cedar Lined
See **Cedar Lined Mahogany and Walnut Chests**
——Chests, Luxor
See **Chests, Luxor-Mahogany**

Mail Advertising Service
See **Direct Mail Advertising Services**

Make-Up and Powder Cases and Tables, Bedroom
See **Bedroom Make-Up and Powder Cases and Tables**

Mansrobes, Bedroom
See **Bedroom Mansrobes**

Mantel Clocks
See **Clocks, Mantel**

Maple, Hard
Illustrated or Described
Northern Hard Maple Manufacturers 388–389

Markets
See **Exhibition Spaces**

Martha Washington Sewing Cabinets and Stands
See **Sewing Cabinets and Stands,** Martha Washington

Mattresses
Illustrated or Described
Anchor Spring & Bedding Co. 393 (Z2)
Mentioned Only
Barcalo Manufacturing Company 393 (Z1)
Chittenden & Eastman Company 377
Hard Manufacturing Co. 404 (Z1)
Northfield Company 122–123

Mayflower or Priscilla Sewing Cabinets and Stands
See **Sewing Cabinets and Stands,** PRISCILLA OR MAYFLOWER

Medicine Cabinets, Bathroom
See **Bathroom, Medicine Cabinets**

Metal
——Beds
Illustrated or Described
Barcalo Manufacturing Company 393 (Z1)
Foster Bros. Mfg. Co. 69
Rome Company, Inc. 70–71
Mentioned Only
Chittenden & Eastman Company 377
Hard Mfg. Co. 404 (Z1)

——Costumers
Illustrated or Described
Hard Mfg. Co. 404 (Z1)
Mentioned Only
Chittenden & Eastman Company 377

——Couches
Mentioned Only
Barcalo Manufacturing Co. 393 (Z1)
Rome Company, Inc. 70–71

——Cribs
Illustrated or Described
Barcalo Manufacturing Co. 393 (Z1)
Foster Bros. Mfg. Co. 69
Hard Mfg. Co. 404 (Z1)
Mentioned Only
Rome Company, Inc. 70–71

——Day Beds
Illustrated or Described
Rome Company, Inc. 70–71

——Divans
Mentioned Only
Rome Company, Inc. 70–71

——Folding Cots
Illustrated or Described
Anchor Spring & Bedding Company 393 (Z2)
Mentioned Only
Chittenden & Eastman Company 377
Rome Company, Inc. 70–71

——Gliding Davenports
Illustrated or Described
Rome Company, Inc. 70–71

——Hammock Stands
Mentioned Only
Rome Company, Inc. 70–71

——Hospital Beds
Mentioned Only
Rome Company, Inc. 70–71

——Office Chairs
Mentioned Only
Empire Chair Company 194–195
Standard Chair Company 239

——Office Desks
Illustrated or Described
Stow-Davis Furn. Co. 76–77

——Porch Beds
Mentioned Only
Rome Company, Inc. 70–71

——Sedanettes
Mentioned Only
Rome Company, Inc. 70–71

Mirror
——and Picture Cords
See **Cords, Mirror and Picture**

——Novelties
Mentioned Only
Chicago Mirror & Art Glass Co. 395 (Z3)

——Plate
Mentioned Only
Chicago Mirror & Art Glass Co. 395 (Z3)

Mirrors
See Also **Bathroom Mirrors; Bathroom Cabinet Mirrors; Bedroom Mirrors; Console Mirrors; Dining Room Mirrors; Hall Mirrors, and Window Display Mirrors**
Illustrated or Described
Chicago Mirror & Art Glass Co. 395 (Z3)
Furst Bros. & Company 78
Hemsing Manufacturing Co. 405 (Z1)
Irwin Company, Robert W. 275
West Michigan Furn. Co. 286–287
ADAM 275
CHIPPENDALE 405 (Z1)
CONVEX, COLONIAL 78
MODERN 78
VENETIAN 395 (Z3)
Mentioned Only
Davis-Birely Table Co. 193
Imperial Furniture Co. 198–205
Showers Bros. Co. 336–341
Stickley, L. & J. G. & Stickley Mfg. Co. 352–353
Williamsport Furniture Co. 358
Norquist Company, A. C. 305
CHEVAL 368
HAND & SHAVING 305

Mirrors *(continued)*
Mentioned Only
MODERN 395 (Z3)
PANEL 78
VENETIAN 78; 377

Mission Chairs
Mentioned Only
Whitney Co., Inc., W. F. 240

Models, Ship
See **Ship Models**

Modern
——Beds
See **Beds,** MODERN
——Benches, Bedroom
See **Bedroom Benches,** MODERN
——Buffets, Dining Room
See **Dining Room Buffets,** MODERN
——Chairs, Arm, Upholstered
See **Arm Chairs, Upholstered,** MODERN
——Chairs, Bedroom
See **Bedroom Chairs,** MODERN
——Chairs, Dining Room
See **Dining Room Chairs,** MODERN
——Chests of Drawers, Bedroom
See **Bedroom Chests of Drawers,** MODERN
——China Cabinets and Closets, Dining Room
See **Dining Room China Cabinets and Closets,** MODERN
——Davenports and Sofas
See **Davenports and Sofas,** MODERN
——Dressers, Bedroom
See **Bedroom Dressers,** MODERN
——Dressing Tables, Bedroom
See **Bedroom Dressing Tables,** MODERN
——Mirrors
See **Mirrors,** MODERN
——Night Tables, Bedroom
See **Bedroom Night Tables,** MODERN
——Pictures and Picture Frames
See **Pictures and Picture Frames,** MODERN
——Servers and Serving Tables, Dining Room
See **Dining Room Servers and Serving Tables,** MODERN
——Silver Cabinets, Dining Room
See **Dining Room Silver Cabinets,** MODERN
——Suites Complete, Bedroom, Including Bench, Chair, Rocker, and Night Table
See **Bedroom Suites Complete (Including Bench, Chair, Rocker, and Night Table),** MODERN
——Suites Complete, Dining Room
See **Dining Room Suites Complete,** MODERN
——Suites, Living Room
See **Living Room Suites,** MODERN
——Tables, Dining Room
See **Dining Room Tables,** MODERN
——Vanities, Bedroom
See **Bedroom Vanities,** MODERN

Mohair
See **Drapery and Upholstery Fabrics, Mohair**

Moires
See **Drapery and Upholstery Fabrics, Moires**

Moquettes
See **Drapery and Upholstery Fabrics, Moquettes**

Mouldings Furniture and Picture
Mentioned Only
Furst Bros. & Company 78

Music Cabinets
Mentioned Only
Century Furniture Company 92
Peterson Art Furniture Co. 164

N

Nails, Upholstery
See **Upholstery Nails**

Needlepoint
——Genuine
See **Drapery and Upholstery Fabrics, Needlepoint,** GENUINE
——Hand Loom
See **Drapery and Upholstery Fabrics, Needlepoint,** HAND LOOM

Nests of
——Chairs
Mentioned Only
Whitney Co., Inc., W. F. 240

——Tables
Illustrated or Described
Furniture Shops 160–161
Imperial Furniture Co. 198–205
JACOBEAN 160–161
Mentioned Only
Century Furniture Company 92
Elite Furniture Co. 146
Hastings Table Company 150–151
Paalman Furniture Company 400 (Z3)
St. Johns Table Co. 236
Schoeck Mfg. Co., Inc. 415 (Z1)
Tillotson Furniture Corp. 258
Yeager Furniture Co. 431 (Z1)

Net, Lace, and Novelty Curtains
See **Curtains, Lace, Net, and Novelty**

Newspaper, Book, and Magazine Racks and Stands
See **Book, Magazine and Newspaper Racks and Stands.** *(See Also* **Reed and Fibre Book, Magazine, and Newspaper Racks and Stands)**

Night Tables, Bedroom
See **Bedroom Night Tables**

Novelties, Mirror
See **Mirror Novelties**

Nursery Furniture
Also See **Infants Furniture**
Mentioned Only
Chittenden & Eastman Company. 377
Conant-Ball Company 191
Standard Chair Company 239
Memphis Furniture Mfg. Co. 303

O

Oak
Illustrated or Described
Hardwood Mfrs. Inst., Oak Service Bureau 384–385

Odd Beds
See **Beds, Odd**

Odd and Occasional
——Chairs
Illustrated or Described
Harden Company, Frank S. 108–109
Indianapolis Chair & Furn. Co. 152
Jamestown Lounge Company 105
Karpen & Bros., S. 112–119
Levin Bros., Inc. 111
Louisville Chair & Furn. Co. 396 (Z2)
Mallen & Company, H. Z. 121
Milne Chair Company 207
Northfield Company 122–123
Phoenix Chair Company 222–235
Sikes Chair Company 288
Spencer-Duffy Company, Inc. 125–127
Tauber Parlor Furn. Co. 402 (Z3)
Thomasville Chair Co. 349
Whitney Co., Inc., W. F. 240
FRENCH STYLE 105
SIR CHRISTOPHER WREN 222–235
Mentioned Only
American Parlor Furniture Co. 91
Chittenden & Eastman Company 377
Conant, Ball Company 191
Conants' Sons, Inc., F. H. 192
Decker, Inc., Isaac C. 96
Fenske Bros. 99
Franklin Furniture Co. 102
Fullerton Furniture Factories 103
Globe Parlor Furniture Co. 106–107
Gunlocke Chair Co., W. H. 401 (Z1)
Irwin Company, Robert W. 275
Memphis Furn. Mfg. Co. 303
Pullman Couch Company, Inc. 128–129
Showers Bros. Company 336–341
Steul & Sons, Henry C. 348
Sultan & Company, William 132
Tauber Parlor Furniture Co. 402 (Z3)
Union Brothers 420 (Z1)
Wellsville Upholstering Co. 423 (Z1)
Wiener Company, E. 406 (Z3)

——Rockers
Illustrated or Described
Phoenix Chair Company 222–235
Mentioned Only
Thomasville Chair Company 349

——Tables
See Also **Reed and Fibre Odd and Occasional Tables**
Illustrated or Described
Bay View Furniture Co. 393 (Z3)
Century Furniture Company 92
Conant, Ball Company 191
Davis-Birely Table Co. 193
Furniture Shops 160–161
Hannahs Manufacturing Co. 197
Hastings Table Company 150–151
Imperial Furniture Co. 198–205
Keystone Table Company 411 (Z1)
Kiel Furniture Company 208–215
Lassahn Furniture 154
Mersman Bros., Corp. 216–221
St. Johns Table Company 236
Schoeck Mfg. Co., Inc. 415 (Z1)
DUNCAN PHYFE 160–161; 150–151
Mentioned Only
American Parlor Furn. Co. 91
Athens Table & Mfg. Co. 190
Aulsbrook & Jones Furn. Co. 242
Chittenden & Eastman Company 377
Colonial Desk Company 138–141
Crocker Chair Company 137
Elite Furniture Company 146
Florence Table & Mfg. Co. 271
Hekman Furniture Co. 398 (Z3)
Indianapolis Chair & Furn. Co. 152
Irwin Company, Robert W. 275
Klamer Furn. Corp. 288–289
Luger Furniture Co. 399 (Z3)
Memphis Furn. Mfg. Co. 303
Michigan Chair Company 162–163
Monitor Furniture Co. 288–289
Peterson Art Furn. Co. 164
Seaburg Mfg. Co. 416 (Z1)
Sultan & Company, William 132

Office and Bank
See **Bank and Office.** *(See Also* **Metal Office Chairs)**

Open Shelf Bookcases
See **Bookcases, Open Shelf**

Organ and Piano Benches
See **Piano and Organ Benches**

Oriental Rugs
See **Carpets and Rugs,** ORIENTAL RUGS

Ottomans and Footstools
See **Footstools and Ottomans.** *(See Also* **Reed and Fibre Footstools and Ottomans)**

Oval Axminster Rugs
See **Carpets and Rugs,** AXMINSTER, OVAL

P

Panel Mirrors
See **Mirrors,** PANEL

Paste and Cement for Linoleum
See **Carpets and Rugs, Linoleum Cement and Paste**

Parlor Furnaces
Illustrated or Described
Allen Mfg. Co. 136

Pedestals
  Illustrated or Described
    Seaburg Mfg. Co.........................416 (Z1)
    Conant, Ball Company.......................191

  Mentioned Only
    Chittenden & Eastman Company.............377
    Hannahs Mfg. Co...........................197
    Peterson Art Furn. Co.....................164

Pembroke Tables: DUNCAN PHYFE
  Illustrated or Described
    Furniture Shops........................160-161

Pergolas
  Mentioned Only
    Rustic Hickory Furniture Co...............68

Phonograph and Radio Cabinets
  See Radio and Phonograph Cabinets

Photograph Frames
  Mentioned Only
    Mages Company, Geo. C.....................80
    Furst Bros. & Co..........................78

Piano
——**and Organ Benches**
  Illustrated or Described
    Seaburg Mfg. Co.........................416 (Z1)

  Mentioned Only
    Empire Chair Company...................194-195
    Harden Company, Frank S................108-109
    Michigan Chair Company.................162-163
    Peterson Art Furniture Co.................164
    Seaburg Manufacturing Company..........416 (Z1)
    Sikes Chair Company......................238

——**Scarfs**
  See Drapery and Upholstery Fabrics, Piano Scarfs

Picture
——**and Furniture Mouldings**
  See Mouldings, Furniture and Picture
——**and Mirror Cords**
  See Cords, Mirror and Picture

Pictures and Picture Frames
  Illustrated or Described
    Furst Bros. & Company.......................78
    Mages Company, Geo. C.......................80
    Lesch, Rudolph..............................79
    MODERN.....................................78

  Mentioned Only
    Chittenden & Eastman Company.............377

Pie Crust Top Tables
  Mentioned Only
    Chittenden & Eastman Company.............377
    Crocker Chair Company....................137
    Kiel Furniture Company.................208-215
    Luger Furniture Co....................399 (Z3)

Pier
——**Bookcases**
  Illustrated or Described
    Conant, Ball Company.......................191

  Mentioned Only
    Imperial Furniture Company.............198-205
    Udell Works, Inc......................419 (Z1)

——**Cabinets**
  Illustrated or Described
    Colonial Desk Company...................138-141
    Crocker Chair Company......................137
    Grand Rapids Upholstering Co............252-253
    Hannahs Mfg. Co............................197
    Rockford National Furn. Co..............324-326
    Rockford Peerless Furn. Co..............168-171
    Skandia Furniture Company...............172-185

  Mentioned Only
    Elite Furniture Company..................146
    Michigan Chair Company.................162-163
    Rockford Standard Furn. Co............327-331
    Udell Works, Inc......................419 (Z1)

Placques
  Mentioned Only
    Furst Bros. & Company.....................78

Plain Kentshah Carpet
  See Carpets and Rugs, KENTSHAH PLAIN CARPET

Plush
  See Drapery and Upholstery Fabrics, Plush

Poplins and Reps
  See Drapery and Upholstery Fabrics, Reps and Poplins

Porch
——**And Lawn**
  See Lawn and Porch. (*See Also* Reed and Fibre Lawn and Porch Swings; Reed and Fibre Porch Chairs, and Rockers; and Reed and Fibre Porch Tables)
——**Beds, Metal**
  See Metal Porch Beds
——**Shades**
  Illustrated or Described
    Automatic Shade Company.....................189

Powder and Make-Up Cases and Tables, Bedroom
  See Bedroom Make-Up and Powder Cases and Tables

Princess Type Dressers, Bedroom
  See Bedroom Dressers, Princess Type

Princess or Mayflower Sewing Cabinets and Stands
  See Sewing Cabinets and Stands, PRISCILLA OR MAYFLOWER

Printed Linen
  See Drapery and Upholstery Fabrics, Printed Linen

Pull Up Chairs
  Illustrated or Described
    Phoenix Chair Company..................222-235

  Mentioned Only
    Conants' Sons, Inc., F. H................192

Pulls, Tassel, and Decorative Carvings for Window Shades
  See Window Shades, TASSEL PULLS AND DECORATIVE CARVINGS FOR

Q

Queen Anne
——**Chairs**
  See Chairs, QUEEN ANNE
——**Chairs, Arm, Upholstered**
  See Arm Chairs, Upholstered, QUEEN ANNE
——**Chairs, Adjustable**
  See Chairs, Adjustable, QUEEN ANNE
——**Chairs, Easy Lounging**
  See Easy Lounging Chairs, QUEEN ANNE
——**Chairs, Wing**
  See Wing Chairs, QUEEN ANNE
——**Cedar Chests**
  See Cedar Chests, QUEEN ANNE
——**Davenports and Sofas**
  See Davenports and Sofas, QUEEN ANNE
——**Suites Complete, Dining Room**
  See Dining Room Suites Complete QUEEN ANNE
——**Tables**
  See Tables, QUEEN ANNE
——**Tables, Coffee**
  See Coffee Tables, QUEEN ANNE
——**Tables, Console**
  See Console Tables QUEEN ANNE

R

Racks
——**And Stands, Book, Magazine and Newspaper**
  See Book, Magazine and Newspaper Racks and Stands. (*See Also* Reed and Fibre Book, Magazine and Newspaper Racks and Stands)
——**And Stands, Luggage**
  See Luggage Racks and Stands
——**Book and Davenport Tables Combined**
  See Davenport Tables, BOOK RACK COMBINATION
——**Clothes Closet**
  Illustrated or Described
    Domes of Silence, Inc......................134
——**Clothes Drying**
  Illustrated or Described
    Domes of Silence, Inc......................134
——**Kitchen Utensil**
  See Kitchen Racks for Utensils
——**Shoe**
  See Shoe Racks

Radio
——**and Phonograph Cabinets**
  Mentioned Only
    Chittenden & Eastman Company.............377
——**Benches**
  Mentioned Only
    Decker, Inc., Isaac C.....................96
    Showers Brothers Company.................188
——**Cabinets and Tables**
  Illustrated or Described
    Colonial Desk Company...................138-141
    Marstall Furniture Co., Inc.............397 (Z2)
    Rockford Peerless Furn. Co..............168-171
    Showers Brothers Company...................188

  Mentioned Only
    Athens Table & Manufacturing Co..........190
    Century Furniture Company.................92
    Chittenden & Eastman Company.............377
    Curtiss & Son, Wm. P..................399 (Z1)
    Davis-Birely Table Company...............193
    Hannahs Mfg. Co..........................197
    Hastings Table Company................150-151
    Imperial Furniture Company............198-205
    Lassahn Furniture Co.....................154
    Luger Furniture Company..................399
    Memphis Furn. Mfg. Co....................303
    Mersman Bros. Corporation............216-221
    Peterson Art Furniture Co................164
    St. Johns Table Company..................236
    Seaburg Mfg. Co.......................416 (Z1)
    Shreve Chair Co., Inc....................237
    Tillotson Furniture Corp.................358
    Udell Works, Inc......................419 (Z1)

Rag Rugs, Colonial
  See Carpets and Rugs, COLONIAL RAG RUGS

Rails, Short, Bed Display
  See Bed Short Rails for Displaying Beds

Ramie Velvets
  See Drapery and Upholstery Fabrics, Velvets, RAMIE

Ranges, Kitchen
  See Kitchen Ranges

Reading Chairs
  Illustrated or Described
    Conants, Sons, Inc., F. H..................192
    SPANISH DESIGN............................192

Reed and Fibre
——**Aquariums**
  Mentioned Only
    Ypsilanti Reed Furniture Co..............135

——**Arm Chairs**
  Illustrated or Described
    Karpen & Bros., S.......................112-119
    Northfield Company......................122-123
    Universal Willow & Reed Ware Co., Inc...422 (Z1)

  Mentioned Only
    Ypsilanti Reed Furniture Co..............135

——**Benches**
  Mentioned Only
    Northfield Company....................122-123

——**Bird Cages**
  Mentioned Only
    Ypsilanti Reed Furniture Co..............135
    FERNERY COMBINATION.......................135

——**Book, Magazine and Newspaper Racks and Stands**
  Mentioned Only
    Northfield Company....................122-123
    Ypsilanti Reed Furniture Co..............135

——**Bookcases**
  Mentioned Only
    Northfield Company....................122-123

——**Breakfast Room Tables**
  Mentioned Only
    Ypsilanti Reed Furn. Co..................135

——**Chairs**
  Illustrated or Described
    Karpen & Bros., S.......................112-119
    Ypsilanti Reed Furniture Co................135

——**Chaise Lounges**
  Illustrated or Described
    Karpen & Bros., S.......................112-119

  Mentioned Only
    Northfield Company....................122-123
    Ypsilanti Reed Furn. Co..................135

——**Console Tables**
  Mentioned Only
    Ypsilanti Reed Furn. Co..................135

——**Couches**
  Mentioned Only
    Ypsilanti Reed Furn. Co..................135

——**Davenette Beds**
  Mentioned Only
    Ypsilanti Reed Furn. Co..................135

——**Davenport Bed Suites**
  Illustrated or Described
    Northfield Company......................122-123

  Mentioned Only
    Ypsilanti Reed Furn. Co..................135

——**Davenport Beds**
  Illustrated or Described
    Northfield Company......................122-123

  Mentioned Only
    Ypsilanti Reed Furniture Co..............135

——**Davenport Tables**
  Mentioned Only
    Ypsilanti Reed Furn. Co..................135

——**Davenports and Sofas**
  Illustrated or Described
    Northfield Company......................122-123
    Ypsilanti Reed Furn. Co...................135

——**Day Beds**
  Mentioned Only
    Ypsilanti Reed Furn. Co..................135

——**Desk Chairs**
  Illustrated or Described
    Karpen & Bros., S.......................112-119

  Mentioned Only
    Ypsilanti Reed Furn. Co..................135

——**Desks**
  Illustrated or Described
    Karpen & Bros., S.......................112-119
    Northfield Company......................122-123

  Mentioned Only
    Ypsilanti Reed Furn. Co..................135

——**End Tables**
  Mentioned Only
    Northfield Company....................122-123
    Ypsilanti Reed Furn. Co..................135

——**Ferneries**
  Illustrated or Described
    Karpen & Bros., S.......................112-119

  Mentioned Only
    Northfield Company....................122-123
    Ypsilanti Reed Furn. Co..................135

——**Fuel Baskets, Fireside**
  Mentioned Only
    Ypsilanti Reed Furn. Co..................135

——**Footstools and Ottomans**
  Illustrated or Described
    Karpen & Bros., S.......................112-119

  Mentioned Only
    Northfield Company....................122-123
    Ypsilanti Reed Furn. Co..................135

——**High Back Chairs**
  Illustrated or Described
    Northfield Company......................122-123

——**Hotel and Club Furniture**
  Mentioned Only
    Ypsilanti Reed Furn. Co..................135

——**Jardineres and Jardinere Stands**
  Mentioned Only
    Ypsilanti Reed Furn. Co..................135

——**Lamps**
  Mentioned Only
    Northfield Company....................122-123
    Ypsilanti Reed Furn. Co..................135

——**Lawn and Porch Swings**
  Mentioned Only
    Ypsilanti Reed Furn. Co..................135

——**Lawn Furniture**
  Mentioned Only
    Ypsilanti Reed Furn. Co..................135

Reed and Fibre
——Library Tables
Mentioned Only
Ypsilanti Reed Furn. Co. 135
——Living Room Tables
Mentioned Only
Ypsilanti Reed Furn. Co. 135
——Lounging Chairs
Illustrated or Described
Karpen & Bros., S. 112-119
——Odd and Occasional Tables
Mentioned Only
Northfield Company. 122-123
——Porch Chairs and Rockers
Mentioned Only
Ypsilanti Reed Furn. Co. 135
——Porch Tables
Mentioned Only
Ypsilanti Reed Furn. Co. 135
——Rockers, Upholstered
Illustrated or Described
Northfield Company. 122-123
Ypsilanti Reed Furn. Co. 135
WITH LOOSE CUSHIONS
Mentioned Only
Ypsilanti Reed Furn. Co. 135
——Settees
Illustrated or Described
Universal Willow & Reed Ware Co., Inc. 422 (Z1)
Mentioned Only
Ypsilanti Reed Furn. Co. 135
——Sewing Baskets
Mentioned Only
Ypsilanti Reed Furn. Co. 135
——Sewing Rockers
Mentioned Only
Ypsilanti Reed Furn. Co. 135
——Smokers' Cabinets and Stands
Mentioned Only
Northfield Company. 122-123
Ypsilanti Reed Furn. Co. 135
——Suites
Illustrated or Described
Karpen & Bros., S. 112-119
Universal Willow & Reed Ware Co., Inc. 422 (Z1)
——Sun Room and Sun Porch Furniture
Illustrated or Described
Northfield Company. 122-123
Universal Willow & Reed Ware Co., Inc. 422 (Z1)
Mentioned Only
Memphis Furn. Mfg. Co. 303
Ypsilanti Reed Furn. Co. 135
——Tables
Illustrated or Described
Karpen & Bros., S. 112-119
Northfield Company. 122-123
Universal Willow & Reed Ware Co., Inc. 422 (Z1)
Ypsilanti Reed Furn. Co. 135
——Tabourets
Mentioned Only
Chittenden & Eastman Company. 377
Ypsilanti Reed Furn. Co. 135
——Telephone Cabinets and Stands
Mentioned Only
Northfield Company. 122-123
Ypsilanti Reed Furn. Co. 135
——Theatre Box Chairs
Mentioned Only
Ypsilanti Reed Furn. Co. 135
——Waste Baskets
Mentioned Only
Ypsilanti Reed Furn. Co. 135
Refectory Tables
Mentioned Only
Baker Furniture Factories, Inc. 243
Century Furniture Company. 92
Hastings Table Company. 150-151
Imperial Furniture Co. 198-205
Limbert Company, Charles P. 281
Reflectors, Table
See Table Reflectors
Refrigerators
Mentioned Only
Chittenden & Eastman Company. 377
Reps and Poplins
See Drapery and Upholstery Fabrics, Reps and Poplins
Restaurant
——Chairs
Mentioned Only
Colonial Furniture Co. 93-95
Conant, Ball Company. 191
Sikes Chair Company. 238
Tell City Chair Company. 403 (Z3)
——Stools
Mentioned Only
Chittenden & Eastman Company. 377
——Tables
Illustrated or Described
Gunn Furniture Co. 396 (Z3)
COMPOSITION TOP. 396 (Z3)
Mentioned Only
Colonial Furniture Co. 93-95

Restaurant Tables (continued)
Mentioned Only
Curtiss & Son, Wm. P. 399 (Z1)
Davis-Birely Table Co. 193
Luger Furniture Company. 399 (Z3)
Mutschler Bros. Company. 74
St. Johns Table Company. 236
Tillotson Furniture Corp. 258
Revolving Trays and Stands
See Trays and Stands, REVOLVING
Rocker and Chair Sets
See Chair and Rocker Sets
Rockers
Illustrated or Described
Colonial Furniture Co. 93-95
Empire Chair Company. 194-195
Indianapolis Chair & Furn. Co. 152
Milne Chair Company. 207
Phoenix Chair Company. 222-235
Stickley, L. & J. G. & Stickley Mfg. Co. .. 352-353
Shreve Chair Company. 237
COLONIAL (Early American). 194-195; 352-353
——And Chairs, Cane Back
See Cane Back Chairs and Rockers
——And Chairs, Cane Back and Seat
See Cane Back and Seat Chairs and Rockers
——And Chairs, Cane Seat
See Cane Seat Chairs and Rockers
——And Chairs, Fibre Seat
See Fibre Seat Chairs and Rockers
——And Chairs, Porch, Reed and Fibre
See Reed and Fibre Porch Chairs and Rockers
——And Chairs, Sewing
See Sewing Chairs and Rockers
——Auto Spring Seat
Illustrated or Described
Milne Chair Company. 207
Mentioned Only
Chittenden & Eastman Company. 377
Crocker Chair Company. 137
Harden Company, Frank S. 108-109
Indianapolis Chair & Furn. Co. 152
Shreve Chair Co., Inc. 237
——Bedroom
See Bedroom Rockers
——Cane Back with Loose Cushions
See Cane Back Rockers with Loose Cushions
——Cane Seat with Loose Cushions
See Cane Seat Rockers with Loose Cushions
——Children's
See Children's Rockers
——Fireside
See Fireside Rockers
——Flag Seat
Mentioned Only
Conants' Sons, Inc., F. H. 192
——Ladder Back
See Ladder Back Rockers
——Lawn and Porch
See Lawn and Porch Rockers
——Odd and Occasional
See Odd and Occasional Rockers
——Reed and Fibre, Upholstered
See Reed and Fibre Rockers, Upholstered
——Roll Seat
Mentioned Only
Standard Chair Company. 239
——Sewing, Reed and Fibre
See Reed and Fibre Sewing Rockers
——Upholstered
Illustrated or Described
Empire Chair Company. 194-195
Phoenix Chair Company. 222-235
Indianapolis Chair & Furn. Co. 152
COLONIAL (Early American). 152
Mentioned Only
Chittenden & Eastman Company. 377
Crocker Chair Company. 137
Delker Bros. Mfg. Co. 97
Furniture City Uph. Co. 104
Harden Company, Frank S. 108-109
Horn & Company, J. P. 410 (Z1)
Levin Bros., Inc. 111
Louisville Chair & Furn. Co. 396 (Z2)
Tauber Parlor Furn. Co. 402 (Z3)
Wellsville Upholstering Co. 423 (Z1)
Whitney Co., Inc., W. F. 240
Yeager Furniture Co. 431 (Z1)
——Windsor
See Windsor Rockers
——Wing
See Wing Rockers
——With Loose Cushions
See Also Reed and Fibre Rockers, Upholstered WITH LOOSE CUSHIONS
Mentioned Only
Chittenden & Eastman Company. 377
Delker Bros. Mfg. Co. 97
Furniture City Upholstery Co. 104
Levin Bros., Inc. 111
Tauber Parlor Furn. Co. 402 (Z3)
——Wood
Illustrated or Described
Colonial Furniture Co. 93-95
Empire Chair Company. 194-195
Shreve Chair Co., Inc. 237
Mentioned Only
Conant, Ball Company. 191
Conants' Sons, Inc., F. H. 192
Crocker Chair Company. 137
Harden Company, Frank S. 108-109
Memphis Furn. Mfg. Co. 303
Sikes Chair Company. 238
Standard Chair Company. 239
Roll
——Seat Rockers
See Rockers, Roll Seat
——Top Desks
Mentioned Only
Hekman Furniture Company. 398 (Z3)

Roman Chairs
See Chairs, ROMAN
Rugs and Carpets
See Carpets and Rugs
Rush Seat
——Chairs
Illustrated or Described
Colonial Furniture Co. 93-95
Whitney Co., Inc., W. F. 240
IN-THE-WHITE. 403 (Z3)
Mentioned Only
Baker Furniture Factories, Inc. 243
Century Furniture Company. 92
Chittenden & Eastman Company. 377
Conant, Ball Company. 191
Empire Chair Company. 194-195
Gunlocke Chair Co., W. H. 401 (Z1)
Memphis Furniture Mfg. Co. 303
Michigan Chair Company. 162-163
Sikes Chair Company. 238
Steul & Sons, Henry C. 348
——Rockers
Mentioned Only
Century Furniture Company. 92
Chittenden & Eastman Company. 377

S

Safes, Kitchen
See Kitchen Safes
Sales
——And Display Rooms, Special for Use of Dealers
Peck & Hills Furn. Co. 392
——Special Conductors of
Norton Sales Service, C. S. 374
Satins and Sateens
See Drapery and Upholstery Fabrics, Satins and Sateens
Savonnerie Rugs
See Carpets and Rugs, SAVONNERIE RUGS
School and Kindergarten Furniture
See Kindergarten and School Furniture
Screens, Fireplace
See Fireplace Screens
Seamless
——Axminster Carpets and Rugs
See Carpets and Rugs, AXMINSTER SEAMLESS
——Chenille Carpet
See Carpets and Rugs, SEAMLESS CHENILLE CARPET
——Wilton Carpet
See Carpets and Rugs, WILTON SEAMLESS CARPET
Seats
——Chair, Upholstered
See Chair Seats, Upholstered
——Home, Upholstered
Mentioned Only
Peterson Art Furniture Co. 164
Wellsville Upholstering Co. 423 (Z1)
——Wagon
See Wagon Seats
Secretary
——Cabinets
Mentioned Only
Imperial Furniture Co. 198-205
——Desks
Illustrated or Described
Bay View Furniture Co. 393 (Z3)
Colonial Desk Company. 138-141
Furniture Shops. 160-161
Hekman Furniture Co. 398 (Z3)
Hemsing Manufacturing Company. 405 (Z1)
Imperial Furniture Co. 198-205
Indianapolis Chair & Furn. Co. 152
Landstrom Furniture Corporation. 290-301
Mechanics Furniture Co. 155
Rockford Chair & Furn. Co. 308-313
Rockford Furniture Co. 314-321
Rockford National Furn. Co. 324-326
Rockford Peerless Furn. Co. 168-171
Rockford Standard Furn. Co. 327-331
Skandia Furniture Company. 172-185
Udell Works, Inc. 419 (Z1)
Union Furniture Co. 186-187
BLOCK FRONT. 138-141
CHIPPENDALE. 405 (Z1)
COLONIAL (Early American). 327-331; 186-187
FRENCH PROVINCIAL. 138-141
GOVERNOR WINTHROP. 138-141; 152; 172-185; 186-187; 308-313; 314-321; 324-326; 327-331
MODERN. 314-321
QUEEN ANNE. 138-141
SHERATON. 160-161; 168-171
STRAIGHT FRONT. 138-141
Mentioned Only
Baker Furniture Factories, Inc. 243
Century Furniture Company. 92
Charlotte Furniture Company. 258
Elite Furniture Company. 146
Hastings Table Company. 150-151
Irwin Company, Robert W. 275
Luger Furniture Company. 399 (Z3)
Steul & Sons, Henry C. 348
Yeager Furniture Company. 431 (Z1)
SWELL FRONT. 138-141
Sectional Bookcases
See Bookcases, Sectional
Sedanettes, Metal
See Metal Sedanettes
Semi Vanities, Bedroom
See Bedroom Vanities, Semi
Serving Tables and Cabinets Combined, Breakfast Room
See Breakfast Room Serving Tables and Cabinets Combined
Serving Trays and Stands
See Trays and Stands, SERVING

Trellises
   Mentioned Only
   Rustic Hickory Furn. Co......................... 68

Troughs
——**Book**
   See **Book Troughs**
——**Book and End Tables Combined**
   See **Book Troughs and End Tables, Combined**

Tub Chairs
   Illustrated or Described
   Michigan Chair Company................162–163

Tudor
——**Chairs, Adjustable**
   See **Chairs, Adjustable,** TUDOR
——**Suites, Complete, Dining Room**
   See **Dining Room Suites, Complete,** TUDOR

Tufted Rugs, Hand, European
   See **Carpets and Rugs,** EUROPEAN, HAND TUFTED RUGS

Tuxedo Davenports and Sofas
   See **Davenports and Sofas,** TUXEDO TYPE

Twin Beds
   See **Beds, Twin**

Typewriter
——**Desk Chairs**
   See **Bank and Office Chairs,** TYPEWRITER DESK
——**Desks**
   See **Bank and Office Desks,** TYPEWRITER
——**Tables**
   See **Bank and Office Tables,** TYPEWRITER

U

Unfinished
   See **In-The-White**

Unframed and Framed Tapestries
   See **Tapestries, Framed and Unframed**

Upholstered Furniture Frames
   See **Frames for Upholstered Furniture**

Upholstery
——**And Drapery Fabrics**
   See **Drapery and Upholstery Fabrics**
——**Leather**
   See **Leather, Upholsterers'**

Utensil Racks, Kitchen
   See **Kitchen Racks for Utensils**

Utility
——**Cabinets**
   Illustrated or Described
   Rockford Peerless Furn. Co.................168–171
——**Desks**
   Illustrated or Described
   Rockford Peerless Furniture Co.............168–171
——**Tables**
   Illustrated or Described
   Keystone Table Company.................411 (Z1)

V

Vanities
——**Full**
   See **Bedroom Vanities**
——**Semi**
   See **Bedroom Vanities, Semi**

Vanity
——**Dressers**
   See **Bedroom Vanity Dressers**
——**Tables**
   See **Bedroom Vanity Tables**

Vases
   Mentioned Only
   Furst Bros. & Company....................... 78

Velours
——**De Gene**
   See **Drapery and Upholstery Fabrics, Velours** DE GENE
——**Linen**
   See **Drapery and Upholstery Fabrics, Velours,** LINEN
——**Plain and Fancy Weaves**
   See **Drapery and Upholstery Fabrics, Velours,** PLAIN AND FANCY WEAVES

Velvets
——**Plain and Fancy Weaves**
   See **Drapery and Upholstery Fabrics, Velvets,** PLAIN AND FANCY WEAVES

Velvets
——**Ramie**
   See **Drapery and Upholstery Fabrics, Velvets,** RAMIE

Venetian
——**Day Beds**
   See **Day Beds,** VENETIAN
——**Mirrors**
   See **Mirrors,** VENETIAN

Virginia Type Living Room Suite
   See **Living Room Suites,** VIRGINIA TYPE

Wagon Seats
   Mentioned Only
   Stickley, L. & J. G. & Stickley Mfg. Co........352–353

Wagons, Tea
   See **Tea Wagons**

Wall
——**Cabinets**
   Illustrated or Described
   Colonial Desk Company....................138–141
   Kiel Furniture Company....................208–215
   Mentioned Only
   Century Furniture Company.................... 92
   Conant-Ball Company....................... 191
   Lassahn Furniture Company.................. 154
   Memphis Furniture Mfg. Co.................. 303
——**Desks**
   Illustrated or Described
   Colonial Desk Company....................138–141
   Hastings Table Company...................150–151
   Landstrom Furniture Corporation..........290–301
   Union Furniture Company.................186–205
   Mentioned Only
   Chittenden & Eastman Company............. 377
   Elite Furniture Company.................... 146
   Imperial Furniture Company...............198–205
   Indianapolis Chair & Furn. Co............. 152
   Lassahn Furniture Company................ 154
   Luger Furniture Company...............399 (Z3)
   Peterson Art Furniture Co.................. 164
   Rockford Standard Furn. Co...............327–331
   St. Johns Table Company................... 236
   Udell Works, Inc........................419 (Z1)
——**Shelves, Corner**
   See **Corner Wall Shelves**
——**Tables**
   Mentioned Only
   Athens Table & Mfg. Co.................... 190
   Hannahs Mfg. Co........................... 197

Walnut
   Illustrated or Described
   American Walnut Mfrs. Assn...............380–381

Walnut and Mahogany Chests, Cedar Lined
   See **Cedar Lined Mahogany and Walnut Chests**

Wandering Tables
   Mentioned Only
   Davis-Birely Table Company................. 193
   Indianapolis Chair & Furn. Co............. 152
   Luger Furniture Company...............399 (Z3)

Wardrobes
——**Bank and Office**
   See **Bank and Office Wardrobes**
——**Bedroom**
   See **Bedroom Wardrobes**

Wash Stands
   Mentioned Only
   Memphis Furn. Mfg. Co..................... 303

Waste Baskets
   See Also **Reed and Fibre Waste Baskets**
   Illustrated or Described
   Stow-Davis Furniture Company...............76–77
   Mentioned Only
   Conant-Ball Company....................... 191
   Imperial Furniture Company...............198–205

Water Benches
   Mentioned Only
   Stickley, L. & J. G. & Stickley Mfg. Co........352–353

Welsh Dressers
——**Breakfast Room**
   See **Breakfast Room Welsh Dressers**
——**Dining Room**
   See **Dining Room Welsh Dressers**

William and Mary
——**Benches, Living Room**
   See **Living Room Benches,** WILLIAM AND MARY
——**Commodes**
   See **Commodes,** WILLIAM AND MARY
——**Suites, Complete, Bedroom**
   See **Bedroom Suites, Complete,** WILLIAM AND MARY
——**Tables**
   See **Tables,** WILLIAM AND MARY

Wilton Seamless Carpet
   See **Carpets and Rugs,** WILTON SEAMLESS CARPET

Window
——**Display Mirrors**
   Mentioned Only
   Chicago Mirror & Art Glass Co.............395 (Z3)
——**Seat Cedar Chests**
   See **Cedar Chests,** WINDOW SEAT TYPE
——**Shades**
   Illustrated or Described
   Automatic Shade Company................... 189
   Western Shade Cloth Company...........405 (Z3)
   TASSEL PULLS AND DECORATIVE CARVINGS FOR.405 (Z3)

Windsor
——**Beds**
   See **Beds, Windsor**
——**Chairs**
   See Also **Breakfast Room Chairs,** WINDSOR *and* **Children's Chairs,** WINDSOR
   Illustrated or Described
   Conant-Ball Company....................... 191
   Empire Chair Company...................194–195
   Colonial Furniture Company...............93–95
   Indianapolis Chair & Furn. Co............. 152
   Karpen & Bros., S......................112–119
   Milne Chair Company...................... 207
   Phoenix Chair Company.................222–235
   Stickley, L. & J. G., & Stickley Mfg. Co......352–353
   Tell City Chair Company................403 (Z3)
   Whitney Co., Inc., W. F.................... 240
   HIGH BACK.............................194–195
   IN-THE-WHITE.........................403 (Z3)
   Mentioned Only
   Chittenden & Eastman Company............. 377
   Crocker Chair Company.................... 137
   Hastings Table Company..................150–151
   Memphis Furn. Mfg. Co.................... 303
   Michigan Chair Company.................162–163
   Shreve Chair Company, Inc................. 237
   Sikes Chair Company...................... 238
   Standard Chair Company................... 239
   Steul & Sons, Henry C..................... 348
——**Rockers**
   See Also **Children's Rockers,** WINDSOR
   Illustrated or Described
   Colonial Furniture Company...............93–95
   Empire Chair Company...................194–195
   Phoenix Chair Company.................222–235
   FIBRE SEAT.............................194–195
   Mentioned Only
   Century Furniture Company.................. 92
   Chittenden & Eastman Company............. 377
   Indianapolis Chair & Furn. Co............. 152
   Michigan Chair Company.................162–163
   Standard Chair Company................... 239

Wing
——**Chairs**
   See Also **Cane Wing Chairs**
   Illustrated or Described
   Grand Rapids Upholstering Co............252–253
   Karpen & Bros., S......................112–119
   Mallen & Company, H. Z.................... 121
   Michigan Chair Company.................162–163
   ENGLISH...............................112–119
   QUEEN ANNE..........................162–163
   Mentioned Only
   Chittenden & Eastman Company............. 377
   Globe Parlor Furniture Co...............106–107
   Sikes Chair Company...................... 238
——**Rockers**
   Mentioned Only
   Chittenden & Eastman Company............. 377
   Fenske Bros............................... 99
   Hebenstreit's, Inc......................397 (Z3)
   Indianapolis Chair & Furn. Co............. 152
   Levin Bros., Inc.......................... 111
   Tauber Parlor Furn. Co.................402 (Z3)
   Wellsville Upholstering Co..............423 (Z1)

Wood
——**Rockers**
   See **Rockers, Wood**
——**Seat Chairs**
   See **Chairs, Wood Seat**

Writing Desks
   Illustrated or Described
   Athens Table & Mfg. Co.................... 190
   Imperial Furniture Co...................198–205
   Hastings Table Company..................150–151
   Rockford Peerless Furn. Co...............168–171

Wrought Iron Console Tables
   See **Console Tables,** WROUGHT IRON

TRADE NAMES INDEX

A

ANTOINETTE—Bedroom Furniture
  Klamer Furniture Corporation..............288-289
  Monitor Furniture Company..............288-289
ARISTOCRAT—Loose Pillow Arm Davenport
  Jamestown Upholstery Co., Inc............ 110
ATO—Electric Clocks
  Miller Clock Company, Herman.............. 144
AUGUSTINE—Dining Room Suites
  Klamer Furniture Corporation..............288-289
  Monitor Furniture Company..............288-289

B

BARONIAL GRAIN—Upholstery Leather
  Eagle Ottawa Leather Company.............. 83
BELLE MEADE—Couch Hammocks
  Anchor Spring & Bedding Company..........393 (Z2)
BELLINI—Dining Room Suites
  Period Cabinet Mfg. Co..................... 307
BERNARD—Dining Room Furniture
  Klamer Furniture Corporation..............288-289
  Monitor Furniture Company..............288-289
BRETON—Dining Room Suites
  Rockford Palace Furniture Co..............322-323

C

CANTERBURY—Bedroom Suites
  Winnebago Manufacturing Company..........368-371
CANTERBURY—Decorative Fabrics
  Marshall Field & Company (Wholesale).......... 87
CASTLE—Broadloom Carpets
  Beattie Manufacturing Company.............. 82
CENTURY—All Products of
  Century Furniture Company.................. 92
CHAMBERS—Dining Room Suites
  Rockford Palace Furniture Co..............322-323
CHARACTER—All Products of
  Thomasville Chair Company................. 349
CHARLOTTE—All Products of
  Charlotte Furniture Company................ 258
CHESTERFIELD—Davenports
  Jamestown Upholstery Co., Inc............. 110
COLBERT—Dining Room Suites
  Rockford Standard Furniture Co..............327-331
COLONIAL—Drapery Fabrics
  Marshall Field & Company (Wholesale).......... 84
COLONIAL GRAIN—Leather
  Eagle Ottawa Leather Company.............. 83
COTTAGE—Shades
  Automatic Shade Company................... 189
CROWN—Box Spring Mattresses
  Anchor Spring & Bedding Company..........393 (Z2)
CURTISS—All Products of
  Curtiss & Son, Wm. P......................399 (Z1)

D

DAISY LINE—All Products of
  Peterson Art Furniture Company............. 164
DE BEDSTA—Bed Stays
  De Boer Manufacturing Company............. 133
DE LUXE—Coil Bed Springs
  Rome Company, Inc.......................70-71
DIXIE QUEEN—Bed Springs
  Anchor Spring & Bedding Co..............393 (Z2)
DIXIE—All Products of
  Dixie Furniture Company................... 263
DOMES OF SILENCE—Furniture Glides
  Domes of Silence, Inc...................... 134
DORAK—Combination Shelf, Tie Rack, Trouser and Coat
  Hanger
  Domes of Silence, Inc...................... 134
DROP HANDLE—Tea Wagons
  Paalman Furniture Company................400 (Z3)

F

FAULTLESS—Mattresses
  Anchor Spring & Bedding Company..........393 (Z2)
FIELDSTON—Radio Cabinets
  Showers Brothers Company.................. 188
FOSTER IDEAL—All Products of
  Foster Bros. Mfg. Co...................... 69

H

HANOVER—Bedroom Suites
  Winnebago Manufacturing Company..........368-371
HANOVER—Dining Room Suites
  Rockford Palace Furniture Company..........322-323
HAPPY HOME—Living Room Suites
  Jamestown Upholstery Co., Inc............. 110

HEIRLOOMS OF TOMORROW—Colonial Four Poster Beds
  Patton-McCray Company..................... 306
HIGHTSTOWN—Rugs
  Hightstown Rug Company.................... 88
HOLLYWOOD—Couch Hammocks
  Anchor Spring & Bedding Company..........393 (Z2)
HOME-CREST—Floor Coverings
  Marshall Field & Company (Wholesale).......... 86
HOME-CREST—Upholstered Furniture
  Marshall Field & Company (Wholesale).......100-101
HOMEWOOD—Dining Room Suites
  Rockford Standard Furniture Co..............327-331
HOT BLAST—Heaters
  Fair Foundry Company, Inc................394 (Z2)

I

IDEAL—Shades
  Automatic Shade Company................... 189
INGLEWOOD—Couch Hammocks
  Anchor Spring & Bedding Company..........393 (Z2)
IVANHOE—Dining Room Suites
  Rockford Standard Furniture Co..............327-331

J

JANEIRO—Bedroom Suites
  Continental Furniture Company..............260-261
JEANETTE—Bedroom Furniture
  Klamer Furniture Corporation..............288-289
  Monitor Furniture Company..............288-289
JEFFERSON—Bedroom Suites
  Continental Furniture Company..............260-261
JOHN BUNNY—Chairs
  Jamestown Upholstery Co., Inc............. 110

K

KENSINGTON—Dining Room Suites
  Empire Furniture Company.................. 268
  Penn Table Company....................... 268
KENTICO—Carpets and Rugs
  Kent-Costikyan............................ 89
KENTSHAH—Carpets
  Kent-Costikyan............................ 89
KINDEL—All Products of
  Kindel Furniture Company..........282-283; 372-373
KNOX
  ——BEAUTY—Stoves and Ranges
  ——BROWNIE—Stoves
  ——CAST—Ranges
  ——CLUB-HOUSE—Portable Grates
  ——CORKER—Stoves
  ——E-Z—Laundry Stove
  ——FRANKLIN—Heaters
  ——HOT BLAST—Heaters
  ——KING—Ranges
  ——METEOR DE LUXE—Ranges
  ——PERFECTION—Ranges
  ——PREMIER—Ranges
  ——PRINCE—Ranges
  ——QUEEN—Stoves
  ——REGENT OAK—Heaters
  ——ROYAL ENAMEL—Ranges
  ——SOUTHLAND—Stoves
  ——VICTOR—Stoves
  ——ZERO BOX—Heaters
  Knox Stove Works.....................395 (Z2)
KUMFORT—Bed Springs
  Anchor Spring & Bedding Company..........393 (Z2)

L

LAKESIDE—Couch Hammocks
  Anchor Spring & Bedding Company..........393 (Z2)
LAZY CHAIRS—Coxwell Chairs
  Wellsville Upholstering Company............423 (Z1)
LAZY SUSAN—Revolving Trays
  R. R. Scheibe...........................414 (Z1)
LEHIGH—Metal Double Day Beds
  Barcalo Manufacturing Company............393 (Z1)
LIFE LONG—All Products of
  Hard Manufacturing Company...............404 (Z1)
LINO—Composition Top Desks, Tables and Bookcases
  Gunn Furniture Company...................396 (Z3)
LUXART—Upholstered Furniture
  Buffalo Lounge Company...................394 (Z1)

M

MADISON—Bedroom Suites
  Winnebago Manufacturing Company..........368-371
MALVERN—Dining Room Suites
  Charles P. Limbert Company................ 281
MATT-REST—Mattresses
  Barcalo Manufacturing Company............393 (Z1)
MASCOT—Day Beds
  Rome Company, Inc.......................70-71

MAYFLOWER—Couch Hammocks
  Anchor Spring & Bedding Company..........393 (Z2)
MERCER—Rugs
  Hightstown Rug Company.................... 88
MONARCH—Coal-Wood and Electric Ranges
  Malleable Iron Range Company.............. 73
MOUNTVILLE—Cedar Lined Walnut Chests
  Mountville Wood Products Co., Inc..........412 (Z1)

N

NORMAN—Radio Cabinets
  Showers Brothers Company.................. 188
NORTHFIELD—Living Room Furniture
  Northfield Company......................122-123

O

OUR SPECIAL—Box Spring Mattresses
  Anchor Spring & Bedding Company..........393 (Z2)

P

PANCORAK—Rack for Kitchen Utensils
  Domes of Silence, Inc...................... 134
PARAMOUNT—Gas and Combination Ranges
  Malleable Iron Range Company.............. 73
PHOENIX—Bedroom and Dining Room Suites
  Robert W. Irwin Company................... 275
PINEHURST—Bed Springs
  Barcalo Manufacturing Company............393 (Z1)
PORCE-NAMEL—Kitchen Furniture
  Mutschler Brothers Company................ 74
PREMIER—Mattresses
  Anchor Spring & Bedding Company..........393 (Z2)
PRIDE OF DIXIE—Mattresses
  Anchor Spring & Bedding Company..........393 (Z2)
PROVINCETOWN—Bedroom Suites
  Estey Manufacturing Company............... 265
PYRAMID LINE—All Products of
  Memphis Furniture Mfg. Co................. 303

R

RADIRAK—Clothes Drying Rack for Radiators
  Domes of Silence, Inc...................... 134
RAYNTITE—Shades
  Automatic Shade Company................... 189
RED ANCHOR—Mattresses
  Anchor Spring & Bedding Company..........393 (Z2)
RED ANCHOR BRAND—All Products of
  Anchor Spring & Bedding Company..........393 (Z2)
RED BIRD—Cedar Chests
  Mountville Wood Products Company, Inc......412 (Z1)
REMRAK—Closet Door Shoe Rack
  Domes of Silence, Inc...................... 134
RESTAWAY—Couch Hammocks
  Anchor Spring & Bedding Co..............393 (Z2)
REST EASY—Bed Springs
  Anchor Spring & Bedding Company..........393 (Z2)
REST EASY—Coxwells
  B. C. Poston Mfg. Co....................401 (Z3)
ROMELINK—Couch Hammocks, Glider Davenports and Beds
  Rome Company, Inc.......................70-71
ROSTAND—Bedroom Furniture
  Winnebago Manufacturing Company..........368-371
ROYAL—Bedroom and Dining Room Furniture
  Robert W. Irwin Company................... 275
ROYAL—Mattresses
  Anchor Spring & Bedding Company..........393 (Z2)

S

SANITIQUE—Cushion Covers
  Spencer-Duffy Company, Inc..............125-127
SARAH SIDDONS—Dining Room Furniture
  Period Cabinet Manufacturing Company....... 307
SHOWERS KITCHEN CABINETS
  Showers Brothers Company.................. 75
SHOWERS RADIO FURNITURE
  Showers Brothers Company.................. 188
SONNY—Cribs
  Barcalo Manufacturing Company............393 (Z1)
SUPERIOR—Ranges
  Fair Foundry Company, Inc................394 (Z2)
SUPREME—Mattresses
  Anchor Spring & Bedding Company..........393 (Z2)
SUPREME LINE—CUSTOM BUILT—All Products of
  American Parlor Furniture Company.......... 91
SURREY—Dining Room Suites
  Rockford Palace Furniture Co..............322-323
SUSANNAH—Bedroom Furniture
  Klamer Furniture Corporation..............288-289
  Monitor Furniture Company..............288-289

T

TABLETWO—Living Room and Dining Room Tables Combined
Imperial Furniture Company....................198–205
TAUBILT—Living Room Suites
Tauber Parlor Furniture Company............402 (Z3)
TAYLOR MADE—Bedroom Furniture
Jamestown Table Company..................... 276
TUDOR-DUPLEX—Tables
Phoenix Chair Company......................222–235

V

VAN FAASEN—Bedroom Suites
West Michigan Furniture Company...........286–287
VERITAS—Bedroom Furniture
Karges Furniture Company.................... 280
VICTOR—Ranges
Fair Foundry Company, Inc..................394 (Z2)
VIKING—Sectional Bookcases
Skandia Furniture Company.................172–185

W

WARREN—Shades
Automatic Shade Company..................... 189

Z

ZION—Lace Curtains and Nets
Marshall Field & Company (Wholesale) 85

1928-1929

WOODS *and* FINISHES

∿∿∿

THE 28 color plates on the seven following pages are exact reproductions of the woods and finishes now most widely used by
furniture manufacturers.

These plates were made from wood panels selected and finished
especially for the Reference Book by Mr. Walter K. Schmidt of
Grand Rapids after consultation with leading designers and other
wood finishing experts.

Manufacturers refer to these plates in their Reference Book
Catalogs. They state how these finishes shown here differ from or
resemble their own finishes.

These plates enable the furniture manufacturer to present his line
to the dealer in all its finishes and woods without the cost of using
color in his catalog. These plates also give the dealers standards to
go by when specifying finishes on original orders or replacements.

In addition to reproducing these "going" woods and finishes, the
Bureau is prepared to furnish manufacturers and dealers with panels
from which these plates were made and also the formulas used in
obtaining these finishes.

A section of this kind will be one of the features of each annual
issue of the FURNITURE DEALERS' REFERENCE BOOK and
each year color plates representing the woods and finishes which
buying tendencies indicate as "Standard" for that year will be included in this section.

In selecting and publishing these woods and finishes each year, it
is not our desire to recommend any one wood or finish over another.
Our only object is to identify the most popular current woods and
finishes so that specifications concerning them will be exact and under-
standable by every one in the furniture business.

No. 1—Standard American Mahogany. Produced with a water stain dark brown filler and finished with varnish or wood lacquer, dull rubbed.

No. 2—Pollard Oak. This is a two stain proposition. The ground color is made with water stain and the shading is done with an oil stain. Usually produced in shades according to the designs and styles of furniture. Finished in wax.

No. 3—Toona Mahogany. Produced with water stain and in order to be correct no wood other than genuine mahogany should be used. Water stained. Finished dull in varnished or wood lacquer.

No. 4—Fumed Oak. This is an open pore finish made either by fuming or staining. Staining should be done with water stain. Usually finished in wax over shellac. The best finishes are made with wax over wood lacquer.

No. 5—Golden Oak. The Golden Oak of the present day must not be confounded with the original as first introduced. This is usually made by thinning an antique filler to such a degree as to produce the desired shade. Finished in shellac and varnish, rubbed dull.

No. 6—Silver Gray on Oak. This is a water stain which after it has dried and has been sanded, is filled with a thin white filler, then shellaced and waxed.

No. 7—Early English. An old favorite produced with an oil stain or a water stain and usually finished dull; either shellac, varnish or wood lacquer, rubbed dull.

No. 8—Persian Maple. A very popular shade made with a water stain ofttimes high-lighted. Usually a shellac finish and dull rubbed.

No. 9—American Walnut—**Light**. Walnut is usually produced with an oil stain, with a dark filler and finished in wood lacquer or varnish, rubbed dull.

No. 10—American Walnut—Dark. This undoubtedly is the most popular of all for walnut. Produced with oil stains as well as water stains, dark brown filler. Varnish or wood lacquer finish.

No. 11—American Mahogany—Dark. Usually made with a water stain, dark brown filler, varnish or lacquer dull rubbed.

No. 12—Amber Birds Eye. This is made with a water stain, usually high-lighted by adding second coat. Finished with sheen coat or thin wood lacquer and rubbed dull.

No. 13—Chateau Brown Birds Eye Maple. A water stain. When desired, high-lighted it is given a second shading coat. This produces a darker effect. Finished in white sheen coat, shellac or thin wood lacquer. Rubbed dull.

No. 14—American Walnut Standard. This is named Standard because it is a shade produced by practically all furniture manufacturers, and in consequence it simplifies the matching of pieces made in various factories. Produced with a water stain, dark brown filler. Varnish or wood lacquer. Rubbed dull.

No. 15—Spanish Walnut. This is a finish produced with a spraying machine. Usually produced by spraying the entire piece and then doing the shading with the second coat. Filled with dark brown filler and finished with wood lacquer. Dull rubbed.

No. 16—Brown Maple. This is supplied in the solid coat, sometimes high-lighted, made with a water stain. Depending upon the shade desired high-lighting can be done by a spraying machine. If a light shade is desired, the high-lighting is done by sanding. Lacquer finish.

No. 17—French Walnut. This is made with a water stain, filled with a transparent filler and where the finish is desired **extremely light**, filler is applied after the shellac coat. Finished with white shellac and rubbed **dull**.

No. 18—Colonial Mahogany. Made with water stain. If made on genuine mahogany, sponge the wood before staining. Fill with dark brown filler, finish with varnish or wood lacquer. Usually flat.

No. 19—Brown Sheraton. This is a mahogany that lacks the red shade. Very popular, can be obtained in a still lighter shade, water stained, varnish or wood lacquer finish.

No. 20—Brown Maple—Dark. Like other maple finishes it may be high-lighted but many times furnished solid. Finished in wood lacquer.

No. 21—Old Mahogany. This is usually produced on genuine mahogany only with a water stain but where gum and birch parts are used these must be stained first, sanded, and then the entire piece stained. Filled with dark brown filler, finished with sheen coat or thin wood lacquer. Dull.

No. 22—Italian Oak. This is a water stain applied after the wood has been sponged. The original was a plain finish but of late it has been given panel effect by applying two coats to certain parts of the job. It is an open pore, wax finished.

No. 23—Gray Maple. This is a water stain and a semi-filled finish, done with a light gray filler. Shellac or sheen coat and topped off with wax.

No. 24—Standard Mahogany—Light. This very popular mahogany finish is made with water stain applied after the wood has been sponged. Can be finished either in varnish or wood lacquer.

No. 25—Dark Mahogany. This finish is continued because much mahogany is in use, made during the period when this dark shade was in style. It is a water stain finish with an extremely dark filler generally known as number 291 and a varnish dull rubbed finish.

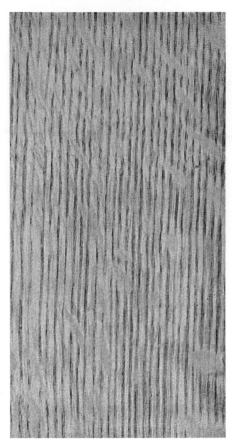

No. 26—Office Oak. This is a natural oak finish produced with filler only, the quality of the finish depending upon the wood and the way the filler is packed into the pores. Usually finished in varnish or shellac.

No. 27—Spanish Oak. A water stain proposition highlighted with sand paper or steel wool. Ofttimes decorated. Finished with wood lacquer.

No. 28—Walnut Eastern. This is a regular walnut finish but as the name implies is a shade that became popular in the East. It is a water stain, has a transparent filler and is finished with thin wood lacquer, rubbed dull.

"HIGH LIGHTS" ON UPPER INTERIOR

1. The wide, unpatterned wall areas and large simple masses and plain coverings of the furniture in this distinguished interior really demand just such a floor as this all-over Black Marble Inlaid linoleum No. 89, one of the latest and most effective of all the long array of successes introduced by the Armstrong Cork Company; Linoleum Division, Lancaster, Penna.

2. This floor is richly decorative, yet simple—patterned, yet tranquil—an ideal background for small, richly colored rugs; but just as successful with no such adornment. Note that while laid in twelve inch tiles, there is a sense of unbroken unity produced by the clever manner in which an all-over effect has been secured.

"HIGH LIGHTS" ON LOWER INTERIOR

1. Three rooms in one: An airy screened porch, a comfortable out-door living room, and a well ventilated sleeping room made possible by these shades made by the Automatic Shade Co., Sauk Rapids, Minn.

2. Made livable under all summer conditions by one feature alone—the roll shade. On burning days it shuts out the sun, providing a cool retreat. Protection from rain storms, also, both by night and by day, is afforded by this same easily handled device.

3. Privacy—another type of protection—is also made possible at small cost and for many seasons by this durable, economical, efficient and decorative roll shade.

"HIGH LIGHTS" ON UPPER INTERIOR

1. Parlor furnace, by The Allen Manufacturing Co., Nashville, Tenn.

2. Made in Period designs to harmonize with furnishings; similar to handsome radio console. Allenamel porcelain finish closely imitates walnut grain.

3. Burns coal or wood; special model for burning gas. Circulates warm moist air throughout the house. Double doors open, giving all the comfort and cheer of real fireplace.

4. Easily and inexpensively installed in rooms or hall.

6. Heat radiating fins double the heating surface and save fuel.

7. Allen's parlor furnace passes the double test of utility and beauty.

"HIGH LIGHTS" ON LOWER INTERIOR

1. Two-piece suite and odd chair by The Buffalo Lounge Co., Buffalo, N. Y.

2. Grace and elegance of Louis XV design combined with typically American characteristics: sturdy construction, simple tasteful ornamentation, real sitting comfort.

3. Exposed frame is built-in, not nailed on after upholstering.

4. Tufted back is exquisitely feminine; lovely satin and damask upholstery fits into home of elegance and refinement.

5. Chair to the right of Queen Anne inspiration; lines and proportions harmonize excellently; upholstery of fine tapestry introduces lively element of color and pattern.

"HIGH LIGHTS" ON UPPER INTERIOR

1. Bedroom furniture by The Conant, Ball Co., Boston, Mass.

2. Individuality in bedrooms achieved through deft use of smaller pieces.

3. Early American pieces always quaint and homelike; permit the use of informal cretonnes, chintzes and other printed goods; also patchwork quilts, braided rugs, etc.

4. Straight Windsor chair might be substituted for rocker; small gateleg or drop-leaf table for bedside table; Cromwellian table by window is a picturesque innovation in the bedroom.

5. These pieces obtainable in walnut, mahogany, maple or painted finish to meet all requirements.

"HIGH LIGHTS" ON LOWER INTERIOR

1. Bedroom furniture, by The Charlotte Furniture Co., Charlotte, Mich.

2. Tudor design: rectangular, sturdy, practical; essentially masculine; also suitable for successful business or scholarly woman.

3. Antique oak: a serviceable wood with much dignity and a noble history, which has "come back" into popular favor.

4. Large size furniture for large room in elaborate home. Oak panelled walls, leaded glass windows, handsome tapestries and oil paintings provide the proper setting.

5. Note clever placing of chest at foot of bed, and chair-and-table group in perfect Period harmony.

"HIGH LIGHTS" ON UPPER INTERIOR

1. Seats, by F. H. Conant's Sons, Inc., Camden, N. Y.

2. Love-seat fits snugly into recess, leaving room for end-table, lamp, smoking stand, etc., at each extremity; invaluable where wall space is limited; also where small groupings are desired for a sense of intimacy.

3. Upholstery: velour or mohair in subdued shade, with reversible down-filled cushions echoing the brighter tones of rug or draperies.

4. Coxwell chair: man-size; strongly braced; tapestry covering richly decorative.

5. End table—natural accompanist of the Coxwell Chair. Excellent Early English design; might also be used as coffee-table.

"HIGH LIGHTS" ON LOWER INTERIOR

1. Dining room suite for small dining room or large breakfast room (Crocker Chair Co., Sheboygan, Wis.).

2. William and Mary influence: hooded top of cabinet; shaped apron of sideboard and table.

3. Spanish setting correct here for four reasons: a. architecture of the room (plaster arches); b. historical association of Spain and Flanders previous to the reign of William and Mary. c. Same sane ideals of sturdiness allied to elegance of lines and proportions. d. Both styles require a plain background treatment and vivid coloring in textiles.

4. Obtainable in walnut and mahogany.

5. Smart stripes in chair seats echo the deep wide grooving in legs.

"HIGH LIGHTS" ON UPPER INTERIOR

1. Overstuffed suite by Isaac C. Decker, Inc., Montgomery, Pa.

2. Three-piece suite used advantageously to brighten large plain uninteresting wall surface.

3. Upholstery fabrics introduce much-needed element of pattern; unusual combination of small conventional all-over pattern with large medallion motif.

4. Great importance given to fabrics in the entire room for a sense of luxurious comfort: large tapestry panel, long draperies, deep-pile rugs, overstuffed furniture, plump cushions, all speak of padded ease.

5. Spanish galleon on cabinet strikes romantic note and justifies lavish use of color.

"HIGH LIGHTS" ON LOWER INTERIOR

1. Leather upholstered chairs and firebench (leather manufactured by Eagle-Ottawa Leather Co., Grand Haven, Mich.).

2. Nothing clumsy about these pieces; dainty enough for background of delicately tinted and paneled walls, yet husky enough to stand hard usage; ideal for home with growing youngsters, as soap and water will keep the covering immaculate.

3. Imagine the dominant hues of patterned rug, wallpaper or drapery fabric,—the blues, russets or greens,—being smartly caught up and intensified into a single splash of color. "Colonial Grain" leather takes on the dye so smoothly too!

4. Patterned areas and small colorful accessories needed for contrast.

"HIGH LIGHTS" ON UPPER INTERIOR

1. Bedroom furniture (Empire Case Goods Co., Jamestown, N. Y.).

2. Complete suite for large room; choice of two or three pieces for apartment or small home.

3. Graceful design, finely matched grain, appeal to feminine taste; sensible proportions win men's approval, also.

4. Careful selection and handling of textiles will enhance the merits of this furniture; spread, rugs and draperies: rich in texture but sober in design; few accessories, where needed to complete a grouping, and each genuinely artistic.

5. Note the rocker: a modern hint in line and coloring.

"HIGH LIGHTS" ON LOWER INTERIOR

1. Bedroom suite (Empire Case Goods Co., Jamestown, N. Y.).

2. Bed set in shallow alcove acquires great dignity from luxurious hangings and medallion-shaped flower picture. Where there is no plaster arch, draperies might be hung from a semi-circular frame.

3. Vanity—following the English idea—is sensibly located where light is best; imparts individuality to commonplace row of windows.

4. This scheme suggests how additional sleeping space may be obtained by converting dining room into unusual bedroom, if large breakfast room or sun parlor can accommodate the family for meals.

"HIGH LIGHTS" ON UPPER INTERIOR

1. Bedroom furniture by Estey Manufacturing Company, Owosso, Mich.

2. Colonial design, with particularly attractive open footboard; youth, grace, daintiness.

3. Chaise-longue, small desk and arm-chairs with end-tables and lamps would create regular bed-sitting-room for adolescent daughters or visiting couple.

4. Wall panels are hung with toile de Jouy in coral, green or lavender; same color selected for carpeting; also dominant in striped rayon spreads, cretonne draperies, braided rugs and upholstery chintzes. Great sense of repose resulting from prevalence of one hue.

"HIGH LIGHTS" ON LOWER INTERIOR

1. Dining room by The Florence Table and Manufacturing Co., Memphis, Tenn.

2. Finish: table—shaded walnut, highlighted or antiqued; buffet and server—Toona mahogany. Veneer panels are center matched to obtain medallion effect. Chairs—walnut; Jacquard velour covers.

3. Decorative set, highly desirable when background is plain. Accent each piece by means of wall decoration: pictures, decorative plates, etc.

4. Server may be placed under row of windows and commonplaceness of the latter transformed by clever draping.

5. Colors of chair upholstery repeated in striped damask curtains.

"HIGH LIGHTS" ON UPPER INTERIOR

1. Bedroom furniture by the Forsyth Furniture Lines, Inc., Winston-Salem, N. C.

2. Exquisitely matched burl walnut panels and applied wood decoration will appeal to the younger people.

3. Composite style fits into most rooms; emphasize by proper setting the desired characteristics:—plaster arches, plain background, woven panels, striped draperies bring out commonsense proportions and fine workmanship typical of Spanish style; cretonne, chintz, patchwork quilt, braided rugs and rocker will combine with Empire design to create American interior; while large colorful areas would develop the hint of modernism latent in beautiful wood combinations.

"HIGH LIGHTS" ON LOWER INTERIOR

1. Living room or library by The Furniture Shops, Grand Rapids, Mich.

2. Essentially masculine interior: great importance given to wood; Jacobean design which favors straight lines; nature of furniture pieces (work table, cabinet secretary or cellarette, smoking table, etc.); also simple draperies and vigorous pattern of couch cover.

3. Suitable for man's den, library, club room, or living room in household where masculine influence dominates. In the latter case, concession to feminine taste may be made through choice of gay, though conventional, rug pattern.

4. Note Chinese Chippendale end-table; clever touch.

"HIGH LIGHTS" ON UPPER INTERIOR

1. Living room couch and chairs (Franklin Furniture Co., Columbiana, O.).

2. Modern adaptation of Louis XV design; more substantial; better suited to American requirements; two or three matching pieces; or different fabrics for each chair.

3. Chair at left called "Sleepy Hollow"—deep seat, soft cushion, padded hugging back will appeal to ease-loving man; covering of plain rose mohair with imported linen frieze back, a temptation to any woman.

4. Chair in foreground, good to sew in; short seat, low arms.

5. Semi-upholstered chair—to pull up to card table, desk or radio.

"HIGH LIGHTS" ON LOWER INTERIOR

1. Bedroom furniture by the Globe-Bosse-World Furniture Co., Evansville, Ind.

2. Fascinating combination of wood veneers for fastidious women in quest of "something different."

3. Bed—solid head-board; low matching foot-board with turned posts and bar.

4. Make bed center of interest of the room; emphasize its importance by placing textile panel and picture above it; plan symmetrical arrangement of furniture and accessories on each side.

5. Proper materials to accompany this suite are dainty silks, taffetas, toile de Jouy, glazed chintz or fine tapestry.

"HIGH LIGHTS" ON UPPER INTERIOR

1. Chairs and benches by the Frank S. Harden Co., McConnellsville, N. Y.

2. Impression of lightness, grace and space created by small-size furniture, in which chairs play a prominent part.

3. Chairs for different purposes; most of them portable; this might be an "efficiency living room," with in-a-door bed, and gateleg table to serve meals for two.

4. Stools, or benches are quaint; contribute individuality; break the monotony of strict wall-line arrangement.

5. Pattern in covering of chairs makes for liveliness and diversity; colors caught and tied together by means of oval rug.

"HIGH LIGHTS" ON LOWER INTERIOR

1. Living room seats by the Frank S. Harden Co., McConnellsville, N. Y.

2. Full-size davenport and easy chairs for the orthodox living room.

3. Tactful choice of upholstery covers essential in distributing plain and patterned areas in a room. Notice alternate use of each in this particular room: plain carpet, figured rug, plain chair and davenport, figured panel, plain wall. Chair with all-over pattern covering is set out on plain carpet; figured bench upholstery is isolated from figured rug by plain band of mohair.

"HIGH LIGHTS" ON UPPER INTERIOR

1. Office furniture by the Gunn Furniture Co., Grand Rapids, Mich.

2. Correct design plus attention to practical details. The kind that men and business women like and that helps to keep their work systematic.

3. Lino tops are exclusive feature, only used on Gunn desks. Wear like iron; are easily cleaned; absorb light and thus save the eyes.

4. Office should be dignified but not bare. A few relevant pictures (posters, maps, photographs, etc.), simply framed to match the wood of office furniture, relieve the plainness of tinted walls.

"HIGH LIGHTS" ON LOWER INTERIOR

1. Kitchen and breakfast room furniture, by the Hoosier Manufacturing Co., New Castle, Ind.

2. Take drudgery out of kitchen work by applying principles of Interior Decoration to kitchen arrangement.

3. Beauty has been sadly neglected for the cause of utility; the Hoosier Manufacturing Co. has proved that beauty of design and coloring is compatible with maximum efficiency.

4. Breakfast chairs in Early American taste, delightfully quaint; Welsh dresser offers opportunity for gay display of peasant chinaware.

5. Select finish of cabinet and breakfast set to harmonize, and repeat colors in linoleum, curtains, small rug and accessories.

"HIGH LIGHTS" ON UPPER INTERIOR

1. Bedroom furniture (B. F. Huntley Co., Winston-Salem, N. C.).

2. Lovely simple lines in Early English fashion.

3. Suitable for married couple, guest or business girl's room.

4. Simplicity, yet a certain fastidiousness, emphasized in decoration: plain walls with drop ceiling; plain polished floor with quaint braided rug; plain bedspread with graceful gathered flounce; plain voile curtains, exquisitely finished with ruffles, valance and tie-backs.

5. A few changes could fit this room for an elderly person: allover carpeting, large easy chair with footstool, quilted spread and imitation crewel work draperies in appropriate colors.

"HIGH LIGHTS" ON LOWER INTERIOR

1. Jenny Lind bedroom suite, manufactured by the Indianapolis Chair and Furniture Co., of Aurora, Ind.

2. Colonial inspiration; quaint and youthful; suitable for girls' or guest room.

3. Three points to observe in planning decorative scheme: 1. Simplicity to bring out charm of spindle and button turnings and of shaped footboard, night-table and bureau apron; 2. colorfulness,—based on the ivory-and-apple-green enamel finish with stripe and hand-painted floral decoration; 3. old-fashioned womanliness,—to emphasize the spirit embodied in the furniture design.

"HIGH LIGHTS" ON UPPER INTERIOR

1. Office furniture de luxe, by the Imperial Furniture Co., Grand Rapids, Mich.

2. Antique chestnut, Gothic design:—square outlines, linenfold motif on carved panels.

3. Furniture of that Period was exclusive privilege of the ruling classes; has retained character of great power and dignity; therefore suitable for man of powerful physique or forceful personality.

4. Oak panelling, leather or dark embossed wall paper tone down the light and will create a proper background.

5. Rug and draperies of rich texture and vigorous coloring tie the lower part of the room to the undecorated upper area.

"HIGH LIGHTS" ON LOWER INTERIOR

1. Davenport, by the Jamestown Upholstery Co., Inc., Jamestown, N. Y.

2. Single unit; conservative design will harmonize with most surroundings; and with the many types of chairs now on the market.

3. Three possible locations: in the fireplace group; as center of interest in the smaller room that has no fireplace (back up against plain wall, with large panel, picture or mirror above and symmetrical decoration on each side); in bay window.

4. Plain upholstery plays important part in color scheme: may be in dominant or complementary color. Create contrast by using patterned rug, draperies and chair coverings.

"HIGH LIGHTS" ON UPPER INTERIOR

1. Office furniture de luxe, by the Imperial Furniture Co., Grand Rapids, Mich.

2. Design of great distinctiveness; embodies business man's ideals: straight lines, plain surfaces stand for honesty; beautiful wood, for optimism, prosperity and vision; massive construction and sensible leather upholstery, for stability and reliability; while decorative features (semi-turned chair legs, reeded columns, matched burl) represent the share of imagination and romance in every business venture.

"HIGH LIGHTS" ON LOWER INTERIOR

1. Office furniture de luxe, by the Imperial Furniture Co., Grand Rapids, Mich.

2. Slightly more ornate, lighter design than the one above, the desk in the foreground is preferable for younger man or one of slender build.

3. Embodies the same ideals, but the optimism of youth is more conspicuous.

4. This is the type of furniture chosen by men accustomed to luxurious home surroundings and by successful business women. The very elegance of the design reveals a mind that is free from financial worries; it speaks of prosperity, not as an occasional experience, but as a life habit.

"HIGH LIGHTS" ON UPPER INTERIOR

1. Bedroom furniture by the Joerns Brothers Furniture Co., Stevens Point, Wis.

2. Illustrates the present tendency to use fine wood grain as a decorative medium; a form of beauty formerly appreciated by few besides cabinet makers; marks the evolution of women's taste towards feminine ideal tinged with masculine qualities.

3. Texture is the point to emphasize in the entire room, as it is the dominant feature in the furniture; velvety wall finish; silk draperies and bedspread; chintz, toile de Jouy and fine tapestry chair coverings; small handtufted rugs in dainty colors over plain carpeting.

"HIGH LIGHTS" ON LOWER INTERIOR

1. Rug by Kent-Costikyan, manufacturers of Hand-woven to Order Rugs, New York, N. Y.

2. Savonnerie (or Chinese) rug in Louis XVI and Adam dining room.

3. Rich, elegant, dainty; silky texture; aristocratic coloring.

4. Discreet pattern of rug echoes tasteful moderation of Adam decoration on cornice, ceiling, mirror and transoms; repeats the pattern of tapestry upholstery; insert in border corresponds to flower motif on backs of chairs; this might be woven in the shape of a medallion, following even more closely the Louis XVI inspiration.

"HIGH LIGHTS" ON UPPER INTERIOR

1. Kindel Double Day-Bed, by The Kindel Furniture Co., Grand Rapids, Mich.

2. Excellent design: spool turned rail and spindle in Cottage Colonial style always quaintly decorative. Appropriate in the informal though tasteful living room.

3. Does not take up any more space than the usual davenport.

4. Covering may be selected to conform with character of the room: denim, cretonne, sateen, tapestry, corduroy, velour or damask.

5. Loose cushions on day-bed should be of a contrasting color; mirror, or combination mirror and picture, most appropriate wall decoration.

"HIGH LIGHTS" ON LOWER INTERIOR

1. Kindel Double Day-Bed, by The Kindel Furniture Co., Grand Rapids, Mich.

2. Simplicity: the change from living room to bedroom function can be worked at a moment's notice in one simple operation; no jerks, no jamming; a child can manage it.

3. Comfort: amazing buoyancy due to special spring construction. Cushions are of high grade aerated Linters cotton with extra heavy tufting which will not bunch.

4. Stands the test of time: no trouble to users; no parts to get out of order.

"HIGH LIGHTS"

1. Quaintness and Distinction—(a contradiction in terms—but a fact none the less)—describes this furniture made by S. Karpen & Bros., part of it the type used in the sumptuous court of Louis XV, part of it a combination of Louis XV and Louis XVI as modified and simplified by the cabinet makers of Brittany and Normandy.

2. The dressing table bench is Louis XV; the panels of the tall wardrobe, with its carvings, mark it as Provincial of the same period. The bedstead—with its substantial, simply turned posts, and curved slat cross-bars, is strictly Provincial, revealing a kinship in its design and construction to American Colonial bedsteads of the seventeenth century. The wing chair is a familiar Normandy design. Its wide deep seat, cushioned arms and protecting wings produce an effect of comfort and shelter and invitation that make this chair a welcome addition to living rooms as a fireside chair.

3. It is the simple straightforward character of the furniture

that saves this most charming bedroom from an atmosphere of artificiality. The somewhat elaborate fabric canopy might produce an effect of pretentiousness, except for the friendly, unassuming design of the furniture. On the other hand there is a decorative charm about the furniture which unites it with its background into a setting which is as delightful as it is characterful.

4. Of course the colors—rose and pale green, with the relieving gray on the painted walls and the green blue on the ruffles of the hangings, play a part in producing the intimate and feminine character of the room.

5. The cost of reproducing this Provincial boudoir is most moderate; the furniture quite inexpensive.

6. The toile de Jouy design of the bed and dressing table hangings as well as the papered wall panel were naturally suggested by the style of the furniture. Green chintz covers the arm chair and bench, while the canopy and draperies are of taffeta.

"HIGH LIGHTS"

1. This interior by S. Karpen & Bros. strikingly reveals the possibilities for correlation between the room and its furnishings, in point of design, scale and color. The interior architecture—Early Georgian—goes back to Sir Christopher Wren in the days of Queen Anne, for its inspiration.

2. The gracious curves and dignified demeanor of the high-backed Queen Anne wing chair is as much an integral part of the room as the pediment above the book shelves; and the rich, warm red of its damask covering provides a splendid foil for the cool green of the paneled walls. Such a chair, in any interior, is the hall-mark of quality.

3. The Coxwell chair—deep seated and low—speaks eloquently of lounging comfort; and its colors—mulberry, gold and green—set the color palette for the room, which colors are repeated in draperies and rug.

4. The third chair—at the desk—not only repeats one of the room colors, but introduces into the setting a line or curve of surpassing beauty. The gracious sweep of the arm terminates in a double curve, prosaically termed a "goose-neck" by the trade, but known to the world of design as "The Hogarth Line of Beauty." All Queen Anne chairs are beautiful but this one is in a class by itself.

5. As a desk chair, occasional chair or a chair for the young lady of the house it should find a welcome in any living room. The pierced splat (fiddle shaped) in the back is another outstanding art creation.

6. The spacious, low tilt-top table "belongs" in such a setting; and for an additional chair or two or a sofa, almost any of Thomas Chippendale's models would be suitable.

"HIGH LIGHTS"

1. This room by S. Karpen & Bros. answers the oft-repeated question "Will modernist furniture fit into conventional settings?"

2. It will, when as in this instance, its design conforms sufficiently to the established styles to prevent it from arousing antagonism. This seating furniture expresses the modern motif most adequately. It should make instant appeal to the crowd that demands the "dernier cri."

3. But while the sofa and chairs are strictly modernique in their structural forms, yet they amply suggest the historical and proper uses of such furniture.

4. Modernism is expressed by the shapes and colors but comfort is written large in the depth of the cushions, rake of the back, slope of the seat and the low slung lines.

5. Color, another insignia of modernism, is found in the brilliant hues of the upholstery fabrics and in the painted tables with their characteristic compartments.

6. When introducing one piece of this type of furniture into a room of the prevailing type of architecture—a chair for instance—it is advisable to supplement it by a table in the same mode, to enhance and strengthen the effect.

7. All these modernistic furnishings, it will be observed, are assembled in a paneled room of the conventional type, but there is no feeling of discord or lack of unity.

8. This is the seating furniture that took the first prize in a national Karpen competition in 1927. The two contrasting chair coverings have a common color note of burnt orange which the mesh window curtains echo.

9. The green is repeated in the screen and vases; the red strip is carried out in the chandelier tassels; the tables and the curtain edging. The rug combines the entire color scheme.

10. It is in interiors such as this—a music room or in sun rooms—that it is most feasible to work out the Modern Mode in an entire ensemble.

"HIGH LIGHTS"

1. Formal dignity, strength and rich decoration are the characteristic qualities of the Late Jacobean, known as Charles Second or Restoration furniture produced by S. Karpen & Bros.

2. The arm chairs are exact replicas of a treasured antique now in the Metropolitan Museum. In these modern reproductions you get the bold, swelling scroll shapes, the rich, deep, pierced carvings and the colorful tapestry coverings of the originals that graced the court of the last of the Jacobean kings.

3. In an entrance hall or as formal chairs in a living room they are unsurpassed. The bench exhibits the same characteristics. Placed before a fireplace or back of a table it would add a note of interest, comfortableness and real distinction to any interior.

4. Richly decorated wood paneled oak or walnut walls are not essential as a background for this noble and dignified furniture. It is equally at home in a plastered or papered room of the more conventional sort.

5. As shown however, this hallway provides a nice study in the art of relating furniture to its architectural background. A nice formality is here achieved by the balanced placing of the chairs; in their height, dignity and richness of decoration they are wholly in accord with the style and proportions of the background. A smile and a warmth of atmosphere are supplied by the color scheme, whose motif is found in the wall tapestry, the blues for the chair coverings, the reds for draperies, bench and warmer tones of the rug.

6. From an earlier period than the furniture comes the wall paneling in fumed oak that proudly displays, above the Gothic door, carved emblems from the days when England's knighthood was in flower.

"HIGH LIGHTS"

1. It is evident from these designs of S. Karpen & Bros. that in ensembles where grace, elegance and distinction are sought there is no type of furniture that is quite so appropriate as that of Louis Quinze.

2. These three qualities are seen in the rhythmic curves which characterize this period type, the delicate rococo carvings, which enhance the beauty of the exposed frames of seating furniture and the damask, needlework and Beauvais tapestries used in the coverings of chairs and sofas.

3. The chair on the right—an authentic fauteuil—has seat and back covered with picture tapestries of the Beauvais type, which are designed and woven to exactly fit the contours of the frames.

4. It is interesting to note that Louis Fifteenth chairs and couches were the first to supply real comfort to their users; a quality which still is characteristic of them.

5. Because of its small proportions, this seating furniture is particularly suitable for use in the rather small rooms which are becoming so prevalent in American homes.

6. The interior above portrays the fine fundamentals of successful living rooms. The interior architecture is Louis XV, matching the furniture. The silk damask on the larger pieces sets the dominant color, vivid yet cool, for repetition in mouldings and draperies. For contrast the occasional chair inspires the warm and subdued hues of the rug. Intimate grouping and luxurious comfort lend the charm of friendliness to a style that is quite formal.

From "Color and Design," by Marshall Field & Company, Wholesale
Colonial Drapery Fabrics department

TRANQUILLITY AND REST IN A BEDROOM OF THE EARLY AMERICAN TYPE

The Early American or Colonial type of house is very dear to our American hearts because of its close association with our early days. Both the stately southern Colonial with its low veranda and tall classic pillars, and the Salem Colonial, characterized always by simplicity, sincerity and restraint, are much in vogue.

Roomy, comfortable, old-fashioned four-posters of mahogany; shining white wood work, frequently with mahogany doors; chintzes or toiles at the windows and often on the upholstery; patchwork quilts; wing or barrel type chairs; skirted dressing tables—all these belong to the Colonial period, and develop charmingly bright, quaint and comfortable rooms today.

This cheer, delightful Early American bedroom, with northern exposure, carries out the motif of its period quite ideally. The walls are papered in a grayed ivory tone, while the dado, which is also a distinguishing mark of the Colonial bedroom, and the woodwork, are painted in ivory white. An all-over carpet of taupe covers the floor, deeply accenting the wall tone, while here and there are Colonial braided scatter rugs. Graceful simplicity of true Colonial character marks the lines of the mahogany furniture. A joyous rosy touch is contributed by the airy Colonial Toile de Jouy draperies, which show a scenic pattern closely following the true manner of the artist J. B. Huet, of a century and a half ago. These are patterned in rose on an ivory ground. The same fabric has been used for the bedspread and upholstered chair, while for a harmonious change the side chair has a box-pleated, slip-covered seat of Colonial Charlton Chintz, Design Rosebud. The Toiles de Jouy, by the way, are adapted from the quaint old fabrics that originated in the little French town of Jouy so many years ago. They were a distinct part of window decoration in our Colonial days; recently they have come back into popularity, and fit gracefully into the Early American rooms now so much favored.

Have you noticed that the dominant color used in this room is a warm one—rose; essential because of the east light it receives? And that because of the light value of this color, there is no feeling of oppressiveness or of crowded space.

From "Color and Design," by Marshall Field & Company, Wholesale
Colonial Drapery Fabrics department

COLOR AND GOOD TASTE ARE EXPRESSED IN THIS LIVING ROOM

Colorful, comfortable, livable—that's the sort of living room most of us want in our homes. And when it is artistic and in good taste, cheerful enough to bring out the joy of living, restful enough to give us the repose we need after strenuous days of activity, then it may well be viewed with pride, as a pleasant task well done. The present-day desire for color explains in great part why the use of cretonnes is so much advocated: they fit so charmingly and easily into our modern life—they offer such relief from the dull drab complexes of a few years ago. The warmth and brilliance of color in these cretonnes enliven our homes during wintry months . . . their radiant flowers and foliage and birds bring the glorious outdoor world into our rooms in all seasons.

The gracious, unpretentious type of living room on this page is the sort the majority of us would like to have. Quiet, restful walls in ivory with panels of grayed ivory; a reproduction of a rare oriental rug in multi-colors, blending with the cretonne hangings. The striking Colonial Town and Country Cretonne draperies, Design Weigelia, wonderfully simulating the fine old-world hand-blocked linens, set the color keynote of the room with their dominant rose-reds, greens and blues on black background. Do you see how the green of them is unobtrusively picked up in the sofa of soft green damask? And how the large Queen Anne wing chair is slip-covered in cretonne, in which green predominates? The rose-red in the draperies is accented by the small upholstered armchair of rose color Colonial Pompadour satin-striped moire, and by the red parchment shade of the wrought iron lamp—all warm tones which counteract the north light which the room receives.

Notice too, how the furniture, though not at all "matched," is in harmony, each piece with the other. For example, the light graceful types, such as Sheraton, Duncan Phyfe and Queen Anne, all combine well, while it would give an extremely bad effect to use with them a ponderous Jacobean or Elizabethan piece.

In the room which is pictured, the walnut drum-top table of Duncan Phyfe style is most harmonious with the Georgian coffee table set with a real Wedgwood service. The Sheraton side chair is a lovely companion for the Queen Anne wing chair.

From "Color and Design," by Marshall Field & Company, Wholesale,
Colonial Drapery Fabrics department

PROBLEM OF A SMALL LIVING ROOM

Small rooms can be charmingly decorated, as you will see by the photograph of the gay little living room on this page. Because this room faced to the west and so received sunlight for a large part of the day, we selected a cool grayish beige for the wall paper; the woodwork is in ivory. The cool blue and green tones of the black-ground rug are harmoniously carried out in the painted green rush-seat chair and the silvery green vase. The glass curtains are sheer and soft, fashioned of Colonial Venetia Gauze, and over them are hung the delightful draperies which give such a joyous atmosphere to the room. For these a beautiful exotic floral pattern of Chinese Chippendale influence was selected. It is Colonial Town and Country Cretonne, quite apparently hand-printed, simulating wonderfully well the interesting hand-blocked linens of olden times. The little love seat is upholstered in the same material, and so provides a desirable note of unity. Colors of the accessories—lamps of brown, ivory, blue . . . books with various hued backs—are in complete accord; and there is a final note of good taste in the mahogany furniture which so nicely con-

trasts and accents the greens and blues which are the dominant colors in the room.

There is an adequate quantity of furniture—tea wagon, Windsor chair, Chippendale desk chair, lovely Governor Winthrop desk, and walnut gate-leg table.

Now let's go back and pick up threads of this description, so to speak, and see wherein this living room, though limited in size, carries out the principles of good decoration.

Being a west room, it required cool shades; witness the green and blue tones. To avoid monotony, spots of complementary color were used in the reddish brown lamp shade, and the rose and ecru in draperies and love seat. The floor or foundation is darkest, the walls lighter, ceiling lightest, as they always should be to avoid a "top-heavy" or unbalanced effect. The pictures and small accessories are well placed, not confusing in arrangement; neither do they cause a crowded appearance.

In short, can you conceive a small living room decorated in a more livable, artistic manner?

"HIGH LIGHTS" ON UPPER INTERIOR

1. Dining room furniture by the Klamer Furniture Corporation, Evansville, Ind.

2. Combines simple sensible structure with tasteful ornamentation; therefore admits of plain or patterned background.

3. Sideboards in two sizes for small or large room; both may be used if wall spaces permit. Have the out-dated built-in buffet or unpopular box seat removed from dining room, and Klamer sideboard placed under row of high windows.

4. China cabinet pleasantly breaks the monotonous low line of average dining room pieces.

5. Butterfly table adds individual and homelike touch.

"HIGH LIGHTS" ON LOWER INTERIOR

1. Bedroom furniture (Klamer Furniture Corporation, Evansville, Ind.).

2. Design conspicuous for remarkably clever handling of long noble curves: headboard, mirror, dresser bench.

3. Give this feature prominence by contrasting it with straight line in decoration: straight curtains and draperies; cornice molding; striped material; square or rectangular pictures; pattern in rug and fabrics should be of the all-over type.

4. Exquisite weave and silky texture of plain spread and draperies bring out beautiful grain of large smooth wood surfaces.

5. If walls are panelled, omit pictures and fabric hanging.

"HIGH LIGHTS" ON UPPER INTERIOR

1. Cedar chest by The Lane Company, Inc., Altavista, Va.

2. Design: a tasteful blending of early English styles; harmonizes with Late Jacobean, William and Mary, Queen Anne furnishings; also fits admirably into Colonial interior.

3. Extra capacity; no stooping; tall feet allow space underneath to be easily dusted. Drawer beneath chest section supplies needed storage space.

4. Can be used in dining room in place of server; in hall or living room for console; in bedroom for dresser. Make it the center of a perfectly symmetrical decorative composition.

5. Outer finish of walnut harmonizes with other furniture pieces.

"HIGH LIGHTS" ON LOWER INTERIOR

1. Upholstered furniture by Levin Brothers, Inc., Minneapolis, Minn.

2. Comfortable seats for every member of the family: Coxwell (right) for father; fireside chair (left), plumply padded, for grandmother; davenport and wing chair on far side of fireplace for use of mother and children; stool for radio fan; Louis XV chair for card table; firebench, always popular.

3. Where there are many upholstered seats, ensure pleasing variety by having some pieces overstuffed, others with the frame exposed; some with plain covering, some with pattern. Tufted back of davenport and matching chair is attractively "different."

"HIGH LIGHTS" ON UPPER INTERIOR

1. Bedroom Suite by The Luger Furniture Co., Minneapolis, Minn.

2. Design is youthful and feminine: graceful curves are emphasized within the limits of good taste; dainty ornamentation appeals to the girl in her teens; yet the set has enough character to please newly-married couple.

3. As the duties of life take up larger portion of time and interests, the more transient elements in the decorative scheme (fabrics and chairs) may be modified accordingly. But while the gay light-hearted mood lasts, taffetas and chintzes are very much in order.

"HIGH LIGHTS" ON LOWER INTERIOR

1. This electric range by The Malleable Iron Range Co., Beaver Dam, Wis., was planned to do away with excessive weight without detriment to strength and durability.

2. Unusually large capacity: six plates, two ovens, for the large family.

3. Extra sockets on side of range provide current for toaster, percolator, hand-iron and other heat units. Thus the electric light bill may be much lowered, as current for range is usually supplied at special rates.

4. Smokeless electric cooking means endless life to aluminum pans that can be kept bright as silver without extra care.

"HIGH LIGHTS" ON UPPER INTERIOR

1. Bedroom suite by The Memphis Furniture Manufacturing Co., of Memphis, Tenn., specialists in gumwood furniture.

2. Gumwood: economical; gives great service; takes a walnut finish beautifully.

3. Dainty design: notice the rounded footboard of the bed; the extra-legs of bed and vanity; the delicate decoration; all these features are exquisitely feminine.

4. Green and orchid, or blue-green and peach are particularly attractive with this wood finish.

5. Extra piece of furniture may be placed in alcove or well-lighted closet; a baywindow is an ideal location for the dressing-table.

"HIGH LIGHTS" ON LOWER INTERIOR

1. Formal French bedroom suite of great dignity, by The Herman Miller Furniture Co., Zeeland, Michigan.

2. Long low lines and wide wood surfaces suggest both the Empire style and the Art Moderne, without any of the eccentricities of the latter.

3. French atmosphere may be created by means of panelled walls, toile de Jouy spread with taffeta flounce, chandelier, Empire table lamp and French etchings.

4. For a suggestion of Art Moderne, the walls should be plain, painted in some silvery color and decorated with large unframed mirrors of geometric design. Lamps, lampshades and wall fixtures in the new mode.

"HIGH LIGHTS" ON UPPER INTERIOR

1. The Northfield Company, Sheboygan, Wis., designed this fiber furniture for the sunroom.

2. Moderately priced, it makes a fine living room suite for the family of modest means who cannot afford high-grade upholstered living room furniture, yet will not be satisfied with inferior goods.

3. A great variety of pieces available, even to telephone stand and magazine racks, to permit grouped arrangements as in orthodox living room.

4. Color is a commodity which costs little: fiber frame and cretonne cushions provide a basis for attractive scheme to be developed through draperies and linoleum floor covering.

"HIGH LIGHTS" ON LOWER INTERIOR

Living Room or Sun Room Suite of hand woven fiber manufactured by the Northfield Furniture Co., Sheboygan Wis., marked by four outstanding characteristics.

1. Elegance and Distinction of Design:
Note the graceful forward and downward sweep of the arms of the davenport and chairs forming the famous "Hogarth Line of Beauty." Also the charming variation in the design of the "weave" itself.

2. Rugged Construction: This furniture is built to give long-time service.

3. A Striking and Artistic Color Scheme: The interweave of colors between the fiber structure and the smartly designed covering is a real achievement.

4. Genuine Comfort: In the substantial filling and well made upholstering.

"HIGH LIGHTS" ON UPPER INTERIOR	"HIGH LIGHTS" ON LOWER INTERIOR
1. The Litchfield dining room suite, by The Period Cabinet Mfg. Co., New Albany, Ind.	1. Colonial dining room suite by The Period Cabinet Mfg. Co., New Albany, Ind.
2. Designed especially for the 100th Market Anniversary; Chippendale inspiration, in memory of remarkable craftsman and masterly carver who was the originator of the Furniture Market idea.	2. Exquisite in every detail, this suite spells lasting attractiveness. Simple elegant lines and sober ornamentation form a tasteful ensemble of which one does not tire. Particularly suitable for people who take a pride in their belongings and cherish them year after year.
3. This "Fitting Furniture" splendidly justifies its makers' slogan. Will fit into average room, large or small, in home or apartment.	3. Quality of material and excellence of workmanship are the most subtle form of luxury and are always indicative of good breeding and fastidious taste.
4. Formerly made exclusively for the elite of society, Chippendale furniture is now within the reach of all who can appreciate its excellence: the aristocrats of taste.	4. Reticence in background treatment and use of accessories expressive of feminine modesty.

"HIGH LIGHTS" ON UPPER INTERIOR

1. Dining Suite by Charles P. Limbert Co., Holland, Mich.

2. A Sheraton group of unusual beauty, true to style in every detail.

3. Graceful in outline and delicate in proportion, yet every piece is strongly constructed, with all posts, rails and stretchers of solid mahogany and all fronts and tops of heavy laminated stock.

4. The fronts are surfaced with beautifully figured crotch mahogany, with inlays of genuine marqueterie.

5. The table top is equipped with equalizing slides and extends to 8 or 10 feet.

6. The chairs, with frames of solid mahogany, have upholstered spring seats.

"HIGH LIGHTS" ON LOWER INTERIOR

1. Living room table, by Mersman Brothers Corpn., Celina, O.

2. Jacobean bulb motif, combined with mellow curve of stretcher suggesting Italian Renaissance influence, and dainty carvings and wood veneers of later date. Typical of modern American tendency in furniture design, which is not to rebel against tradition, but to blend elements of various Periods susceptible of association.

3. Window grouping: one of the many possible treatments of the table in living room decoration. Windows with draperies provide high lines; table with flanking chairs glorifies a rather trite architectural conception.

"HIGH LIGHTS" ON UPPER INTERIOR

1. Small tables by Mersman Brothers Corpn., Celina, O.

2. "Each chair group must contain at least one table," is an axiom in modern Interior Decoration.

3. Size of table should be proportionate to that of chair next to which it is placed; gateleg table exactly qualified to associate with davenport; octagonal table also excellent.

4. Rectangular table next to chair of rectilinear design; one equipped with drawers particularly convenient; for instance, small objects left about may be collected there and sorted out once a week, saving many trips across the house.

"HIGH LIGHTS" ON LOWER INTERIOR

1. Tables by Mersman Bros. Corpn., Celina, O.

2. Davenport table of exquisite Duncan Phyfe inspiration; typically American; graceful, aristocratic. Notice quaint medallion reminiscent of old-fashioned fire-screens.

3. Location back of davenport, in center of room, where the eye falls upon it as soon as one enters, is justified by excellence of design, texture and workmanship.

4. Tables next to fireside chairs: not only convenient, but support decorative accessories which play important part in fireplace grouping, as they introduce joyous elements of color and pattern: books, lamp, vases, flowers and trinkets.

"HIGH LIGHTS" ON UPPER INTERIOR

1. Tables by Mersman Bros. Corpn., Celina, O.

2. Davenport table in the French manner (Louis XVI): light, vertical, slender; delicately matched veneers; great attention to details.

3. Though surroundings are not French, they express the same spirit of elegance, and exquisiteness: no heavy chairs, violent colors or large patterns.

4. This table is the jewel of the room, therefore occupies the center of the floor; but is backed up against the davenport because a table must always: (1) serve a useful purpose, (2) be related to some other furniture pieces.

"HIGH LIGHTS" ON LOWER INTERIOR

1. Tables by Mersman Bros. Corpn., Celina, O.

2. Long narrow table used as console; central motif in wall composition of great decorative interest; suitable base for large oil painting: slightly heavier and darker, gives stability to the ensemble.

3. Notice that chairs are placed close by, so that table may serve its logical purpose.

4. Octagonal tables: richly carved; suitable complements to davenport group; a pair needed to ensure absolute symmetry.

5. Table at left: for a man's use, next to large chair, probably a Coxwell: sturdy construction, vigorous design, solid top.

"HIGH LIGHTS" ON UPPER INTERIOR	"HIGH LIGHTS" ON LOWER INTERIOR
1. Chair and table group, by The Phoenix Chair Co., Sheboygan, Wis.	1. Chair and table group by The Phoenix Chair Co., Sheboygan, Wis.
2. Entirely composed of early American pieces, delightfully quaint, yet serviceable, too; might be a reading and writing corner in the really lived-in living room, where every bit of space has utility and significance; probably part of a girl's bedroom.	2. Fully illustrates the "living-room trinity": chair, table and lamp. By day, the window fulfills function of the latter.
3. Like words in a sentence, each piece of furniture contributes something to the completeness of the group. Chair and table, in particular, have become inseparable, and lamp completes the "trinity" which is the basis of good decoration.	3. Various elements of the group are related together: chair is made of Select Birch, finished Walnut; patterned fabrics conform to simple homelike ideal of early American design; colors of upholstery pattern are repeated in draperies and echoed in book bindings; lamp is tall enough and placed to permit reading in perfect comfort.

"HIGH LIGHTS" ON UPPER INTERIOR

1. Left: Occasional chair.

2. A charming group that is both serviceable and decorative. The table, though a gem in itself, needed to fill this bare corner, would not be complete without a seat. Chair is form-fitting, gaily upholstered, inviting.

3. Right: A genuine reading nook requires good light, books and magazines near at hand *and a comfortable chair*.

4. Nagging never did keep a man at home, but a good fireside chair is an irresistible argument.

"HIGH LIGHTS" ON LOWER INTERIOR

1. Tasteful though inexpensive living room. In Early American design, simplicity is utilized as a basic artistic element.

2. Chairs hold a permanent invitation to stay awhile, therefore are powerful allies against modern tendency of young folks to seek entertainment outside of home.

3. Group chairs with other pieces, to suggest some form of activity and thus give them their full significance.

4. Colorful upholstery echoes hues of draperies; lively, cheerful; permits use of inexpensive plain background and practical all-over carpeting.

Write to "American Homes Bureau" for information on where to secure the furnishings shown.

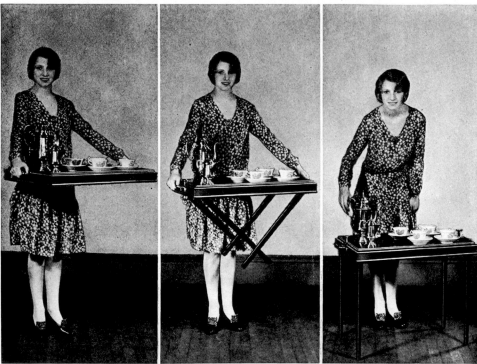

"HIGH LIGHTS" ON UPPER INTERIOR

1. Living room pieces by The Phoenix Chair Co., Sheboygan, Wis.

2. Chairs: early American inspiration; quaint, home-like, each with a charm and individuality of its own. Yet reasonably priced.

3. Genuinely comfortable, too: note the form-fitting design.

4. Fireside chair of exceptional merit: low seat, slanting backward; low arms; back that corresponds exactly to human anatomy and gives real support.

5. Book case: makes books seem more accessible, more lived-with, more chummy than when aligned in neat rows on built-in shelves. Can also serve as china cabinet in dining room.

"HIGH LIGHTS" ON LOWER INTERIOR

1. Convertible Table-Tray, solid Mahogany or colored Lacquer Enamel, by R. R. Scheibe, Somerville, Mass.

2. This is an attractive and novel furnishing, useful in small apartments or more pretentious homes, or in Clubs and Hotels.

3. Can be spread with doily and tea service, carried before guests as a tray, and served from as a table. When removing, table is converted into tray without disarrangement of the service.

4. Either change made in three seconds, by merely pressing lightly on thumb latches while holding clear of the floor.

5. Economical of space and combines the purposes of two articles, a separate table and the usual serving tray.

"HIGH LIGHTS" ON UPPER INTERIOR

1. Fabrics imported by M. H. Rogers, Inc., New York City.

2. Harmonious use of colorful materials imparts to a room interest, character and a sense of comfort.

3. Many different types of fabrics may be used in one room if related through texture and color scheme.

4. Love-seat at left:—silk velours de Genes;—silk, chenille and tinsel embroidery used for piano scarf and two cushion tops; —sofa and chairs upholstered in brocade, gold silk damask and needle-point;—draperies of gold silk, damask to match sofa;—gauze curtains.

"HIGH LIGHTS" ON LOWER INTERIOR

1. Dining room furniture sold by Peck and Hills Furniture Co., Chicago, Ill.

2. Early English: the more decorative features of several closely related styles have been skillfully combined to produce this richly aristocratic suite.

3. Large Elizabethan table and Late Jacobean sideboard fit into large room and call for sumptuous background.

4. Chairs meet modern demand for comfort: slanting backs, upholstered seats are improvements on original specimens of the Period.

5. High china cabinets with doors were not made in the 17th century, but the one shown here embodies the best characteristics of Early English design and harmoniously completes the set.

"HIGH LIGHTS" ON UPPER INTERIOR

1. Pullman Couch, by The Pullman Couch Co., 3759 So. Ashland, Chicago, Ill. A davenport bed that successfully conceals its utilitarian function.

2. No visible structural difference between this and the usual davenport. Straight and curved lines, plain and figured fabrics harmoniously combined. Designed to blend in pleasingly with most Period designs.

3. Natural center of interest in average room.

4. Opens quickly and easily into double bed. Special set of springs ensures sleeping comfort. You do not sleep on the same springs you sit on.

"HIGH LIGHTS" ON LOWER INTERIOR

1. Pullman Couch and chair, manufactured by The Pullman Couch Co., 3759 So. Ashland, Chicago, Ill.

2. Highly suitable for small living room, but also at home in larger interior because of rich decorativeness. Louis XV design.

3. Ideal to impart character to bare nondescript background.

4. Colorfulness of linen frieze covering suggests a Spanish setting: rough plastered walls, arched windows, striped draperies hung from poles, heraldic panel over mantel.

5. Proportions of furniture and rich carvings on frame call for details both colorful and exquisite: note paintings, banjo clock and smaller accessories.

"HIGH LIGHTS" ON UPPER INTERIOR

1. Dining room furniture by The Rockford Standard Furniture Co., Rockford, Ill.

2. Louis XVI influence, indicated by use of medallions in chair backs and in center of furniture pieces. Differs essentially from Louis XVI in size, mass and proportions. This modification rendered necessary by requirements of American Home-life which tends toward solidity and durability.

3. Highly ornate, will fit into large bare room of non-descript character and strike a note of opulence.

4. Few accessories needed to complete decorative scheme, as suite provides both pattern and color in abundance.

"HIGH LIGHTS" ON LOWER INTERIOR

1. Dining room suite, by The Rockford Standard Furniture Co., Rockford, Ill.

2. Massive table, legs arranged in pairs, plus business-like central support: stability and solidity made visible; renders practical service and creates a restful state of mind.

3. Chairs: rich, comfortable, colorful; seats and back upholstered.

4. Cabinet has height, pattern and color, three elements that are precious in creating a distinctive interior.

5. Substantial and elaborate buffet requires wall decoration of vigorous pattern and rich coloring.

6. Glitter of gold in picture and mirror frames brings out exotism of Chinese decoration on cabinet.

"HIGH LIGHTS" ON UPPER INTERIOR	"HIGH LIGHTS" ON LOWER INTERIOR

"HIGH LIGHTS" ON UPPER INTERIOR

1. Dining room suite, by The Rockford Furniture Co., Rockford, Ill.

2. Art Moderne influence is felt in geometric conception of chair backs and decorative panels.

3. To incorporate into American settings, temper the rigidity of design by use of floral rug, floral picture and accessories featuring the curve. Plain draperies and plain light-colored plain walls, however, are consistent with this style of furnishing.

4. Oddness of decorative panels might prove less aggressive if the traditional American atmosphere were renounced altogether and rug, draperies, pictures, accessories and light fixtures planned according to modernistic tenets. Must be done right, however, as clumsy attempt easily results in grotesque effects.

"HIGH LIGHTS" ON LOWER INTERIOR

1. Dining room suite by The Rockford Furniture Co., Rockford, Ill.

2. Colonial inspiration: suggests large, hospitable and gracious interiors of pre-revolutionary days. Details are noteworthy: straight cabinet top with pediment reminiscent of Chippendale; slender vase motif of chair backs characteristic of Sheraton; Duncan Phyfe sweep of table legs; all combine into harmonious ensemble of great distinction.

3. The background is consistently plain, to emphasize the elegant restraint of the furniture design, with the one exception of the sideboard group which is artistic in conception, coloring, discrimination and symmetrically balanced arrangement.

"HIGH LIGHTS" ON UPPER INTERIOR

1. Dining room suite, by The Rockford Furniture Co., Rockford, Ill.

2. Spanish design: rectangular outlines; arched contour of chair backs at top and bottom; brass nails and finials; wrought iron under-bracings; arch and column decorative motif.

3. Gives individuality to plain, characterless walls. Typical striped draperies with wrought iron poles are very much in harmony with such furniture, but illustration shows how a plain fabric hanging from a cornice molding may be effectively substituted.

4. Rich colorful rug on plain dark carpeting, tile floor or linoleum in tile pattern.

"HIGH LIGHTS" ON LOWER INTERIOR

1. Dining room furniture by Henry C. Steul and Sons, Inc., Buffalo, N. Y.

2. Italian Renaissance design: substantial, artistic, richly decorative. Furniture of that Period was designed for palaces; still conveys suggestion of sumptuousness and aristocracy.

3. In scale with large room, in prosperous, hospitable home.

4. Individual pieces are all harmonious, yet vary enough in detail so that they do not become monotonous.

5. Upholstered backs of chairs add charm and comfort to this pattern.

6. Few accessories needed, but should be of good size and unquestionable artistic merit.

Early American
BUILT BY
STICKLEY
OF FAYETTEVILLE, N.Y.

Early American
BUILT BY
STICKLEY
OF FAYETTEVILLE, N.Y.

"HIGH LIGHTS" ON UPPER INTERIOR

1. Early American furniture built by L. & J. G. Stickley, Inc., of Fayetteville, N. Y.

2. Woods are the same as found in original Early American pieces: cherry, hickory, maple, pine.

3. Rich soft mellow tone of rare old pieces, particularly right for this type of furniture, duplicated in Stickley Finish. When placed with other furniture, it strikes a note of perfect harmony and in addition brings interest and variety to a room.

4. At least a few Early American pieces should be in every home, as this style was born and developed on our own soil and conveys, therefore, a peculiarly significant message.

"HIGH LIGHTS" ON LOWER INTERIOR

1. Bedroom furniture by L. & J. G. Stickley, Inc., Fayetteville, N. Y.

2. Wood combinations in each piece are studied carefully so as to create the most authentic and effective Early American furniture outside of genuine antiques.

3. Spirit of the early 1700's embodied in this furniture, between the time when the most vital need was for rough shelter, and the later era of preciosity when leisure and wealth led settlers to covet the magnificence of European homes.

4. Principal characteristics of original models express ideals that are close to our own today: durability, comfort with simplicity; beauty without ostentation.

"HIGH LIGHTS" ON UPPER INTERIOR

1. Furniture by The Stow-Davis Furniture Co., Grand Rapids, Mich. Suitable for office, bank, library or club room.

2. Italian design, modern in execution, being devoid of carvings and other sculptural decorations. Smooth polished surfaces and massive proportions suggest business man's ideals of commonsense, straightforwardness, stability and prosperity.

3. Same ideals should be embodied in background: oak panelled walls, adorned with large oil paintings; massive panelled doors, handsome parquet floor and dignified velour draperies.

4. Linoleum floor covering in parquet design or all-over carpeting also very satisfactory.

"HIGH LIGHTS" ON LOWER INTERIOR

1. Office furniture by The Stow-Davis Furniture Co., Grand Rapids, Mich.

2. Strictly business-like: rectangular, unadorned, massive; yet artistic: the lines are excellent, the texture and tone of the wood are beautiful.

3. Comfortable: roomy desk, with plenty of drawer space; semi-upholstered chairs; davenport.

4. Usual principles of Interior Decoration apply to office rooms as well as homes, with stress on suitability. Furniture placed for convenience, but also for correct effect; dark tones of wall panelling create proper atmosphere for concentration; long straight-hanging draperies obviate the usual bare look of office windows without offending masculine taste.

"HIGH LIGHTS" ON UPPER INTERIOR

A tasteful room after the Italian Renaissance, with interest centered in the Beautiful Streit Slumber Chair (The C. F. Streit Mfg. Company, Cincinnati, O.).

1. Note how the Queen Anne design of the Streit Chair harmonizes perfectly with the other furnishings.

2. Note how the graceful arms of the chair invite you to come and "sit down."

3. And how the deep, rich upholstering conveys a sense of luxurious comfort.

4. The matched footstool, too, adds a touch of smartness and enables a man to take his ease like a gentleman.

"HIGH LIGHTS" ON LOWER INTERIOR

A charming living-room group, built around another model of the Beautiful Streit Slumber Chair (The C. F. Streit Mfg. Company, Cincinnati, O.).

1. Here, the Florentine design of the Streit Chair was selected to add a contrasting note to the severity of the Post Colonial furnishings.

2. Grace of line and perfect proportions contribute to the authentic beauty of this chair.

3. Its unique features and luxurious depths supply just the soul-satisfying comfort a man yearns for.

4. A woman's chair for looks—a man's for use!

"HIGH LIGHTS" ON UPPER INTERIOR

1. Elaborate bedroom suite No. 455, by the Union Furniture Co., Batesville, Ind.

2. Serpentine outlines, ornate carvings suggestive of Louis XV Period, make this furniture feminine in the extreme. Suitable for the woman of leisure who likes to surround herself with the symbolism as well as the substance of luxury.

3. Fragility of Louis XV style here more apparent than real: proportions are massive though decoration creates illusion of lightness; typical cabriole legs have been modified to vertical construction with fluted columns and finials.

4. Fine grain effects are typical of Union Furniture.

"HIGH LIGHTS" ON LOWER INTERIOR

1. The White Furniture Co., of Mebane, N. C., created this charming bedroom suite.

2. Severity of rectilinear design is graced with discreet curves in mirrors and head board, while cut-out footboard with posts represents the fanciful element, strictly disciplined and kept within bounds.

3. Suitable for young couple; but what a delightful room it would make for the business girl! Small writing table, simple rocking chair suggest just such an occupant, active, efficient.

4. Simple though tasteful wall panelling is most adequate; long straight draperies in excellent harmony. Feminine taste revealed in many mirrors, dainty boudoir lamps and French pastel reproductions.

"HIGH LIGHTS" ON UPPER INTERIOR

1. Decorative function of Cedar Chest, illustrated by The West Branch Novelty Co., Milton, Pa.

2. There is room for more than one chest in every home. Here is one at home in living room, rendering service as end table to the persons using either chair.

3. Cedar lining is masked by handsome walnut Plywood exterior, harmonizing with usual living room woods. Four knobs suggest an upper drawer; railing at back gives effect of a box seat.

4. Simple tasteful design and unadorned surface contrast excellently with patterned panel and upholstery fabric.

"HIGH LIGHTS" ON LOWER INTERIOR

1. Cedar chest in location that saves wall space for taller pieces (The West Branch Novelty Co., Milton, Pa.).

2. Design and decoration are exquisitely feminine.

3. Seat arrangement, with footboard of bed as back rest; emphasized by cushion and small rug.

4. Chest as useful as a table to set down wraps and packages when entering the room. Whole grouping is stamped with the seal of woman's resourcefulness.

5. Walnut Plywood with maple overlays and wood turnings fit this chest for the Colonial room; while heavy scroll legs make it just as suitable for Spanish interior.

"HIGH LIGHTS" ON UPPER INTERIOR

1. "The Lawrence" bedroom suite. Produced by the West Michigan Furniture Co., Holland, Mich.

2. Fine example of excellent construction and workmanship priced very low.

3. Beautiful butt walnut veneers carefully selected for their color and figure—skillfully laid and matched. Clusters of flowers hand-painted on background of shaded jade green lending a tone of color that is most pleasing and restful. Trimmings of Old English Antique brass.

4. The painted motif may serve as guide in building up color scheme. Emphasize the floral note in draperies and rug, using green for background.

"HIGH LIGHTS" ON LOWER INTERIOR

1. Bedroom suite (West Michigan Furniture Co., Holland, Mich.).

2. Solid maple, with rich hue of old amber maple blended with antique shading; hand painted clusters of flowers in low tones give each piece that peculiar touch that stamps it with individuality.

3. Practical, yet artistic. Imagine the delight and pride of a boy or girl with a room all their own, furnished with pieces of this type.

4. Large enough, however, to accommodate adult. Just right for small bedroom that needs color; inexpensive but tasty combination for guest room.

5. Single or double bed available.

"HIGH LIGHTS" ON UPPER INTERIOR

1. Occasional chair, by W. F. Whitney Company, Inc., So. Ashburnham, Mass.

2. Staunch graceful design; homelike charm due to lively pattern and gay coloring.

3. Type of upholstery on seat and back only cuts down price considerably, yet produces a chair that is comfortable, serviceable and decorative.

4. Particularly effective when grouped with small table possessing great individuality, such as early English design shown here.

5. Use this as master's chair in quaint dining room suite composed of: large gateleg table, five fiddle-back windsor chairs, Welsh dresser and Colonial corner cabinet.

"HIGH LIGHTS" ON LOWER INTERIOR

1. Bedroom furniture by The John Widdicomb Co., Grand Rapids, Mich.

2. Tasteful combination of 18th century English styles; elegantly simple; fine wood grain and contrasting inlays suggest the modern mode without disturbing the perfect harmony of old masters' conception.

3. Such a room might look on to a lovely old-fashioned English garden; a hint of this is embodied in the floral medallions which decorate each piece and further developed through use of charming wallpaper with naturalistic hollyhock motifs; oval rug with flower wreath and natural bouquet on highboy.

"HIGH LIGHTS" ON UPPER INTERIOR	"HIGH LIGHTS" ON LOWER INTERIOR

"HIGH LIGHTS" ON UPPER INTERIOR

1. Window shades and window shade decorations by The Western Shade Cloth Co., Chicago, Ill.

2. *Luxor* window shades—made of unfilled translucent fabric, treated with exquisite color tones in pure, non-fading oil colorings.

3. *Arabesk Carvings*—affixed to the lower edge of shades. Unusual delicate hand-tinted effects. Several color combinations to harmonize with draperies and Luxor shade cloth colors.

4. New style *Tassel Pulls*—with composition ovals in colors to blend with Arabesk Carvings and Luxor shade cloth.

5. *Luxor* shades, *Arabesk Carvings* and *Tassel Pulls* form a complete harmonizing decorative unit which, with variations of colored, will fit into the decorative scheme of any room.

"HIGH LIGHTS" ON LOWER INTERIOR

1. Bedroom furniture by The Widdicomb Furniture Co., Grand Rapids, Mich.

2. Lovely Georgian (English) suite: dignity and restraint in design; quiet beauty and grace for a lifelong appeal.

3. Panelled wall background, finished in delicate pastel tint, corresponds to sober elegance of the furniture and permits an occasional readjustment of the decorative scheme.

4. For youthful occupants or a gay summery ensemble, use small rugs in colorful patterns and a floral fabric for draperies. A more formal setting to conform with the English design calls for plain chenille carpeting, damask draperies with festooned valances, crystal chandeliers and wall fixtures, and taffeta bedspreads.

"HIGH LIGHTS" ON UPPER INTERIOR

1. Sunroom furniture in the Modern mode (Ypsilanti Reed Furniture Co., Ionia, Mich.). Comfort combined with cool simplicity and ultra-smart colorfulness.

2. Square massive design particularly felicitous wherever man-size chairs are desired.

3. Modernistic patterns of upholstery fabrics best displayed against severely plain though colorful background. Try unusual tones, such as primrose yellow, henna, silver mauve, ashes of roses or periwinkle blue.

4. Small end-table of matching design just as essential to comfort here as in living room.

5. Modern lamps, shades and wall fixtures would put finishing touch to tasteful fashionable ensemble.

"HIGH LIGHTS" ON LOWER INTERIOR

1. Living room or hall furniture, by E. Wiener Company, Milwaukee, Wis.

2. An exquisite wall composition for entrance hall; also suitable for living room.

3. Early English design (chairs), formal and decorative; tempered by French influence noticeable in lines of cabinet.

4. Strictly symmetrical arrangement creates an impression of dignity and restfulness suited to the character of the furniture.

5. Mirror essential to hall decoration, as light supply is seldom adequate.

6. Cabinet might serve as telephone stand.

7. Walls might be: 1. plain; 2. papered in a space-making climbing vine pattern; or 3. a Chinese design.

As Shown by Venturus, John Wanamaker, New York

An interesting portion of one of the Venturus interiors with its divan in black and white lacquer by L. and Maurice Jallott, the Primavera Bookcase in palissandre, and the decorative doors in gold, black and silver lacquer by L. and Maurice Jallott. Hand tufted "Floreal" rugs.

THE MODERN PERIOD

BY HELEN GARDNER

A new style has suddenly appeared in our midst. It is called by various names, "Modern," "Modernistic," "Design moderne," "Post impressionism," "French decorative art of the modern school," "Contemporary furniture," "The new decorative art," "Modernique," etc.

To understand the new style it is necessary to understand what the modern spirit means in every phase of life. It would be absolutely impossible to understand the new furniture without first knowing the causes that have produced it.

WHAT IS IT?

A *new style* for a *new age*. Not a new fancy, a passing fad, nor a manufacturer's whim. A period style that will be recognized by future ages just as we recognize the period styles of the past. It is a style that *represents us*. We are modern people, with modern manners and clothes and ways of living, and modern expression in the furnishing and decorating of our homes follows. The whole world has changed and it is illogical for the people of today to live against backgrounds that are of the past, in which the spirit is dead and gone as the days of the Louis's and George's are dead and gone. We are in a new and wonderful age of our own.

This is an age of machinery and steel, of gasoline and electricity, of swift motion, of congestions, of democracy. An age not dictated to by the historian but by artisans who are using the new tools. In this new era we are beginning to be governed by ideas of fitness. timeliness, and creative imagination instead of imitation of other periods. Truth is being measured in new ways. Other ages expressed mysticism, or elegance, or sentimentality, today we are fascinated by *facts*, by science, by the way things work. And this is what the new decorative art expresses.

The basis of the whole modern style is a *new spirit*. It is our response to the new order of things. Life has changed and there is no turning back.

WHY IS IT?

The modern style is not difficult to understand if we get at the *cause* of its development.

Art is the mirror of life. Each age of history was dominated by peculiar influences of its own. These furnishings gave birth to peculiar forms of architecture and art and furnishings which interpreted the civilization of that age. Each period had its own kind of beauty. Until the modern style began to take form, art styles had had no sound basis in general living conditions since the Georgian

(Continued on next page)

61

Designed and executed by Barker Bros., Los Angeles, for their "Modes and Manners Shop."

"Stock" table. Ivory enamel with flame color interior. May be used against the wall or against a large chair as an end table.

Designed and executed by Barker Bros., Los Angeles, for their "Modes and Manners Shop."

Chair. Silver leaf. Upholstery of almond green brocade. French table in silver leaf with mirror top.

era. Up to that time there had always been a sound relation between the thought and life of the times and the architecture and furniture and hangings and so forth.

The beauty of our era then is expressing itself upon the *interests of the men of today*, not upon what interested their ancestors. The revolution wrought by the machine age is at the bottom of it. It is based upon industrialism as the key-note of modern civilization.

WHAT DOES IT MEAN?

The *Ladies Home Journal* for May, 1928, says editorially, "This sudden swing to a modernistic tendency in furniture and rugs and fabrics, in china and silver and glassware, is quite the most interesting and entertaining new development that has come into home decoration in many years. . . . Furniture stores that put in a few pieces for display have found in this new style a new best seller, and some of the American manufacturers are preparing to ride in on the wave of popular enthusiasm for something new. . . . Except for the ungainly "craftsman" furniture of a generation ago this is the first new design in furniture in more than a century. . . . One thing it proves —and this is an element in the greatness of our country and our time—*that style is never static*. And the excitement over a new vogue in home furnishings gives further point to the remark of some wise man that *change is progress* and *progress is change*.

WHAT IS ITS HISTORY?

When the machine age began in the nineteenth century the products of the machine were almost universally ugly. As a revolt against this in 1860 in England, William Morris started a movement to get back to the old beauty of handicraft. This movement had a wide following in Germany and America. Elbert Hubbard's Roycrofters at East Aurora, N. Y., were exponents of it in this country. It was a sincere and high-minded movement but wrong fundamentally. It is impossible to set up old handicraft styles as models of beauty in a machine age.

ART NOUVEAU. About 1896 in Germany and Austria and France it began to be felt that *beautiful objects* could be produced by *machinery*. The Art Nouveau furniture was a deliberate attempt to use the new tools to create a new style. The results were not good. There was too much decoration and it was often monstrously ugly. Peculiar curves were used that made for weak design.

EXPOSITIONS. In 1904 the St. Louis exposition displayed furniture and objects d'art from Austria and Germany which showed what they were doing in developing the new art.

In 1910 the Brussels exposition made a great showing of what was being done in the modern manner.

In 1925 occurred the Paris exposition. France had been much interested in the modern displays at the Brussels exposition and decided to have an exhibit of her own in 1915. Due to the war, however, it was not ready until 1925. The modern things shown there at that time interested the whole world. The eccentricities of the Art Nouveau had been discarded and a new and elegant and simple style evolved. From the Paris Exposition has come the great impetus to modern furnishings of the last few years. France is organized to set styles, and this manner of furnishing that she has developed and which is closely related to her modern life, is exported by her to other countries.

GERMANY. At the very start of the new movement schools for artisans began to spring up in Germany, starting first at Munich.

They have a method in Germany of bringing artist and manufacturer together. In exhibitions of arts and crafts a designer will create designs for some certain factory which then produces sample articles, exhibiting them at the same time.

AMERICA. The modernistic style is used extensively all over Europe but is just beginning in America. Older nations have deeper art traditions and therefore were the first to develop an art with the new tools to meet the new conditions. The skyscrapers of America are a modernistic development but Europeans were the first to notice their beauty. America was not represented at the Paris Exposition because there seemed to be no designers at that time who could do work not based on the period styles. Until very recently we have been using machinery merely to copy the styles of bygone days that were made by hand and no effort has been made toward anything creative. American designers are so accustomed to copying bits from here and there that it is hard for them to realize that we are in the second epoch of civilization—that of *machinery*.

As yet American furniture manufacturers have not become much interested in producing the modern designs. Their plants are fitted for making reproductions of the standardized period styles. But the new style is beginning to "take" and eventually they will have to make the change. France is supplying the impetus for the new styles but America will have to do the quantity production. Competent designers of the new styles are beginning to be known in the larger cities.

THE HOME FURNISHING ARTS of America have developed as follows:

1. Early settlers on the east coast—developed hand-made decorative arts of their own fitted to their life.
2. The pioneers of the west were torn loose from European ways. They were thrown on their own resources and developed household arts like those of primitive people. Such still exist in some of the southern mountain districts.
3. Era of power-driven machinery.
    a. Period of wood-turning. 1870.
    b. Period of compo carving.
    c. Reproductions of period styles.
    d. Modern period based on machinery conditions.

HOW IS MODERNISM EXPRESSING ITSELF?

We find modernism being expressed in every phase of life. In the FINE ARTS—in the seemingly queer forms of some modern poetry and literature and drama—in futuristic and cubistic painting and sculpture—in the work of modern composers such as Debussy—in the rhythms of jazz.

CLOTHING. Women's attire has changed greatly. The short skirts and general comfort of their clothes, together with bobbed hair meet the demands of this fast-moving, practical age. Everywhere on the newest styles are seen geometrical and futuristic ornamentation.

JEWELRY. Jewelry was one of the first arts to display the modern note in this country. It seems to be easier to introduce a new style in small things such as jewelry.

ADVERTISING. A new dress for advertising—it has suddenly become geometric and expressionistic. Used in newspaper advertising and in brilliant colors on magazine covers and bill boards. The display windows of some of the high class stores have begun to blaze with gay, strangely designed, bizarre dressings.

ART IN TRADES CLUB. A "get-together" of manufacturers, designers, buyers. They have exhibitions and hold competitions.

ARCHITECTURE. Always the first to show the new ideas of an age. Modern architecture based on engineering and the new use of materials—steel framework with thin coverings of concrete or brick. *Flatness* the note—windows not recessed. Started with the American skyscraper. In Europe a new domestic architecture has grown up founded on the same geometric principles—applying the virtues of skyscrapers, factories, steamers and automobiles to the building of houses. *Lightness* an important factor as contrasted with the thick walls of old architecture. Also larger windows used and more of them. The new houses are severely plain, constructed of cement, with plain iron railings. Windows may run all the way around a corner. Some are built as one large room with moveable partitions.

MUSEUMS. The Metropolitan Museum in New York City has recognized the new style to the extent of having a permanent exhibit of modern furnishings.

In 1926 a loan exhibit of modern furnishings from France toured the country and was shown at various museums.

STORES. The American department store caters to popular demand. So there is a reason when it begins to feature modernistic furnishings. Wanamaker's in New York have a department of modern furniture; Lord and Taylor have an exhibit of modern French furnishings—next year they plan to have an All-American modern exhibit. The International Exposition of Arts and Trades was held at Macy's in New York—American designers competing with foreign for the first time. The Abraham and Straus Co. in Brooklyn have a model home decorated throughout in modern style. Marshall Field and Co. in Chicago are featuring modern furniture under the trade name of "Dynamique Creations." Barker Bros. in Los Angeles have had for several years a shop devoted to the most advanced modern furnishings and featuring the creations of Kem Weber, who has become well-known as a modernistic designer.

(Continued on next page)

Designed and executed by Barker Bros., Los Angeles, for their "Modes and Manners Shop."

Bed-room piece. In black and silver leaf. Hand carving.

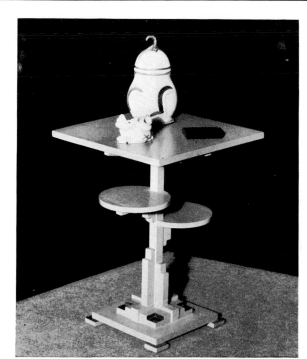

Designed and executed by Barker Bros., Los Angeles, for their "Modes and Manners Shop."

Smoking table. Decorated in different tones of solid color.

Designed and executed by Barker Bros., Los Angeles, for their "Modes and Manners Shop."

Beds in black and silver leaf.

Designed and executed by Barker Bros., Los Angeles, for their "Modes and Manners Shop."

Love seat. Woodwork of dusty pink. Upholstery in silk moire to match. Extremely low coffee table.

HOTELS. Many high class hotels and restaurants, especially abroad, are decorated in the new style. The new Hotel Lincoln in New York is decorated throughout in the modern manner—rugs, hangings and furniture. Also the Bismark Hotel in Chicago.

OCEAN LINERS. One of the great new French liners is decorated entirely in the most modernistic manner.

THE STAGE. The stage settings of modernistic designers like Joseph Urban have had a sweeping influence. Also the well-known "Chauve Souris" of the Russian, Balieff.

MOTION PICTURES. Extracts from the Los Angeles *Times*, April, 1928: "Films Set New Furniture Mode. Bold, Modernistic Style Coming into Vogue. Architecture, Decorations, Affected. Will Probably Influence All Home Furnishings. A new, boldly symbolic style of furnishings and decorations, as modern as next season's automobile has been adopted for the embellishment of some forthcoming screen offerings. That it will influence strongly the home furnishings of this country as other innovations have done in the past, is deemed inevitable by art directors of Hollywood motion-picture studios.

Cedric Gibbons, a master craftsman of motion-picture design, says, "This is what might be called the modernistic period and this decorative change in motion-picture settings follows naturally. Motion pictures set the vogue in wearing apparel styles. So it is with architectural and decorative styles. The screen designer must search them out—be the first to use them."

In "The Dancing Girl" (Metro-Goldwyn-Mayer), the modernistic sets and their furnishings—every piece designed and constructed within the studio—attracted home builders and furniture manufacturers who sought to compare the Gibbons designs with their own creations. Throughout the modernist motif employed by Gibbons, sweeping curves, abrupt angles and almost futuristic compositions are featured. Gold and silver, enriched by solid blacks, provide the central color scheme.

The furniture is of skyscraper design, and sharp, yet evenly balanced squares predominate. Full-length mirrors are triplaned and set at angles that reflect striking postures. Great, circular rugs.

Van Nest Polglaze has designed an exotic and modern setting for "The Magnificent Flirt" (Paramount). "Hollywood is fast becom-

Large coffee or "lounge" table. In colored enamels and gold-leaf.

ing the world's architectural center," Polglaze explains. "If one could but glimpse at some of the letters I receive from architects throughout the world regarding some certain design utilized in a picture, one would *appreciate the power of the silver sheet.*"

THE HOME. American architects have designed and built Norman and Spanish and English houses and thus led to a demand for "period" furniture and textiles to use in them. In "House Beautiful," May, 1928, Simon de Vaulchier says, "Completely different in aim and feeling is the modern idea of what goes to decorate a house. *The home is the last place to adopt a change*, it succumbs reluctantly to the mode of life lived outside the home and it is the public exigency that finally moulds the private life. The home at one time faintly reflected the splendors of the cathedral—later it was the rich display of the state that captured the imagination of the house-builder— each man strove to construct his own Versailles. Now the home is reflecting the factory and the machine. The mechanical, the mathematical is the obvious source of our present interior architecture and furniture."

Note: Detailed descriptions of the modern furniture are given later.

DRAPERIES AND WALL PAPER. To meet the need for modern wall paper, upholstery and drapery fabrics, designers have applied the principles of the new art. Restraint and geometrical patterns predominate.

OBJETS D'ART. In the smaller art objects the attempt is to *get the essential characteristics of things*. Hence the very much simplified figure and bird and animal contours.

Lalique, the great French glassware designer, has brought a new spirit of modernism into *glassware* and his productions are famous for their beauty.

SILVERWARE. Modernisticism finds expression in recently shown silver services. Coffee pot, creamer and sugar, each shaped upon the acutely angular lines of modernistic art.

Some makers are even expressing the modern love of color by using colored enamels as decorative parts of silverware.

Chaise longue! Typical simplified lines. "Powder table" of glass.

(Continued on next page)

RUSTIC HICKORY FURNITURE CO.

Manufacturers of Chairs, Rockers, Settees, Tables, Swings and Outdoor Rustic Work

LA PORTE, INDIANA

PRODUCTS

MANUFACTURERS OF
SUMMER HOME AND GARDEN
  FURNITURE including
BEDS
DRESSERS
GOLF BENCHES
ENAMELED FURNITURE
PERGOLAS
SUMMER HOUSES
TRELISSES
RUSTIC FENCES AND GATES

RUSTIC HICKORY FURNITURE THE MOST UNIQUE SUMMER FURNITURE IN AMERICA

Rustic Hickory Furniture has been the most popular summer furniture made for over a quarter century. It is hand-built of selected, second growth Northern hickory—the last word in comfort, beauty and durability. Made in 130 different styles for cabins, resorts, country clubs, urban porches, lawns and garden spots.

Send for complete catalog.

PRICES

The prices shown on this page are list or retail and subject to change without notice.

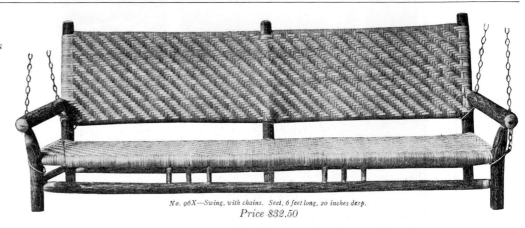

No. 96X—Swing, with chains. Seat, 6 feet long, 20 inches deep.
Price $32.50

No. 104X—Table. Height, 31 inches. Oak top, 36 inches in diameter. Golden Oak finish.
Price $16.00

No. 66X—Settee. Seat, 40 inches long; 16 inches deep; height of back from seat, 20 inches.
Price $20.00

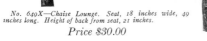

No. 649X—Chaise Lounge. Seat, 18 inches wide, 49 inches long. Height of back from seat, 21 inches.
Price $30.00

No. 522X—Chair. Seat, 17 inches wide; 15 inches deep; height of back from seat, 20 inches.
Price $11.00

No. 523X—Rocker. Seats 17 inches wide; 15 inches deep. Height of back from seat, 20 inches.
Price $12.00

FOSTER BROS. MFG. CO.
Steel Beds and Bed Springs
Main Office and Factory 807 Broad St., UTICA, N. Y.
Western Office and Factory
ST. LOUIS, MO.

No. 1165—Steel Bed. A very desirable
number with square tubing, solid steel
panel finished in two tone Walnut, hand
colored decoration, with cross grained
posts. Walnut or Mahogany. See Plates
Nos. 11 and 14.

No. 1727—Steel Bed. A beautiful large
panel bed with moulded tubing, spindle
fillers, finished in two-tone Walnut, hand
colored decoration. Walnut or Mahogany.
See Plates Nos. 11 and 14.

No. 187—Toe Trip Crib. An
appealing design in moulded tubing with solid panel, hand decorated, spindle fillers. Equipped with
the famous Foster toe trip attachment allowing ease of operation.
Walnut or Mahogany. See Plates
Nos. 11 and 14.

No. 1079—Glide Over Double
Day Bed. An attractive pattern
with coil spring construction,
square tubing, solid steel panel ends
finished in two tone Walnut, hand
decorated. Walnut or Mahogany,
See Plates Nos. 11 and 14.

PRODUCTS
Manufacturers of

Metal Beds
Coil and Fosterlink Bed-
springs
Metal Day Beds
Toe Trip Cribs
Davenport Bed Fixtures
Upholstery Spring Con-
structions
Upholstery Springs for all
purposes
Spring Filling for mattresses.

The Foster IDEAL Spring.
True and perfect spine support
without sag. Relaxation for nerves
and muscles. Better comfort—
rest—and sleep.

TRADE NAME
"Foster Ideal"—registered trade-mark and trade name used to
define products manufactured by this company.

GENERAL INFORMATION
Foster Bros. Mfg. Co., represents *over* half a century of spe-
cialized spring and metal bed construction. Its products are
known from coast to coast and are conceded by well informed furniture experts to be second to none.

OUR AIM IS TO SERVE YOU RIGHT
And we are at all times ready to quickly supply you with any
data or information that you may desire relative to our line or
our business. Write, wire or telephone.

Foster Bros. Mfg. Co.
Foster IDEAL
Utica. N.Y.-St.Louis.Mo.

FEATURES OF
FOSTER PRODUCTS
Foster Ideal Beds are made
of metal tubing — round,
square, or Victorian—in a
comprehensive assortment of
designs. They are finished in
white or ivory decorated enamel, or the more modern wood
finishes similar to plates
11 and 14, in the Woods and
Finishes Section preceding page
9 of this Reference Book.

Foster Toe Trip Cribs are sturdily made little beds with a patented Foster Toe Trip feature and a Foster Sliding Side.

Foster Ideal Springs are known, advertised and sold throughout the country as "The Bedspring that Supports the Spine." It
is made of 120 super-tempered spirals, with an interlocked and
chain linked top—flexible band center supports—and a swedged
(not cut) bar foundation.

Foster Glide Over Day Beds are 100% Foster built. Modern
wood finishes similar to plates 11 and 14, shown in the Woods
and Finishes Section preceding page 9 of this book.

Foster Spring Mattress Filling and Foster Davenport Bed Fixtures are used by many of this country's fine furniture makers.
The same holds true of Foster Upholstery Springs.

THE ROME COMPANY, INC.

Manufacturers of Bed Springs and Metal Furniture

3601-3617 So. Racine Ave., CHICAGO, ILL.

FACTORIES AT

CHICAGO, ILL., 3601-17 So. Racine Ave.　　　　BOSTON, MASS., 176 Portland Street
LONG ISLAND CITY, N. Y., Meadow St. and Anable Ave.　　　BALTIMORE, MD., 617 W. Pratt Street
ROME, N. Y., Northern Rome Division

Complete Stocks at all Times Carried in the Following Rome Warehouses:

Abilene	Chicago	High Point	Milwaukee	Phoenix	San Francisco
Albany	Cincinnati	Houston	Minneapolis	Pittsburgh	Seattle
Atlanta	Columbus	Indianapolis	Newark	Pocatello	Sioux City
Augusta	Dallas	Jacksonville	New Haven	Portland	Spokane
Baltimore	Denver	Kansas City	New Orleans	Providence	Springfield, Mass.
Bangor	Des Moines	Long Island City	Oklahoma City	Richmond	St. Louis
Boston	Detroit	Los Angeles	Omaha	Rochester	Toledo
Buffalo	El Paso	Louisville	Peoria	Rome, N. Y.	Wilkes-Barre
Butte	Grand Rapids	Memphis	Philadelphia	Salt Lake City	Worcester

---

PRODUCTS

MANUFACTURERS OF

BED-SPRINGS
—De Luxe, the Bed Spring Luxurious
—Hinge-Tied coil springs
—Helical-top coil springs
—Link fabric springs
—Cable fabric springs
BEDS
—Cribs (steel)
—Day Beds "Mascot"
—Day Beds coil springs
—Steel (Regular and twin sizes)
—Institution
—Bunks, Institution, contractors

COTS AND COUCHES
—Cots folding steel
—Couches, Sanitary, Steel
—Divans
—Porch Beds
HAMMOCKS AND GLIDERS
—Couch Hammocks, steel, upholstered
—Hammock stands, steel
—Hammock awnings
—Gliding Davenports
—Sedanettes

TRADE NAMES

"De Luxe" Coil Bed Springs; "Mascot" Day Beds and "Rome-Link" Couch Hammocks and Glider Davenports and Rome Beds identify the products of the Rome Company.

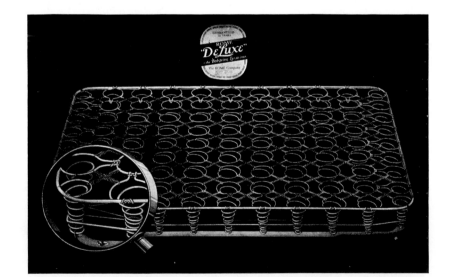

ROME
"DeLuxe"
- the Bedspring Luxurious
Trade Mark

SOLD UNDER POLICIES THAT PROTECT YOUR INTERESTS

There are good reasons for the outstanding success of Rome De Luxe Bedsprings—

To begin with, the product is right. You can offer it to your customers with full assurance of satisfaction. No other bedspring in the world offers the unique features of the exclusive De Luxe free-coil construction. It brings a new degree of comfort . . . sounder, more refreshing sleep.

Most widely advertised bedspring. Ready sales are made easier for you by extensive advertising. Practically every cus-

tomer who comes into your store already knows this famous bedspring . . . is partly sold already.

The Rome De Luxe is the most widely and heavily advertised bedspring on the market today!

Rome dealers are also provided with effective displays and local tie-ups to make this advertising work for *them*.

Your interests protected. Moreover, Rome De Luxe Bedsprings are sold under policies that protect the dealer's interests and position in every way. They are profitable items to sell.

THE ROME COMPANY, Inc.

No. 3745—*Automatic Coil Spring Day Bed. Its simplicity of operation, with large storage space for bedding, is very appealing. It has natural seat height for day use and standard bed height when opened as full size bed. Has heavy steel tubular ends with wide steel center and bottom panels, both of which carry attractive decorations and striping. Has one shaped wood spindle each side of center panel. Mattress is heavy all cotton filled, roll edge, button tufted. End shown is one of a wide variety of steel and wood ends which can be furnished.*

No. 0415—*Gliding Davenport. Back mattresses cotton filled, with slip cover drawn over pad; covered back. Seat mattress three cotton filled reversible cushions, box edge, no tufts. Fringed valance across front. Furnished only in coil spring constructions. Ends and arms swing over the top of supporting stand. Broad, comfortable reed arms, with cloth covering entire end construction.*

FINISHES

New combinations of Wood finishes and decorations have been worked out, with larger decals and marquetry designs used to give some of the patterns a more striking and more highly decorative appearance. You, of course, realize what Rome Wood Finish is and it is needless to say that there is not a wood finish on metal beds today which reproduces the natural grain of the wood as accurately as the Rome Process of Wood Finishing. In addition to the following finishes, it is now possible to obtain Bird's Eye Maple, Antique Maple and others that may be required to match up special finishes:

Bird's Eye Maple, resembling plate *13* Woods and Finishes Section.

Antique Maple, resembling plate *16* Woods and Finishes Section.

Mahogany, resembling plate *11* Woods and Finishes Section.

American Walnut, resembling plate *10* Woods and Finishes Section.

Persian Maple, resembling plate *8* Woods and Finishes Section.

French Walnut, resembling plate *17* Woods and Finishes Section.

Colonial Mahogany, resembling plate *18* Woods and Finishes Section.

The Woods and Finishes Section precedes page 9 of this book.

Special Enamel Finishes. To meet the demands of the many color schemes carried out in the home, a line of Special Enamel Finishes is now available on patterns in the line of Rome Beds. All of these finishes have been studied to a point where every detail of harmony in decoration and coloring has been carried out. Decorations are delicately colored flower designs, gold stripings, shaded effects, etc., have been worked out on each finish to a point of perfection in color schemes.

For your selection we have: Red — with Japanese decorations and gold and black striping; Jade Green—of two tones, making a most pleasing combination; Eb-

ony—ornamented with gold decorations and striping; Green and Ivory Combination—posts and filler tubing in Green, with Ivory panel, ornamented with harmonizing decoration and striping; Ebony and Ivory Combination—posts and filler tubing in Ebony, with Ivory panel, ornamented with harmonizing decoration and striping; Parchment—richly shaded with panels carrying attractive decorations in color.

INTERESTING NEW ROME PATTERNS

With the addition of the new patterns for 1928—there has never before been a line of Metal Beds that has as many unusual selling features as the Rome Line.

There is a variety of the Oval Bend, the Rome-craft and the Rome Gothic—the latter being in both the round, and inch and a half square tubing. In addition, we have included some patterns of inch and a half round tubing, some of which have the special shaped spindles and make very attractive designs. We have also included a number of very striking and attractive Windsor designs—combinations of solid panels with decorations, and special shaped steel spindles—which put these patterns in a position exceeding any past efforts in metal bed designing.

A new and complete line of Cribs has been developed—some having the square tubing throughout—with solid and decorated panels; others made with round tubing and the Oval Bend in the ends. The special shaped steel spindles have also been used in the Crib Line. Here again we have given you a large variety of patterns to select from.

No. 5781—*Twin Steel Beds. Head end 48 inches high; foot end, 33 inches high; square steel tubing. Has 24-inch wide solid steel panels in head and foot ends, all of which carry decorative striping, enamel border and floral decoration in center. Finished regularly in Walnut. Also furnished in Ebony, Red, Green or Parchment, with suitable striping and decorations. Made in twin size only. (3/3)*

THE HOOSIER MANUFACTURING CO.

Kitchen and Breakfast-room Furniture

28 Ashton Street, NEW CASTLE, IND.

EXHIBITS AND SHOWROOMS

CHICAGO, ILL., Space 1025 American Furniture Mart   SAN FRANCISCO, CALIF., The Hoosier Pacific Bldg.

No. 2842. A popular low-priced Hoosier. Finishes, Golden Oak or Grey Enamel.

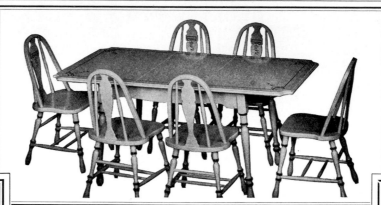

Extension Table No. 830. Chair No. 818. Silver or Antique Oak; Wedgwood Green or Grey Enamel.

A 36-inch model No. 2836. Available in Golden Oak or Grey Enamel.

Hoosier Highboy No. 2877. Available in five finishes, beautifully decorated in contrasting colors.

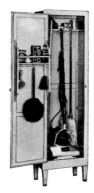

Broom Unit No. 8003. Available in all cabinet finishes.

Shelf Unit No. 8004. Available in all cabinet finishes.

Hoosier Beauty No. 2855. Available in five finishes, beautifully decorated in contrasting colors.

No. 828 Table. No. 818 Chair. Navajo—Beautiful two-tone grey oak.

No. 825 Table. No. 818 Chair. Antique—Rich brown oak, highlighted, decorated in green and yellow.

No. 827 Table. No. 818 Chair. Italian—A two-tone greyish-brown oak.

PRODUCTS

MANUFACTURERS OF

A complete line of Kitchen Cabinet and Breakfast-room Furniture. The line consists of Kitchen Cabinets—four patterns and five finishes—Broom and Shelf Storage Units, Stepladder-Stool, Porceliron top tables in both solid and drop-leaf types, and a variety of Breakfast-room Furniture in Oak and Enamel finishes, consisting of drop-leaf and extension tables, Buffets, Welsh Cupboards, Servers and Chairs.

NEW VARIETY—COLOR—CONVENIENCE
Modern Ideas That Are Building Sales

A type of kitchen equipment to suit any requirement, with exclusive features designed for convenience and efficiency . . . beauty that will delight any woman.

HOOSIER

Saves Time
Advertised Slogan

In kitchen cabinets, in supplementary units, in breakfast sets, Hoosier brings you ideas and improvements that attract today's buyer.

A powerful nation-wide advertising program backs every Hoosier item in your stock. Dealer tie-ups last year brought tremendous success to thousands of merchants from coast to coast.

Write today without obligation for full information concerning Hoosier's lively new plans for 1928.

MALLEABLE IRON RANGE COMPANY

Manufacturers of Coal, Wood, Gas and Electric Ranges

110 Lake Street, BEAVER DAM, WIS.

Paramount Gas No. 637—Bake oven, 17x20¼x13 inches. Broiler, 17x20¼x7½ inches. Cooking top, 22½x24 inches. Equipped with super heated oven and oven heat control. 43 inches long.

Monarch, Coal-Wood, No. 7000V. Cooking top, 35½x24 inches. Oven, 19x21 or 17x21 inches. Total length, 35½ inches. Total width, 24 inches. Warming closet, 35½x9x12½ inches. With water heating equipment if desired. Full enamel finish.

Monarch Electric No. 27A—Bake oven, 17x14x18 inches—two 1500 watt units. Pastry oven, 17x8x18 inches—one 1500 watt unit. Equipped with time and temperature controls. Four top units, one 1500, one 1250, one 1000, one 750 watts. 47 inches long.

Paramount Gas No. H637—With built-in kitchen heater. Bake oven, 15x20½x13 inches. Broiler, 15x20¼x7½ inches. Cooking top, gas, 20¼x20 inches. Coal, 11x24 inches. Equipped with superheated oven and oven heat control. 50 inches long.

Monarch Electric No. 16A—Oven, 16x15x18 inches; two 1500 watt units. Equipped with Time and Temperature controls. Four top units, one 1500, one 1250, one 1000, one 750 watts. 48 inches long.

PRODUCTS

Manufacturers of

"Monarch"

—Coal-Wood Ranges
—Electric Ranges
—Combination Coal-Wood and Electric Ranges
—Hotel Coal-Wood and Electric Ranges
—Coal-Wood Kitchen Heaters

Trade-mark identifying Coal-Wood and Electric Ranges.

—Electric Hot Plates and Tables

"Paramount"

—Combination Coal, Wood and Gas Ranges
—Gas Ranges, Superheated
—Gas Ranges with Kitchen Heaters
—Combination Refuse Burners and Heaters with Gas Kindler

Trade-mark identifying Gas and Combination Ranges.

—Gas Hot Plates and Table Stoves

MANUFACTURERS OF A LINE OF RANGES THAT WILL MEET EVERY REQUIREMENT

Consider the advantages in carrying a line of ranges that offer you a complete assortment of models for use with any of four types of fuel, and sizes and types of equipment to fill every request.

As illustrated, the MONARCH and PARAMOUNT line of cooking devices furnishes four distinct types of ranges; coal, wood, electric, gas, or combination, gas and coal or electric and coal. MONARCH and PARAMOUNT ranges are also furnished in attractive but conservative tints of enamel to meet the demand for colored equipment in the kitchen.

The illustrations are representative of the entire line, which consists of over 400 various models. There are over 150 various models of MONARCH Electric ranges alone.

Types of equipment of every size and style, from the small, compact, apartment units to heavy duty, commercial ranges. Catalogs and prices as well as details of our agency proposition will be furnished on request. In writing, kindly furnish us with details of types of fuel most commonly used in your community, and if gas or electricity is available, information regarding your local rates will facilitate forwarding complete information regarding operating costs and installation.

MUTSCHLER BROTHERS COMPANY
Manufacturers of Kitchen Equipment and Breakfast Room Furniture
NAPPANEE, INDIANA
EXHIBITS
CHICAGO, ILL., Space 1017, American Furniture Mart

Dropleaf Table, Model 407 with pinch back chair.

PRODUCTS
MANUFACTURERS OF

KITCHEN EQUIPMENT including:

Kitchen Cabinets, bases, tables, dish cupboards, broom cupboards, auxiliary cupboards, sink cupboards.

LINOLEUM TOP CAFETERIA OR LUNCHROOM TABLES.

PORCELAIN TOP TEA ROOM OR CAFETERIA TABLES.

TABLES for offices, directors' rooms, or display rooms.

TABLES for school or kindergarten.

TELEPHONE STANDS.

AN UNEXPLOITED FIELD OF PROFIT

No longer is it necessary for the room where the soul-satisfying delicacies of the table are prepared to be dressed in the drab garb of the hospital; no longer is the kitchen a mere workshop, for color and life have come into it—the same color that makes the living-room the center of the family group.

PORCE-NAMEL handy-roomy kitchen furniture offers to the dealer an unexcelled field of

PORCE-NAMEL
handy-roomy
KITCHEN FURNITURE
★
Kitchen Tables-Cabinets
Cupboards-Breakfast Sets

profit in the only unexploited room in the home—the kitchen. Here it is that the present day decorators are recommending color—color that makes the kitchen as livable as the library—color that takes the housewife's mind off her task, and makes the necessity of cooking less a burden. Think of it—tables, chairs, kitchen cabinets, broom closets—all finished in lustrous golden ivory, delicate jade greens, and smooth French greys, and all equipped with the practical time-and labor-saving features that have made the name of Mutschler Brothers synonymous with household efficiency.

Finish? Certainly—table tops in special vitreous enamels that will neither buckle nor bulge—enamels that are easily cleaned. All models are finished in beautiful satin enamel with decorations of a most appropriate nature.

Prices? They will surprise you with their reasonableness, and the possibilities they open for a tremendous volume of business, for every home is a prospect.

Write us for the details of the Mutschler PORCE-NAMEL sales plan, and when you are at the Mart, call upon us, and let your own judgment convince you that what we say is true.

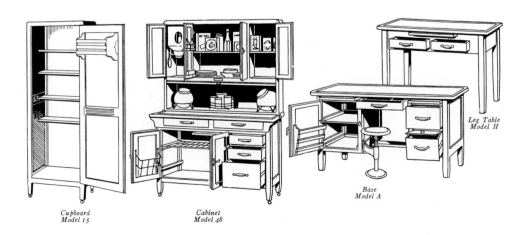

Cupboard Model 15

Cabinet Model 48

Base Model A

Leg Table Model H

SHOWERS BROTHERS COMPANY
KITCHEN CABINETS
Bedroom and Dining Room Furniture, Radio Furniture, Occasional Chairs
BLOOMINGTON, INDIANA

Factories: BLOOMINGTON, IND., BLOOMFIELD, IND. and BURLINGTON, IOWA
Exhibits: Space 1501, American Furniture Mart, CHICAGO, and Space 1607-9-11, New York Furniture Exchange, NEW YORK

PRODUCTS
MANUFACTURERS OF
KITCHEN CABINETS

For other products see Case Goods Catalog, pages 336 to 341 and Radio Furniture Catalog, page 188.

TRADE NAMES

"SHOWERS KITCHEN CABINETS" is used in connection with the regular Showers trade mark on our complete line of cabinets.

GENERAL INFORMATION

White, gray, green or ivory enamel on hardwood, with attractive stenciled decorations on top doors. (Order by number to indicate finish.)

The symbol of 60 years of manufacturing furniture of honest value—profitable to handle.

Ends, backs, partitions and drawer bottoms are of three-ply built-up stock. Solid ends in top sections. Interiors of top sections finished in enamel to match exteriors.

Wire panracks on base compartment doors, and wire shelves in all base compartments. Metal shelves in top sections. Metal bread box with perforated ventilating lid in lower drawer, resting on self-supporting side hangers.

The sliding curtains are of stickered construction and operate in a new type routed track. The curtains are easily removed for cleaning. A new center guide construction is used on all drawers which makes them slide easily and prevents tipping of drawers when extended. All cabinets equipped with breadboards.

Hardware made rust-resisting by new "utelite" process. Angle-brace construction throughout.

No. 9727—Showers Cabinet.

No. 9727—White Enamel. Height, 65 inches. Sliding porcelain top, 25x41½ inches. Top size extended, 33x41½ inches. Shipping weight, 205 lbs. Tilting flour bin.
No. 9727½—Same in Gray Enamel.
No. 9027—Same in Golden Oak.
Price, $41.00.

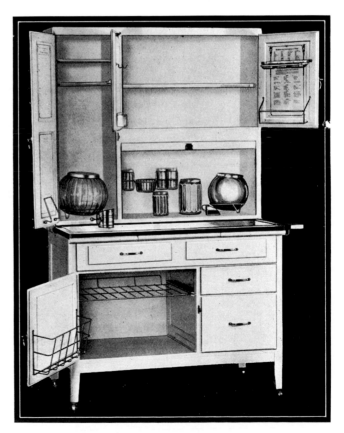

No. 9735—Showers Cabinet.

No. 9735—White Enamel. Height, 72 inches. Sliding porcelain top, 25x41½ inches. Work space, top closed, 27x41½ inches. Work space, top extended, 32½x41½ inches. Shipping weight, 275 lbs. Glass flour jar with hand sifter included.
No. 9735½—Same in Gray Enamel.
No. 9735¼—Same in Ivory Enamel.
No. 9035—Same in Golden Oak.
No. 9735¾—Same in Green Enamel.
This can also be furnished in the tilting type flour bin.
Price, $70.00.

STOW-DAVIS FURNITURE COMPANY
Manufacturers of Bank and Office Furniture
70 to 138 Front Ave., GRAND RAPIDS, MICH.
OWNERS AND OPERATORS OF THE GRAND RAPIDS DESK COMPANY

A Directors' Room of the Colonial Trust Company, Pittsburgh, Pennsylvania, equipped with Stow-Davis Directors' Table No. 471-S; and Chairs No. 472-S.

The motif of this table and chairs blends itself subtly with the dignity which a room of this character should bear.

PRODUCTS

MANUFACTURERS OF

BANK AND OFFICE FURNITURE including:

CHAIRS, Straight and Swivel Types, Wood only or upholstered in leather.

DAVENPORTS

DESKS, Office and Typewriter

FILING CABINETS

TABLES, Office and Directors'

TELEPHONE CABINETS AND STANDS

WARDROBES

WASTE BASKETS

GENERAL INFORMATION

Stow-Davis Furniture does not ask for comparisons. We leave it to our product to find its own niche in the estimation of those who are naturally accustomed to the better things of life. If this high appraisal were to have as a corollary unreasonable expenditure, these suites would lose some of their practicability, but that is not so. They are commercial as well as worthy.

WOODS AND FINISHES

The best designed piece will lose some of its beauty if it has not a finish comparable with its character and purpose and will lose in worth if its original finish will not be preserved for an indefinite time under all conditions. Woods and finishes employed in the building of Stow-Davis Furniture resemble plates 1 and 28 as shown in the Woods and Finishes section preceding page 9 of this book.

PRICE RANGES

The Stow and Davis line offers a wide price range, from a sixty-inch desk listing at $220.00 to $790.00 for a seventy-two inch Florentine. Each line complete with chairs, tables and the various small pieces necessary.

The Grand Rapids Desk Co's. line, which is the commercial line in conjunction with the above, is made complete in a three and four drawer desk, listing from $96.00 to $168.00 with typewriter desks from $114.00 to $123.00 list.

Prices subject to change without notice.

STOW-DAVIS FURNITURE COMPANY

INTRODUCING THE LATEST DEVELOPMENT IN THE FURNITURE INDUSTRY
A Steel and Wood Desk

An interior framework of steel, rustproof finished, enclosed by wood, five-ply veneered panels, fitting tightly into steel moldings. Conventional wood drawers, dove-tailed construction and five-ply veneered tops. All contact working surfaces of wood. The only metal showing being the base molding around the bottom and the small steel molding between the panels and drawers which are grained to match the wood. Combining the good points of steel and the superior advantages of wood, where nature's graining is always the best, and a contact surface for the user ever warm and agreeable. No sharp corners anywhere, rounded end corners on all panels and tops. All flush pulls, finished antique brass color. Steel sockets case hardened. An ideal desk for large corporations. Adoption of the automotive assembly production methods, in both the finishing room and final assembly make possible the low price at which it is offered.

Dealers carrying this line will have no competition. Made in a

Illustration of Steel and Wood Desk, No. 160-F; Top measurement, 60x34 inches. List price, $114.00.

three and four drawer desk, all sizes and a complete line of typewriter desks. Also two grades of tables to match.

Send for illustrations and prices to Grand Rapids Desk Co.

VICTORIAN COLONIAL OFFICE SUITE No. F5200

This particular suite is neither New York, Pennsylvania nor Louisiana Colonial, but is rather the pure Victorian type. Our designers have taken advantage of the latitude offered by the peculiar historical facts pertaining to Colonial styles and have injected ideas of their own. The beauty and quiet dignity and the air of serviceableness of this suite speak for themselves. Finish resembles plate 28 as shown in the Woods and Finishes section preceding page 9 of this book; and is priced at $682.00 for six pieces. Additional arm chairs at $100.00, list. Desk 60 inches long.

Prices subject to change without notice.

LOMBARDY ITALIAN OFFICE SUITE No. G6000

The motif for this suite is taken from museum pieces that were produced in Lombardy and Tuscany early in this period. There are, of course, adaptations to make this suite fit modern requirements, but losing none of the beauty of this historic period. In spite of its intricate carvings, it has an air of simple richness, combined with a dignity that seems to be inherent. Finish resembles plate 28 as shown in the Woods and Finishes section preceding page 9 of this book; and is priced at $1324.00 for six pieces. Additional arm chairs at $132.00, list. Desk 66 inches long.

Prices subject to change without notice.

FURST BROS. & COMPANY

Manufacturers of Mirrors, Pictures, Frames, Furniture Novelties, Tapestries, Art and Gift Wares

38 Hopkins Place, BALTIMORE, MD.

BRANCH OFFICES AND EXHIBITS

CHICAGO, ILL., The American Furniture Mart, 666 Lake Shore Drive   PHILADELPHIA, PA., E. H. McGowan, 730 Cherry St.

NEW YORK, N. Y., A. E. Hickock, 225 Fifth Ave.   HIGH POINT, N. C., Furniture Building

PRODUCTS
MANUFACTURERS OF

MIRRORS
—Authentic Reproductions
—Modernistic Designs
—Semi-Venetian
—Venetian
—Panel
—Buffet
—Console
—Dressing Table
—Hall
—Bathroom
PICTURES
—Framed Pictures of
   Every Description
FRAMES
—Picture Frames of
   Every Description
—Photo
MOULDINGS
—Picture
—Mirror
—Panel
—Wall
—Chair

MEDICINE CABINETS
FURNITURE NOVELTIES
—Ship Models
—Fireside Screens
—Accessories of Every
   Character
—Serving Trays
TAPESTRIES
—Framed and Unframed
ART AND GIFT WARES
—Vases
—Book Ends
—Placques
—Ash Trays
CLOCKS
—Reproductions
—Chime
—Mantel
—Kitchen

No. 4217 —Authentic Colonial Reproduction. Size, 21x16 inches. Convex mirror 12-inch diameter. Frame burnished antique gold finish. 13 balls represent 13 original states. Each, $35.00.

GENERAL INFORMATION

Furst Brothers Mirrors and Pictures are individually designed and finished in the most artistic manner.

For 45 years we have been leaders in the manufacture of Mirrors, Pictures and Art Novelties.

This year we present a complete line of Modernistic Designs and Authentic Reproductions now so much in demand.

"Furst Line Second To None" has come to be known as the trade mark for fine quality merchandise.

For your convenience we maintain comprehensive sample displays in five cities as listed above.

FURST LINE
Second to None

Trade Mark

No. 24269—Modern Picture. Size, 28x16 inches. Glass, 26x14 inches. Black frame decorated with red line. Four assorted subjects of attractively colored block prints. Each, $10.00.

No. 42169—Modernistic Design. Size, 27x18 inches overall; mirror plate, 24x14 inches. Frame finished in burnished silver, mottled black. Each, $25.00.

No. 24302 — Framed Tapestry. Size, 54x18 inches. Framed in antique burnished finish. Assortment of twelve subjects. Each, $12.00.

Revere Banjo Clock.

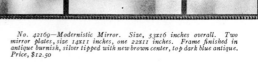

No. 42169—Modernistic Mirror. Size, 53x16 inches overall. Two mirror plates, size 14x11 inches, one 22x11 inches. Frame finished in antique burnish, silver tipped with new brown center, top dark blue antique. Price, $12.50.

REVERE BANJO CLOCK

Pictured at right. Size, 35½x10 inches. Polished mahogany finish case. Convex glass, 6-inch Ivoroid dial. Eight-day movement. Each $23.50.

WRITE US

We shall be glad to furnish you with full information regarding our lines if you will address us at 38 Hopkins Place, Baltimore, Md.

FURNITURE NOVELTIES

We manufacture and import furniture novelties and accessories of every character. In addition to this we import a wide variety of individual art and gift pieces. In fact, novelties of every character necessary to complete the decoration of every home.

The illustrations on this page are merely representative of the articles we manufacture. It would take over a hundred pages like this to list all the items we manufacture.

RUDOLF LESCH
FINE ARTS
Publishers of Finer Pictures
225 Fifth Ave., NEW YORK, N. Y.

PRODUCTS

COLOR PRINTS
FRAMES
PAINTINGS: Floral
PAINTINGS: Reproductive After Old Masters

PICTURES: Framed and Unframed
SHEET PICTURES
SHIPMODELS

"Iris"
By Vincent Van Gogh

"Paris—Notre Dame Bookstalls"
By Max Pollak

PICTURES
WITH THE MODERN TOUCH

The increased use of modern furniture has brought the decorator face to face with the problem of providing the proper background.

The obvious solution is the use of modern pictures. One need not search far to find them.

Whether one seeks a group to serve as a background or a single fine example to use for a daring note, the destination should be the same.

For we have a selection of moderns in which you will find the very type you seek.

COLOR ETCHINGS
IN LIMITED EDITIONS

For those who choose the more exclusive limited edition color etching, we have a wide variety to offer.

Proofs from the best artists in France, in Belgium, and elsewhere may be had within a range of subject matter which will satisfy any requirement.

A series of handbooks for the dealer is being prepared. From time to time, brochures on prominent artists will be distributed. May we send them to you as they are published?

A visit to our showrooms will be a most interesting one and a cordial welcome awaits you.

Trade Mark

GEO. C. MAGES COMPANY

Manufacturers of Pictures, Moldings and Frames

1750 Fulton Street, Corner Wood Street, CHICAGO, ILL.

PERMANENT EXHIBIT
CHICAGO, ILL., Room 627, American
Furniture Mart, 666 Lake Shore Drive

Trade Mark

SHOWROOM
CHICAGO, ILL., 1750 Fulton Street,
Corner Wood Street

No. 2029F-1—Promise
of Spring—Carl W. Raw-
son. Glass size, 21 x 26½
inches. Frame is profusely
gold burnished and toned
in soft harmonizing color.
High grade color facsimile.
List price, $20.00.

No. 2005F-1—A New
England Fishing Village.
Glass size, 16 x 22 inches.
Print in colors. Frames
gold burnished with hand
laid corner ornaments.
Toned in perfect harmony
with picture. List price
$12.00.

PRODUCTS

MANUFACTURERS OF

—Picture Cords
—Photograph Frames
—Framed Pictures

DISTRIBUTORS OF

—Pictures

No. 2028F-3—A Night in June—by Webster.
Glass size, 17 x 21 inches. A charming subject
in delicate colorings and fancy tinted mat. Frame
gold burnished. Blue tone and hand mounted
ornaments. List price, $11.00.

No. 2023F—The Man in Armor—Van Dyke.
Glass size, 18½ x 20½ inches. Imported high grade
color type and framed in gold burnished antique
frame and hand laid ornaments. List price, $17.50.

PICTURES IN THE DECORATIVE SCHEME

You can sell more furniture through discriminating use of good pictures. Group your furniture in a more or less orderly manner and place a few pictures on the wall above them and watch results. Pictures form an indispensable part of every decorating scheme,

and Mages pictures are produced with the idea of creating the proper setting for every type of interior, whether in period style or in the ultra-modern.

Notice some of the display ideas shown here—not only is the value of the pictures emphasized but the furniture and rug are set off to the best possible advantage. A similar

effective display is carried out in the desk group. Arrangements such as these strategically placed in your store will bring you more business—not only in pictures but furniture and other auxiliary furnishings.

A great variety of items can be found in the Mages Line—pastels, colored wood blocks, and many other novelty prints, also fine landscapes in a variety of sizes . . . all in the latest framings.

The ways of using pictures to beautify your store displays are legion—but you can sell more pictures at a profit if you use them to increase the appeal of your merchandise.

ARMSTRONG CORK COMPANY
LINOLEUM DIVISION
Manufacturers of Linoleum and Felt-Base Rugs and Floor Covering
LANCASTER, PA.
BRANCH OFFICES

ATLANTA, 1229 Candler Building
CHICAGO, 1206 Heyworth Building
CLEVELAND, 716–718 Keith Building
CINCINNATI, 538 Dixie Terminal Building
DALLAS, 706 Santa Fe Building

DENVER, 720 Symes Building
KANSAS CITY, 504 Huntzinger Building
MEMPHIS, 1104 First National Bank Building
MINNEAPOLIS, 912 Plymouth Building

NEW ORLEANS, 524 Bienville Street
NEW YORK, 295 Fifth Avenue
SAN FRANCISCO, 180 New Montgomery Street
SEATTLE, 803 Terminal Sales Building
ST. LOUIS, 1102–03 Ambassador Building

PRODUCTS
MANUFACTURERS OF

ARMSTRONG's LINOLEUM—Marble Inlaid, Plain, Jaspé, Embossed Plain, Inset Plain, Inset Jaspé, Oak Plank Inlaid, Parquetry Inlaid, Granite, Straight Line Inlaid, Embossed Inlaid, Moulded Inlaid, Arabesq, Printed
ARMSTRONG's CORK CARPET
ARMSTRONG's QUAKER-FELT AND STANDARD-FELT PIECE GOODS
ARMSTRONG's RUGS—Inlaid, Jaspé, Printed, Quaker-Felt, Standard-Felt
ARMSTRONG's LINING FELT
ARMSTRONG's WATERPROOF CEMENT
ARMSTRONG's LINOLEUM PASTE—Paste and Liquid
ARMSTRONG's LINOLEUM WAX—Paste and Liquid
ARMSTRONG's LINOLEUM LACQUER

GENERAL INFORMATION

The Armstrong Line for 1928 includes 428 patterns—a design and quality for every taste and every purse, from the finest of Handmade Marble Inlaid Linoleum through to inexpensive felt-base. The entire line, with the exception of a limited group of low-cost printed and felt-base patterns, is protected by the new Accolac finish, a dirt-resistant lacquer. It is a quality line, carefully made of tested ingredients to meet a high standard and backed by strong, all-year-round advertising in prominent magazines and farm papers and a spring and fall newspaper campaign.

The Armstrong Line is sold through wholesale distributors who carry extensive warehouse stocks at practically every jobbing center in the United States. Names of wholesale distributors furnished promptly to any retailer upon request.

DESCRIPTIONS

Plain and Jaspé Linoleum—Armstrong's Plain and Battleship Linoleum is made by the Walton process only and more than meets the U. S. Government standard. It is manufactured 2 yards wide in 7 gauges and 8 colors. Armstrong's Jaspé Linoleum is a two-tone finely grained material, made in 4 gauges and 7 colors. Embossed Plain, in which recessed lines catch the play of light and shadow over the floor, and Inset Plain and Inset Jaspé, in which occasional figures break up the monotony of the plain expanse, are artistic variations designed for large floor space.

One of the figures inserted in Armstrong's Inset Jaspé Linoleum

A typical design in Armstrong's Embossed Inlaid Linoleum

Inlaid Linoleum—The Armstrong Inlaid Lines include Handmade Marble Inlaid, a handsome dignified floor for fine residence and business installations; Embossed Inlaid, a floor of unusual texture in popular flagstone, cobblestone, handcraft and pebblestone tile and mosaic designs; Oak Plank Inlaid, Parquetry Inlaid, clean-cut tile designs in 3 gauges of Straight Line Inlaid and attractive handcraft, flagstone, mosaic, Dutch tile and carpet effects in 2 gauges of Moulded Inlaid. There are designs for every taste within a wide price range—handsome floors for any room in the house, or for office, store, or public building. All Inlaid Linoleum has the Accolac finish.

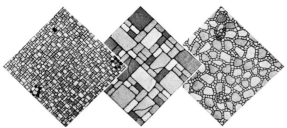
Three of the new pebblestone and flagstone effects in Armstrong's Inlaid Linoleum

Arabesq Linoleum—An exclusive Armstrong product in which the ground color of the linoleum forms part of the design which is overlaid in heavy oil paints.

Printed Linoleum—Dutch tile, wood block, marble, carpet, floral and shaded tile effects in Printed Linoleum, protected by the Accolac finish, and a few low-priced designs known as "Standard Finish Printed Linoleum," which are not lacquered.

Quaker-Felt—Armstrong's Quaker-Felt and Quaker-Felt Rugs, in original patterns created by the artists who design Armstrong's Linoleum, carefully printed with durable paint on a heavy rag felt and finished in Accolac, represent high quality at a reasonable price. Each Armstrong's Quaker-Felt Rug is protected by a money-back guarantee. Armstrong's Quaker-Felt is manufactured in 2- and 3-yard widths and the rugs are made in 10 sizes, from 18 x 36 inches to 9 x 15 feet.

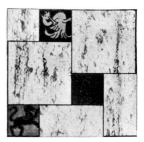
One of the marbleized designs in Arabesq Linoleum

An Armstrong's Quaker-Felt Rug

Linoleum Rugs—Jaspé Linoleum Rugs, in which attractive tile and floral borders and figures are overlaid on a base of two-tone Jaspé Linoleum, protected by the Accolac finish, are suitable for living-rooms, dining-rooms and bedrooms, and are especially durable and easy to clean. They are made in 6 sizes, from 6 x 9 to 12 x 15 feet. In Armstrong's Inlaid Linoleum Rugs, made in 3 sizes, 6 x 9, 9 x 12 and 12 x 12 feet, the pattern colors go through to the burlap back. Armstrong's Printed Linoleum Rugs include a variety of unusual figured tile and floral designs, in heavy oil paints, protected by the new Accolac finish. They are made in 6 sizes, from 6 x 9 to 12 x 15 feet.

SELLING POINTS

Linoleum floors, properly cemented over deadening felt, are:
1. Attractive—harmonious, colorful backgrounds for rugs and furnishings in any room.
2. Durable—properly laid and protected, linoleum is a serviceable floor, which never requires refinishing.
3. Quiet—a permanent linoleum floor deadens sound and muffles footsteps.
4. Comfortable—linoleum is resilient and restful to the foot, comfortable to walk and stand upon.
5. Sanitary—the germicidal action of its oxidized linseed oil content makes the linoleum especially sanitary. There are no cracks to collect germ-breeding dust and the new Accolac finish seals the pores and affords a smooth surface, delightfully easy to clean. Linoleum materially lowers upkeep costs in business buildings.

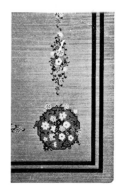
A Jaspé Linoleum Rug

ADVERTISING HELPS

The merchant who sells Armstrong's Linoleum and Quaker-Felt is invited to write for free electros for newspaper advertising, window displays, motion picture film and slides, store display cards and signs, booklets and other advertising materials. The Armstrong Advertising Department will also be glad to prepare suggested form letters, newspaper advertising copy, plans for special stunts and contests and assist the merchant in every way to build up his Armstrong sales.

BOOKLETS ON REQUEST

Write for any of the following material in which you are interested:
1. 1928 Armstrong Catalog, a 9 x 12-inch handbook in which all of the patterns in the Armstrong Line are illustrated in colors.
2. Linoleum Layer's Handbook which describes in detail the modern method of laying linoleum by cementing it permanently to the floor over a lining of deadening felt, and also contains directions for cleaning and maintaining linoleum floors.
3. "Making Them Say Yes," a book for the salesman on the floor and the linoleum buyer, containing a variety of ideas for speeding up sales.

THE BEATTIE MANUFACTURING CO.

Castle Broadloom Carpets

295 Fifth Avenue, NEW YORK, N. Y.

BRANCH OFFICE
CHICAGO, ILL., 228 So. Wabash Ave.

MILLS
LITTLE FALLS, N. J.

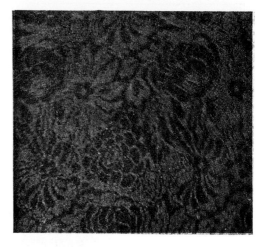
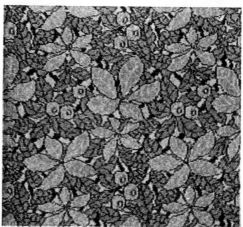

PRODUCTS

MANUFACTURERS OF
RUGS AND CARPETS
CASTLE CARPET
—27 inches wide
—9 feet wide
—12 feet wide
—Any length.

"CASTLE BROADLOOM" CARPETS

This is a figured drum printed fabric made with an exceptionally high pile and woven in one piece.

The quality is constructed especially for good hard wear and made in colorings to harmonize with all decorations.

We can highly recommend this carpet for all fine homes. Living rooms, libraries, dining rooms and chambers, and for "Contract departments" in the furnishing of hotels, clubs, theatres and offices.

It is made 9 feet and twelve feet wide, without a seam, any length, and with 27-inch width to match.

"Castle Broadloom" Carpets can be purchased either by the roll or in "cut order" quantities from any of the following wholesale jobbers of floor coverings. Price for cut quantity, $10.00 per square yard East of the Mississippi River and $10.50 per square yard West of the Mississippi River.

Prices subject to change without notice.

These illustrations represent but four of our fifteen patterns. Other Samples on request.

JOBBERS HANDLING "CASTLE BROADLOOM" CARPETS WHERE CUT ORDER QUANTITIES CAN BE SECURED

C. W. Rollins Co., Boston, Mass.
H. D. Taylor Co., Buffalo, N. Y.
O. W. Richardson & Co., Chicago, Ill.
George F. Otte Co., Cincinnati, Ohio.
Cousins & Fern, Columbus, Ohio.
Barrar Floor Covering Co.,
    Dayton, Ohio.
Wm. Volker & Co., Denver, Colo.
Burnham Stoepel Co., Detroit, Mich.
Herpolsheimer Co.,
    Grand Rapids, Mich.
Ros-Lange Carpet Co.,
    Indianapolis, Ind.
Wm. Volker & Co., Kansas City, Mo.
Wm. Volker & Co., Los Angeles, Calif.
Neidhoefer & Co., Milwaukee, Wis.
Geo. W. Snaman & Co., Pittsburgh, Pa.
Adam H. Bartel Co.,
    Richmond, Indiana.
Howe & Rogers Co., Rochester, N. Y.
Finch-Van Slyck-McConville,
    St. Paul, Minn.
Wm. Volker & Co.,
    Salt Lake City, Utah.
Wm. Volker & Co.,
    San Francisco, Calif.
Youngstown Dry Goods Co.,
    Youngstown, Ohio.

EAGLE-OTTAWA LEATHER CO.

The World's Largest Tanners of Fine Upholstery Leathers

GRAND HAVEN, MICHIGAN

BRANCH OFFICES

CHICAGO, ILL., 912 West Washington Blvd.; NEW YORK, N. Y., 74 Gold St.; SAN FRANCISCO, CALIF., 569 Howard St.

The Spanish, Italian and Early English interiors which have become so popular require rugged beauty and warmth of color which can be adequately supplied only by the use of leather.

PRODUCTS

TANNERS OF
UPHOLSTERY LEATHERS

"COLONIAL GRAIN" LEATHER LENDS ITSELF TO COLOR HARMONY

The use of color is the outstanding factor today in home decoration. The question of how to produce more perfect effects of color harmony is uppermost. The makers of "Colonial Grain" have recognized this need of colorful material and are producing a wonderful variety of textures, tints, shades and combinations to harmonize with every possible color scheme of rugs, draperies, walls and floors.

INCREASINGLY POPULAR WITH DESIGNERS AND DECORATORS

Designers of good furniture are using it with a most brilliant effect. Makers of good furniture are exhibiting its ingenious use in the loveliest of screens, tables, wall hangings, beds, couches, and chairs. And decorators are using more and more of this product to put the necessary life and color in rooms of every type.

Designed by the late Mr. Tom Handley.

PRACTICAL, DURABLE, AND SANITARY

As upholstery material "Colonial Grain" is the most sanitary, dust-proof and moth-proof material usable. For the home where there are children, it presents a surface which can be kept fresh and new by washing with Castile Soap and water, when muddy feet and soiled hands will ruin fabrics.

Its durability cannot be surpassed. Its extreme pliability makes for ease in upholstering. These important qualities warrant the use of "Colonial Grain" leather by all manufacturers of upholstered furniture.

BIG BUYERS PROVE WORTH OF "COLONIAL GRAIN"

Some recent installations using "Colonial Grain" include Detroit Masonic Temple, the Cadillac Athletic Club of Detroit, the Palmer House of Chicago, Stevens Hotel, Tribune Tower and the Elks Memorial Building of Chicago; also the State Capitol, Olympia, Washington. These people selected "Colonial Grain" after thorough researches into various upholstery materials embracing beauty and durability.

"BARONIAL GRAIN"— A NEW CREATION

Our latest creation "Baronial Grain" a soft and beautiful piece of steer hide, is now being offered in conjunction with our already famous "Colonial Grain."

Art Moderne leathers in bright, rich, striking, colorful effects showing the new French styles of reptile grains and other bizarre innovations for upholstery leathers.

COLONIAL DRAPERY FABRICS
PRODUCED BY
MARSHALL FIELD & COMPANY, WHOLESALE

Adams, Quincy, Franklin & Wells
CHICAGO, ILL.

Madison Avenue at 35th Street
NEW YORK, N. Y.

The standard of excellence in American Printed and Dyed Drapery Fabrics, including a wide variety of popular priced materials for "over the counter selling," suitable for draperies, curtains, upholstering, pillows, bedspreads and fancy articles.

The damask illustrated above is one of our 50-inch damask numbers known as Drusilla No. 152. This design comes in a full variety of the most popular selling colors. It is a typical French period pattern produced in this inexpensive and practical cloth.

The design Jacobean, No. 30431, illustrated above, is one of our Town and Country Newton Cretonnes. In design and color it is an ultra-modern adaption of an antique Jacobean linen. It is especially suitable for the decorative schemes of today.

PRODUCTS

Listed below are a few of the fabrics included in the Colonial Drapery line:

COLONIAL TOWN AND COUNTRY CRETONNES, including
—Berkshire Cretonnes
—Newton (Part-Linen) Cretonnes
—DeLuxe Printed All-Linen
—Granville Hand-Printed Cretonnes
—Permafast Cretonnes (guaranteed fast colors)
COLONIAL PARKVIEW CRASH
COLONIAL TORKINGTON CRASH
COLONIAL CHARLTON CHINTZ
COLONIAL GREENLEAF CRETONNE

COLONIAL GLASS CURTAIN GAUZES
COLONIAL FURNITURE AND SLIP COVERINGS
COLONIAL WOVEN NOVELTY ART CRASHES
COLONIAL DRAPERY DAMASKS (in all-over and striped effects)
COLONIAL DRAPERY TAFFETAS (both plain and change-able)
COLONIAL NOVELTY DRAPERY FABRICS (both figured and plain)

Comforter materials including Standard Silkoline and down-proof Sateens, and Art Tickings.

GENERAL INFORMATION ON COLONIAL DRAPERY FABRICS

The designs in all Colonial Drapery Fabrics are original and exclusive with Marshall Field & Company, Wholesale, producers and sole distributors. The wide variety of fabrics and designs included in this line makes it possible to secure at moderate prices materials to fit in with almost any decorative plan.

All Colonial Drapery Fabrics are sold in piece lots only.

USE THE NEW COLONIAL DRAPERY BOOK "COLOR AND DESIGN" TO INCREASE YOUR DRAPERY BUSINESS

This new authoritative book on home decoration has been prepared and advertised to help the merchant increase his business in Colonial Drapery Fabrics. It treats in a direct and authentic manner the various phases of home decoration with special emphasis on window treatments. This book is already in the homes of hundreds of women all over the country. It is being extensively advertised in a large group of home magazines. It should be in your store. We will supply it to you at $12.50 a hundred, to be sold to your customers at 25c a copy. It will call attention to your store as a source of authentic information on home decoration. Write for further information on this important book.

Pages 20 and 21 of the New Colonial Drapery Book "Color and Design." See pages 30, 31, and 32 of this edition of the Reference Book for reproductions of three of the color plates in this booklet.

ZION LACE CURTAINS AND NETS
PRODUCED BY
MARSHALL FIELD & COMPANY, WHOLESALE

Adams, Quincy, Franklin & Wells
CHICAGO, ILL.

Madison Ave. at 35th St.
NEW YORK, N. Y.

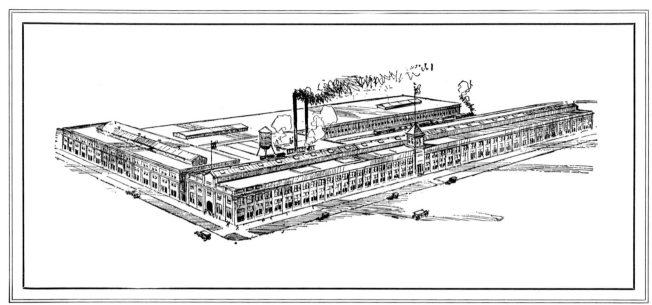

THE ZION LACE MILLS, ZION CITY, ILL.

The Zion Lace Curtain Mills where every operation in the manufacture of curtains is done under one roof.

Trade Mark

PRODUCTS
of the Zion Lace Industries, Zion City, Ill.
MANUFACTURERS OF

RAYON LACE CURTAINS AND CURTAIN NETS
Made in Shadow, Filet and Combination Weaves.

COTTON LACE CURTAINS AND CURTAIN NETS
ALSO procurable in Shadow, Filet and Combination Effects in both fringed and tailored.

RAYON LACE CURTAINS AND CURTAIN NETS

Emphasize the need of suitable curtains for each room in the house. Very few of your customers show consideration for this important feature of home adornment.

The neat, dainty designs of our collection which are enhanced by subtle tints of ecru, bronze and antique gold will help you to not only give your clientele a suitable curtain but also a curtain suitable to the atmosphere of the client's home.

All our Rayons are fringed and reasonably priced.

COTTON LACE CURTAINS AND CURTAIN NETS

Similar patterns that we carry in silk merchandise are also reproduced in cotton, so as to enable you to meet the demands of some of your trade who may desire curtains of this material. These curtains are furnished in either the fringed or tailored effects.

NOVELTY CURTAINS
Fringed and Tailored Styles

You are well aware of the modernistic trend that is sweeping the country today and its tremendous effect on furniture and furnishings. It will pay you to carry curtains of this style to satisfy the tastes of your customers.

Our line is most complete carrying many tasteful designs that are neatly finished.

DON'T BUY TILL YOU SEE OUR NEW SAMPLES
OF CURTAINS AND NETS

Our salesmen are constantly touring the country with complete samples of our curtain line and will be glad to call on you upon request.

HOME-CREST FLOOR COVERINGS

MANUFACTURED AND DISTRIBUTED BY
MARSHALL FIELD & COMPANY, WHOLESALE

Adams, Quincy, Franklin, Wells
CHICAGO, ILL.

HOME-CREST
FLOOR
COVERINGS
Trade Mark

Madison Avenue at 35th Street
NEW YORK, N. Y.

Pattern No. 1667. Home-Crest Marabia Wilton Rug.

Pattern No. 5145. Home-Crest Creston Wilton Rug.

PRODUCTS
MANUFACTURERS AND DISTRIBUTORS OF

WILTON RUGS AND CARPETS
—Super Marabia
—Super Creston
—Durbar Wilton
SEAMLESS AXMINSTER RUGS
—Florentine Seamless
—Homecrest Venetian
SALEM OVAL RUGS, Fringed,
    Plain and Figured Carpets
ORIENTAL RUGS
LINOLEUMS
NARROW AND BROAD LOOM CARPETS

Home-Crest Salem Oval Rug Pattern No. 215.

GENERAL INFORMATION

Home-Crest Floor Coverings are manufactured at mills in Philadelphia and Leaksville, N. C., owned and operated by Marshall Field & Company, Wholesale.

Designs and patterns for these floor coverings are created by the company's own artists who go to the leading art centers all over the world for their inspirations.

Marshall Field & Company Wholesale exclusively controls the distribution of Home-Crest Floor Coverings.

WILTON RUGS AND CARPETS
Produced at the Home Crest Mill in Philadelphia

Super Marabia—the very finest quality domestic worsted Wilton rug. Made in a very large range of authentic antique Oriental designs. The line also contains a wide range of modern decorative adaptations of oriental effects and strictly modernistic designs. This very fine standard quality is made in a very complete assortment of sizes, and also can be had in special large sizes.

Super Creston—a heavy quality worsted Wilton made in strictly Oriental designs of bright Oriental colorings. Ground colors include blue, rose, taupe, warm tan, and ecru.

Durbar Wilton—a heavy grade wool Wilton made in a large range of well-covered designs suitable to modern decorative schemes.

SEAMLESS AXMINSTERS
Produced at the Home Crest Mill in Leaksville, N. C.

Florentine Seamless Axminster—considered the standard of excellence for the heaviest quality of domestic Axminster rugs. Designs are well-covered Persian, Old English and strictly modernistic effects. In coloring and variety these are considered as leaders in the floor covering decorative field.

Home-Crest Venetian Seamless Axminster Rugs—a fine standard quality. Made in a great range of designs and color combinations suitable for all types of interiors.

SALEM OVAL RUGS, FRINGED
Produced at our Mill in Leaksville, N. C.

The Salem Oval Rug, Fringed, is made in the following sizes: 26x38 inches, 26x48 inches, 35x54 inches, 4 feet 4 inches x 6 feet 8 inches, 5 feet 10 inches x 9 feet.

The Salem Oval Rug is in very great demand for use in bedrooms, sun parlors, breakfast rooms, and as occasional rugs in living rooms, libraries and dining rooms.

The Salem rug is brought out in a large variety of striking bright color combinations. Ground colors are red, lavender, jade green, orange, rose, orchid, and black.

There are also many designs with a mass of bright top colors on grounds of rose and tan.

PLAIN AND FIGURED CARPETS

Marshall Field & Company Wholesale also manufactures and distributes plain and figured carpets. There is in stock at all times a complete range of figured and plain carpets in Axminster, Wilton and Velvet qualities. A cut order service is maintained for the benefit of furniture merchants who do not carry complete stocks of carpets, and sample lines from which the retailer may make his sales are furnished at a nominal cost.

A complete color range of two heavy qualities of Broadloom Velvet is always in stock in 27-inch, 36-inch, 9-foot, 10-foot 6-inch, 12-foot, and 15-foot widths.

Oriental Rugs and Linoleums—Our wide range of Oriental Rugs gathered from all corners of the world will interest as well as our selection of Linoleums. There is a pattern and a color to suit the taste of any of your customers.

CANTERBURY DECORATIVE FABRICS
EXCLUSIVE IMPORTATIONS
MARSHALL FIELD & COMPANY, WHOLESALE

CHICAGO, ILL. PHILADELPHIA, PA. BOSTON, MASS. NEW YORK
Adams, Quincy, Franklin, Wells 1602 Finance Bldg. 420 Boylston St. Madison Ave. at 35th St.

Pattern No. 6038, 52-inch Lampas. Colors: 9-Red, 2-Green, and 12-Gold. An exact reproduction made from a fine museum document produced during the Louis XVI period.

Trade Mark

PRODUCTS
IMPORTERS OF

BROCADES,
 BROCATELLES,
 AND DAMASKS
—Cotton
—Silk
—Wool
FRIEZES
—Silk
—Linen
—Wool
MOQUETTES
PLUSHES
TAPESTRIES
—Cotton
—Wool

VELVETS AND VELOURS
—Plain Weaves
—Fancy Weaves
CASEMENTS
—Silk
—Cotton
—Rayon
—Mohair
CRETONNES
CHINTZES
PRINTED LINENS
SLIP COVER FABRICS
EMBROIDERED DECORA-
 TIVE FABRICS
REPS AND POPLINS
GAUZES
DRAPERY SILKS

TAFFETAS
—Plain
—Figured
MOIRES
SATINS AND SATEENS

TAPESTRY PANELS
PIANO SCARFS
TABLE RUNNERS
FANCY PILLOWS
INDIA PRINTS

GENERAL INFORMATION

A comprehensive collection of decorative fabrics for drapery and upholstery uses, selected from the best of the world's markets and comprising many faithful reproductions of the finest period styles and adaptations from them.

Canterbury Decorative Fabrics are sold in any required yardage and are recognized by the leading interior decorators, furniture manufacturers, and all retailers of decorative drapery fabrics and furniture.

Samples sent on request.

THE HIGHTSTOWN RUG CO.

Established 1886

Manufacturers of Rugs and Carpets

HIGHTSTOWN, N. J.

SALES OFFICE

NEW YORK, N. Y., 295 Fifth Avenue

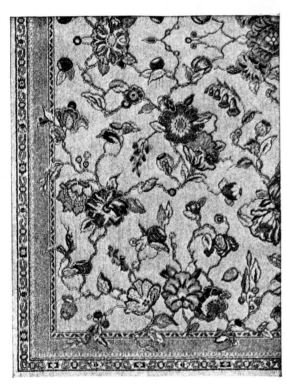

"Mercer" Seamless Axminster Pattern No. 540—
Made in 34 Regular sizes; also special sizes.

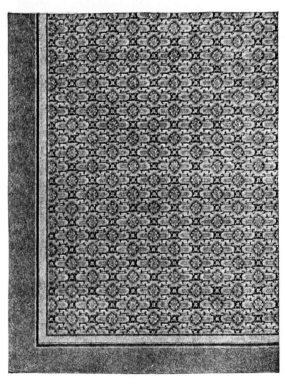

"Mercer" Seamless Pattern No. 541.

PRODUCTS

MANUFACTURERS OF

CARPETS AND RUGS
OVAL AXMINSTER RUGS (Fringed)
SEAMED AXMINSTER RUGS
SEAMLESS AXMINSTER RUGS
EXTRA SEAMLESS AXMINSTER RUGS

TRADE NAMES

"HIGHTSTOWN"—Oval, Seamed, and Extra Seamless Axminster Rugs.
"MERCER"—Seamless Axminster Rugs.

HIGHTSTOWN QUALITY

For a period of 42 years the Hightstown Rug Company has maintained an enviable reputation as Axminster specialists. This specialization has brought perfection. All of the yarns used in the weaving of our rugs and carpets are dyed in our own mills, thus giving us full control of our colors. The "Mercer" (Seamless) and the "Hightstown" (Seamed) rugs have a high pile, 5⅔ rows of yarn to the inch. Customers like the down tread of these rugs.

During the past year a high grade Axminster, known as "Hightstown" Extra Seamless has been added to our line. Harmony of color is given first consideration in these new rugs.

Pattern 140
"Hightstown Oval" Axminster
(Fringed). Made in six sizes.

STYLES AND SIZES

Our Axminsters are made in three styles—"Mercer" (Seamless), "Hightstown" (Seamed), and "Hightstown" (Extra Seamless). There are 34 regular sizes in the "Mercer" line for your selection. In addition to this wide assortment, rugs can be made special-to-order if desired. New patterns are constantly being added to keep our offerings up to the minute.

WE OFFER EVERY FURNITURE DEALER A REAL PROPOSITION

Many dealers are increasing their rug sales by selling odd sizes and special sizes to order. Your ability to serve your trade can be greatly augmented by using our weekly stock sheets and lithographs in connection with your regular stock patterns. This is a practical and effectual way of stimulating rug sales without adding to your stock investment. Let us put your store on our mailing list to receive our weekly stock sheets and lithographs. We make no charge for this.

DIRECT FROM MILL TO YOU

No jobber's profit—"Hightstown" rugs are sold to you direct from the mill. You do not need to carry large stocks. Every dealer is quoted the same price—a low one. Your mark up is practically all profit. Write for information and illustrations of patterns and sizes available for immediate delivery.

KENT·COSTIKYAN
Manufacturers of Handwoven-to-Order Rugs
Importers of Oriental Rugs

Second Floor, 485 Fifth Avenue (Opposite Public Library)   Telephone Murray Hill 0115
NEW YORK, N. Y.

BRANCH OFFICES

PHILADELPHIA, PA., 1520 Locust St.   CHICAGO, ILL., 1811 Heyworth Bldg.
SAN FRANCISCO, CALIF., 251 Post St.   LOS ANGELES, CALIF., 816 So. Figueroa St.   BOSTON, MASS., 420 Boylston St.

Antique Fereghan Rug in Panelled English Living Room   *"Kentshah" Plain Carpet in Bed Room*

PRODUCTS
MANUFACTURERS AND IMPORTERS OF

Seamless Wilton Plain Carpets; Seamless Chenille Plain Carpets; Kentshah Plain Carpets; Bordered Plain Carpets; Colonial Rugs; Hooked Rugs; Spanish Rugs; Emblem Rugs for Clubs, Lodges, etc.; European Handtuft Rugs; Aubusson and Savonnerie Rugs; Chinese Rugs; Chenille Rugs; Imported Oriental Rugs.

Trade Mark

TRADE NAMES

"Kentico": Name given to our imported Scotch Wilton and Chenille, characterized by an unusual artistic texture and the long wearing quality of the Scotch Wool. Carried in stock for immediate delivery in widths, 9, 12, 15 and 20 feet in four standard neutral shades.

"Kentshah": Name given to our handwoven lustrous carpet, seamless up to 21 feet wide. 30-day delivery in any color (dyed to match). Blends with Oriental Rugs; will not show footprints.

KENT-COSTIKYAN SPECIAL-TO-ORDER SERVICE

For the interior decorator in a store, as well as for the rug department, Kent-Costikyan offers a special to-order service which will help you in filling orders for rugs you do not carry in stock, for unusual sizes or colors, or for rugs to fit special rooms. If you use this service to supplement your rug department you can make substantial profits without increased investment. We can satisfy your customer—whether for home, bank, club, hotel or office.

We carry in stock over 1000 room size rugs, running up to 40 feet long and 20 feet wide, or we fill any orders—having the rugs handwoven in Europe and the Orient. If the order is large enough to warrant it, we will be glad to send one of our salesmen to co-operate with you on the sale. If the rugs cannot be delivered by the time they are needed, we will lend suitable rugs to use until they are ready.

HOW TO ORDER KENT-COSTIKYAN RUGS

Look through our stock list and then write us for full descriptions and photographs of the rugs which appear to be suitable,

at the same time giving us all possible information as to number and size of rooms, predominating color, general style of decoration, and approximate appropriation for rugs.

DESIGNS

We have accumulated several thousand designs in colors. Any of these may be modified by our designers to suit the decorator or the owner. For plain carpets, we have stock border designs, and others may be woven on order. Samples suitable to show to prospective customers, complete in colors and qualities carried, will be sent on request. They are standard size, three feet by two feet, and after serving their use as samples may be used in alcoves or doorways. If kept over 30 days, we charge for samples in accordance with the prices mentioned. This will be refunded at any time if the samples are returned in good condition.

Rugs can be seen at any time at our New York showroom, our branch offices, or at the Architects Samples Corporation, 101 Park Avenue, New York, and at the Architects Exhibit Corporation, 11 Beaver Street, Boston. If your customers are coming to New York give them a letter of introduction to us and assure them of the advantage of our forty years of experience. We will give them careful attention and your profit will be assured by billing the merchandise through your store.

SEND FOR FREE BOOKLETS

HB1 Stock lot of 1000 large Oriental Rugs.

HB2 Booklet giving summary of our departments and type of rugs suitable for different rooms.

HB3 Form for specifying floor coverings.

HB4 Color chart and price list of Seamless Plain Carpets and specially made-to-order rugs.

HB5 Booklet on "Care of Your Oriental Rugs."

M. H. ROGERS, INC.
Imported Drapery and Upholstery Fabrics
One Park Avenue, at Thirty-Third St., NEW YORK CITY

BRANCH OFFICES

SAN FRANCISCO, CALIF., 442 Post St.   BOSTON, MASS., Berkeley Bldg.
LOS ANGELES, CALIF., Fine Arts Bldg.   SEATTLE, WASH., Terminal Sales Bldg.
CHICAGO, ILL., Room 1112, Heyworth Bldg.

A complete display at Space 620, American Furniture Mart, 666 Lake Shore Drive, Chicago, Ill.

Illustrating a sectional view of M. H. Rogers, Inc., show rooms devoted to the introduction and display of fine imported upholstery goods, located in our new quarters at One Park Avenue, which is situated next to the new Furniture Exchange and within easy distance of all railroad terminals and principal points of interest and business.

PRODUCTS
IMPORTERS OF

Upholstery Fabrics, Seats and Backs, and Decorative Drapery Materials of all kinds, including:
Linen Friezes
Velours de Gene
Fine Silk Friezes
Brocades
Flemish and Aubusson Tapestry Panels
Flemish, Aubusson and Genuine and Hand Loom Needlepoint
   Seats and Backs
Taffetas
Damasks
Curtain Materials
"Rogers Quality" Tapestry Panels
Velvet Wall Panels

Table Runners and Scarfs
Cushion Tops
Couch Covers and PARISRUGS
and many other distinctive imported fabrics suitable for furniture covering and draperies.

VISIT OUR SHOW ROOMS

We extend a cordial invitation to buyers of upholstery and drapery fabrics to visit our beautifully equipped show rooms, so conveniently located with respect to hotels and transportation centers. Here you will find a wide range of imported fabrics of the finest quality, especially designed for furniture coverings and decorative purposes.

AMERICAN PARLOR FURNITURE CO.

Manufacturers of High Grade Upholstered Furniture

421-431 No. Lincoln St., CHICAGO, ILL.

EXHIBITS

CHICAGO, ILL., Space 1605-9, American Furniture Mart, 666 Lake Shore Drive

No. 958—Davenport—Length, 76 inches; height, 33 inches and depth, 31 inches. Chair furnished in same pattern.

PRODUCTS

MANUFACTURERS OF

UPHOLSTERED FURNITURE including:

BENCHES, Living Room	CHAISE LOUNGES
CHAIRS	DAVENETTE BEDS, Settee Style
—Arm	DAVENPORT BEDS AND SUITES
—Coxwell	DAY BEDS equipped with bed
—Easy	fixtures
—High Back	LIVING ROOM SUITES
—Leather Upholstered	LOVE SEATS
—Living Room	ROCKERS, Fireside
—Odd	SUN ROOM FURNITURE

ALSO manufacturers of Enameled Tables, End Tables, and Occasional Tables.

TRADE NAME

"The Supreme Line—Custom Built"—Trade Mark and Trade Name appearing on Silk Label on every product made by the American Parlor Furniture Company.

FEATURES OF "THE SUPREME LINE"

1. Every piece of upholstered furniture bears a silk label stating what the filling consists of, and each statement is guaranteed.

2. The tailoring of the suite is as perfect as high skilled mechanics can produce.

3. The upholstering work is done only by specially trained men who have served their apprenticeship and proven their ability to produce workmanship worthy of the "Supreme Line."

4. The frames are made of the very best grade of Mexican or Honduras Mahogany, thoroughly kiln dried.

5. Our carving department is composed of only the most skillful hand carvers and the designs produced are absolutely "Supreme" as can be readily seen from the illustrations on this page.

6. The finish on these frames is known throughout the trade as one of the best produced.

7. Every piece of furniture bearing the "Custom Built" label is carefully inspected in every stage of its manufacture by highly competent foremen.

No. 955—Arm Chair—Length, 34 inches; depth, 29 inches and height, 35 inches. Davenport furnished in same pattern.

CENTURY FURNITURE COMPANY

Manufacturers of Dining Room, Living Room, Library and Hall Furniture

Ionia and Prescott Avenues, GRAND RAPIDS, MICHIGAN

Shop Mark

PRODUCTS

MANUFACTURERS OF

BEDROOM
—Bench, Chair, and Rocker Sets for Odd Suites
—Boudoir and Slipper Chairs
—Cane Seat Benches, Chairs, and Rockers
—Desks
—Dressing Tables and Vanity Dressers
DINING ROOM SUITES COMPLETE AND DINING ROOM
—Buffets and Colonial Buffets
—Chairs
—China and Silver Cabinets, Servers, Sideboards, and Welch Dressers
BREAKFAST ROOM SUITES COMPLETE AND BREAKFAST ROOM
—Chairs in-the-white for decorating or special finish
—Buffets and Cabinets, Chairs, Servers, Tables, and Extension Tables

Furniture for the Library and Hall—Benches—Bookcases (Glass Door, or Open Shelves)—Bookcases and Desks Combined—Book, Magazine and Newspaper Racks and Stands—Card Tables—Chairs; Arm (Wood only and Upholstered)—Chairs, Cane and Wood—Chairs, Leather Upholstered—Chairs, Rush Seat—Chaise Lounges—Chests of Oak, Mahogany, or Walnut (not Cedar lined)—Coffee Tables—Console Cabinets, Tables, and Mirrors—Corner Closets—Couches—Curio Cabinets—Davenports — Davenport Tables—Desk Chairs—Desks, Cabinet Style and Kidney Shaped—Drop Leaf Tables—End Tables—Foot Stools and Ottomans—Hall Chairs and Mirrors—Library Desks and Table Desks—Living and Dining Tables Combined — Love Seats — Music Cabinets—Piano and Organ Benches—Radio Cabinets — Refectory Tables — Rockers, Rush Seat—Screens, Folding and Fireplace — Secretary Desks — Sewing Rockers—Smoking Cabinets and Stands—Sofas—Tables, Nested—Tilt Top Tables—Telephone Benches, Cabinets, and Desks—Wall Cabinets—and Windsor Rockers.

ALSO Manufacturers of Children's Chairs—Commodes—Directors' Tables—Furniture Coverings—Hotel and Club Chairs—Make-up Vanity Cases—Manicure Tables—Mirror Frames—Office Desks—Pictures—and Vanity Tables.

TRADE NAMES

"Century" Products usually referred to as "Century Productions." Name "Century" or "Century Furniture Company" invariably associated with "Grand Rapids, Michigan," as "Century, Grand Rapids," or "Century Furniture Company of Grand Rapids," or "A Century, Grand Rapids, Production."

GENERAL INFORMATION

All Century Productions are reproductions of the world's masterpieces in furniture, or original creations based on historic and classic motifs. No restrictions whatever, either in time or materials, are placed on the designing and building of this furniture. Nothing is left undone that will make Century furniture as flawless as furniture can be built. Such furniture is suited to the finest homes.

DESIGNS

Century Productions embrace all beautiful and suitable designs, including, not only the styles of Chippendale, Hepplewhite, The Brothers Adam, Sheraton in England, but Daniel Marot, and other great French designers, as well as our own Duncan Phyfe. In Century Productions there are examples of the Early Egyptian, Greek, Roman, Gothic, Tudor, Elizabethan, Spanish, Jacobean, Queen Anne, William & Mary, Dutch, Italian Empire, Louis Quatorze, Louis Quinze, Louis Seize, French Empire, Colonial, Early American and Modern. In addition there are many adaptations and creations which betray the general characteristics of the locality at the time the style was prevalent. In all—too varied to enumerate.

CO-OPERATION

A catalog of Century Productions will be sent to any representative dealer or decorator who is interested in this class of furniture. Brochures concerning various suites have been prepared which illustrate and describe in brief the actual pieces of the suite and present a brief resumé of the historical background that gives it existence.

"Furniture" is the name of a 256-page volume which briefly, concisely and interestingly covers all the leading furniture periods and furniture designers in history. Thousands of copies have been distributed to teachers, students, furniture dealers, furniture lovers, artists, architects, decorators, libraries and others. Booklets, valuable in themselves, describing the contents of the volume "Furniture" will be supplied dealers, who are interested, to circularize their better trade. It is illustrated with Century furniture. Write for complete information.

COLONIAL FURNITURE COMPANY
Manufacturers of Windsor and Upholstered Chairs
Using a Famous LOCK-JOINT in All Chairs
1430 So. Main St., HIGH POINT, N. C.

PRODUCTS

Manufacturers of
100 Different Designs of Wind-sor and Colonial Chairs for Homes, Hotels, Cafeterias, Churches and Club Rooms.
Custom Made Goods
Upholstered Chairs for Hotels
Tables for Cafeterias
Dining Chairs for Hotels

GENERAL INFORMATION

Rocker to right numbered at all vital points which are locked with a Steel Split Rivet. Views illustrate in detail how the joints would look if cut open. Note the Fish Hook action. These rivets bear the same relation to the constructional features of a chair as Steel Reinforcements do to Concrete.

Our Chairs second to none.

All Chairs constructed with the greatest care for perfection, and are correctly reproduced.

WOODS AND FINISHES

All Colonial Chairs made of select Northern Birch, and finished in the following rich finishes of Duco.

Finishes

Brown Mahogany similar to Plate No. 18.
Red Mahogany similar to Plate No. 24.
American Walnut similar to Plate No. 14.
Spanish Walnut similar to Plate No. 15.
Amber Maple similar to Plate No. 8.
Brown Maple similar to Plate No. 16.
Early English Oak similar to Plate No. 7.
Venetian Walnut.—A beautiful shade between Walnut and Mahogany—One of our Standard recommended finishes.

The above mentioned plates are in the Woods and Finishes Section preceding Page 9 of this Reference Book.

(Continued on next page

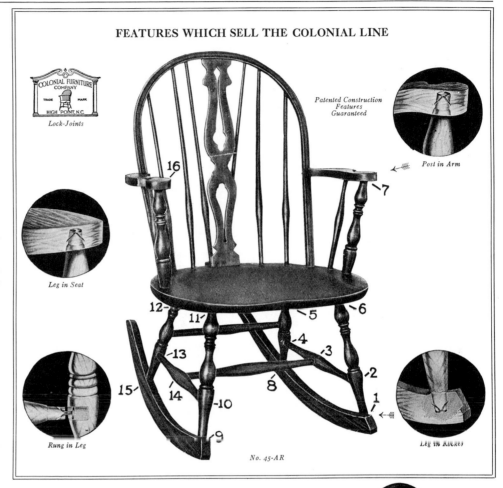

FEATURES WHICH SELL THE COLONIAL LINE

Lock-Joints

Patented Construction Features Guaranteed

Post in Arm

Leg in Seat

Rung in Leg

Leg in Rocker

No. 45-AR

No. 122-ACF—Width of seat, 17 inches; Depth of seat, 15½ inches; Height of back above seat, 17¾ inches.

No. 122-CF—Width of seat, 17 inches; Depth of seat, 15½ inches; Height of back above seat, 17¾ inches.

No. 94-CR—Side Chair to match No.94-C. Width of seat, 17 inches; Depth of seat, 16 inches; Height of back above seat, 19½ inches.

No. 98-C—Rocker to match No. 98-CR. Width of seat, 17 inches; Depth of seat, 16 inches; Height of back above seat, 19 inches.

No. 50-AC—Arm Rocker to match No. 50-AR. Width of seat, 19 inches; Depth of seat, 15½ inches; Height of back above seat, 23¾ inches.

No. 50-ARF—Arm Chair to match No. 50-ACF. Width of seat, 19 inches; Depth of seat, 15½ inches; Height of back above seat, 23¾ inches.

No. 50-CRF—Side Chair to match No. 50-CF. Width of seat, 19 inches; Depth of seat, 15½ inches; Height of back above seat, 23¾ inches.

No. 50-C—Side Rocker to match No. 50-CR. Width of seat, 19 inches; Depth of seat, 15½ inches; Height of back above seat, 23¾ inches.

No. 35-C—Width of seat, 17 inches; Depth of seat, 16 inches; Height of back above seat, 17 inches.

No. 24-C—Width of seat, 17 in.; Depth of seat, 16 in.; Height of back above seat, 17 inches.

No. 55-CR—Side Chair to match No. 55-C. Width of seat, 17 inches; Depth of seat, 16 inches; Height of back above seat, 19 inches.

No. 34-AR—Arm Chair to match No. 34-AC. Width of seat, 21 inches; Depth of seat, 17 inches; Height of back above seat 20¼ inches.

No. 136-C—Width of seat, 17 inches; Depth of seat, 16 inches; Height of back above seat, 20 inches.

No. 79-AR—Arm Chair to match No. 79-AC. Width of seat, 21 inches; Depth of seat, 17 inches; Height of back above seat, 27½ inches.

No. 45-CF—Width of seat, 17 inches; Depth of seat, 16½ inches; Heigh of back above seat, 21¼ inches.

No. 48-AR—Arm Chair to match No. 48-AC. Side Chair to match No. 48-C. Width of seat, 19 inches; Depth of seat, 15½ inches; Height of back, above seat, 23½ inches.

No. 44-ARF—Arm Chair to match No. 44-ACF. Width of seat, 21 inches; Depth of seat, 16 inches; Height of back above seat, 21¾ inches.

No. 44-AC—Arm Rocker to match No. 44-AR. Width of seat, 21 inches; Depth of seat, 16 inches; Height of back above seat, 21¾ inches.

No. 42-ACF—Arm Rocker to match No. 42-ARF. Width of seat, 21 inches; Depth of seat, 16 inches; Height of back above seat, 21½ inches.

No. 42-AR—Arm Chair to match No. 42-AC. Width of seat, 21 inches; Depth of seat, 16 inches; Height of back above seat, 21½ inches.

No. 45-AC—Arm Rocker to match No. 45-AR. Width of seat, 21 inches; Depth of seat, 17 inches; Height of back above seat, 22½ inches.

No. 45-ARF—Arm Chair to match No. 45-ACF. Width of seat 21 inches; Depth of seat, 17 inches; Height of back above seat, 22½ inches.

No. 37-AC—Arm Rocker to match No. 37-AR. Width of seat, 21 inches; Depth of seat, 17 inches; Height of back above seat, 22½ inches.

No. 27-AR—Arm Chair to match No. 27-AC. Width of seat, 21 inches; Depth of seat, 17 inches; Height of back above seat 22½ inches.

No. 97-CF—Width of seat, 16¾ inches; Depth of seat, 15½ inches; Height of back above seat, 20¾ inches.

No. 121-CF—Width of seat, 16¾ inches; Depth of seat, 15½ inches; Height of back above seat, 23½ inches.

No. 124-CF—Width of seat, 18 inches; Depth of seat, 18 inches; Height of back above seat, 27½ inches.

No. 124-ACF—Width of seat, 19¾ inches; Depth of seat, 18 inches; Height of back above seat, 27½ inches.

ISAAC C. DECKER, INC.

Manufacturers of Davenport Bed Suites, Overstuffed Suites and Couches

MONTGOMERY, PENNA.

No. 1152 SUITE—3-piece as shown $272.00

Pillow Arm and Swell Front Overstuffed Suite. Spring edge, removable spring cushions, spring back and removable pillows on arms. Length of davenport overall, 90 inches. Pillows are of same covering on both sides. Arm underneath each pillow is covered in same material. Pillows are filled with special mixture of silk floss and down. Suite illustrated is covered in good grade of small check Jacquard Velour with backs, reversible cushions and both sides of pillows in a good grade of Moquette. No. 3 Footstool, as shown, size 18x22 inches; 16 inches high. Spring seat.

PRODUCTS

Manufacturers of

DAVENPORT BED SUITES with Seng Bed Iron
—Overstuffed Bed Suites with ¾ width bed and also long bed ranging in price from $153.00 to $400.00
—Frame-End Bed Suites in either oak or mahogany finish starting in price with imitation leather at $78.00, muleskin at $82.50 and genuine leather at $102.50

OVERSTUFFED LIVINGROOM SUITES ranging in price from $119.00 on up to $800.00

GENUINE LEATHER OVER-STUFFED SUITES FOR OFFICES AND HOTELS
CHAIRS
—Coxwell
—Occasional
—Button Back
—John Bunny
BENCHES
—Fireside
—Radio
FOOTSTOOLS
COUCHES starting in price with imitation leather or velour $23.50 on up to $72.50.

GENERAL INFORMATION

We have been manufacturing a medium and high grade line of davenport bed suites and livingroom furniture for twenty-three years.

The suite illustrated above is just one of a wide selection of suites made by Isaac C. Decker, Inc. Each suite represents the same amount of care and craftsmanship in its construction so that you can offer our furniture feeling assured that your customer is receiving a real value.

Send for our catalog and price list illustrating other attractive numbers. No obligation.

Prices shown are subject to change without notice.

DELKER BROS. MFG. CO.
Upholstered Living Room Furniture
HENDERSON, KENTUCKY

Davenport. Length, 80 inches; Depth 32½ inches; Height 36¼ inches Seat, 65 by 23 inches.

Davenport. Length, 76 inches; Depth, 33 inches; Height, 34 inches; Seat, 61 by 21 inches.

Fireside Chair. Width, 34 inches; Depth, 34 inches; Height, 38½ inches. Seat, 23 by 19 inches.

Chair. Width, 34 inches; Depth, 34 inches; Height, 34½ inches and Seat, 23 by 19 inches.

No. 181, Suite—Exposed Parts. Solid Mahogany. Web Bottom. Web Back and Full Spring Edge. Nachman Springs in Cushions.

Fireside. Width, 34 inches; Depth, 33 inches; Height, 36 inches; Seat, 21 by 19 inches.

Chair. Width, 34 inches; Depth, 33 inches; Height, 34 inches; Seat, 21 by 19 inches.

No. 36, Suite—Steel Bottom. Full Spring Edge. Nachman Springs in Cushions.

PRODUCTS
MANUFACTURERS OF

BENCHES
—Fireside
—Upholstered Living Room
CANE LIVING ROOM SUITES
CHAIRS
—Arm, Upholstered
—Coxwell
—Fireside
—Living Room, Upholstered
DAVENPORT BED SUITES
DAVENPORTS
—Bed
—Cane
—Overstuffed
—Stationary
—Upholstered
FOOT STOOLS
ROCKERS
—Cane Back
—Cane Back with
   Loose Cushions
—Upholstered
—With Loose Cushions

Davenport. Length, 76 inches; Depth, 31½ inches; Height, 34 inches; Seat, 67½ by 21 inches.

Chair. Width, 30 inches; Depth, 35 inches; Height, 34½ inches. Seat 21½ by 21 inches.

No. 177, Suite—Exposed Parts. Solid Mahogany. Web Bottom. Full Spring Edge. Nachman Springs in Cushions.

GENERAL INFORMATION

Delker suites have three definite qualities that make them outstanding values—and quick sellers. Designs developed to appeal to your customers, sturdy construction, and always the *newest* coverings.

Delker has been in business for 26 years. That is your guarantee of satisfaction and service.

COVER FABRICS AND RETAIL PRICE RANGES

All the popular fabrics of domestic and foreign inspiration are available in Delker Furniture—Mohairs, Plain Velours, Velours, Tapestries, Cretonnes and so on. Delker suites vary in price from $130.00 to $700.00 depending on the grade of upholstery. Davenport Bed Suites range from $160.00 to $588.00.

Prices subject to change without notice.

Open View of Davenport Bed.

Fireside Chair. Width, 30½ inches; Depth, 34 inches; Height, 30 inches; Seat, 23 by 19 inches.

Chair. Width, 30½ inches; Depth, 34 inches; Height, 33½ inches and Seat, 23 by 19 inches.

Davenport. Length, 87 inches; Depth, 34 inches; Height, 37 inches and Seat, 74 by 25 inches.

No. 844, Davenport Bed Suite—Full Spring Edge. Nachman Springs in Cushions. Coil Spring Bed Fixture.

DUNBAR FURNITURE MANUFACTURING CO.

Manufacturers of Upholstered Living Room Furniture

BERNE, INDIANA

PERMANENT EXHIBITS

CHICAGO, ILL., Space 944, American Furniture Mart Bldg., 666 Lake Shore Drive

No. 3049—Chair. Height, 34 inches. Inside width, 20 inches. Outside width, 33 inches. Inside depth, 23 inches. Outside depth, 35 inches.

No. 3049—Fireside. Height, 38 inches. Inside width, 20 inches. Outside width, 33 inches. Inside depth, 23 inches. Outside depth, 37 inches.

No. 3040—Height, 34 inches. Inside width, 20 inches. Outside width, 35 inches. Inside depth, 22 inches. Outside depth, 31 inches.

No. 3040—Height, 38 inches. Inside width, 21 inches. Outside width, 29 inches. Inside depth, 23 inches. Outside depth, 34 inches.

No. 3049—Davenport. Height, 34 inches. Inside length, 66 inches. Outside length, 80 inches. Inside depth, 23 inches. Outside depth, 35 inches.

No. 3040—Height, 34 inches. Inside length, 64 inches. Outside length, 80 inches. Inside depth, 22 inches. Outside depth, 31 inches.

No. 3033—Height, 34 inches. Inside length, 62 inches. Outside length, 92 inches. Inside depth, 23 inches. Outside depth, 35 inches.

No. 3033. Height, 34 inches. Inside width, 23 inches. Outside width, 33 inches. Inside depth, 23 inches. Outside depth, 37 inches.

No. 3057—Height, 34 inches. Inside length, 69 inches. Outside length, 70 inches. Inside depth, 24 inches. Outside depth, 36 inches.

No. 3057—Height, 33 inches. Inside width, 22 inches. Outside width, 32 inches. Inside depth, 22 inches. Outside depth, 33 inches.

PRODUCTS

MANUFACTURERS OF

LIVING ROOM SUITES, Overstuffed or Exposed Wood Frames, including DAVENPORT SUITES

—Davenport   —Fireside, Coxwell, or
—Arm Chair   —High Back Chair

Individual pieces sold separately:

DAVENPORT   LOVE SEATS
COUCHES   FOOT STOOLS
BENCHES   COXWELL CHAIRS
HIGH BACK CHAIRS   FIRESIDE CHAIRS

ALSO Furniture for Lodges, Hotels, and Clubs.

DESIGNS

The expression of the best thought of an eminent American designer and the manufacturing skill of the Dunbar Furniture Manufacturing Company have produced designs that have so appealed to the general consumer taste as to make them remarkable for unprecedented turnover on the dealer's floor.

Dunbar designs have their characteristic and individual motif.

FRAMES AND SPRINGS

Quite as much as is required in the planning of a building, engineering specifications are needed to insure substantial and durable construction in furniture frames. All Dunbar frames are made of kiln dried hardwood, dowelled with hickory dowels set in hot glue and corners blocked. All web bottom frames are built of L. M. C. webbing, double tacked, insuring maximum wear. Springs are of Premier wire and tied in eight knots with a pure Italian flax twine. When steel construction is used with the frames, they are reinforced with wood slats.

FILLINGS

In moss filled suites the finest grade of multi-ginned sanitary moss is used. High grade, clean, white felted cotton is employed in every piece. All filling materials used in Dunbar Furniture are new, sanitary and free from impurities. Down used is of the highest grade and is of the quality to be found only in quality upholstery.

SHIPPING FACILITIES

The Dunbar Factories are strategically located on the Pennsylvania R. R. insuring prompt shipments in all directions.

FRANCHISE

The prestige and good will of Dunbar makes a selling franchise of real value to the merchant selling the line. This reputation has been built upon the "Mark of Enduring Service."

FENSKE BROS.

Manufacturers of Upholstered Furniture

1666 McHenry Street, CHICAGO, ILL.

PERMANENT SHOWROOMS

CHICAGO, ILL., Space 212-221 American Furniture Mart,

and Fenske Building, 1313-1317 S. Michigan Avenue

No. 4697 Chair.   *No. 4697 Davenport.*

No. 4697 Three Piece Living Room Suite

This suite is made with a closely woven base webbing. Springs securely hand tied. Loose spring filled seat cushions and fine
upholstered spring backs. The frames are of solid mahogany, neatly carved. Can be had in a wide assortment of coverings to
suit any desired taste or color scheme.

Spring Edge Construction in No. 4697 Two Piece Suite.

PRODUCTS

MANUFACTURERS OF

BENCHES
—Fireside
—Living Room, Up-
    holstered
CHAIRS
—Arm
—Arm, Upholstered
—Arm, Wood
—Cane Back
—Coxwell
—Easy
—Easy, Upholstered
—Fireplace
—Fireside
—Hall, Home
—Leather, Uphol-
    stered
—Library
—Living Room, Up-
    holstered
—Odd, Upholstered
—Upholstered Seats
COUCHES
DAVENPORT BED
    SUITES

DAVENPORT BEDS
—Overstuffed
—Wood Ends
DAVENPORTS
—Stationary
—Upholstered
DAY BEDS EQUIPPED
    WITH BED FIX-
    TURES
FOOT STOOLS, UP-
    HOLSTERED
LIVING ROOM SUITES
—Cane
—Upholstered
LOVE SEATS—UP-
    HOLSTERED
ROCKERS
—Cane Back
—Cane Back with
    Loose Cushions
—Fireside, Up-
    holstered
—Upholstered
—Wing, Upholstered

No. 4618 Coxwell Chair.

SLOGAN

"Fashioned by Fenske" has been used in connection with Fenske Furniture as a guarantee to retailers that the furniture is of good quality and craftsmanship, at a fair price.

DESIGNS

Fenske Designers have conceived patterns that are reminiscent of the William and Mary, Louis XV, Queen Anne and Spanish Periods, but yet carrying a distinct stamp of originality that is decidedly Fenske.

CONSTRUCTION

Fenske takes especial pride in the interior construction of each piece of furniture. Each frame is built of solid, healthy lumber that has been properly air seasoned and kiln dried. Each joint is carefully reinforced to give lasting durability. Your customer buys *good* furniture when she selects Fenske Fashioned Furniture.

YOU AND FENSKE

The durability of Fenske Frames coupled with the high grade stuffings, and outstanding covers, present to you an opportunity of making real profits. Send for a complete catalog of our entire offering with price list.

MARSHALL FIELD & COMPANY, WHOLESALE

Manufacturers of "Home-Crest" Upholstered Furniture

219 West Adams Street, CHICAGO, ILL.

PRODUCTS

MANUFACTURERS OF

UPHOLSTERED FURNITURE FOR LIVING ROOM
AND LIBRARY, including
BENCHES, FOOT STOOLS, AND OTTOMANS

CHAIRS	DAVENPORTS	LIVING ROOM SUITES,
—Coxwell	COUCHES	two and three-piece
CHAISE LOUNGES	SOFAS	LOVE SEATS

FIELD QUALITY **HOME-CREST** FURNITURE MANUFACTURED BY MARSHALL FIELD & COMPANY WHOLESALE

This Trademarked Label Appears
On Every Piece of "Home-Crest" Furniture

For information on other products see catalogs of floor coverings, page 86, upholstery and drapery fabrics, pages 84 and 87, and curtain materials, page 85.

No. 622—Mahogany finished Birch frame—two-piece suite,
$200.00. Davenport, Length, 81 inches; Height, 35 inches.
A—Moqutte (part linen)—Inside back and cushions, balance
in a linen filler to match.
B—All over in Rose Taupe or Walnut Mohair with reverse
cushions of moqu tes, linens or linen friezes. Samples sent on
request.

No. 645—Semi-Overstuffed Suite. Mahogany finished Birch
frame. Davenport, Length, 78 inches; Height, 35 inches.
A—Shown in standard coverings, Walnut, Green, Burgundy,
Red, black or Rose Taupe Mohair all over with Linen Frieze
reverse cushions. Two-piece suite, $250.00.

"HOME-CREST" FURNITURE

Unless otherwise specified "Home Crest" furniture carries the following points of construction:

Designs

A minimum of 25 styles to meet all requirements of decoration. Some plain, some elaborate, wood frames and overstuffed, but all emphasizing comfort with full sized deep seats with fully upholstered backs and arms.

Construction

All exposed parts are of birch, walnut or mahogany.
Frames are doweled, and reinforced with heavy corner blocks.
All carving is clean distinct wood carving.
The materials used are the best obtainable. Each piece carries a full web construction. Springs tied eight ways with best Italian twine. Standard filling is double cleaned 4XXXX Moss.
Deep spring edge, soft spring back, Nachman spring filled cushions, well padded on all sides. Backs are full spring and webbing construction, insuring greatest comfort and long life.

Workmanship

All hand work by expert craftsmen, tailoring of the upholstery is the best.
Finish is a soft tone, hand rubbed and well high-lighted.

Fabrics

We can offer you the full line of high grade exclusive decorative Canterbury fabrics as coverings for any piece.

All prices are subject to change without notice.

No. 301—Coxwell of Birch finished Mahogany. Inside back and cushion in fine Linen Frieze, Mohair arms, balance in Velour. Silk ball fringe. (This is representative of our Coxwell Chair line ranging from $60.00 to $150.00.)

No. 737½—Chaise Lounge. Solid Mahogany carved frame with a full reversible down cushion. One of several types of Chaise Lounges ranging in price from $170.00 to $380.00.

No. 49—One type of Ottoman with a pillow top. $20.00 to $35.00.

No. 1012—Club Chair to match Lawson.

No. 106—Solid Mahogany carved Easy Chair. Massive, distinctive and comfortable. According to the covering, $110.00 to $180.00.

No. 1012—English Lawson. This Davenport may be had with three separate sections in the back or the back may be made in one piece. As shown the back is hair filled and the cushions are down filled. A most comfortable custom made piece. One of the best proven sellers, because of its simplicity of line which lends so readily to any decorative scheme. Two pieces, $300.00 to $500.00.

May we have your request for samples and more detailed information about particular pieces or about the line in general?

"HOME-CREST" FURNITURE must look well, wear well and be comfortable.

THE FRANKLIN FURNITURE CO.

Manufacturers of Upholstered Furniture

COLUMBIANA, OHIO

Trade Mark

Coxwell, No. 325—Height 37 inches; Width, 25 inches; Depth, 20 inches. As shown—Linen Frieze Back and Down Cushion. Balance in Plain Green Mohair.

Arm Chair, No. 223—Height 35 inches; Width, 29 inches; Depth, 23 inches. As shown—Plain Wine Mohair Seat with imported Frieze Back.

Davenport of three-piece Suite No. 1170—Height, 37 inches; Length, 86 inches; Between Arms, 65 inches; Depth 23 inches. As shown—with Plain Rose Taupe Mohair with Linen Frieze Reversible Cushions.

PRODUCTS

MANUFACTURERS OF

UPHOLSTERED AND CUSTOM BUILT LIVING ROOM FURNITURE as follows:

—TWO AND THREE PIECE LIVING ROOM SUITES
—ODD DAVENPORTS AND SOFAS IN DOWN OR SPRING CONSTRUCTION

—ODD CHAIRS	—LOVE SEATS
—OCCASIONAL CHAIRS	—BENCHES
—HALL CHAIRS	—OTTOMANS
—SLEEPY HOLLOW CHAIRS	—STOOLS

EXCLUSIVE DESIGNS

On suites illustrated in our catalog the exposed surfaces of frames are all of choice solid mahogany from Central America. These suites are of exclusive designs, made especially for us, by celebrated designers, and are fabricated completely in our own shops.

FRANKLIN A-GRADE COLUMBIANA, OHIO.

Name Plate
Attached
to Every Piece
of Franklin Furniture

A-GRADE CONSTRUCTION THROUGHOUT

All Fine Franklin Furniture is of strictly *A-Grade* construction. For frames we use only selected, sound, thoroughly-seasoned hard wood, so firmly put together that generations of use will find them still in the best of shape. Seat bottoms are of fine webbing upon which are firmly sewed double-cone Premier steel wire springs, the tops of which are tied eight times with six-ply Italian twine, covered with ten ounce new burlap. The outside of the backs are covered with burlap and cotton wadding over which the covers are blind tacked and hand sewed.

ATTRACTIVE COVERINGS

The coverings of exquisite patterns and texture, come from the finest looms of Europe and America embracing a line of foreign and domestic friezes, jacquards, mohairs, tapestries, and other coverings of almost unlimited choice.

ATTRACTIVE SELLING FEATURES

The unusually attractive selling features of Fine Franklin Furniture enable you to offer to your customers something different—suites, davenports and chairs that are individual in design and workmanship; built completely in our own plant by expert craftsmen.

Write for our catalog and price list.

FULLERTON FURNITURE FACTORIES
ESTABLISHED 1892
Manufacturers of Upholstered Living Room Furniture
FULLERTON, PENNA.

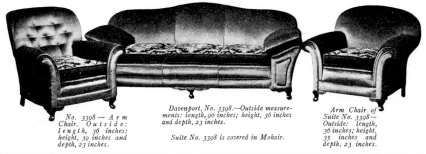

No. 3398 — Arm Chair. Outside: length, 36 inches; height, 30 inches and depth, 23 inches.

Davenport, No. 3398.—Outside measurements: length, 90 inches; height, 36 inches and depth, 23 inches.

Suite No. 3398 is covered in Mohair.

Arm Chair of Suite No. 3398— Outside: length, 36 inches; height, 35 inches and depth, 23 inches.

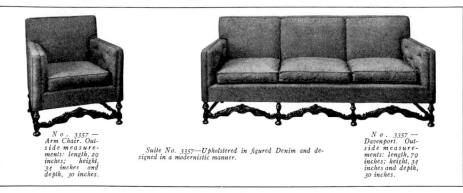

No. 3357 — Arm Chair. Outside measurements: length, 29 inches; height, 34 inches and depth, 30 inches.

Suite No. 3357—Upholstered in figured Denim and designed in a modernistic manner.

No. 3357 — Davenport. Outside measurements: length, 79 inches; height, 34 inches and depth, 30 inches.

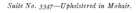

Arm Chair, No. 3347—Outside: length, 35 inches; height, 34 inches and depth, 27 inches.

Davenport, No. 3347— Outside: length, 82 inches; height, 34 inches and depth, 27 inches.

Suite No. 3347—Upholstered in Mohair.

Coxwell of Suite No. 3347—Outside: length, 25 inches; height, 36 inches and depth, 30 inches.

PRODUCTS

MANUFACTURERS OF

UPHOLSTERED LIVING ROOM FURNITURE including:
BENCHES
CHAIRS
—Arm
—Cane Back or Cane Back and Seats
—Wing, Cane
—Coxwell
—Fireplace and Fireside
—High Backed
—Odd and Occasional
—Cushions, Kapok
DAVENPORT BED CONSTRUCTION
DAVENPORT BEDS, CANE BACK OR ARMS
DAVENPORTS AND SOFAS
FRAMES FOR UPHOLSTERED FURNITURE

Love Seat, No. 3336—Outside measurements: length, 51 inches; height, 37 inches and depth, 26 inches. Upholstered in Linen.

IT'S MADE ITS WAY—THE WAY IT'S MADE SINCE 1892

The construction and durability of Fullerton Furniture has long been known to the industry. There is a decided stamp of serviceability in all Fullerton creations that has given it a nation-wide appeal—a serviceability that is not only apparent but an inherent part of every Fullerton offering. You offer your trade a real home adornment when you sell Fullerton.

INFORMATION ON DESIGNS

All designs are embued with a modernistic tone subtly blended with many of the periods. There are many patterns that are representative of Fullerton alone. Examine the patterns on this page and draw your own conclusions as to their merit.

WOODS, FINISHES AND FABRICS

Thoroughly seasoned hardwoods are employed in the construction of Fullerton Frames which are further rigidly reinforced. A good grade of spring which is covered with muslin before the final cover is put on. Fullerton fabrics are numerous and you can satisfy the varying tastes of any of your clientele. Finishes on all exposed parts are durable and in keeping with the fabric.

RETAIL PRICE RANGES

Fullerton Suites range in price from $180.00 to $1800.00. This is a price commensurate with the quality of the merchandise offered. You will realize substantial profits and good will through Fullerton.

FURNITURE CITY UPHOLSTERY CO.

Manufacturers of Upholstered Furniture

140-208 Front Ave., S. W., GRAND RAPIDS, MICH.

WESTERN FACTORY
DENVER, COLORADO, 1215 12th Street

Suite No. 952—Davenport measurements, Outside: Length, 80 inches; Height, 35 inches; Depth, 40 inches.

No. 152½—Chair. Measurements, Outside: Height, 38 inches; Width 33 inches Depth, 40 inches.

No. 931½—Arm Chair. Measurements, Outside: Height, 35 inches; Width, 36 inches; Depth, 43 inches.

Davenport of Suite No. 931—Measurements, Outside: Length, 84 inches; Height 35 inches; Depth, 44 inches.

No. 403¾—Fireside Chair of Suite No. 931. Measurements, Outside: Height, 46 inches; Width, 35 inches; Depth, 36 inches.

"The Quality Line"

Trade Mark

PRODUCTS

MANUFACTURERS OF

BENCHES, LIVING ROOM
—Upholstered

CHAIRS
—Arm, Upholstered
—Coxwell
—Easy, Upholstered
—Fireside
—Leather Upholstered
—Living Room, Upholstered
—Sleepy Hollow
—Upholstered, Odd

CLUB HOUSE FURNITURE
DAVENPORTS—Stationary
—Upholstered
DAVENPORT BEDS
—Upholstered
FOOT STOOLS
LODGE FURNITURE
OTTOMANS—Upholstered
—Foot Stool
ROCKERS—Upholstered
—With Loose Cushions

GENERAL INFORMATION

In handling the Furniture City Line you are assured of upholstered furniture of quality. On frames of selected woods, strong, closely woven webbing is interlaced and tacked on, over which a full quota of the best tempered and tested springs are placed. These springs are supported by eight individual twins to the spring. An exclusive feature of the line is the full floating type of seat, with spring edge completely around seat, front, sides and back. For filling, only the best black cypress moss and curled hair together with pure cotton felt are used—tow, excelsior, and other inferior fillings are prohibited in the Furniture City Factory.

With our new modern and well-equipped factory we are in a position to give service; heavy stocks are maintained with prompt shipments made of all orders. The co-ordination of design, construction and moderate prices has rightly earned the Furniture City product the reputation of a "Quick Turnover Line."

JAMESTOWN LOUNGE COMPANY

Upholstered Living Room Furniture

JAMESTOWN, N. Y.

PRODUCTS

MANUFACTURERS OF

DAY BEDS

BENCHES
—Fireside
—Living Room,
    Upholstered

CHAIRS
—Arm
—Arm, Upholstered
—Arm, Wood
—Bedroom
—Cane Back
—Coxwell

CHAIRS
—Easy
—Easy, Upholstered
—Fireside
—Hall
—Home
—Leather,
    Upholstered
—Library
—Living Room,
    Upholstered

CHAISE LOUNGES

DAVENPORTS,
    Stationary
FOOT STOOLS AND
    OTTOMANS,
    Upholstered
SOFAS
LODGE FURNITURE
LOVE SEATS,
    Upholstered
HOTEL AND CLUB
    FURN., Upholstered
OFFICE FURNITURE

GENERAL INFORMATION

These pieces are some of our new creations in serviceable merchandise. Study this furniture and you will note immediately the unmistakable finished look of a real piece of home equipment. There is embued in each a staunch—comfort-inviting—atmosphere that stamps all Jamestown Lounge Furniture as a product apart.

In spite of the fact that we employ nothing but the best grade of materials in the manufacture of our furniture, we are able to offer our merchandise at a profitable basis to you. For the interests of your business, you owe it to yourself to see our merchandise.

WOODS, FINISHES AND CONSTRUCTION

The wood used in the construction of these pieces is solid Mahogany and finished in the shade shown in Woods and Finishes Section, preceding page 9 of this book, plate 21. They are covered with linen frieze and mohair throughout. The workmanship and neat tailoring are evident.

DESCRIPTION OF ILLUSTRATED PIECES

In the chair shown to our left the subtle French influence is readily detectable. While retaining all the gracefulness and beauty of the age it represents, there is strength and durability that makes it an ideal home furniture.

The spacious, comfortable suite illustrated below speaks for itself. This type pillow-arm sofa has for the past seven or eight years been a constant repeater on the retail floors of our customers. It is a large, roomy, comfortable sofa that will fit into any interior.

Odd Chair, No. 1010 of French Inspiration.

Sofa of Suite No. 728½—Linen Frieze and Mohair.

Arm Chair of Suite No. 728½—Real apparent comfort.

GLOBE PARLOR FURNITURE CO.

Upholstered Furniture

HIGH POINT, N. C.

ASSOCIATE FACTORY
HIGH POINT, N. C., Globe Manufacturing Company

EXHIBITS
CHICAGO, ILL., Space 511, American Furniture Mart   NEW YORK, N. Y., Space 611, New York Furniture Exchange
HIGH POINT, N. C., East Half, 4th Floor, Southern Exposition Building

PRODUCTS
MANUFACTURERS OF

LIVING ROOM SUITES
—Overstuffed
—Exposed Carved Frames
—Cane Back
DAVENPORT BED SUITES
—Overstuffed
—¾ Beds, Overstuffed
—Cane Back
—Davenette Suites

LOVE SEATS
—Single Loose Cushion (Down filled)
BENCHES
—Overstuffed
—Spring Seat
—Pad Seat
—Boudoir
—Foot Stools

Trade Mark

CHAIRS
—Coxwell
—Spot
—Easy
—Hall
—Throne
—High Back
—Low Back
—Wing Back
—Boudoir
—Occasional

CHAIRS
—Overstuffed
—Cane Back
SOFAS
—Virginia
—Duncan-Phyfe
—Lawson
—Spanish
—Cane Back
—Overstuffed
—Chesterfield
—Moderne

GENERAL INFORMATION

In addition to emphasizing individuality of design, Globe Parlor Furniture has all the characteristics that go to make durable and lasting furniture. This is but natural when one considers the staunch frames and reinforcements, the quality of the fabrics, the luxuriousness of the springs and fillings . . . facts to be seen and felt.

We invite you to inspect our merchandise at any of the above showrooms—our representatives will be glad to have the opportunity of showing you around. If not convenient to do this —write for further information and price list.

The beauty of simplicity is obviously manifested in this Virginia Sofa. Its striking beauty may be attributed to its lack of ornamentations and to its wealth of grace. It is an exact reproduction of an old original Virginia Sofa. This sofa has a webb bottom, and a solid mahogany frame. The finish is shaded Antique Mahogany.

*Davenport, No. 1556—
Length, 78 inches; Width,
30 inches. Inside length,
65 inches.*

*Club Chair of Suite
No. 1556—Seat, 29 x 22
inches. Height from floor,
17½ inches.*

*Spot Chair of Suite
No. 1556—Seat, 24 x 19
inches.*

SUITE NO. 1556

Suite No. 1556 is representative of the many new exposed carved frame suites recently brought out by Globe.

Here the heavy hand-carved back rails are cut from solid mahogany wood. The feet and front rails are also elaborately carved from solid mahogany. The arm rails, running along the outer edge of the arms, do not take from the comfort qualities of the full overstuffed, yet this feature gives the suite the well proportioned beauty of the exposed frame.

The spot chair, upholstered in linen frieze and mohair, makes the optional third piece to this suite. It too is of solid mahogany, and while it perfectly matches the suite, it serves an excellent means of deviating from the usual three pieces. At the same time it has an additional use for grouping purposes.

*The Love Seat. The Down filled reversible cushion gives this love seat unusual comfort for
furniture of this type. The carved legs, and all exposed wood, is of solid mahogany. The price of
this piece makes possible its very extensive use.*

THE FRANK S. HARDEN COMPANY

Chair Makers for Forty Years
Also Manufacturers of Library and Living Room Furniture
McCONNELLSVILLE, N. Y.

Factories at McCONNELLSVILLE, N. Y. and CAMDEN, N. Y.

SHOWROOMS

GRAND RAPIDS, MICH., Manufacturers Bldg.   NEW YORK, N. Y., 206 Lexington Ave.

CHICAGO, ILL., Space 1746, American Furniture Mart

No. 62—Bench. Height, 18 inches. Length, 28½ inches. Width, 15½ inches.

No. 745—Arm Chair. Height 38 inches. Width, 24 inches.

No. 287½—Seat. Height, 32 inches. Length 53 inches.

No. 770—Arm Chair. Height, 37 inches. Width, 24 inches.

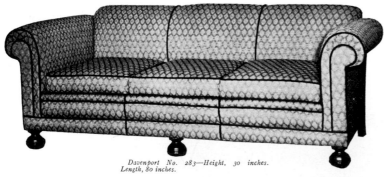

Davenport No. 283—Height, 30 inches. Length, 80 inches.

No. 283-BB—Chair. Height, 35 inches. Width 36 inches.

PRODUCTS
Manufacturers of

DISTINCTIVE
HARDEN FURNITURE
DEPENDABLE
Chair Makers for Forty Years

Trade Mark

BEDROOM CHAIRS AND ROCKERS, Upholstered
BENCHES, Upholstered
BENCHES for Pianos and Organs
COXWELL CHAIRS
EASY OR LOUNGING CHAIRS
FIRESIDE CHAIRS
HALL CHAIRS for Home
HOTEL AND CLUB CHAIRS
LIBRARY AND LIVING ROOM CHAIRS, Upholstered and Not Upholstered
SLEEPY HOLLOW CHAIRS

AUTO SPRING SEAT ROCKERS
SEWING ROCKERS
UPHOLSTERED ROCKERS and
PLAIN WOODEN ROCKERS
DAVENPORT BED CONSTRUCTION
DAVENPORT BED SUITES
DAVENPORT BEDS
DAVENPORTS
OTTOMANS AND FOOT-STOOLS

Bench No. 50—Top, 22x1 inches. Height, 19 inches.

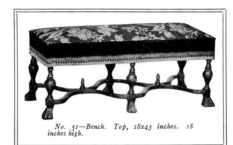

No. 51—Bench. Top, 18x43 inches. 18 inches high.

No. 48—Stool. Top, 13x20 inches. 10 inches high.

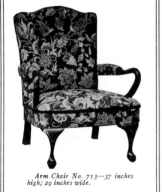

Arm Chair No. 713—37 inches high; 29 inches wide.

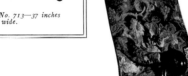

No. 761—Chair. Height, 38 inches and width, 28 inches.

No. 744—Arm Chair. 38 inches high; 24 inches wide.

Side Chair No. 780—Height, 34¼ inches; width, 18 inches and depth, 16½ inches.

No. 740—Arm Chair. 38 inches high and 28 inches wide.

No. 772—Chair. Height, 37 inches and width, 29 inches.

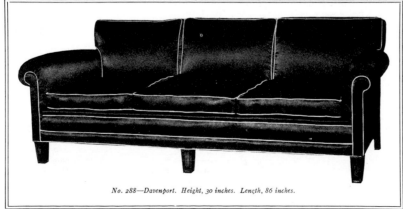

No. 288—Davenport. Height, 30 inches. Length, 86 inches.

JAMESTOWN UPHOLSTERY COMPANY, INC.

Manufacturers of Upholstered Furniture

300 Crescent Street, JAMESTOWN, N. Y.

EXHIBITS

GRAND RAPIDS, MICH., Fourth Floor, Manufacturers Bldg.
During January and July

JAMESTOWN, N. Y., 7th Floor, Manufacturers Bldg.
During May and November

PRODUCTS

MANUFACTURERS OF

Upholstered Living Room Furniture including:

CHAIRS, UPHOLSTERED
—Arm
—Coxwell
—Leather
—Lounging
—Sleepy Hollow
—Slipper
DAVENPORTS AND SOFAS, UPHOLSTERED
OTTOMANS, UPHOLSTERED
HOTEL AND CLUB FURNITURE, UPHOLSTERED

DESIGNS

Most of the popular designs are reproduced in "The Best Made Line in America", including many period styles such as the Italian Renaissance, Chippendale and Queen Anne. We specialize in roomy, luxurious, lounging pieces.

TEXTILES USED AND COLOR COMBINATIONS OF COVERS

Only 100 per cent Mohair is used on "The Best Made Line in America." These are offered in many different shades. Imported Linens, Linen Friezes and like materials offer durable and attractive covers. Many combinations of covers can be effected to please the varied tastes of your clientele.

PRICE INFORMATION

The price range of the upholstered living room suites is from $370.00 to $1400.00. All prices include back linings and reversible cushions with moss-edging. Prices also include a freight allowance as far as New York East, Chicago West, and Cincinnati South.

Prices subject to change without notice.

The "John Bunny Chair" has amazing comfort. Known the country over. This chair is included with the Chesterfield and Loose Pillow Aristocrat Suites.

Suite No. E2612. "The Happy Home Suite." Length of Davenport, 87 inches. Over 8,000 homes made happy by this Suite. A perfect design at a reasonable price.

GENERAL CONSTRUCTION

Frames—the frames are made strong and rugged—will not fall apart. They are built carefully of selected kiln-dried maple dressed both sides. (Using kiln-dried hardwood lumber eliminates the possible incubation and breeding of wood worms and vermin often found in softwood and cheaper lumber.) All joints and corners of frames are doweled with hickory dowels set in hot glue—reinforced with screwed inside corner blocks—super-reinforced with corrugated metal fasteners. The rails are 1¼ inches thick because to them must be tacked the webbing which supports not only the springs and super-structure, but which bears a large share of the weight and jolts imposed on the finished piece. Tacks will not pull out of hardwood.

Webbing—four-inch two-ply imported webbing—the best obtainable is used to support the springs. This is so closely interlaced that it practically forms one continuous surface with no space between the webbing. Each strip is tacked, redoubled and double tacked to maple rails with six tacks at one end and nine at the other (alternating tack groups are staggered to prevent possibility of splitting rail), thus forming a very strong yet resilient foundation for the base springs in davenport or chair. Two reinforcing slats or stringers further strengthen the base of Davenports and give added support to the webbing. Bottoms built this way serve for years and never fall out.

Springs—in the base and back are of the individual type (not unit type) and of the finest oil tempered, rust-proof steel—double cone in shape and of scientifically determined weight and size. Each spring is sewed to the webbing in four places with strong flax twine specially stitched. Tops of springs are tied eight ways. Thirty-six to forty springs are used in the base or seat part of the Davenport (depending on size) and a like number go into the back.

Filling—only the finest grade of triple ginned Sanitary Moss is used. This is the only vegetable material that is moth and insect proof and has the resiliency of animal hair.

Exposed Parts—all exposed parts of frames and seats are made of either solid Mahogany or solid Walnut and finished with a beautiful Italian combination to match the cover.

ORDER A TRIAL SUITE

The above factors explain why "The Best Made Line in America" is a good investment and the cost is truly low in proportion to the long life, lasting beauty and luxurious comfort obtainable from it—you sell something else besides upholstered furniture—satisfaction, plus. Select one of these suites for a trial order.

Suite No. 2628. The "Loose Pillow Arm Aristocrat." Length of Davenport, 98 inches. Also a Junior Aristocrat, 85 inches long. The "John Bunny Chair" illustrated above is included in this Suite.

Suite No. 2528. Chesterfield Davenport. Length, 85 inches. Truly "The Shrine of the Home." The "John Bunny Chair" illustrated above is included in this Suite.

LEVIN BROTHERS, INC.

Manufacturers of Upholstered Furniture

29 Main St., S. E., MINNEAPOLIS, MINN.

PRODUCTS

MANUFACTURERS OF

BENCHES
—Fireside
—Living Room, Upholstered
CHAIRS
—Arm, Upholstered
—Bedroom
—Bedroom, Upholstered
—English Easy
—Fireplace
—Hotel and Club
—Leather Upholstered
—Living Room, Upholstered
—Odd, Upholstered
—Sleepy Hollow

ROCKERS
—Bedroom, Upholstered
—Upholstered
—Wing
—With Loose Cushions
CHAISE LOUNGES
DAVENPORT
—Beds
—Beds, Overstuffed
UPHOLSTERED
—Davenports
—Love Seats
—Ottomans
—Foot Stools
HOTEL AND LODGE FURNITURE

TRADE NAME

On every piece of furniture leaving the Levin Plants, will be found a small piece of metal (see illustration below center) which is your assurance and your customer's that the furniture she is buying is quality clear through. Behind it is the experience of thirty-two years.

DESIGNS

A wide galaxy of pleasing designs are available in such periods as—

Louis XV	Italian Renaissance	Tuxedo
Spanish Renaissance	English Colonial	William and Mary
Chippendale	Louis XVI	Empire
Jacobean	Queen Anne	Art Moderne
	Tudor	

GENERAL INFORMATION

In the 32 years of upholstered furniture manufacture experienced by Levin Brothers, not a year has passed without showing definite growth. From a tiny beginning the organization has grown to a dominant figure in the industry. The main factory building is a five-story structure. More than 144,000 square feet of floor space are utilized in this one building.

The new woodworking plant has added tremendously to our facilities. Both plants contain complete equipment for the manufacture of fine upholstered furniture. All wood employed in Levin merchandise has been thoroughly seasoned and kiln dried.

The national demand for Levin products is a worthy incentive to maintain the high quality of materials and workmanship for which Levin Brothers Upholstered Furniture is recognized.

No. 7047, Chaise Lounge "Queen Anne." Height, 36 inches; Width, 31 inches; Depth, 68 inches.

No. 7049, Side Chair. Height, 37 inches; Width, 29 inches; Depth, 37 inches.

No. 7075, English Easy Chair. Height, 36 inches; Width, 35 inches; Depth, 41 inches.

No. 7001, Coxwell Chair "Louis XV." Height, 35 inches; Width, 28 inches; Depth, 36 inches.

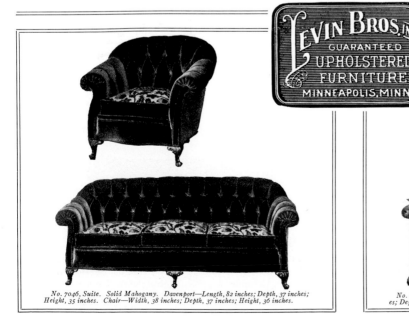

No. 7046, Suite. Solid Mahogany. Davenport—Length, 82 inches; Depth, 37 inches; Height, 35 inches. Chair—Width, 38 inches; Depth, 37 inches; Height, 36 inches.

No. 7012, Suite. Solid Mahogany. Davenport—Length, 80 inches; Height, 35 inches; Depth, 32 inches. Chair—Height, 33 inches; Width, 36 inches; Depth, 31 inches.

S. KARPEN & BROS.

Designers and Manufacturers of Upholstered Furniture
Fiber Furniture, Dining and Bedroom Furniture,
Public Building Furniture and Transportation Seating Facilities

636-678 W. 22nd St., CHICAGO, ILL.

Trade Mark

FACTORIES
CHICAGO, ILLINOIS
LONG ISLAND CITY, N. Y.
MICHIGAN CITY, INDIANA
LOS ANGELES, CALIFORNIA
(Huntington Park P. O. Box o)

SALESROOMS
CHICAGO—801-11 S. Wabash Ave.
NEW YORK—37th & Broadway
SAN FRANCISCO—
180 New Montgomery St.

PRODUCTS
MANUFACTURERS OF

UPHOLSTERED FURNITURE

MATCHED SUITES

—Period Reproductions
and Adaptations
—Overstuffed Styles
—Modern Designs
—Enameled and
Decorated

DAVENPORT BEDS

DAY BEDS

CHAISES LONGUES

CHAIRS
—Formal Chairs
—Coxwell Chairs
—Lounging Chairs
—Occasional Chairs
—Windsor Chairs
—Ladderback Chairs

CUSTOMBUILT FURNITURE
—Suites and individual pieces in temporary coverings

HANDWOVEN FIBER FURNITURE

HANDWOVEN ARTFIBRE FURNITURE
Matched suites and accessories including
—Tables and Desks   —Chaises Longues
—Day Beds and Lamps   —Ferneries

DINING & BEDROOM FURNITURE
(Made at Los Angeles, Calif.)
Matched suites and individual pieces

CONTRACT FURNITURE for
—Clubs, Hotels, Lodges and Public Buildings

TRANSPORTATION SEATING FURNITURE for
—Motor Coaches   —Railroad Club and
—Electric Cars   Dining Cars

Typical Karpen Construction

SPECIAL SERVICE
Lay-outs and estimates for complete decorating and furnishing schemes prepared by experts without charge. Address Contract Department in Chicago, New York or Los Angeles.

GUARANTEE
Effective as of July 1, 1924, Karpen guarantees all coverings against damage by *moths* for three years from date of shipment from factory.

TYPICAL KARPEN CONSTRUCTION

A standard Karpen construction is herewith illustrated and described. All Karpen furniture is guaranteed to be as good or better than this standard of manufacture.

Frames. Inner frames of seasoned hardwoods, doweled, screwed and glued; reinforced with fitted corner blocks screwed and glued in place. Outer frames as may be specified.

Webbing. Red-striped webbing closely interwoven on seats; black striped webbing on arms and backs.

Springs. High carbon premier wire springs throughout. 32 or more double cone coil springs to a sofa seat; 12 or more in chair seats. 160 or more Karpenesque springs in sofa backs and 55 or more in chair backs. 133 Karpenesque springs in sofa cushions; 48 or more in chair cushion.

Seat springs tied 8 to 11 times with unfinished American hemp twine and securely anchored to frame. Karpenesque springs each encased in separate muslin pocket and sewed across two ways into units. All springs sewed to webbing below and burlap above.

Burlap. Covers all springs and outside backs and arms.

Fillings. Genuine curled hair throughout. No moss or inferior fillings of any kind. A layer of cotton covers the hair, and the outside back and arms. Down cushions where specified.

KARPEN FORMAL FURNITURE

The Karpen line abounds in splendid examples of the wood carver's art. Every great period of design is represented. Fabrics of rich texture and coloring and luxurious cushioning are in complete harmony with the beautiful frames. Photographs and samples will be sent upon request. Also, suggestions and plans for the furnishing of fine residences will be prepared without charge. The illustration below is reproduced from the original color painting by Edgar W. Jenney whose drawings distinguish Karpen national advertising. Karpen pieces 938, 939, 940, 941 and 942, Louis XV Period.

(Continued on next page)

No. 151—Charles II Chair. Walnut. 55 inches high.

No. 152—Louis XIV Chair. Walnut. 44 inches high.

The Karpen Nameplate marks furniture of intrinsic worth.

No. 153—Venetian Chair. Mahogany. 35 inches high.

No. 154—Cromwellian Chair. Mahogany. Down cushion.

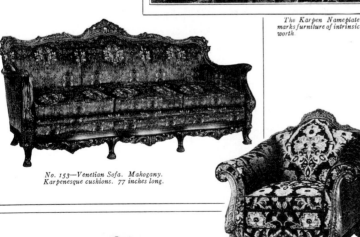

No. 153—Venetian Sofa. Mahogany. Karpenesque cushions. 77 inches long.

No. 155—Italian Adaptation Sofa and Chair. Mahogany. Karpenesque cushions.

No. 154—Cromwellian Sofa. Mahogany. Down cushions. 78 inches long.

No. 149—Queen Anne Sofa. Walnut. 84 inches long.

No. 156—Modern Sofa, Club Chair, Ottoman and Book-
stand. Birch painted and decorated. Other pieces to match.

No. 159—Modern Chair. Walnut.
Down cushion.

No. 159—Modern Love Seat. Walnut. Down cushion.
55 inches long.

KARPEN MODERNE

Many models showing the modern trend in modified form are a part of the new line. They meet the deep and growing demand for new art in furniture without going to extremes. Let our decorating department help you in the selection of such furniture.

DECORATING SERVICE

For dealers who render a decorating service, Karpen offers hundreds of unusual pieces in every mode and the services of professional decorators. "Beautiful Interiors" is a practical book on decorating and furnishing which is gladly sent for the asking.

No. 158—Chippendale Sofa. Walnut. Down cushions. 77 inches long.

No. 161—French Provincial Suite.
Antique Maple on birch. Reversible
Karpenesque cushions.

No. 160—Queen Anne Love Seat. Mahogany.
Down cushions. 47 inches long. Chair made to match.

No. 162—Chippendale Chair.
Mahogany. 39 inches high.

No. 157—Early American Sofa. Mahogany. 78 inches long.

No. 170—Lounging Chair.
Mahogany. Down cushion.

Karpen Sofa No. 211 in antique velour was made to order for the library (left) of the Modern Priscilla Proving Plant, Boston. Delineator and Good Housekeeping have likewise used Karpen pieces in furnishing their Studio rooms.

Custombuilt KARPEN FURNITURE CHICAGO—NEW YORK

KARPEN CUSTOMBUILT FURNITURE

No. 163—Custombuilt Chair.
Down cushion. 42 inches high.

No. 165—Custombuilt Chair.
Down cushion. 35 inches high.

To meet the modern mode in decoration which demands different yet harmonizing coverings for a room ensemble, Karpen offers a wide line of custombuilt patterns in temporary coverings. With these the dealers are showing large cuts of the newest fabrics. Women appreciate the privilege of ordering coverings to fit their preference and decoration scheme. Many dealers are featuring the plan with signal success. Any piece of Karpen furniture, of course, can be covered to order. All Karpen overstuffed furniture is particularly adaptable to this plan whether exhibited in temporary or permanent upholstery fabrics.

(Continued on next page)

No. 164—Custombuilt Sofa. Down cushions.
55 inches long.

No. 160—Chair. 35 inches high.
Down cushion and back.

No. 169—Sofa. 87 inches long. Down cushions and back.

No. 166—Custombuilt Sofa and Chair. Birch legs. Down cushions.

No. 168—Chair. 35 inches high.
Down cushion.

No. 171—Sofa. Karpenesque. Mahogany. 73 inches long.

No. 171—Arm Chair. Mahogany.
35 inches high.

No. 171—High Back Chair. Mahogany.
46 inches high.

No. 173—Sofa. Karpenesque. Mahogany. 79 inches long.

No. 173—Chair. Mahogany. 37 inches high.

DEPENDABLE MERCHANDISE

Quick turnover and volume sales may both be realized without risking the reputation of your house for dependable merchandise. The Karpen line starts with an unlimited variety of "values" (all having the Karpen standard construction) which will build profits and prestige—good will and confidence. Every season brings a bigger and better line of these business-building Karpen leaders for Karpen dealers. Visit any one of our three permanent salesrooms and compare values—and prices—and construction.

CLINCHING A SALE

Pointing out the Karpen nameplate helps close a sale.

No. 172—Sofa. Karpenesque Mahogany. 80 inches long.

No. 172—Tufted Back Chair.
Mahogany. 36 inches high.

No. 172—Arm Chair. Mahogany.
36 inches high.

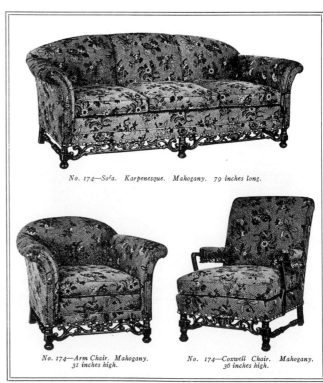

No. 174—Sofa. Karpenesque. Mahogany. 79 inches long.

No. 174—Arm Chair. Mahogany.
31 inches high.

No. 174—Coxwell Chair. Mahogany.
36 inches high.

No. 180—English Wing Chair. Mahogany. Down cushion.

No. 187—Coxwell. Karpenesque.

No. 188—English Club Chair. Mahogany. Down cushion. 36 inches high.

No. 186—Coxwell. Down cushion.

Another view of the Modern Priscilla library shows Karpen Wing Chair No. 212 with box Ottoman to match in printed linen.

CHAIRS

An endless variety of chairs is included in the Karpen line. Chairs for every need; for every decorative plan; for every purse. Period chairs, modern chairs. Formal chairs, lounging chairs. A style and price range unequalled by any other manufacturer. Send for illustrations, prices, and samples of coverings.

(Continued on next page)

No. 179—Louis XVI Chair Walnut. 37 inches high.

No. 178—Louis XV Chair. Walnut. 36 inches high.

No. 181—Queen Anne Chair. Mahogany. 46 inches high.

No. 184—Normandy Chair. Birch, antique mahogany.

No. 177—Occasional Chair. Mahogany. 35 inches high.

No. 189—Ladderback. Antique mahogany on birch. Handwoven fiber seat.

No. 190—Windsor.

S. KARPEN & BROS.

No. 195—Louis XVI Chaise Longue.
Mahogany. Floss cushion. 64 inches long.

No. 193—Early American Day Bed. Antique mahogany
on birch. 78 inches long. Opens into full size bed.

No. 192—Cedar Box Couch. 76 inches long.
Tufted spring seat.

No. 191—Karpen Inner-Mattress Sofa Bed.
Gumwood finished mahogany. 92 inches long.

No. 196 and No. 197—Leather Chairs matching sofas illustrated at right.

DIVERSIFY YOUR DISPLAY

The diversity of the Karpen line is augmented by specialty pieces of this type. Karpen Davenport Beds and Day Beds are sold to those who want a piece of quality furniture combining the convenience and economy of the invisible bed. The boxcouch shown has been a staple pattern for more than twenty-five years. Every well appointed bedroom or boudoir offers opportunity for a chaise longue sale. The one shown in the young girl's bedroom above, furnished by Butterick Studios, is Karpen model No. 213.

No. 196—Leather Sofa. 75 inches long.
Mahogany legs. Down cushions.

No. 197—Leather Sofa. 82 inches long.
Karpenesque. Birch legs.

KARPEN LEATHER FURNITURE

The demand for leather furniture is gradually increasing and the fine reputation which Karpen genuine leather furniture enjoyed during its earlier vogue is reflected in the present volume of business. Many models in Karpen Sterling and Spanish leathers and genuine Morocco. These leathers used in combination with Karpenesque spring construction and down cushions in many styles, provide luxurious ease. Most appropriate and serviceable for clubs, hotels, lodges and public buildings.

No. 214—Chair and Ottoman and No. 215—Desk and Chair
above show the new type of weaving.

SMART—DECORATIVE—INEXPENSIVE

Karpen Handwoven Fiber and Artfibre furniture is enjoying an unprecedented patronage this year. New designs in the modern vogue, new weavings of unusual beauty, striking color schemes, and the best line of covers ever shown are reasons for its leading all other lines in sales. Let us send you illustrations and prices. Suites are matched with such accessories as tables, desks, ferneries, ottomans, lamps and other novel pieces.

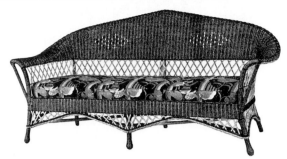

No. 204—Artfibre Sofa. 73 inches long.

No. 204—Arm Chair.

No. 204—Fernery. 28 inches long.

No. 200 Arm Chair. 30 inches high.

No. 200—Chair. 38 inches high.

No. 200—Artfibre Sofa. 75 inches long.

No. 202—Table. 31 inches high.

No. 205—Chair. 41 inches high.

No. 204—Ottoman.

No. 201—Lounging Chair.

No. 204—Desk. 34 inches wide.

No. 204—Desk Chair.
36 inches high.

No. 204—Chaise Longue. 60 inches long.

JOHN J. MADDEN MFG. CO.

Upholstered Furniture

Sherman Drive at 16th St., INDIANAPOLIS, IND.

SHOWROOMS

CHICAGO, ILL., Space 1032-35 American Furniture Mart

Davenport, 907S—Inside dimensions: Height, 19 inches; Width, 77 inches and Depth, 24 inches.

Style No. 907S has all exposed surfaces finished in Duco—Gum Mahogany. Overstuffed arms and back of plain velour.

Arm Chair of Suite No. 907S.

High Back Arm Chair or Fireside Chair of Suite No. 907S.

Davenport, No. 644S—Inside measurements: Height, 18 inches; Width, 64 inches and Depth, 23 inches.

Style No. 644S—Finish: Duco—Gum Mahogany. Outside arms and back plain velour.

Arm Chair of Suite No. 644S.

The Madden Quality

Trade Mark

High Back Arm Chair or Fireside Chair of Suite No. 644S.

PRODUCTS

MANUFACTURERS OF

Stationary and Bed Davenport Suites, Coxwell Chairs and Ottomans, and showing a comprehensive line of coverings ranging from the conventional two-toned Jacquard Velours to the finest Friezes.

GENERAL INFORMATION

The two numbers illustrated have proven to be the most popular in our very extensive line and are characteristic of the value built in all of our suites. An inquiry regarding prices will prove beneficial.

H. Z. MALLEN & COMPANY
Manufacturers of Upholstered Furniture
346 St. Johns Court, CHICAGO, ILL.
EXHIBITS
CHICAGO, ILL., Spaces 145-6-7 American Furniture Mart

No. 3675—Wing Chair.

No. 3700— Occasiona Chair.

No. 3573 — Occasiona Chair.

Lounging Chair No. 3726.

No. 3282 — Occasiona Chair.

PRODUCTS
MANUFACTURERS OF
HIGH GRADE UPHOLSTERED FURNITURE including

BENCHES	CHAISE LOUNGES
OTTOMANS	LOVE SEATS
LIVING ROOM CHAIRS	SETTEES
BOUDOIR CHAIRS	BANK AND OFFICE CHAIRS, and
HALL CHAIRS (Home)	DAVENPORTS
DAY BEDS	SUN ROOM FURNITURE
DAVENPORTS	

ALSO Console Tables with Mirrors—Cane Back and Seat Chairs and Rockers—Drop Leaf and Library Tables.

GENERAL CONSTRUCTION
It is effective to talk to your customer about all exposed frames being made of solid Mahogany or solid Walnut and the balance of Birch and Ash. When you demonstrate the full spring construction of the seats—how the springs come clear to the edge, and set in the best webbing money can buy, you convince your prospect the sofa or chair is made to last. When you relate that the filling used is all hair covered with the best white cotton felting and all pieces made up on muslin before final cover, you make your customer understand why it will last for years.

Considering Quality and Design, Mallen's big production gives you the advantage of a line which builds business, stimulates recommendation at prices which make your products *move*.

No. 3673—Sun Room Sofa.
7(by 33 inches.

No. 3684¾—Georgian Sofa.
82 by 33 inches.

Love Seat, No. 3723
39 by 49 inches.

Queen Anne Sofa. No.
3687—86 by 36 inches.

Kidney Love Seat, No.
3668—56 by 33 inches.

THE NORTHFIELD COMPANY
Makers of Good Living Room Furniture
SHEBOYGAN, WISCONSIN
EXHIBIT AND SALESROOM
CHICAGO, ILL., Space 1420, American Furniture Mart, 666 Lake Shore Drive

Bed-Davenport No. 1678. 83½ inches long over all.

Arm Chair No. 678C. Seat size, 20x 20½ inches; Height of back from floor, 30½ inches.

Coxwell Chair No. 678W. Seat size, 23x 22½ inches; Height of back from floor, 36½ inches.

Davenport No. 2960. 83 inches long over all.

Arm Chair No. 960C. Seat size, 20x 21½ inches; Height of back from floor, 33 inches.

Odd Chair No. 960W. Seat size, 22½x22½ inches; Height of back from floor, 36½ inches.

Davenport No. 2962. 84 inches long over all.

Arm Chair No. 962C. Seat size, 19½x20 inches; Height of back from floor, 33 inches.

Old Chair No. 962W. Seat size, 18x19 inches; Height of back from floor, 35 inches.

Davenport No. 2966. inches long over all.

Arm Chair No. 966C. Seat size, 19x 22½ inches; Height of back from floor, 34¼ in.

Odd Chair No. 966W. Seat size, 19x21 inches; Height of back from floor, 31 inches.

Davenport No. 2957. 83½ inches long over all.

Arm Chair No. 957C. Seat size, 20x 22 inches; Height of back from floor, 34 in.

Arm Chair No. 957W. Seat size, 21½x21½ inches; Height of back from floor, 37½ inches.

Coxwell Chair No. 104W. Seat size, 24x 23½ inches. Height of back from floor, 37 inches.

Coxwell Chair No. 106W. Seat size, 24x 22½ inches. Height of back from floor, 35½ inches.

PRODUCTS

MANUFACTURERS OF

LIVING ROOM AND SUN ROOM SUITES—
—Stationary (Upholstered)
—Stationary (Fibre)
—Davenport Bed (Upholstered)
—Davenport Bed (Fibre)
—Davenport Bed (Oak)
—Davenport Bed (Period Designs)
BENCHES, Fibre
BOOK CASES, Fibre
BOLSTERS
BRIDGE LAMPS, Fibre
CHAISE LOUNGES, Fibre
COXWELL CHAIRS, Upholstered
DESKS, Fibre
END TABLES, Fibre
FERNERIES, Fibre
FOOTSTOOLS, Fibre

LAMPS, Fibre
MAGAZINE RACKS, Fibre
OCCASIONAL TABLES, Fibre
ODD CHAIRS, Upholstered
OTTOMANS, Fibre
PILLOWS
SMOKERS, Fibre
TABLES, Fibre
TELEPHONE STANDS, Fibre

TRADE NAME

"Northfield Living Room Furniture" is used in connection with all furniture manufactured by this company.

UPHOLSTERED FURNITURE

The Northfield line is designed, styled and built for the "Middle-of-the-road" class. And it is moderately priced, to make it possible for a family of modest means to own a fine living room suite, properly and attractively styled with regard to both design and cover, and perfectly tailored.

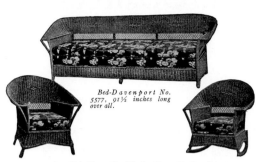

Bed-Davenport No. 5577, 91½ inches long over all.

Arm Chair No. 577C and Rocker No. 577R. Seat size, 20 x 20½ inches; Height of back from floor, 34 inches.

Davenport No. 2553. 75 inches long over all.

Arm Chair No. 553W. Seat size, 20x21½ inches; Height of back from floor, 38½ inches.

Arm Chair No. 553C. Seat size, 20x21 inches; Height of back from floor, 40½ inches.

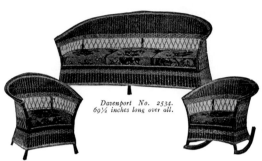

Davenport No. 2534. 69¼ inches long over all.

Arm Chair No. 534C and Rocker No. 534R. Seat size, 18 x 22 inches; Height of back from floor, 32 inches.

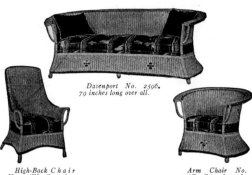

Davenport No. 2596. 79 inches long over all.

High-Back Chair No. 596W. Seat size, 20 x 20½ inches; Height of back from floor, 41½ inches.

Arm Chair No. 596C. Seat size, 18x 24 inches; Height of back from seat, 29 in.

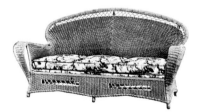

Arm Chair No. 585C. Seat size, 20x 20½ inches. Height of back from floor, 41½ inches

Davenport No. 2585. 78½ inches long over all.

Arm Chair No. 585W. Seat size, 20x20½ inches. Height of back from floor, 44½ inches.

FIBRE FURNITURE

Northfield *fibre furniture* is hand-woven in beautiful, artistic designs over wood frames of good grade, well-seasoned lumber. The finishes and coverings available in the fibre line are selected with great care to carry out the harmonious combination of design, finish and covering, and the large variety offers selections for any color scheme desired.

Chair No. R070. Seat size, 15x16½ inches; Height of back from floor, 33½ inches. Desk No. R073. Top size, 23x36 inches; Height over all, 34 inches.

Chair No. R099W. Seat size, 21½x21½ inches; Height of back from floor, 29 inches.

Davenport No. R5099 76 inches long over all.

Chair No. R099C. Seat size, 20½x23 inches; Height of back from floor, 32½ inches.

Chair No. R096C. Seat size, 24x22 inches; Height of back from floor, 32½ inches.

Table No. R060. Top size, 26x26 inches; Height over all, 30 inches.

NATIONAL FURNITURE COMPANY
Manufacturers of Bedroom Furniture
MOUNT AIRY, N. C.
EXHIBIT
GRAND RAPIDS, MICH., Fifth Floor, South Half, Klingman Building

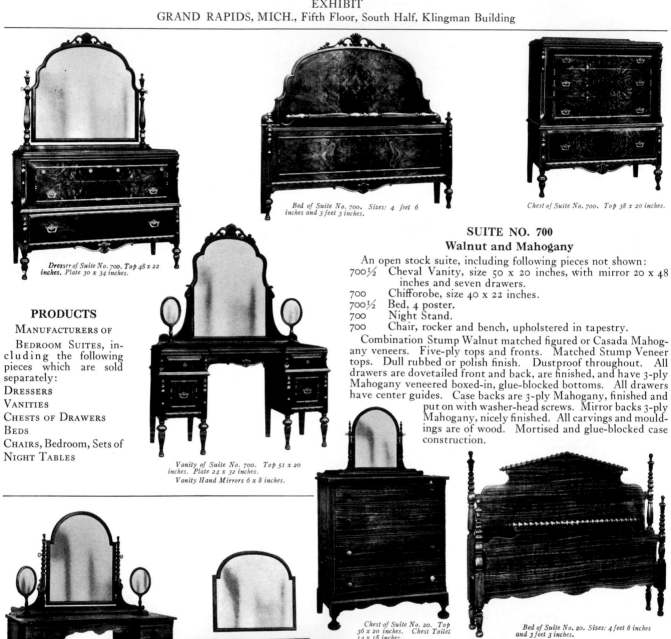

Dresser of Suite No. 700. Top 48 x 22 inches. Plate 30 x 34 inches.

Bed of Suite No. 700. Sizes: 4 feet 6 inches and 3 feet 3 inches.

Chest of Suite No. 700. Top 38 x 20 inches.

Vanity of Suite No. 700. Top 51 x 20 inches. Plate 24 x 32 inches. Vanity Hand Mirrors 6 x 8 inches.

PRODUCTS
MANUFACTURERS OF

BEDROOM SUITES, including the following pieces which are sold separately:

DRESSERS
VANITIES
CHESTS OF DRAWERS
BEDS
CHAIRS, Bedroom, Sets of
NIGHT TABLES

SUITE NO. 700
Walnut and Mahogany

An open stock suite, including following pieces not shown:

700½   Cheval Vanity, size 50 x 20 inches, with mirror 20 x 48 inches and seven drawers.
700   Chifforobe, size 40 x 22 inches.
700½   Bed, 4 poster.
700   Night Stand.
700   Chair, rocker and bench, upholstered in tapestry.

Combination Stump Walnut matched figured or Casada Mahogany veneers. Five-ply tops and fronts. Matched Stump Veneer tops. Dull rubbed or polish finish. Dustproof throughout. All drawers are dovetailed front and back, are finished, and have 3-ply Mahogany veneered boxed-in, glue-blocked bottoms. All drawers have center guides. Case backs are 3-ply Mahogany, finished and put on with washer-head screws. Mirror backs 3-ply Mahogany, nicely finished. All carvings and mouldings are of wood. Mortised and glue-blocked case construction.

Vanity of Suite No. 20. Top 48 x 20 inches. Plate 22 x 28 inches. Vanity Hand Mirrors 6 x 8 inches.

Dresser of Suite No. 20. Top 45 x 21 inches. Plate 22 x 28 inches.

Chest of Suite No. 20. Top 36 x 20 inches. Chest Toilet 14 x 18 inches.

Bed of Suite No. 20. Sizes: 4 feet 6 inches and 3 feet 3 inches.

EARLY AMERICAN COLONIAL SUITE NO. 20
Mahogany, Walnut, Blue Enamel, Decorated, or Curly Maple

Other pieces in this Colonial grouping may be had as follows—

20   Dresser, as above except with swinging mirror, size 22 x 28 inches.
20   Highboy, size 30 x 20 inches, with seven drawers.
20   Lowboy, size 45 x 21 inches, with five drawers, 3 long and 2 at top.
20   Writing Table, size 30 x 20 inches.
20   Night Table.
20   Chair, rocker and bench, upholstered in tapestry.

Combination broken stripe Mahogany, Sliced Walnut, or Curly Maple veneers. Enamel over Maple veneers. Five-ply tops and fronts, dull rubbed finish. Dust-proof throughout. All drawers are dovetailed front and back, are finished, and have 3-ply Mahogany veneered boxed-in, glue-blocked bottoms. All drawers have center guides. Wood mouldings. Mortised and glue-blocked case construction.

Write or wire us for prices or illustrations of other suites.

THE SPENCER-DUFFY COMPANY, INC.

Designers and Manufacturers of Upholstered Furniture

Factory and Permanent Exhibit
GRAND RAPIDS, MICH.

PRODUCTS

MANUFACTURERS AND DESIGNERS OF

UPHOLSTERED FURNITURE in leather and fabric.

OFFICE SUITES in leather.

LIVING ROOM, BOUDOIR, HALL AND SOLARIUM FURNITURE.

HOTEL, LODGE ROOM AND CLUB ROOM FURNITURE and special upholstered furniture of involved detail and design—Makers of furniture frames for the trade—Jobbers of upholstery fabrics.

DAVENPORTS, ARM CHAIRS, SIDE CHAIRS, SOFAS, SETTEES.

LOVE SEATS, ROMAN CHAIRS, CHAISE LONGUES, FIRESIDE CHAIRS.

FOOT STOOLS, OTTOMAN HASSOCKS AND BENCHES UPHOLSTERED.

LUXURIOUS LOUNGING CHAIRS.

CUSHIONS on special contract for church and hall seating white muslin first cover and equipped with the celebrated Sanitique Demountable upholstery covers.

The "SANITIQUE" Fastener

The "Sanitique" fastener is a patented device which opens the cover in a single stroke—zipp. Refastening the cover, is equally as easy. No wrinkles or slackness. Non-visible when cushions are in place. The device is patented—obtainable in Spencer-Duffy Furniture.

TRADE NAME

"SANITIQUE"—An invisible, hookless, fastener device which opens or closes upholstery covers in a single stroke. Copyrighted by the Spencer-Duffy Company.

"SANITIQUE" CUSHION COVERS

As illustrated "Sanitique" covers are quickly detached from the cushion. This convenience makes them easier to keep clean. A clean cover looks better and lasts longer. "Sanitique" covers are interchangeable. They make it possible to sell the customer who likes a certain upholstered piece but prefers a different cover on the cushions. All cushions

No. 552—Howlett Chair. Width, 20 inches; depth, 36 inches; height, 31 inches.

and pillows are made in a first cover of white muslin — demount the covers — cushion centers exposed to sun and air restores original fullness throughout the life of the furniture.

No. 554—Howlett Chair. Width, 28 inches; depth, 30 inches; height, 31 inches.

EXCLUSIVE FRANCHISE

The Spencer-Duffy Agency which carries the "Sanitique" feature is an exclusive franchise and can be offered to but one dealer in your locality.

No. 540—Davenport. Length, 78 inches; depth, 34 inches; height, 33 inches.

No. 540—Chair. Width, 30 inches; depth, 34 inches; height, 32 inches.

No. 531—Chair. Width, 32 inches; depth, 30 inches; height, 33 inches.

No. 531—Davenport. Length, 78 inches; depth, 31 inches; height, 34 inches.

THE SPENCER-DUFFY COMPANY, INC.

No. 24448—Chair.
Width, 31 inches;
depth, 26 inches;
height, 34 inches.

No. 22358 — A r m
Chair. Width, 28 inches;
depth, 29 inches; height,
39 inches.

A Corner View of the elaborate Spencer-Duffy permanent showrooms at Grand Rapids.

AMERICA'S FINEST EXHIBITION OF UPHOLSTERED FURNITURE

Our New Exhibition building with its splendid facilities embraces every refinement for the successful display and sale of *better furniture*.

These wholesale display rooms are open throughout the year with admission restricted; for dealers and their properly sponsored clients.

Trade opinion has generously pronounced this the finest and most complete Exhibition of upholstered furniture in America.

No. 24528—Decorated Chair.
Width 24 inches; depth, 24 inches; height, 35 inches.

No. 21818—S i d e Chair.
Height, 35 inches; width, 15 inches; depth, 15 inches.

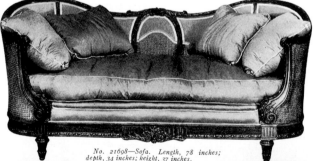

No. 21608—Sofa. Length, 78 inches;
depth, 34 inches; height, 37 inches.

No. 25008—Sofa. Length, 81
inches; depth, 43 inches; height, 33
inches.

No. 21888—A r m
Chair. Width, 29
inches; depth, 31 inches; height, 38 inches.

No. 24108—Sofa. Length, 72
inches; depth, 35 inches; height, 40
inches.

No. 22348—Chinese Chippendale Chair. Width, 26
inches, depth, 31 inches and
height, 38 inches.

*No. 25308—Lobby Unit—Three Seat Section.
Length, 125 inches; depth, 81 inches; height, 31
inches. Also made in Two Seat Section.*

*No. 23848—Chair. Depth, 30
inches; width, 30 inches; height, 32
inches.*

*No. 23318—
Bench. Length,
53 inches; width,
30 inches; height,
28 inches.*

*No. 25578—Chair. Width, 33
inches; depth, 34 inches; height, 35
inches.*

*No. 21368—Chair. Width, 27
inches; depth, 31 inches; height, 55
inches.*

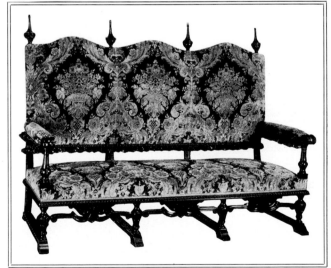

*No. 21348—Tri Seat (Also made in Two Seat
Sections). Length, 74 inches; depth, 32 inches,
height, 55 inches.*

CLUB, HOTEL, AND LODGE FURNITURE

The distinctiveness of Spencer-Duffy Furniture needs no long drawn out statement of convincing facts. The furniture has all the characteristics and charm that is an inherent trait of all well made furniture.

We invite you to our showrooms—you will be convinced that Spencer-Duffy Furniture is the kind you want to sell and have on your floors.

PULLMAN COUCH COMPANY, INC.

Manufacturers of Davenport Bed Suites, Living Room, Decorated Furniture

General Offices and Factory, 3759 So. Ashland Ave., CHICAGO, ILL.

EXHIBITS

CHICAGO, ILL., 12th Floor, American Furniture Mart   NEW YORK, N. Y., 2nd Floor, One Park Ave. Bldg.

Offices and Warehouses   **Factories**
BOSTON, MASS., 197 Friend St.   CHICAGO, ILL., 3759 So. Ashland St.
DALLAS, TEX., 316 No. Preston St.   LONG ISLAND CITY, N. Y., Meadow and Pearson Sts.

PRODUCTS
MANUFACTURERS OF
CUSTOM BUILT SUITES AND OCCASIONAL CHAIRS
COIL SPRING DAVENPORT BEDS AND SUITES
COIL SPRING DAY BEDS
LIVING ROOM SUITES

There are three distinct departments in the Pullman factory—the living room furniture department, the day bed and davenport bed suite department, and the custom built department. Each department has its own foreman and is entirely separate from the others.

PULLMAN CUSTOM BUILT FURNITURE

Pullman custom built furniture is the last word in beauty of design and coverings, in superiority of materials and workmanship. This quality group is made with solid mahogany exposed wood, moss and hair filling, webbed bottoms, sides and backs, and springs tied eight times.

Chairs which are beautiful and distinctive are part of the Pullman custom built line. Unusual hand carved solid mahogany frames and rich coverings. Large production on Pullman custom built furniture makes the prices amazingly low.

This is the tag found on every piece of Pullman custom built furniture.

PULLMAN COIL SPRING DAY BEDS

The Pullman line of day beds is very complete and most attractive in design and materials. They have the same coil spring construction as the Pullman davenport beds, and therefore are unusually comfortable both as beds and as couches.

PULLMAN MERCHANDISER

The "Pullman Merchandiser" is a monthly publication prepared for the benefit of all Pullman dealers. Each issue contains suggested advertisements written by experts, original ideas on how to increase your business, and discussions of vital topics.

Another of the beautifully designed and constructed Pullman custom built chairs. The great value of this line allows you an excellent markup.

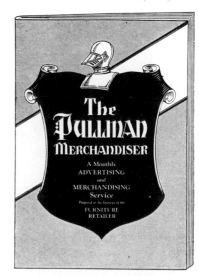

PULLMAN COIL SPRING DAVENPORT BEDS

The exceptional charm and comfort of Pullman davenport bed suites will instantly appeal to your customers. The fashionable designs and beautiful coverings fit these suites for any living room. During the daytime no one would ever suspect that the big, extremely comfortable davenport holds a bed. Night time arrives, and in an instant the davenport is converted into a full size, regular coil-spring bed, as comfortable as the finest bed.

The pictures below show how easily and simply the Pullman works. These beautiful photographs are available to Pullman dealers free of charge, in the form of large cards for window or store display.

FOR FASHIONABLE HOMES

Pullman davenport bed suites are so fashionable in design and beautiful in finish that they are suitable for the finest homes. Any piece of Pullman furniture can be supplied in a wide variety of handsome covers.

COMFORTABLE! BEAUTIFUL!

By day the Pullman is a handsome davenport, fit to grace any living room. Deep, cozy seats—soft, comfortable cushions. Your customers will instantly appreciate the beauty and comfort of the Pullman.

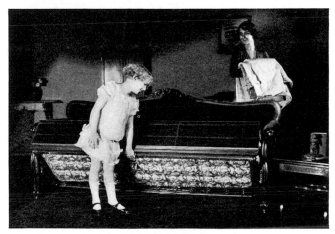

REVOLVES QUICKLY, EASILY

Night time arrives, and the Pullman offers the convenience of an extra full-size bed. A child can open it—the revolving seat of the Pullman has powerful balancing springs which do most of the manual work of opening the bed.

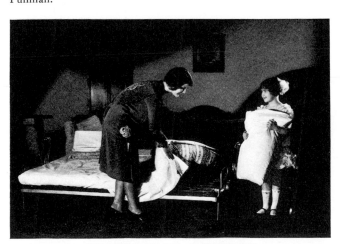

HOLDS A 25-LB. MATTRESS

The Pullman has coil springs just like the finest beds. You do not sleep on the same springs as you sit on. Opened, the davenport bed takes a double-size 25-pound mattress and makes up just like a regular bed.

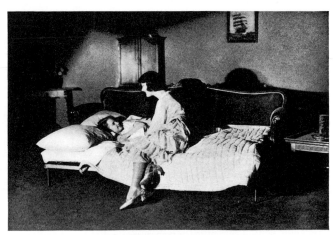

A PERFECT DOUBLE BED

The Pullman davenport bed is quickly convertible into a perfect double bed. Full length, comfortable, convenient. Good value from every standpoint.

THE C. F. STREIT MFG. COMPANY
The Beautiful Streit Slumber Chair
1110 Kenner Street, CINCINNATI, OHIO

Since 1871, makers of fine upholstered furniture

Permanent display of complete line at New York Furniture Exchange and at the American Furniture Mart, Chicago

PRODUCTS

MANUFACTURERS OF

The Beautiful Streit "Slumber" Chair, in a variety of models including the following period designs:

English Coxwell
Queen Anne
Tudor
Heppelwhite
Modern Overstuffed
Florentine
Modified Coxwell

The C. F. Streit Co. also manufacture Bed-Davenports and a complete line of high-grade upholstered furniture.

TRADE NAME

"The Beautiful Streit Slumber Chair," used in connection with the triangular name-plate shown above, which is attached to every chair. The chair, itself, has been patented in the United States, Canada, and Argentina.

GENERAL INFORMATION

The eight popular period models of the Beautiful Streit Slumber Chair illustrated here are authentic designs—rich in coloring, truly patrician. There is one among them that will fit into any decorative scheme.

WOOD

The Beautiful Streit Slumber Chair is made only of the finest woods—carefully selected and well seasoned.

GUARANTEE

The following guarantee accompanies every chair:

"The workmanship and material in this Beautiful Streit Slumber Chair are of the highest quality, and are fully guaranteed. If you are not perfectly satisfied with the chair, you may return it, at our expense. The C. F. Streit Manufacturing Company, Cincinnati, Ohio."

English Coxwell
No. 1520 Upholstering—Moquette in tan background, pattern in crimson, blue, lavender and sienna. Arms and trimmings, soft crimson mohair.
Retail Price—complete with stool—$114.50.

Queen Anne
No. 1522 Upholstering—Jacquard Velour dark red background, raised patterns of black background, raised patterns of black and dark pearl.
Retail Price—complete with stool—$71.00.

A CHAIR OF BEAUTY AND SUPERLATIVE COMFORT

It isn't often that a chair appeals to both men and women, for men think of chairs in terms of comfort, while women think of them in terms of beauty. But the Beautiful Streit Slumber Chair supplies just this wanted combination. Women purchase it every day as a smart occasional chair. And men—well, once a man sinks into it for an after-dinner smoke, it's *his* for life.

The reason for this superlative comfort is the exclusive Streit feature. The back tilts with the seat to just the angle a man's tired body likes best. No slipping forward, no "krick" at the small of the back—the chair offers support at every point. Thick cushions snuggle up to the small of the back, the head is supported, even the feet have a soft-padded footstool to rest upon. In all the world there is no chair like this.

And the chair is just as durable as it is comfortable. Made in our own factories of seasoned woods and selected materials, the Streit Chair will stand up under the hardest usage.

FREE SLIP-COVERS

Merchants are authorized to include, free of charge, a well-tailored, perfectly-fitting Streit slip-cover with every chair delivered. The cover is of excellent material and workmanship, of a quality selling at from $5 to $7 in most stores.

Further information regarding the Beautiful Streit Slumber Chair will be gladly sent on request. Write today!

Prices shown are subject to change without notice.

In the Beautiful Streit Slumber Chair, notice how seat and back tilt as one to form a comfortable pocket for the work-weary body.

This man strives vainly for comfort by trying to make his body fit his chair.

Modern Overstuffed
No. 1528 Upholstering—Jacquard Velour, multi-colored design. Arms and trimmings in small, vari-colored patterns.
Retail Price—complete with stool—$101.00.

Tudor
No. 1532 Upholstering—Arms and trimmings in small-checked Jacquard Velour. Back and seat in Jacquard Velour also—warm maroon, blue, gray and brown hues.
Retail Price—complete with stool—$90.00.

Florentine
No. 1525 Upholstering—Ratine Tapestry—dark cream background, soft-relief floral pattern in blended browns, blues, dark red, and burnt orange. Arms and trimmings in plain Velour.
Retail Price—complete with stool—$75.50.

Queen Anne
No. 1517 Upholstering—Arms and trimmings, dark brown mohair. Back and seat, flowered Linen Friezé.
Retail Price—complete with stool—$166.00.

Hepplewhite
No. 1510 Upholstering—Arms and trimmings, dark brown Mohair. Back and seat in Linen Friezé—floral pattern in tan, brown, azure and old rose.
Retail Price—complete with stool—$180.50.

Modified Coxwell
No. 1533 Upholstering—Arms and trimmings in plain gray Velour. Back and seat in rich, flowered Ratine Tapestry—blended blue-greens, siennas and browns or background of deep cream.
Retail Price—complete with stool—$85.00.

WILLIAM SULTAN & COMPANY

Manufacturers of Upholstered Furniture

732-740 North Morgan Street, CHICAGO, ILL.

PERMANENT EXHIBIT

CHICAGO, ILL., Spaces 1237-38, American Furniture Mart, 666 Lake Shore Drive

No. 648 — Davenport. Louis XVI design, solid Walnut imported frame. Length, 68 inches; Height, 42 inches; Depth, 32 inches.

No. 648—Chair. Louis XVI design. Solid Walnut. Length, 30 inches; Height, 39 inches; Depth, 31 inches.

PRODUCTS

MANUFACTURERS OF

BENCHES
—Fireside
—Living Room, Upholstered

CHAIRS
—Antique Mahogany
—Arm, Upholstered
—Arm, Wood
—Bedroom
—Bedroom, Upholstered
—Coxwell
—Desk, Upholstered
—Easy, Upholstered
—Fireside
—Leather, Upholstered

CHAIRS
—Living Room, Upholstered
—Lounging, Odd
—Slipper
—Upholstered Seat

CHAISE LOUNGES

FOOT STOOLS

HOTEL AND CLUB FURNITURE

LOVE SEATS, Upholstered

TABLES
—Console
—Occasional

No. 521½—Love Seat. Louis XV design. Solid Walnut imported Frame. Length, 48 inches; Height, 35 inches; Depth, 27 inches.

THE CREED OF SULTAN

To deliver to the American household upholstered furniture of authentic design, proper construction and perfectly matched coverings, at a price within everyone's reach; is and always has been the aim of this company.

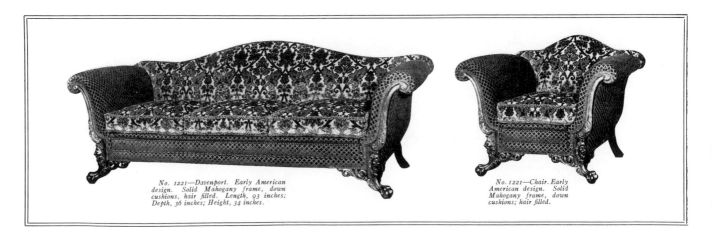

No. 1221—Davenport. Early American design. Solid Mahogany frame, down cushions, hair filled. Length, 93 inches; Depth, 36 inches; Height, 34 inches.

No. 1221—Chair. Early American design. Solid Mahogany frame, down cushions; hair filled.

DE BOER MANUFACTURING CO.

Manufacturers Since 1909

South State Street at Woodland Avenue, SYRACUSE, N. Y.

BED RIGID   *The* DEBEDSTA

MOVES CONVENIENLY   **WAY**

THE OLD WAY
– Bed Racks

PRODUCTS
MANUFACTURERS OF
BED STAYS
ADJUSTABLE SHORT BED RAILS for Displaying Beds

TRADE NAME
"DEBEDSTA"—Bed Stays made by the De Boer Manufacturing Company.

THE DEBEDSTA MAKES POOR BEDS GOOD
GOOD BEDS BETTER

Every bed needs a bed stay. It makes no difference who made the bed or the kind of bed locks used on the bed rail.

The adjustable DeBedsta Bed Stay is *adjustable* so that it can be quickly attached to any size or make of wood bed. A simple little twist of one thumb-screw with two adjustable castings on the end of a steel rod, four wire cables and eight hooks unite the four corners and side rails of the bed firmly together, making an easy rolling, rigid piece of furniture that can be conveniently moved without racking. The adjustable DeBedsta Bed Stay keeps the slats of the bed from falling and strengthens the corner locks so that the bed cannot break down and pull to pieces. They also increase the durability and add to the value of any wood bed.

PRICES AND TERMS

$15.00 per dozen Bed Stays. 20% Discount on Gross Orders. Terms: 60 days net; 2% discount if paid in 30 days from date of invoice. F. O. B. Factory. These prices are not subject to any discount except as stated here.

PATENTS PENDING

Every Bed Needs a Bed Stay

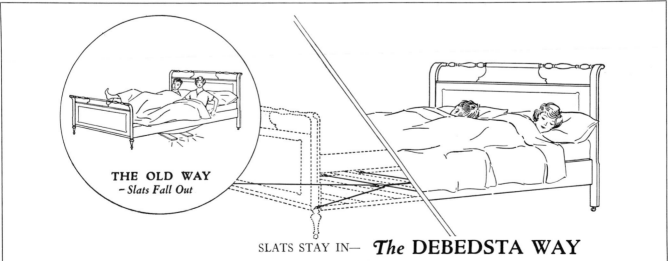

THE OLD WAY
– Slats Fall Out

SLATS STAY IN— *The* DEBEDSTA WAY

DOMES OF SILENCE, INC.
Manufacturers of Furniture Glides
Also Racks for Clothes, Shoes and Kitchen Utensils
21 Pearl Street, NEW YORK, N. Y.

PRODUCTS
MANUFACTURERS OF
FURNITURE CASTERS
COMBINATION SHELF AND CLOTHES CLOSET
RACKS
SHOE RACKS
CLOTHES DRYING RACKS for use on Radiators
RACKS for Kitchen Utensils.

We also manufacture all grades of sliding casters, Felt Slides, Felt Feet for Radio, Upholstery Nails, Celluloid Tacks, etc.

TRADE NAMES

"DOMES OF SILENCE"— Patented trade name and Registered Trade Mark for all furniture glides made by Domes of Silence, Inc., New York, N. Y.

"DORAK"—a combination shelf, tie rack, trouser and coat hanger.

"REMRAK"—a shoe rack.

"RADIRAK"—a small clothes drying rack for attachment to radiator.

"PANCORAK"—a rack for Kitchen Utensils.

PUT THIS DISPLAY
IN YOUR WINDOW

Taking all the people who come into your store—buyers and inquirers alike—how much is each customer worth to you? Would you like more people to come in? Could you sell them furniture? Here's a way to attract people into your store: Display Domes of Silence in your window. Nationally advertised and sold by some stores to the amount of a gross sets a day, you can count on them to

No. D10—Assortment. Packed 1/2 gross sets. One dozen each of 1/2-inch, 5/8-inch, 3/4-inch, and 7/8-inch. $9.00 per gross sets.

bring customers in. $9.38 will give you a full gross stock and a display cabinet combined—a $9.38 investment to secure ten or more potential furniture customers every week!

PUT THIS DISPLAY IN YOUR
STORE

The new metal Display-stock Cabinet—Assortment D-20—costs $9.38 and sells for $15. Contains a gross sets as follows: 1 dozen each of 3/8-inch and 1 1/8-inch; 2 1/2 dozen each of 1/2-inch, 5/8-inch, 3/4-inch and 7/8-inch.

INSIST ON GENUINE DOMES
OF SILENCE

The furniture retailer especially is deeply concerned with imitation —the public is quick to discover inferiority. Domes of Silence are being imitated, and although vigorous steps will be taken to protect Domes of Silence patent rights as we protect their quality we believe retailers should be cautioned to look for the name, "Domes of Silence," and the patent number 995,758. Specify genuine Domes of Silence. Then you will get the genuine.

Front view as the customer sees it.

Back view: Showing arrangement of packages.

WE ALSO MANUFACTURE ALL GRADES OF SLIDES AT COMPETITIVE PRICES

Doubles Closet Space

Dorak for Clothes $6.00 Retail

Remrak for Shoes $2.00 Retail

FOR QUICK DRYING

IN USE

SLIDES DOWN WHEN NOT IN USE

Radirak $3.00 Retail

DORAK

A shelf, place for ties, trousers and eight coat hangers. Hang from top of door, or reverse arms and attach to wall or door by nails or screws.

REMRAK

For your shoes. Steel, beautiful bronze or black telephone finish, 10-inch for small doors, 24-inch for usual size doors.

"Everything Handy when you Open Door."

RADIRAK

Can be instantly attached to radiator at any height. Three ex-

tension arms moving in any direction make Radirak a wonderful convenience for drying hosiery, handkerchiefs, etc.; arms tuck inside when not in use. Brass, nickel-plated. Rust-proof. Nothing to get out of order.

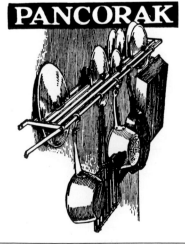

PANCORAK

Pancorak $3.00 Retail

Pancorak holds five pots or pans and 12 pot lids, or covers can be used for shelf. Attached to wall or door by four nails or screws. Steel, beautiful bronze, enamel finish. Patent applied for. Holds heaviest weight.

Dorak, Remrak, Radirak, Pancorak, all come complete, folded flat, one in a box, with screws.

Regular dealer discount on these four articles.

YPSILANTI REED FURNITURE CO.

Manufacturers of Reed and Fibre Furniture

IONIA, MICHIGAN

PERMANENT EXHIBITS

NEW YORK, N. Y. No. 1, Park Avenue   CHICAGO, ILL., American Furniture Mart

January and July Exhibits—GRAND RAPIDS, MICH., Klingman Furniture Exchange

S8788F5—*Fibre Davenport. Spring filled cushion over spring seat. Seat 60 inches wide between arms. Back, 24 inches high. Price in Tapestry, $86.00.*

PRODUCTS

MANUFACTURERS OF

A complete line of Reed and Fibre Furniture for Living Room, Sun Parlor and Porch. Distinctive designs, attractive finishes, high grade upholstery.

AQUARIUMS
BASKETS
—Fireplace for wood
—Sewing or Work
—Waste Paper
BIRD CAGES, AND
BIRD CAGES WITH FERNERIES COMBINED
BOOK, AND MAGAZINE RACKS AND STANDS
CHAIRS
—Arm
—Ladies' Desk
—Porch
—Theatre Box
—Chairs with Upholstered Arms and Seats
CHAISE LOUNGES
COUCHES

DAVENETTES
DAVENPORT BED SUITES INCLUDING DAVENPORT AND TWO CHAIRS
DAVENPORT BEDS
DAVENPORTS
DAY BEDS, EQUIPPED WITH BED FIXTURES
DESKS, LADIES', FOR BEDROOMS
FERNERIES
FOOT STOOLS
HOTEL AND CLUB FURNITURE
JARDINIERES, AND
JARDINIERE STANDS

LAMPS
—Bridge
—Desk
—Floor
—Table

LAMP SHADES, PARCHMENT
LAWN FURNITURE
ROCKERS
—Porch
—Sewing
—Upholstered
—With Loose Cushions
SETTEES
SMOKERS' STANDS
SUN ROOM AND SUN PORCH FURNITURE
SWINGS, LAWN, PORCH, ETC.
TABLES
—Breakfast
—Console
—Davenport
—End
—Library and Living Room
—Porch
TABOURETS
TELEPHONE STANDS

GENERAL INFORMATION

Only the best reed is used in our reed line. The fibre cord and steel wire centered stakes for our fibre furniture are made in our own plant to insure a constant quality. Specially constructed looms produce the fibre webbing that goes on our Loom Woven Fibre line. Designs are modish and mechanically correct. Complete catalog on request.

Prices shown are subject to change without notice.

S8788D—*Fibre Rocker. Spring filled cushion over spring seat. Seat 19 inches wide. Back, 25 inches high. Price in Tapestry, $40.80.*

No. 8788G—*Table. Veneered Top. Size of Top, 18 by 34 inches. Height, 30 inches. Price, $24.50.*

No. 8788C—*Fibre Chair. Spring filled cushion over spring seat. Seat, 19 inches wide. Back, 25 inches high. Price in Tapestry, $40.80.*

ALLEN MANUFACTURING COMPANY

Stove Specialists for a Quarter Century

NASHVILLE, TENNESSEE

WAREHOUSE STOCKS CARRIED IN THE FOLLOWING CITIES

BOSTON   DES MOINES   HARRISBURG   SPOKANE   MILWAUKEE   PORTLAND   SEATTLE   NASHVILLE
SYRACUSE   DALLAS   MINNEAPOLIS   ST. JOSEPH   MISSOULA   GRAND RAPIDS   COLUMBUS   SAN FRANCISCO

PRODUCTS

MANUFACTURERS OF

ALLEN'S PARLOR FURNACE—A most efficient above-the-floor warm-air furnace. Made in two sizes—No. 500 and No. 600.

Also a special model for burning gas—No. 800.

THE ORIGINAL PARLOR FURNACE

The name ALLEN has been identified for more than a generation with the best heating equipment. Thousands of Allen Stoves and Parlor Furnaces have been giving satisfaction for many years in every section of the country.

When the requirements of the modern home dictated improved heating systems, Allen developed the now famous Parlor Furnace, which combines the efficiency of a twentieth century heating system and the cheerfulness of the old-fashioned fireplace.

Allen's heats by circulating clean, healthful, moist warm air throughout the house. As the air is heated by Allen's it expands and becomes lighter than the cool air. The light warm air, rising naturally, displaces the cool air which falls by gravity and circulates to the furnace to be reheated and recirculated. Thus a constant circulation of air currents is set in motion. Extra heating capacity is provided by the exclusive Allen heat radiating fin construction. Burns coal or wood.

Allen's is easily installed in a room or hall without expense. Requires minimum floor space. Its classic design appeals to good taste. Due to superior manufacturing methods, the porcelain Allenamel finish used on the entire outer casing is of very fine quality and faithfully reproduces the natural effect of walnut grain and color. It is easily dusted and retains its lustre indefinitely.

Model 800—For gas only.

FASTEST SELLING ABOVE-THE-FLOOR FURNACE ON THE MARKET

Allen's Parlor Furnace with Oldtime Fireside Cheer—our latest achievement—met with instant success. Everywhere Allen Dealers have enjoyed unprecedented sales.

Model 500 or 600—Open view.

Model 500 or 600—Closed view.

The phenomenal yearly sales growth is attributable to the unique design—Allen's patented and exclusive features (Oldtime Fireside Cheer and Heat Radiating Fins)—Allen's consistent national advertising and liberal co-operative dealers' local sales and advertising plan.

OLDTIME FIRESIDE CHEER

When the outer doors swing open Allen's gives all the comfort and cheer of the old-fashioned fireplace. With the doors closed, Allen's resembles a piece of beautiful period furniture. Harmonizes with finest furnishings.

HEAT RADIATING FINS

This exclusive Allen construction doubles the heating surface, strengthens and prolongs the life of the heating unit, adds greatly to heating capacity, saves fuel.

SPECIFICATIONS

Made in two sizes—No. 500 and No. 600. Supplied with either Tri-Bar Revolving Grates or Duplex Rocker Grates.

No. 500—Height, 45″; Width, 28″; Depth, 22″; Weight Crated, 490 lbs—net 425 lbs.

No. 600—Height, 47″; Width, 28″, Depth, 24½″; Weight Crated, 565 lbs—net 490 lbs.

Patent numbers 69,731—1,604,869—16,677. Trademark Number 202,578.

ALLEN'S SALES AND ADVERTISING PLANS

Allen helps you to get your share!

Allen's 1928 Advertising Campaign, including leading national, sectional and state publications, eclipses all previous efforts. This tremendous campaign will carry the Allen messages to more than 50,000,000 readers.

Allen also offers a very liberal co-operative Dealer Sales and Advertising Plan. In addition to supplying various forms of literature and a number of dealer helps of proven worth, either free or at actual cost, we pay one-half the cost of your local newspaper advertising campaign, direct-by-mail campaign and bill board advertising—a vitally important factor in developing local sales. Full details will gladly be sent on application.

CROCKER CHAIR COMPANY

Dining Room and Breakfast Room Furniture; Occasional Tables and Novelties; Odd Chairs, Office Chairs, Rockers and Stools

SHEBOYGAN, WISCONSIN
PERMANENT EXHIBIT
CHICAGO, ILL., Space 1424, American Furniture Mart

Dining Room Table, No. A230. Top, 36 by 48 inches. Extends to 6 feet. Finished in Antique Walnut and Maple.

China Cabinet, No. A236. Base, 16 by 36 inches. Finished in Antique Walnut and Maple.

No. A234—Buffet. Top, 17 by 54 inches. Silver drawer. Finished in Antique Walnut and Maple.

PRODUCTS
MANUFACTURERS OF

BREAKFAST ROOM FURNITURE including Sets and Complete Suites. Also: Buffets; Chairs; Tables; and Extension Tables; Serving Tables and Cabinets combined. Also Chairs and Tables in the white for Decoration or Special Finishes.

DINING ROOM FURNITURE including Dining Suites Complete and Apartment (or Junior Size) Dining Suites. Also: Buffets; Upholstered Chairs; China Cabinets; Servers; and Tables.

A complete line of Chairs including the following types:—

—Arm (Wood or Upholstered Seat)	—Children's	—Living Room, Upholstered
—Bank, Upholstered	—Coxwell	—Office
—Bathroom	—Desk, Home (Wood or Upholstered Seats)	—Office, Upholstered
—Bedroom (Wood or Upholstered Seat)	—Folding	—Slip Seat Leather
—Bentwood	—Hall, Home	—Tablet Arm
—Bow Back	—High	—Typewriter
—Cane Seat	—Kitchen	—Windsor (Wood or Upholstered Seat)
	—Ladder Back	
	—Leather Upholstered	

We also manufacture special-to-order chairs.
Rockers: Auto Spring Seat; Upholstered; Wood.
Stools: Bathroom; Kitchen; Office; Store.

TELEPHONE: CABINETS; SETS; STANDS.

Also manufacturers of: Upholstered Foot Stools; Grip Stands; Settees for Home and Office; Console Mirrors; Wood Costumers; and Hotel, Club, Hospital and Institution Furniture.

Tables for every use including the following types:

—Butterfly	—Davenport	—Enameled or Enameled Tops
—Coffee	—Drop Leaf	
—Console (With and without Mirrors)	—End	
—Hall	—Library	—Pie Crust Top
—Kitchen	—Occasional	—Tilt Top
—Extension	—Gateleg or Gateleg Extension	

WOODS AND FINISHES

The Crocker Line is built of a good grade of Walnut, Mahogany and combinations with selected Birch woods. The quality of Crocker merchandise is further enhanced by attractive suitable finishes that appeal most favorably to the eye.

GENERAL INFORMATION

Crocker Furniture has all the predominant characteristics that enter into the creation of distinctive pieces. The pieces illustrated on this page all carry that "finished" appearance which can only be effected by sound workmanship. The finishes, too, are durable and play a dominant part in the sale of any of these pieces.

You can realize profits and good will through the Crocker Line. Order a few of these pieces today.

Drop Leaf Table, No. 8882. Top closed, 12 by 36 inches; Top, open, 42 by 36 inches. Finished in Walnut. Old Walnut Finish.

No. 8872—Magazine Stand. Height, 25 inches; Width, 9¾ inches; Finished in variety of Decorated Finishes in pleasing tones.

No. 8880—Gateleg Table. Top, closed, 12 by 36 inches. Top, open, 32 by 36 inches. Finished in Walnut, Old Walnut Finish.

Drop Leaf Table, No. 9030. Top, closed, 11 by 48 inches. Top, open, 40 by 48 inches. Finished in Birch. Walnut Decorated No. 4 and Walnut Decorated No. 6.

Pier Cabinet, No. 8866. Height, 70 inches; Width, 17 inches. Finished in Birch, in Decorated Finishes.

Magazine Basket, No. 8861. Height, 21 inches; Width, 15¼ inches. Finished in variety of decorated finishes in pleasing tones.

No. 8869—Underfold Davenport Table. Top, 24 by 48 inches, closed. Open, 39 by 48 inches. Finish: Walnut, Old Walnut Finish.

COLONIAL DESK COMPANY
Makers of Fine Furniture
ROCKFORD, ILL.
EXHIBITS
GRAND RAPIDS, MICH., Second Floor, Klingman Building

PRODUCTS

MANUFACTURERS OF

HIGHBOYS, Colonial

LOWBOYS, Colonial

CHESTS
—Luxor
—Queen Anne

SECRETARIES
—Cabinet
—Swell Front
—Desk
—Colonial
—Straight Front
—Queen Anne
—French Provincial
—Governor Winthrop

DESKS
—Governor Winthrop
—John Hancock
—Straight Front
—Wall
—Ladies'
—Spinet
—Secretary
—Cabinet
—Swell Front

BOOKCASES
—One, Two, and
    Three Door Style
—Open Shelf
CABINETS
—Silver
—Linen
—China
—Corner
—Pier
TABLES
—Console
—Occasional
—Coffee
—Carved
COMMODES, William
    and Mary Mar-
    quetry
CHAIRS
—Odd Desk
—Dining
DINETTE SUITES,
    Complete, includ-
    ing Buffet, China,
    Table and Chairs.
ALSO sold as sepa-
rate pieces.

Trade Mark

No. 29

FINISHES

We finish our goods in the regular Mahogany and Walnut shades, but in response to demands we furnish these finishes in various shades, and in order to convey just about what these different finishes may be, we have listed them below, and opposite have indicated by number which plates they most closely resemble in the Woods and Finishes Section preceding Page 9 of this book. The finishes shown in those pages are not, of course, exactly the shade we use, but they are somewhat similar and for that reason show, in a measure, just what we feature.

Special finishes can be matched.

Colonial Red Mahogany....No. 1
Brown Mahogany..........No. 24
Antique Mahogany........No. 21
Early American Mahogany..No. 3
American Walnut..........No. 14
Regular Maple............No. 8
Amber Maple.............No. 12

No. 25

WOODS

"Colonial" Furniture is built chiefly of Mahogany—the modernistic Furniture primarily of Walnut. The woods used in individual pieces are specified in the brief explanations accompanying illustrations. Many fancy veneers are used in combination with regular Cabinet Woods, as on drawer fronts, overlays, etc. Several pieces may be had in Castano in combination with Birch. A few numbers are made in combination of Mahogany and Gumwood, and Walnut and Gumwood.

GENERAL INFORMATION

All furniture built by us is very sturdily and carefully constructed of the best materials obtainable. All cases are dust-proofed throughout, and all drawers are dove-tailed. All interiors are very well made and all given an unusually thorough and fine finish which gives them a very neat and trim appearance. We feature our interior work.

Quality of workmanship and construction is paramount and we spare no efforts to make our furniture of the best to sustain a reputation well earned by us. We feature only medium and high grade furniture for the living room, dining room, and library—which, coupled with unusual designs and best workmanship possible, enables us to present a large line of merit and distinction for all good dealers.

It is not possible for us to illustrate and describe in these pages each and every piece built by us, but we have shown some numbers of each type to indicate the scope of our manufacture, and we are ready at all times to supplement these descriptions by supplying you with immediate information concerning our line of furniture, should you so desire.

We wish to co-operate as closely as possible with our dealer friends, and ask that you write us for any information desired.

All prices shown in this catalog are subject to change without notice.

HIGH BOYS AND LOW BOYS

High Boys and Low Boys made in Mahogany-Colonial. Retail Price Range, *$90.00 to $194.00.*

No. 25—High Boy—(see illustration). Colonial-Mahogany. Size: Height, 84 inches; Width, 38 inches; Depth, 18 inches. Price, *$194.00.*

No. 26—Colonial Low Boy— (Same as base of High Boy, No. 25 illustrated). Size: Height, 32 inches; Width, 38 inches; Depth, 18 inches. Price, *$90.00.*

CHESTS

Chests, in addition to No. 28 and No. 29 illustrated—available in Mahogany with Crotch Mahogany front. Late Queen Anne style. Size: Height, 52 inches; Width, 38 inches; Depth, 17 inches. Price, *$100.00.*

No. 28—Luxor-Mahogany—(See illustration). Entire front Hollywood Marquetry. Cross banded drawer edges in Mahogany. Size: Height, 48 inches; Width, 35 inches; Depth, 15 inches. Price, *$170.00.*

No. 29—Mary—(1780). Adam School (see illustration). Inlaid Satinwood Commode. Entire front in Marquetry: Kingwood Emboina, Holly, Pearwood, Ebony, Hairwood. Size: Height, 33 inches; Width, 45 inches; Depth, 23 inches. Price, *$250.00.*

No. 103   No. 102   No. 101   No. 107

No. 105   No. 119   No. 117   No. 114

SECRETARIES

Our manufacture includes a large number of Secretaries—available in Mahogany, Walnut, Satinwood and Walnut, Satinwood and Mahogany, Mahogany and Gum, Maple, Castano and Birch, also with Marquetry fronts. Imported fancy veneers are used in combination in practically all numbers. Doors can be had with scrolls or solid panel, and some with mirrors. Most cases have full drawer space, 3, 4 and 5 drawers.

All pigeon holes have satinwood drawer fronts and frieze. All are made very complete and trim, and are given a very thorough and smooth finish. We give interior work particular attention. Sizes range from Height, 67 inches; Width, 32 inches; Depth, 16 inches to Height 87 inches, Width, 41 inches, Depth 21 inches. Retail price range, *$53.00 to $236.00.*

Most Secretary bases can be had separately as desks. See Secretary Desks on next page.

No. 101—*Straight front. In Mahogany and select Gumwood (see illustration). Can also be had decorated. Size: Height, 76 inches; Width, 32 inches; Depth, 15 inches. Price, $63.00.*
No. 101¾—*Desk (base of No. 101 Secretary. Illustrated on next page). In Plain Mahogany and Crotch Mahogany fronts. Price, $45.00 and $57.00.*
No. 102—*Straight front. In Mahogany and select Gumwood (see illustration). Blister Mahogany top. Can also be had decorated. Size: Height, 83 inches; Width, 32 inches; Depth, 17 inches. Price, $79.00.*
.. 102¾—*Desk. May be had separately. Price, $53.00.*
.. 103—*Genuine Governor Winthrop Secretary. In Mahogany (see illustration). Size: Height, 87 inc. s; Width, 41 inches; Depth, 21 inches. Price, $170.00.*
N.. 103½—*Desk. May be had separately. Price, $114.00.*
▶ *Governor Winthrop Secretaries and Desks also in sizes from 38-inch width to 33-inch width. Genuine Mahogany throughout. To combination Mahogany and Gum. With Crotch Mahogany front also. Price Range: Secretaries, $95.00 to $150.00—Desks, $72.00 to $102.00.*
No. 105—*Straight front in Satinwood and Walnut. Open top with silk damask back (see illustration). Height, 80 inches; Width, 30 inches; Depth, 18 inches. Price, $114.00.*
No. 105½—*Desk (base of Secretary). May be had separately. Price, $79.00.*

No. 114—*Genuine Mahogany with Blister Mahogany drawer fronts (see illustration). Size: Height 86 inches; Width, 34 inches; Depth, 19 inches. Price, $138.00.*
No. 114½—*Desk (base of Secretary). Height, 43 inches; Width, 34 inches; Depth, 19 inches. Price $98.00.*
No. 117—*Queen Anne (see illustration). Mahogany-crotch Mahogany front. With Maidou burl. Hand decorated head. Size: Height, 80 inches; Width, 33 inches; Depth, 20 inches. Price, $160.00.*
No. 117½—*Desk (base of Secretary). Size: Height, 43 inches; Width, 33 inches; Depth, 20 inches. Price, $104.00.*
No. 119—*Mahogany (see illustration). Size: Height, 82 inches; Width, 33 inches; Depth, 18 inches. Price, $95.00.*
No. 107—*John Hancock Secretary (see illustration). Mahogany. Top of Blister Mahogany. Pigeon hole front of redwood burl. Automatic Slide. Size: Height, 88 inches; Width, 38 inches; Depth, 21 inches. Price, $235.00.*
No. 107½—*Desk (base of Secretary). Size: Height, 43 inches; Width, 38 inches; Depth, 21 inches. Price, $165 00.*

(Continued on next page)

COLONIAL DESK COMPANY

No. 214

No. 201

SECRETARY DESKS

No. 101¾

Straight Front and Swell Front—In Mahogany, Walnut, Satinwood and Mahogany, Satinwood and Walnut, Mahogany and Gum, Castano and Birch. Some cases have fronts of Crotch Mahogany, others of Mottle Mahogany, and others of Marquetry. Most of them with full drawer space. Interiors very complete and trim and have a thorough and smooth finish. Range in sizes: from Height, 45 inches; Width, 41 inches; Depth, 21 inches; to Width, 32 inches; Depth, 18 inches. Retail price, $45.00–$165.00.

No. 101¾—Desk—(see illustration). Mahogany front, also Crotch Mahogany front. Select Gumwood ends. Interior same as No. 101. Size: Height, 43 inches; Width, 31 inches; Depth, 17 inches. Mahogany front, $45.00—Crotch Mahogany front, $57.00.

No. 116½—Desk—Mahogany, Blister Mahogany base (see illustration). Size: Height, 43 inches; Width, 37 inches; Depth, 20 inches. (Same interior as No. 114 Secretary illustrated on preceding page.) Price, $106.00.

No. 116½

WALL DESKS

Walnut in combination with fancy veneers—as Maple, Maidou Burl, Crotch Walnut and Marquetry Desks. Also in Mahogany (Duncan Phyfe). Have full size from: Height, 45 inches; Width, 29 inches; Depth, 15 inches; to Height, 54 inches; Width, 40 inches; Depth, 16 inches. Retail price, $47.00 to $170.00.

No. 208

No. 214—Desk—(see illustration). Walnut, carved front and mouldings, Marquetry inlay. Fall lid. Size: Height, 49 inches; Width, 40 inches; Depth, 16 inches. Price, $170.00.

No. 201—Desk—Walnut, Walnut overlays (see illustration). Size: Height, 46 inches; Width, 33 inches; Depth, 17 inches. Price, $75.00.

No. 208—Desk—Walnut with Crotch Walnut drawer fronts, top drawers, and fall band of Maidou Burl (see illustration). Size: Height, 54 inches; Width, 37 inches; Depth, 16 inches. Price, $175.00.

SPINET DESKS

Spanish influence. Walnut in combination with Maple Burl fronts. Hand decorations. Full interiors with pull-out writing bed. Partitioned drawers. Price, $50.00 to $97.00.

No. 306   *No. 304*   *No. 308*   *No. 312*

BOOK CASES

In Mahogany and in Walnut, also in Castano and Birch, in combination with fancy veneers. In both open and closed type. Some with drawers or compartments at base. One, two, and three-door style. Retail price, $46.00 to $90.00.

No. 304—Mahogany or Walnut—Double door (see illustration). Size: Height, 48 inches; Width, 45 inches; Depth, 14 inches. Price, $90.00. Also in Single Door style—No. 303—Mahogany or Walnut. Size: Height 48 inches; Width, 28 inches; Depth, 14 inches. Price, $70.00.

No. 306—Mahogany—Double Door (see illustration). Size: Height, 54 inches; Width, 45 inches; Depth, 14 inches. Price, $75.00. Also in Single Door—Mahogany, No. 305—Size: Height, 54 inches; Width, 29 inches; Depth, 14 inches. Price, $55.00.

No. 308—Mahogany or Walnut—Double Door (see illustration). Drawer below. Size: Height, 49 inches; Width, 46 inches; Depth, 13 inches. Price, $73.00. Also in Single Door—Mahogany or Walnut, No. 307—Drawer below. Size: Height, 49 inches; Width, 28 inches; Depth, 13 inches. Price, $53.00.

No. 312—Mahogany or Walnut—Double Door (see illustration). Compartment below, doors decorated, or in Butt Walnut veneer, or Blister Mahogany. Size: Height, 49 inches; Width, 44 inches; Depth, 14 inches. Price, $74.00. Decorated, $82.00. Also in Single Door—Mahogany or Walnut, No. 311—Door decorated or in Walnut or Mahogany veneer. Size: Height, 49 inches; Width, 28 inches; Depth, 14 inches. Price, $54.00. Decorated, $58.00.

No. 51   No. 69   No. 59   No. 63

WALL CABINETS

Cabinets—Wall. (Silver and Linen) in Walnut and in Mahogany. Fancy woods as Redwood Burl, Butt Walnut, Crotch Mahogany, used on fronts. Some with carved fronts. Others have hand decorations. Sizes: Height, 55 inches; Width, 32 inches; Depth, 16 inches; to Height, 65 inches; Width, 40 inches; Depth, 16 inches. Retail prices, *$64.00 to $190.00.*

No. 51—Cabinet—Linen or Silver (see illustration). Walnut, carved front, four doors. Size: Height, 60 inches; Width, 42 inches; Depth, 18 inches. Price, *$150.00.*

No. 69—Wall Cabinet—Mahogany (see illustration). Crotch Mahogany front, Imported Carved Mouldings. Hand decorations on doors. Size: Height, 62 inches; Width, 40 inches; Depth, 18 inches. Price, *$176.00.*

CORNER CABINETS

Corner Cabinets—In Walnut, and in Mahogany in combination with Crotch Mahogany. Solid doors and grill doors. Some with Desk arrangements. Sizes: Height, 72 inches; Width, 34 inches; Depth, 19 inches; to Height, 75 inches; Width, 38 inches; Depth, 20 inches. Retail prices, *$80.00 to $120.00.*

PIER CABINETS

Pier Cabinets—In Maple, Finished Maple, Mahogany, or Walnut. Hand decorations. One with Desk arrangement. Sizes: Height, 64 inches; Width, 18 inches; Depth, 15 inches; to Height, 74 inches; Width, 18 inches; Depth, 16 inches. Retail prices, *$30.00 to $40.00.*

CABINET-DESKS

Cabinet-Desks—Walnut in combination with Curly Maple trimming. Have shelf space above and below. Some have carved fronts, some with full desk arrangement. Also in Mahogany with Satinwood front, with draw desk arrangement. Size, Height, 55 inches; Width, 32 inches; Depth, 16 inches; to Height, 71 inches; Width, 37 inches, Depth, 19 inches. Retail price, *$70.00–$158.00.*

No. 59—Cabinet-Desk—Walnut with Curly Maple veneer trimmings. (See illustration). Two doors above—drop below. Size: Height, 58 inches; Width, 34 inches; Depth, 16 inches. Price, *$154.00.*

Also with four doors as Cabinet No. 66. Same size and same woods. Price, *$146.00.*

No. 63—Cabinet-Desk—(see illustration). In Mahogany-Satinwood front. Hand decorations. Has writing bed which pulls out. Compartments above and below. Size: Height, 71 inches; Width, 37 inches; Depth, 19 inches. Price, *$158.00.*

No. 62 Walnut Cabinet-Desk—Similar to No. 63. Size: Height, 63 inches; Width, 36 inches; Depth, 18 inches. Price, *$70.00.*

RADIO CABINETS

Many of our Desks and Cabinets may be used for Radios—most any set is readily installed.

No. 503¼

No. 501¼

CHINA CABINETS

These Cabinets are from two of our four Dinette Suites. Any piece can be purchased separately. In Mahogany, Walnut, Walnut and Oak. Fancy fronts of Crotch Mahogany, Satinwood, and Redwood Burl, English Oak Swirls. Hand decorations in combination. Sizes: Height, 62 inches; Width, 40 inches; Depth, 18 inches; to Height, 77 inches; Width, 38 inches; Depth, 18 inches. Retail prices, *$124.00 to $194.00.*

No. 501¼—Cabinet—(See illustration). China Cabinet for Duncan Phyfe Dinette Suite. Mahogany in combination with Satinwood and Redwood Burl—Marquetry inlays. Suites may be had complete or pieces individually. Size: Height, 74 inches; Width, 36 inches; Depth, 18 inches. Price, *$154.00.*

No. 503¼—Cabinet—(see illustration). China Cabinet of Dinette Suite. In Walnut with combination of Crotch Mahogany and Redwood Burl. Hand decorations on doors and drawers. Suites may be had complete or separately. Size: Height, 75 inches; Width, 40 inches; Depth, 18 inches. Price, *$194.00.*

DINETTE SUITES

We manufacture several Dinette Suites of high grade—the Cabinets of two are illustrated above. The suites can be had complete or pieces individually. Tables extend to full width, having full apron fillers in addition to drop leaves.

No. 501—Suite—Duncan Phyfe—Genuine Mahogany with Crotch fronts in combination with Satinwood and Redwood Burl —Marquetry inlays. Table has drop leaves. Arm and Side Chair—Full upholstered. Price, *$670.00.*

No. 504—Suite—In Walnut and Oak with select Gumwood. In Walnut with English Oak fronts and ends, Gum legs. Has Refec-

tory Table. Side Chair—Slip seat. Price, 9 pieces, *$460.00.*

No. 503—Suite—Genuine Walnut in combination with Crotch. In Walnut and Mahogany—with Crotch Mahogany fronts. One Suite has arm and side chair full upholstered—others only side with slip seat webbed bottom. Has Refectory Table. Side Chair —Slip seat. Price, 9 pieces, *$574.00.*

No. 505—Suite—Genuine Mahogany. With Crotch Mahogany fronts. Side Chair only—slip seat. Table has drop leaves. Price, 9 pieces, *$542.00.*

COLONIAL MANUFACTURING CO.
World's Largest Makers of Hall Clocks
ZEELAND, MICHIGAN

EXHIBIT
GRAND RAPIDS, MICH., Keeler Building

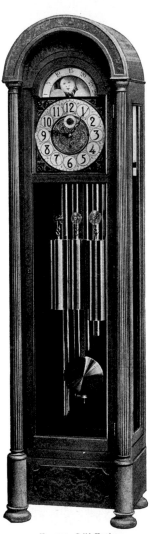

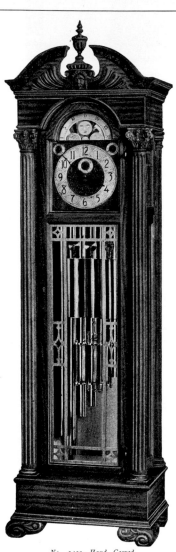

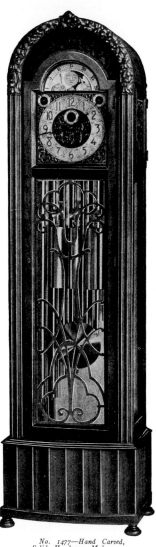

No. 1430—Hand Carved, Solid Honduras Mahogany. Height, 85 inches; Width, 25 inches; Depth, 16 inches.

No. 1347—Solid Honduras Mahogany, overlaid with Redwood Burl. Height, 70 inches; Width, 22 inches; Depth, 16 inches. Beveled Plate Glass.

No. 1477—Hand Carved, Solid Honduras Mahogany. Height, 83 inches; Width, 23 inches; Depth, 17 inches. Inlaid with Maple. Beveled Plate Glass in Sides.

PRODUCTS AND RANGE OF PRICE

A COMPLETE LINE OF HALL CLOCKS, designed in all the historic and modern furniture styles, with cases of Solid Honduras Mahogany, and equipped with the finest imported movements. Selling prices range from $70.00 to $1800.00 to fit the requirements of every home—from the simplest bungalow to the most palatial mansion.

ALSO a distinctive line of secretaries, desks, and other home furnishings, with a price range as broad as the great market for better furniture.

POINTS TO STRESS IN SELLING COLONIAL CLOCKS

Every Colonial Clock has a case of Solid Honduras Mahogany, no matter how low the price.

Every Colonial Clock has an Imported Movement of the finest workmanship.

The line of Colonial Clocks is by far the largest in the world. There is a style and a price for every taste.

In every price division Colonial Clocks are the finest obtainable, easily giving the most value in every respect.

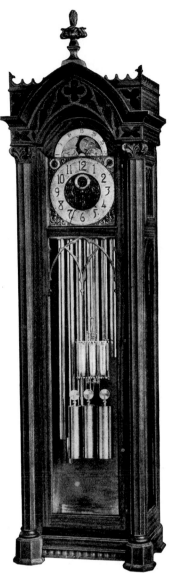

No. 1453—Hand Carved, Solid Honduras Mahogany. Height, 102 inches; Width, 28 inches; Depth, 18 inches.

No. 1216—Solid Honduras Mahogany. Height, 87 inches; Width, 21 inches; Depth, 15 inches. Beveled Plate Glass.

No. 1466—Solid Honduras Mahogany. Height, 79 inches; Width, 21 inches; Depth, 12 inches.

GENERAL INFORMATION

Through a consistent program of national advertising and the constant creation of new patterns to meet modern trends in furniture styles, Colonial leadership in both style and price is stronger today than ever before. There's no better way of keeping pace with an ever broadening market for fine hall clocks, and the profits it assures, than to capitalize on the unprecedented opportunities offered by the present Colonial line.

All Colonial Clocks—no matter what the price—are made of Solid Honduras Mahogany—the supreme wood because of its superiority in ruddy color, marvelous figure, firm texture and warmth of feeling. All cases are Duco finished. Colonial's imported movements are the finest obtainable; record perfect time; and measure their length of service not by years, but by generations.

All Colonial Clocks are assembled in the Colonial Factory at Zeeland—the largest of its kind in the world—by craftsmen who make an art of their tasks, and are satisfied with nothing short of perfection in every detail.

From whatever angle you may judge hall clock value . . . style leadership, precision movement, conscientious workmanship, sales potentialities . . . or dealer profits, the Colonial Line is well in the forefront . . . safely ahead of all competition.

THE HERMAN MILLER CLOCK CO.

Clocks of Character

ZEELAND, MICHIGAN

PERMANENT EXHIBIT
GRAND RAPIDS, MICH., Keeler Building

No. 130—Height, 11½ inches; Width, 22 inches; Depth, 6 inches. Case: Solid Honduras Mahogany. Front: Maple Burl. Movement: Imported 8-day Westminster Rod Chime.

No. 125—Height, 9½ inches; Width, 22 inches; Depth, 6½ inches. Case: Solid Honduras Mahogany. Front: Mahogany. Movement: Imported 8-day Westminster Rod Chime.

No. 136—Height, 12 inches; Width, 11½ inches; Depth, 6½ inches. Case: Solid Honduras Mahogany. Front: Exquisitely hand carved floral design—modern French treatment. Movement: Imported 8-day Westminster Rod Chime.

No. 306—Height, 21 inches; Width, 12 inches; Depth, 7 inches. Case: Solid Honduras Mahogany. Front: Maidou Burl overlay on Mahogany crest; hand painted glass door. Dial: Special, hand decorated. Movement: Imported 8-day, half and hour strike.

No. 502—Height, 41 inches; Width, 12 inches; Depth, 6 inches. Case: Solid Honduras Mahogany, Front: Amboyna Burl; Sheraton marquetry inlays. Carved mouldings cut from Solid Mahogany. Dial: Special; Roman numerals. Movement: Imported 8-day, half hour and hour strike.

PRODUCTS AND PRICE RANGES

A COMPLETE LINE OF CLOCKS, including more than 100 Mantel, 50 Banjo, 50 Electric and a wide variety of small occasional patterns. Priced to sell from $12 to $400.

GENERAL INFORMATION

One of the features that accounts for the unusual salability of Herman Miller Clocks is their originality and freshness of design. Differing widely in individuality, they appeal to all tastes.

Another feature that appeals strongly to dealers who cater to a discriminating public, is the obvious superiority in all details of structural excellence. They have imported movements of marvelous precision. The tick is so silent you can scarcely hear it. They have a reserve power which safely carries over the customary slackening around the eighth day. Where chimes are used, they, too, are imported. So are the jewelry-like dials. The cases are of

Solid Honduras Mahogany, Duco finished, and skillfully adorned with precious woods.

In selling Herman Miller clocks, you can do so with the assurance that they are not only America's most beautiful clocks, but likewise the most reliably accurate. There's a surprisingly large market for clocks of this character.

ATO ELECTRIC CLOCKS

The new line of ATO Electric Clocks is offered in a wide variety of models—over 50 designs to select from—all with the skillful blending of design and precious woods for which Herman Miller has long been famous in the clock industry.

Exhaustive tests have proved the Ato movement using the electro-magnetic principle to be the finest of its kind. Winding and wiring is entirely eliminated. Accurate. Silent. Simple. The foremost line of Electric Clocks in America.

THE HERMAN MILLER FURNITURE CO.

Makers of Fine Furniture

ZEELAND, MICHIGAN

PERMANENT EXHIBIT
GRAND RAPIDS, MICH., Keeler Building

PRODUCTS AND PRICE RANGES

The Herman Miller Furniture Company confines itself exclusively to the production of BEDROOM SUITES in the best traditional and modern designs. Selling prices range from $300.00 to $1600.00.

GENERAL INFORMATION

Advanced quality in every detail of construction accounts in part for the constantly increasing popularity of Herman Miller bedroom suites among dealers who feature furniture above the commonplace. But an even more important factor in explaining this popularity is the rare knowledge displayed of what is most appealing in design . . . a knowledge that manifests itself in each creation.

Every Herman Miller suite is created with the definite purpose of making a distinct and permanent contribution to the art of furniture design. Herman Miller artisans are never led by a servilely imitative spirit in the interpretation of a traditional or of a modern style. There is always a constant endeavor to add individuality and value to each creation. That's why Herman Miller suites are so well abreast of changing tastes.

In the newer Herman Miller creations the refined modernism of the French School is sympathetically interpreted. That Herman Miller has caught and expressed the beauty of the modern style trend in a way most appealing to fastidious buyers is evidenced by the remarkable popularity of the suite illustrated below. Several markets ago it was introduced in anticipation of a growing demand for refined modernism—one of the first Art Moderne bedroom suites. Today it is admittedly a style leader, and the demand for it is constantly increasing.

To invest in Herman Miller suites is not only a matter of keeping your store out in front as a style leader . . . it's likewise a matter of enjoying larger profits than the merely commonplace allows.

The No. 2069 suite here pictured was introduced several markets before furniture began to go modern. Now it can be seen in all the important exhibits—and it still walks away with honors, largely because of its adherence to the refined style of the Modern French School. This suite is certainly a remarkable illustration of the point that each new Herman Miller offering is a departure from the commonplace; a forecast of what will be followed by others a year or so hence.

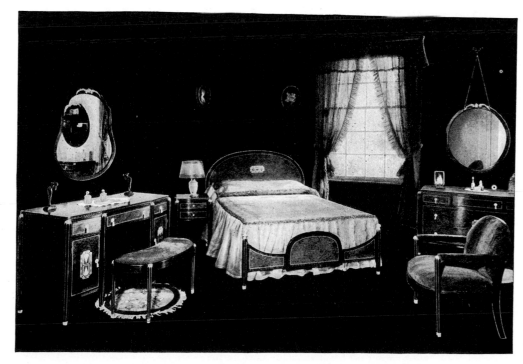

THE ELITE FURNITURE COMPANY
Living Room Tables and Occasional Pieces
JAMESTOWN, N. Y.

EXHIBIT
JAMESTOWN, N. Y., Manufacturers' Bldg.

PRODUCTS
MANUFACTURERS OF

TABLES
—Library
—Davenport
—Desk
—Folding Console
—Coffee
—End
—Drop Leaf
—Extension
—Gateleg
—Nested

TABLES
—Bedroom
—Center
—Tilt Top
—Console
—Occasional including a great many unusual designs

DESKS
—Wall
—Secretary
—Table

CONSOLE MIRRORS
CABINETS
—Sewing
—Pier
STANDS
—Magazine
—Smoking
TELEPHONE SETS
CELLARETTES
TABORETTES
BOOK TROUGHS

WHY THIS FURNITURE IS MADE SO WELL

The Elite organization formed in 1909 by master craftsmen in furniture building is really a furniture guild of the most skilled artisans. The thought uppermost in the minds of each of these workers is not to make more furniture, or more profit, but the sincere desire to make furniture more beautiful, more sturdy, and more worthy of a place in finest American homes.

FOLDING CONSOLE TABLES

The Elite folding console tables, of which the Duncan Phyfe design illustrated on the right is a splendid example, have the mark of quality which distinguishes them in any store. The display ranges from those of heavy colonial style to many graceful slender leg designs.

TILT TOP TABLES

There is quite a large selection of tilt top tables in this line, and this one with its top inset with genuine marquetry is an example of the great beauty to be found in all of them.

Two things are impressed most forcibly upon everyone who examines Elite furniture. Designs are good—so wholly pleasing in every detail that they dominate any display in which they are found. And the construction! Such attention to detail! Such painstaking care that everything be perfection!

ELITE FURNITURE IS FOR YOUR VERY BEST CUSTOMERS

An immense production brings this unusually high quality to a rather low price level. Yet in its charm and in its richness it will be preferred by those of your customers who need not consider price. It is significant that when executives of furniture stores and departments choose furniture for their own homes, they are invariably drawn to the Elite display.

GATELEG TABLES

No. 693 gateleg table which we show above opens to dining table size. Others in the display range down to those smaller gateleg tables which find such ready sale for occasional use in living rooms.

DESKS AND TABLES

Library tables and desk tables in the Elite display offer almost a bewildering array. Tables elaborate enough to take a prominent place in a hotel lobby or simple enough to grace a small apartment room.

GRIFFITH FURNITURE WORKS
Manufacturers of Smokers' Furniture and Auxiliary Furniture
2019 E. Willard Street, MUNCIE, INDIANA

EXHIBITS

CHICAGO, ILL., American Furniture Mart   NEW YORK, N. Y., Furniture Exhibition Building

HIGH POINT, N. C., Furniture Building

No. 282

No. 231

No. 228

DESCRIPTION OF ILLUSTRATED PIECES

No. 282—Smokers' Table—Made from Red Gum. Finished in Tudor Mahogany. Top, 12½ by 23½ inches. Height, 25 inches. Packed in corrugated carton. Weight, one carton, 15 pounds. A serviceable and graceful table with a very convenient smokers' drawer.

No. 252—Smokers' Stand—Height, 27 inches. Top, 12 by 12 inches. Finishes Mahogany and Walnut.

No. 263—Smokers' Stand—With Humidor made of Red Gum and finished in Tudor Mahogany. Top, 11 by 13 inches, height, 26½ inches. Packed in corrugated carton. Weight of one carton, 23 pounds. Practicable for the smoker and attractive for the home.

No. 252

No. 263

No. 228—Book and Magazine Table—Made from Red Gum and finished in Tudor Mahogany. Top, 11½ by 15 inches. Height, 28½ inches. Packed in corrugated carton. Weight, one carton, 20 pounds. A most practicable and popular furnishing.

No. 234—Small Table with Book Trough—Made from Red Gum and finished in Tudor Mahogany and decorated Mahogany. Top, 12½ by 21½ inches. Height, 24½ inches. Packed in corrugated carton. Weight, one carton, 18 pounds. A serviceable product that lends taste to the furnishings of a room.

PRODUCTS

MANUFACTURERS OF

BOOK TROUGHS
WOOD TELEPHONE DESKS
HUMIDORS
SMOKERS' NOVELTIES
BOOK RACKS
MAGAZINE RACKS
SMOKERS' SETS
SEWING CABINETS
SLIDES FOR EXTENSION TABLES

SMOKERS' CABINETS
SMOKERS' STANDS
MAGAZINE STANDS
SEWING STANDS
END TABLES
SMOKERS' TABLES
TELEPHONE SETS
TELEPHONE STOOLS

GENERAL INFORMATION

The wise dealer knows that he gets the benefit of quantity production in his prices when he buys furniture from the manufacturer who concentrates on a line of goods in one field only, and who produces his line in large quantities.

The dealer who is guided by this intelligence in his buying, will investigate the production facilities of the manufacturer, and his reputation in his field.

For six years, The Griffith Furniture Works has concentrated on the production of cleverly designed, firmly constructed and attractively finished useful furniture.

Our plant is equipped throughout with modern machinery and labor-saving devices to enable us to obtain mass production and quality at low costs.

We are constantly on the alert, developing new methods and special equipment to enable us to progress still farther in improving our line and manufacturing it in greater quantities at lower costs. We are therefore able to provide our customers with high quality merchandise at prices not even expected of cheaper grades.

You will be delighted with the individuality of our designs, the quality of our workmanship, the beauty of our finishes, and the amazing attractiveness of our prices. No matter what your requirements may be, we have numbers covering a range of prices, finishes, and designs, that will meet your demands and delight your customers.

We invite your attention to our new line for 1928—send for your catalog and our proposition.

TUDOR MAHOGANY FINISH

The pieces illustrated on this page are all finished in Tudor Mahogany. This finish is very similar to plate No. 21—Old Mahogany, in the Woods and Finishes Section preceding Page 9 of this Reference Book.

HANSON CLOCK COMPANY, INC.

Manufacturers of High Grade Hall Clocks

ROCKFORD, ILL., U. S. A.

PERMANENT EXHIBITS

CHICAGO, ILL., Space 624, American Furniture Mart   NEW YORK, N. Y., Space 403, New York Furn. Exchange

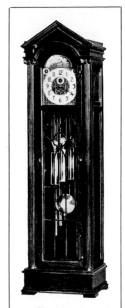

No. 807—Equipped with movement DU. 5 tube Westminster Chime, $500.00; equipped with movement FU. 7 tube Westminster and St. John's Chimes, $540.00. Height, 85 inches; width, 23½ inches; depth, 18 inches. Mahogany.

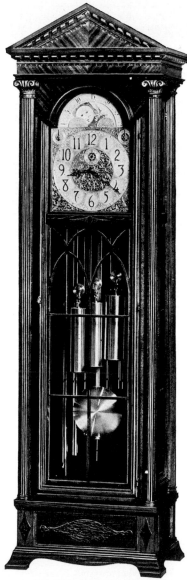

No. 1200—Equipped with movement E. 9 tube Westminster, Whittington and St. John's Chimes, $697.00. Height, 87 inches; width, 24 inches; depth, 16 inches. Mahogany.

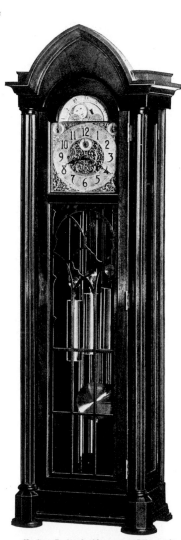

No. 800—Equipped with movement DU. 5 tube Westminster Chime, $450.00; equipped with movement FU. 7 tube Westminster and St. John's Chimes, $490.00. Height, 82 inches; width, 23 inches; depth, 16 inches. Mahogany.

No. 705 — Equipped with movement A Cathedral Gong, $160.00; equipped with movement S Divina Gong, $180.00; equipped with movement C Westminster Chime, $230.00. Height, 87 inches; width, 19 inches; depth, 12 inches. Mahogany.

PRODUCTS

MANUFACTURERS OF HALL CLOCKS

GENERAL INFORMATION

Hanson Hall Clocks are not only beautiful to the eye—they are also as near trouble proof as it is possible for a clock to be. Built by experienced clock makers.

Finest workmanship, attractive styles, rich in tone, the ability to give life-long service—Hanson Clocks are quick to be admired—long to be enjoyed.

It is not only their appeal of rich beauty and timely designs, but also their evident usefulness that gives the Hanson Line its ready sale.

You can safely add your endorsement to them and know your customers' final satisfaction will further increase your prestige.

DESCRIPTION OF MOVEMENTS

Movement A. Hour and half-hour strike Hall Clock movement. It strikes the hour and half-hour on a deep tone Cathedral Gong of exceptionally beautiful tone. Heavy solid brass plates, Graham escapement, eight day, steel-cut pinions, brass chain wind, two brass weights. A special beat adjustment is provided for adjusting the beat without disturbing the position of the clock.

Movement S. Divina Gong is the same general construction as movement A. It strikes the hour and half-hour on five rods—Bim-Bam. The first on two, the second on three rods, very fine tunes, eight day.

Movement C. Westminster Chime three-weight chain movement striking on eight musical tuned rods. Steel-cut pinions, eight day. Automatic correction of the chimes within one hour, preventing same from getting out of adjustment. Graham escapement. This movement chimes on the one-quarter, one-half, three-quarter and four-quarter on four rods, strikes the full hour on one accord on four rods. A chime that is of high quality in tone. Special device is provided for adjusting the beat without disturbing the position of the clock.

Movement CR. Westminster Chime striking on six musical tuned rods, each quarter, also on the hour. Eight-day spring wind. Automatic correction of the chimes within one hour, preventing same from getting out of adjustment. Large barrels fitted with best quality main springs, all three attachable in a new and simple manner, thus, broken springs can be easily replaced without taking the entire movement apart.

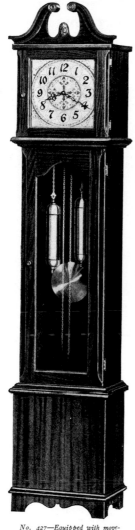
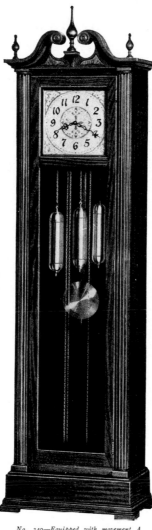
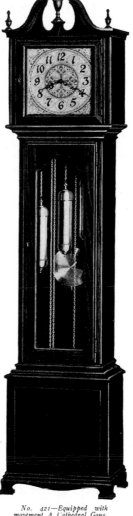
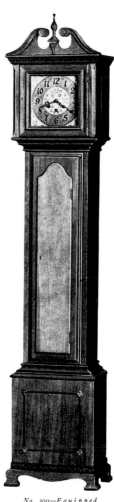

No. 315 — Equipped with movement CR Westminster Chime, $135.00. Height, 67 inches; width, 11 inches; depth, 16 inches. Mahogany.

No. 427—Equipped with movement A Cathedral Gong, $100.00; equipped with movement S Divina Gong, $120.00; equipped with movement C Westminster Chime, $170.00. Height, 80 inches; width, 16 inches; depth, 12 inches. Mahogany.

No. 340—Equipped with movement A Cathedral Gong, $120.00; equipped with movement S Divina Gong, $140.00; equipped with movement C Westminster Chime, $190.00. Height, 83 inches; width, 21 inches; depth, 13 inches. Mahogany.

No. 421—Equipped with movement A Cathedral Gong, $131.00; equipped with Movement S Divina Gong, $151.00; equipped with movement C Westminster Chime, $191.00. Height, 82 inches; width, 17 inches; depth, 11½ inches. Mahogany.

No. 300—Equipped with movement CR Westminster Chime, $150.00. Height, 75 inches; width, 15½ inches; depth, 9½ inches. Mahogany.

Movement D. Westminster Chime, large full-size tubular movement, eight day, three train, extra heavy brass plates, dead beat escapement, maintaining power. All wheels of hard brass, pinions of hardened and tempered steel. Renders the Westminster Chime on the quarter, half, three-quarter and on hour on five tubes.

Movement DX. Westminster Chime, small five-tube movement, arch moon dial, eight day, three train, extra heavy brass plates, dead beat escapement, maintaining power. All wheels of hard brass, pinions of hardened and tempered steel. Renders the Westminster Chime on the quarter, half, three-quarter and on hour on five tubes.

Movement DU. Westminster Chime, large five-tube movement, arch moon dial, eight day. Same general construction as Movement D. It plays the Westminster Chime on five tubes.

Movement FU. Westminster and St. John's Chime, large movement, arch moon dial, eight day. Strikes on seven tubes, each quarter, also on hour. This movement plays either the Westminster Chime or the St. John's Chime, and is equipped with seven tubes. Either one of the chimes may be played at the option of the owner and chime desired is obtained by merely moving an indicator on the dial. Also by moving other indicators the chimes may be entirely silenced or the strike may be silenced, or both if desired.

Movement E. Westminster, Whittington and St. John's Chime, large movement, strikes on nine tubes, each quarter, also on the hour. Any one of the chimes, Westminster, Whittington or St. John's, may be played at the option of the owner. The chime desired is obtained by merely moving an indicator on the dial. Also by moving other indicators the chimes may be entirely silenced or the strike may be silenced, or both. This movement is of particularly high-grade quality in construction and has the same general construction as movements D, DU, and FU.

All our tubular movements are also equipped with the automatic correction of the chimes within one hour, preventing same from getting out of adjustment.

SEND FOR CATALOG

The pieces illustrated on this page represent but a small part of the variety of clocks that can be obtained from us. We invite you to write for our complete catalog and price list.

All prices shown are subject to change without notice.

HASTINGS TABLE CO.

Manufacturers of Living Room Tables and Desks
HASTINGS, MICH.
SALES OFFICE AND DISPLAY ROOMS
GRAND RAPIDS, MICH., Keeler Building

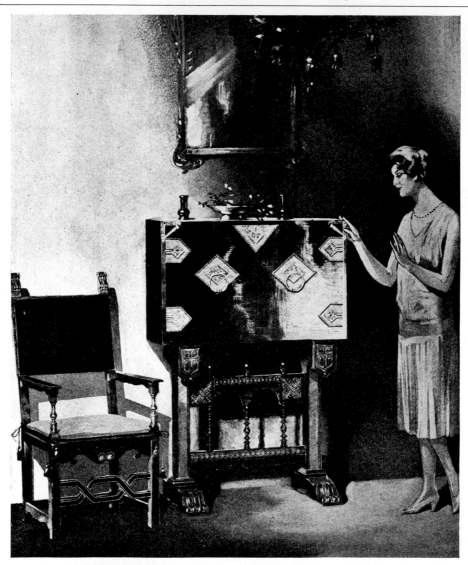

This striking Vargueno desk and chair form a grouping that is particularly attractive for modern apartments and homes where smartness must go hand in hand with compactness.

Hastings pieces lend themselves exceptionally well to this present day living requirement—re-creating the finest beauty of famous periods of the past in a manner that is widely adaptable and in a price range within the reach of all.

A rich treatment of details features this Vargueno desk. The chair has a scarlet mohair back and tasseled cushion.

PRODUCTS
MANUFACTURERS OF

BOOK STANDS
BREAKFAST ROOM SETS
BREAKFAST ROOM SUITES, Complete
BUFFETS, Breakfast
CABINETS
—Console
—Living Room
—Radio, End Table
CHAIRS
—Arm
—Breakfast Room
—Desk, Home
—Dining Room
—Spinet

CHAIRS
—Windsor, Wood Only
CHINA CABINETS
CHINA CLOSETS
CLUB ROOM FURNITURE
DESKS
—Ladies'
—Library
—Library Table
—Secretary
—Spinet
—Telephone
—Wall
DINING ROOM BENCHES
DINING ROOM FURNITURE

DINING ROOM SUITES, Complete
RADIO AND PHONOGRAPH CABINETS, Interchangeable
TABLES
—Breakfast Room
—Breakfast Room, Extension
—Butterfly
—Card
—Centre
—Coffee
—Console
—Davenport
—Desk
—Dining, Combination Living Room
—Dining Room
—Directors'

TABLES
—Drop Leaf
—End
—Extension
—Gate-Leg
—Gate-Leg, Extension
—Library
—Nested
—Occasional
—Refectory
—Smokers'
TEA WAGONS
TELEPHONE
—Cabinets
—Stands
—Stools
—Tables

Stately and magnificent, this fine Elizabethan table in walnut or oak lends an air of dignity to a large room. No. 281.

A writing table and bench of refreshingly different design. The desk has a compartment for stationery and two drawers below. No. 125C.

An Italian cabinet—useful in a score of places in the home. In walnut, with tooled leather panel. No. 508.

Authentic in every detail is this reproduction of a Colonial Card or Console table in fine inlaid crotch mahogany. No. 250.

An exquisitely proportioned Duncan Phyfe design in rosewood and mahogany for the living room. No. 375.

A fine Spanish end table, enriched with rusty wrought iron, handsome antiqued carvings in old gold, and tooled leather top. No. 111.

This butterfly table is an authentic reproduction in walnut of a fine old piece in Granada, Spain. No. 268.

An Italian chair with a back which folds down cleverly to form an attractive magazine or elbow table. No. 125C.

HASTINGS FURNITURE

Trade Mark

GENERAL INFORMATION

Hastings' ability to create the distinctive and unusual in design is clearly shown in the variety of pieces pictured here.

Each creation is original in conception, authentic in detail, and cleverly adapted to the needs of modern homes and apartments.

Construction and finish are most effective in bringing out the beauties of the design, and carry on the fine tradition of worthy craftsmanship which has always characterized Hastings productions.

Write for photographs and prices of other equally as attractive patterns built in the Hastings way. No obligation.

INDIANAPOLIS CHAIR AND FURNITURE CO.

Manufacturers of Chairs and Furniture

AURORA, INDIANA

EXHIBIT

CHICAGO, ILL., Space 1603-4, American Furniture Mart

No. 1825—Bench. All exposed wood parts made of Gum or Hardwood. Web Bottom Seat. Height, 18 inches. Seat, 17 by 41 inches.

No. 1516— Rocker. All exposed wood parts made of Maple. Web Spring Seat. Height of Back, 35 inches. Depth of Seat, 19½ inches. Width of Seat, 21½ inches.

No. 140—Governor Winthrop Secretary. Genuine Mahogany Doors. Heavy Carved Feet. Five-ply figured Mahogany Drop Lid, Drawer Fronts and Sides. Gum Drawer Rails and Feet. Mahogany Drawer Bottoms. Quartered Sycamore Drawer Sides and Backs. Genuine Mahogany Desk Compartments. High grade Locks and Hardware. A high grade Secretary in every respect, especially suitable where a Colonial or Early American decorative scheme is carried out.

No. 1204-F—Windsor Chair—Fibre Seat. Made of Hardwood. Height of Back, 39½ inches. Width of Seat, 19 inches. Depth of Seat, 15 inches.

No. 1202—Windsor Chair. Made of Hardwood. Height of Back, 38½ inches. Width of Seat, 19 inches. Depth of Seat, 15 inches.

PRODUCTS
MANUFACTURERS OF

BREAKFAST SETS, COMPLETE

BEDROOM AND DINING ROOM SUITES COMPLETE, including the following pieces sold separately:

BEDS
—Bow End, Straight End
—Colonial, Four Poster
—Twin
BENCHES
—Bedroom, Upholstered
—Cane Seat
—Desk, Dressing Table
—Toilet Table
—Living Room, Upholstered

BOOKCASES, Combination Desk
—Book Shelves, Stands, Troughs
CABINETS
—Breakfast Room
—Curio, Wall
—Living Room
CHAIRS
—Arm, Upholstered
—Arm, Wood

CHAIRS
—Bedroom, Upholstered; Sets of
—Breakfast Room
—Cane Back; Cane Seat
—Cane Back and Seat
—Cane, Wing
—Coxwell
—Desk, Home
—Dining Room
—Easy, Fireside

CHAIRS
—Hall, Home
—Hotel, Club, etc.
—Living Room, Not Upholstered and Upholstered
—Odd, not Upholstered
—Slip Seat, Leather
—Special-to-Order
—Seats, Upholstered
—Windsor, Fibre Rush Seats; Wood only
CHESTS OF DRAWERS
CHIFFONIERS

CHIFFORETTES
CHIFFOROBES
DESKS
—Bedroom
—Cabinet
—Ladies'
—Library; Secretary
—Spinet
—Telephone, Wood
—Wall
DRESSERS
RACKS, Magazine; Stands
ROCKERS
—Auto Spring Seat
—Bedroom
—Cane Back; Cane Seat
—Cane Back with Loose Cushions
—Cane Seat and Back
—Cane Seat with Loose Cushions
—Windsor
—Wing; Wood Seat
SERVERS
—Breakfast Room
SERVING TABLES
SERVING TABLES and Cabinets Combined for Breakfast Room
SMOKERS' CABINETS, Stands, Novelties

SOMNOES
SUN ROOM AND SUN PORCH FURNITURE
TABLES
—Breakfast Room
—Coffee
—Console
—Davenport
—Davenport, Extension
—Desk
—Dining, Combination Living Room
—Drop Leaf Dressing
—End
—Flip Top
—Library
—Library, Extension
—Night
—Occasional
—Smokers'
—Tea
—Tilt Top
—Tilt Tray
—Wandering

TELEPHONE CABINETS, Stands, Stools, Benches and Tables

VANITIES; Semi-Vanities

No. 1514—Chair. All exposed wood parts made of Gum or Hardwood. Spring Cushion Seat. Height of Back, 40½ inches. Depth of Seat, 24¼ inches. Width of Seat, 29 inches.

No. 1501—Chair. All exposed wood parts made of Walnut. Carved Top and Arms. Spring Seat. Height of Back, 39 inches. Depth of Seat, 21 inches. Width of Seat, 24 inches.

No. 1075—Chair. All exposed wood parts made of Gum or Hardwood. Button Sag Seat. Height of Back, 34½ inches. Depth of Seat, 20¾ inches. Width of Seat, 19½ inches.

No. 1518—Chair. All exposed wood parts Solid Mahogany. Web Spring Seat. Height of Back, 40 inches. Depth of Seat, 21 inches. Width of Seat, 26 inches.

THE LANE COMPANY, INC.
World's Foremost Cedar Chest Makers
ALTAVISTA, VIRGINIA
DISPLAY ROOMS

CHICAGO, ILL., American Furniture Mart   NEW YORK, N. Y., New York Furniture Exchange

SAN FRANCISCO, CALIF., San Francisco Furniture Exchange

Warehouses in Altavista, Virginia and Chicago, Illinois

PRODUCTS
MANUFACTURERS OF

a complete line of cedar chests including all popular designs and sizes both in the full cedar and cedar with exteriors of walnut, mahogany and other woods used in the manufacture of furniture.

Lane Cedar Chests with hardwood exterior veneers matching other fine furniture—follow the same government recommendations in their construction. In this respect Lane "hardwood" chests are unique. No others afford such a combination of beauty and moth damage protection. Every Lane Chest is certified as to its authentic construction and bears a certified label to that effect.

GENERAL INFORMATION

Lane Cedar Chests have the distinction of being built in accordance with the U. S. Government recommendations for moth-killing cedar chests—i.e., with seventy per cent of the chest construction, or back, ends, bottom and front, built of aromatic red cedar heartwood, three-quarters of an inch thick.

Not only do the chests therefore contain a sufficient natural *content* of aromatic cedar oil, the aroma of which is combative to the moth miller and fatal to the undeveloped larvae, but the chests are built with permanent, snug fitting lids, and inseparably interlocked joints, as airtight as chests can be built. Hence the Lane holds in the aroma and protection given is lasting.

No. 48865—48x19x23
Genuine Walnut Veneered top, 5-ply stock. Genuine Walnut Veneer on ¾-inch Cedar panels, front and ends. Solid ¾-inch Cedar back and bottom. American Walnut finish. Rubbed and polished top.

NATIONAL ADVERTISING AND RESALE HELPS

Lane stands foremost among national advertising cedar chest manufacturers, having adopted a steady policy of national advertising which for years has been appearing at regular and dependable intervals in leading national magazines including *The Saturday Evening Post*. Behind the fixed policy of national advertising goes also a campaign of resale helps including local newspaper advertisements, special sale campaigns, window display material, etc. that dealers are finding of great value.

LANE CHESTS NOW BUILT WITH AROMA-TITE TOPS
(Pat. Pending)

These new tops preclude all chance of escape of aroma. Original strength of aroma is hence maintained and greater moth killing efficiency is a result.

No. 44839—44x19x20¾
Extreme height, 26 inches. Genuine Walnut Veneered top. 5-ply stock, with reproduction of 4-piece Butt design. Genuine Walnut Veneer on ¾-inch Cedar panels, front and ends. Solid ¾-inch Cedar back and bottom. American Walnut finish. Rubbed and polished top.

No. 48920—48x20x33
Walnut Veneered top, 5-ply stock. Walnut Veneer on ¾-inch Cedar panels, front and ends. Solid ¾-inch Cedar back and bottom. American Walnut finish.

No. 44867—44x20x27
Genuine Walnut Veneered top, 5-ply stock. Genuine Walnut Veneer on ¾-inch Cedar panels, front and ends. Solid ¾-inch Cedar back and bottom. American Walnut finish. Rubbed and polished top.

No. 48794—48x21x25
Top is of Genuine 4-piece Matched Butt Walnut Veneers, 5-ply stock. Front and ends are Genuine Walnut Veneer on solid ¾-inch Cedar panels. Back and bottom are solid ¾-inch Cedar. American Walnut finish. Rubbed and polished top.

LASSAHN FURNITURE COMPANY
Manufacturers of Novelties of Character
Smokers, End Tables, Secretaries, Telephone Sets, Tea Wagons, etc.

1214-1218 North Wells Street, CHICAGO, ILLINOIS
EXHIBITS
CHICAGO, ILL., Space 525, American Furniture Mart, 666 Lake Shore Drive

PRODUCTS
MANUFACTURERS OF

BOOK TROUGHS
CABINETS
—Telephone
—Wall
DESKS
—Cabinet
—Ladies'
—Library
—Spinet
—Telephone
—Wall
SMOKERS'
—Cabinets
—Stands

HUMIDORS
TABLES
—Coffee
—Console
—Desk
—End
—Gateleg
—Library
—Occasional
—Smokers'
—Tea
TELEPHONE
STANDS
TEA WAGONS

DESCRIPTION OF ILLUSTRATED ITEMS

No. 708A—Smoking Cabinet. Humidor lined with copperized metal. Walnut or Mahogany finish. Size, 24x10 inches; Height, 30 inches. Each, $17.00.

No. 150A—End Table. 5-ply Walnut top. Walnut or Mahogany finish. Top, 13x20 inches; Height, 25 inches. Each, $15.00.

No. 802A—Occasional Table. Solid Walnut, hand carved. Genuine Black and Gold marble tops. Top, 30x20 inches; Height, 29 inches. Each, $121.50.

No. 151A—End Table. 5-ply Walnut top. Walnut or Mahogany finish. Top, 12x24 inches; Height, 24 inches. Each, $9.50.

No. 718A—Smoking Cabinet. Metal lined Humidor. Brown Mahogany or Walnut finish. Red or Green highlighted, $14.00. Colors, each, $15.00.

No. 606A—Telephone Set. 5-ply Walnut door hand carved. Walnut or Mahogany finish. Top open, 17½x18 inches; Closed, 17½x11 inches; Height, 52 inches. Each, $36.00.

No. 716A—Smoking Cabinet. Metal lined Humidor. Brown Mahogany or Walnut finish. Red or Green highlighted. Top, 12½x11¾ inches; Height, 28 inches. Mahogany or Walnut, each, $10.60. Colors, each, $11.60.

No. 705A—Smoking Stand. Top, 24x12 inches; Height, 25 inches. 5-ply Walnut top. Metal lined. Mahogany or Walnut, $16.00. Decorated, $18.50.

No. 700A—Smoking Set. 5-ply top. Size 24x12-Height 24 inches. Metal lined. Mahogany or Walnut, $25.00. Mahogany or Walnut Decorated, $27.50.

No. 802A

No. 150A

No. 606A   *No. 705A*   *No. 151A*

No. 716A   *No. 718A*   *No. 708A*   *No. 709A*

MECHANICS FURNITURE CO.

Manufacturers of Desks, Secretaries, Cabinets,
Highboys and Dining Room Furniture
ROCKFORD, ILL., U. S. A.

No. 21—Secretary. Height, 74 inches; width, 28 inches. Mellowtone finish. List price, $77.00. Legs and ends Red Gum. Wrought iron stretcher. Blistered maple veneer on drop lid. Butt walnut veneer on drawer fronts.

No. 401—High Boy. Open. Salem finish. Height, 74 inches. Width, 30 inches. Legs and top turning solid Mahogany. Crotch Mahogany veneers on entire front. Front and ends 5-ply construction. When closed appearance is as of eight drawers. Contains six drawers and desk feature. List price, $150.00.

No. 56—Secretary. Height, 81 inches; width, 36 inches. Salem finish. Crotch Mahogany veneered fronts of 5-ply construction. Equipped with our Duo strength drop lid support which automatically extends into place with the lowering of the drop lid. Drawers have outward swelled fronts. List price, $141.00.

No. 203—Desk. Height, 48 inches; width, 40 inches. Mellowtone finish. Top, ends and legs quarter sawed Red Gum. Butt Walnut veneer on drawer fronts. KoKo veneer on edges and center of doors. Light fixture includes eight feet of cord, bulb and plug. Ready for use when shipped. Left hand compartment large enough to contain telephone. Three shelves in right hand compartment. List price, $90.00.

No. 306—Silver Cabinet. Height, 80 inches; width, 42 inches. Top drawer slightly open. Mellowtone finish. Legs and stretcher solid Walnut. Ends 5-ply construction. Walnut veneer on door panels. Medallions on door panels genuine imported German Marquetry. Hand carving and crotch Walnut veneer on drawer which also swells outwards. Plumes at top hand-carved. When closed there is nothing to indicate the secret drawers at the top. Two shelves in compartment. List price, $245.00.

No. 55—Desk. Salem finish. Height, 40 inches; width, 36 inches. Crotch Mahogany veneered fronts of 5-ply construction. Equipped with our Duo strength drop lid support which automatically extends into place with the lowering of the drop lid. Drawers have outward swelled fronts. List price, $104.00.

PRODUCTS
Manufacturers of

Corner Closets
Desks
—Combination Bookcase types
—For Ladies
Secretary Desks
Highboys
Silver Cabinets

For information on Dining Room Furniture see page 302.

Trade Mark

RETAIL PRICES

The Retail Selling Prices of the furniture shown on this page are as follows:

No. 21, Secretary, $77.00.

No. 55, Desk. As shown, $104.00—Walnut veneered front, $98.00.

No. 56, Secretary. As shown, $141.00—Walnut veneered front, $135.00.

No. 203, Desk, $90.00.

No. 306, Silver Cabinet, $245.00.

No. 401, Highboy, $150.00.

All prices subject to change without notice.

THE LUCE FURNITURE COMPANY
DIVISION OF THE LUCE FURNITURE SHOPS
Bedroom and Dining Room Furniture
779 Godfrey Ave., GRAND RAPIDS, MICH.

PRODUCTS
MANUFACTURERS OF

DINING ROOM SUITES
—Tables
—Buffets
—China Cabinets
—Serving Tables
—Chairs

BEDROOM SUITES
—Beds

BEDROOM SUITES
—Dressers
—Dressing Tables
—Vanity Dressers
—Chests
—Night Stands
—Chairs
—Benches
—Mirrors

Trade Mark

DESIGNS

While the Luce Furniture Company retains in its line of dining room and bedroom suites, the best of the historical designs, it is devoting its principal efforts in 1928 to the development of "the Modern Art." In doing so, the Luce organization feels that it is keeping in step with the times. That for a long time to come there will be a great and increasing demand for this new type of furniture, so characteristic of the age in which it is being produced. For this reason these four Luce pages in the 1928-1929 Furniture Dealers' Reference Book are devoted entirely to "Art Moderne."

GENERAL INFORMATION

The Luce Furniture Company manufactures dining room and bedroom furniture of high and medium grades. The range of designs is sufficiently wide to provide patterns to please all tastes. All the great periods of furniture history are painstakingly reproduced, or carefully adapted to modern requirements. New creations of Luce designers are constantly being offered the trade. The realm of Art Moderne is represented by a number of graceful dining room and bedroom suites which, while well reflecting this new trend, are carefully designed along lines that will not offend the time honored standards of fine furniture.

WOODS AND FINISHES

All the American and imported woods desirable for furniture manufacturing are used in the construction of Luce suites, each selected according to the character of the suite of which it is to be a part.

No. 2180—China Cabinet. Base, 16x30 inches. Height, 64 inches.

No. 2180—Table. Base, 32x50 inches. Height, 31 inches.

Side Chair No. 2180.

No. 2180—Serving Table. Base, 20x48 inches. Height, 47 inches.

CONSTRUCTION OF LUCE SUITE No. 2180

Exterior—Top of extension table and tops and ends of cases are figured 5-ply East Indian satinwood veneer. Buffet and cabinet drawer of English harewood with oval inlaid panel of satinwood, white holly and Macassar ebony banded with tulipwood. China cabinet door and extension table rim are 5-ply English harewood. Wood back of buffet is solid maple, with center panel of 5-ply English harewood inlaid with marquetry banded with tulipwood. Pilasters of buffet and cabinet are solid maple with hand carved tassels. Legs of buffet, cabinet and table are lami-

nated maple. Chairs solid maple with front rails of 5-ply English harewood.

Interiors—Drawer interiors are quarter sawed solid white oak with bottoms of 3-ply quarter sawed oak veneer. Buffet drawer has lined, removable silver tray. Case work of full, dust proof construction.

Chairs—Upholstered in figured silk damask.

Finish—Lacquer, hand rubbed to a low sheen.

No. 540—Bed. Slat, 4 feet 6 inches. Height, 54 inches. Macassar Ebony.

No. 540—Dresser. Base, 22x50 inches. Mirror, 30x32 inches. Height, 71 inches.

No. 540¾—Dressing Table. Base, 19x48 inches. Mirror, 22x26 inches. Height, 66 inches.

No. 540—Night Stand. Base, 11x16 inches. Height, 28 inches.

No. 540—Side Chair.

No. 540—Bench Chair.

No. 541½—Chest of Drawers. Base, 21x40 inches. Mirror, 12x12 inches. Height, 69 inches.

CONSTRUCTION OF LUCE SUITE No. 540

Exterior—Tops, ends, drawer fronts of cases and bed panels are 5-ply Macassar ebony veneer. Center drawers and decorative portions of bed panels are 5-ply maple veneer, inlaid with marquetry of rare woods in an English Harewood background. Vanity mirror frame and removable chiffonier mirror frame are of 5-ply English Harewood veneer. Posts, stretchers and other exposed solid parts are selected white maple.

Interior—Drawer interiors are of quarter sawed solid white oak. Drawer bottoms quarter sawed 3-ply oak veneer. Dresser drawer equipped with sliding pin tray of quarter sawed oak.

Chairs—Upholstered, the backs in figured green silk and the seats in green mohair.

Finishes—Lacquer, hand rubbed and polished. Mouldings, turnings and edges hand striped in ivory and black.

(Continued on next page)

CONSTRUCTION OF LUCE SUITE No. 2185

Rare Laurel wood and Walnut, with refined ornamental motifs of celluloid distinguish Luce Dining Suite No. 2185. It typifies Art Moderne at its best. The shoes of the legs are of genuine ivory, of special design and craftsmanship. The closed silver cabinet is eminently practical. The tub shaped chairs, with their alluring, restful contour, round out a delightful ensemble. Drawer interiors quarter sawed white oak. Chairs upholstered in mohair. Buffet drawer has lined removable silver tray. Lacquer finish hand rubbed to a smooth dull gloss.

No. 2185—Buffet. Base, 21x72 inches. Height, 36 inches.

No. 2185—Extension Table. Base, 42x60 inches. Height, 31 inches.

No. 2185—Silver Cabinet. Base, 16x35 inches. Height, 61 inches.

No. 2185—Server. Base, 18x38 inches. Height, 34 inches.

No. 2185—Side Cha

No. 2185½—Arm Chair.

CONSTRUCTION OF LUCE
SUITE No. 590

This graceful chamber suite, No. 590 of the Luce line, is the creation of a noted French designer. It embodies the European conception of Art Moderne. Rare Bubinga wood and imported English Harewood are the principal woods. Ornamental features are genuine marquetry central motifs and friezes in the French manner. Unusual mirror shapes distinguish the vanity and dresser. Drawer interiors quarter sawed white oak. Full dust proof construction. Chair and Bench with upholstered slip seats of silk damask. Lacquer finish hand rubbed to a smooth dull gloss.

No. 590—Twin Beds. Width, 3 feet 3 inches. Height, 50 inches.

No. 590—Bench.

No. 590—Night Table. Base, 14x15 inches. Height, 29 inches.

No. 590½—Chest. Base, 21x36 inches. Height, 52 inches.

No. 590—Chair.

No. 590—Dresser. Base, 21x48 inches. Height, 69 inches.

No. 590¼—Vanity Dresser. Base, 17x53 inches. Height, 65 inches.

THE FURNITURE SHOPS
DIVISION OF THE LUCE FURNITURE SHOPS
Everything for the Living Room, Library and Hall
840 Monroe Ave., GRAND RAPIDS, MICH.

PRODUCTS
MANUFACTURERS OF

BOOK CASES
BREAKFAST ROOM
  SUITES
CABINETS
CELLARETTES
CHESTS
CONSOLES AND MIR-
  RORS
DESKS
HUMIDORS
MAKE-UP CASES

TABLES
—Coffee
—Desk
—End
—Gateleg
—Nested
—Occasional
—Tea
SECRETARIES
STANDS
—Magazine
—Telephone

No. 2449—Sheraton Secretary.

GENERAL INFORMATION

The pieces illustrated are but a small part of a complete line of furniture for the living room, library and hall, manufactured by The Furniture Shops. A dealer's requirements are amply covered by a range from the most merchantable end tables for special sales, to the more pretentious reproductions, and our own designers' interpretations of the Art Moderne. These pieces are all well constructed, in accordance with The Furniture Shops' established policy, yet you will find them invariably moderate in price. Catalogs semi-annually.

No. 2305—Duncan Phyfe Swing Top Table.

No. 2137—Sheraton Book Rack.

No. 2407—Duncan Phyfe Lamp Table.

No. 1828—Canterbury Magazine Rack.

No. 2006—Sheraton Console Cabinet.

No. 1972—Duncan Phyfe Drum Table—four-piece top.

No. 1993—Duncan Phyfe Pembroke Table. Exact reproduction of one in Metropolitan Museum of Art.

No. 2402—Duncan Phyfe Coffee Table.

No. 2400—Queen Anne
Coffee Table.

No. 1784—Jacobean Desk Table.

No. 2422—Italian Seven-
teenth Century Coffee Table.

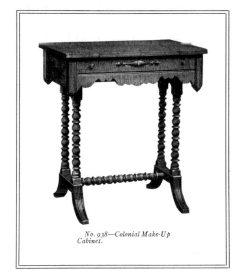

No. 2049—Jacobean Nest
Table.

No. 938—Colonial Make-Up
Cabinet.

No. 1760—Early American
Butterfly Table.

No. 2670—Colonial Scalloped Edge
Gateleg Table.

No. 2515—Sheraton End
Table.

No. 2216—Queen Anne Console Table.

MICHIGAN CHAIR COMPANY
DIVISION OF THE LUCE FURNITURE SHOPS
Manufacturers of Chairs and Upholstered Furniture
803 Godfrey Ave., GRAND RAPIDS, MICH.

PRODUCTS
MANUFACTURERS OF

APARTMENT DINING SUITES
BEDROOM CHAIRS, ROCKERS AND BENCHES.
LIVING ROOM BENCHES
BREAKFAST SUITES
BOUDOIR CHAIRS
CHAISE LOUNGES
CONSOLE TABLES AND MIRRORS
COXWELL CHAIRS
DINING CHAIRS
EARLY AMERICAN MAPLE CHAIRS
HIGH CHAIRS

HIGH BACK CARVED CHAIRS
HIGH BACK UPHOLSTERED CHAIRS
LIVING ROOM CHAIRS
LIVING ROOM SUITES
LOUNGING CHAIRS
LOVE SEATS
OTTOMANS
PIER CABINETS
PIANO BENCHES
RUSH SEAT CHAIRS
SUN ROOM SUITES
TABLES
—Coffee
—End
—Occasional
—Tilt Top
WALL RACKS
WINDSOR CHAIRS AND ROCKERS

GENERAL INFORMATION

The Michigan Chair Company Division of Luce Furniture Shops manufactures a very large and varied line of high grade upholstered furniture for the Living Room and Library, chairs for the Dining Room and Bed Room, upholstered piano benches for the music room, consoles with mirrors, Ottomans and other distinctive furniture. Soundness in construction and grace and beauty in design have been the fundamental policies of the company since its establishment in 1883. Many patterns are hand carved, Upholsteries and coverings are painstakingly selected with a view to giving the final purchaser a wide selection of color to match the individual home decorative scheme. Permanent exhibit, fourth floor Luce Furniture Shops Exhibition Galleries, in Godfrey Ave., Grand Rapids, Mich.

WOODS AND FINISHES

Mahogany pieces are finished in Verona; Maple pieces in Amber; Oak pieces in Italian Oak; Walnut, no prescribed finish.

No. D-770¼—Italian Oak, High Back Carved Arm Chair Charles II period.

No. K-128—Italian Oak Console Table with mirror, Charles II period.

No. D-770—Italian Oak High Back Carved Side Chair, Charles II period.

No. A-157¼—Verona Mahogany Queen Anne Chair.

No. A-67—Walnut William and Mary Bench.

No. A-260¼—Verona Mahogany Tub Chair.

No. L-127—Verona Mahogany Sheraton Settee.

No. A-228¼—Verona Mahogany Georgian Arm Chair.

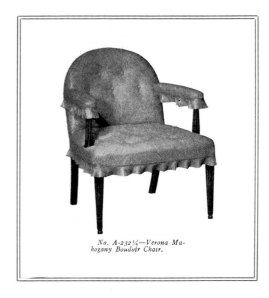

No. A-232¼—Verona Mahogany Boudoir Chair.

No. A-250¼—Verona Mahogany Heppelwhite Arm Chair.

No. A-223¼—Verona Mahogany Queen Anne Tufted Easy Chair.

No. S 455—Verona Mahogany Settee

PETERSON ART FURNITURE CO.

Manufacturers of Living Room, Library and Den Furniture

708 W. 5th St., FARIBAULT, MINN.

EXHIBITS
CHICAGO, ILL., Space 1003, American Furniture Mart

Bookcase No. B-3179. Height, 54 inches and width, 42 inches. Finished in high-lighted Old Mahogany. Priced at $58.00.

Suite No. 150 has gained the stamp of approval from retailers in various parts of the country. Built from Sycamore and Mahogany and finished in Mahogany, resembling Old Mahogany (Plate No. 21, Woods and Finishes Section), shaded into Light Mahogany (Plate No. 24, Woods and Finishes Section), its value is further enhanced by the reasonable price of $230.00 for eight pieces. Silver Chest, $66.00.

PRODUCTS

MANUFACTURERS OF

BENCHES
—Desk
—Piano and Organ
BOOKCASES
—Combination Desk
—Library, Glass Doors
—Open Shelves
BOOK ENDS
CABINETS
—Bathroom and Medicine
—Console
—Music Roll and Player Piano
—Radio
—Sheet Music
—Smokers'
CHAIRS
—Desk, Home
COSTUMERS
—Wood

DESKS
—Bedroom, Ladies'
—Library
—Telephone
—Wall
MAGAZINE RACKS
MIRRORS, CONSOLE
PEDESTALS
PHONOGRAPHS
—Console
—Upright
SEATS
—Hall and Home
TABLES
—Breakfast Room
—End
—Library
—Night
—Occasional
—Tilt Top
TELEPHONE SETS

Smoking Cabinet No. S-75. Measures 14 x 14 inches and is 29 inches high. Finished in high-lighted Old Mahogany. Priced at $24.00.

Desk No. D-379. Measurements: 14 x 48 x 48 inches. Finished in high-lighted Old Mahogany. Priced at $64.00.

TRADE NAME

"The Daisy Line" covers all of the products manufactured by this company.

GENERAL INFORMATION

The Peterson Art Furniture Company, established in 1865, is one of the oldest manufacturers of auxiliary (so-called novelty) furniture in the United States, with six plants—four in Faribault and two in Waterville, Minnesota. Our policy is to manufacture auxiliary furniture of moderate price which will nevertheless harmonize with the most expensive furniture as well as low priced furniture. In carrying out this policy we select for our designs those forms which have proven most suitable for the decoration of American homes, such as the Early American and Early English motifs.

Prices shown are subject to change without notice.

BOOKCASES AND DESKS

We specialize in home desks of every kind, bookcases both open shelf and glass doors, and combination bookcases and desks. Many patterns of desks are made to match our bookcase designs.

WOODS AND FINISHES

Peterson Art Furniture is built chiefly of Walnut and Mahogany with some combinations of selected gumwoods of good grade. Finishes resemble plates No. 21, and No. 24, as shown in the Woods and Finishes Section preceding page 9 of this Reference Book.

ROCKFORD CEDAR FURNITURE CO.
Manufacturers of Cedar and Period Chests
ROCKFORD, ILL.

No. 504—Length, 46 inches; Height. 28 inches; Width, 21 inches.

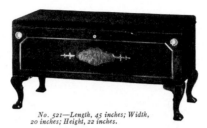

No. 521—Length, 45 inches; Width, 20 inches; Height, 22 inches.

No. 501—Length, 48 inches; Width, 21 inches; Height, 29½ inches.

No. 502—Length, 48 inches; Width, 20 inches; Height, 30 inches.

No. 510—Length, 44 inches; Width, 19 inches; Height, 21½ inches.

No. 506—Length, 46 inches; Width, 21 inches; Height, 28 inches.

No. 503—Length, 48 inches; Width, 20 inches; Height, 30 inches.

No. 523—Length, 47 inches; Width, 20 inches; Height, 26 inches.

No. 505—Length, 48 inches; Width, 21 inches; Height, 30 inches.

No. 525—Length, 46 inches; Width, 20 inches; Height, 20 inches.

No. 508—Length, 45 inches; Width, 20 inches; Height, 23½ inches.

No. 527—Length, 42 inches; Width, 18 inches; Height, 19 inches.

PRODUCTS
MANUFACTURERS OF
All Styles of Period Cedar Chests including such patterns as:
WINDOW SEAT   CONSOLE

CONSTRUCTION
Above chests except Nos. 525 and 527 have 5-ply Walnut tops, fronts and ends. Gum posts. Cedar lined interiors of selected stocks. Interlocking corners. Our chests are carefully finished in a mellow, soft Brown color which we call our Van Dyke Finish. Order a few of these chests today.

ROCKFORD EAGLE FURNITURE CO.

Manufacturers of Cedar Chests

ROCKFORD, ILL.

EXHIBIT
CHICAGO, ILL., Space 201, American Furniture Mart

*No. 16648—Length, 48 inches; Width, 21 inches;
Height, 32 inches.*

*No. 18646—Length, 46 inches; Width, 21 inches;
Height, 31 inches.*

*No. 18448—Length, 48 inches; Width, 21 inches;
Height, 31 inches.*

PRODUCTS

MANUFACTURERS OF

SOLID RED CEDAR CHESTS, including all Period Designs in Walnut
  or Mahogany and the following styles:

CONSOLE

WINDOW SEATS

GENERAL INFORMATION

There is a finished craftsmanship apparent in all Rockford
Eagle Designs—this is the result of expert concentration on a line
of Cedar Chests that would vie for a place in the home furnishing
scheme. Each design is pleasing in tone and finish as is apparent
by the illustrations on this page. A hasty glance will show you
inspirations from the Queen Anne, Spanish, Italian Renaissance
and Jacobean Periods.

Rockford Eagle invites you to inspect their merchandise at the
factory or showrooms. Examine the woods, the construction, and
durable finishes—you will need no further arguments to show you
why these cedar chests sell—and sell profitably.

The pieces illustrated represent but a small part of the many
patterns and designs that are available. We invite you to write
for additional illustrations and price list.

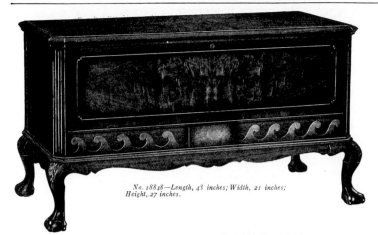

No. 18848—Length, 48 inches; Width, 21 inches; Height, 27 inches.

MADE IN
ROCKFORD
ILLINOIS
ROCKFORD EAGLE FURN. CO. INC.

Trade Mark

No. 1954-3—Length, 45 inches; Width, 20 inches; Height, 28 inches.

No. 17046—Length, 46 inches; Width, 21 inches; Height, 22 inches.

No. 19048—Length, 48 inches; Width, 21 inches; Height, 27 inches.

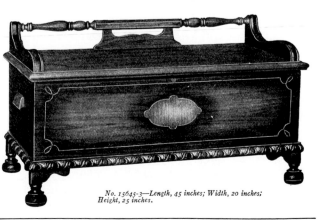

No. 15645-3—Length, 45 inches; Width, 20 inches; Height, 25 inches.

ROCKFORD PEERLESS FURNITURE CO.

Manufacturers of Lamps, Shades, Cabinets, Chests of Drawers, Desks, Secretaries, Tables, and Dinette Suites

11th St. and 20th Ave., ROCKFORD, ILL.

PRODUCTS
MANUFACTURERS OF

CABINETS
—Silver, 18th Century English
—Italian Renaissance
—Spanish
—Louis XVI
—Radio
—Utility
—Pier

DUTCH CABINETS
—English—Louis XIV
—Sheraton
—Jacobean
—Gothic
—Hall type
—Elizabethan

DESKS
—Utility
—Louis XVI
—Adam Combination
—Gothic
—English
—Writing
—Spanish
—Ladies', Writing

SECRETARY DESKS
—Sheraton

CORNER CABINETS
CHAIRS
—Louis XVI
—Adam
—Gothic
—English
—Spanish

CHESTS OF DRAWERS
BENCHES
DINETTE SUITES
—Buffets
—China Cabinets
—Tables
—Chairs

TELEPHONE SETS
—Louis XVI
—Gothic
—Hand Decorated

CONSOLE TABLES AND MIRRORS to match
TABLES
—Italian Renaissance
—Jacobean End

TABLES
—French End
—Louis XIV Coffee
—Octagon Center
—Occasional (Wood or Marble Tops)
—End
—Gateleg
—Gateleg Extension
—Davenport
—Spanish Coffee (Wood or Marble Tops)

BRIDGE LAMPS
—Junior (Small Size) Floor Lamps
—Table Lamps
—Boudoir Lamps
—Silk Shades
—Parchment Shades

Trade Mark

THE LINE OF A HUNDRED MASTERPIECES

Popular demand and the large number of requests which we have received from our clientele has urged us to present these illustrations of our latest designs. We wish to express our appreciation of your patronage and assure you that it is ever our earnest desire to co-operate with you and render real service.

Therefore, it is with a feeling of pride that we present a selection from our "line of a hundred masterpieces." Pride that comes with the making of a thoroughly good product, built by a company with years of experience and by craftsmen who are peerless in the industry.

Coupled with craftsmanship we have installed in our plant the most modern machinery in order to fulfill the very important item of dependable, quick and efficient service which can always be relied upon by the dealers handling our product. We sincerely invite your further inquiries.

All prices shown are subject to change without notice.

No. 122—Bell Shape. Height, 13 inches. Taffeta silk, silk lined, trimmed with fancy braid and hand made flowers. Wired complete. Retail price, $11.00.

No. 27—Basket. Height, 13 inches. Taffeta silk silk lined, fancy braid, hand made flowers. Wired complete. Retail price, $13.00.

No. 177—Height, 17 inches. Fancy dome shade. Taffeta silk, silk lined, trimmed with fancy braid and hand made flowers. Wired complete. Retail price, $12.00.

No. 429/12—Polychrome Iron Lamp with No. 12 Shade. Height, 14 inches. Taffeta silk and silk lined. Wired complete. Retail price, $8.50.

No. 123—Two-Light Lamp. Height, 12 inches. Taffeta silk, silk lined, trimmed with fancy braid. Wired complete. Retail price, $17.00.

LAMPS AND SHADES

Our modern lamp department is equipped to turn out a very fine line of lamps and shades, where skilled labor and the best of materials are used to make a first class article. We specialize in lamps of walnut or mahogany and shades of silk or parchment carrying a wide variety of designs and colors.

We illustrate above a few of our popular novelties for the boudoir to show the general design of our line. Illustrations of bridge, junior, table, boudoir, torchiere and bed lamps will be sent upon application.

Lamp stands are finished plain or polychromed and are wired complete with cord, plug and sockets. Shades can be furnished in any color combination desired. Parchment shades are furnished in a variety of designs and colors suitable for any room.

Write us for further illustrations.

No. 18—Height, 16 inches. Stretched silk shade, silk lined, wires trimmed with fancy braid. Wired complete. Retail price, $9.00.

No. 19—Height, 17 inches. Stretched silk shade, silk lined. Wires trimmed with fancy braid. Wired complete. Retail price, $10.00.

CABINETS
Descriptions and Prices of Numbers Not Shown

Ten of our cabinets are illustrated described, and priced on the opposite page. Descriptions and prices of other numbers in our cabinet line are as follows:

No. 1277—Cabinet. Height, 76 inches; Width, 41 inches; Depth, 20½ inches. Italian Renaissance of all Walnut with Maple overlays and drawer fronts, decorated Butt Walnut in center of doors. Two shelves. Retail price, $255.50.

No. 1231—Hutch Cabinet. Height, 58 inches; Width, 37 inches; Depth, 18 inches. All Walnut, hand carved, hand painted marine scene in door panels. Two shelves. Retail price, $196.00.

No. 1261—Elizabethan Cabinet. Height, 56½ inches; Width, 34 inches; Depth, 17 inches. All Walnut with Butt Walnut Veneer on doors, Maple overlay, hand decorated floral design. Two shelves. Retail price, $105.50.

No. 1256—Spanish Cabinet. Height, 70 inches; Width, 41 inches; Depth, 18 inches. All Walnut, hand carved, blistered Maple overlays, door panel finished in blue, green or champagne lacquer with floral decoration. Two shelves. Retail price, $228.00.

No. 1275—Louis XVI Cabinet. Height, 57½ inches; Width, 36 inches; Depth, 18 inches. All Walnut and satinwood combination, hand decorated with floral design. Two shelves. Retail price, $180.00.

No. 1403—Corner Cabinet. 74 inches high, 25 inches wide, 14 inches deep. Mahogany finish similar to plate No. 1 Woods and Finishes Section preceding page 9. Hand decorated. Also furnished in colored lacquer, decorated. Three shelves. Retail price in Mahogany, $70.00; in colors, $80.00.

No. 1230—English Hutch Cabinet. 61 inches high, 44 inches wide, 20 inches deep. Carved base finished in Antique Gold or Walnut Polychrome. Top lacquered in green or burnt orange crackled. Hand decorations. Two shelves. Retail price, $395.50.

No. 1269—Eighteenth Century English Silver Cabinet. 76 inches high, 45½ inches wide, 19 inches deep. Walnut, Satinwood, and Rosewood combination. Hand decorated panels. Hand carved. Two shelves. Retail price, $550.00.

No. 1404—Corner Cabinet. 74 inches high, 25 inches wide, 14 inches deep. Mahogany finish similar to plate No. 1 Woods and Finishes Section preceding page 9. Hand decorated. Also furnished in colored lacquer, decorated. Three shelves. Retail price in Mahogany, $80.00; in colors, $90.00.

No. 1268—Spanish Cabinet. 60 inches high, 38 inches wide, 18 inches deep. All Walnut, hand carved, Redwood burl borders with Spanish red decorated embossed panels. Two shelves. Retail price, $300.00.

No. 1284—Utility Cabinet. 78 inches high, 34 inches wide, 18 inches deep. All Walnut and Walnut Veneered. Finish similar to plate No. 14 Woods and Finishes Section preceding page 9. Butt Walnut Veneered panel in door. Also furnished with glass and grill in door. Two shelves. Retail price, $124.00.

No. 1265—Pier Cabinet. 69 inches high, 18 inches wide, 11 inches deep. Walnut and Maple combination, decorated doors. Three shelves. Retail price, $56.00.

No. 1282—Sheraton Hutch Cabinet. 61 inches high, 38 inches wide, 10 inches deep. All Mahogany. Finish similar to plate No. 1 Woods and Finishes Section preceding page 9. Crotch Mahogany Veneered fronts. Two shelves. Retail price, $96.00.

No. 1201—Hall Hutch Cabinet. 52 inches high, 36 inches wide, 17 inches deep. All Walnut carved with polychrome finish. One shelf. Retail price, $119.50.

CABINETS (Continued)

No. 1274—Louis XVI Cabinet. Height, 57 inches; Width, 37 inches; Depth, 18 inches. All Walnut and Satinwood combination with marqueterie trim, hand decorated floral design. Two shelves. Retail price, $240.00.

No. 1227—Hutch Cabinet. Height, 60 inches; Width, 36 inches; Depth, 17 inches. Combination Walnut and Mahogany finished, hand decorated. Also furnished in red, green or black decorated lacquer. Two shelves. Retail price, $150.00.

No. 1281—Gothic Hutch Cabinet. Height, 59 inches; Width, 39 inches; Depth, 18 inches. All Walnut and Walnut Veneered, hand carved. Two shelves. Retail price, $215.00.

No. 1221—Hutch Cabinet. Height, 56 inches; Width, 28 inches; Depth, 18 inches. All Walnut, hand carved, furnished in polychrome finish or plain. One shelf. Retail price, $164.00.

No. 1254—Radio Cabinet. Size as No. 1221. Furnished with or without radio chassis, grilled panel with loudspeaker and doors in back. Cabinet can be furnished equipped with panels and doors in back only for installation of instrument. Equipped for Radio including machine, loudspeaker, but no tubes or batteries, $360.00.

No. 1258—Louis XIV Silver Cabinet. Height, 66½ inches; Width, 35½ inches; Depth, 18 inches. All Walnut and Maple combination, hand carved, hand decorated floral design. Two shelves. Retail price, $249.00.

(Continued on next page)

No. 1253—Radio Cabinet. 54 inches high, 28 inches wide, 18 inches deep. All Walnut. Hand carved. Polychromed finish. Also furnished plain. Retail price equipped for radio with machine, loudspeaker, but no tubes nor batteries, $330.00.

CHESTS OF DRAWERS

No. 1229—Chest of Drawers. 41 inches high, 18 inches wide, 12½ inches deep. Mahogany. Finish similar to plate No. 1 Woods and Finishes Section preceding page 9. Hand decorated. Also furnished in red, green, or black lacquer, plain or crackled, hand decorated. Retail price in Mahogany, $70.00; in colors, $75.00.

No. 1235—Chest of Drawers. 32 inches high, 42 inches wide, 20 inches deep. All Walnut and Veneered. Hand decorated. Inside furnished with three cedar lined drawers. Retail price $146.00.

No. 1271—Adam Combination Desk and Chair. Desk—45½ inches high, 48 inches wide, 18 inches deep. Mahogany, Satinwood, and Rosewood combination. Hand decorated floral designs. Marqueterie trim. Retail price, $170.00. Chair furnished with upholstered tapestry seat. Retail price, $24.00.

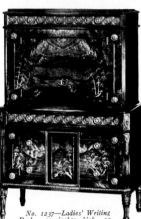

No. 1211—Writing Desk. 46½ inches high, 32 inches wide; 14½ inches deep. All Walnut or Mahogany. Finishes similar to plates Nos. 1 or 14 Woods and Finishes Section preceding page 9. Retail price of desk with light, $62.00. Without light, $54.00.

No. 1237—Ladies' Writing Desk. 53 inches high, 35 inches wide, 18 inches deep. All Walnut and Veneered. Hand decorated. Retail price $230.00.

No. 1248—Secretary Desk. 79 inches high, 30 inches wide, 17 inches deep. All Walnut. Finish similar to plate No. 14 Woods and Finishes Section preceding page 9. Hand carved. Decorated top. Two shelves. Retail price, $136.00

No. 1278—Sheraton Secretary Desk. 82 inches high, 31 inches wide, 16 inches deep. All Mahogany with combination of imported marquetries inlaid on panels. Two shelves. Retail price, $250.00.

SECRETARIES
Descriptions and Prices

No. 1278—(See illustration above).

No. 1248—(See illustration above).

No. 1267—Secretary Desk. Height, 81½ inches; Width, 32 inches; Depth, 17 inches. All Walnut and Maple combination, hand decorated. Two shelves. Retail price, $157.00.

No. 1223—Secretary Desk. Height, 81 inches; Width, 32 inches; Depth, 19 inches. All Walnut and Maple combination. Two shelves. Retail price, $148.00.

No. 1224—Secretary Desk. Height, 86 inches; Width, 36 inches; Depth, 20 inches. All Walnut Maple trim, furnished with light. Two shelves. Retail price, $196.00.

No. 1263—Secretary Desk. Height, 82 inches; Width, 33 inches; Depth, 18 inches. All Walnut with Maple fronts, hand decorated. Two shelves. Retail price, $140.00.

No 1276—Secretary Desk. Height, 77 inches; Width, 32 inches; Depth, 15 inches. All Mahogany with Crotch Mahogany Veneered fronts. Also furnished in all Walnut with Butt Walnut Veneered. Retail price, Striped or Plain Mahogany, $75.50; Mottled or Figured Mahogany, $84.00; Crotch Mahogany, $98.00; Butt Walnut, $98.00.

No. 1206—Secretary Desk. Height, 72 inches; Width, 27 inches; Depth, 17 inches. All Walnut and Walnut Veneered. Two shelves. Retail price, $148.00.

DESKS AND CHAIRS
Descriptions and Prices

No. 1271—Desk and Chair (see illustration).

No. 1211—Desk (see illustration).

No. 1237—Desk (see illustration).

No. 1247—Desk (see illustration).

No. 1272—Louis XVI Desk and Chair. Desk—Height, 35 inches; Width, 37 inches; Depth, 17 inches. Walnut, Satinwood and Rosewood, combination furnished with brass rail only. Chair furnished with upholstered tapestry seat. Retail price of desk, $150.00. Retail price of Chair, $27.00.

No. 1279—English Desk. Height, 30½ inches; Width, 46 inches; Depth, 21 inches. All Mahogany with fancy burl drawer fronts. Retail price of desk, $104.00.

No. 1279—Chair to match. Mahogany furnished with slip seat No. 145 tapestry shown. Retail price of chair, $18.00.

No. 1280—Gothic Desk. Height, 30½ inches; Width, 47½ inches; Depth, 21 inches. All Walnut, hand carved. Retail price of desk, $134.00.

No. 1280—Chair to match. Upholstered seat and back. Retail price of chair, $37.00.

No. 1202—Writing Desk. Height, 43 inches; Width, 32 inches; Depth, 17½ inches. All Walnut, hand carved base, two-tone Walnut top. Retail price, $90.00.

No. 1214—Writing Desk. Height, 49 inches; Width, 36 inches; Depth, 18 inches. All Walnut or Mahogany with blistered Maple fronts. Retail price, $124.00.

No. 41—Chair. All Walnut, carved. Retail Price, $32.50.

No. 42—Chair. All Walnut furnished with slip seat. Retail price, $24.00.

No. 1264—Spanish Desk. Height, 44 inches; Width, 32 inches; Depth, 17 inches. Walnut and Maple combination, decorated. Retail price, $85.00.

No. 1266—Chair. Walnut and Maple polychromed. Slip seat. Retail price, $24.00.

No. 1247—Utility Desk. 76 inches high, 35 inches wide, 17 inches deep. All Mahogany and Mahogany Veneered. Finish similar to plate No. 1 Woods and Finishes Section preceding page 9. Also furnished in red, green, or black decorated lacquer. Two shelves. Retail price in Mahogany, $97.00; in colors, $127.00.

No. 712—Gateleg Extension Table. Top, 44x22 inches, 70 inches extended. Combination Mahogany or Walnut finish similar to plates Nos. 1 or 14 Woods and Finishes Section preceding page 9. Retail price, $79.00.

No. 927—French End Table. 24½ inches high; Top, 26x12½ inches. All Walnut. Finish similar to plate No. 14 Woods and Finishes Section preceding page 9. Hand carved. Top and rims fancy burl Walnut. Retail price, $72.00.

No. 919—Octagon Center Table. 30 inches high, Top, 30x30 inches. All Mahogany Veneered top. Finished similar to plate No. 1 Woods and Finishes Section preceding page 9. Hand carved. Retail price, $63.50.

No. 1239—Console Table. 32 inches high, 35 inches wide, 18 inches deep. Furnished in all Walnut with Walnut decorated fronts or all Walnut with Satinwood fronts decorated. Retail price, $120.00.
No. 1222—Mirror. Frame, 32 inches high and 18 inches wide. Retail price, $37.50.

No. 926—Italian Renaissance Table. 30½ inches high; Top, 29½ x 29½ inches. All Walnut. Finish similar to plate No. 14 Woods and Finishes Section preceding page 9. Hand carved. Imported French burl Walnut top. Retail price, $180.00.

No. 903—Davenport Table. 24 inches wide. All Walnut or Mahogany. Finishes similar to plates Nos. 1 or 14 Woods and Finishes Section preceding page 9. Hand carved. Veneered top. Retail price, 72-inch length, $112.00; 60-inch length, $104.00.

TABLES AND TELEPHONE SETS
Descriptions and Prices
TABLES

No. 1239—Console Table and Mirror. (See illustration.)
No. 712—Gateleg Extension Table. (See illustration.)
No. 927—French End Table. (See illustration.)
No. 919—Octagon Center Table. (See illustration.)
No. 926—Italian Renaissance Table. (See illustration.)
No. 903—Davenport Table. (See illustration.)
No. 46-47—Telephone Set. (See illustration.)
No. 44—Bench. (See illustration.)
No. 929—Louis XIV Coffee Table. (See illustration.)
No. 1243—Console Table. Height, 37 inches; Width, 40 inches; Depth, 17 inches. All Walnut, hand carved. Retail price, $79.00. For description, illustration and price of No. 1222 mirror to match this table see illustration of No. 1239 Console Table and Mirror.
No. 1262—Console Table with Mirror. Height, 32 inches; Width, 40 inches; Depth, 17 inches. Mirror frame—Height, 41 inches; Width, 26 inches. All Walnut and Maple combination, hand decorated. Retail price, Console Table, $108.00; Mirror to match, $55.50.
No. 928—Jacobean End Table. Height, 24½ inches; Top, 26x12½ inches. All Walnut, hand carved with butt Walnut top. Retail price, $48.00.
No. 920—End Table. Height, 24 inches; Top, 12x26½ inches. All Walnut or Mahogany. Veneered top. Retail price, $16.00.
No. 916—End Table. Height, 25 inches; Top, 13x26 inches half round. All Walnut or Mahogany. Veneered top. Retail price, $14.00.
No. 915—End Table. Height, 25 inches; Top, 13x26 inches half round. All Walnut or Mahogany. Veneered top. Retail price, $14.00.
No. 923—Occasional Table. Height, 27½ inches; Top, 17x25 inches. All Walnut, polychrome finish, furnished with Walnut or Black and Gold Marble top. Retail price, Marble top, $96.00; Wood top, $43.00.
No. 922—Occasional Table. Height, 27½ inches; Top, 25 inches round. All Walnut, polychrome finish, furnished with Walnut or Black and Gold Marble top. Retail price, Marble top, $104.00; Wood top, $49.00.
No. 918—End Table. Height, 24 inches; Top, 12x26½ inches. All Walnut or Mahogany. Veneered top. Retail price, $18.00.
No. 924—Spanish Coffee Table. Height, 24 inches; Top, 26x18 inches. All Walnut decorated. Veneered top, furnished in either Walnut or imitation Marble top. Retail price, $24.00; Formica Marble Top, $37.50.
No. 716—Gateleg Table. 36x14x50 inches. All Walnut or Mahogany. Veneered tops. $53.50.

No. 46-47—Telephone Set. Cabinet, 42 inches high, 18 inches wide, 14 inches deep. Furnished in red, green, or black, hand decorated. Also furnished Walnut or Mahogany decorated. Retail price, $45.00.

No. 44—Bench. All Walnut. Finish similar to plate No. 14 Woods and Finishes Section preceding page 9. Furnished with cane or upholstered tapestry seat. Retail price, $17.00.

No. 929—Louis XIV Coffee Table. 19 inches high; Top, 24x16 inches. All Mahogany. Finish similar to plate No. 1 Woods and Finishes Section preceding page 9. Hand carved. Imported French burl Walnut top. Retail price, $59.00.

DINETTE SUITES
Descriptions and Prices

No. 1413—Duncan Phyfe Dinette Suite. (See illustration.)
No. 1409—Dinette Suite. All Walnut and Veneered, Maple trim with hand decorations.
Buffet, 39 inches high, 48 inches wide, 18 inches deep.
China, 63 inches high, 32 inches wide, 15 inches deep.
Table top 34x48 inches, 66 inches extended. Height, 30 inches.
Slip Seat Chair. Retail price complete with 4 chairs, $336.00. Retail prices of individual pieces: Buffet, $94.00; China, $94.00; Table, $76.00; Chairs, each, $18.00.
No. 1405—Dinette Suite. Walnut and Maple combination, hand decorated.
No. 1405—Buffet. Height, 38½ inches; Width, 49 inches; Depth, 18 inches.
No. 1406—China. Height, 62 inches; Width, 31 inches; Depth, 15 inches.
No. 1407—Table. Top, 32x48 inches; Height, 31 inches. Extended, 32x66 inches.
No. 1408—Chair. Slip seat. Retail price complete with 4 Chairs, $310.00. Retail prices of individual pieces: Buffet, $90.00; China, $86.00; Table, $70.00; Chair, $16.00.

No. 1413—Buffet. 38 inches high, 48 inches wide, 18 inches deep. Retail price, $70.00.

No. 1416—Chair. Slip seat. Retail price, $18.00.

No. 1415—Table. Top, 32x42 inches, 60 inches extended. All Walnut. Retail price, $70.00.

No. 1414—China. 72 inches high, 30 inches wide, 15 inches deep. Retail price, $80.00.

No. 1413—Duncan Phyfe Dinette Suite. All Mahogany. Finish similar to plate No. 1 Woods and Finishes Section preceding page 9. Crotch Mahogany Veneered fronts. Retail price including four chairs $292.00.

SKANDIA FURNITURE COMPANY
Manufacturers of Desks, Bookcases, and Dining Room Furniture

Factory and General Offices
No. Second Street, ROCKFORD, ILL.

PERMANENT EXHIBITS
NEW YORK, N. Y., New York Furniture Exchange   GRAND RAPIDS, MICH., Klingman Building

No. 1920. Mission Style Sectional Bookcase

Reg. Trade Mark
Skandia Furniture

Reg. Trade Mark
Sectional Bookcases

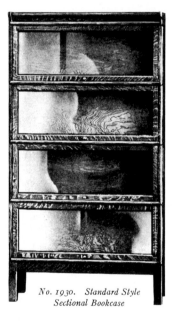

No. 1930. Standard Style Sectional Bookcase

No. 1900. Colonial Style Sectional Bookcase

PRODUCTS

MANUFACTURERS OF

MEDIUM AND HIGH GRADE LIBRARY AND DINING ROOM FURNITURE

BENCHES, Desk	DESKS
BOOKCASES	—John Hancock
—Open Shelf	—Ladies'
—Sectional	—Library
CHESTS OF DRAWERS	—Secretary
CORNER CABINETS	—Spinet
AND CLOSETS	—Wall
DESKS	HIGHBOYS
—Cabinets	PIER CABINETS
—Governor Winthrop	

For information on Dining Room Furniture see pages 342 to 345.

TRADE NAMES

The upper trade mark at the top center of this page appears on every Skandia product except our sectional bookcases. "The Viking" trade name and lower trade mark illustration identifies all sectional bookcases made in our shops.

"THE VIKING" SECTIONAL BOOKCASES

The Sectional Bookcase has demonstrated its indispensability within the last twenty years.

Its practically unlimited adaptability, its elasticity and building up feature make the sectional bookcase, beyond question, the modern repository for books in the home or office library.

"The Viking" Sectional Bookcase represents the very highest development of the sectional idea, embodying the best features of modern construction. They are designed in the three styles shown, Mission, Standard, and Colonial, of Plain and Quartered Oak (Golden finish), Birch (Mahogany finish), Walnut and Mahogany.

The complete catalog of "The Viking" line of sectional bookcases should be in the hands of every dealer. This catalog, illustrating and describing each "Viking" pattern, will be mailed to you at your request.

GENERAL INFORMATION

Since the establishment of the Skandia Furniture Company in 1889, the painstaking care of true craftsmen has been reflected in the furniture which we have produced.

There are workmen in our shops who received their first training from their fathers and grandfathers in the Scandinavian countries, ever known for their excellence in the wood-working arts. Other Skandia workmen are sons and grandsons of such men.

The fact that Skandia Furniture is built by these men who are finished masters of the furniture craft is an important consideration to the dealer who wants assurance of the best workmanship in the furniture he recommends to his customers.

This catalog gives specific buying information on many of the pieces comprising the Skandia line. Further information of any kind which you consider necessary or desirable before ordering will be furnished immediately upon receipt of your inquiry.

All prices shown in this catalog are subject to change without notice.

WOODS AND FINISHES

All Skandia products are finished in body lacquer with the exception of sectional bookcases which are varnished.

No. 1293½W—Width, 33 inches; Height, 41 inches. Mahogany Veneer and Gum. Walnut Veneer and Gum. Automatic Sliding Lid Supports.

No. 1299½W—Width 37 inches; Height, 41 inches. Mahogany Veneer and Gum. Automatic Sliding Lid Supports.

No. 1210½—Width, 38 inches; Height, 40½ inches. Mahogany Veneer and Mahogany. Automatic Sliding Lid Supports.

No. 1293½—Width, 33 inches; Height, 41 inches. Mahogany Veneer and Gum. Automatic Sliding Lid Supports.

No. 1208½. Width, 39 inches; Height, 42 inches. Crotch Mahogany Veneer and Mahogany. Butt Walnut Veneer and Walnut. Automatic Sliding Lid Supports.

No. 1208½W—Width, 37 inches; Height, 40 inches. Mahogany Veneer and Gum. Automatic Sliding Lid Supports.

No. 1221½—Width, 37 inches; Height, 40 inches. Mahogany Veneer and Gum. Automatic Sliding Lid Supports.

No. 1208½. Width, 37 inches; Height, 40 inches. Mahogany Veneer and Gum. Automatic Sliding Lid Supports.

This group ranges in price from $73.50 to $119.00. Top and Center Rows, Governor Winthrop Desks. Bottom Row, Block Front Desks.

In order to locate the panels in the Woods and Finishes Section preceding page 9 of this Reference Book which approximate the color and tone of Skandia finishes refer to the table on the right.

First, in the left hand column, locate the finish or finishes specified under the illustration. In the second column you will find the number and name of the plate which most nearly approximates the finish we specify.

By viewing this color plate you will have a good general idea of the grain of the wood and the color of the finish in which this particular number is available.

This table does not include the several Skandia items finished in colored lacquer with hand decorations.

Finish in Skandia Furniture	No. and Name of Plate in Woods and Finishes Section preceding page 9 of this book which Approximates This Finish
Antique Mahogany	21. Old Mahogany
Brown Mahogany	19. Brown Sheraton
Colonial Red Mahogany	1. Standard American Mahogany
Salem Mahogany	24. Standard Mahogany—Light
American Walnut	14. American Walnut—Standard
Antique Walnut	10. American Walnut—Dark
Commercial Oak	26. Office Oak
Golden Oak	5. Golden Oak
Fumed Oak	4. Fumed Oak

(Continued on next page)

SKANDIA FURNITURE COMPANY

GENERAL RETAIL PRICE RANGE OF SKANDIA FURNITURE

Desks.......from $23.00 to $180.00
Secretaries.......from 47.00 to 269.00
Bookcases.......from 27.00 to 168.00
Highboys.......from 99.00 to 171.50
Corner Cabinets.......from 50.00 to 150.00

Pier Cabinets.......from $ 31.50 to $ 53.00
Chest of Drawers.......from 56.00 to 95.00
Dining Room Suites.......from 430.00 to 810.00
Terms: 2% thirty days, net sixty days, f. o. b. Rockford, Illinois.

THIS GROUP OF DESKS RANGES IN PRICE FROM $45.00 TO $95.00

No. 1412—Width, 34 inches; Height, 41 inches. Mahogany Veneer and Gum. Walnut Veneer and Gum. Automatic Sliding Lid Supports.

No. 1415. Width, 34 inches; Height, 41 inches. Mahogany Veneer and Gum. Walnut Veneer and Gum.

No. 1415G. Width, 34 inches; Height, 41 inches. Plain Green Lacquer Decorated.

No. 1220½. Width, 34 inches; Height, 40½ inches. Mahogany Veneer and Gum. Walnut Veneer and Gum. Automatic Sliding Lid Supports.

No. 1422—Width, 32 inches; Height, 40 inches. Crotch Mahogany Veneer and Gum. Butt Walnut Veneer and Gum. Also Maple Veneer and Maple.

No. 1219½—Width, 35 inches; Height, 40 inches. Crotch Mahogany Veneer and Gum. Butt Walnut Veneer and Gum.

No. 1220½—Width, 34 inches; Height, 40½ inches. Maple Veneer and Maple. Automatic Lid Supports.

No. 1219½. Width, 35 inches; Height, 40 inches. Maple Veneer and Maple.

SKANDIA FURNITURE COMPANY

THIS GROUP OF DESKS RANGES IN PRICE FROM $23.00 TO $44.50

No. 1418—Width, 31 inches; Height, 39 inches. Mahogany Veneer and Gum. Walnut Veneer and Gum.

No. 1419. Width, 31 inches; Height, 38 inches. Mahogany Veneer and Gum. Walnut Veneer and Gum.

No. 1420—Width, 31 inches; Height, 39 inches. Mahogany Veneer and Gum. Walnut Veneer and Gum.

No. 1423—Width 29½ inches; Height, 39 inches. Maple Veneer and Maple. Mahogany Veneer and Gum. Walnut Veneer and Gum.

No. 1450—Width, 27 inches; Height, 30 inches. Mahogany Veneer and Gum.

No. 1452—Width, 31 inches; Height, 38 inches. Mahogany Veneer and Gum.

No. 1451—Width, 26 inches; Height, 30 inches. Mahogany Veneer and Gum.

THREE WALL DESK SELECTIONS
WALL DESKS RANGE IN PRICE FROM $38.00 TO $76.00

No. 1445—Width, 34 inches; Height, 40 inches. Mahogany Veneer and Mahogany. Walnut Veneer and Walnut also with Modified Decoration. Equipped with Electric Light Fixture Complete.

No. 1446—Width, 26 inches; Height, 40 inches. Mahogany Veneer and Gum also Lacquer in Colors. Equipped with Electric Light Fixture Complete.

No. 1437G—Width, 30 inches; Height, 42½ inches. Mahogany Veneer and Gum. Walnut Veneer and Gum; also Green Lacquer Decorated. Equipped with Electric Light Fixture Complete.

(Continued on next page)

SKANDIA FURNITURE COMPANY

THIS GROUP OF DESKS RANGES IN PRICE FROM $98.50 TO $180.00

No. 1200½—Width, 42 inches; Height, 41 inches. Crotch Mahogany and Mahogany Automatic Sliding Lid Supports.

No. 1300—Top, 28x54 inches. Height, 30 inches. Crotch Mahogany Veneer and Mahogany Double Faced Desk.

No. 1454—Width, 48 inches; Height, 44 inches. Mahogany Veneer and Mahogany. Walnut Veneer Border on Lid. Automatic Sliding Lid Supports.

No. 1421—Width, 38 inches; Height, 41 inches. Walnut Veneer and Gum. Automatic Sliding Lid Supports. Electric Light Fixture Complete.

No. 1205½—Width, 38 inches; Height, 41 inches. Butt Walnut Veneer and Walnut. Automatic Sliding Lid Supports. Electric Light Fixture Complete.

No. 1281½—Width, 40 inches; Height, 41 inches. Mahogany and Rosewood Veneer and Mahogany. Marquetry Inlay. Automatic Sliding Lid Supports. Electric Light Fixture Complete.

No. 1218½—Width, 36½ inches; Height, 41 inches. Maple Veneer and Maple. Crotch Mahogany Veneer and Mahogany. Butt Walnut Veneer and Walnut.

No. 1216½—Width, 35 inches; Height, 39 inches. Crotch Mahogany Veneer and Mahogany. Butt Walnut Veneer and Walnut. Swell Front.

No. 1217½—Width, 36 inches; Height, 40 inches. Crotch Mahogany Veneer and Gum.

No. 1701—Width, 44 inches; Height, 38 inches. Walnut and Maple Veneer and Gum, also with Modified Decoration.

SPINET DESKS RANGE IN PRICE FROM $35.00 TO $110.00

No. 1701½—Bench. Width, 24 inches; Height, 19 inches. Walnut Veneer and Gum.

No. 1700—Width, 45 inches; Height, 35 inches. Walnut and Maple Veneer and Gum, also with Modified Decoration.

THIS GROUP OF SECRETARIES
RANGES IN PRICE FROM $93.00 TO $173.00

No. 1298—Width, 38 inches;
Height, 80 inches. Mahogany
Veneer and Gum. Automatic
Sliding Lid Supports.

No. 1299W—Width, 38 inches;
Height, 81 inches. Mahogany
Veneer and Gum. Automatic Slid-
ing Lid Supports.

No. 1299—Width, 38 inches;
Height, 81 inches. Mahogany
Veneer and Gum. Automatic
Sliding Lid Supports.

No. 1208—Width, 39 inches;
Height, 82 inches. Crotch Ma-
hogany Veneer and Mahogany.
Butt Walnut Veneer and Walnut.
Automatic Sliding Lid Supports.

No. 1210—Width, 38 inches;
Height, 83 inches. Mahogany
Veneer and Gum. Automatic Slid-
ing Lid Supports.

No. 1293. Width, 35 inches;
Height, 78 inches. Mahogany
Veneer and Gum. Automatic Slid-
ing Lid Supports.

No. 1293W—Width, 35 inches;
Height, 78 inches. Mahogany
Veneer and Gum. Walnut Veneer
and Gum. Automatic Sliding Lid
Supports.

(Continued on next page)

No. 1276—Width, 33 inches; Height, 71 inches. Mahogany Veneer and Gum. Walnut Veneer and Gum.

No. 1296—Width, 34 inches; Height, 77 inches. Mahogany Veneer and Gum. Walnut Veneer and Gum.

No. 1296G—Width, 34 inches; Height, 77 inches. Red or Ivory Crackle with Hand Decoration, also Plain Green Lacquer with Hand Decoration.

No. 1297D—Width, 35 inches; Height, 78 inches. Mahogany Veneer and Gum. Walnut Veneer and Gum, also with Modified Decoration.

No. 1219—Width, 36 inches; Height, 82 inches. Crotch Mahogany Veneer and Gum. Butt Walnut Veneer and Gum.

No. 1219—Width, 36 inches; Height, 82 inches. Maple Veneer and Maple.

No. 1220—Width, 34 inches; Height, 81 inches. Maple Veneer and Maple. Automatic Sliding Lid Supports.

No. 1220—Width, 34 inches; Height, 81 inches. Mahogany Veneer and Gum. Walnut Veneer and Gum. Automatic Sliding Lid Supports.

THIS GROUP OF SECRETARIES RANGES IN PRICE FROM $61.00 TO $133.50

No. 1217—Width, 38 inches; Height, 73½ inches. Crotch Mahogany Veneer and Gum.

No. 1205—Width, 38 inches; Height, 81 inches. Butt Walnut Veneer and Walnut. Automatic Sliding Lid Supports. Electric Light Fixture Complete.

No. 1207—Width, 35 inches; Height, 78 inches. Walnut Veneer and Gum, also with Modified Decoration. Automatic Sliding Lid Supports.

No. 1200—Width, 42 inches; Height, 86 inches. Crotch Mahogany and Maple Veneer and Mahogany. Automatic Sliding Lid Supports.

No. 1216—Width, 37 inches; Height, 83 inches. Crotch Mahogany Veneer and Mahogany. Butt Walnut Veneer and Walnut. Swell Front.

No. 1281—Width, 40 inches; Height, 76 inches. Mahogany and Rosewood Veneer and Mahogany. Marquetry Inlay. Automatic Sliding Lid Supports. Electric Light Fixture Complete.

No. 1281¼—Width, 40 inches; Height, 76 inches. Mahogany and Rosewood Veneer and Mahogany. Marquetry Inlay. Automatic Sliding Lid Supports. Electric Light Fixture Complete.

No. 1218—Width, 36½ inches; Height, 86 inches. Maple Veneer and Maple. Crotch Mahogany Veneer and Mahogany. Butt Walnut Veneer and Walnut.

THIS GROUP OF SECRETARIES RANGES IN PRICE FROM $102.50 TO $269.00

(Continued on next page)

No. 1215—Width, 25½ inches; Height, 76 inches. Crotch Mahogany Veneer and Gum.

No. 1211—Width, 25 inches; Height, 73½ inches. Crotch Mahogany Veneer and Mahogany.

No. 1212—Width, 42 inches; Height, 75 inches. Crotch Mahogany Veneer and Mahogany.

No. 1202—Width, 26 inches; Height, 74 inches. Mahogany Veneer and Gum. Automatic Sliding Lid Supports.

No. 1290—Width, 31 inches; Height, 74 inches. Mahogany Veneer and Gum.

No. 1203—Width, 30½ inches. Height, 63 inches. Mahogany and Maple Veneer and Gum. Walnut and Maple Veneer and Gum.

No. 1265½—Width, 22 inches; Height, 71½ inches. Walnut Veneer and Gum.

THE SECRETARIES SHOWN ABOVE
AND THE GROUP ON THE NEXT PAGE RANGE IN PRICE FROM $48.00 TO $176.00

No. 1284—Width, 28 inches; Height, 68 inches. Mahogany Veneer and Gum. Automatic Sliding Lid Supports. Electric Light Fixture Complete.

No. 1284¼R—Width, 28 inches; Height, 68 inches. Red Crackle Lacquer Decorated. Automatic Sliding Lid Supports. Electric Light Fixture Complete.

No. 1286—Width, 30 inches; Height, 72 inches. Walnut and Maple Veneer and Gum. Automatic Sliding Lid Supports.

No. 1283½—Width, 32 inches; Height, 75 inches. Mahogany Veneer and Gum.

No. 1287—Width, 30 inches; Height, 60 inches. Walnut and Maple Veneer and Gum. Automatic Sliding Lid Supports. Electric Light Fixture Complete.

No. 1292—Width, 35 inches; Height, 78 inches. Mahogany Veneer and Gum. Walnut Veneer and Gum.

(Continued on next page)

SKANDIA FURNITURE COMPANY

THIS GROUP OF
LIBRARY BOOKCASES
AND THE THREE AT THE TOP
OF THE NEXT PAGE
RANGE IN PRICE FROM
$36.00 TO $168.00

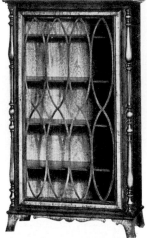

No. 1556½—Width, 31 inches; Height, 53 inches. Maple Veneer and Gum. Walnut Veneer Grille. Walnut or Mahogany Finish.

No. 1557½—Width, 40 inches; Height, 53 inches. Maple Veneer and Gum—Walnut Veneer Grille. Walnut or Mahogany Finish.

No. 1531½—Width, 44 inches; Height, 53 inches. Gum—Mahogany Veneer Grille and Overlay. Walnut or Mahogany Finish.

No. 1530½—Width, 27 inches; Height, 53 inches. Gum—Mahogany Veneer Grille and Overlay Walnut or Mahogany Finish.

No. 1553½—Width, 27 inches; Height, 51 inches. Red Gum—Mahogany Veneer Grille. Walnut or Mahogany Finish.

No. 1554½—Width, 45 inches; Height, 51 inches. Red Gum—Mahogany Veneer Grille. Walnut or Mahogany Finish.

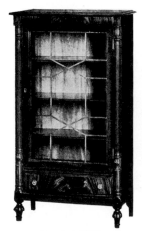

No. 1569½—Width, 25 inches; Height, 44½ inches. Crotch Mahogany Veneer and Gum. Butt Walnut Veneer and Gum. Solid Mahogany or Solid Walnut Top.

No. 1570½—Width, 37 inches; Height, 44½ inches. Crotch Mahogany Veneer and Gum. Butt Walnut Veneer and Gum. Solid Mahogany or Solid Walnut Top.

No. 1573½—Width, 37½ inches; Height, 42 inches. Red Gum—Mahogany Veneer Grille. Mahogany or Walnut Finish.

No. 1572½—Width, 27 inches; Height, 42 inches. Red Gum—Mahogany Veneer Grille. Mahogany or Walnut Finish.

SKANDIA FURNITURE COMPANY

No. 1568½—Width, 69 inches;
Height, 54 inches. Crotch Mahogany Veneer and Mahogany.

No. 1566½—Width, 31
inches; Height, 54 inches.
Crotch Mahogany Veneer
and Mahogany.

No. 1567½—Width, 50
inches; Height, 54 inches.
Crotch Mahogany Veneer
and Mahogany.

THIS GROUP OF PIER CABINETS RANGES IN PRICE FROM $31.50 TO $49.50

No. 1561D—Width, 19
inches; Height, 61 inches.
Mahogany Veneer and
Gum, also with Modified
Decoration.

No. 1562—Width, 18
inches; Height, 62 inches.
Mahogany Veneer and
Gum, also with Modified
Decoration.

No. 1563—Width, 19
inches; Height, 66 inches.
Mahogany Veneer and
Gum; also with Modified
Decoration.

No. 1564D—Width, 19
inches; Height, 62 inches.
Maple Veneer and Gum,
also with Modified Decoration.

No. 1564I—Width, 19
inches; Height, 62 inches.
Ivory Crackle with Hand
Decoration.

(Continued on next page)

DUTCH CABINETS
RANGE IN PRICE
FROM $99.50 TO $140.00

CABINETS
RANGE IN PRICE
FROM $51.50 TO $70.50

No. 181¼—Width, 38 inches; Height, 81 inches. Crotch Mahogany Veneer and Mahogany.

No. 175½G—Width, 23 inches; Height, 72 inches. Walnut Veneer and Gum, also Green or Ivory Lacquer Decorated.

No. 175I—Width, 23 inches; Height, 72 inches. Ivory Crackle Decorated.

No. 175G—Width, 23 inches; Height, 72 inches. Plain Green Lacquer Decorated.

No. 175—Width, 23 inches; Height, 72 inches. Walnut Veneer and Gum.

No. 176D—Width, 32 inches; Height, 70 inches. Walnut Veneer and Walnut, also with Modified Decoration.

No. 178—Width, 27 inches; Height, 77 inches. Butt Walnut and Maple Veneer and Gum. Crotch Mahogany Veneer and Mahogany.

THIS GROUP OF CORNER CABINETS RANGES IN PRICE FROM $50.00 TO $92.00

No. 1128—Width, 25 inches; Height, 65 inches. Crotch Mahogany Veneer Front and Ends, Balance Solid Mahogany.

No. 1129—Width, 36 inches; Height, 77 inches. Maple Veneer and Maple.

HIGHBOYS RANGE IN PRICE FROM $99.00 TO $171.50

No. 1100—Width, 27 inches; Height, 44 inches. Maple and Walnut Veneer and Gum.

No. 1101—Width, 20 inches; Height, 43 inches. Maple and Walnut Veneer Front, Ends and Legs Gum, Balance Solid Walnut.

No. 1102—Width, 27 inches; Height, 45 inches. Walnut Veneer and Walnut.

No. 1103—Width, 38 inches; Height, 48 inches. Maple and Walnut Veneer Front, Ends and Top, Balance Gum.

CHESTS OF DRAWERS RANGE IN PRICE FROM $56.00 TO $95.00

UNION FURNITURE COMPANY

Manufacturers of Library Furniture

18th Avenue, ROCKFORD, ILL.

PERMANENT EXHIBITS

CHICAGO, ILL., Space 1108-1109, American Furniture Mart   GRAND RAPIDS, MICH., 5th Floor, Manufacturers Exhibition Bldg.
SAN FRANCISCO, CALIF., 180 New Montgomery St.   NEW YORK, N. Y., Space 1514, 206 Lexington Ave.

No. 553½—Desk. Width, 30 inches; Height, 29 inches. Drawer fronts and fall of 5-ply Mahogany veneer 2 sides. Drawer bottoms of 3-ply Mahogany veneer, balance of quartered sawed Gum. Full automatic slide supports. Finished in Brown and Red Mahogany. List price $63.00.

No. 553—Secretary Bookcase. Width, 30 inches; Height, 77 inches. Drawer fronts and fall of 5-ply Mahogany veneer 2 sides. Back of bookcase unit and drawer bottoms of 3-ply Mahogany veneer, balance of quartered Red Gum. Full automatic slide supports. Finished in Brown and Red Mahogany. List price, $83.00.

No. 540—Colonial Secretary Desk. Width, 30 inches; Height, 75 inches. Made with 5-ply Walnut or Mahogany veneer front. Ends of quartered sawed Gum. Drawer bottoms and back of 3-ply Mahogany. Can be furnished in any of the Mahogany or Walnut finishes. List price, $67.00.

No. 544—Desk Table. Top, 27x54 inches. Front, back, ends and top of 5-ply Walnut veneer. Legs of quartered sawed Gum. Drawer bottoms of three-ply Mahogany. Finished in Antique Walnut on all four sides. Back is the same as front. List price $119.00.

No. 552—Secretary Bookcase. Width, 37 inches; Height, 80 inches. Entire front of beautifully figured and matched Butt Walnut veneers —5-ply construction. Ends of 5-ply Walnut veneers. 6-drawer writing interior. Back of book unit and drawer bottoms of 3-ply Mahogany veneer. Full automatic slide supports. List price, $150.00. For desk only, No. 552½— List price, $100.00.

No. 541—Secretary Bookcase. Width, 33 inches; Height, 77 inches. Fall of 5-ply matched Butt Walnut veneers. Drawer fronts and gallery of 5-ply Blistered Maple. Doors of 5-ply Walnut veneers. Legs, stretcher, and all mouldings of solid Walnut. Back of book unit and drawer bottoms of 3-ply Mahogany veneer, balance in quartered Gum. Finished in antique Walnut. List price, $98.00. For desk unit, No. 541½ same materials as above, list price, $73.00.

UNION FURNITURE COMPANY

Trade Mark

No. 524½—*Governor Winthrop Design Desk. Width, 30 inches; Height, 41 inches. Drawer fronts, fall, fall bed and ends of 5-ply Mahogany veneer, 2 sides. Top, interior writing arrangement, drawer sides and back of solid Mahogany. Drawer bottoms, 3-ply Mahogany. Ball claw feet of quartered sawed Gum. Full automatic slide supports. Finished in Red and Brown Mahogany. List price, $106.00.*

No. 524—*Governor Winthrop Design Secretary Bookcase. Width, 30 inches; Height, 85 inches. Drawer fronts, fall, fall bed and ends of 5-ply Mahogany veneer 2 sides. Gallery, doors, drawer sides and backs, and drawer bottoms of 3-ply Mahogany veneer. Ball claw feet of quartered sawed Gum. Full automatic slide supports. Finished in Red and Brown Mahogany. List price, $150.00.*

No. 538—*Wall Desk. Width, 29 inches; Height, 48 inches. Drop front of 5-ply Walnut veneer, 2 sides. Cut out ornaments on drop front of Mahogany and Maple. Balance in quartered sawed Gum Finished in Antique Walnut. Hinges and Escutcheon finished in Antique Bronze. List price, $43.00.*

No. 607½—*Open Front Bookcase. Width, 36 inches; Height, 44 inches. Made in quartered sawed Gum. 3-ply Mahogany back. Can be furnished in any of Mahogany finishes. List price $30.00.*

No. 607¾—*Open Front Bookcase. Width, 48 inches; Height, 44 inches. Made in quartered sawed Gum. 3-ply Mahogany back. Can be furnished in any of Mahogany finishes. List price, $30.00.*

No. 607—*Open Front Bookcase. Width, 24 inches; Height, 44 inches. Made in quartered sawed Gum. 3-ply Mahogany back. Can be furnished in any of Mahogany finishes. List price, $23.00.*

SHOWERS BROTHERS COMPANY
RADIO FURNITURE
Bedroom and Dining Room Furniture, Kitchen Cabinets, Occasional Chairs
BLOOMINGTON, INDIANA

Factories: BLOOMINGTON, IND., BLOOMFIELD, IND. and BURLINGTON, IOWA
Exhibits: Space 1501, American Furniture Mart, CHICAGO, and Space 1607-9-11, New York Furniture Exchange, NEW YORK

PRODUCTS
MANUFACTURERS OF

RADIO BENCHES
CONSOLE RADIO CABINETS
RADIO TABLES
RADIO MIRRORS

For information on other products see Case Goods Catalog, pages 336 to 341, and Kitchen Cabinets Catalog, page 75.

The symbol of 60 years of manufacturing furniture of honest value—profitable to handle.

WOODS AND FINISHES

Precious wood veneers and overlays mark the entire line of Showers Radio Furniture. Blistered Maple, Zebrawood, Oriental Walnut, Satinwood, and many others are used over selected American Gumwood or Poplar cores. Hand rubbing gives a smooth, velvety surface to the finish. All carvings and ornamentations are blended, high-lighted and hand-wiped.

TRADE NAMES

"SHOWERS RADIO FURNITURE" is used in connection with the regular Showers trade mark on our complete line of cabinets.

GENERAL INFORMATION

The quality of Showers Radio Furniture has always been above the average. We have again been appointed the manufacturers of the official Crosley Cabinets. These cabinets, of course, are sold only through authorized Crosley dealers. The regular line of Showers Radio Furniture can be obtained through authorized jobbers. Write us today. We will put you in touch with our nearest jobber.

All prices shown are subject to change without notice.

No. C3—Showers Crosley Radio Cabinet.

SHOWERS CROSLEY RADIO CABINET
Number C 3

Sold only through authorized Crosley dealers. Walnut veneer with carved ornamentation. American Gum or Poplar legs, rails and cores. Legs and rails in Walnut finish. Top, 14 inches by 21 inches—height, 38 inches. Price, equipped with Dynacone speaker, $60.00.

No. J45—Showers Radio Cabinet.

PRECIOUS WOOD OVERLAYS MARK THIS CABINET
"The Fieldston"
Model J 45

Pleasing proportions, graceful carvings and a hand-rubbed finish make this cabinet an addition to any well furnished home. The finish is antique Walnut. The top banding Zebrawood. Striking Blistered Maple overlays on the doors and rails enhance the beauty of this cabinet. Designed to fit any standard receiving set. Sold only through Showers dealers. Price with Showers speaker, $50.00.

No. D100—Showers Radio Cabinet.

HOLDS ANY STANDARD RECEIVING SET
"The Norman"
Model D 100

A beautiful Console Cabinet designed to hold any standard receiving set. Doors five-ply laminated matched Oriental Walnut veneer over selected hardwood core. Blistered Maple and Zebrawood overlays. All carvings hand-rubbed and high-lighted. Walnut finish. American Gumwood or Poplar legs, rails and cores. Sold only through authorized Showers dealers. Price with Showers speaker, $50.00.

AUTOMATIC SHADE COMPANY
Manufacturers of Wooden Slat Porch Shades
401-411 Summit St., SAUK RAPIDS, MINN.
BRANCH OFFICES AND EXHIBITS
MINNEAPOLIS, MINN., J. A. Evers, Sales Agent, 740 Washington Ave..No.
and Bromley Advertising Agcy., 712 Sixth Ave. So.

PRODUCTS
MANUFACTURERS OF
WOODEN SLAT SHADES for use on Outdoor or Glazed-in Porches, or on Windows of Schools, Offices, Factories, Institutions, Hotels, etc. This entire line of Shades bears the name "Warren's Shades."

TRADE NAMES
Warren's Shades are divided into four general groups: Warren's "RAYN-TITE" Shade, Warren's "IDEAL" Shade, Warren's "COTTAGE" Shade and Warren's "INDUSTRIAL" Shade (for offices, factories, shops, etc.).

GENERAL INFORMATION
Warren's Shades are sold through jobbers in certain sections of the country, and through house-furnishing and department stores in every state in the Union. Dealers are finding that the agency for Warren's Shades is a very definite asset in their business.

WOODS, COLORS, FINISHES
Warren's Shades are made from selected Basswood, oil-stained after emerging from the loom. The slats are given a velvety smooth finish before being woven, and after staining, are waterproof, and to a very large extent, sunfast as well.

SPECIFICATIONS
Warren's "Rayn-tite" Shade is the only shade of its kind in America. The slats are ¾ inch wide, with beveled edges in place of straight edges (see illustrations below). The effect of this is that the shade is Rainproof, Sunproof, and Sightproof, yet admits ample ventilation. Widths are 3 to 12 feet, drop either 6 or 7 feet. Simple hanging device and non-whip stretchers come with each shade.

Each shade enclosed in heavy kraft paper bag, then packed in bundles in burlap.

Warren's "Ideal" Shade is of the same selected Basswood, with ⅞ inch slats; also finished in oil-stain colors, and furnished in 3 to 12 foot widths, 6 or 7 foot drop. Slats of this shade have straight edges. Burlap and kraft paper wrapped for shipment. Sold throughout America and very popular with your "medium class trade."

Warren's "Cottage" Shade, also of Basswood, but not selected. Supplied in the same widths, drops and colors as the other 2 numbers. Burlap wrapped only. Fully equipped for hanging. Made to meet the demand of the "price shopper," and a splendid value for the money.

OUR NATIONAL ADVERTISING
You will find Warren's Porch and Window Shades advertised this year in "Furniture Record," "Furniture Age," "Furniture Reporter," "Southern Furniture Journal" and "Furniture Digest." Also, to stimulate a demand you can supply, we are represented in "Better Homes & Gardens," "Good Housekeeping," "House Beautiful" and "Dairy Farmer." All of this publicity makes every sale that much easier and more satisfactory. In a widespread manner, dealers are cashing in on this national advertising.

DEALER'S SALES STIMULATORS
To help you re-sell Warren's Shades, we will supply street car or counter cards, display cutouts, package or envelope inserts (imprinted if desired), newspaper mats or cuts, colored folders, lantern slides imprinted, actual miniature samples of shades, and suggested retail price cards.

DEPENDABILITY
Quality, Durability, Service, are all woven into Warren's Shades. It would be very easy to make them cheaper; we could use cheaper lumber—selected Basswood is expensive. We could forget to give the slats that smooth velvety finish. We could use a much cheaper warp-cord in weaving. We could find many lower priced stains. We could omit doubling the warp, and the two wire stitches holding it. We could use cheaper hardware. We might leave out the non-whip stretchers.

But such practices would lower the quality, decrease the durability and shorten the service; in short you'd not want to recommend Warren's Shades to your most particular trade, as you now can. Warren's Shades are made somewhat better than you'd expect, and will continue to be.

Our schedule of very moderate prices, our terms and quantity discounts, as well as freight equalization arrangements, and our prompt shipment facilities, are matters with which you ought to be familiar. Write us for these details. You will turn them into new and additional sales.

JUST A FEW DETAILS OF CONSTRUCTION THAT MAKE WARREN SHADES SUPERIOR

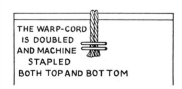

THE WARP-CORD IS DOUBLED AND MACHINE STAPLED BOTH TOP AND BOTTOM

Details of Slat Construction
Illustration at left shows why the warp-cord holds firmly across the entire top, where the strain is heaviest. On the right is shown sectional view of Warren's "Ideal" Shade.

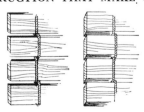

The slightly overlapping edge of the slat in Warren's new "Rayn-tite" Shade is shown in illustration at left: a feature providing a Rainproof, Sunproof, Sightproof shade with free ventilation. Picture at right shows section of moulding with double slat reinforcing, which runs across entire top of shade, affording strength to withstand strains.

HEAVY MOULDING PREVENTS SAGS AND BREAKAGE

ATHENS TABLE & MANUFACTURING CO.
Manufacturers of Living and Dining Room Tables
ATHENS, TENNESSEE

PERMANENT SHOWROOMS
CHICAGO, ILL., 5th Floor, American Furniture Mart.

No. 584—Butterfly Table. Hardwood, finished
Imitation Mahogany or Walnut Antique. Top
open, 30 by 32 inches; Height, 25 inches. Shipped
K. D. one in a crate. Weight about 50 pounds.
List price, $15.00.

No. 827—Apartment Table. Imitation Walnut or Mahogany on
Hardwood. Top closed 32 by 44 inches; extended 32 by 64 inches.
Shipped K. D. two in a crate. Weight about 75 pounds. The legs
are 2 inches at the square. List price, $19.00.

No. 669—Writing Desk. A desk
of this type is adaptable for use in
any place, especially for hotels,
boarding houses, bedrooms, etc.
Finished in imitation mahogany or
walnut. Height, 29 inches. List,
$15.00.

PRODUCTS

MANUFACTURERS OF

TABLES
—Breakfast Room
—Davenport
—Dining, Combination Living
   Room
—Dining Room
—End
—Extension
—Library
—Occasional
—Wall
—Radio
—Console

No. 681—Davenport Table with Book
Racks. Provides storage room for
books, magazines, humidors, etc. Early
American turnings on spindles and
legs. Imitation mahogany on hardwood. Top, 18 by 48 inches. List,
$19.00.

TWENTY YEARS OF TABLE BUILDING

Athens has been specializing
in the manufacture of tables
for twenty years. This inten-
sive experience is our guarantee of dependable materials
and construction.

You should make it a point
to investigate these offerings
before stocking your next order
of tables.

Prices shown are subject to
change without notice.

No. 963—Extension. This dining table is just
a hint of the exceptional merit of our entire showing. Simplicity of charm and selling appeal are
features which have been expertly combined in
this combination walnut. List, $37.00.

No. 250—Double Duty. Whatever may be
your customers' requirements in a table, you
will find that need embraced in our assortment. This attractive number embodies every
worthwhile feature in convenience, style, finish and construction. List, $48.00.

CONANT-BALL COMPANY

Manufacturers of Chairs, Cottage Dining Room Suites
Living Room and Bedroom Furniture

Executive Office and Sample Rooms, 76-100 Sudbury St., BOSTON, MASS.
Factory at Gardner, Mass.
EXHIBIT
GRAND RAPIDS, MICH., 7th Floor, Manufacturers Building

No. 2054-10 — Bench. Height, 8 inches; top, 9x14 inches.

No. 1749-4.

No. 1743½-5 — Windsor.

No. 2058-5 — Arm Chair. Height, 36 inches; Width between arms, 20 inches; Depth of seat, 19 inches.

No. 1665-5 — Ladder-Back.

No. 1763-4.

199C — Chest of Drawers. Top, 16x31 inches; Height, 33 inches.

No. 232-C — Height, 47¾ inches; Width, 14 inches; Depth, 8 inches.

No. 212-CS — Height, 26 inches; Top 13 inches.

No. 214 — Height, 30 inches; Top, 14x14 inches closed; 24x14 inches extended.

No. 242-B — Height, 31 inches; Width outside rails, 36 inches; Length of rails, 75 inches.

No. 224-T — Top, 38x24 inches; Height, 27 inches.

No. 199-B — Sizes, 3 feet 3 inches, or 4 feet 6 inches.

PRODUCTS

MANUFACTURERS OF

APARTMENT (or small)
SIZE DINING ROOM
SUITES
DINING ROOM CHINA
CABINETS
COLONIAL BUFFETS
WELSH DRESSERS
SERVERS
TABLES
BEDROOM FURNITURE,
including
Bench, Chair and
Rocker Sets for
Odd Suites
Benches, Cane Seat and
Upholstered
Boudoir Chairs, Up-
holstered
Chairs and Chair Sets
Chests of Drawers

Dressing & Toilet
Table Benches
Night Tables
BREAKFAST ROOM SUITES
Complete, and
BREAKFAST ROOM FUR-
NITURE, including
Chairs and Tables in
the white (unfinished)
Chairs
Buffets
Cabinets
Servers
Serving Tables and
Cabinets, Combined
Tables
Extension Tables
BOOK, MAGAZINE, AND
NEWSPAPER RACKS
AND STANDS

CHAIRS
—Arm
—Assembly Hall
—Baby
—Children's
—Cane Seat
—Cane Back
—Desk, Home
—Easy
—Fireplace and
Fireside
—Hall
—Hotel and Club
—Ladderback
—Library and
Living
Room
—Restaurant

CHAIRS
—Mother
—Nursery
—Odd and
Occasional
—Rush Seat
—Slip Seat
—Splint
—Tablet Arm
—Windsor
—Wood Seat
ROCKERS
—Cane Seat
—Rush Seat
—Wood
—Windsor
TABLES
—Butterfly
—Cafe

BOOK SHELVES
CHURCH CHAIRS
CORNER WALL SHELVES
WALL CABINETS
WASTE BASKETS
FOOT STOOLS AND
OTTOMANS
FRAMES FOR UPHOL-
STERED FURNITURE
SMOKERS' STANDS AND
TABLES
MIRRORS, Console and
Hall
FURNITURE for Hospitals,
Institutions, Hotels,
Clubs, Tea Rooms

TABLES
—Center
—Coffee
—Console
—Dining and
Living
Room,
Combined
—Drop Leaf
—End
—Flip Top
—Gateleg
—Gateleg
Extension
—Hall
—Odd and Occa-
sional

TABLES
—Side
—Tuckaway

CONANT-BALL CO. BOSTON — C-B — Trade Mark

GENERAL INFORMATION

For more than three quarters of a century CONANT-BALL has been a name known wherever good furniture was sold.

For quality of materials used, workmanship that acknowledges no superiority, and finish of unquestioned dependability, CONANT-BALL products have always enjoyed an enviable reputation.

Pioneers in the introduction of Windsor and Colonial Chairs, as well as in the revival and manufacture of COLONIAL REPRODUCTIONS, their fame has become national.

"CONANT-BALL" COLONIALS are made in our own factory, in the Colony of Revolutionary Days—*Massachusetts*—the home of the Pilgrims.

Free from the touch of the restorer—CONANT-BALL build into every Colonial piece they make, and without change or alteration of lines—that rare Beauty of proportion—genuine Simplicity—and the matchless Charm that distinguishes the authentic Early Colonial.

FINISHES

Our No. 26 finish is similar to plate No. 24. Our No. 64 is similar to plate No. 8. Our No. 44 is similar to plate No. 15. Our No. 41 is similar to plate No. 14 and our No. 27 finish is similar to plate No. 1. See Woods and Finishes Section preceding page 9 of this book.

RETAIL PRICE RANGES

Chairs—
Windsor	$ 9.50 to $26.00
Colonial	12.50 to 37.00
Settees	48.00 to 53.50
Boudoir	18.00 to 55.00
Wing	47.00 to 189.00
Occasional	38.00 to 184.50
Dining	22.00 to 43.00

Tables—
Gateleg	37.50 to 52.00
Tuck-A-Way	14.00 to 24.00
Drop Leaf	25.50 to 72.00
Dining	41.00 to 52.00
Chests and Cabinets	24.00 to 58.50
Mirrors	17.00 to 24.00

Novelties—
Tables, Racks, Stands, etc.	$4.00 to $50.00

Beds—
Regular Colonial	42.00 to 46.00
Day Beds	24.00 to 38.00

All prices shown are subject to change without notice.

F. H. CONANT'S SONS, INC.

Established 1851

Chairs, Rockers and Benches

CAMDEN, NEW YORK

EXHIBIT

GRAND RAPIDS, MICH., First Floor, Waters Klingman Building

No. 21—Fireside Bench. 12½x19x19¼ inches high. Mahogany. Price $34.00.

No. 20—Fireside Bench. 13x20x19½ inches high. Mahogany. Price $31.00.

No. 611—After the Spanish Manner. Upholstered in Figured Denim. Price $59.00. Up to $97.00 depending on Covers. This chair is usually called a Reading Chair.

No. 830—English Club Chair. Mahogany with Gumwood Back Legs. Price $58.50. Figured Denim. Up to $110.50.

No. 935—Coxwell. Upholstered in Tapestry. Mahogany-Walnut, Gumwood Back Legs. Price $54.00. Up to $90.00.

PRODUCTS

MANUFACTURERS OF

CHAIRS
—Coxwell, with Spring or Down Cushions
—Reading, with or without Loose Cushions
—Occasional and Pull-up, with Upholstered or Wood Back
—And Rockers, Wood and Flag Seats to match Love Seats
BENCHES, Fireside
FOOT RESTS
LOVE SEATS, Double Seat, Loose Cushions filled with down or springs

DESIGNS

Conant Chairs as a whole follow such popular periods as the Spanish, Italian Renaissance, Queen Anne, Empire and the Early English. In each piece of Conant Furniture there is apparent an individualistic touch that sets it apart . . . that speaks well for the ingenuity of Conant designers.

WOODS AND FINISHES

Each piece of wood entering into Conant merchandise has been thoroughly kiln-dried and seasoned and is to a very marked extent free from defect. The better grades of hardwoods are employed, with Walnut and Mahogany the outstanding specie. Finishes on Conant Furniture resemble plates 11, 21, 10, and 15 as shown in the Woods and Finishes Section preceding page 9 of this book.

RETAIL PRICE RANGES

Coxwell Chairs vary from $43.50 to $133.50.
Reading Chairs, $43.50 to $131.00.
Chairs, Rockers, Wood and Flag Seat, $15.00 to $44.00.
Occasional and Pull-up Chairs, $24.50 to $102.50.
Chairs to match Love Seats, $59.00 to $150.50.
Love Seats, $87.50 to $203.50.
Benches, Fireside, $29.00 to $64.50.
Foot Rests, $3.00 to $39.00.
All prices shown are subject to change without notice.

CONSTRUCTION

Frames—All frames are made of selected hardwoods, air dried and then kiln dried. Only the best grades of Mexican Mahogany and American Walnut are used. Finished with Lacquer and hand rubbed.

Upholstery—Only curled hair, moss and cotton are used for filling. Springs are sewed to webbing bottoms, no steel construction being used.

Cover Fabrics—The coverings used are Tapestries, Velours and Mohairs which are selected from the best makers in this country and abroad. All Mohairs are specially treated to make them moth proof.

SELECT ONE OF THESE NUMBERS

Pick out several of these numbers now . . . the price is right, and Conant construction will help you build up a satisfied clientele. We shall be glad to send you photographs of other Conant numbers that are equally as interesting.

No. 283—Arm Chair in the Spanish Manner. Upholstered in Tapestry. Gumwood, Mahogany arms. Price $31.00. Up to $49.00.

No. 617—Fireside Chair. Mahogany, Gumwood Back Legs. Upholstered in Denim. Price $65.00. Up to $107.50.

No. 263—Arm Chair in Spanish Manner. Upholstered in Tapestry. Price $34.00. Up to $49.00.

DAVIS-BIRELY TABLE COMPANY

Manufacturers of Tables and Auxiliary Furniture

SHELBYVILLE, INDIANA

EXHIBIT
GRAND RAPIDS, MICH., 2nd Floor, Fine Arts Bldg.

No. 6003—Size, 36x32 inches. Mahogany or Walnut Veneer on Quartered Gum. Crated, 110 lbs.

No. 6418—Size, 23x23 inches. Height, 25 inches. Figured Mahogany Veneer on Quartered Gum. Colonial Finish. Crated, 65 lbs.

No. 5186—Size, 32x26 inches. Mahogany or Walnut Veneer on Quartered Gum. Crated, 80 lbs.

No. 1077—Size, 48x26 inches. Five drawers. Mahogany or Walnut Veneer on Quartered Gum. Crated, 160 lbs.

No. 6008—Size, 34x20 inches. Mahogany Veneer on Quartered Gum. Colonial Finish. Crated, 60 lbs.

PRODUCTS
MANUFACTURERS OF

BOOK ENDS
BOOK TROUGHS
CABINETS
—Radio End Table
—Sewing
—Sewing, Martha Washington
CHAIRS, DESK, HOME
DESKS
—Kidney Shaped
—Ladies'
—Library Table
—Telephone, Wood
HOTEL FURNITURE

MIRROR FRAMES
MIRRORS, CONSOLE
RACKS
—Book
—Magazine and News-paper
STANDS
—Grip
—Magazine
—Trunk
TABLES
—Arm
—Butterfly
—Cafe

TABLES
—Center
—Coffee
—Console with Mirrors
—Davenport
—Art Moderne

TABLES
—Davenport, Extension
—Desk
—Dining and Living Room Combination
—Drop Leaf (Not a Gate-leg Table)
—Enameled Finish
—End, Radio Cabinet
—Flip Top
—Gate Leg
—Hall
—Hotel
—Library
—Lunch Room
—Night

TABLES
—Occasional
—Pie Crust Top
—Radio
—School
—Sewing
—Tea
—Tilt Top
—Wandering
TELEPHONE
—Sets
—Stands
—Stools
—Tables

Trade Mark

EVERY KIND OF TABLE FOR YOUR TRADE

Davis-Birely Designs embrace all the popular periods with the William and Mary, Early English, Early American, Queen Anne and Sheraton predominating.

The wide range of Davis-Birely products does not permit us to give a detailed description of each and every piece—a comprehensive catalog will be sent to you upon request with prices. Write for the Davis-Birely proposition today.

Table No. 303—Top, 48x60 inches. List Price, $58.00.

Arm or Host Chair No. 303A—List Price, $15.50.

No. 301A—Arm or Host Chair. List Price $12.50.

Table No. 301—Top, 42x54 inches. List Price, $48.00.

China Cabinet No. 303—Top, 18x40 inches. Height, 66 inches. List Price, $54.00.

Server No. 303—Top, 38 inches. List Price, $32.00.

Server No. 301—Top, 36 inches. List Price, $24.00.

China Cabinet No. 301—Height, 62 inches; width, 38 inches. List Price, $49.00.

Side Chair of Suite No. 303—List Price, $11.50.

No. 303—Buffet. Top, 66 inches. List Price, $76.00.

Buffet No. 301—Top, 60 inches. List Price, $55.00.

Side Chair No. 301—List Price, $8.50.

Suite No. 303 has Bird's-Eye Maple Apron and Pencil Stripe Walnut Overlay on the Buffet, Server and China. List Price, $282.00.

Suite No. 301—Built of Combination Walnut Veneer and reasonably priced at $231.00 List.

TUDOR AND JACOBEAN DESIGNS
In Walnut and Gum

Empire Suites follow two popular periods—Tudor and Jacobean. The charm of these two periods is further enhanced by the burl walnut fronts, walnut tops and ends. Suites are combinations of gum and walnut. Genuine carvings are used. Chairs have walnut backs and fronts.

HANNAHS MANUFACTURING COMPANY

"Hannahs Tables"

KENOSHA, WISCONSIN

PERMANENT EXHIBITS AND SALESROOMS
CHICAGO, ILL., Suite 1116-1117, American Furniture Mart

PRODUCTS
MANUFACTURERS OF

TABLES
—Butterfly
—Center
—Chair
—Console
—Davenport
—Desk
—Double Utility
—End
—Gateleg
—Gateleg Extension
—Library
—Living Room

TABLES
—Night
—Occasional
—Tilt Top
—Wall
BOOK TROUGHS
MAGAZINE BASKETS
PEDESTALS
CABINETS
—Pier
—Radio
TABOURETTES
WALL RACKS

No. 2716—Magazine Rack.
Length, 16¼ inches; Height, 21
inches. Constructed entirely of
hard wood.
Finish: Imitation Mahogany;
Imitation Walnut; Red shaded
with Black and Gold; Green shaded
with Black and Gold.

No. 2723—Magazine Basket.
Length, 19 inches; Width, 10 inches;
Height, 23 inches. Columns of 5-ply
stock surfaced in Mahogany or
Walnut. Balance of hard wood and
finished in Imitation. Mahogany
or Walnut.

No. 2868—Occasional Table. Top,
30 by 30 inches; Height, 28 inches.
Top is 5-ply center matched Butt Walnut
or center matched Swirl Mahogany.
Underneath parts in other hard woods
finished in Imitation. Mahogany overlay on rail.
Finish: Mahogany or Walnut.

No. 2700—Pier Cabinet.
Width, 16 inches; Depth, 8½
inches; Height, 64 inches.
Constructed entirely of hard
wood.
Finish: Imitation Mahog-
any; Imitation Walnut; Red
shaded with Black and Gold;
Green shaded with Black and
Gold.

No. 2865—Gateleg Table. Size,
opened, 38 by 54 inches; Size, closed,
38 by 18 inches. Top and leaves are
5-ply surfaced in Mahogany or Walnut.
Underneath parts in other hard woods
finished in Imitation.
Finish: Mahogany or Walnut.

No. 2738—End Table. Top,
12 by 28 inches; Height, 24
inches. Top is 5-ply surfaced
in Mahogany or Walnut.
Underneath parts in other
hard wood finished in Imitation.
Finish: Mahogany or Wal-
nut.

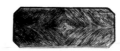

No. 2886—Living Room Table. Top, 20 by 50 inches. Top is 5-ply center matched
Butt Walnut or center matched Swirl Mahogany. Underneath parts in other hard
woods finished in Imitation.
Finish: Mahogany or Walnut.

No. 2735—Chair Table. Size, 10 by
22 inches; Height, 26 inches. Constructed entirely of 5-ply stock surfaced
in Mahogany or Walnut excepting the
brackets which are of other hard wood
and finished in Imitation.
Finish: Mahogany or Walnut.

IMPERIAL FURNITURE COMPANY
Manufacturers of Tables of All Kinds

Factory and Offices, GRAND RAPIDS, MICHIGAN

Showrooms at the Factory

Imperial Tabletwo
Library and Dining

Imperial Tables
Grand Rapids

Trade Marks

PRODUCTS
MANUFACTURERS OF

APARTMENT DINING GROUPS
BENCHES
BOOK END TABLES
BOOK TABLES
BOOKCASES
BUFFETS
BUTTERFLY TABLES
CABINETS
CELLARETTES
CHESTS
CHESTS OF DRAWERS
CHINA CABINETS
CHECK DESKS
CONSOLE TABLES
COSTUMERS
COFFEE TABLES
DESKS
DESK TABLES
DROP LEAF TABLES
END TABLES
EXTENSION TABLES
FOLDING TOP CONSOLES
GATELEG TABLES

EXTENSION GATELEG TABLES
HUMIDORS
KIDNEY DESKS
LIVING ROOM TABLES
MARTHA WASHINGTON SEWING CABINETS
MIRRORS
NESTS OF TABLES
NESTS OF COFFEE TABLES
OCCASIONAL TABLES
OFFICE SUITES
PIER BOOKCASES
RADIO TABLES
REFECTORY TABLES
SERVERS
SEWING CABINETS
SEWING TABLES
SECRETARIES
STANDS
SECRETARY CABINETS
TABLETWO COMBINATION TABLES
TEA CARTS

TELEPHONE SETS
TELEPHONE DESK SETS
TELEPHONE STANDS
TILT TOP TABLES
WASTE BASKETS
WELSH CUPBOARDS
WELSH CABINETS
WALL DESKS

TRADE NAMES

"IMPERIAL TABLES" "IMPERIAL TABLETWO" "CERTIFIED TABLES"

WOODS AND FINISHES

The woods used in Imperial furniture include mahogany, walnut, oak, chestnut, maple, pine, gumwood, and various decorative woods such as hurawood, satinwood, Pollard oak, macassar ebony, etc. Each article of furniture carries a tag stating the woods used in its manufacture. Standard finishes are Tudor mahogany high lighted, Walnut high lighted, Brown mahogany not high lighted, Chestnut high lighted, Maple high lighted, Pine high lighted. Genuine water-proof lacquer finish.

CERTIFIED TABLES

Each piece of furniture shipped from the Imperial Factory carries a tag certifying to the woods used in its manufacture. This assists the store salesman and establishes the confidence of the customer in the goods.

CATALOG

An Imperial catalog is issued to dealers annually and a mid-year supplement, also. All Imperial dealers are supplied. ·

GENERAL INFORMATION

The Imperial Furniture Company has for many years enjoyed the reputation of being the *World's Greatest Table Makers*. The company is 25 years old and has grown consistently until it is now one of the largest of the Grand Rapids factories. It specializes on tables, and its Grand Rapids craftsmen have become expert table makers capable of high quality work. Its factory is an outstanding example in the industry of efficient production. Time-saving methods and specially designed machines are features. Large scale output and purchasing of materials enable exceptional values while strictly upholding standards of quality. In design and originality of ideas it has always been a leader. The trade has become accustomed to looking to Imperial at each market for the new ideas in living room furnishings.

IMPERIAL MAGAZINE ADVERTISING

The advertising of Imperial Tables has been carried on continuously in leading magazines for a period of many years, until Imperial Tables are the best known tables in America today. This makes Imperial an easy selling line, capable of quick turnover. The furniture store salesman should always point out the Imperial crown and green shield trademark on the furniture, because in most cases the customer will be familiar with it and it will make the sale easier.

IMPERIAL NEWSPAPER MAT SERVICE

Imperial furnishes dealers with an attractive newspaper ad mat showing the same furniture advertised in the magazines. Stores insert these ads in their newspapers at about the time the magazine advertising appears, thus connecting their stores with Imperial Tables directly. We also furnish mats of nearly every pattern in the Imperial line to dealers on request. Dealers should keep their mat files up-to-date with Imperial mats covering every piece on order or in stock.

IMPERIAL MESSENGER

The 16-page Messenger is issued monthly to dealers and the salesmen, and is filled with merchandising and advertising suggestions. It is one of the oldest and best known house organs in the trade.

SEMI-MONTHLY STOCK SHEET

Twice each month Imperial dealers are mailed a stock sheet showing just the condition for shipment of all patterns. By means of this the dealer can determine when numbers can be obtained. This will enable him to keep at all times a well-balanced assortment of Imperial merchandise on hand, and makes the Imperial one of his strongest merchandising lines.

No. 1670—Living Room Table, Five-ply laminated construction richly figured top with crotch mahogany veneer with burl maple border. Selected American gumwood base. Moulded rim and decorative base.

Selling Price $

LIVING ROOM TABLES

Although the popularity of the small table is steadily increasing, it has not displaced the need of the large living room table which exists in every home. The living room table, of impressive proportions and dignified character, is one of the principal articles of furnishing in the home, and must be of commendable design because of the conspicuous part it plays in the ensemble. Imperial has always given studious attention to the development of the living room table and its line embraces an extensive assortment of beautiful patterns covering the various woods and periods. The broad top of the large table affords opportunity for the artistic craftsman to arrange figured woods in striking effects.

OCCASIONAL TABLES

The occasional table has been developed into one of the most useful and decorative articles in the modern home. The classification is broad and embraces a wide variety of styles and designs. Today the properly furnished home must possess a number of small tables. Placed artistically at strategic points about the living room, they contribute much to its charm and attraction. Dainty tables are needed for books and magazines, for flowers and pottery, for games and writing, for smoking materials, for photographs and plants, for a hundred and one requirements in the modern home. And how beautiful they have become, with the grace and originality of design manifest by the designers of today, and the choice of so many rare and beautiful woods available. Imperial has given long study and thought to the development of the occasional table into varied delightful forms.

Selling Price $

No. 1466—Occasional Table, octagon shape top, 30x30 inches, richly figured crotch mahogany, butt walnut or Pollard oak veneered top with burl maple border and gumwood base.

Selling Price $

No. 1741—Table Desk. Five-ply figured mahogany or walnut veneer top, 26x48 inches. Veneered drawer fronts and table sides, gumwood posts and stretchers. Drawer overlays of maple burl. Double drawer in right hand pedestal.

TABLE DESKS

The Table Desk has been developed by Imperial to serve a double purpose in the home which has only a limited amount of space and yet which needs both a roomy table and a writing desk. In the Imperial line will be found a variety of handsome designs in different styles and woods, in which selected surfaces of rare figure are a prominent part of the enrichment.

(Continued on next page)

COTTAGE COLONIAL GROUP IN PINE

No. 1107—Desk with curious over-hanging top presumably to give the writer knee room.

Selling $
Price

This furniture has unusual attraction because of its quaint forms and the antique appearance of the wood. It will give a room marked individuality and distinction. The designs represent an interpretation of the Adam style by early Colonial craftsmen, who were accustomed, in their elementary way, to fashion their own creations from the inspiration derived from elegant Adam's originals which were brought across the sea by the wealthier colonists.

Pine was much used by the early furniture makers because it was near at hand, a domestic wood that was both workable and accessible. These

Imperial pieces have been skillfully made of Northern Pine to match the aged appearance of prized heirlooms found in the museums.

These Cottage Colonial pieces will interest people who seek to introduce original ideas in their home appointments. They are charming and old-fashioned, and refreshingly different from conventional types. The group includes an extension table, a buffet, two china cabinets, a book case, a secretary, a cabinet, a desk, an occasional table, an end table and a coffee table, side and arm chairs.

No. 1106—Secretary.
Selling $
Price

No. 87-C—Side Chair.
Selling $
Price

No. 1687—Octagon Table. Top, 36x36 inches, chestnut throughout with quaint antique finish and worn edge to give the appearance of age and use.

CHESTNUT FURNITURE

Chestnut pieces afford variety and interest in home furnishings. Chestnut is particularly appropriate for reproductions and adaptations of Early English styles as the broad grained wood can be treated to give the appearance of age and use. The Imperial Chestnut line consists of living room tables, occasional tables, end tables, book stands, chests, humidors, cellarettes, apartment groups and office suites. Some of the designs are modified reproductions of prized antiques in English homes and museums which have come down from the 16th and 17th centuries. These Imperial pieces show every indication of age. Parts are worn smooth as though from much use. The finish is rich and mellow. Their unique character makes them objects of interest in the home.

CONSOLE TABLES AND MIRRORS

Imperial offers the dealer one of the most varied assortments of console tables and mirrors in the trade. The line ranges from narrow consoles of the pedestal type with slender mirrors for between windows and under stairways, to tall and imposing sets for broad wall spaces and large halls. Only a small percentage of homes have consoles and mirrors, and the market is promising for the dealer who will develop it. The console and mirror is one of the most decorative articles of furniture available to the home.

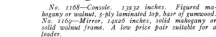

No. 1168—Console. 13x32 inches. Figured mahogany or walnut, 5-ply laminated top, base of gumwood. No. 1160—Mirror, 14x26 inches, solid mahogany or solid walnut frame. A low price pair suitable for a leader.

No. 721—Folding Top Console. Duncan Phyfe lyre design with leafage carving, richly figured mahogany veneer top and rails, balance solid mahogany.

FOLDING TOP CONSOLES

The folding top console may be used with or without a mirror to make a pleasing wall effect in the living room. The fold over leaf, when opened against the wall to show the beauty of its figured wood, is a conspicuous decorative touch. The Duncan Phyfe table at the left, with its octagon top and handsome lyre pedestal, indicates the decorative possibilities of this particular article of furniture.

(Continued on next page)

APARTMENT DINING GROUPS

Imperial groups for the small dining room range from the dignified and conservative type of design to the smartly original and unconventional. They are made in oak, chestnut, maple, mahogany and walnut veneers, and also decorated. The styles include various English and American motifs, including the Duncan Phyfe. The market for this type of dining room furniture of smaller dimensions is constantly growing, owing to the tendency to build smaller homes and an increasing number of apartments. The low price of these groups compared with conventional size dining furniture makes the Imperial Apartment Groups attractive to a wide market.

No. 91C—Dining Chair.

Selling $
Price

No. 452—China Cabinet. All flat surfaces veneered with stripe mahogany or walnut, balance of selected American gumwood.

Selling $
Price

No. 450—Extension Table. Top, 36x50 inches, extends six feet, selected mahogany or walnut, veneered top and fillers.

Selling $
Price

No. 91A—Dining Chair.

Selling $
Price

No. 451—Buffet. 19x56 inches. Top, front and ends of stripe mahogany or walnut veneer. Base of American gumwood. Silver tray in top drawer.

Selling $
Price

| Selling $
Price |
|---|

No. 429—Tabletwo. Closed, 22x50 inches, opened, 38x50 inches. Mahogany and gumwood or walnut and gumwood. Top and leaves are five-ply laminated with figured mahogany or walnut facing. Base of selected gumwood.

| Selling $
Price |
|---|

No. 88—Tea Wagon, with shelf and removable tray. When the leaves are raised it becomes a roomy luncheon table, 27x40 inches. Automatic leaf supports, artillery wheels, drop handle. Figured veneer of selected walnut or mahogany top. No. 88½ is the same design with a drawer.

IMPERIAL TABLETWO

The objection to the combination table has always been that its appearance is marred by the necessity of having the top divided in the center. No such objection prevails with the Imperial Tabletwo, which in appearance is a handsome living room table giving no hint of its dual purpose. Yet it can be enlarged in a moment to accommodate six people for dining. A hinged leaf is concealed under each side. These leaves can be raised by simply reaching under and touching the spring which releases them. They work on the same principle as the leaves of a gateleg table. Tabletwo thus does away with the need of removing things from the top of table to enlarge it. There are no separate leaves to lift in and out. Retail price range $36.00 to $150.00.

TEA CARTS

Years ago Imperial sponsored the tea cart and has always been foremost in its development. It perfected its mechanical efficiency, improved its design and made it a suitable article of furniture for any home, and then by immense production reduced its cost, putting it within the reach of the average home. Such features as the artillery wheel, the pivoted small wheel, the automatic leaf support, the removable tray, the disappearing handle, are traceable to Imperial inventive genius. Imperial's line embraces a wide variety of tea carts.

No. 1345—Extension Gateleg. Top, 48x48 inches; open, 48x72 inches. Handsome round top of richly figured mahogany or walnut veneer, beveled edge, eight graceful Colonial turned legs. Has three veneered fillers. Suitable either for dining table or extra large living room table. Mahogany and gumwood, or walnut and gumwood.

| Selling $
Price |
|---|

No. 1484—Oblong gateleg table with two drop leaves, 34x48 inches, suitable either for dining or living room table, or both in an apartment. One drawer. Top of choice mahogany or walnut veneer, balance gumwood.

| Selling $
Price |
|---|

IMPERIAL GATELEGS

The Imperial family of gatelegs has always been known for its leadership in design and price, and the quality has always been strictly maintained in a highly competitive field. Patterns range from the tiny gateleg for the corner to the big extension gateleg.

Tops are round, oval, oblong and octagonal. Imperial gatelegs are distinguished by more gracefully turned legs, shaped rims, thorough workmanship and beautiful veneers.

(Continued on next page)

TILT TOPS

The Imperial line of tilt tops consists of a delightful variation of graceful tops, round, oval and oblong, some with raised pie crust edge, others with various artistic shapings. The tops are made of either solid mahogany or choice mahogany and walnut veneers carefully selected for the exceptional character of the figure.

Selling Price $

No. 632—Tilt Top Table. Top, 28x28 inches, solid mahogany.

No. 1143—End Table. Top, 12x26 inches, mahogany and gumwood or walnut and gumwood. Figured top.

Selling Price $

END TABLES

Imperial makes an extensive line of end tables covering a wide range of designs and woods, with and without drawers and shelves. Some patterns have book troughs underneath, some have disappearing glass ash trays. End tables make suitable merchandise for leaders and specials, because of their low price and their usefulness in every home. The verage living room in fact could well accommodate two or three end tables, by the side of davenport and chair arms or by the wall.

BOOK TABLES

Imperial book tables and magazine stands embrace a variety of dainty designs, with numerous shelves and book troughs, and some with drawers. Included in the line are low price numbers suitable for specials.

Selling Price $

No. 1392—Book Table with unique double book trough, top, 16x30 inches, selected mahogany or walnut veneer, gumwood base.

Selling Price $

No. 1171—Nest of Tables. Top of largest table 16x26 inches. Made of selected mahogany or walnut veneered top, gumwood base, or hurawood veneered top and maple base.

TELEPHONE STANDS

Our line of telephone sets includes simple and inexpensive stands, decorative cabinets in which the instrument is entirely concealed, and roomy desks with chairs. Some of our more simple designs are admirable for specials and hour sales.

Selling Price $

No. 1176—Telephone Set. Top, 16x20 inches. Made of solid maple, posts turned from 2-inch stock. Shelf will accommodate three directories.

NESTS OF TABLES

Table Nests are entitled to a wider use in well arranged homes because of their great utility. The Imperial nests include a number of appealing designs in which figured veneers have been used with striking effect.

THE AMBASSADOR

This is Imperial office group No. 938. It will impart a distinguished appearance to an executive's environment. The Doric columns of ancient Greek architecture have been chosen as the keynote of the design. This furniture is made in walnut, with the employment of butts of rare figure to enrich the broad surfaces of the pieces.

IMPERIAL OFFICE GROUPS

A new and profitable field for sales and profits has developed for the furniture store—that of furnishing the business office. The man of affairs today realizes that it is a valuable asset to have his office create the proper impression of good taste and character.

Imperial has created a number of noteworthy suites of office furniture to enable the furniture merchant to obtain this profitable business. Besides THE AMBASSADOR pictured above, there is THE CHANCELLOR in choice American walnut, in which a modified Doric column and classic mouldings are employed as decorative details; THE LORD BACON, in both oak and walnut,

Pollard Oak of interesting figure and historic background being used for decorative purposes in the oak group; THE FROBISHER in chestnut, an Elizabethan design adapted from antiques giving a flavor of individuality and taste to the business office. Individual pieces such as desks of dignified design, imposing cabinets, humidors, costumers and waste baskets, are also shown in the Office Furniture catalog, which will be sent on request.

See pages 21 and 22 for illustrations and descriptions of other Imperial office suites.

THE KIEL FURNITURE COMPANY
Manufacturers of Living Room Tables
32nd and Center Streets, MILWAUKEE, WIS.

PRODUCTS

MANUFACTURERS OF

BENCHES, FIRESIDE
TABLES
—Center
—Coffee, Wood or Marble
    Tops
—Console, Wood or
    Wrought Iron
—Davenport, Wood or
    Wrought Iron
—Davenport, Extension
—Desk Type

TABLES
—Dining Room and Living
    Room Combination
—Direcots
—End, Wood or Wrought
    Iron
—Flip Top
—Library
—Odd and Occasional
—Pie Crust Tilt Top
—Tilt Top
TELEPHONE SETS

Reg. Trade Mark

Striking full-page advertisements read by millions of subscribers to the most powerful magazines, make the Kiel Trademark a sure source of profits for you.

TRADE MARK

Every Kiel Table is trade marked as a guarantee of quality and service. Underneath each table the trade mark is branded into the top. Each table is further identified by an attractive tag with provision for your stock number and price.

NATIONALLY ADVERTISED

Kiel Tables are nationally advertised and intensively merchandised. Full page and half page advertisements will be used throughout the year in such leading publications as the *Ladies' Home Journal* and the *Saturday Evening Post*. This advertising is prestige and inquiry-creating of the most productive character. You get full advantage of this advertising.

CONSTRUCTION OF "KIEL" TABLES

All tables are constructed of veneered stock in combination with genuine American gumwood and other hardwoods, except those designated as "Solid" or "Badger." All veneered tops are of 5-ply construction, insuring the best lasting results.

No. 4570—Wall Cabinet. Mahogany veneer front, top and sides. Size, 36 inches wide, 60 inches high. Finish: English Antique Mahogany. Approximate shipping weight, S. C., 125 lbs.

WALL CABINETS

Wall cabinets and writing desks range from $50 to $100, subject to change without notice. There are eight new desks and cabinets in our 1928 line.

WOODS AND FINISHES

Finishes in which Kiel Tables are available are as follows:

English Antique Walnut
Badger Butt Walnut
Badger Brown Mahogany, Two-Tone

Each illustration has the finish in which it is available printed beneath it.

"Badger"—A name adopted by us many years ago as indicating an imitation finish. These pieces are made of solid gumwood and the finish is built up just as carefully as though solid mahogany or butt walnut were being used. Kiel's "Badger finish" in mahogany is famous as being exceptionally fine and our newest finish. "Badger" butt walnut is unmatched for its faithful reproduction of the genuine.

Special Finishes—On orders for special finishes there is a charge of 10% above the list price and such orders are not subject to cancellation.

KIEL STYLES BRING PRESTIGE AND PROFIT

Your customers are learning the importance of the right table in the right place. Striking full-page advertisements like the one reproduced on the opposite page make them realize their homes are table shy. They want the distinctive beauty and exquisite style we build into Kiel tables.

You need these famous tables in your store. They bring both prestige and profits with them. Designs range from the highly decorative to simpler ones in a wide variety of styles.

Here is a representative group of eighteen Kiel tables. Show them on your floors and in your windows. You'll get a good fast turnover.

Merchandising Plans and the material to make them completely successful are furnished to every Kiel dealer. This makes it easy for you to tie up to the powerful "Table Shy" Campaign.

Keep our catalog always at hand. Complete stocks are warehoused conveniently. Tables are shipped K. D. to cut Freight costs.

No. 7001—End Table. Size, 26x12 inches. Genuine, 5-ply, Walnut veneer top. Finish: English Antique Walnut. Approximate shipping weight, S. C., 40 lbs.

No. 4589—Drop Leaf End Table. (With Drawer.) Size closed, 10x14 inches. Open, 33x14 inches. Finish: English Antique Mahogany. Approximate shipping weight, S. C., 45 lbs. Shipped set up.

No. 7000—End Table. Size 26x12 inches. Genuine, 5-ply Mahogany veneered Top. Finish: English Antique Mahogany. Approximate shipping weight, S. C., 40 lbs. Shipped set up.

No. 4501—End Table. Size, 24x12 inches. Height, 26 inches. Finish: Badger Butt Walnut. Approximate shipping weight, D. C., 35 lbs., S. C., 20 lbs.

END TABLES

Twenty-three end tables including Drop Leaf and Butterfly types ranging in resale price from $6 to $50, subject to change without notice.

(Continued on next page)

No. 4420¼—End Table. Size, 28x14 inches. Height, 26 inches. Genuine, Butt Walnut veneer top. Finish: English Antique Walnut. Approximate shipping weight, D. C., 80 lbs., S. C., 45 lbs.

No. 4535¼—End Table. Size, 24x14 inches. Height, 26 inches. Genuine, 5-ply, Hand Matched, Butt Walnut top with Curly Maple Banded edge. Marquetry inlay on rail. Finish: English Antique Walnut. Approximate shipping weight, S. C., 43 lbs. Shipped set up.

No. 4503—Console Table. Size, 28x13 inches. Height, 31 inches. Genuine, 5-ply, Figured Walnut veneer top. Overlay of Bird's Eye Maple on rail. Finish: English Antique Walnut. Approximate shipping weight, S. C., 40 lbs.

No. 4501—Console Table. Size, 20x10 inches. Height, 31 inches. Genuine, 5-ply, Matched Butt Walnut top. Finish: English Antique Walnut. Approximate shipping weight, S. C., 35 lbs.

No. 4505—Console Table (with Drawer). Genuine, 5-ply, Mottled Mahogany veneer top and rail. Finish: English Antique Mahogany. Approximate shipping weight, S. C., 50 lbs.

CONSOLE TABLES

Fourteen approved patterns in Console Tables for you to choose from. These sell to your trade from $10 to $40, subject to change without notice.

No. 4582—Magazine Trough End
Table. Size, 26x14 inches. Genuine,
5-ply, Butt Walnut veneer top. Panels
are 5-ply, Walnut veneer. Finish:
English Antique Walnut. Approximate
shipping weight, S.C., 40 lbs. Shipped
set up.

MAGAZINE TROUGH END TABLES

Range in Retail Price from $10 to $50, subject to change without notice.

No. 5004—Occasional Table (All
Walnut). Size, 35x28 inches. Top is
four-piece Matched English Oak Swirl
veneer. Madrone Burl veneer on rail.
Finish: English Antique Walnut. Approximate shipping weight, S. C., 90
lbs. Shipped set up.

No. 4624—Occasional Table. Size,
30x30 inches. Genuine, 5-ply Hand
Matched Walnut top with Ebony inlay.
Finish· English Antique Walnut. Approximate shipping weight, S.C., 85 lbs.

OCCASIONAL TABLES

Thirty-eight designs in occasional tables comprise this year's line of occasional tables. Retail Prices range from $15 to $100, subject to change without notice.

(Continued on next page)

No. 4614—Occasional Table. Size, 30x30, inches. Finish: Badger Butt Walnut. Approximate shipping weight S. C., 70 lbs. Shipped set up.

No. 4623—Occasional Table. Size, 30x30 inches. Genuine, 5-ply, Hand Matched Butt Walnut. Finish: English Antique Walnut. Walnut top. Approximate shipping weight, S. C., 85 lbs.

No. 5000—Occasional Table. Size, 30x30 inches. Genuine, 5-ply, Hand Matched Butt Walnut veneer top. Finish: English Antique Walnut. Approximate shipping weight, S. C., 70 lbs. Shipped set up.

No. 5005—Occasional Table. Size, 30x30 inches. Top is 6-piece Matched Butt Walnut. Finish: English Antique Walnut. Approximate shipping weight, S. C., 70 lbs. Shipped set up.

No. 5006—(All Mahogany) Occasional Table. Size, 28x28 inches. Top is Hand Matched Fauxsatine with Fiddleback Mahogany Banding. Finish: English Antique Mahogany. Approximate shipping weight, S. C., 70 lbs. Shipped set up.

No. 5002—Occasional Table. Size, 30x30 inches. Genuine 5-ply Butt Walnut veneer top. Finish: English Antique Walnut. Approximate shipping weight, S. C., 80 lbs. Shipped set up.

No. 4538—Occasional Table. Size, 30x30 inches. Genuine, Hand Matched, Butt Walnut. Veneer top with Curly, Maple Banded edge. Finish: English Antique Walnut. Approximate shipping weight, S. C., 100 lbs. Shipped set up.

No. 5001—Occasional Table. Size, 30x30 inches. Genuine 5-ply Butt Walnut veneer. Walnut veneer shelf. Finish: English Antique Walnut. Approximate shipping weight, S. C., 70 lbs. Shipped set up.

(Continued on next page)

No. 5007—Occasional Table. Size, 34x22 inches. Hand Matched Brazilian Rosewood top. Finish: English Antique Walnut. Approximate shipping weight, S. C., 90 lbs. Shipped set up.

No. 1003—Davenport Table. Size, 44x16 inches. 5-ply, Mahogany veneer top, Curly Maple on rail. Finish: English Antique Mahogany. Approximate shipping weight, D. C., 110 lbs., S. C., 70 lbs.

No. 4616—Davenport Table. Size, 54x18 inches. Genuine, 5-ply, Mahogany veneer top. Bird's-Eye Overlay on stretcher. Finish: English Antique Mahogany. Approximate shipping weight, D. C., 120 lbs., S. C., 70 lbs.

No. 4530—Davenport Table. Size, 46x18 inches. Finish: Badger Butt Walnut. Approximate shipping weight, D. C., 110 lbs., S. C., 70 lbs.

DAVENPORT TABLES

Line consists of seventy-one numbers ranging in retail selling price from $14 to $100, subject to change without notice.

No. 4445—Davenport Table. Size, 48x18 inches. Genuine, 5-ply, Mahogany veneer top. Finish: English Antique Mahogany. Approximate shipping weight, D. C., 100 lbs., S. C., 65 lbs.

No. 4438—Davenport Table. Size, 44x18 inches. Finish: Badger Brown Mahogany. Two-tone. Approximate shipping weight, D. C., 110 lbs., S. C., 60 lbs.

No. 4527—Davenport Table. Size, 60x20 inches. Genuine, 5-ply, Butt Walnut veneer top. Finish: English Antique Walnut. Approximate shipping weight, D. C., 180 lbs., S. C., 110 lbs.

DAVENPORT EXTENSION TABLES

This attractive line of tables ranges in price from $30.00 to $140.00, subject to change without notice.

No. 1005—Davenport Table. Size, 48x18 inches. 5-ply, Mahogany veneer top. Finish: English Antique Mahogany. Approximate shipping weight, D. C., 115 lbs., S. C., 75 lbs.

THE MERSMAN BROS. CORPORATION

Manufacturers of Tables

Main Offices and Factory, CELINA, OHIO

PERMANENT EXHIBIT AND SALES ROOMS

NEW YORK—206 Lexington Ave., Between 32nd and 33rd Streets Spaces 1213-1215. In charge of M. I. Miller. Telephone Caledonia 7332.

BOSTON—112 Canal Street. In charge of Warren T. Simpson.

CHICAGO—9th Floor, American Furniture Mart, 666 Lake Shore Drive. In charge of A. Hallenstein.

HIGH POINT—Southern Furniture Exposition. In charge of H. D. Martin whose permanent address is 216 S. Mendenhall St., Greensboro, N. C.

SAN FRANCISCO—San Francisco Furniture Exchange, 947 Brannan St., San Francisco, Cal. Care of Myers & Schwartz.

MINNEAPOLIS—Furniture Sales Company.

WAREHOUSES

Main Office for Warehouse in New York City, N. Y. M. I. Miller, 206 Lexington Ave., Space 1213-15, New York City, N. Y. (Warehouse located in New York City.)

Warehouse in Kansas City, Mo. Minturn Bros., 1302 Union Ave., Kansas City, Mo.

Warehouse in Milwaukee, Wis. Lahl & Kidney, 315 E. Water St., Milwaukee, Wis.

Main Office for Warehouse in Chicago, Ill. A. Hallenstein, 666 Lake Shore Drive, Chicago, Ill., 9th Floor, Space 924.

Warehouse in San Francisco, Cal. Myers & Schwartz, 947 Brannan St., San Francisco, Cal.

Warehouse in Boston, Mass. W. T. Simpson, 112 Canal St., 6th Floor, Boston, Mass.

Warehouse in Los Angeles, Cal. Myers & Schwartz, 1207-11 E. 6th St., Los Angeles, Cal.

Warehouse in Minneapolis, Minn. Furniture Sales Co., 718 Central Ave., Minneapolis, Minn.

PRODUCTS
MANUFACTURERS OF

TABLES	TABLES
—Library	—Consoles with or
—Davenport	without mirrors
—Davenport	—Gate Leg
Extension	—Decorated
—End	—Coffee
—Occasional	—Radio Table Cabinets

GENERAL INFORMATION

Our tables are designed to meet the demand in popular, medium and fine grades. We operate under one of the largest production schedules in the country and it has been our constant aim to bring prices down while maintaining thoroughly dependable grades. We were among the first to subscribe to the government code of honest listing of woods and finishes, on which basis are all the listings on the following pages. All prices shown are subject to change without notice.

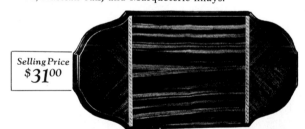

Mersman Tables

Trade Mark

WOODS AND FINISHES

All table tops are of five-ply construction, cross-banded to prevent warping. Genuine woods and any imitations used are truly listed in each case. Finishes and coloring accord with prevailing fashion and in many cases rich wood veneers in great variety are combined to give colorful effects on table tops. Among the woods most used for table top veneers and trims are: brown mahogany, plain, burl, rotary cut and butt jointed walnut, rosewood, blistered maple, birds-eye maple, zebra veneers, ebony, redwood burls, satinwood, Russian oak, and Marqueterie inlays.

Selling Price $31.00

No. 4001—Davenport Table. Brown mahogany, dull finish. Top, 18x48 inches. 5-ply genuine mahogany, Marqueterie inlay and blue rosewood veneered top. Center panel and stretcher bracket rosewood veneered. Rails, mahogany veneered. Base, selected gum, mahogany finish. Weight: One in a crate, 70 lbs.; two in crate, 120 lbs.

Selling Price $39.50

No. 988—End Table. Walnut dull Finish. Top, 14x28 inches. One drawer. 5-ply genuine ebony, Marqueterie inlay and rosewood veneered top. Drawer front and false drawer front veneered, rosewood finished end rails, butt walnut veneered. Stretcher, walnut veneered. Legs, selected gum, walnut finish. Height, 25 inches. Weight: One in crate, 25 lbs.

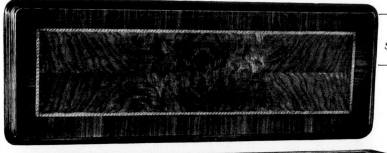

Selling Price
$65⁵⁰

No. 995—Davenport Table. Walnut, dull finish. Top, 22x60 inches. One drawer is within top. Five-ply genuine butt joint walnut, marqueterie inlay and rosewood veneered top. Drawer front and false drawer front, butt walnut veneered. Stretcher ornament, rosewood veneered. Ends and stretcher, selected gum, walnut finish. Weights: One in crate, 85 lbs.; two in crate, 140 lbs. This table is also made as a Davenport Extension Table, style No. 4028.

GUARANTEE

The following liberal guarantee applies to every table we manufacture: "This table is inspected during each manufacturing process and also before crating for shipment,—but if, at any time, defects in material or workmanship should develop, we will furnish a new table without charge." We unqualifiedly stand back of every item we manufacture.

DAVENPORT TABLES

On this and the preceding page, we have illustrated four patterns in Davenport Tables out of a line that embraces 139 different numbers. A representative showing of Davenport Extension Tables is included also.

Retail Price Range—*$12.00 to $80.00.*

GATELEG, RADIO, AND COFFEE TABLES

While not pictured in the Reference Book, because of lack of room, we manufacture a very attractive collection of Gate Leg Tables and a limited line of Radio and Coffee Tables. On Gate Legs, the

Retail Price Range—*$18.50 to $55.50.*

(Continued on next page)

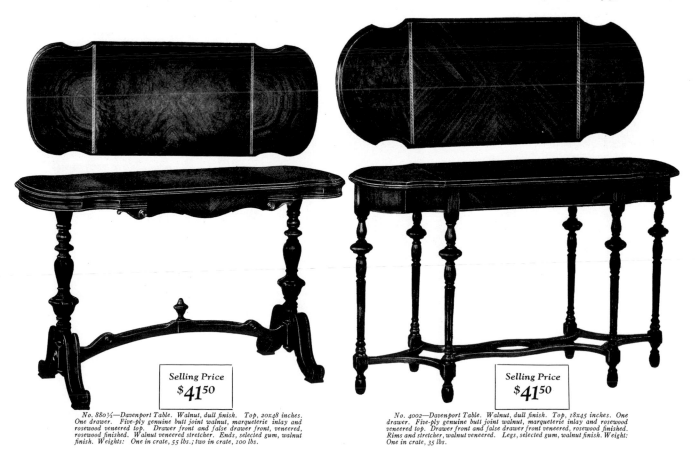

Selling Price
$41⁵⁰

No. 880¼—Davenport Table. Walnut, dull finish. Top, 20x48 inches. One drawer. Five-ply genuine butt joint walnut, marqueterie inlay and rosewood veneered top. Drawer front and false drawer front, veneered, rosewood finished. Walnut veneered stretcher. Ends, selected gum, walnut finish. Weights: One in crate, 55 lbs.; two in crate, 100 lbs.

Selling Price
$41⁵⁰

No. 4002—Davenport Table. Walnut, dull finish. Top, 18x45 inches. One drawer. Five-ply genuine butt joint walnut, marqueterie inlay and rosewood veneered top. Drawer front and false drawer front veneered, rosewood finished. Rims and stretcher, walnut veneered. Legs, selected gum, walnut finish. Weight: One in crate, 35 lbs.

OCCASIONAL TABLES

Merchants who are alert to sales possibilities have discovered an ever growing market in Occasionals. Nearly every home in America is a prospect for this class of furniture. As this book goes to press, we are producing 51 different patterns and are continually bringing out new, fast-selling designs.

Retail Price Range—*$13.00 to $66.00.*

Selling Price
$4550

No. 4004½—Occasional Table. Walnut, dull finish. Top, 30x30 inches. Five-ply genuine butt joint walnut veneered top. Rails and stretcher, walnut veneered. Legs and turnings, selected gum, walnut finish. Height, 30 inches. Weights: One in crate, 55 lbs.; two in crate, 100 lbs.

Selling Price
$5500

No. 970—Occasional Table. Walnut, dull finish. Top, 32x32 inches. Five-ply genuine mahogany veneered top, amber finished, with 5-ply genuine butt joint walnut center and marqueterie inlay. Rails veneered, rosewood finished Burl walnut veneered ends. Walnut veneered end stretchers. Base, selected gum, walnut finish. Height, 30 inches. Weights: One in crate, 60 lbs.; two in crate, 110 lbs.

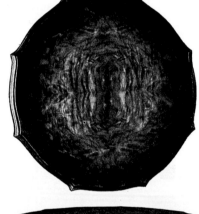

Selling Price
$2550

No. 965½—Occasional Table. Walnut, dull finish. Top, 28x28 inches. Five-ply genuine butt joint walnut veneered top. Walnut veneered stretcher. Legs, selected gum, walnut finish. Height, 27 inches. Weights: One in crate, 45 lbs.; two in crate, 80 lbs.

Selling Price
$3550

No. 979—Occasional Table. Walnut, dull finish. Top, 28x28 inches. Five-ply genuine butt joint walnut, marqueterie inlay and rosewood veneered top. Stretcher, walnut veneered. Legs, selected gum, walnut finish. Height, 30 inches. Weight: One in crate, 35 lbs.

Selling Price
$5100

No. 960—Occasional Table. Walnut, dull finish. Top, 30x30 inches. Five-ply genuine butt joint walnut, marqueterie inlay and Russian oak veneered top. Rails and stretcher, walnut veneered. Legs, selected gum, walnut finish. Height, 30 inches. Weights: One in crate, 55 lbs.; two in crate, 100 lbs.

CONSOLE TABLES

17 Patterns in Consoles give the dealer wide choice of designs. These tables are offered with or without harmonizing mirrors. **Retail Price Range**—*$7.50 to $33.50* (without mirrors).

Descriptions

No. 16—Mirror. Plate, 16x26 inches. No. 876—Console Table. Brown mahogany, dull finish. Top, 15x34 inches. Five-ply genuine mahogany veneered top. Front and back panel, center panel and stretcher, overlay Zebra veneer. Legs, selected gum, mahogany finish. Height, 30 inches. Weight: One in crate, 35 lbs.

No. 15—Mirror. Plate, 16x26 inches. No. 989—Console Table. Brown mahogany, dull finish. Top, 13x28 inches. Five-ply genuine mahogany veneered top. Front rail veneered, rosewood finished. Brackets, mahogany veneered. Base, selected gum, mahogany finish. Height, 30 inches. Weight: One in crate, 20 lbs.

No. 980—Console Table. Walnut, dull finish. Top, 16x38 inches. Five-ply genuine butt joint walnut, marqueterie inlay and ebony veneered top. Stretchers, walnut veneered. Legs, selected gum, walnut finish. Height, 30 inches. Weight: One in crate, 30 lbs.

No. 975—Console Table. Walnut, dull finish. Top, 16x36 inches. Five-ply genuine butt joint walnut and rosewood veneered top. Rails, rosewood veneered. Base, selected gum, walnut finish. Height, 30 inches. Weight: One in crate, 40 lbs.

(Continued on next page)

No. 16 Mirror
No. 876 Console Table
Selling Price Without Mirror $25⁵⁰

No. 15 Mirror
No. 989 Console Table
Selling Price $16⁰⁰ Without Mirror

No. 975 Console Table
Selling Price $33⁵⁰

No. 980 Console Table
Selling Price $32⁵⁰

END TABLES

End Tables, like Occasionals, can be counted on to produce many extra sales. They "fit in" most acceptably in the modern scheme of home decoration. 32 Patterns in a wide variety of designs and woods.

Retail Price Range—*$5.00 to $37.00.*

Selling Price $22⁵⁰

No. 906—End Table. Brown mahogany, dull finish. Top, 14x24 inches. One drawer. Five-ply genuine mahogany veneered top. Drawer front, walnut and Zebra veneered. Base, selected gum, mahogany finish. Height, 24 inches. Weight: One in crate, 25 lbs.

Selling Price $19⁰⁰

No. 987—End Table. Walnut, dull finish. Top, 13x28 inches. Five-ply genuine butt joint walnut, marqueterie inlay and rosewood veneered top. Front rails and scrolls, walnut veneered. Legs and base, selected gum, walnut finish. Height, 25 inches. Weight: One in crate, 20 lbs.

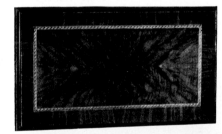

Selling Price $14⁵⁰

No. 900—End Table. Brown mahogany, dull finish. Top, 13x28 inches. Five-ply genuine mahogany veneered top. Front panel veneered, rosewood finished. Legs and stretchers, selected gum, mahogany finish. Height, 25 inches. Weight: One in crate, 20 lbs.; two in crate, 35 lbs.

Selling Price $37⁰⁰

No. 978—End Table. Walnut, dull finish. Top, 15x28 inches. One drawer. Five-ply genuine butt joint walnut, marqueterie inlay and rosewood veneered top. Front and back rails veneered, rosewood finish. End rails, aprons, ends and shelf, walnut veneered. Height, 25 inches. Weights: One in crate, 45 lbs.; two in crate, 85 lbs.

Selling Price $25⁰⁰

No. 977—End Table. Walnut, dull finish. Top, 13x28 inches. Five-ply genuine butt joint walnut, marqueterie inlay and rosewood veneered top. Scroll and base, walnut veneered. Height, 25 inches. Weight: One in crate, 30 lbs.

NEWSPAPER CUT SERVICE ON MERSMAN TABLES

The dealer who stocks Mersman Tables can have newspaper illustrations on any or all of these tables, upon request. Mats or electros, as may be desired, are furnished without cost. Furthermore, we are always glad to make suggestions for special sales or other special advertising.

Immediately below we show the style of illustrations provided.

By comparison it will be seen that these are the same numbers as those catalogued on the preceding page. We do not hamper the dealer in the use of these cuts by attaching a trade-mark but have executed the illustrations in a style and size most used in the average store's advertising. The pattern number and top size that appear under each cut are for reference only and are not a part of the electro or mat furnished.

No. 900
Top, 13 inches x 48 inches

No. 906
Top, 14 inches x 24 inches

No. 987
Top, 13 inches x 28 inches

No. 978
Top, 15 inches x 28 inches

No. 977
Top, 13 inches x 48 inches

HOW WE ARE HELPING FURNITURE MERCHANTS TO INCREASE BUSINESS IN EVERY DEPARTMENT OF THEIR STORES

Some two years ago, we came to the conclusion that the manufacturer might do many things to boost the furniture business generally that no furniture dealer could readily undertake on his own hook. We might call our attitude "enlightened selfishness." The retailer's welfare is our welfare. If we can help him succeed, then we will reap a great success ourselves. If we can help him sell more dining room suites or more rugs or more refrigerators, his added sales will be reflected back to us by increased sales in tables, also. If we can show a merchant a better system of collections than he now uses, his store will enjoy greater prosperity. If we can offer any valuable hints to the retail salesmen of this country, the net result will be favorable to the furniture industry.

That is why we came to issue "The Mersman Idea Book," which is now in the hands of more than three thousand furniture retailers,—a service that is supplemented by many new bulletins monthly.

This Idea Book is a loose-leaf bulletin service, planned to help retailers in all departments of the modern furniture store. We make no attempt to promote the sale of tables, particularly. Sales and merchandising plans are presented, also information of value to retail salesmen, notes relative to accounting and record systems, newspaper advertising introductories, letter campaigns, etc., etc.

This service is freely offered to all who want it, providing the firms are our customers. There are no strings to this offer, no stipulations that a certain volume of orders must be placed, no obligation whatever.

If you want The Idea Book, providing of course you are not already receiving it, be sure to request this item when placing an order for tables.

Aside from these regular services, our organization is pleased to co-operate with the trade in any and every way that is proper and practical. Many retailers write outlining their local trade problems and in reply our service bureau makes merchandising recommendations and, when feasible, prepares individual sales and advertising campaigns. We have evidence that our efforts have often been of considerable value.

The Mersman organization is engaged in making good tables at the right price; in backing this product to the limit, and in supporting its dealers in the sale of this merchandise. On this foundation of dependable tables and outstanding service, we base our bid for your patronage.

A complete catalog of the Mersman Line will be sent anywhere on request.

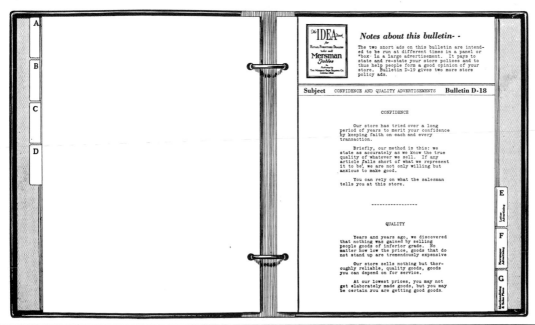

Sample page from the Mersman Idea Book showing the indexed binder that is furnished with this service.

PHOENIX CHAIR COMPANY

"BUSY SINCE 1875"

Manufacturers of Chairs, Rockers, Tables,
and Complete Suites for Breakfast and Apartment Dining Rooms

SHEBOYGAN, WIS.

PERMANENT DISPLAYS

CHICAGO, ILL., American Furniture Mart   SHEBOYGAN, WIS., at Factory

---

PRODUCTS

MANUFACTURERS OF

APARTMENT AND DINING ROOM SUITES
BREAKFAST ROOM SUITES
—Tudor Duplex Tables   —China Cupboards
—Equalizer Tables   —Buffets
—Drop Leaf Tables   —Chairs

CHAIRS AND ROCKERS, Upholstered

—Occasional Chairs   —Fireside Chairs   —Bedroom Chairs
—Hall Chairs   —Coxwell Chairs   —Slipper Chairs

Trade Mark

CHAIRS AND ROCKERS, Wood Seat
—Windsors   —Juvenile
—Desk   —Rockers—Oak
—High Chairs

HOTEL CHAIRS AND TABLES

TRADE NAME

"TUDOR-DUPLEX"—the table that opens and closes like a drawer. Patented March 29, 1927.   U. S. Letters Patent 1622544.   Other Patents Pending.

(Continued on next page)

Home of the Phoenix Chair Co., Sheboygan, Wis.
Largest Chair Factory in the World Under One Roof

No. 772-14

No. 772 XT—Height, 30 inches. Top closed, 32 by 42 inches. Top extended, 32 by 70 inches.

No. 772 DLT—Height, 30 inches. Top closed, 38 by 23 inches. Top open, 38 by 42 inches.

No. 772-14

SOLID OAK SUITES

Are always in demand.   *Finished:* Acorn Walnut
London Smoke
Salmon

No. 773-14

No. 773XT—Top closed, 32 by 42 inches. Top extended, 32 by 70 inches. Height, 30 inches.

No. 773-14

No. 773DLT—Top closed, 38 by 24 inches. Top open, 38 by 42 inches. Height, 30 inches.

Solid Oak. Finished Ash Grey, Seal Brown or Fawn.

RELIABLE AND QUICK SELLING
BREAKFAST ROOM SUITES

(Continued on next page)

PHOENIX CHAIR COMPANY

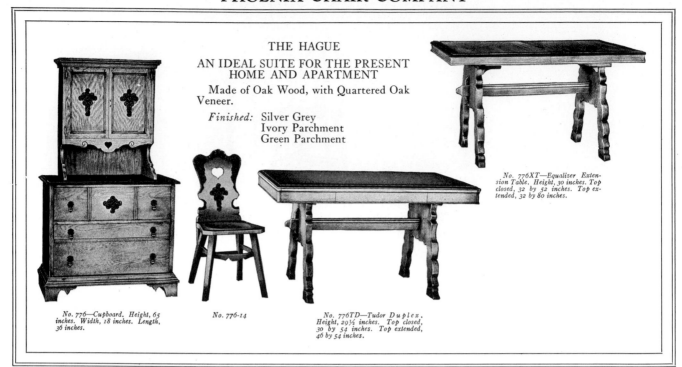

THE HAGUE
AN IDEAL SUITE FOR THE PRESENT HOME AND APARTMENT

Made of Oak Wood, with Quartered Oak Veneer.

Finished: Silver Grey
Ivory Parchment
Green Parchment

No. 776XT—Equalizer Extension Table. Height, 30 inches. Top closed, 32 by 52 inches. Top extended, 32 by 80 inches.

No. 776—Cupboard. Height, 65 inches. Width, 18 inches. Length, 36 inches.

No. 776-14

No. 776TD—Tudor Duplex. Height, 29½ inches. Top closed, 30 by 54 inches. Top extended, 46 by 54 inches.

No. 779TD—Tudor Duplex. Height, 29½ inches. Top closed, 30 by 54 inches. Top extended, 46 by 54 inches.

Note the sectional Silver Drawer which does not interfere with the opening and closing of the table.

Patented March 29, 1927. U. S. Letters Patent 1622544. Other Patents Pending.

THE FLAMINGO

Made of Birch Wood, with Curly Maple Veneer.

Finished: Ivory Parchment
Green Parchment
Walnut

No. 779-38

No. 779C—Cabinet. Height, 70 inches. Width, 18 inches. Length, 34½ inches.

No. 779XT—Equalizer Extension Table. Height, 30 inches. Top closed, 32 by 52 inches. Top extended, 32 by 80 inches.

No. 779B—Buffet. Height, 38 inches. Width, 18 inches. Length, 59 inches.

No. 779-18

No. 742-14

No. 742XT—Equalizer Extension Table.
Height, 30 inches. Top closed, 32 by 42
inches. Top extended, 32 by 70 inches.

No. 742-14

No. 742DLT—Drop Leaf Table. Height,
30 inches. Top closed, 38 by 26 inches.
Top open, 38 by 48 inches.

ATTRACTIVELY DESIGNED AND STURDILY CONSTRUCTED

Made of Select Birch.
Finished: Violet Shaded or rich Mahogany.

THE PHOENIX "TUDOR DUPLEX" DINETTE-APARTMENT SUITE IS ATTRACTING UNUSUAL ATTENTION WHEREVER IT IS SHOWN

It is graceful, beautifully proportioned and skillfully executed in every detail; it will appeal to the most discriminating tastes.

A slight outward pull on either side of the Table and automatically two hidden leaves are added to the one-piece top.

No. 742TD—Open View

Fully covered by United States Patent 1622544, dated March 29, 1927.

"Opens and closes like a drawer." Made of Birch Wood, with Birch Veneer Table Top. Finished: Shaded Violet, or Mahogany, decorated.

No. 742-14

No. 742C — Cupboard.
Height, 54 inches. Width,
18 inches. Length, 38
inches.

No. 742TD—T u d o r Duplex.
Height, 29½ inches. Top closed,
30 by 54 inches. Top open, 46 by
54 inches.

No. 742B—Buffet.
Height, 30 inches.
Width, 18 inches.
Length, 38 inches.

(Continued on next page)

46 by 54 inches Open

No. 763-14

No. 763TD—30 by 54 inches Closed

No. 763C—Height, 72 inches. Width, 17 inches. Length, 34½ inches.

THE MANCHESTER

Made of Birch Wood, with Genuine Mahogany or Walnut Veneer.
Finish: Mahogany or Walnut Hi-lighted.

Place a trial order and convince yourself of the true merits of this beautiful suite.

No. 762C—Cupboard. Height, 72 inches. Width, 18 inches. Length, 48 inches.

No. 762-17—Chair

No. 762TD—Table. 46 by 54 inches open; 30 by 54 inches closed.

THE DUNCAN PHYFE

Made of Birch Wood, with Genuine Mahogany Veneer and Rosewood Overlay.
Finish: Mahogany Hi-lighted.

No. 777C—Height, 64 inches.
Width, 36 inches. Depth, 18 inches.

No. 777-14

No. 777TD—Tudor Duplex. 46 by 54 inches open;
30 by 54 inches closed.

THE NORMANDY

Made of Birch Wood, with Curly Birch Veneer.

Finish: Old Maple, Walnut, or Orange Parchment, decorated.

No. 774XT — Equalizer Extension Table.
Height, 30 inches. Top closed, 32 by 42 inches.
Top extended, 32 by 70 inches.

No. 774DLT—Drop Leaf Table.
Height, 30 inches. Top closed, 38 by 24 inches. Top open, 38 by 48 inches.

The Equalizer and Drop Leaf Tables are made of solid oak.

No. 774C—Height, 56 inches.
Width, 17 inches. Length, 36 inches.

No. 774-14

No. 774TD—30 by 54 inches closed; 46 by 54 inches open.

THE SEVILLE

Made of Oak Wood, with Quartered Oak Veneer.

Finish: Pearl Grey or Baronial Oak, decorated.

(Continued on next page)

No. 777—Cupboard is illustrated on the preceding page.

No. 777-14

No. 777XT—Equalizer Extension Table. Height, 30 inches. Top closed, 32 by 52 inches. Top extended, 32 by 80 inches.

Finish: Old Maple, Walnut or Orange
Parchment, decorated.

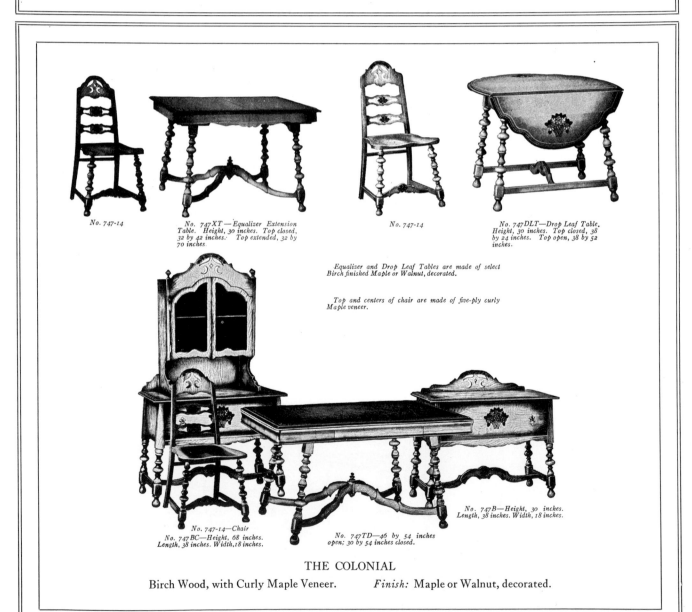

No. 747-14

No. 747XT—Equalizer Extension Table. Height, 30 inches. Top closed, 32 by 42 inches. Top extended, 32 by 70 inches.

No. 747-14

No. 747DLT—Drop Leaf Table. Height, 30 inches. Top closed, 38 by 24 inches. Top open, 38 by 52 inches.

Equalizer and Drop Leaf Tables are made of select Birch finished Maple or Walnut, decorated.

Top and centers of chair are made of five-ply curly Maple veneer.

No. 747-14—Chair

No. 747BC—Height, 68 inches. Length, 38 inches. Width, 18 inches.

No. 747TD—46 by 54 inches open; 30 by 54 inches closed.

No. 747B—Height, 30 inches. Length, 38 inches. Width, 18 inches.

THE COLONIAL

Birch Wood, with Curly Maple Veneer.   *Finish:* Maple or Walnut, decorated.

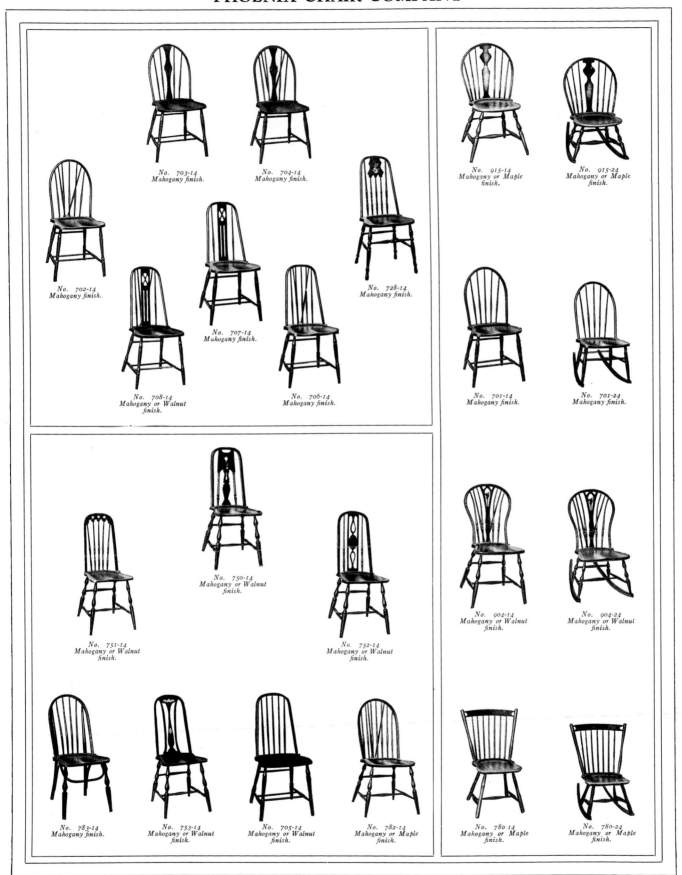

No. 703-14
Mahogany finish.

No. 704-14
Mahogany finish.

No. 702-14
Mahogany finish.

No. 707-14
Mahogany finish.

No. 728-14
Mahogany finish.

No. 708-14
Mahogany or Walnut
finish.

No. 706-14
Mahogany finish.

No. 915-14
Mahogany or Maple
finish.

No. 915-24
Mahogany or Maple
finish.

No. 701-14
Mahogany finish.

No. 701-24
Mahogany finish.

No. 750-14
Mahogany or Walnut
finish.

No. 751-14
Mahogany or Walnut
finish.

No. 752-14
Mahogany or Walnut
finish.

No. 904-14
Mahogany or Walnut
finish.

No. 904-24
Mahogany or Walnut
finish.

No. 783-14
Mahogany finish.

No. 753-14
Mahogany or Walnut
finish.

No. 705-14
Mahogany or Walnut
finish.

No. 782-14
Mahogany or Maple
finish.

No. 780-14
Mahogany or Maple
finish.

No. 780-24
Mahogany or Maple
finish.

CHAIRS SUITABLE FOR THE DESK, BEDROOM, OR THE ODD CORNER

(Continued on next page)

PHOENIX CHAIR COMPANY

No. 156—Elm Gloss

No. 35—Elm Gloss

Nos. 35 and 156 are reinforced with Steel Rods.

No. 2-14—Elm Gloss.
White Enamel.

No. 504RY—Oak Gloss.
Mahogany finish.

No. 1782-13—Mahog-
any finish.

No. 1929-33—Mahog-
any finish.

No. 1702-13—Mahog-
any finish.

FIBRE SEAT CHAIRS

No. 799-14—Mahogany
or Walnut finish.

No. 997-14—Mahogany
or Walnut finish.

LOW IN PRICE
BUT PHOENIX QUALITY

No. 728-34—Mahogany
finish.

No. 728-44—Mahogany
finish.

No. 783-34—Mahogany
finish.

No. 929-34—Mahogany
finish.

No. 915-34—Mahogany
or Maple finish.

No. 961-34—Mahogany
finish.

No. 962-34—Mahogany
finish.

No. 904-34—Mahogany
or Walnut finish.

No. 751-34—Mahogany
or Walnut finish.

No. 960-34—Mahogany
finish.

No. 780-34—Mahogany
or Maple finish.

No. 961-44—Mahogany
finish.

No. 962-44—Mahogany
finish.

No. 904-44—Mahogany
or Walnut finish.

No. 751-44—Mahogany
or Walnut finish.

No. 960-44—Mahogany
finish.

No. 780-44—Mahogany
or Maple finish.

PHOENIX CHAIR COMPANY

INCREASE YOUR SALES AND PROFITS BY FEATURING
PHOENIX "LINDY" CHAIRS AND ROCKERS
Our extremely low prices will surprise you.

No. 872-38BB478—Tapestry. Color combination of red, blue and black with grey background.

No. 872-48BB484—Tapestry. Floral design consisting of soft shades of lavender, pink, orange and blue. Light brown background.

No. 877-38BB405—Tapestry with "real life." Predominating colors being various shades of red and green. Light green background.

No. 877-48B352—Jacquard Velour. Floral design. Flower is deep red, foliage taupe.

No. 876-38AA221—Tapestry. Rich in texture, A multitude of colors, yet they harmonize wonderfully.

No. 876-48AA220—Tapestry. Flower design—Red, lavender and brown with green foliage. Background of circle—grey. Background between circles—black.

No. 878-38D744 and D745—Moquette. Motif design—just a touch of red, brown, black and yellow. Small flowers are in lavender, green and brown.

No. 878-48C560—Tapestry. Multi-colored. Predominating colors—blue, pale green and light red with light grey background.

No. 875-38BB463—Tapestry. Red, blue and green flowers. Grey background. All soft shades harmoniously blending together.

No. 875-48BB405—Tapestry. Predominating colors being various shades of red and green. Light green background.

No. 873-38BB484—Tapestry. Color combination of lavender, blue and green with light brown background.

No. 873-48B352—Jacquard Velour. Red and taupe with light grey background.

No. 871-38CC659—Jacquard Velour. Oval design—light and dark green. Floral design in center of oval—red with light and dark green foliage.

No. 871-48BB415—Tapestry. Color combination consisting of varying shades of red, green and black with light grey background.

No. 874-38AA204—Tapestry. Red and green flower design. Brown background.

No. 874-48F1109—Linen-Velour. Deep brown, gold and old rose with just a touch of blue. One of the best velours we have in our line.

(Continued on next page)

PHOENIX CHAIR COMPANY

FAST SELLING OCCASIONAL CHAIRS AND ROCKERS
Made of Select Birch, Finished Walnut.

No. 1383½-38EE1019 —Figured Mohair.

No. 1383½-48DD822 —Moquette.

No. 1384½-38F1106-F1107—Imported Frieze.

No. 1384½-48DD847-DD848—Linen-Velour.

No. 1384-38D752—Tapestry back, CC603 Green Mohair Seat.

No. 1384-48D749—Tapestry Back, Taupe Mohair Seat.

No. 1385½-38EE1026 —Frieze.

No. 1385½-48H1511— Frieze.

No. 1385-38C560—Tapestry. Green Mohair Seat.

No. 1385-48G1310— Frieze Back, Walnut Mohair Seat.

No. 1386½-38D757— Cotton Frieze on Back and Seat.

No. 1386½-48DD853 —Moquette on Back and Seat.

No. 1386-38GG1407— Frieze. Green Mohair Seat.

No. 1386-48DD860— Frieze. Walnut Mohair Seat.

No. 1383-38DD840— Linen Velour. Green Mohair Seat.

No. 1383-48GG1408— Frieze. Taupe Mohair Seat.

No. 327-CC500—Jacquard Velour.

No. 299B352—Jacquard Velour.

No. 1375-38BB415— Velour Back and Reversible Cushion. Balance BB413 Velour.

No. 419-39H1506— Frieze, Back and Seat. Balance Velour.

No. 684-38CC667—Tapestry Back, Seat, Inside Arms. Balance Velour.

No. 479½-38G1310—
Frieze, Walnut Mohair
Seat.

No. 480½-38BB463—
Tapestry.

No. 387-38C567—Tapestry. This pattern is also made with Oak Frame.

No. 469-38DD839—
Moquette.

No. 394-38BB491—
Tapestry.

No. 2387-38GG1402—
Frieze Back. Taupe Mohair Seat.

No. 467-38BB403—
Tapestry.

No. 466-38DD852—
Tapestry.

No. 870-38BB105—
Tapestry Back. BB413—
Velour Seat.

No. 397-38F1101—
Tapestry. Walnut Mohair Seat.

COMFORTABLE OCCASIONAL CHAIRS
Frames are Birch Finished Walnut.

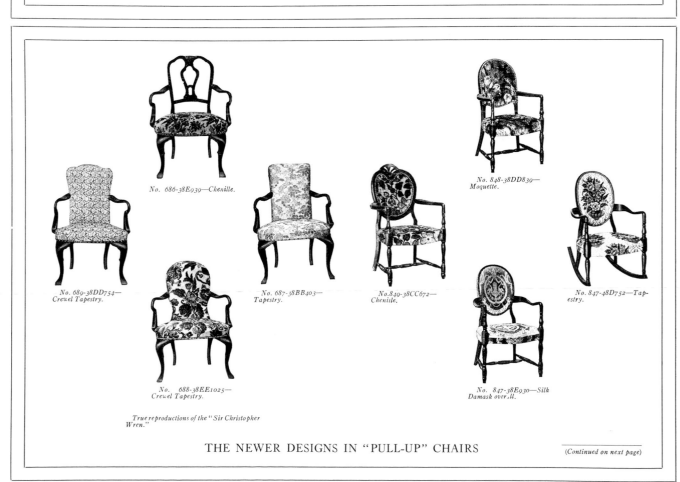

No. 686-38E939—Chenille.

No. 848-38DD830—
Moquette.

No. 689-38DD754—
Crewel Tapestry.

No. 687-38BB403—
Tapestry.

No. 849-38CC672—
Chenille.

No. 847-48D752—Tapestry.

No. 688-38EE1025—
Crewel Tapestry.

No. 847-38E930—Silk Damask over .ll.

True reproductions of the " Sir Christopher Wren."

THE NEWER DESIGNS IN "PULL-UP" CHAIRS

(Continued on next page)

PHOENIX CHAIR COMPANY

No. 1377-38CC604—
Red Mohair Overall.

No. 1376-38B348—Do-
ver Cloth.

No. 443-19—P l a i n
Black, Red, Taupe or
Mulberry Mohair.

No. 443-39—P l a i n
Black, Red, Taupe or
Mulberry Mohair.

No. 1382-38GG1425—
Frieze Back. Balance
Green Mohair.

No. 682-38GG1402—
Frieze Back. Taupe Mo-
hair Seat. Velour back of
Back.

No. 1379-38GG1425—
Frieze Back and Reversi-
ble Cushion. Balance
Green Mohair.

No. 441-18—P l a i n
Black, Red or Taupe
Mohair.

No. 441-38—P l a i n
Black, Red or Taupe
Mohair.

No. 694-38

No. 861-38H1506—
Frieze Back. Red Mo-
hair Seat.

No. 862-38CC640—
Jacquard Velour Back.
Walnut Mohair Seat.

No. 693½-78

No. 693½-38

Upholstered in Art Moderne Damask. G1309.

Finished-Ebony

TRUE "MODERNISTIC" FURNITURE

The three patterns of "Art Moderne" Furniture shown here are fine examples of the latest developments in this field.

No. 361-38I—
CC Grade Tapestry.

No. 860-38DD844—
Crewel Tapestry.

PHOENIX CHAIR COMPANY

SETTEE AND PULL-UP CHAIR
THAT CAN BE USED IN THE HOME, HOTEL OR CLUB
In fact—wherever furniture of the better type is needed.

No. 681-78GG1402—Frieze Back. Balance Taupe Mohair.

No. 681-38GG1422—F r i e z e Back, Seat and Inside Arms. Balance Red Mohair.

NEW AND ATTRACTIVE
Upholstered in colorful cretonnes.
Write for "A Complete Sales Plan."

No. 811—C o v e r Combination X-1.

Cover Combination X-3.

Size of seat, 13¼ by 14 inches. Height of back, 28 inches. Height of seat, 17 inches.

PHOENIX
SAFE AND SANITARY HIGH CHAIRS

No. 961-54SAT—Ivory, Mahogany, Ivory and Blue. *No. 961-54Y—Ivory, Mahogany, Ivory and Blue.* *No. 186-51SAT—Putty.* *No. 184-54SAT—Blue.*

No. 190-54SAT—Mahogany, Walnut, Ivory, Ivory and Blue. *No. 192-54SAT—Ivory, Mahogany or Ivory and Blue.* *No. 50-54SAT—Elm Gloss, Fumed.*

No. 195-54SAT—Pink, Blue, Green or Grey. *No. 107-54SAT—Maize, Grey, Green or Ivory.* *No. 171-54SAT—Red, Blue, Orchid, Ivory or Walnut.* *No. 185-54SAT—Black.*

CHILD'S WINDSOR CHAIR AND ROCKER

No. 1961-54—Ivory, Mahogany, Ivory and Blue. *No. 1961-64—Ivory, Mahogany, Ivory and Blue.*

MISSES' CHAIR AND ROCKER

No. 961-54—Ivory, Mahogany, Ivory and Blue. *No. 961-64—Ivory, Mahogany, Ivory and Blue.*

No. 50-64—Elm Gloss.

No. 197-64—Maize, Grey, Green or Ivory. *No. 195-64—Pink, Blue, Green or Grey.*

ST. JOHN'S TABLE COMPANY
Manufacturers of Tables, Dinette and Breakfast Suites
CADILLAC, MICH.
PERMANENT EXHIBITS AND SALESROOMS
CHICAGO, ILL., American Furniture Mart   NEW YORK, N. Y., New York Furniture Exchange
BOSTON, MASS., 90 Canal St.

*No. 3574—Top, 28x28 inches. Top,
5-ply, Butt Walnut, Veneered; Base,
Gumwood: Finished Antique Walnut.*

*No. 3335—Top, 18x48 inches. Top,
5-Ply Mahogany, Veneered; Base,
gumwood; finished Antique Mahogany.*

*No. 1355-B—Buffet.
Top, 18x46 inches.*

*No. 1355-T—Table. Top, open
54x32 inches; Top, closed 42x32
inches.*

*No. 1355-C—Chair.
Antique Walnut fin-
ish; Slip seat of
Figured Velour or
genuine leather, red.*

*Tops, 5-ply Walnut, Veneered; Bases, gumwood: Finished Antique
Walnut. This suite also made in solid oak, finished Cathedral Brown.*

PRODUCTS
MANUFACTURERS OF

APARTMENT DINING ROOM SUITES
BREAKFAST ROOM SETS AND SUITES
BREAKFAST ROOM TABLES AND EXTENSION TABLES
BREAKFAST ROOM TABLES IN THE WHITE
BREAKFAST ROOM CHAIRS
BREAKFAST ROOM SERVERS AND SERVING TABLES
BREAKFAST ROOM SERVING TABLES AND CABINETS COMBINED
DINING ROOM TABLES
DINING AND LIVING ROOM TABLES COMBINED
BENCHES FOR DESKS AND TELEPHONES
BOOK TROUGHS
BOOK, MAGAZINE AND NEWSPAPER RACKS AND STANDS
DESKS, WALL
FIREPLACE SCREENS
RADIO CABINETS AND TABLES
TELEPHONE TABLES, STANDS AND SETS
BUTTERFLY TABLES
CENTER TABLES
COFFEE TABLES
CONSOLE TABLES, WOOD

DAVENPORT AND DAVENPORT EXTENSION TABLES, WOOD
DROP LEAF TABLES
END TABLES
FLIP TOP TABLES
GATELEG AND GATELEG EXTENSION TABLES
LIBRARY AND LIBRARY EXTENSION TABLES
NESTS OF TABLES
ODD AND OCCASIONAL TABLES
 Also Hotel Desks, and Tables; School and Kindergarten Tables;
Office, Typewriter and Work Tables; and Restaurant Tables.

GENERAL INFORMATION
Ours is the largest table factory in the world. We produce
tables and dinette furniture of good quality, authentic design and
fine finish in great variety at reasonable prices.

RETAIL PRICE RANGES
Living Room Tables retail from $4.50 to $50.00.
Radio Tables from $10.50 to $60.00.
Breakfast and Dining Tables from $9.00 to $44.00.
Breakfast and Dinette Sets and Suites from $48.00 to $77.00.
School and Kindergarten Tables from $11.00 to $22.00.
Office and Hotel Tables from $10.00 to $50.00.

THE SHREVE CHAIR COMPANY, INC.

Manufacturers of Chairs and Tables

UNION CITY, PENNA.

PERMANENT EXHIBIT
CHICAGO, ILL., 5th Floor, American Furniture Mart

No. 94

No. 94½

No. 56

No. 150

No. 1550—Extension Table

PRODUCTS

MANUFACTURERS OF

BREAKFAST ROOM FURNITURE
CHILDREN'S CHAIRS
FERNERIES
OFFICE REVOLVING CHAIRS
RADIO TABLES

SPRING SEAT ROCKERS
STOOLS
TELEPHONE STANDS
WINDSOR CHAIRS
WOOD SEAT CHAIRS

GENERAL INFORMATION

The pieces shown on this page represent but a few of the many attractive patterns that can be obtained in our line. We invite you to write for our complete catalog and price list.

SIKES CHAIR COMPANY
Manufacturers of Chairs Since 1859

500 Clinton St., BUFFALO, N. Y.
BRANCH OFFICES AND SALESROOMS
PHILADELPHIA, PA., 23rd St. and Passyunk Ave.—NEW YORK, N. Y., 110 W. 34th St.
GRAND RAPIDS, MICH., Keeler Building

No. 5071—Georgian Arm Chair.

No. 5028—English Wing Chair.

No. 1731½. Queen Anne Arm Chair.

No. 5049—Rip Van Winkle Chair.

No. 1455—Side Chair. Colonial influence quite marked.

No. 2216—Desk Chair. Duncan Phyfe influence.

No. 1850½—Leather Lounging Chair. Colonial influence.

PRODUCTS
MANUFACTURERS OF

BENCHES
—Bedroom
—Cane Seat
—Dressing Table
—Fireside
—Living Room
—Upholstered

CHAIRS
—And Rockers, Bedroom
—Arm
—Bank
—Bedroom
—Breakfast
—Club
—Coxwell

CHAIRS
—Desk, and Ladies' Desk
—Easy, or Lounging
—Fireplace
—Hall
—Hotel
—Leather, Upholstered
—Library and Living Room
—Lunchroom and Restaurant
—Odd and Occasional
—Office
—Rip Van Winkle
—Rush Seat
—Sleepy Hollow

CHAIRS
—Upholstered Wing
—Windsor

ROCKERS
—Bedroom
—Rush Seat
—Windsor

ROCKERS
—Wood Seat

PIANO STOOLS

DAVENPORTS, BANK AND
OFFICE

COUCHES

FOOT STOOLS

And other Upholstered Furniture for the Home, Office, Bank, Hotel and Club.

GENERAL INFORMATION
Every year finds Sikes offering retailers a wider and wider range of attractive patterns that not only appeal to the eye but purse of the buying public.

The design and construction of Sikes chairs together with reasonable prices give you an opportunity to carry a popular line of chairs that will sell at a profit and add materially to the prestige of your store. Order a few of these numbers today.

STANDARD CHAIR COMPANY
Manufacturers of Wood Seat Chairs
UNION CITY, PENNA.

PERMANENT EXHIBIT
CHICAGO, ILL., Space 1529, American Furniture Mart

A bird's-eye view of the Standard Chair Company plants—here is a real, dependable source of supply.

Breakfast Room Chair.

Breakfast Room Chair.

PRODUCTS
MANUFACTURERS OF

BENCHES
—Bedroom
—Toilet Table
BREAKFAST ROOM CHAIRS in
the White for Decorating or
Special Finish
CHAIRS
—Arm, Wood
—Bow Backs
—Breakfast Room
—Children's

CHAIRS
—Desk, Home
—High
—Kitchen
—Knock-Down
—Living Room, Not Upholstered
—Nursery
—Windsor, Wood Only
—Wood Seat, Bedroom
—Wood Seat, Desk (Home)
—Office, Iron and Swivel

ROCKERS
—Bedroom
—Plain, Wooden
—Roll Seat
—Sewing
—Windsor
—Wood Seat

STOOLS
—Bath Room
—Factory
—Kitchen
—Office and Store

GENERAL INFORMATION
Standard Chairs are obtainable in all the popular finishes and designs. The merit of these chairs has been measured again and again by the rigid construction and selected woods. Prices, too, are reasonable and will enable you to realize a fair mark-up. We invite you to write for our price list.

W. F. WHITNEY COMPANY, INC.

Manufacturers of Windsor Chairs, Upholstered Chairs and Breakfast Sets

SOUTH ASHBURNHAM, MASS.

BRANCH OFFICES AND EXHIBITS

LONG ISLAND CITY, N. Y., Teepe-Whitney Corporation, Vernon and Nott Avenue

CHICAGO, ILL., Space 823, American Furniture Mart, 666 Lake Shore Drive

No. 664. Ladder Back. Rush Seat. Height, 42 inches. Seat, 14⅝ inches deep; 18½ inches wide. Weight per dozen, 125 pounds. Birch. Selling Price, $18.50.

No. 640F-2. Governor Hancock Arm Chair. Rush Seat. Height, 40¾ inches. Seat, 21¾ inches deep; 20 inches wide. Weight per dozen, 180 pounds. Selling Price, $29.00.

No. 50-2. Governor Bradford Arm Chair. Height, 43¼ inches. Seat, 17 inches deep; 21 inches wide. Weight per dozen, 204 pounds. Birch. Selling Price, $21.50.

No. 35F. Barbara Side Chair. Height, 35½ inches. Seat, 20 inches deep; 17 inches wide. Weight per dozen, 144 pounds. Selling Price, $13.00.

No. 4140. Upholstered Chair with Grade G combination covering. Seat, 20½ inches deep; 19½ inches wide. Height of back, 21½ inches. Height of seat from floor, 15 inches. Weight, 20 pounds. Exposed wood Birch. Selling Price, $38.00. Price range depending on covering used, $26.00 to $54.00.

No. 425. Coffee Table. Height, 23 inches. Top, 23½ inches diameter. Weight, 16¾ pounds. Birch. Selling Price, $16.00.

No. 608. Butterfly Table. Height, 23½ inches. Width, 12¼ inches leaves down; 28½ inches leaves up. Length, 26¼ inches. Leg, 1½ inches diameter. Decorations to order. Weight, 24 pounds. Birch. Selling Price, $21.00.

No. 4131. Upholstered Chair with Grade E combination covering. Seat, 19 inches deep; 19 inches wide. Height of back, 25 inches. Height of seat from floor, 16½ inches. Weight, 20½ pounds. Exposed wood Birch. Selling Price, $31.00. Price range depending on covering used, $25.00 to $53.00.

PRODUCTS

MANUFACTURERS OF

WINDSOR CHAIRS, BREAKFAST CHAIRS, BREAKFAST SETS AND SMALL TABLES.

BEDROOM CHAIRS, ROCKERS AND BENCHES, as separate items or in sets for odd suites.

CHAIRS OF OTHER TYPES INCLUDING

—Arm (Wood and Upholstered); Bathroom

—Children's; Desk (home); Dining; High (Children's)

—Hotel, Club, etc.; Kitchen; Living Room (Wood and Upholstered)

—Mission Style; Nested; Odd (Wood and Upholstered); Office

—Spinet; Tablet.

ROCKERS (with either Wood or Upholstered)

FACTORY STOOLS

STEP STOOLS

TEA ROOM FURNITURE

ESTABLISHED · 1868

WHITNEY · CHAIRS

Trade Mark

FINISHES

Windsor Chairs and Tables are finished in Mahogany, Walnut or Maple, plain or antique. Also plain enamel. On upholstered Chairs, exposed wood surfaces are finished Mahogany or Walnut.

Our finishes resemble the following plates in the Woods and Finishes Section preceding page 9 of this book: Mahogany, plate No. 1—Standard American Mahogany; Walnut, plate No. 14—American Walnut Standard; and Maple, plate No. 8—Persian Maple.

ATLAS FURNITURE COMPANY
Manufacturers of Bedroom Furniture
JAMESTOWN, N. Y.
EXHIBITS
JAMESTOWN, N. Y., Jamestown Furniture Market Association

PRODUCTS
MANUFACTURERS OF
BEDROOM SUITES, COMPLETE, including BENCH, CHAIR, ROCKER and NIGHT TABLE.

GENERAL INFORMATION
Atlas prices represent values which appeal to a constantly growing group of Dealers—not because Atlas quality is skimped for looks—but because the Atlas organization can and does achieve quality workmanship on an economical basis.

The Atlas organization is directed by the workers themselves who own and operate the two big plants. Everybody works. There isn't a cent of non-pro-ductive overhead. The President and other officers, the heads of the various departments and a majority of the workers in the Atlas Plants are stockholders. Their main interest lies in keeping quality up and costs down.

Atlas is Every Dealer's Line. A Line to depend on—a Line that always sells. It pays to keep informed on Atlas offerings. Write for photos and prices today.

DESCRIPTION OF SUITE ILLUSTRATED BELOW
Suite No. 399—Is a very attractive number having figured Butt Walnut fronts (matched four ways) relieved and beautified with Rosewood overlays.

The construction is dustproof throughout. The drawer bottoms are mahogany. The drawer sides are sycamore. A high grade, beautifully finished suite reflecting the highest standards of workmanship.

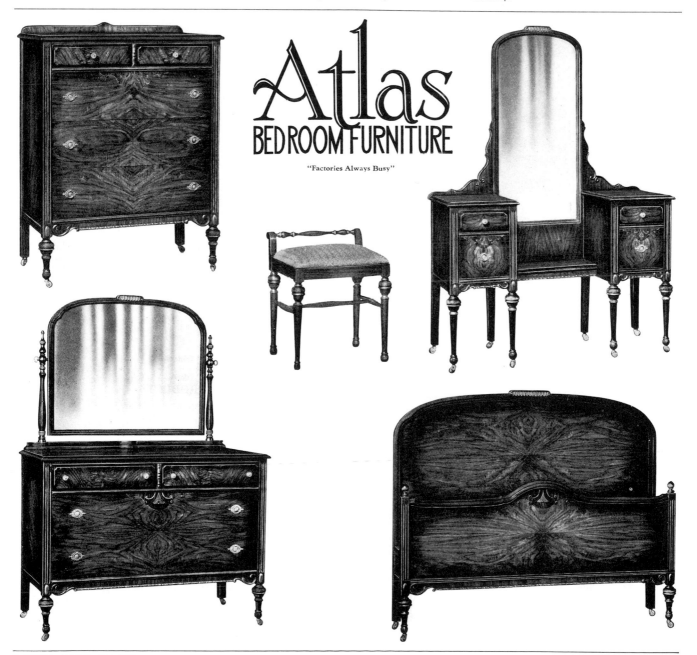

Atlas
BEDROOM FURNITURE
"Factories Always Busy"

THE BASIC FURNITURE CO.
WAYNESBORO, VA.
J. L. WITZ FURNITURE CORPORATION
STANTON, VA.

Manufacturers of Dining Room Suites, Odd Buffets and Tables

PERMANENT EXHIBITS
NEW YORK, N. Y., New York Furniture Exchange   CHICAGO, ILL., American Furniture Mart
SAN FRANCISCO, CALIF., Furniture Exchange

Illustrating a very popular Suite, No. 241.

PRODUCTS
MANUFACTURERS OF
DINING ROOM FURNITURE in Complete Suites and Separate Pieces sold on order as follows:

BUFFETS	CHINA CABINETS	SERVERS
CHAIRS		TABLES

Also Odd Dining Tables and Odd Buffets.

CONSTRUCTION
"The Basic Line" is constructed from a good grade of Walnut in combination with hardwood. Five-ply built-up tops and fronts with three-ply ends. Boxed-in, dust-proof, drawers with three-ply bottoms. In the buffets are sliding silver drawers as well as side compartments. Flush end construction. Every piece of lumber entering into the Basic Products has been well seasoned and kiln dried assuring your customer of furniture that will not warp or crack.

ODD BUFFETS
Basic Odd Buffets can be made up to match your customer's present suites in any period or style. Each is well-made and reasonably priced—prices ranging from $40.00 to $80.00 depending on period design selected.

DESIGNS
"The Basic Line" has confined itself to a large extent to the reproduction of furniture depicting the Queen Anne and Early English periods. Some of the patterns show the influence of the more modern times and thus create a product that has the charm of the Old World as well as the New.

FINISHES
The appeal of this furniture is further enhanced by the durable attractive finishes. All the popular shades are obtainable including Duco.

PRICES
Ten-Piece Suites
The price range of "The Basic Line" is between $146.00 and $500.00 for ten pieces. These prices will permit you a substantial profit and make the merchandise appealing to your customer. Order a few of Basic number now.

ODD TABLES
The advantages of being able to buy dining room tables separately is readily appreciated by furniture dealers. Two sizes are obtainable—45 by 54 inches and 45 by 60 inches. Each is supplied with extension leaves. Prices range from $36.00 to $80.00.

BLACKHAWK FURNITURE COMPANY
Manufacturers of Bedroom Furniture
ROCKFORD, ILLINOIS
PERMANENT EXHIBIT
CHICAGO, ILL., Space 1647, American Furniture Mart, 666 Lake Shore Drive

PRODUCTS

MANUFACTURERS OF
BED ROOM SUITES Complete including the
following pieces which are sold separately:

CHAIRS, Bedroom Sets of	DRESSERS
	VANITIES
BEDS	BENCHES
—Bow End	NIGHT TABLES
—Four Poster	CHESTS OF DRAWERS

Bed. Height, 50 inches; Width, 54 inches. List price, $106.00.

Vanity. Height, 31 inches; Width, 50 inches; Depth, 19 inches. Mirror, 26x32 inches. List price, $136.00.

Chest of Drawers. Height, 56 inches; Width, 38 inches. Depth, 21 inches. List price, $127.00.

Dresser. Height, 35 inches; Width, 50 inches; Depth, 23 inches. Mirror, 32x34 inches. List price $142.00.

SUITE NO. 146

5-ply Butt Walnut fronts and 5-ply tops and ends with Maple Burl Veneer on top drawers. Hand wood carvings. Dust-proof. Center drawer guides. List price, 4-piece suite, $511.00. List price on pieces not illustrated—Chair, $25.00; Bench, $25.00, and Night Stand, $37.00

Dresser. Height, 35 inches; Width, 50 inches; Depth, 23 inches. Mirror, 32x34 inches. List price, $148.00.

GENERAL INFORMATION

The Van Dyke finish, which is a mellow, soft Brown color together with the exclusive Blackhawk designs, makes a furniture that is truly distinctive. Walnut and Gum chiefly are used in the construction of our bedroom suites which are sometimes set off by rare woods, such as Zebra and Carpathian Elm. Carvings are usually by hand unless otherwise specified.

All prices shown are subject to change without notice.

Bed. Height, 51 inches; Width, 54 inches. List price, $103.00.

Chest of Drawers. Height, 48 inches; Width, 37 inches; Depth, 20½ inches. List price, $134.00

Vanity. Height, 33½ inches; Width, 40¾ inches; Depth, 18 inches. List price, $150.00.

SUITE NO. 144

5-ply veneered Faux Satine fronts and 5-ply veneer Butt Walnut tops. Center drawer guides: dust-proof construction. List price, 4-piece suite, $535.00.

Chest of Drawers. Height, 47 inches; Width, 37 inches; Depth, 20½ inches. List price, $82.00.

Vanity. Height, 31 inches; Width, 48 inches; Depth, 18 inches. Mirror, 24x36 inches. List price, $92.00.

Dresser. Height, 35 inches; Width, 48 inches; Depth, 21 inches. Mirror, 30x34 inches. List price, $98.00.

Bed. Height, 49 inches; Width, 54 inches. List price, $78.00.

Trade Mark

SUITE NO. 145

5-ply Butt Walnut veneer fronts with 5-ply Walnut tops and ends. Center drawer guides; dust-proof construction. List price, 4-piece suite, $250.00. List price on pieces not shown —Chair, $20.00; Bench, $18.00, and Night Table, $23.00.

Vanity. Height, 35 inches; Width, 52 inches; Depth, 20 inches. Mirror, 26x30 inches. List price, $180.00.

Bench. List price, $28.00.

Night Stand. List price, $42.00.

Chair. List price, $32.00.

Chest of Drawers. Height, 51 inches; Width, 40 inches; Depth, 20 inches. List price, $140.00.

SUITE NO. 135

5-ply Butt Walnut fronts and tops with Maple Burl Veneer on top drawers. Solid Wood Carvings. Van Dyke finish. List price, 4-piece suite, $624.00.

Bed. Height 53 inches; Width 56 inches. List price, $124.00.

Dresser. Height, 35 inches; Width, 54 inches; Depth, 23 inches. List price, $190.00.

(Continued on next page)

Dresser. Height, 35 inches; Width, 54 inches; Depth, 23 inches. Mirror, 32x40. List price, $170.00.

SUITE NO. 141
Butt Walnut Veneer fronts with 5-ply Striped Walnut tops and ends. Carpathian Elm and Zebra wood veneer on top, drawer fronts. List price, 4-piece suite, $588.00.

Bed. Height, 52 inches; Width, 54 inches. List price, $114.00.

Chest of Drawers. Height, 56 inches; Width, 30 inches; Depth, 21 inches. List price, $134.00.

Vanity. Height, 31 inches; Width, 50 inches; Depth, 18 inches. Mirror, 32x32. List price, $170.00.

Night Stand. Top, 14x16 inches. Height, 28 inches. List price, $36.00.

Bench. List price, $32.00.

Chair. List price $32.00.

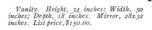

Bench. List price, $24.00.

Chair. List price, $24.00.

Night Stand. Top, 14x16 inches. Height, 28 inches. List price, $39.00.

Vanity. Height, 34 inches; Width, 50 inches; Depth, 18 inches. Mirror, 28x32 inches. List price, $150.00.

Bed. Height, 52 inches; Width, 54 inches. List price, $98.00.

Chest of Drawers. Height, 50 inches; Width, 38 inches; Depth, 20 inches. List price, $130.00.

Dresser. Height, 35 inches; Width, 52 inches; Depth, 22 inches. Mirror, 34x32 inches. List price, $152.00.

SUITE NO. 143
5-ply Butt Walnut veneer on fronts and tops. Japanese Ash on bottoms. Dust-proof construction. Center drawer guides. List price, 4-piece suite, $530.00.

BERKEY & GAY FURNITURE COMPANY
Bedroom and Dining Room Furniture
440 Monroe Ave., GRAND RAPIDS, MICH.

THE BERKEY & GAY FACTORY

The Berkey & Gay factory, now in its 75th year, has become one of the largest of its kind in the country devoted exclusively to the production of highest quality furniture. There are five factories, showrooms, and warehouses with a combined floor space of thirty acres! 2800 highly skilled craftsmen are employed continually, and are supervised by experts in every phase of furniture designing and building. The factory uses 2372 horse power daily, is equipped with the most modern machinery and devices for the making of furniture; and manufactures and ships a complete suite every 4½ minutes.

(Continued on next page)

**THE NATIONALLY KNOWN
BERKEY & GAY SHOP MARK**

This Shop Mark, inset in every Berkey and Gay piece, has been nationally advertised for more than forty years. It is the consumer's assurance of finest craftsmanship. Furniture bearing this distinguished mark is handled exclusively by only the finest furniture and department stores in the country.

BERKEY & GAY FURNITURE COMPANY

THE FURNITURE

Berkey & Gay make bedroom suites and dining room suites exclusively, and the same designers create the living room pieces for the Grand Rapids Upholstering Company.

The "Goddard." One of the suites created to commemorate Berkey & Gay's 75th Anniversary.

Two pieces of the "Burgos." A Spanish design autographed on silver by the designer and decorator.

THE GREAT CHOICE IN BERKEY & GAY DESIGNS

Over 150 separate and distinct suite designs offer a complete variety of fashionable furniture in every conceivable style. Every need or whim, from the new modern creations to authentic reproductions of masterpieces of the past, can be met in Berkey & Gay furniture.

Each season a vast number of new designs make the display of still greater interest and beauty.

THE PRICE RANGE

Berkey & Gay bedroom and dining room suites are offered in an unusually wide price range. There are suites for people of refined tastes at prices for those in either the modest, small apartment, or those who require furnishings for the palatial home.

THE CONSTRUCTION OF BERKEY & GAY FURNITURE

For 75 years Berkey & Gay have been synonymous with the finest furniture construction. Here are just a few interesting reasons for this furniture's sturdiness.

Five-Ply Panels

All broad surfaces, such as doors, drawer fronts, tops, sides and ends of cabinets and tables, are of a five-ply laminated veneered construction that will not warp or pull out of shape—stronger and more durable than a single piece of wood of equal thickness. Curved, bow, and serpentine surfaces are frequently of an eleven-ply construction to prevent the possibility of coming out of shape.

Interior Construction

Posts and legs are of one continuous piece of wood. The framework of each cabinet piece is secured by dowel construction, considered the best by Berkey & Gay after years of study and experience, since dowels do not tend to weaken the frame as a mortise and tenon joint, and because dowels offer resistance crosswise

with the grain of the wood. Properly executed and with everyday usage, they should not pull apart or loosen. Three-ply, dust-proof panels between all drawers are fitted by tongue and groove to a heavy frame. A center drawer glide adds rigidity to the frame and prevents jamming of the drawer. The corner blocks, secured with screws, give added strength and minimize breakage during shipment.

Close-up circle shows the moving functions of the center drawer glide. Hard maple runner below; grooved mahogany track above, on the underside of the drawer bottom.

(Continued on next page)

Sectional view showing interior construction of Berkey & Gay Furniture.

THE BEAUTY OF BERKEY & GAY FURNITURE

Practically every Berkey & Gay suite or piece is an original creation, unless purposely copied, reproduced from a museum piece. Period and modern pieces alike receive that attention to each detail that assures furniture of distinction and originality. Each year Berkey & Gay creations tend to establish the prevailing vogue in furniture.

Here are seven important points that reflect the beauty and excellence to be found in this furniture.

HAND MATCHED VENEERS

Veneers and elaborately figured woods are carefully matched to produce the beautiful and interesting panels for doors, drawers, tops, and broad surfaces generally. These rare woods come from the four corners of the earth.

HAND CARVING

All carving on Berkey & Gay pieces, whether simple or elaborate, is of wood individually cut by hand. Substitutes or compositions are never used.

HAND PAINTED DECORATIONS

All color decorations on Berkey & Gay suites are hand-painted by artists, using palette and brush just as a portrait or landscape is painted. Substitutes, such as decalcomanias and transfers, are never used.

MARQUETRY WORK

All marquetry on Berkey & Gay furniture is designed and produced in our own factories, painstakingly executed by hand in combinations of rare cabinet woods selected for their natural colorings to harmonize best with the particular piece on which they are used.

DECORATIVE MOLDINGS

All moldings and applied turnings are of wood, especially selected from a natural color and texture standpoint to make possible best color harmony and decorative elements for the piece in question. Many of these decorative moldings are individually designed.

HIGH LIGHTING, SHADING

The mellow shading and soft high-lighting on Berkey & Gay pieces, especially for carvings, moldings, fluted legs, and the like, are the result of skillful and patient hand-work.

HAND FINISHING

Extremely careful methods in hand-coloring and finishing harmonize and equalize the uneven color tones invariably existing in highly figured woods. The natural beauty of these colorings and figurings are, moreover, intensified and protected. Painstakingly all surfaces are hand-rubbed to a deep mellow richness.

BERKEY & GAY FURNITURE COMPANY

THE CONVENIENCE OF BERKEY & GAY FURNITURE

Berkey & Gay suites are rich in the kind of convenience features that women welcome, and which help in the sale of the suites. Everything is done to make pieces handy and convenient to use—to add to the joy of possession.

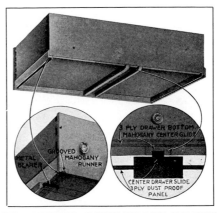

TRAYS FOR TRIFLES

Most bedroom bureaus and chiffoniers have a small tray with jewelry box of solid mahogany, carefully smoothed and finished. Many have removable velvet pads.

EASY GLIDING, DUST-PROOF DRAWERS

All drawer sides and ends are of solid mahogany carefully smoothed and finished. The bottoms are three-ply to prevent warping. They are hand-fitted to assure easy gliding, to prevent sticking and binding. The circle to the left shows the grooved runner which glides on a metal bearer, minimizing friction. In the right hand circle is a closeup of the center drawer glide. This assures easy gliding, prevents jamming, and acts as a stop. The special flanged sloping of the top of the drawer minimizes binding.

SILVER TRAYS

Most sideboards are equipped with an all-mahogany tray, plush-lined and conveniently partitioned for silver. Handles make it easy to carry when removed from the sideboard.

COSMETIC TRAYS

The upper right hand drawer of most Berkey & Gay vanity or toilet tables has a sliding tray of heavy plate glass. Cosmetics, perfumes, etc., if placed on this tray during the toilet will not disfigure the piece with stains or alcohol.

TABLE LEAVES

All dining room extension tables have three leaves—two with aprons. These leaves are veneered, finished, and fitted to match the top in every detail.

LINEN TRAYS

Sideboards are equipped with deep mahogany drawers or two removable mahogany trays for linen. Dust-proof and carefully finished, they prevent soiling or wrinkling.

(Continued on next page)

GRAND RAPIDS UPHOLSTERING COMPANY

Furniture for the Living Room

440 Monroe Ave., GRAND RAPIDS, MICH.

PERMANENT DISPLAY
GRAND RAPIDS, MICH., 6th Floor, Berkey & Gay Exhibition Bldg.

Created by Berkey & Gay designers, made by our own skilled cabinet workers, and decorated by our wood carvers and artists. Each piece is an example of the great artistry and perfection that are possible when exacting standards are made almost a religion. There is an air of permanence about this furniture.

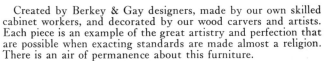

PRODUCTS

The Grand Rapids Upholstering Company makes a complete line of Cabinet and Upholstered Pieces for the Living Room, the Library and the Hall.

GENERAL INFORMATION

The Grand Rapids Upholstering Company is under the same control and direction as the Berkey & Gay Furniture Company.

GRAND RAPIDS UPHOLSTERING COMPANY

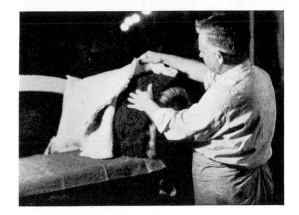

CONSTRUCTION
Springs
Steel wire; oil tempered, Japanned. Tied eight ways to each other and to the maple frame with flax twine.

Filling
Curled hair over which is set a top layer of cotton felt.

CONSTRUCTION (Continued)
Frames
Hardwoods with heavy oversize maple rails. Doweled. Reinforced with brackets.

Webbing
Non-sag closely woven webbing throughout.

HAND TAILORED
A perfect hand-tailoring is evident in every upholstered piece. Years of use only serve to make evident the in-built quality of materials and workmanship that lie hidden beneath the covering.

PRESTIGE FOR YOUR STORE
There is an added selling value in any piece about which you may say "Created by Berkey & Gay Designers." The same beauty which marks each Berkey & Gay suite and has made that line the outstanding one in the entire industry is found in all products of the Grand Rapids Upholstering Company. A selection of this furniture on your floor will gain for your store a valuable prestige and a preference among those people with whom highest quality is the rule.

A WIDE STYLE RANGE
Everything from the popular selling patterns to those that follow the strict period motifs and which are found more often in the decorator's studio, is included in this furniture created by Berkey & Gay designers.

A WIDE PRICE RANGE
Prices, too, range from the lower popular-selling level all through the price scale. Each store will find many pieces to suit its particular clientele.

CENTRAL FURNITURE COMPANY
Manufacturers of Dining Room Furniture
Race and Mill Streets, ROCKFORD, ILL.

PERMANENT EXHIBITS

CHICAGO, ILL., Spaces 1519-22, American Furniture Mart   ROCKFORD, ILL., at Factory

PRODUCTS
MANUFACTURERS OF

DINING ROOM SUITES, Regular Size and Apartment (or Small) Size

Also separate dining room pieces as follows:

BUFFETS AND COLONIAL BUFFETS
CHAIRS, Arm and Side
CHINA CABINETS AND CLOSETS
SERVERS
TABLES

GENERAL INFORMATION

The Central Furniture Company, established in 1872, is a pioneer in the manufacture of dining room furniture. The selected and seasoned woods combined with sturdy construction and beautiful, durable finishes are ingredients of every Central Furniture Company product.

RETAIL PRICE RANGES

Complete ten-piece suites from $316.00 to $1280.00. Buffets from $65.00 to $250.00. Chairs from $70.00 to $360.00 per set of one arm chair and five side chairs. Servers from $50.00 to $120.00. Tables from $70.00 to $250.00. China Cabinets from $60.00 to $160.00. All prices are subject to change without notice.

Buffet. Top, 22x66 inches.

Arm Chair, 27½ inches wide and 40 inches high.

Chair. Side, 20 inches wide and 38½ inches high.

Dining Room Table. Top. 44x60 inches. Extends to 8 feet with 3 leaves.

China Cabinet. Width 42 inches; Height, 66 inches.

Server. Top, 19x38 inches.

DESCRIPTION OF DINING ROOM SUITE No. 501

Construction. Full frame construction throughout. Drawers dust-proof partitions and bottoms, full thickness 5-ply ends, interior solid quarter sawed white oak with 3-ply quarter sawed white oak bottoms. All corners dovetailed and set in guides to insure smooth operation.

Legs, stretchers, bases and frames, solid Walnut. Tops, ends, fronts and aprons on table 5-ply construction with striped Walnut veneer. Fronts of large drawer in Buffet and China Cabinet of Butt Walnut veneer. Panels on either side of China Cabinet door and doors on Buffet and Server veneered with striped Walnut veneer, with overlay of Ash swirl veneer. Solid Walnut mouldings and carvings.

Chairs solid Walnut throughout with 5-ply stock veneered with Walnut on center panels. Regular slip seats.

Table has two-piece six-leg base, top equipped with standard Maple slides on regular dividing frame.

Hardware. Brass finish.

Finish. Non-fading stain thoroughly filled and finished with three coats of lacquer rubbed smooth. A Van Dyke Brown finish similar to Plate No. 10 in the Woods and Finishes Section of this Book.

Server. 38 inches wide, 36 inches high, 19 inches deep.

Side Chair. 21 inches wide, 38 inches high.

China Cabinet. 38 inches wide, 66 inches high, 15 inches deep.

Arm Chair. 26 inches wide, 41½ inches high.

Buffet. 66 inches wide, 37 inches high, 22 inches deep.

Table. Top 44x60 inches. Extends to 8 feet with 3 apron fillings.

DESCRIPTION OF DINING ROOM SUITE No. 494

Style and Characteristic Features. A true Sheraton period design combining features of Shearer and Hepplewhite influences. Slender forms, graceful lines, perfect balance and proportions. Serpentine front on Buffet, serpentine ends on table, and fluted posts and legs. Legs turned and carved with authentic details. Veneer inlay on posts. Shield back chairs with authentic Sheraton design carvings. Hand painted designs on drawers and table aprons supply the principal ornamentation.

Construction. Full frame construction throughout. Dust-proof partitions and bottoms, full thickness 5-ply ends, drawer interiors solid quarter sawed White Oak with 3-ply quarter sawed White Oak bottoms, all corners dovetailed and set in guides to insure smooth operation. End drawers of Buffet lined with green felt for silver storage.

Legs, bases, frames and stretchers of solid Walnut. Top, ends, fronts and table aprons, 5-ply construction. Tops and ends striped Walnut veneer. Center Buffet and Server drawers and China Cabinet drawer of crotch Walnut veneer. Top drawers of Buffet and Server, Buffet doors, side panels on Server and China Cabinet veneered with highly figured Carpatheon Elm Burl. Border of Buffet doors, border of side panels on Server, border of panels on China Cabinet and China Cabinet head veneered with striped Walnut. All mouldings of solid Walnut, and Hand Carvings throughout. Aprons on Table veneered with Carpatheon Elm Burl with Crotch Walnut veneer on corners.

Table has ten-leg base with 2 center legs stationary. Top equipped with standard Maple slides built on dividing frame.

Chairs solid Walnut throughout. Hand carved panels and backs. Carpatheon Elm Burl on bottom of back panel. Regular spring seat construction. Arm chair in either upholstered or panel back.

Hardware. Authentic Sheraton style with designs in center and on edges. Brass in a subdued silver color.

Finish. Non-fading stain thoroughly filled and finished with one coat of shellac and three coats of lacquer. Rubbed smooth and even. Walnut veneers and all solid wood stained a Van Dyke Brown similar to Plate No. 14 in the Woods and Finishes Section of this Book. Elm Burl veneers are finished reddish brown yet lighter in color than the other surfaces. Small mouldings on doors, panels, and on bottom of corner aprons on table are stained black. The black pencil line designs on top drawers and table apron are hand painted.

(Continued on next page)

Buffet. 68 inches wide, 44 inches high, 22 inches deep.

Server. 38 inches wide, 30 inches high, 19 inches deep.

China Cabinet. 42 inches wide, 73 inches high, 29 inches deep.

Table. Top, 44x60 inches, 8-foot extension with three leaves.

DESCRIPTION OF DINING ROOM SUITE No. 495

Construction. All legs, stretchers and frames of solid quartered Red Gum. Cases have 5-ply Maple veneer front bases and 5-ply striped Walnut veneer tops and ends. Doors of Buffet and Server and corner of Table rims of highly figured Elm Burl. Front of Buffet linen drawer and China drawer 5-ply Butt Walnut veneer. Front of top drawer in Buffet 5-ply Zebra wood bordered with small figured moulding. Center Buffet drawer and front panels on either side of China door 5-ply Maple veneer. All drawers of quarter sawed White Oak Dust-proof construction. The top drawer of the Buffet is divided into four sections and lined with green felt for the storage of silver. Stationary base and tops of table equipped with equalizer slides. Seats of Chairs are regular spring seats upholstered in red mohair and heavily designed back.

Side Chair. 21 inches wide, 42 inches high.

Arm Chair. 27 inches wide, 44 inches high.

Finish. Lacquer. General color effect, Van Dyke Brown. All Elm Burl and Maple veneers are stained in a lighter shade which gives a pleasing two-tone effect. See Plate No. 14 in the Woods and Finishes Section of this Book for the basic color of this finish.

Buffet. 74 inches wide, 43 inches high, 22 inches deep.

Server. 34 inches high, 44 inches wide, 18¾ inches deep.

China Cabinet. 38 inches wide, 61 inches high, 16 inches deep.

Table. Top, 42x66 inches. Extends to 101 inches. Also in 8-foot extension with 6-leg construction.

DESCRIPTION OF DINING ROOM SUITE No. 483

Construction. Full frame construction throughout. Drawers dust-proof partitions and bottoms, full thickness 5-ply ends, interiors of solid quarter sawed White Oak, with 3-ply quarter sawed White Oak bottoms, all corners dovetailed and set in guides to insure smooth operation.

Legs, stretchers, and base of frames of Red Gum. Tops and ends 5-ply construction veneered with striped Walnut. Drawers of solid quarter sawed White Oak construction with lined silver tray in top drawer of Buffet. Large Buffet drawer veneered with striped Walnut and Butt Walnut in the arches, the small Buffet drawer Maple veneer and trimmed with Gum moulding and rosettes. Buffet,

China Cabinet and Server doors are Walnut with Maple veneer overlay and a diamond shaped Butt Walnut overlay on top of the Maple, with composition carvings and Gum rosettes. Moulding on Buffet is Maple. Spindle carving on base and head rail of Buffet.

Chair of Walnut and Gum.

Side Chair. 21 inches wide, 41 inches high.

Arm Chair. 25 inches wide, 45 inches high.

Table has stationary platform base with refectory top. Extension leaves operated with lever allowing easy opening and closing without scratching top. Base of quartered Red Gum. Center top, leaves, and aprons of 5-ply construction veneered with striped Walnut veneer. Maple veneer on apron of Table with moulding and rosette trimming.

Hardware. Brass with knobs and round pulls.

Finish. Non-Fading stain thoroughly filled and finished with two coats of shellac, sanded and waxed. Color, Van Dyke Brown similar to Plate No. 14 in the Woods and Finishes Section of this Book.

Server. 38 inches wide, 38 inches high, 18 inches deep.

Buffet. 72 inches wide, 38 inches high, 22 inches deep.

China Cabinet. 40 inches wide, 64 inches high, 18 inches deep.

Arm Chair. 26 inches wide, 41½ inches high.

Side Chair. 21 inches wide, 38 inches high.

Table. Top, 60x38 inches. Extended length, 92 inches.

DESCRIPTION OF DINING ROOM SUITE No. 497

Construction. Full frame construction throughout. Drawers dust-proof partitions and bottoms, full thickness 5-ply ends, interiors solid quarter sawed White Oak with 3-ply quarter sawed White Oak bottoms. All corners dovetailed and set in guides insuring smooth operation.

Legs, stretchers, bases and frames of solid Walnut. Tops and ends 5-ply construction veneered with striped Walnut. Drawers of Buffet and China Cabinet and doors of Server 5-ply construction veneered with quarter sawed White Oak with border around edge of 5-ply construction veneered with Zebra veneer. Solid Walnut center pieces between Buffet drawers and doors on Buffet and China Cabinet. Solid Walnut doors on Buffet and China Cabinet. All mouldings solid Walnut and Oak turnings on fronts of cases. Hand carved designs on doors and bases in solid Walnut. Spindle carvings on legs.

Chairs solid Walnut throughout. Hand carved designs on back. Side chair with full upholstered saddle seat. Arm chair full upholstered saddle seat and upholstered back.

Table has stationary platform base with refectory top. Extension leaves operated with lever allowing easy opening and closing without scratching top. Edges slightly rounded. Base solid Walnut. Center top, leaves, and apron 5-ply construction veneered with striped Walnut. Rims solid quarter sawed White Oak. Hand carvings and Oak turnings on stretchers.

Hardware. Brass with pendulum type pulls.

Finish. Non-fading stain thoroughly filled and finished with two coats of shellac, sanded and waxed. Color is yellowish brown, darker than golden Oak—similar to Plate No. 10 in the Woods and Finishes Section of this Book.

Server. 36 inches wide, 37 inches high, 18 inches deep.

Buffet. 66 inches wide, 42 inches high, 22 inches deep.

China Cabinet. 40 inches wide, 67 inches high, 18 inches deep.

Arm Chair. 27½ inches wide, 40 inches high.

Side Chair. 20 inches wide, 38½ inches high.

Table. Top, 60x42 inches. Extends to 8 feet with 3 leaves.

DESCRIPTION OF DINING ROOM SUITE No. 498

Construction. Full frame construction throughout. Drawers dust-proof partitions and bottoms, full thickness 5-ply ends, interior solid quarter sawed White Oak with 3-ply quarter sawed White Oak bottoms. All corners dovetailed and set in guides to insure smooth operation.

Legs, stretchers, bases, and frames, solid Walnut. Tops, ends, fronts and aprons on Table 5-ply construction with striped Walnut veneer. Fronts of center drawer in Buffet and China Cabinet drawer of Butt Walnut veneer. Doors on Buffet and Server Burl Walnut veneer. Walnut overlay on Buffet linen drawer with Walnut center carving. Panels on either side of China Cabinet door are striped Walnut veneer with Walnut overlay and solid Walnut center carvings. Scrolled panel on glass door of 3-ply Walnut. Solid Walnut mouldings and carvings.

Chairs solid Walnut throughout with 5-ply stock veneered with Walnut on center panels. Regular slip seats.

Table has two-piece six-leg base, top equipped with standard Maple slides on regular dividing frame.

Hardware. Brass finish.

Finish. Non-fading stain thoroughly filled and finished with three coats of lacquer rubbed smooth. A Van Dyke Brown finish similar to Plate No. 10 in the Woods and Finishes Section preceding page 9 of this book.

THE CHARLOTTE FURNITURE CO.

Reproductions and Adaptations of Antique Furniture
for the Bedroom, Living Room and Hall

CHARLOTTE, MICHIGAN

EASTERN OFFICE
NEW YORK, N. Y., 216 E. 45th St., 3rd Floor

EXHIBIT
GRAND RAPIDS, MICH., 4th Floor, Keeler Bldg.

No. 61 Oak Dresser and Glass

No. 48 Smoky Pine Bed

No. 63 Oak Dressing Table and Glass

No. 57 Mahogany Chest and Desk

No. 63 Oak Night Table

PRODUCTS
MANUFACTURERS OF

BEDS
BENCHES
CHAIRS
CHESTS
CHEST TOILETS
DESKS
DRESSERS
HANGING MIRRORS

HIGH BOYS
LINEN CHESTS
SECRETARIES
TABLES
—Night
—Makeup
—Toilet

Trade Mark

TRADE NAMES

"CHARLOTTE FURNITURE" used in connection with trade mark here illustrated on all furniture of our manufacture.

GENERAL INFORMATION

Our products are reproductions and adaptations of prized antiques made in the following designs and woods:

Early American in Smoky Pine, Plain and Crotch Mahogany; Antique Maple, Oak and Cherry.

Early English in Antique Oak and Crotch Mahogany.

Provinçal French in Smoky Oak and Beech.

FINISHES

Our finishes closely resemble those shown in the Woods and Finishes Section preceding page 9 of this book.
Duxbury Mahogany, see plate No. 24.
Antique Oak, see plate No. 4.
Early English Oak, see plate No. 4. Our finish is darker.
Antique Topaz Maple, see plate No. 8.
Smoky Pine, see plate No. 28. Our finish is lighter.

HEIRLOOMS OF TOMORROW

Charlotte Furniture carries in "House and Garden" and "House Beautiful" educational advertisements stressing the advantages of antique reproductions of Period Furniture—you as a distributor should increase your profits by tying up with this program and becoming an authorized Charlotte representative.

RETAIL PRICE RANGES

Our four piece bedroom suites range in price to consumers $368 to $1080, subject to change without notice.

CHATTANOOGA FURNITURE COMPANY
Manufacturers of Dining Room Furniture

Chestnut & Fourteenth St., CHATTANOOGA, TENN.

PERMANENT EXHIBITS
CHICAGO, ILL., Space 744, American Furniture Mart
GRAND RAPIDS, MICH., First Floor, Manufacturers Bldg.

Side Chair No. 172. Seat upholstered in Tapestry or Velour.

Dining Room Table No. 174. Top, 45x60 inches. Equipped with equalizing slides.

Host Chair No. 173. Tapestry or Velour seat.

PRODUCTS
MANUFACTURERS OF
DINING ROOM FURNITURE SOLD AS SUITES OR AS SEPARATE PIECES
including
—CHAIRS, ARM AND SIDE   —CHINA CABINETS
—TABLES   —BUFFETS   —SERVERS

DESIGNS
The designs in Chattanooga Furniture are modernistic in their scope. While in some pieces the influence of European Periods is apparent the versatility of Chattanooga designers have imbued these with other characteristics that are distinctly individual.

CONSTRUCTION OF CHATTANOOGA FURNITURE

The construction of Suite No. 173 illustrated (with the exception of the China Cabinet) on this page incorporates the principles found in all Chattanooga numbers. Tops, Fronts and Ends of five-ply Walnut with posts of Gumwood. The interiors are of Oak with deep velvet finish. A suitable compartment for silver is provided. Drawers have the boxed-in dovetail construction and are thoroughly dust-proof. This suite is durably built to give many years of genuine satisfaction. The handsome carved moldings add much to the charm.

Write for our prices.

Buffet. Two sizes:—No. 173—Width, 66 inches
No. 174—Width, 72 inches.

Server No. 173. Width, 44 inches.

THE CONTINENTAL FURNITURE CO.
Manufacturers of Bedroom Furniture
HIGH POINT, NORTH CAROLINA

EXHIBITS

CHICAGO, ILL., Space 726 American Furniture Mart   HIGH POINT, N. C., 3rd Floor Exposition Building

No. 600—Bench.
Fiber Seat, 25x15 inches.

No. 600—Chest. Base 40 inches with or without Deck.
With or without Standing Mirror 18x16 inches.

No. 601—Chest.
Base 28 inches. With or
without Wall Mirror
18x16 inches.

No. 600—Rocker.
Fiber Seat.

No. 600—Night Table.
Top 16x16 inches.

No. 600—Highboy.
Base 42 inches.

No. 600—Chest. Base 40 inches with or without Deck.
With or without Standing Mirror 18x16 inches.

No. 600—Chair.
Fiber Seat.

No. 600—Dresser. Base 50 inches.
Mirror 34x30 inches.

No. 600—Bed. (54 inches.
(Twin Bed 39 inches.)

No. 605—French Vanity.   Base 50 inches.
Mirror 32x26 inches.

"THE JEFFERSON" BEDROOM SUITE No. 600
Genuine and Solid Mahogany

This attractive American Colonial design has merited a selection of very best materials for its construction. Genuine and Solid Mahogany material is used throughout. Solid brass hardware, of authentic Colonial design, is in keeping with other decorative motifs that lend distinction to the entire group. This production is one of the richest of our line, and meets the present demand for character that differentiates from the every-day plainness of the older types of this same period. The Continental trade mark guarantees superior quality in every detail of construction and finish. This will be maintained in the line as a permanent open stock design.

No. 800—Night Table.
Top, 18x14 inches.

No. 800—Bed (54 inches).

No. 800—Chair.

No. 800—Desk. Base 36 inches.

No. 800—Bed (39 inches).

No. 800—Bed, 39 inches.

No. 805—French Vanity. Base, 48 inches.
Mirror, 36x22 inches.

No. 800—Chest. Base, 38 inches.

No. 800—Bench. Seat 24x14 inches.

No. 800—Dresser. Base 50 inches.
Mirror 32x30 inches.

No. 800—Chest. Base 38 inches.
Standing Mirror, 16x14 inches.

"THE JANEIRO" BEDROOM SUITE No. 800
Genuine Brazilian Rosewood

A departure from the usual in this new Continental Bedroom design will be instantly recognized by dealers who know good selling value. Homes too, where the better type of furniture is appreciated, will be looking for such quality and conservative cost. Genuine Brazilian Rosewood veneers in glowing finish of natural golden brown on all flat surfaces. Frames, posts and other solid parts of selected woods finished in antique brown walnut tones to harmonize. Hand spindle moldings and carvings are of beautifully grained solid wood. Hardware appropriately finished in old gold. Interiors of Solid and Genuine Mahogany, finished with usual Continental skill.

PRODUCTS

MANUFACTURERS OF

BEDROOM SUITES COMPLETE,
  including Bench, Chair,
  Rocker and Night Table
BEDROOM BENCH, CHAIR,
  ROCKER for Odd Suites
BEDROOM FURNITURE, Odd
  Pieces

BEDS
—Bow End
—Straight End
—Four Poster
BENCHES
—Bedroom
—Dressing and Toilet Table

**CONTINENTAL
SUPERIOR QUALITY
C F Co**

Trade Mark

CHAIRS, Bedroom, Sets of
CHESTS OF DRAWERS
CHIFFONIERS
CHIFFORETTES
CHIFFOROBES
COSTUMERS, Wood
DESKS, Bedroom
DRESSEROBES

DRESSERS
DRESSERS, Vanity
DRESSERS AND WARDROBES
  Combined
DRESSING TABLES
HOTEL FURNITURE
ROCKERS, Bedroom
TABLES, Night

DAVIS FURNITURE CORPORATION
Manufacturers of Bedroom and Dining Room Furniture
JAMESTOWN, N. Y.

PRODUCTS

MANUFACTURERS OF

BEDROOM SUITES, Complete, including Bench, Chair, Rocker and Night Table.

Also the following furniture for the bedroom sold separately on order:

BENCHES   NIGHT TABLES
CHAIRS AND ROCKERS   TWIN BEDS
FOUR POSTER BEDS

DINING ROOM SUITES, Complete or Separate Pieces as follows:

BUFFETS   EXTENSION TABLES
CHAIRS   SERVERS

BEDROOM FURNITURE

Davis Bedroom Furniture has the characteristics that sell—that is evident.

The finish is durable and attractive and aids materially in giving the necessary touch to an already attractive design.

FOUR POSTER BEDS

Davis carries a full line of four poster beds that will appeal and sell to your profit. All the popular designs are carried in this line and you will have a wide variety to select from.

Colonial Four Poster Bed No. 400.—4 ft. 3 in. or 3 ft. 3 in. slats. Walnut or Mahogany.

DINING ROOM FURNITURE

Dining Room Furniture to sell must combine utility and comfort with durability. Perhaps in no other direction has Davis exerted more effort in creating a furniture that would embrace these features in addition to being salable. The latest improved methods of construction are employed with reinforcements wherever practical.

CONSTRUCTION AND FINISHES

All fronts, tops and end panels are five-ply Butt Walnut. Flush End construction is used throughout. Drawers are boxed in with three-ply bottoms, oak interiors and sides, fully dustproof.

Mahogany—Salem Red Colonial and Walnut—rich High-light Brown.

Trade Mark

DESCRIPTIVE LITERATURE

Write for prices and other descriptive literature on the Davis line. Our offerings will interest you.

Highboy No. 500.—Top, 40 by 20 inches. Walnut or Mahogany.

Vanity No. 309.—Top, 48 by 20 inches. Mirror, 28 by 22 inches. Walnut or Mahogany.

Dresser No. 90.—Top, 48 by 22 inches. Mirror, 30 by 26 inches. Walnut or Mahogany.

DIXIE FURNITURE COMPANY
Manufacturers of Bedroom Furniture
LEXINGTON, N. C.

SALES AND SHOWROOMS

CHICAGO, ILL., Space 529, American Furniture Mart   HIGH POINT, N. C., Southern Furniture Exposition Bldg.
NEW YORK, N. Y., Louis J. Doran Co.

Dresser No. 90.

Trade Mark

Vanity No. 90.

PRODUCTS

MANUFACTURERS OF

BEDROOM SUITES COMPLETE, INCLUDING:
—Bench Chair, Rocker, and Night Table
BEDROOM SUITES, four pieces only.
Also separate Bedroom Pieces, including:

BOW END BEDS	NIGHT TABLES
TWIN BEDS	CHESTS OF DRAWERS
BENCHES	CHIFFOROBES
CHAIRS	DRESSERS
ROCKERS	VANITY DRESSERS

TRADE NAMES

"DIXIE"—used in connection with all products of this company. See illustration of trade mark seal which is tagged to each piece of "DIXIE" furniture.

WOODS AND FINISHES

"DIXIE" furniture is finished in Mahogany or Walnut similar in appearance to plates Nos. 1 and 14 in the Woods and Finishes Section preceeding page 9 of this book.

RETAIL PRICE RANGES

Bedroom Suites Complete range from $195 to $265. Four piece Suites from $160 to $200. Beds from $40 to $80. Chests of Drawers and Chifforobes from $35 to $75. Dressers and Vanities from $45 to $90. Chairs, Rockers, and Benches from $10 to $17.50. Night Tables from $7.50 to $12.

The foregoing prices are subject to change without notice, terms 2% ten days, 30 days net.

Bed No. 101.

EBERT FURNITURE CO.

SINCE 1854

Manufacturers of Dining Room Furniture

RED LION, PENNA.

SHOWROOMS

RED LION, PA., at Factory   PHILADELPHIA, PA.   NEW YORK, N. Y.   CHICAGO, ILL.
BOSTON, MASS.   SAN FRANCISCO, CAL.   HIGH POINT, N. C.

PRODUCTS

MANUFACTURERS OF COMPLETE DINING ROOM SUITES; ALSO OAK CHINA CLOSETS in various styles and sizes.

Buffet, Top 22x66 inches. List price, $76.00.

Side Chair of Suite No. 1045. Set of six chairs including five side chairs and one arm chair, list price, $56.00.

No. 1045—Arm or Rest Chair. Set of six chairs including five side chairs and one arm chair, list price, $56.00.

SUITE No. 1045

Suite of 4 pieces—list price, $216.00. Suite of ten pieces which includes six chairs, list price, $272.00.

Suite No. 1045½ which has a canopy on the China Cabinet, retailing for $61.00 with prices on other pieces the same as No. 1045, can be obtained, four pieces, $223.00, and ten pieces for $279.00.

Dining Table of Suite No. 1045. Top, 60x42 inches. List price, $55.00.

No. 074—Plain Oak Closet. Gloss finish. Height, 62 inches; Width, 36 inches; Weight, one in a Crate, 120 pounds; Weight, two in a crate, 200 pounds. Price for one, $27.00. Two shipped in one crate at one time, $52.00.

No. 056—China Closet. Plain Oak gloss. Height, 61 inches; Width, 36 inches. List price, $38.50. Weight crated, 150 pounds.

WOODS AND FINISHES

The Woods used in the building of Ebert China Closets are chiefly Plain Oak; while the Dining Room Furniture is constructed of Walnut veneers primarily.

The Plain Oak finishes resemble plate No. 5—Golden Oak; Walnut is close to plate No. 14—American Walnut Standard—see Woods and Finishes Section preceding page 9 of this book.

GENERAL INFORMATION

Ebert furniture is conscientiously built to give enduring service. Reasonably priced it is an opportunity for you to increase your business in this direction.

In the production of Ebert furniture, quality of construction has not been overlooked. Wherever it was possible or practical we have doubly reinforced the joints to add to the rigidity.

Limited space does not permit us to illustrate all the styles and types of furniture that Ebert is able to supply you. Write for descriptive literature or see our furniture at the various exhibits mentioned on the top of this page.

All prices are subject to change without notice.

ESTEY MANUFACTURING CO.
Bedroom Furniture
Cass and Elm Sts., OWOSSO, MICH.

Dresser, Top, 50x22 inches. Mirror, 30x38 inches. List price, $116.00.

No. 1051—Dresser with top 42x22 inches. Mirror, 22x28 inches. List price, $85.00.

Chiffonier, Top, 36x21 inches. Toilet Glass, 12x16 inches. List price: Base, $80.00; Mirror, $19.00.

Bed. Height, 50 inches. Slat, 4 feet 6 inches or 3 feet 3 inches. List price, $48.00.

Dressing Table, Top, 46x20 inches. Plate 20x24 inches. List price, $68.00.

Bench, Top, 24x14 inches. List price, $17.00.

Night Table, Top, 18x14 inches. List price, $28.00.

 *(side chair)*

Side Chair. Standard size. List price, $18.00.

PRODUCTS

MANUFACTURERS OF

BEDROOM SUITES COMPLETE, including Benches, Chairs and Night Tables
SEPARATE PIECES FOR THE BEDROOM, including:

—Four Poster, Straight End and Twin Beds
—Benches, Upholstered and Cane Seats
—Chairs, Cane

Seat and Upholstered
—Chiffoniers
—Ladies' Desks
—Dressers, Vanity Dressers and Semi-Vanities

—Dressing Tables
—Night Tables —Wardrobes
ALSO manufacturers of Highboys and Hotel Furniture.

THE PROVINCETOWN
Mahogany and Gum

There is no doubt that there will always be a demand for Colonial Furniture and that it will increase. Closely associated with the early-history of our country, Colonial Furniture has certain characteristics found in no other period or style.

The Provincetown is the work of a designer who has absorbed the spirit of the period and expressed it with surety and grace in this suite. The deep warm tones of Mahogany enhance the charm of the lines. A fine four post bed is the keynote of The Provincetown. List price of complete suite, $394.

WOODS AND FINISHES

Mahogany, Curly Maple, Maple, Crotch Mahogany in combinations with Gum are the chief woods used in the construction of Estey Furniture. Finishes are durable and in keeping with the furniture.

RETAIL PRICE RANGE

Bedroom Suites range from $190.00 to $800.00. These prices include Benches, Chairs, Rockers and Night Tables. Prices of individual pieces range in proportion. All prices subject to change without notice.

POINTS OF SUPERIORITY TO EMPHASIZE WHEN SHOWING ESTEY BEDROOM FURNITURE

If the average customer understood the value of sound construction in furniture, there would be less tendency to buy cheap furniture. Bring out the following points when showing Estey furniture, to impress on your customers that "Estey" furniture is worth its price and will give them complete satisfaction.

Drawers Cannot Stick nor Jam

The Estey method of drawer construction is illustrated on the right. Drawers are the working parts of Dressers and every one will appreciate this "Kant-stick" construction which prevents sticking and jamming.

Case Backs Screwed on— Not Nailed

This costs a little more but it makes the cases stronger and more lasting.

Special Reinforcements on Case Backs

See the drawing on the right illustrating this. Extra pieces at top and bottom, points A and B, make the whole frame strong and rigid.

Detailed Drawer Construction. Note 2-point Suspension and minimum frictions

Illustrating special reinforcements on case backs at points A and B

Dowels are fully sunk. Dovetailed parts are accurately joined. Result—Estey Furniture stands squarely on the floor. You can't "rock" it by pushing down on one end.

Veneer Allowed to Season

Veneered panels are air dried for ten days. This prevents curling and warping and makes the panels last as long as the furniture is in use.

Five Inspections Before Shipping

Nothing defective leaves our plant. Impress this fact on your customers. It is their assurance, and yours, that every piece of Estey Furniture is guaranteed to satisfy.

EMPIRE CASE GOODS COMPANY
Manufacturers of Bedroom Furniture
122 Foote Ave., JAMESTOWN, N. Y.

EXHIBITS

CHICAGO, ILL., Space 1601, American Furniture Mart   JAMESTOWN, N. Y., Exposition Building
NEW YORK, N. Y., Space 913, New York Furniture Exchange

PRODUCTS
Manufacturers of

BEDROOM SUITES COMPLETE, including Bench, Chair, Rocker and Night Table.

BEDROOM SUITES, Four Pieces Only, including Bed, Dresser, Vanity and Chest.

Also the following Bedroom Pieces sold separately on order:

BEDS, Wood, Colonial	CHIFFOROBES, Cedar lined
BENCHES	DESKS
—Bedroom	DRESSERS
—Dressing Table	—Standard
—Toilet Table	—Vanity
CHAIRS	DRESSING TABLES
CHESTS OF DRAWERS	NIGHT TABLES
CHIFFOROBES	ROCKERS

ALSO manufacturers of Hotel Bedroom Furniture

GENERAL INFORMATION
Designs

The predominant characteristics in the designs of the Empire Case Goods Furniture are Colonial. The charm of this pattern is further enhanced by subtle touches of other equally attractive Period Designs, such as Jacobean and Empire.

Construction

The latest improved methods of assembling are employed in all Empire products. Dust-proof and dovetail construction throughout. Wherever decorations appear you can be assured of quality as each is hand carved.

The Empire Case Goods Company has been long known as one of the largest and most reliable manufacturers of medium price bedroom furniture in the country. You are offered a wide range of patterns at prices enabling you to give excellent value to your trade. Further illustrative and descriptive literature of the line will be sent to you upon request.

Suite No. 571—Colonial Influence—finished in a lustrous shade of Mahogany resembling plate No. 1 in Woods and Finishes Section preceding page 9 of this book, and made in combinations to fill the requirements of every customer.

Dresser No. S61¾—Top, 49 by 23½ inches. Mirror, 30 by 32 inches.

Vanity No. S62—Top, 49 by 20½ inches. Mirror, 22 by 32 inches.

Bed No. X65—4 feet 6 inches and 3 feet 3 inches sizes available.

No. 68¾—Chest of Drawers. Top, 37 by 20½ inches.

No. 61 BEDROOM SUITE
Construction
Five-ply tops and fronts. Face veneer of Butt Walnut. All solid parts such as frames, rails and posts are made of Gumwood. Dust-proof Mahogany drawer bottoms, and Sycamore drawer sides throughout. Dovetail construction. Decorations wood hand carvings and cut moldings.

Finish
Interior of drawers finished in two coats of flat varnish. Exterior of case three coats of high grade varnish rubbed to dull effect. Plate No. 14 American Walnut Standard in the Woods and Finishes Section preceding page 9 of this Reference Book illustrates the finish of this suite.

Pieces Comprising this Suite
This No. 61 suite consists of 45-inch and 49-inch Dressers, in either swinging or stationary mirror. Full Vanity with swinging mirror, triplicate mirrors, or stationary mirror. Semi-Vanity with stationary mirror; Chifforobe; Two Straight End Beds;

Bench No. 60B—Upholstered in Blue-Gray Denim.

Spindle Four-Post Bed or Panel Four-Post Bed; Vanity Table and Night Table. Two types of Chest—Portable Mirror. Bench, Chair and Rocker can be ordered in any combination desired.

WOODS AND FINISHES
Butt Walnut, Walnut and Mahogany veneers are the three chief woods used in the building of Empire Furniture. The beauty of this wood is further brought out by the finishes which resemble plates 14, 15, 1, 3, as shown in the Woods and Finishes Section preceding page 9 of this book.

PRICE RANGE
Complete Bedroom Suites vary from $200 to $250; while four-piece suites range from $160 to $290. These prices help you make attractive offerings to your trade yet realize a substantial profit. All prices subject to change without notice.

EMPIRE FURNITURE CO.
PENN TABLE COMPANY

Manufacturers of Complete Dining Room and Apartment Suites

HUNTINGTON, W. VA.

EXHIBITS

CHICAGO, ILL., Space 1645-6, American Furniture Mart   NEW YORK, N. Y., Space 913, Furniture Exchange

GRAND RAPIDS, MICH., 2nd Floor, Waters-Klingman Bldg.

PRODUCTS

MANUFACTURERS OF

COMPLETE DINING ROOM AND APARTMENT SUITES, DESKS AND SECRETARIES

Penn Table Products—DINING ROOM TABLES AND EXTENSION TABLES

DINING ROOM CHAIRS

GENERAL INFORMATION

In the "KENSINGTON" suite illustrated, the definite and staunch constructional features have a decided Jacobean origin. In this modern interpretation of the Jacobean, the designer has succeeded in retaining the true atmosphere of the period and adapted it to the requirements of the American Home. Note the predominating buffet, the solid table and the attractively ornamented s i d e - board.

There's something about it your trade will like—it combines true craftsmanship with productive efficiency. It also combines beauty and excellence of finish with superiority of design, seldom, if ever, found in a line so moderately priced.

NICHOLSON-KENDLE FURNITURE CO.
Bedroom Furniture and Odd Dressers
HUNTINGTON, W. VA.

PRODUCTS
MANUFACTURERS OF

BEDROOM SUITES COMPLETE
BEDS
—Bow End
—Four Poster
—Odd
—Straight End
BENCHES
—Bedroom
CHAIRS
—Bedroom
CHIFFONIERS

CHIFFORETTES
CHIFFOROBES
DRESSERS
DRESSERS
—Vanity
DRESSING TABLES
HIGHBOYS
LOWBOYS
ROCKERS
—Bedroom
NIGHT STANDS

GENERAL INFORMATION

The general quality and salability of Nicholson-Kendle Furniture has long been known to the industry. To the retailers not yet thoroughly familiar with the merits of this line, an investigation will be to your lasting benefit.

The Furniture we offer you is built and priced to sell—at a profitable mark-up within a short time. You should take this opportunity and increase your business.

DESCRIPTION OF SUITE No. 520

The peculiar appeal of furniture of the William and Mary Period needs no detailed explanation. The Nicholson-Kendle designers have deftly interpreted into this Suite No. 520 the outstanding characteristics that makes this furniture livable and adaptable for the bedroom.

*Dresser No. 525—Top, 46 inches.
Mirror, 24x30 inches.*

No. 527-½—Top, 42 inches.

*Bed No. 519—Height, 53 inches; Width ,4 feet,
6 inches.*

FANCHER FURNITURE CO.

Manufacturers of Breakfast and Dining Room Furniture

SALAMANCA, N. Y.

Suite No. 431—Finished in Walnut.

Suite No. 430—Finished in W .ln t.

Suite No. 429—Finished in Mahogany and Walnut.

Suite No. 428—Finished in Walnut.

PRODUCTS

MANUFACTURERS OF DINING ROOM AND BREAKFAST ROOM SUITES, complete, constructed to meet present-day demand for reasonably priced furniture.

GENERAL INFORMATION

Highly skilled mechanics and large cuttings of a few beautifully designed Dining Room Suites are the fundamental reasons behind the fact that we can, and do, sell Quality Furniture at prices which enable the retailer to get quick turnovers and satisfactory margins—at the same time building a good reputation for dependable merchandise.

Any of the numbers shown above is a value that will appeal favorably to your discriminating trade. Look them over.

Suite No. 426—Finished in Mahogany.

AN OPPORTUNITY

Here is an opportunity to stock the kind of furniture that will sell. Each suite has the characteristics that make ideal home fixtures—within the means of your trade. Write us for photogravures and price list.

OTHER FANCHER SUITES

We regret the necessity of omitting from these illustrations our more recent numbers including a genuine reproduction of an Early American Crotch Mahogany suite having posts and exposed solid parts of Solid Mahogany. Also a Duncan Phyfe suite in Mahogany and a beautiful Walnut suite in English design very attractively priced.

We are also adding another Dinette suite which we believe will rival in popularity our No. 429 which has met with such a pronounced success. We will soon be supplied with group photogravures of these suites which we will be glad to furnish dealers on request.

FLORENCE TABLE
AND MANUFACTURING CO.

Tables, Dining and Breakfast Room Furniture

Mallory Station, MEMPHIS, TENN.

EXHIBITS

CHICAGO, ILL., Space 538, American Furniture Mart

No. 85—Side Chair.

*No. 85—Table. Top, 45x60 inches. 6, 8,
10 or 12-foot lengths may be had.*

No. 85—Arm Chair.

PRODUCTS

MANUFACTURERS OF

BREAKFAST SETS (Tables and Chairs).

COMPLETE BREAKFAST SUITES (Tables, Chairs and Buffets).

INDIVIDUAL PIECES FOR THE BREAKFAST ROOM as follows:
—Buffets
—Chairs
—Tables

DINING ROOM SUITES AND ODD PIECES for the Living Room including the following:
—Buffets
—Tables
—China Cabinets
—Servers
—Chairs
—Odd and Occasional Tables
—Console Tables
—Davenport Tables
—End Tables
—Library Tables
—Side Tables
—Dining-Living Combination Tables
—Drop Leaf Tables

*No. 85—China Cabinet.
42 inches wide.*

No. 85—Buffet. 66 inches long.

No. 85 Suite illustrated above is only one of several patterns. We have more inexpensive as well as better ones.

PERHAPS NO NAME MEANS MORE TO THE FURNITURE INDUSTRY THAN "FLORENCE"

26 Years of Full Production

Our designers may be correctly termed enthusiasts. Our success can be attributed entirely to the nation's acceptance of the quality, beauty and fair prices of our product.

The good reputation we have among the furniture dealers has been earned through years of meritorious service. Devoted to high ideals and principles as you are, Florence quality and values will gain your respect and bring us your patronage.

Trade Mark

Our prestige in the furniture industry is known; we have increased our quality and enlarged our facilities for better service each year. The Florence line is diversified and embodies such creations as will interest the greatest purchasing class; hence, we reason your volume will ultimately be ours.

May this for the present serve as our "Knight of the Grip." While in Chicago visit our space and compare our merchandise. Mail all inquiries to our Memphis address.

FORSYTH FURNITURE LINES, INC.

Dining Room, Bedroom and Breakfast Room Furniture

WINSTON-SALEM, NORTH CAROLINA

PERMANENT SHOW-ROOMS

CHICAGO, ILL., Spaces 1212-13-14, American Furniture Mart   NEW YORK, N. Y., Space 416, New York Furniture Exchange

HIGH POINT, N. C., Ninth Floor, High Point Market

WAREHOUSE POINTS

BROOKLYN, N. Y.   BALTIMORE, MD.   DALLAS, TEXAS   CHICAGO, ILL.   DETROIT, MICH.

Vanity, Suite No. 350.

Dresser, Suite No. 450.

Buffet, from Suite No. 45.

PRODUCTS

MANUFACTURERS OF

DINING ROOM SUITES Complete; Breakfast Room Sets Complete; and Bedroom Furniture, Complete Suites, including Bench, Chair, Rocker and Night Table.

BEDROOM FURNITURE

Ranging from $55 to $160

Suite No. 450—The last word in superb, well-balanced design, selection of woods and thorough craftsmanship in the matching of veneers and handling of decorations catches the spirit of the younger generation. Composed of ten pieces, comprising Double and Twin Straight-Foot Beds, Dresser, as shown, French Vanity, Chest with or without mirror standard, Night Table, Stool, Chair and Rocker.

Specifications—Tops and Fronts, five-ply Walnut Veneers with three-ply end panels. Top drawers, Burl Walnut Veneers; overlays, Bird's-Eye Maple; half turnings of posts at the top give added effect. Drawer bottoms, three-ply Mahogany veneer; interior construction dust-proof.

Suite No. 350—offers a wide selection in its range of Twin Beds, Chifforobe, Chest, Rocker, Chair, Stool, Night Table, Two-size Dressers, Full Vanity and French Vanity. This number will find ready appeal in large metropolitan centers.

Specifications—Tops and Fronts, five-ply Walnut Veneers; End Panels, three ply; Center Panels, Burl Walnut Veneers; Overlays on standards, Burl Walnut. Each piece has decorations set in receding panel with decorations of applied wood on all standards. Drawer bottoms, three-ply Mahogany; all interiors thoroughly dust proof.

Other Numbers—can be seen at any Forsyth Permanent Showroom, or you can get complete information by writing to us direct.

DESIGNS, WOODS AND FINISHES

Forsyth has developed designs distinctly modernistic in character and appeal which are copied in suites built chiefly of Walnut. Finished resemble plates No. 1—Standard American Mahogany; No. 14—American Walnut Standard; No. 19—Brown Sheraton; No. 15—Spanish Walnut, and No. 28—Walnut Eastern, as shown in the Woods and Finishes Section preceding page 9 of this Reference Book.

DINING ROOM FURNITURE

Ranging from $45 to $245

Suite No. 45—is a Forsyth Period Adaptation with gleaming center matched Burl Walnut surfaces, handsome beading and decorations, and distinctive hardware. Suite consists of Buffet, China, Server, Arm Chair and five Side Chairs, two Tables, Six-leg and Pedestal.

Specifications—Double tops on all pieces, five-ply Walnut veneers. Fronts, five-ply center matched Butt Walnut veneer. Butt Walnut veneered Chair panels and Table rims. Heavy paneled doors on chifforobe and china have top overlays of diamond-matched Walnut; also used on center panel of server and top rail of chair backs. Decorative molding motif on back rails of cases is also applied to octagon table corners. Drawers have center guides, dovetailed, boxed-in drawers, dust-proof, three-ply Walnut veneered ends and three-ply case backs. Removable lined silver tray in buffet top drawers. Interiors, three-ply Walnut veneered ends and three-ply case backs; Mahogany carefully finished. Two tables, pedestal and six-leg, both extension, can be furnished. Chairs have oversized seats.

Other Dining Room Numbers—A representative line is on display at the Forsyth Permanent Show Rooms or complete information may be obtained by writing direct.

BREAKFAST ROOM FURNITURE

Forsyth Breakfast Room Suites are real furniture—dinette designs that are suitable for either small dining rooms or breakfast rooms. These suites are also on exhibition at our permanent show rooms or full details concerning them may be obtained by writing us direct. All prices shown are subject to change without notice.

GLOBE-BOSSE WORLD FURNITURE CO.

Manufacturers of Bedroom and Dining Room Furniture, Kitchen Cabinets, Cupboards and Wardrobes

9th Ave. and Maryland St., EVANSVILLE, INDIANA

PERMANENT EXHIBITS

CHICAGO, ILL., Space 919-920, American Furniture Mart   NEW YORK, N. Y., Space 1214-1216, N. Y. Furniture Exchange
EVANSVILLE, IND., Fifth Floor, Furniture Building

No. 1599—Host Chair. Up-holstered in Jacquard. $24.00.

Side Chair No. 1598. Up-holstered in Jacquard. $17.50.

No. 1595—China. Top, 16x42 inches. $64.50.

Buffet No. 1593. Top, 23x66 inches. $73.00. Also another size, No. 1591, Top, 23x72 inches. $79.00.

No. 1590—Table. Top, 45x60 inches. $58.00.

Server No. 1597. Top, 17x40 inches. $39.00.

PRODUCTS

MANUFACTURERS OF

BEDROOM SUITES COMPLETE, DINING ROOM SUITES COMPLETE, including the following pieces sold separately:

KITCHEN CABINETS
SAFES
CUPBOARDS, KITCHEN
WARDROBES
DRESSING TABLES
CHIFFONIERS
CHIFFOROBES
CHINA CLOSETS
CHINA CABINETS
KITCHEN CLOSETS
SERVERS
BEDS, WOOD

BEDS
—Bow End
—Four Poster
—Straight End
BENCHES
BUFFETS
CHEST OF DRAWERS
DRESSEROBES
DRESSERS
—Vanity
DRESSING TABLES
TABLES,
      DINING ROOM

SUITE 1590 ILLUSTRATED

This suite is built of Combination Walnut Veneer and Gum. Butt Walnut, Curly Maple and Zebrano Veneers. Blended Brown Walnut polish finish. Prices shown are subject to change without notice.

CATALOG ON REQUEST

Write for our complete catalog showing the entire Globe-Bosse-World Line—no obligation.

B. F. HUNTLEY FURNITURE CO.

Manufacturers of Bedroom and Dining Room Furniture

WINSTON-SALEM, NO. CAR.

PRODUCTS

MANUFACTURERS OF

BEDROOM FURNITURE,
    including
BENCHES
—Bedroom
—Dressing Table
BENCHES, CHAIRS, AND
    ROCKERS for Odd
    Suites
BEDS
—Bow End
—Twin
CHAIRS
—Bedroom
—Cane Seat
—Sets of
CHESTS OF DRAWERS
CHIFFONIERS
CHIFFORETTES
CHIFFOROBES
DESKS
—Bedroom
—Ladies' Bedroom
DRESSERS
DRESSERS, VANITY

HOTEL BEDROOM FURNI-
    TURE
NIGHT
—Stands
—Tables
ROCKERS
SUITES, Complete, includ-
    ing B e n c h, Chair,
    Rocker and Night
    Table
VANITY
—Cases for Make-Up
—Tables
WARDROBES
WARDROBE
—Chests
—Chiffoniers
DINING ROOM FURNITURE,
    including
BUFFETS
CHAIRS
CHINA CLOSETS
SUITES COMPLETE
SERVERS
TABLES

Also Manufacturers of Grip Stands, Highboys, and Lamp Stands.

Reg. Trade Marks

MIXED CAR LOADINGS

Every successful store is planning its merchandising line-up to give maximum turnover. The Huntley line has been planned to give the retail store the answer to these trends and conditions. You can buy your bedroom and dining room requirements in mixed cars, shipped from the same factory. There is a wide range of style from which to choose. In each design there are optional groupings which provide a wide range of price.

Regardless of price, there is only one Standard of Quality in Huntley style, construction and finish.

HUNTLEY QUALITY STANDARD

An element of style, a beauty of finish, plus Huntley craftsmanship make this line an outstanding value.

The beautiful Huntley finishes, Plymouth, Mahogany, and Bressing Walnut, are a fitting background for the decorations and distinctive hardware that are a feature of Huntley quality. Real style and elegance are rare in moderate priced suites—here you will find both these qualities to an unusual degree. And they mean a lot to people who buy furniture.

CRAFTSMANSHIP
—FROM FOREST TO HOME

Back of the entire Huntley organization lies the heritage and spirit of the master craftsmen of Old Salem, who worked in the rich walnut and mahogany of our Colonial days on fine replicas of English and Flemish designs, brought to the colonies by a few wealthy land-holders.

With its own timber tracts, operating its own logging crews and sawmills, the great Huntley organization carries economy and craftsmanship from raw material to your customers. Thus the Huntley factories are protected against speculative markets in raw material and Huntley costs are based on actual production and not on fluctuating markets.

In every department of the Huntley organization, has been thoroughly instilled the idea that no furniture transaction is complete until the furniture is re-sold from the retail store, and in the hands of a satisfied customer.

With this thought in mind, Huntley designers plan merchandise, not to sell at a certain price, but to fill a certain market requirement, planned to have a particular and definite appeal. In design, construction, finish, and in range of groupings, Huntley merchandise shows a far-sighted planning from the retail point of view.

Every manufacturer is able to talk quality and price. Huntley merchandise talks resale value, profits and turnover.

ROBERT W. IRWIN COMPANY
Manufacturers of ROYAL *and* PHOENIX *Furniture*
Salesrooms, 23 Summer Ave., GRAND RAPIDS, MICH.

PRODUCTS
MANUFACTURERS OF
DINING ROOM AND BEDROOM SUITES, and LIVING ROOM FURNITURE supplying two distinct markets with prices in keeping with the character of the productions.

TRADE NAMES
"ROYAL" and "PHOENIX" are the trade names that designate the two lines, being productions from two distinct factories owned by and operated under the corporate name, Robert W. Irwin Company.

Trade Marks

GENERAL INFORMATION
The Robert W. Irwin Company serves two markets and the needs of two classes of homemakers. The "Royal" line is composed of the more limited and exclusive creations while the "Phoenix" line is the more commercial, popular production. Owing to the resources of this Company, its buying power, and the co-operation between the two plants, exceptional values are offered in both lines.

Royal Furniture for the living room and library—a newly enlarged line—now includes beautiful specimens of upholstered pieces, chairs, sofas, love seats, benches, stools, longues, as well as tables of various types and uses, desks, secretaries, book cases, shelves and cabinets. This line is complete for dealers who cater to the better trade.

Co-related groupings is a feature of these new products.

All prices shown are subject to change without notice.

ROYAL
"Royal" bedroom and dining room suites are made without restrictions of time, labor, money or materials. The finest woods of the world are drawn upon. Period designs and adaptations, hand carving, marquetry, hand painting, and custom fabrication go into these unsurpassed creations. Frankly, this furniture is made for persons of large incomes who demand a distinguished home environment of culture and refinement beyond reproach.

"Royal" living room furniture is fashioned in the same lavish taste, with the same prodigal hand. Tables, consoles, chairs, and various odd pieces compose these products.

Royal Furniture stamps a dealer as a leader in his community, automatically gives him a standing, and attracts to him a powerful clientele.

PRICE RANGES
"Royal" Bedroom and Dining Room Suites are priced from $1000.00 up to $11,000.00, and Royal Living Room Pieces from $60.00 up.

Reproduction of a satinwood commode of about 1770. The marquetry is a beautiful assemblage of satinwood, amaranth and tulipwood.
The mirror is an Adam design, handsomely carved.

PHOENIX
"Phoenix" bedroom and dining room suites are made for that ever-growing class of moderately well-to-do persons who want furniture of beauty and charm but who cannot pay the prices usually associated with and asked for the products of limited and exclusive manufacture.

Phoenix Furniture possesses the same unique distinction in its field as "Royal" does in the narrower appeal. It is commercial furniture only by comparison with "Royal," and by the fact that it is made by production methods which permit lower selling costs. But it is not cheap furniture in any sense and will add character to a vast majority of homes.

ART MODERNE
Recent productions of "Royal" living room and library furniture in the moderne spirit displays an interpretation and understanding of this new vogue which characterizes every product of the organization.

PRICE RANGES
"Phoenix" Bedroom and Dining Room Suites, reveal some remarkable values from $450.00 up to about $1800.00.

JAMESTOWN TABLE COMPANY
Manufacturers of Bedroom Furniture
JAMESTOWN, N. Y.
EXHIBITS
JAMESTOWN, N. Y., Furniture Manufacturers Building   GRAND RAPIDS, MICH., Waters-Klingman Building

Trade Mark

Dresser No. 308.

Chest of Drawers of Suite No. 308.

Vanity No. 308.

PRODUCTS
MANUFACTURERS OF
BEDROOM SUITES

GENERAL INFORMATION

We make bedroom suites exclusively—and a good, sound, salable variety of patterns known for the quality that goes into every detail.

The tremendous demand for Taylor-Made bedroom furniture naturally, as is the case whenever there is mass production, brings prices down to a minimum.

QUALITY

The Taylor-Made line is a quality line. All cases have five-ply tops and fronts. End panels are three ply. Drawers have three-ply mahogany bottoms, and are very carefully finished. They are equipped with center drawer guides. All case and mirror backs are of three-ply veneer—stained and lacquered. Dust-proof interiors. Hand rubbed finishes. And a great many niceties in decoration which are found ordinarily only in the very high priced furniture.

POLICY

In all our forty years of business life, we have always contended that it is at least far more satisfaction to make quality furniture of which we can be proud. And perhaps, if we can price it down to a minimum, the added volume will take care of our profit. We put everything we know how into the furniture we make. It is clean-cut, attractively designed, and made not merely to sell but to stay sold and to satisfy after it is in the customer's home. More and more dealers are turning to Taylor-Made products when it comes to medium priced bedroom furniture.

A smart design is suite No. 308. It uses Butt Walnut graining to decorate its ideally proportioned fronts and tops. Attractive floral panels are used for their daintiness.

JOERNS BROS. FURNITURE CO.
Manufacturers of Bedroom Furniture
STEVENS POINT, WIS.

PRODUCTS
MANUFACTURERS OF
Complete BEDROOM SUITES including Bench, Chair, Rocker and Night Table.

Also separate pieces as follows:

STRAIGHT RETURN END BEDS	CHIFFORETTES
FOUR POSTER BEDS	CHIFFOROBES
BEDROOM AND DRESSING TABLE BENCHES	DRESSERS
	VANITY DRESSERS
BEDROOM CHAIRS	LOWBOYS
CHESTS OF DRAWERS	NIGHT TABLES

Trade Mark

CONSTRUCTION OF SUITE No. 220

Every Joerns case, regardless of price, has the Keystone construction as described for the No. 460 suite. All drawers are boxed in and finished with two coats. Every dust partition is three ply.

This Keystone construction is a decided advantage today, when some furniture is moved every May 1st. The wedged construction at every joint, means a solid, square case.

Materials—Butt Walnut fronts overlayed with Selano, plain Walnut tops and ends. All the scroll work is Selano faced. The carvings are all hand made by our own craftsmen. The whole suite is finished in American Walnut and blended.

DESCRIPTION OF SUITE No. 460

Construction—Cases have full frame under each drawer. All joints are dove-tailed instead of the usual mortise joints. This is an exclusive Joerns feature—the joint is wedged instead of the straight joint depending upon glue for its strength. Drawers are dovetailed throughout and are completely boxed in. Sides and backs are Sycamore with Mahogany bottoms. All drawers have center guides.

Materials—Top: matched butt Walnut. End panels: selected sliced Walnut. Large drawer fronts: matched butt Walnut—overlay surface on center of drawer: Prima Vera. Overlay background: Maple with Mahogany scroll work. Top drawers: Fiddleback Mahogany.

Finish—This suite is finished in American Walnut with the exception of the posts which are finished in Sienne, hilited with Vandyke brown.

GENERAL INFORMATION

The quality and salability of Joerns Products has long been known in the Furniture Industry. The famous Keystone construction is an inherent part of every Joerns suite. The attractiveness of the finishes is a known fact.

When you stock Joerns Furniture—you stock a furniture that has been primarily designed to sell—and to sell at a profit to you. Write for our proposition or better yet place an order now and start selling Joerns.

A. J. JOHNSON & SONS FURNITURE CO.

ESTABLISHED 1869

Manufacturers of Dining and Bedroom Furniture

517 Noble Street, CHICAGO, ILL.

FACTORIES		EXHIBITS
CHICAGO, ILL., 517-537 Noble Street		CHICAGO, ILL., 545-546 American Furniture Mart
927-945 N. Wood Street		1338 S. Michigan Ave.

Trade Mark

PRODUCTS
MANUFACTURERS OF
COMPLETE DINING AND BEDROOM SUITES

Suite No. 604—Walnut—Heppelwhite. Buffet—Width, 72 inches; Height, 37 inches. China Cabinet—Width, 46 inches; Height, 66 inches. Service Cabinet—Width, 45 inches; Height, 35 inches. Side Chair—Height, 38 inches; Arm Chair—Height, 40 inches. Extension Table—45x60 inches—8-foot extension.

Suite No. 627—Oak, Walnut—Jacobean. Buffet—Width, 78 inches; Height, 37 inches. China Cabinet—Width, 42 inches; Height, 72 inches. Service Cabinet—Width, 48 inches; Height, 35 inches. Side Chair—Height, 41 inches; Arm Chair—Height, 44 inches. Refectory Table—40x66 inches—9-foot extension.

Suite No. 234—Walnut—Louis XV. Twin Beds—30 inches; Height, 51 inches. Full Size Bed—54 inches; Height, 51 inches. Dresser—24x54 inches; Height, 32 inches; Mirror, 26x34 inches.

Chifforette—22x41 inches; Height, 51 inches; Dressing Table—22x52 inches; Height, 30 inches; Mirror, 26x34 inches. Foot Stool—14x14 inches; Chair, 16x17 inches; Bench—17x22 in. Night Table—14x17 in.

Suite No. 243.—Mahogany, Walnut. Early American. Twin Beds—30 inches; Height, 51 inches. Full Size Bed—54 inches; Height, 51 inches. Dresser—22x50 inches; Height, 34 inches.

Mirror, 32x22 inches. High Boy—22x35 inches; Height, 65 inches. Dressing Table—18x48 inches Height, 31 inches. Mirror—32x22 inches. Chair—16x19 in. Bench—15x24 in. Night Table—15x20 in

Suite No. 241—Walnut—French Colonial. Twin Beds—30 inches; Height, 60 inches. Full Size Bed—54 inches; Height, 60 inches. Dresser—22x54 inches; Height, 77 inches. Mirror—32x22 inches.

Chifforette—21x41 inches; Height, 56 inches. Vanity, 21x52 inches. Height, 74 inches. Mirror—32x22 inches. Chair—16x16 inches. Bench—17x22 inches. Night Table—16x20 inches.

THE KARGES FURNITURE COMPANY
Manufacturers of Bedroom Furniture
300 West Maryland St., EVANSVILLE, IND.
PERMANENT EXHIBITS

CHICAGO, ILL., Space 1146, American Furniture Mart   NEW YORK, N. Y., 12th Floor, New York Furniture Exchange

No. 820 Bed. 4 feet 6 inches.

No. 860 Bed. 4 feet 6 inches, or 3 feet 3 inches.

No. 850 Bed. 4 feet 6 inches, or 3 feet 3 inches.

No. 812 Bed. 4 feet 6 inches, or 3 feet 3 inches.

PRODUCTS
MANUFACTURERS OF
BEDROOM SUITES Complete, including Bench, Chair, Rocker, and Night Table.

BEDROOM SUITES, four pieces only.

Also the following pieces of bedroom furniture sold individually:

BEDS	CHAIRS	DRESSING TABLES
—Bow End	—Bedroom, Sets of	HIGHBOYS
—Straight End	—Wood Seat	LOWBOYS
—Twin	CHESTS OF DRAWERS	MIRROR FRAMES
BENCHES	CHIFFORETTES	—Plain
—Bedroom	CHIFFOROBES	—Decorated
—Dressing Table	DESKS	NIGHT TABLES
—Toilet Table	DRESSEROBES	ROCKERS
CHAIRS	DRESSERS	VANITIES
—Bedroom	DRESSERS, VANITY	VANITIES, SEMI

VANITY BUREAUS	WARDROBES	WARDROBES
WARDROBE	—Combination	—Standard
CHIFFONIERS	Dresser	

TRADE NAME
"VERITAS" meaning Truth is applied to all products of our manufacture, being indicative of our desire not to misrepresent.

GENERAL INFORMATION
We specialize on unusual and unique designs and finishes, staying away entirely from the competitive market thereby affording the dealer the possibility of a good profit and we eliminate the necessity of "cut throat" methods by protecting loyal customers.

Send for the information about the pieces that match these beds.

CHARLES P. LIMBERT COMPANY
Dining Room Furniture in Period Styles
Factory and Main Office, HOLLAND, MICH.
SALESROOMS
GRAND RAPIDS, MICH., Eighth Floor, Pantlind Exhibition Building

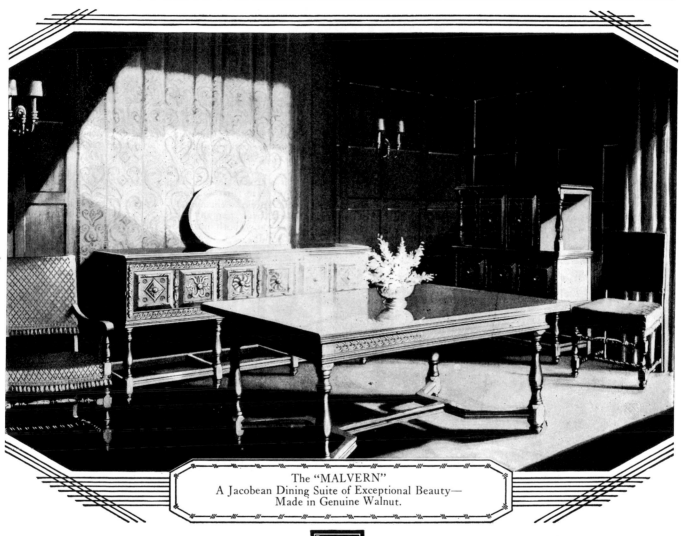

The "MALVERN"
A Jacobean Dining Suite of Exceptional Beauty—
Made in Genuine Walnut.

PRODUCTS
MANUFACTURERS OF
COMPLETE DINING ROOM SUITES, including:

ARM AND SIDE CHAIRS. (Slip Seats, Spring Seats, Upholstered or Wood Backs.)

SIDEBOARDS

CHINA AND SILVER CABINETS

SERVING TABLES

COMBINATION DINING ROOM AND LIVING ROOM GROUPS

EXTENSION TABLES

REFECTORY TABLES

Also Dining Furniture for Hotels and Clubs, including Chairs, Tables, and Folding Tray Stands, on special order.

PERIOD DESIGNS
We feature all the popular period styles such as the Elizabethan, Jacobean, Georgian and more modern English; also American and English Colonial as well as French, English and American Art Moderne.

WOODS AND FINISHES
We use solid Walnut, Mahogany, Oak, Maple and Gumwood in combination with many rare domestic and foreign veneers, carefully selected for beauty of figure and texture. All pieces are finished in genuine "Duco" lacquer The style of a suite is carefully considered in selecting finish and the most appropriate finish is applied. We are showing a number of new and interesting designs and finishes this year.

Our Cabinet work is held to the high standard maintained by the CHARLES P. LIMBERT CO., since 1889.

WEST MICHIGAN FURNITURE COMPANY
Manufacturers of Medium and High Grade Bedroom Furniture
HOLLAND, MICHIGAN
SHOWROOMS
GRAND RAPIDS, MICH., First Floor, Fine Arts Building

PRODUCTS
MANUFACTURERS OF

COMPLETE BEDROOM SUITES—medium and high grade, BEDS, DRESSERS, DRESSING TABLES, CHIFFONIERS, BENCHES, NITE TABLES, CHESTS OF DRAWERS and CHAIRS.

For information on Colonial Cases to harmonize with Kindel Beds, see preceding Pages 284 and 285.

Trade Mark

GENERAL INFORMATION

The West Michigan Furniture Company was established in 1889. Its products consist of medium and high grade groups of furniture for the bedroom, and Colonial cases to harmonize with Kindel beds. Its craftsmen are Holland descent in whom the pride of creative workmanship is traditional. West Michigan products are notable for the character of design and sound and enduring construction. Complete details regarding the line will be furnished on request.

"VAN FAASEN" SUITE No. 604

This charming design will have an enduring appeal for the discriminating home lover. Practical utility, combined with rare beauty of design and finish, gives this unusual Chamber Suite a distinctiveness that compels admiration and creates a desire for possession. It is presented for the purpose of meeting the steadily increasing demand for low priced furniture that is free from all appearance of cheapness and bad taste.

Beautiful Veneer effects is one of the outstanding features of the "Van Faasen." Only the finest of Butt Walnut Veneers are laid on this suite. The oval overlay is of Carpathian Burl, a very rare and beautiful wood that lends to the charm of this design.

Carvings are very fine in detail and are tooled from solid wood. Note the graceful curves of the mirror frames, which are very generous in their proportions.

The Dressing Table with its rounded corners makes an unusually attractive piece.

This suite comes in lacquer finish rubbed to a smooth velvety appearance.

Hardware is Old English Antique Brass.

"THE DE PREE" SUITE No. 600

All of the earnest efforts that are made to create particularly pleasing suites are unfortunately not always successful, but this fact adds glory to the designs that do meet the demand of beauty and utility. Such is the case of this lovely pattern. The proportion of the pieces, the design of the beds, the beautiful contours of the mirrors are all remarkably artistic and pleasing. The rich finish of the fine combination of woods and carefully executed detail of the hand carvings do much to enhance the beauty of this set.

The fronts of the cases are all veneered with selected Butt Walnut. The top drawers and mirror standards are trimmed in Red Wood Burl which, in combination with the Walnut, is very effective.

Our famous Dutch craftsmen worked with much pride and skill in executing this production. Its precise detail of cabinet work and carving gave them a real opportunity to show their best.

The modern homemaker is wonderfully privileged in being able to obtain furniture of this splendid character at ordinary commercial cost.

KLAMER FURNITURE CORPORATION
MONITOR FURNITURE CO.

Manufacturers of Bedroom, Dining Room, and Novelty Furniture

EVANSVILLE, INDIANA

PERMANENT EXHIBITS

EVANSVILLE, IND., Klamer Building   CHICAGO, ILL., American Furniture Mart
NEW YORK, N. Y., Furniture Exchange   SAN FRANCISCO, CAL., 180 New Montgomery St.

Five Large Factories at EVANSVILLE

PRODUCTS
MANUFACTURERS OF

BEDROOM SUITES—High grade period designs as represented by No. 1585, down through different grades to the popular quick selling suites.

DINING ROOM SUITES—A variety of grades and designs—merchandise suitable for any dealer and any class of trade. Also making several unique designs in dinette suites and breakfast suites.

NOVELTY FURNITURE

End Tables	Chairs
Davenport Tables	Rockers
Occasional Tables	Console Tables
Coffee Tables	Sewing Cabinets
Smokers	Daybeds
Book Racks	Davenette Suites

The great variety of case goods is made possible by factories being equipped to make special grades of furniture. High grade merchandise is made in a factory where the workmen are trained to careful workmanship—likewise other factories and workmen produce popular and low priced furniture on a competitive basis.

THE KLAMER GUARANTEE

To give you perfect confidence in the quality of Klamer furniture, the manufacturers attach a special guarantee tag to every piece of furniture sent from the factory. Each tag tells truthfully the kind of wood, workmanship, and finish, which goes into the construction of each particular piece it represents. When you buy Klamer furniture, you buy with absolute confidence. Watch for the "Tag That Tells."

The above trade mark will be found on every piece of Klamer furniture—it's the dealer's guarantee of reliable merchandise.

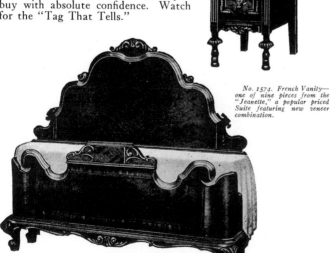

No. 1574. French Vanity—one of nine pieces from the "Jeanette," a popular priced Suite featuring new veneer combination.

No. 1111. For those who seek the atmosphere of the Early American, the "Susannah" will please. Ask for prints of the entire Suite—it is one of the quickest selling suites we ever made.

HELPING THE DEALER SELL MORE FURNITURE

The Klamer plan for merchandising and selling furniture has been adapted from the plans of the large national advertisers in other lines. It is based on the assumption that the manufacturer should continue his interest in the merchandise until in the hands of a satisfied customer.

A DEFINITE ADVERTISING PLAN

Klamer is not satisfied that he has done his part by furnishing "dealer helps" but has devised a plan that if followed will sell real quantities of furniture. The upper section of the opposite page is a reprint of a page from a handsome consumer booklet, printed in two colors, which illustrates and describes three dining room suites, three bedroom suites, dinette suites, daybeds and novelties. The booklet is imprinted with the dealer's name and carries the dealer's ad on the back cover. Besides the booklet, Klamer furnishes newspaper ads, window trims, window hangers, show cards, price tags, etc., and a plan for using them that is a known sales producer.

KLAMER WILL HELP RELIABLE FURNITURE DEALERS

Within the Klamer organization are specialists whose duty it is to help worthy dealers merchandise and plan their sales. Right now competition is keen and will be more so in the future, and chain stores and buying syndicates will crowd out the dealer who is not "on his toes." The live dealer will not weaken, but take advantage of modern methods and meet the conditions as they arise. Klamer wants to help you!

No. 1585. The Bed from a fine Louis XV design. The "Antoinette"—a design that pleases furniture connoisseurs.

KLAMER FURNITURE CORPORATION—MONITOR FURNITURE CO.

A DINING SUITE OF DISTINGUISHED HOSPITALITY— THE "AUGUSTINE"

Dining hospitality has never been outlawed—and never will be! Tradition has it that the function of dining shall be slightly formal, but people who truly enjoy the luxury of good foods insist upon a full measure of grace and beauty in their dining rooms. In the "Augustine" you have a happy compromise of formal dignity and easy grace. The distinctive beauty, the individual style of this Klamer creation, will satisfy your every desire for all that is fine in dining room furniture.

The drawer fronts are faced with beautiful Selano wood, and a heavy circular stump Walnut overlay surmounts the inner edge of each. The cupboard drawers are faced with stump Walnut, and the small silver drawer is faced with mahogany. The moldings, carvings, hand decoration, and unusual overlays of imported woods, give to this suite individuality and distinction. Full dust proof construction. Drawers have Mahogany bottoms and center guides. Finished in nut brown Walnut, beautifully blended.

Ask to see Suite No. 1441. This Suite consists of ten pieces. A large 72-inch Buffet, China, Server, Table, Arm Chair, and five Side Chairs. Sold complete or you may select just the pieces you desire.

No. 1471. Illustrating the Buffet from a L'art Moderne design—a conservative yet popular suite.

The above illustrations and descriptions of Klamer Furniture comprise one page of a handsome two-color booklet which our dealers supply to their customers. See paragraph entitled "A Definite Advertising Plan" on the preceding page.

WHY KLAMER FURNITURE HAS A PRICE ADVANTAGE

The five large factories are amalgamated into one buying and selling organization. This reduces manufacturing and selling costs and permits either a lower price on definite grades or a greater value by using better materials and workmanship. Contrast this enviable organization with the smaller ones that must buy in small quantities with overhead costs distributed on the product of one factory.

SALES AND DISTRIBUTION

Klamer salesmen cover the entire United States. Also semi-annually a portfolio of new designs is issued. If a salesman does not call on you when merchandise is needed, you can safely order from the portfolio. The price list gives complete information and there is nothing to be gained by waiting for the salesman to call. Klamer factories are located in Evansville—conceded to be the best shipping point in the United States.

No. 441. From the "Bernard," a quick selling Dining Room Suite—a most attractive design.

LANDSTROM FURNITURE CORPORATION
Manufacturers of Bedroom, Dining Room, and Living Room Furniture
ROCKFORD, ILLINOIS
PERMANENT EXHIBITS
CHICAGO, ILL., Space 1519, American Furniture Mart, 666 Lake Shore Drive

No. 208½—Semi-Vanity.
Top, 19x50 inches. Plate,
26x32 inches. List price,
$130.00.

No. 208—Bench. Damask.
List price, $28.00.

No. 208—Night Table.
Top, 15x15 inches; Height,
30 inches. List price,
$25.00.

No. 208½—Wardrobe. Top,
2 x40 inches; Height, 57 inches.
List price, $120.00.

PRODUCTS
MANUFACTURERS OF
BEDROOM AND DINING ROOM SUITES COMPLETE, including the following pieces which are sold separately:

DRESSERS
VANITY DRESSERS
WARDROBES
CHIFFOROBES
TOILET TABLES
CHESTS OF DRAWERS
BEDS
—Four Poster
—Bow End
—Straight End
CHAIRS, Dining Room
CHAIRS, Bedroom Sets of

DINING ROOM EXTENSION
   TABLES
BUFFETS
SERVERS
CHINA CABINETS
SECRETARIES
SECRETARY-DESKS
—John Hancock
—Governor Winthrop
DESKS
—Spinet
—Ladies'

Information on Dining Room Furniture, see pages 254, 255, 256 and 257—Central Furniture Company which operates in conjunction with this organization in the production of good furniture.

TRADE MARK
The trade mark as illustrated above is an identifying mark of all Landstrom made furniture. It appears in the top left hand drawer of every piece of case goods. Look for it when the furniture arrives, it is your guarantee of inspected merchandise.

CONSTRUCTION FEATURES
Bedroom Furniture: 5-ply throughout. Tops, fronts and ends, 5-ply. All drawers dove-tailed. Dust-proof between each drawer. Center drawer guides on every drawer. Grooved drawer bottoms. Glue blocks give more rigidity. All decorations hand painted—enhanced by the lacquer body found in all Landstrom finishes.

In selling Landstrom Furniture be sure to point out and emphasize the dust-proof construction. This you will note has the

Trade Mark

bottoms grooved in on all sides of the drawers—glued and not wedged in. This is a real dust-proof construction designed to give years of wear and satisfactory service.

Secretaries all have solid Mahogany Ends with other construction features similar to those found in our Bedroom Suites.

See pages 254, 255, 256 and 257 for details on Dining Room Furniture.

WOODS AND FINISHES
Landstrom Bedroom Suites are constructed of combination Quarter Sawed Red Gum and Walnut; Genuine Mahogany and Genuine Walnut. Secretaries built of Genuine Walnut and Mahogany.

Finishes applied on Landstrom Furniture have characteristics that are similar to plates appearing in the Woods and Finishes Section preceding page 9 of this book.

No. 1 Standard resembles our Colonial Red.

No. 21 Old Mahogany resembles our Antique Mahogany.

No. 24 Standard Mahogany resembles our Salem Mahogany.

No. 14 American Walnut Standard resembles our American Walnut.

No. 10 American Walnut resembles our Antique Walnut.

GENERAL INFORMATION
The quality and workmanship of Landstrom Furniture does not need any long drawn out eulogy. It is evident that being located in the City of Rockford—a center long known for its good furniture—that only the best and most suitable furniture would be built to interest the American Public.

Order a few of these numbers today and enjoy the satisfaction of being able to offer your trade furniture that is well-built, well-finished, well-designed and reasonably priced.

The pieces illustrated on these pages are but a few of the other attractive numbers that we have to offer. We invite you to write for Black print illustrations and prices.

All prices shown are subject to change without notice.

No. 208—Chair. Cane back with upholstered slip seat. List price, $28.00.

No. 208—Rocker. Cane back with upholstered slip seat. List price, $30.00.

No. 208—Dresser. Top, 24x54 inches; Plate, 44x30 inches. List price, $130.00.

No. 208—Chest of Drawers. Top, 21x38 inches, Height, 48 inches. List price, $100.00.

No. 208—Vanity. Top, 19x50 inches; Plate, 12x32 inches; Plate, 20x50 inches. List price, $140.00.

No. 208—Bed. Slat, 4x6 inches. List price, $90.00.

BEDROOM SUITE No. 208

The truly individual design of this suite has met with favor wherever displayed. Its simplicity is a direct step to the so-called "modern" furniture prevalent in the minds of all home-owners today.

Built of Genuine Walnut with Butt Walnut Tops, Fronts and Ends of 5-ply.

(Continued on next page)

No. 171—Bench. Black and Gold Damask slip seat. List price, $28.00.

No. 171—Chair. Black and Gold Damask slip seat. List price, $28.00.

No. 171—Rocker. Black and Gold Damask slip seat. List price, $29.00.

No. 171—Chest of Drawers. Height, 48 inches; Top, 21x40 inches. List price $100.00.

No. 171—Night Table. Height, 30 inches; Top, 16x16 inches. List price $33.00.

No. 171¼—Four Poster Bed. Slat 4x6 inches. List price, $90.00.

No. 171—Dresser. Plate, 34x30 inches; Top, 50x23 inches. List price, $130.00.

No. 171—Vanity. Plate, 12x30 inches; Plate, 20x50 inches; Top, 18x52 inches. List price, $130.00.

No. 203—*Chair. Green striped Moire slip seat. List price, $33.00.*

No. 203—*Bench. Green striped Moire slip seat. List price, $32.00.*

No. 203—*Dresser. Top, 48x22 inches. Plate, 26x32 inches. List price, $135.00.*

No. 203—*Night Table. Top, 14x18 inches. Height, 30 inches. List price, $37.00.*

No. 203—*Chest of Drawers. Top, 36x22 inches; Height, 46 inches. List price, $115.00.*

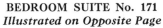

No. 203—*Bed. Slat, 3x3 inches —4x6 inches. List price, $100.00.*

No. 203½—*Vanity. Top, 50x18 inches; Plate, 22x32 inches. List price, $150.00.*

BEDROOM SUITE No. 171
Illustrated on Opposite Page

This suite has all the grace and appeal of the Colonial Period. Constructed of Genuine Mahogany. The appeal of this furniture never diminishes but increases as the years go by. Emphasize to your customers the lasting charm of these Colonial pieces—their suitability to any environment.

BEDROOM SUITE No. 203
Illustrated Above

Genuine Mahogany with Inlaid Marquetry together with the Early American design helps to make this pattern of distinguished appearance. All the pleasing motifs of the Colonial times are apparent and do much to enhance the value of this suite in its appeal to your trade.

(Continued on next page)

LANDSTROM FURNITURE CORPORATION

BEDROOM SUITE No. 206

Here is a suite that will help you to sell many combinations—to meet the requirements of the large and small home owner—yet keep your valuable floor space occupied to a minimum.

Combination Walnut, durably finished forms a good background for the simple, sturdy design that is national in its appeal. The number of suites carried by retailers—the number that is constantly being sold—is concrete evidence of the popularity of this number.

Place one of these suites on your floor now.

No. 206¼—Hi-boy. Top, 21x37 inches; Height, 52 inches. List price, $80.00.

No. 206½ — Chifforobe. Top, 22x41 inches; Height, 59 inches. List price, $80.00.

No. 206—Bed. Slat, 4x6 inches. List price, $50.00.

No. 206¾—Four Poster Bed. Slat, 3x3 inches—4x6 inches. List price, $50.00.

No. 206¼—Bed. Slat, 4x6 inches. List price $50.00.

No. 206—Bench. Cane
seat. List price, $17.00.

No. 206 — Chair.
Cane seat. List price,
$17.00.

No. 206 — Chest of Drawers.
Top, 20x37 inches; Height, 48
inches; Plate, 14x16 inches. List
price, $70.00. Mirror, list price
$25.00.

No. 206—Dresser. Top, 22x46
inches; Plate, 28x32 inches. List
price, $90.00.

No. 206 — Night
Table. Top, 15x15
inches; Height, 30
inches. List price,
$24.00.

Semi-Vanity. Top, 20x48 inches; Plate, 26x32 inches. List price,
$90.00.

No. 206½—Dresser. Top, 50x32
inches; Plate, 30x36 inches. List
price, $100.00.

(Continued on next page)

No. 221—Chest of Drawers. Top, 20x36 inches; Height, 50 inches. List price, $60.00.

No. 221—Bench. Cane seat. List price, $13.50.

No. 221—Night Table. Top, 15x15 inches; Height, 30 inches. List price, $15.00.

No. 221—Chair. Cane seat. List price, $14.00.

No. 221—Semi-Vanity. Top, 18x46 inches; Plate, 22x34 inches. List price, $65.00.

No. 221¼—Hi-boy. Top, 21x36 inches; Height, 52 inches. List price, $60.00.

No. 221—Bed. Slat, 4x6 inches —3x3 inches. List price, $47.00.

No. 221—Dresser. Top, 21x46 inches; Plate, 30x30 inches. List price, $65.00.

BEDROOM SUITE No. 221

Combination Walnut and Mahogany is employed in the building of this pleasing number. The design is reminiscent of the Jacobean Era and which is further evidenced by the squat, inviting pieces so appropriate for the home atmosphere of the American people.

It will suit the tastes of the more sober minded who seek simple, ornate furniture in preference to the sumptuous.

LANDSTROM FURNITURE CORPORATION

No. 220—Chest of Drawers. Top, 21x38 inches; Height, 51 inches. List price, $70.00.

No. 220 — Night Table. Top, 15x15 inches; Height, 30 inches. List price, $17.00.

No. 220—Chair. Cane seat. List price, $16.00.

No. 220—Bench. Cane seat. List price, $15.00.

BEDROOM SUITE No. 220

This suite has the charming grace of Sheraton and the sumptuousness of Chippendale. A happy combination that cannot help but please the most discriminating of your trade.

Combination Walnut and Mahogany. Japanese Ash Veneer overlays on top drawers add a finishing touch to an already distinctive design.

If you are interested in offering your trade a pattern of real merit, we would suggest that you order this suite now.

(Continued on next page)

No. 220—Semi-Vanity. Top, 19x38 inches; Plate, 26x32 inches. List price, $85.00.

No. 220½ — Semi-Vanity. Top, 18x48 inches; Plate, 24x34 inches. List price, $85.00.

No. 220—Bed. Slat, 4x6 inches— 3x3 inches. List price, $50.00.

No. 220—Dresser. Top, 21x48 inches; Plate, 30x34 inches. List price, $85.00.

LANDSTROM FURNITURE CORPORATION

No. 219—Bench. Green tapestry. List price, $54.00.

BEDROOM SUITE No. 219

The design of this charming suite has been influenced to a marked extent by the Louis Periods. Genuine Walnut and Satinwood are used in the construction of Suite No. 219.

The richness of this distinctive style and its pronounced decorative values make this suite equally desirable and appropriate for the more formal rooms.

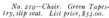

No. 219—Chair. Green Tapestry, slip seat. List price, $54.00.

No. 219—Chest of Drawers. Top, 21x40 inches; Height, 54 inches. List price, $171.00.

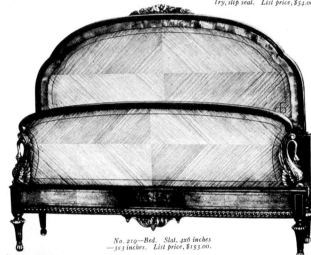

No. 219—Bed. Slat, 4x6 inches —3x3 inches. List price, $153.00.

No. 219—Night Table. Top, 14x17 inches; Height, 30 inches. List price, $54.00.

No. 219—Semi-Vanity. Top, 20x54 inches; Plate, 20x34, inches. List price, $175.00.

No. 219—Dresser. Top, 22x52 inches; Plate, 30x32 inches. List price, $175.00.

LANDSTROM FURNITURE CORPORATION

LANDSTROM SECRETARIES HAVE SOLID MAHOGANY ENDS

In our Secretaries you will find an extremely wide range of selection. Our patterns are designed to meet the varied tastes of your clientele. Such periods as Queen Anne, Chippendale, Colonial, Early American, William and Mary, Spanish Renaissance are found at their best in the well-balanced pieces that we manufacture. A few of these pieces on your floor will bring you more than your share of business in this line.

(Continued on next page)

No. 370—Secretary. Height, 80 inches; Depth, 16 inches; Width, 32 inches. Genuine Mahogany. List price, $115.00.

No. 370—Secretary. Closed view.

No. 374½ — Secretary Desk. 17x22 inches. Genuine Walnut. List price, $40.00.

No. 374—Secretary. Height, 76 inches; 17x22 inches. Genuine Walnut. List price, $69.00.

No. 346—Secretary. Height, 71 inches; 16x32 inches. Genuine Mahogany. List price, $69.00. Genuine Walnut, List price, $73.00.

No. 346½—Secretary Desk. Height, 42 inches; Width, 31 inches. Genuine Mahogany. List price, $55.00. Genuine Walnut. List price, $59.00.

No. 388½ — Secretary Desk. 19x36 inches. Genuine Mahogany. List price, $105.00.

No. 388—Secretary. Height, 85 inches; 19x36 inches. Mahogany. List price, $150.00.

No. 387—Desk. Height, 77 inches; 17x31 inches. Mahogany. List price, $77.00.

No. 367½ — Secretary Desk. Width, 28 inches; Depth, 17 inches. Mahogany. List price, $75.00.

No. 367—Secretary. Height, 78 inches; Depth, 17 inches; Width, 28 inches. Mahogany. List price, $97.00.

No. 387½—Desk. 17x31 inches. Mahogany. List price, $57.00.

No. 376½—Desk. 18x30 inches. Genuine Walnut. List price, $69.00

No. 382½—Desk. 18x37 inches. Mahogany. List price, $93.00.

DESKS

Secretary Desks are ready for shipment within twenty-four hours after receipt of your order. Our service will enable you to meet the urgency of any of your customers.

Many of our Secretary Desks have features that are distinctly of our own device and will help you sell more easily.

No. 376½—Desk. Closed view.

No. 382½—Desk. Closed view.

No. 380½—Desk. Closed view.

No. 380½—Desk. 18x32 inches. Mahogany. List price, $90.00.

No. 379½—Desk. 19x33 inches. Mahogany. List price, $90.00.

No. 379½—Desk. Closed view.

No. 378½ — Desk.
Closed view.

No. 377½ — Desk.
Closed view.

No. 381½ — Desk.
Closed view.

No. 378½. Desk. 19x37 inches.
Mahogany. List price, $105.00.

No. 377½—Desk. 18x30 inches.
Mahogany. List price, $65.00.

No. 381½—Desk. 18x34 inches.
Mahogany. List price, $78.00.

SPINET DESKS

The distinctiveness of Landstrom Spinet Desks do not need further description to you as a buyer of the better grade of merchandise. The pieces illustrated on this page speak for themselves — Landstrom Spinet Desks have that stamp of individuality that lifts them out of the commonplace.

However, the pieces shown are merely representative — we have many more that may better suit your requirements. Write for photographs and prices of our other patterns.

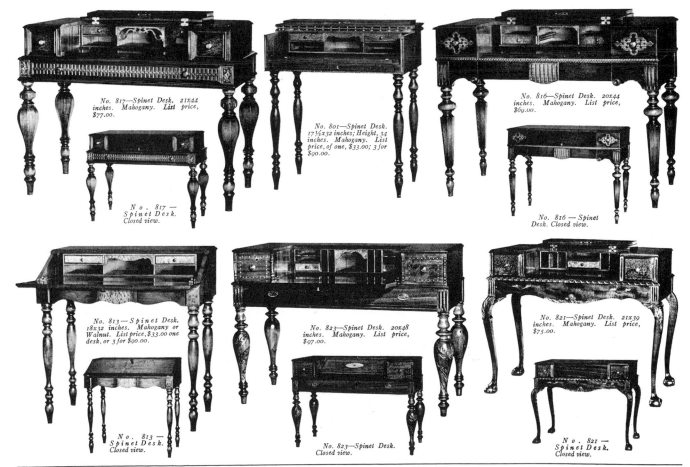

No. 817—Spinet Desk. 21x44 inches. Mahogany. List price, $77.00.

No. 817 — Spinet Desk. Closed view.

No. 801—Spinet Desk. 17½x32 inches; Height, 34 inches. Mahogany. List price, of one, $33.00; 3 for $90.00.

No. 816—Spinet Desk. 20x44 inches. Mahogany. List price, $69.00.

No. 816 — Spinet Desk. Closed view.

No. 813—Spinet Desk. 18x32 inches. Mahogany or Walnut. List price, $33.00 one desk, or 3 for $90.00.

No. 813 — Spinet Desk. Closed view.

No. 823—Spinet Desk. 20x48 inches. Mahogany. List price, $97.00.

No. 823—Spinet Desk. Closed view.

No. 821—Spinet Desk. 21x39 inches. Mahogany. List price, $75.00.

No. 821 — Spinet Desk. Closed view.

MORGANTON FURNITURE COMPANY
Manufacturers of Bedroom and Dining Room Furniture
MORGANTON, N. C.

PERMANENT EXHIBITS

NEW YORK, N. Y., 206 Lexington Ave.
CHICAGO, ILL., American Furniture Mart Building

BOSTON, MASS., 197 Friend Street
SAN FRANCISCO, CAL., The Furniture Exchange

PRODUCTS

MANUFACTURERS OF

BEDROOM SUITES COMPLETE
BEDS
—Bow End
—Twin
BUFFETS
CHESTS OF DRAWERS
CHIFFOROBES
CHINA CLOSETS
DINING ROOM FURNITURE

DRESSERS
DRESSERS, VANITY
HIGHBOYS
SERVING TABLES
TABLES
—Dining Room
—Extension
—Night
WARDROBE CHIFFONIERS

GENERAL INFORMATION

In Morganton Furniture the predominant characteristics of manufacture are the simplicity of design, rigid construction and durable finishes.

Bedroom and Dining Room Furniture shows the same careful workmanship and thought. Morganton Furniture is built to sell and sell with a minimum of sales resistance. We invite you to write for our price list and illustrations of other numbers.

No. 2626—Dining Table. Top 42x58x70 inches.

No. 2631—Server. Top, 38x18 inches.

No. 2602—Buffet. Top, 66x22 inches.

No. 2611—China Cabinet. 40x16 inches. 78 inches high.

DESCRIPTION OF ILLUSTRATED SUITE

There is a graceful simplicity about this suite that is reminiscent of the Queen Anne or Sheraton Periods yet distinctly a design truly representative of modern America.

Standard construction is prevalent throughout every Morganton Suite and many embrace features that are distinctly of our own initiative.

THE A. C. NORQUIST CO.
Manufacturers of Bedroom Furniture
415 Chandler St., JAMESTOWN, N. Y.
EXHIBITS
JAMESTOWN, N. Y., 4th Floor, Furniture Exposition Building—CHICAGO, ILL., 8th Floor, American Furniture Mart
SAN FRANCISCO, CALIF., 7th Floor, Furniture Exchange

Four Poster Bed No. 650. Slats, 4 feet 6 inches and 3 feet 3 inches. Price $69.00.

Night Table No. 650. Top 17 by 14 inches. Price $21.50

Dressing Table No. 650. Top, 45 by 19 inches. Price $39.00. Wall Mirror can be furnished, $19.50.

Chest of Drawers No. 650. Top, 32 by 19 inches. Mirror, 16 by 12 inches. Price: $74.00 and Mirror Stand, 16 by 12 inches, $15.50.

Dresser No. 650. Top, 42x21 inches; Mirror, 26x19 inches. May be had with attached mirror. Dresser $78.00 and Wall Mirror $19.50. Dresser and Wall Mirror $97.50. Dresser with attached mirror $97.50.

Suite No. 650 illustrated is a pure Colonial Reproduction even to the finish which is a rich Mahogany similar to plate No. 18 Colonial Mahogany in the Woods and Finishes Section preceding page 9 of this Reference Book. The Colonial cut out designs of the movable mirror stand on the Chest of Drawers and of the Wall Mirror above the Dresser are replicas of the best Early American Patterns. This suite can be furnished in Curly Maple Veneer and Maple.

QUALITY **SERVICE**
THE A.C. NORQUIST CO.
MANUFACTURERS OF FURNITURE OF CHARACTER
JAMESTOWN, N.Y.
EST. 1881

Trade Mark

DRESSERS
—Standard
—Vanity
HIGHBOYS
MIRRORS
—Hand
—Shaving

NIGHT TABLES

ROCKERS
—Bedroom
—Upholstered
—Cane Seat

WARDROBES

GENERAL INFORMATION

The Norquist line of bedroom furniture is a splendid assortment of highly salable numbers. Though well within the medium price range, they are brilliantly designed and finely executed.

Make it a point to visit our showrooms when in Jamestown, Chicago, or San Francisco, and see the entire Norquist line.

RETAIL PRICE RANGES

The prices shown beneath the illustrations are retail. Other retail prices include this No. 650 suite complete at $317.00; bedroom suites, three pieces, $158.00 to four pieces up to $536.00. Beds from $43.00 to $98.00; Chairs and Rockers and Benches, from $11.50 to $21.00; Bureaus, Dressers, and Vanities from $64.00 to $136.00; Chiffoniers, Chifforettes, Chifforobes, and Wardrobes, from $49.00 to $128.00; Dressing Tables from $39.00 to $101.00; Highboys from $51.00 to $139.00; Mirrors from $15.00 to $29.50; and Night Tables from $15.50 to $37.00. All prices are subject to change without notice.

WOODS AND FINISHES

In addition to the Colonial Mahogany finish of Suite No. 650, we also employ the following finishes:

No. 9, American Walnut, Light. No. 11, American Mahogany, Dark. No. 20, Brown Maple. See Woods and Finishes Section preceding page 9 of this Reference Book.

PRODUCTS
MANUFACTURERS OF

Bedroom Suites Complete, including Bench, Chair, Rocker and Night Table. Bedroom Suites, four pieces only. Individual pieces sold on order as follows:

BEDS
—Straight End
—Colonial
—Four Poster
—Odd
—Bow End
—Twin

BENCHES
—Bedroom
—Dressing Table
—Toilet Table
—Upholstered
BUREAUS

CHAIRS
—Bedroom
—Bedroom, Sets of
—Upholstered
—Cane Seat
CHIFFONIERS
CHIFFORETTES

THE PATTON-McCRAY COMPANY
Manufacturers of Colonial Four Poster Beds
805 West Washington St., BLUFFTON, IND.
EXHIBIT
CHICAGO, ILL., Space 415, American Furniture Mart, 666 Lake Shore Drive

No. 151—Massive Poster Bed with Pineapple Finials; 4-inch stock; Head, 60 inches high; Foot, 52 inches high. Gumwood combined with either Mahogany or Walnut. Price, $65.00.

No. 315—Attractive pattern with foot panel. Gumwood combined with Mahogany or Walnut. Post stock, 3 inches; Height posts, 54 inches. Price, $48.00.

No. 325—Charming pattern at a popular price. Gumwood combined with Mahogany or Walnut; 3-inch stock; Height head, 48 inches; Height foot, 42 inches. Price, $33.00.

No. 321—Graceful pineapple design; Gumwood combined with Mahogany or Walnut; 3-inch post stock; Height head, 53 inches; Height foot, 45 inches. Price, $45.00.

No. 320—Spool Bed of artistic design. Gumwood finished in Mahogany or Walnut. Can also be supplied in genuine Mahogany or Walnut; Height head, 40 inches; Height foot, 32 inches. Price, $32.00.

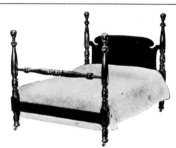

No. 150—Heavy posts from 4-inch stock; Mahogany or Walnut combined with Gumwood; Height head, 60 inches; Height foot, 52 inches. Price, $61.00.

No. 329—Attractive design with molded panel. Gumwood combined with Mahogany or Walnut. Posts, 2½-inch stock; Height head, 49 inches; Height foot, 43 inches. Price, $32.00.

No. 340—Made in Genuine Mahogany only. Beaded posts pineapple design. 3-inch post stock. Height head, 60 inches; Height foot, 52 inches. Price, $90.00.

No. 330—Cottage Bed with low foot board. Mahogany or Walnut in combination with Gumwood. Decorated or plain. Height head, 43 inches; Height foot, 25 inches. Price, $32.00.

PRODUCTS
MANUFACTURERS OF
COLONIAL FOUR-POSTER BEDS, Double and Twin.

SLOGAN
"HEIRLOOMS OF TOMORROW" is used to identify Patton-McCray merchandise. The product is everything that this slogan stresses—it is built not only for today but for the tomorrow.

PRICES
The prices shown beneath each bed are retail prices. A liberal discount will be allowed for pieces supplied unfinished.

CONSTRUCTION AND SIZES
All Patton-McCray beds are supplied with wood side rails of five-ply construction. Side rails are 74 inches long. All beds are made in the full size 54-inch slat length and the twin size 39-inch slat length. Four foot beds can be supplied on special order. Beds are packed and shipped two to a crate.

WOODS AND FINISHES
Finishes are Brown Mahogany resembling plate No. 21—Old Mahogany; Dark Red Mahogany resembling plate No. 25—Dark Mahogany; American Walnut resembling plate No. 10—American Walnut. See Woods and Finishes section preceding page 9 of this book.

Any pattern can be supplied in enamel on special order or in-the-white for decoration or special finish.

PERIOD CABINET MFG. CO.
Dining Room Furniture
Eighth and Shelby, NEW ALBANY, IND.

PERMANENT DISPLAYS AND SALESROOMS, GRAND RAPIDS, MICH., Sixth Floor, Fine Arts Building

Selling Connections

Eastern: Royal B. Smith, 105 W. 40th St., New York City   *Central:* H. C. Canfield, Batesville, Ind.   *Southern:* L. C. Voss, Louisville, Ky.   *Western:* T. F. McConnell, 6459 Odin St., Hollywood, Calif. McCann-Pleas Co., Furniture Exchange, San Francisco, Calif.

PRODUCTS

MANUFACTURERS OF
DINING ROOM FURNITURE as follows:
APARTMENT SIZE SUITES AND REGULAR SIZE SUITES

BUFFETS	SERVERS
CHAIRS	TABLES
CHINA CABINETS	EXTENSION TABLES

CHINA CLOSETS

See Period "Litchfield" and Colonial "Suites" in the Home Furnishing and Decoration Section, page 38.

PERIOD POLICY

Period has established a new price-class. It is the development of a definite manufacturing and sales plan adopted by the Period organization in January, 1924. To give you each season one outstanding value of authentic design, instantly recognizable as definite Medium-Grade—which you can sell at a price noticeably lower than its appearance would lead the shopper to expect. The "Bellini" is this season's "special offering." Write for particulars.

THE SARAH SIDDONS (SHERATON)

Where find a more appropriate name or sentiment for this exquisite Sheraton? Fellow laborers in the expression of art. One declaiming in the famous old Drury Lane Theatre, renowned no less for its fostering of genius than for its influence upon a people, and one wrought in that famous nearby shop, renowned no less for its creation of new forms of beauty to gladden the eye, than that they should endure to inspire the effort of later ages. Here in the exquisitely beautiful woods and master craftsmanship of the present day, Period artisans have faithfully recreated the classic style of the gifted Sheraton. Pictures and words cannot adequately portray the dainty, graceful charm of this beautiful Sheraton, or more than hint at the wealth of glowing color in its exquisite panels. It is worthy of the "honor space" in your display, and worth its cost just to hear pretty women shoppers exclaim in delight over its intriguing beauty.

Materials—Pin stripe Mahogany is used for the tops, drawer fronts, back boards, door stiles and sides of the cabinet pieces, and on the aprons of the table. Crotch Mahogany is used on all doors. All posts and moldings of selected quarter-sawed red gum.

Finish—Period Mahogany only, lacquer finish. Two coats of lacquer dull rubbed. Tops, fronts and overlays beautifully blended. Drawer interiors are finished natural and dull rubbed.

Trimmings—English antique knobs and pulls on all drawers and doors. Caster slides on all pieces.

PERIOD CONSTRUCTION

All panel stock is of five-ply construction. Dovetailed construction throughout every piece. Three-quarter inch end panels in buffet, server and china. All drawers are dovetailed and boxed-in. Dust-proof construction. Drawer sides are made of selected plain oak and bottoms of three-ply quartered white oak veneer. Each drawer is fitted with center guides. In the top of the left compartment of the buffet is fitted a portable silver tray of generous proportions, plush lined. All tables are regularly furnished in eight foot extension with one apron filler.

THE BELLINI—ITALIAN RENAISSANCE

In a rich and sumptuous day, when Venice furnished endless material and abundant color for her artists, there arose one Giovanni Bellini to live a beautiful and useful life in the shadow of St. Mark's Cathedral. One of the most gifted and fascinating painters of the fifteenth century, he later became known as the founder of the Venetian School of Painting. A colorist of the first order, he did much to impart the marvelous golden tone of Venetian painting, and he has left to the world many a lovely picture. Comes Period with an offering as authentic, as glowing and as lovely as a Bellini painting, every piece portraying the distinguishing characteristics of the colorful art of its period. The accentuation of low, straight line effects, massive turned legs, wide moldings and characteristic heavy underbracing are assembled into a substantial solidity of notably fine proportions and home-like style. Feathery Walnut panels, shaped to the graceful arches of Bellini's beloved St. Mark's, framing matched Oak of exquisite grain and glowing amber tint. The "Bellini," too, is a masterpiece.

Materials—The veneers are selected stump and sliced Walnut and native White Oak, all carefully matched for grain and natural beauty. Solid Walnut of selected grain and coloring is used in all door frames, backboards, and banisters of chairs. Posts, stretchers, moldings and turnings are of selected Quarter-sawed Red Gum.

Finish—Done in Period's distinctive Stratford Walnut only. Wax finish. The tops, fronts, moldings, turnings, legs and stretchers are exquisitely shaded. Drawer interiors are finished natural and dull rubbed.

Trimmings—Antique pulls and plates on all drawers and doors. Period shoes on all pieces.

The Sarah Siddons Sheraton Dining Suite. Buffet, 66 by 21 inches; Table, 60 by 42 inches by 6 feet; China, 60 by 39 by 18 inches; Server, 38 by 18 inches; Chairs Lattice Banister. Upholstered seats.

The Bellini Italian Renaissance Dining Suite. Buffet, 66 by 22 inches; Table, 60 by 45 inches by 6 feet; China, 60 by 40 by 18 inches; Server, 40 by 19 inches; Chairs, Panel Back. Upholstered Seats.

ROCKFORD CHAIR & FURNITURE CO.

Manufacturers of Dining Room Suites, Bookcases, Desks and Secretaries

920 Ninth Street, ROCKFORD, ILL.

EXHIBITS
GRAND RAPIDS, MICH., Manufacturers Bldg.

Dining Room Table. Top, 44x60 inches.

Buffet. Top, 20x66 inches.

China Cabinet. Height, 67 inches; Width, 38 inches.

Suite No. 1775 is built of selected Walnut veneer and Gumwood. Finish is of Antique Walnut. Price upon application.

Server. Height, 41½ inches; Width, 38 inches.

Side Chair upholstered in Tapestry or Velour of good grade.

Arm or Host Chair. Seat of Tapestry or Velour of good grade.

Dining Room Table. Top, 42x60 inches.

Buffet. Top, 21x66 inches.

China Cabinet. Height, 67 inches; Width, 38½ inches.

Suite No. 1778 is built of selected Walnut veneer and Gumwood. Finish is of Antique Walnut. Price upon application.

Server. Height, 40 inches; Width, 36 inches.

Side Chair. Upholstered in Haircloth.

Arm or Host Chair. Seat of Haircloth.

No. 231—Secretary Desk. Height, 75 inches; Width, 32 inches. Mahogany Veneer and Gumwood.

No. 0193—Secretary Desk. Height, 78 inches; Width, 35 inches. Mahogany Veneer and Gumwood.

No. 0150—Secretary Desk. Height, 85 inches; Width, 38 inches. Mahogany Veneer and Mahogany

No. 0188—Secretary Desk. Height, 84 inches; Width, 42 inches, Mahogany Veneer and Mahogany.

No. 241—Secretary Desk. Height, 79 inches; Width, 36 inches. Mahogany Veneer and Gumwood.

Trade Mark

PRODUCTS

MANUFACTURERS OF

BOOKCASES, Library
BUFFETS
CHAIRS, Dining Room
CHAIRS, Living Room
CHINA CLOSETS
DAVENPORTS, Upholstered
DESKS
—Ladies'
—Library
—Secretary
DINING ROOM FURNITURE
TABLES, Dining Room

GENERAL INFORMATION

We are offering you merchandise that is built according to the best principles of furniture construction. The furniture illustrated on these pages is the kind that will appeal to the most discriminating of your trade.

Order a few of these numbers today. The prestige and good will that this furniture will bring to your store is worthwhile your serious interest.

(Continued on next page)

No. 0198—Desk. Height, 41 inches; Width, 42 inches. Mahogany Veneer and Mahogany.

No. 233—Desk. Height, 40 inches; Width, 33 inches. Mahogany Veneer and Gumwood.

No. 0203—Desk. Height, 39 inches. Width, 35 inches. Mahogany Veneer and Gumwood.

No. 0164—Desk. Height, 40 inches; Width, 38 inches. Mahogany Veneer and Gumwood.

No. 232—Desk. Height, 41 inches; Width, 32 inches. Mahogany Veneer and Gumwood.

No. 246.—Bookcase-Desk.
Height, 54 inches; Width, 50
inches. Mahogany Veneer and
Mahogany.

No. 237.—Bookcase-Desk.
Height, 51 inches; Width, 48
inches. Walnut Veneer and
Gumwood. Mahogany Veneer
and Gumwood.

No. 0342—Bookcase. Height, 56
inches; Width, 56 inches. Mahogany
Veneer and Walnut. Walnut Veneer
and Mahogany.

No. 0345—Bookcase. Height, 54 inches; Width, 60 inches. Walnut Veneer
and Walnut. Mahogany Veneer and
and Mahogany.

No. 0343—Bookcase. Height, 54
inches; Width, 55 inches. Mahogany
Veneer and Mahogany. Walnut Veneer
and Walnut.

No. 0341—Bookcase.
Height, 49 inches; Width,
30 inches. Walnut Veneer
and Gumwood.

No. 341-2—Bookcase. Height, 48
inches; Width, 44½ inches. Walnut
Veneer and Gumwood.

No. 0328—Bookcase.
Height, 56 inches; Width,
28 inches. Gumwood.

No. 0328-2—Bookcase. Height,
56 inches; Width, 41 inches. Gumwood.

No. 0317-3—Bookcase. Height, 56 inches; Width, 60 inches. Mahogany Veneer and Gumwood.

No. 0317—Bookcase. Height, 56 inches; Width, 26 inches. Mahogany Veneer and Gumwood.

No. 0334-3—Bookcase. Height, 48 inches; Width, 60 inches. Mahogany Veneer and Gumwood.

No. 0334—Bookcase. Height, 48 inches; Width, 25 inches. Mahogany Veneer and Gumwood.

No. 0317-2. Height, 56 inches; Width, 44 inches. Mahogany Veneer and Gumwood.

No. 0344-2. Height, 53 inches; Width, 47 inches. Walnut and Mahogany Veneer and Gumwood.

No. 0334-2. Height, 48 inches; Width, 44 inches. Mahogany Veneer and Gumwood.

No. 261. Height, 44 inches; Width, 24 inches. Gumwood.

No. 0344-3. Height, 54 inches; Width, 64 inches. Walnut and Mahogany Veneer and Gumwood.

No. 0344. Height, 53 inches; Width, 26 inches. Walnut and Mahogany Veneer and Gumwood.

No. 0321. Height, 53 inches; Width, 25 inches. Mahogany Veneer and Gumwood.

No. 262. Height, 44 inches; Width, 35 inches. Gumwood.

No. 266. Height, 44 inches; Width, 48 inches. Gumwood.

No. 0321-3. Height, 48 inches; Width, 60 inches. Mahogany Veneer and Gumwood.

No. 0321-2. Height, 53 inches. Width, 36 inches. Mahogany Veneer and Gumwood.

(Continued on next page)

No. 132—Secretary Desk. Height, 72 inches; Width,, 26 inches. Mahogany Veneer and Mahogany.

No. 218—Secretary Desk. Height, 70 inches; Width, 26 inches. Mahogany Veneer and Gumwood.

No. 256—Secretary Desk. Height, 70 inches; Width, 22 inches. Mahogany Veneer and Gumwood.

No. 221—Secretary Desk. Height, 75 inches; Width, 26 inches. Walnut Veneer and Gumwood.

No. 265—Desk. Height, 45 inches; Width, 30 inches. Genuine Mahogany.

No. 250—Desk. Top, 26x52 inches. Height, 30 inches. Walnut Veneer and Gumwood.

No. 216—Secretary. Height, 50 inches; Width, 26 inches. Walnut Veneer and Gumwood.

No. 249—Desk. Top, 26x52 inches. Height, 31 inches. Walnut Veneer and Gumwood.

No. 0154—Secretary. Height, 50 inches; Width, 29 inches.

No. 251—Desk. Top, 26x52 inches. Walnut Veneer and Gumwood.

No. 102—Desk. Height, 42 inches; Width, 30 inches.

No. 253—Desk. Height, 40 inches; Width, 30 inches. Mahogany and Walnut Veneer and Gumwood.

No. 252—Desk. Height, 40 inches; Width, 30 inches. Mahogany and Walnut Veneer and Gumwood.

No. 101—Desk. Height, 42 inches; Width, 31 inches.

No. 260—Desk. Height, 38 inches; Width, 38 inches. Mahogany Veneer and Gumwood.

No. 254—Desk. Height, 41 inches; Width, 30 inches. Mahogany and Walnut Veneer and Gumwood

No. 196—Secretary Desk. Height, 40 inches; Width, 36 inches.

No. 248—Desk. Height, 40 inches; Width, 38 inches. Walnut Veneer and Gumwood.

No. 240-1—Desk. Height, 41 inches; Width, 45 inches. Walnut Veneer and Gumwood.

EACH ONE OF THESE PATTERNS A MERCHANDISING OPPORTUNITY

The quality, construction and design of Rockford Chair Furniture is such that you can with a minimum amount of sales effort not only thoroughly sell your customer but also realize a real substantial profit.

Each piece of furniture presents a merchandising opportunity.

With Rockford-made Furniture you are offering your clientele the best that can be manufactured with present day methods.

Place a few of these on your floor today and start enjoying the prestige that all dealers carrying Rockford-made Furniture throughout the country have been for years.

ROCKFORD FURNITURE COMPANY
Manufacturers of Dining Room Suites, Desks, and Secretaries
1009 W. Jefferson Street, ROCKFORD, ILL.
OWNERS AND OPERATORS OF THE ROCKFORD DESK COMPANY
PERMANENT DISPLAYS
CHICAGO, ILL., Space 201, American Furniture Mart   ROCKFORD, ILL., at Factory

Arm or Host Chair. List price, $17.00.

Dining Room Table. Top, 44x60 inches. List price, $64.00.

Side Chair. List price, $13.00.

China Cabinet. Height, 67 inches; Width, 42 inches. List price, $70.00.

Server. Top, 10x30 inches. Height, 39 inches. List price, $40.00.

Buffet. Top, 21x66 inches. Height, 42 inches. List price, $100.00.

B-12 DINING ROOM SUITE
See Information below on Construction of "B" Line

In the "Pendleton" is seen a splendid modern adaptation of the English styles of the latter part of the 17th Century. The decoration is simple in character, a feature much appreciated in the modern home. To split turnings, mouldings and Curly Maple overlays is left the duty of embellishing the Figured Walnut veneer fronts. Pieces are quite large and offer generous silver and linen space in their cupboards and drawers. Table has a disappearing 12-inch leaf that is raised into position easily, and two extra 12-inch leaves may be had to make an 8-foot table. List price, ten pieces, $356.00.

PRODUCTS
Manufacturers of
Complete Dining Room Suites including the following pieces also sold separately:

Buffets	Serving Tables
Chairs	China Cabinets
Servers	Tables

Trade Marks

Also Desks and Secretaries manufactured by the Rockford Desk Company, owned and operated by the Rockford Furniture Company.

DINING ROOM SUITES IN TWO CLASSES
Our dining room suites are in two classes, the "A" line and the "B" line. Every "A" line suite has the same features and the same standard construction. "B" line suites are also uniform as to construction features. Our furniture although moderate in price is of the highest quality throughout.

"A" Line Construction Features
With the exception of ornamentation, all exposed solid parts are Genuine Walnut. Waterproof glue is used in construction of flat surfaces which are laminated five-ply with selected Walnut or Mahogany veneer on surface. An unusual feature is noted in the use of Genuine Walnut or Mahogany for core stocks in important parts such as tops of Buffet, Server and Table. Interiors faced with

Walnut or Mahogany veneer and finished. Drawer sides and ends are Mahogany, dovetail joints, bottom three-ply Mahogany face panel. The drawers are equipped with center guides to insure perfect operation. Inside face of China back matched Mahogany veneer—shelves solid Walnut. The artistic finish of lacquer assures maximum durability. Slip seats in chairs upholstered with ample padding.

"B" Line Construction Features
Flat surfaces are laminated five-ply construction using waterproof glue. All exposed solid parts are of select Red Gum. Drawers are dovetailed, three-ply Mahogany faced bottom and carefully fitted center guides to insure smooth operation. Dust-proof construction with solid partition—high grade lacquer finish. One 12-inch folding leaf is standard equipment for table which is equipped with 8-foot slide. The rich tone of stain is finished with lacquer for lasting qualities.

RETAIL PRICE RANGES
Dining Room Suites (10 pieces)—"A" line—range from $340.00 to $2300.00. "B" line suites (10 pieces) range from $245.00 to $356.00. Desks range from $42.00 to $108.00. Secretaries range from $58.00 to $95.00. All prices are subject to change without notice. An additional charge is made for special coverings on chairs, depending upon the quality of material selected.

ROCKFORD FURNITURE COMPANY

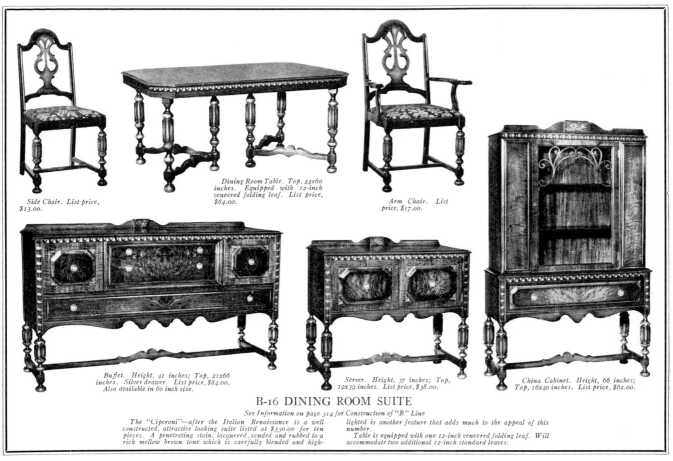

Side Chair. List price, $13.00.

Dining Room Table. Top, 44x60 inches. Equipped with 12-inch veneered folding leaf. List price, $64.00.

Arm Chair. List price, $17.00.

Buffet. Height, 41 inches; Top, 21x66 inches. Silver drawer. List price, $84.00. Also available in 60 inch size.

Server. Height, 37 inches; Top, 19x39 inches. List price, $38.00.

China Cabinet. Height, 66 inches; Top, 16x40 inches. List price, $62.00.

B-16 DINING ROOM SUITE
See Information on page 314 for Construction of "B" Line

The "Ciperani"—after the Italian Renaissance is a well constructed, attractive looking suite listed at $330.00 for ten pieces. A penetrating stain, lacquered, sanded and rubbed to a rich mellow brown tone which is carefully blended and high-lighted is another feature that adds much to the appeal of this number.

Table is equipped with one 12-inch veneered folding leaf. Will accommodate two additional 12-inch standard leaves.

China Cabinet. Top, 16x38½ inches; Height, 67 inches. List price, $60.00.

Side Chair. List price, $12.00.

Dining Room Table. Top, 44x60 inches. List price, $82.00.
Also Table with six legs. List price, $58.00.

Arm Chair. List price, $16.00.

Buffet. Top, 21x66 inches. Height, 39½ inches. List price, $76.00. Also available in 60 inch size.

Server. Top, 19x39 inches. Height, 36½ inches. List price, $31.00.

B-17 DINING ROOM SUITE
See Information on page 314 for Construction of "B" Line.

In the simplicity of design of this suite lies the greatest charm that makes it suitable for any home. It will find its background in the simple tastes of the sedate as well as the more elaborate requirements of the modern homes.

It is reasonably priced at $304.00 for ten pieces and offers you an opportunity to use this suite as a leader in many of your sales programs. Finished in a deep reddish brown tone which is blended and high-lighted.

(Continued on next page)

Side Chair. Padded seat with panel bottom. List price, $17.00.

Dining Room Table. Top, 44x60 inches. List price, $90.00.

Arm Chair. List price, $23.00.

China Cabinet. Top, 16x39 inches. Height, 63 inches. List price, $88.00.

Server. Top, 18x38 inches. Height, 36 inches. List price, $44.00.

Buffet. Top, 22x66 inches. Height, 40 inches. List price, $110.00.

No. 702 DINING ROOM SUITE
See Information on page 314 for Construction of "A" Line

The "Germain" is a Louis XVI style developed from the architecture of Rome and Greece, would possibly appear freakish in the modern home, but the application used on suite illustrated has been carefully designed to overcome this objection and still retain its characteristics, such as, for instance, authentic legs and stretchers. The antique style is also given life by the use of beautiful matched butt walnut veneer and finely proportioned body. To the rather plain lines has been given dignity and life. List price, ten pieces, $440.00.

Side Chair. List price, $17.00.

Table. Top 44x60 inches. List price, $104.00.

Arm Chair. List price, $24.00.

China Closet. Top 16x39 inches. Height, 64 inches. List price, $106.00.

Server. Top, 18½x39 inches. Height, 34 inches. List price, $56.00.

Buffet. Top, 22½x68 inches. Height, 38½ inches. List price, $124.00.

No. 703 DINING ROOM SUITE
See Information on page 314 for Construction of "A" Line

This suite inculcates some of the advanced modernistic trends that are sweeping the country. It is a number that has unusual appeal because of this fact and you should be able to realize a sales volume that will warrant you carrying several of these suites on your floor.

Fronts mitered satinwood and rosewood veneers. Buffet and Table tops Walnut core. Two extra 18-inch leaves of 5-ply, veneered to match table top furnished with suite. List price, ten pieces, $499.00.

Side Chair. List price, $18.00.

Dining Room Table. Top, 44x60 inches. List price, $90.00.

Arm Chair. List price, $24.00.

Buffet. Top, 22x66 inches; Height, 39 inches. List price, $114.00.

Server. Top, 18x30 inches; Height, 36 inches. List price, $48.00.

China Cabinet. Top, 16½x40 inches. Height, 65 inches. List price, $94.00.

No. 704 DINING ROOM SUITE
See Information on page 314 for Construction of "A" Line

This suite called the "Ware" of Jacobean inspiration displays excellent character and grace. The carving is low relief, the deeply moulded doors, shallow body, graceful legs and carved mouldings clearly reflect the feeling of the beginning of the 17th Century in England. Chests instead of china closets were popular at that time.

Development of the chest produced the Court cupboard, which in turn developed into the present day china closet. The design of entire suite has been carefully carried out to retain authenticity, and still blend itself into a modern home. List price, ten pieces, $460.00.

China Cabinet. Height, 68 inches; Width, 40 inches. List price, $96.00.

Side Chair. List price, $22.00.

Dining Room Table. Top, 44x66 inches. List price, $110.00.

Arm Chair. List price, $32.00.

Server. Height, 36 inches; Width, 40 inches. List price, $60.00.

Buffet. Top, 22x72 inches. Height, 41 inches. List price $132.00.

No. 781 DINING ROOM SUITE
See Information on page 314 for Construction of "A" Line

The predominant note of this pleasing pattern is after the manner of Chippendale—the graceful legs are reminiscent of Sheraton. The well-placed inlays add the finishing touch. The simplicity of this suite makes it readily adaptable for any modern

home. The chairs have the comfortable Sheraton swoop that one never tires of—yet a style in keeping with modern tastes. List price, ten pieces, $540.00.

(Continued on next page)

ROCKFORD FURNITURE COMPANY

Arm Chair. List price, $24.00.

Dining Room Table. Top, 44x60 inches. List price, $94.00.

Side Chair. List price, $18.00 each.

China Cabinet. Height, 69 inches; Width, 45 inches. List price $103.00.

Server. Top, 19x40 inches; Height, 38 inches. List price, $62.00.

Buffet. Top, 22x70 inches. Height, 43 inches. List price, $125.00.

No. 793 DINING ROOM SUITE
See Information on page 314 for Construction of "A" Line

The "Tyndoll" is designed in the Renaissance style, subtly interwoven with Elizabethan details that add a touch of refinement to the rather heavy frame work. In the finely carved details, the sublimated relief of foreign craftsmen, as compared to the rather crude work of the English, is distinctly noted. List price, ten pieces, $498.00.

Side Chair. List price, $22.00.

Dining Room Table. Top, 44x 66 inches. List price, $120.00.

Arm Chair. List price, $32.00.

China Cabinet. Height, 73 inches; Width, 41 inches. List price, $98.00.

Server. Top, 19x41 inches; Height, 37 inches. List price, $64.00.

Buffet. Top, 22x72 inches. Height, 41 inches. List price, $136.00.

No. 795 DINING ROOM SUITE
See Information on page 314 for Construction of "A" Line

The "Traner" follows the Sheraton motif which is nicely set off by the Duncan Phyfe Table. Satinwood and dainty black and white inlay border the doors and drawers. List price of ten pieces, $560.00. When selling this suite emphasize the pleasing proportions of the chairs which display Sheraton motifs at their best.

Side Chair. List price, $44.00 each.

Dining Room Table. Top, 46x66 inches. List Price, $166.00.

Arm Chair. List price, $54.00.

China Cabinet. Height, 71 inches; Width, 46 inches. List price, $200.00.

Server. Top, 20x44 inches; Height, 39 inches. List price, $130.00.

Buffet. Top, 23x76 inches. Height, 44 inches. List price, $220.00.

No. 796 DINING ROOM SUITE
See Information on page 314 for Construction of "A" Line

The "Bellevue" Suite No. 796 following the Louis XVI motif has many characteristics indicative of that Period noticeable quite readily in the straight fluted legs. The artistic hand-painted scrolls on Buffet, Server and China together with beautiful borders of Rosewood and Marqueterie and the blended Satinwood veneer on China closet door accentuate the beauty of design and figured veneers. List price, ten pieces, $990.00.

Side Chair. List price, $17.00.

Dining Room Table. Top, 44x60 inches. List price, $90.00.

Arm Chair. List price, $25.00.

China Cabinet. Height, 69 inches; Width, 41 inches. List price, $88.00.

Server. Top, 19x40 inches; Height, 38 inches. List price, $52.00.

Buffet. Top, 22x66 inches; Height, 42 inches. List price, $110.00.

No. 797 DINING ROOM SUITE
See Information on page 314 for Construction of "A" Line

The "Branford" after the manner of the Elizabethan is listed at $450.00 for ten pieces. Overlays of Curly Maple veneer on doors of Buffet, Server and grill of China Cabinet, together with highly figured matched Walnut veneers add a delightful touch of color to the rather somber motifs of the period.

(Continued on next page)

Side Chair. List price, $24.00 each.

Dining Room Table. Top, 44x60 inches. List price, $116.00.

Arm Chair. Lis price, $34.00.

China Cabinet. Height, 76 inches; Width, 30 inches. List price, $118.00.

Server. Top, 19 x 30 inches; Height, 40 inches. List price, $50.00.

Buffet. Top, 22x72 inches. Height, 45 inches. List price, $152.00.

No. 798 DINING ROOM SUITE
See Information on page 314 for Construction of "A" Line

The "Wickford" although predominantly an Early American Suite is relieved by the reeded pilasters of Sheraton. The result is a most pleasing example of what is today termed Colonial design. List price, ten pieces, $590.00.

Side Chair. List price, $15.00.

Dining Room Table, style as shown, 44x60 inches. List price, $84.00. Also Refectory Dining Room Table. 42x60 inches. List price, $78.00.

Arm Chair. List price, $23.00.

China Cabinet. Height, 65 inches; Width, 38 inches. List price, $70.00.

Server. Top, 19x38 inches. Height, 36 inches. List price $44.00.

Buffet. Top, 22x66 inches; Height, 39 inches. List price, $94.00.

No. 799 DINING ROOM SUITE
See Information on page 314 for Construction of "A" Line

The "Wimbledon" has features that make it quite reminiscent of the Periods. The Refectory Table and Yorkshire Chairs are in the manner of the Jacobean. List price, ten pieces, $384.00 with table illustrated. List price, ten pieces, with four-legged table, not illustrated, $378.00.

ROCKFORD FURNITURE COMPANY

No. 108—Desk. Top, 24x52 inches. The heritage of many epochs of furniture design which had come down to the cabinet makers of the latter part of 18th Century was brought to a luxuriant flowering by the Adam Brothers, Heppelwhite and Sheraton. The result of this condition was the conscious creation of furniture styles which were differentiated each from the other by studied use of decorative motifs and design combined in characteristic ways. The design of the desk illustrated is influenced from the works of the period described. List price, $90.00.

No. 111—Desk. Width, 29 inches; Height, 54 inches. After the manner of Sheraton's later designs this desk shows a distinct style all his own. All in all his designs are the very last word in fine cabinet work of the 18th Century in England, containing the essence of all the new ideas which had come into being during the last quarter of the century. List price, $55.00.

No. 105—Secretary. Width, 30 inches; Height, 74 inches. Sheraton was a cabinet maker by trade and a designer by profession, and, therefore, of unusual importance in educational influences in the art crafts at the end of the 18th Century. This desk is a copy of Sheraton's graceful designs. Characteristic of this designer's work, it is unusually well proportioned. List price, $58.00.

No. 110—Combination Desk. Width, 50 inches; Height, 45 inches. The use of Crotch Mahogany with a rather restrained feeling of decorative treatment indicates that the design is of the late 18th Century English inspiration. Furniture of this period showed a lightening of proportions. The vertical supports such as the legs of this desk were designed upon the basis of the classic fluted column. List price, $108.00.

No. 106½—Secretary Desk. Width, 30 inches; Height, 42 inches. Also available in a secretary style, No. 106. Exposed solid parts on all pieces Gum. All veneered parts 5-ply with Walnut or Mahogany face, fronts veneered with Butt Walnut or Crotch Mahogany. Drawer sides Red Gum, 3-ply drawer bottoms, Mahogany face, dovetail construction. Pigeon hole interior of Red Gum. List price, $47.00.

No. 103—Secretary. Height, 81 inches; Width, 30 inches. Also furnished in Secretary Desk only. Walnut finish. Exposed solid parts on all pieces gum. All veneered parts 5-ply with Walnut or Mahogany face; fronts veneered with Butt Walnut. Drawer sides Red Gum, 3-ply drawer bottoms, Mahogany face, dovetail construction. Pigeon hole interior of Red Gum. List price, $76.00.

No. 112—Secretary. Width, 30 inches; Height, 71 inches. The beauty of modern furniture designs resides in the simplicity and purity of its lines and the quality of material used in construction. The design of this "Modern French" Secretary is a logical outgrowth of the French decorative art and is characterized by elegance of line and proportion, the use of rare wood and fine finish. List price, $85.00.

No. 112½—Secretary Desk. Width, 30 inches. Height, 43 inches. See description under Secretary No. 112. List price, $62.00.

No. 100—Secretary. Height, 82 inches; Width, 33 inches. The "scrutoire" quite common in New England at one time was built with a reverse serpentine curve on front of desk with a ball and claw foot leg. Pigeon holes were copied after the true Governor Winthrop type, curved outline being left out and also the vertical paper drawers on each side of center door. These secretaries are plain, the lattice work in doors of top part being also of simple straight line design. Mahogany finish. Now made with claw foot. List price, $95.00

DESKS AND SECRETARIES
MADE BY THE ROCKFORD DESK COMPANY

ROCKFORD PALACE FURNITURE COMPANY

Manufacturers of Distinctive Period Dining Room Furniture, Desks, Bookcases and Radio Cabinets

1724 Woodruff Ave., ROCKFORD, ILL.

EXHIBITS

GRAND RAPIDS, MICH., 5th Floor, Keeler Bldg.   NEW YORK, N. Y., New York Furniture Exchange

and Showrooms at Factory in Rockford

No. 46—Arm or Host Chair. Upholstered in Tapestry or Damask. Seat, 19x22 inches. Height, 40 inches. List price, $46.00.

No. 46—Table. Top, 44x60 inches. Height, 30 inches. Eight-foot extension. List price, $130.00.

No. 46—Side Chair. Seat, 18x19½ inches. Height, 38 inches. Upholstered in Tapestry or Damask. List price, $36.00.

No. 46—China Closet. Top, 34x16 inches. List price, $125.00.

No. 46—Server. Top, 17x40½ inches. Height, 38½ inches. List price, $84.00.

No. 46—Buffet. Top, 20x66 inches. Height, 41½ inches. List price, $179.00.

Suite No. 46—The "Hanover"

The "Hanover" Suite here illustrated is in the style most frequently associated with Chippendale. In the early days of his rise to fame the current style of furniture inclined towards heaviness and an emphasis of strength. The Master carver managed to invest his designs with grace and charm, without ever losing the essential qualities of stability and dignity.

All solid exposed parts such as legs and stretchers are made of Genuine Mahog-

any. Tops, ends and fronts 5-ply selected veneers. Beautiful Crotch Mahogany veneers on fronts. Satinwood veneers overlaid with Mahogany veneers used for ornamentation. Hand carved. Finished in Antique Mahogany resembling plate No. 24—Standard Mahogany in the Woods and Finishes Section preceding page 9 of this Reference Book. List price, ten pieces, $744.00. Nine-piece suite for $660.00. Eight-piece suite for $535.00.

No. 44—Arm or Host Chair, upholstered in Tapestry or Damask. List price, $45.00.

No. 44—Dining Room Table. Top, 44x60 inches. List price, $144.00.

No. 44—Side Chair. Upholstered in Tapestry or Damask. List price, $36.00.

No. 44—China Closet. Height, 71 inches; width, 37 inches. List price, $165.00.

No. 44—Server. Height, 39 inches; width, 40 inches. List price, $105.00.

No. 44—Buffet. Height, 42 inches. Width, 72 inches. List price, $210.00.

Suite No. 44—The "Chambers"

Some of Chippendale's most charming pieces were in the Chinese manner. Sir William Chambers, an architect who was a powerful influence in the artistic world, had visited China and had brought back many new ideas in decoration from the East. With remarkable skill Chippendale adapted these designs of the Orient for use in homes of the West.

All solid exposed parts, such as, legs, stretchers, etc., of Genuine Mahogany.

Tops, ends and fronts 5-ply selected Mahogany veneers. Beautiful Crotch Mahogany veneers on fronts. List price for ten pieces, $849.00. Nine piece suite, $744.00 and eight piece suite for $579.00. Mohair, $2.00 per chair additional. Chairs illustrated are upholstered in damask or tapestry. Finish: Mahogany resembles plate No. 1 in the Woods and Finishes Section preceding page 9 of this Reference Book.

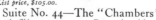

ROCKFORD PALACE FURNITURE COMPANY

No. 45—Side Chair. Seat, 17x21 inches. Height, 36½ inches. Upholstered in Tapestry or Damask. List price, $40.00.

No. 45—Dining Room Table. Top, 44x60 inches. Height, 30 inches. List price, $158.00.

No. 45—Arm or Host Chair. Seat, 17x21 inches. Height, 36½ inches. Upholstered in Tapestry or Damask. List price, $46.00.

No. 45—China Closet. Top, 40x16½ inches. Height, 68½ inches. List price, $197.00.

No. 45—Server. Top, 19x40 inches. Height, 30½ inches. List price, $100.00.

No. 45 — Buffet. Top, 21x72 inches. Height, 39½ inches. List price, $229.00.

Suite No. 45—The "Breton"

During the days of its glory, when the French Court was cultivating art and beauty with lavish expenditures, it was natural that furniture design should reflect the general tone . . . but it was too elaborate for the simpler homes of the provinces. Rural cabinet makers learned much from skilled Parisian craftsmen and invested their work with quiet simplicity and strong individual character.

All solid exposed parts such as legs, stretchers, etc., genuine Solid Walnut. Tops, ends, and fronts 5-ply selected Walnut veneers. Butt Walnut fronts. Hand carving. Finish: Walnut, resembles plate No. 1 in Woods and Finishes Section preceding page 9 of this Reference Book. Price for suite, ten pieces, list price, $930.00. Nine-piece suite for $830.00. Eight-piece suite for $633.00.

No. 48—Arm or Host Chair. Seat, 19x23 inches. Height, 39 inches. Upholstered in Tapestry or Damask. List price, $40.00.

No. 48—Dining Room Table. Top, 44x60 inches. List price, $190.00.

No. 48—Side Chair. Seat, 18x21 inches. Height, 39 inches. Upholstered in Tapestry or Damask. List price, $33.00.

No. 48—China Closet. Top, 37½ inches by 18 inches. List price, $145.00.

No. 48—Server. Top, 40x17 inches. Height, 38 inches. List price, $115.00.

No. 48—Buffet. Top, 24x72 inches. Height, 40½ inches. List price, $195.00.

Suite No. 48—The "Surrey"

George Heppelwhite, whose work flourished in the latter half of the 18th Century, shared with the Adam Brothers a love of simplicity, but his designs had none of the severity which is sometimes found in their designs. Note the clear cut lines and delicacy of ornament.

A most beautiful Walnut is used in this Heppelwhite Suite with genuine

Marqueterie Inlays, Burl Walnut fronts and Genuine walnut legs and stretchers. Rosewood border and Butt Walnut top on Table. Tulip-Wood Inlay. Finish: Walnut, resembles plate No. 10 in Woods and Finishes Section preceding page 9 of this Reference Book. List price for ten-piece suite, $850.00; nine-piece suite, $735.00; eight-piece suite, $590.00.

PRODUCTS

MANUFACTURERS OF

DINING ROOM SUITES, Complete, including the following pieces which are sold separately: SECRETARY DESKS, RADIO CABINETS, and BOOKCASES (Open Shelf and Glass Door Closed Types.)

AUTHENTIC PERIOD FURNITURE

Chinese Chippendale, French Provincial, Heppelwhite, Adam, Sheraton, English Chippendale, Colonial and Tudor periods.

MADE IN
ROCKFORD
ILLINOIS
ROCKFORD PALACE FURNITURE CO.

Trade Mark

GENERAL RETAIL PRICE RANGE

Complete Dining Room Suites average from $400.00 to $1400.00. Desks, from $120.00 to $200.00. Bookcases from $15.00 to $100.00 and Radio Cabinets, from $98.00 to $200.00. All prices shown are subject to change without notice. Terms—2% 30 days, net 60 days, F. O. B. Factory.

OTHER ATTRACTIVE SUITES

Complete catalog and price list will be sent upon request which illustrates other numbers not shown on these pages.

ROCKFORD NATIONAL FURNITURE CO.
Manufacturers of Dining Room and Library Furniture
2300 Kishwaukee, ROCKFORD, ILL.

Dining Room Table. Top, 42x60 inches.

Side Chair.

Arm Chair.

China Cabinet. Height, 64 inches; Width, 42 inches.

Server. Height, 37 inches; Width, 41 inches.

Buffet. Height, 42 inches; Width, 66 inches.

DINING ROOM SUITE No. 91

Suite No. 91. This suite is made both in Walnut veneer and Gum combination and Walnut and Walnut veneer. The veneer used on the drawer fronts of the Buffet and the side panels of the China is of highly figured butt Walnut veneer, and the veneer used on the doors of the buffet, server and the drawer front of the China is imported English Pollard Oak. The mouldings on this suite are of Oak, also. The interiors of the drawers in this suite are of Mahogany.

Dining Room Table. Top, 42x66 inches.

Side Chair.

Arm Chair.

Buffet. Height, 30 inches; Width, 79 inches.

China Cabinet. Height, 71 inches; Width, 42 inches.

Server. Height, 35 inches; Width, 46 inches.

DINING ROOM SUITE No. 95

Suite No. 95. This suite is Gum in combination with several kinds of veneers. The doors are of straight striped matched Walnut Veneer with a border of Redwood Burl. The top drawer is veneered in Zebra wood, as are the base aprons under the doors. The lower drawer of the Buffet is veneered in Butt Walnut and the ends and tops are veneered in straight striped Walnut. The posts and carvings are in Gum in this suite to enable us to get effect in the finishing, which we are not able to get using Walnut. The drawer construction is of Mahogany, also.

Dining Room Table.
Top, 42x60 inches.

Side Chair.

Arm Chair.

China Cabinet. Height,
60 inches; Width, 41 inches.

Buffet. Height, 41 inches; Width, 66 inches.

Server. Height, 38 inches. Width, 39 inches.

DINING ROOM SUITE No. 98

Suite No. 98. This suite is described as genuine Walnut or Walnut and Walnut Veneer. The ornamental veneers used on this Suite are Butt Walnut mainly, with a little Oak veneer used under the carving on the top drawer of the Buffet and the door of the China. Oak is also used on the head-rail of the Serving Table. The carvings, mouldings, etc., are Walnut and the drawer construction is of Mahogany.

Dining Room Table.
Top, 42x58 inches.

Side Chair.

Arm Chair.

China Cabinet. Height, 61 inches; Width, 40 inches.

Server. Height, 30 inches; Width, 38 inches.

Buffet. Height, 43 inches; Width, 66 inches.

DINING ROOM SUITE No. 100

Suite No. 100. This Suite is made in Walnut and Walnut Veneer, using highly figured Butt Walnut Veneer for the ornamental effect on the fronts. The posts, stretchers, etc., are of Walnut and the carved ornaments are of Walnut also. The interior construction of the drawers is Mahogany. The construction as to materials, of the China, Serving Table and Chairs corresponds to that of the Buffet, except that Chairs are solid Walnut thru-out. This is a low priced Suite.

PRODUCTS

MANUFACTURERS OF

DINING ROOM, DINETTE, and BREAKFAST ROOM SUITES comprising the following pieces also sold separately:

BUFFETS and COLONIAL BUFFETS   CHAIRS, ARM and SIDE
CHINA CABINETS and CLOSETS   SERVERS and SERVING TABLES
TABLES, EXTENSION

LIBRARY FURNITURE including:

BOOKCASES	SECRETARY DESKS
BOOKSHELVES	WALL DESKS
PIER CABINETS	TABLE DESKS

(Continued on next page)

Bookcase No. 17. Height, 48 inches; Width, 43 inches. Is a two section size of a three-piece series, all of which are 40 inches high—single door section is 23 inches wide; two door section is 43 inches wide, and the three door section is 61 inches. This series is made in Walnut combination.

Bookcase No. 20. Height, 44 inches; Width, 42 inches. Is a two-door section of a two-piece series, made up of a single door and two-door side bookcase. The single door side is 23 inches wide and 44 inches high and the double door is 42 inches wide and 44 inches high. This is a genuine mahogany piece with a Myrtle Burl base.

Bookcase No. 22. Height, 48 inches; Width, 43 inches. This is a two-door bookcase in a two-piece set, made up of a single and two door side bookcase. The double door piece is 43 inches wide and 48 inches high. The single door piece is 23 inches wide and 48 inches high. This series is genuine mahogany with Burl frieze and drawer front.

Table Desk No. 711. Top, 26x48 inches; Height, 30 inches. This desk has gum posts and stretchers, with Butt Walnut drawer fronts and top. The overlay on one of the drawers is Carpathian Elm Burl. The interior construction of this desk is Mahogany, with boxed-in drawers, and other features of the desk construction are up to the usual high grade standards of construction of Rockford-made furniture.

Secretary No. 507. Height, 77 inches; Width, 29 inches. This is a genuine Walnut Secretary, ornamented on the fall and drawer fronts with Butt Walnut veneer, and on the apron base, top and side panel of the Secretary is Myrtle Burl. The mouldings and carvings used on this piece are genuine Walnut and the decoration on the panel in the door is hand painted. This is a very beautiful piece of furniture and it is sold either with the top section as a Secretary or without as a Desk.

WOODS AND FINISHES

Plates Nos. 1, 8, and 14 in the Woods and Finishes section preceding page 9 are approximately the same tone finishes which we employ for our Mahogany, Maple and Walnut finishes.

RETAIL PRICE RANGES

Rockford National Dining Room Suites retail from $250.00 to $950.00; Dinette and Breakfast Suites from $125.00 to $300.00; Bookcases from $40.00 to $80.00; Pier Cabinets from $30.00 to $65.00; Secretary Desks from $75.00

Secretary No. 500. Height, 76 inches; Width, 28 inches. This Secretary is made either in Butt Walnut fronts or Mahogany, both in combination with gum posts. The drawer interiors and the panel back of the secretary is of Mahogany. The desk section is sold separately.

Secretary No. 510. Height, 87 inches; Width, 39 inches. Number 510 Secretary is a genuine Mahogany authentic Governor Winthrop Secretary. It has the correct pigeon hole interior and automatic fall supports, correct grill and feet.

Pier Cabinet No. 908. Height, 73 inches; Width 19 inches. An all Maple pier with two cupboards, a drawer and a desk fall, behind which is pigeon hole work. This pier cabinet is sold either plain or decorated.

Secretary No. 508. Height, 78 inches; Width, 33 inches. This Secretary is made either in Gum combination with Mahogany veneer fronts or Gum with combination Walnut veneer fronts. This is a low priced Secretary, but is exceedingly well made with Mahogany interiors. We also made a desk section in the same design as the lower part of the Secretary to match.

to $250.00; Wall Desks from $40.00 to $110.00; and Table Desks from $80.00 to $165.00.

Prices of products illustrated in this catalog will be furnished on request.

All prices are subject to change without notice.

GENERAL INFORMATION

The charm and dignity of Rockford National-made Furniture is too apparent to be ignored—the quality of materials and construction too craftsmanly to be slighted—in all you have a furniture that is built to adorn the home. Emphasize this truth at all times and you will be pleased with results.

ROCKFORD STANDARD FURNITURE CO.

Manufacturers of Desks, Bookcases, and Dining Room Furniture

Factory and General Offices, Eleventh Street, ROCKFORD, ILL.

PERMANENT EXHIBITS

NEW YORK, N. Y., Furniture Exchange, 206 Lexington Ave.   CHICAGO, ILL., American Furniture Mart, 666 Lake Shore Drive

Trade Mark

PRODUCTS
Manufacturers of
Medium and High Grade Library and Dining Room Furniture

BOOKCASES
—Open Shelf
CHESTS OF DRAWERS
DESKS
—Cabinet
—Governor Winthrop

DESKS
—Ladies'
—Library
—Secretary
—Spinet
—Wall
PIER CABINETS

TRADE MARK

The Rockford Standard Furniture Company line has always been identified by the trade mark of the "Standard bearer mounted on horseback" in an octagon shape trademark as shown in the top center of this page.

GENERAL INFORMATION

This company was established in 1886 and ever since its inception has manufactured a medium and high grade line of quality furniture. The illustrations shown on these pages comprise only a small part of our line and we will be glad to furnish photographs and prices or any other information required upon receipt of your inquiry.

WOODS AND FINISHES

All Rockford Standard products are finished in body lacquer with the exception of our Oak Library Bookcases which are varnished. Any numbers in our line may be ordered in any particular special finish desired. If finish is not specified, the standard finishes being used are applied.

GENERAL RETAIL PRICE RANGE OF "STANDARD" FURNITURE
Catalog and Price List on Request

Desks......................................Retail from $27.00 to $125.00
Secretaries...............................Retail from 45.00 to 150.00
Bookcases.................................Retail from 23.00 to 110.00
Pier Cabinets.............................Retail from 29.00 to 49.00
Dining Room Suites (10 pieces)............Retail from 300.00 to 1750.0

All prices shown above and elsewhere on these pages are subject to change without notice. Terms: 2% thirty days, net sixty days, f. o. b. Rockford, Illinois.

China Cabinet. Height, 68 inches; Width, 40 inches. List price, $90.00.

Arm or Host Chair. Upholstered in Tapestry or Velour. List price, $22.00. Mohair seat $2.00 extra per chair.

Buffet. Height, 42 inches; Width, 66 inches. List price, $118.00.

Dining Room Table. Top 48x60 inches. 8-foot extension. List price, $110.00. 6-foot extension. List price, $100.00.

Server. Height, 37 inches; Width, 40 inches. List price, $75.00

Side Chair upholstered in Tapestry or Velour. List price, $16.00. Mohair seat $2.00 extra per chair.

No. 856 Suite "THE HOMEWOOD"

Fashioned in a handsome Walnut combination, this charming Suite has a note of simplicity and dignity that marks it out from the crowd. It is beautifully designed, gathering inspiration from several popular periods. The best things that we know of today in furniture are brought down to us from the past either as tangible objects or as an inspiration. The requisites of a piece of furniture in historical periods were usefulness and beauty. In this modern and extreme age, this principle has not changed in the least. Modern science has replaced old methods but not the principle. The handsome crotch Walnut veneers and the four-way matched drawers of butt Walnut veneer of this Suite make its beauty as unquestioned as its utility. Hand carving used extensively on this Suite.

Suite complete as shown $495.00, with 6-foot table, $485.00.

(Continued on next page)

Buffet. Height, 44 inches; Width, 66 inches. List price, $108.00.

Server. Height, 36 inches; Width, 40 inches. List price, $66.00.

China Cabinet. Height, 71 inches; Width, 42 inches. List price, $90.00.

Dining Table. Top, 45x60 inches. 8-foot extension. List price, $108.00. 6-foot extension. List price, $98.00.

Diner. Upholstered in Tapestry or Velour. List price, $16.00. Mohair seat, $2.00 extra per chair.

Arm Chair. Upholstered in Tapestry or Velour. List price, $24.00. Mohair seat, $2.00 extra per chair.

No. 850 Suite "DUNCAN PHYFE"

This is a Mahogany combination Suite with crotch Mahogany fronts and cross-mottle Mahogany tops. This Suite is proportioned to give an effect of slenderness and lowness and while inexpensive is exceedingly well adapted for that type of house which has elegant simplicity for its keynote. Duncan Phyfe style has but recently been revived but its slender forms and elegant simplicity have made it immensely popular. Suite complete as shown $476.00, with 6-foot table, $466.00.

China Cabinet. Height, 63 inches; Width, 39 inches. List price, $105.00.

Server. Height, 36 inches; Width, 38 inches. List price, $79.00.

Buffet. Height, 39 inches; Width, 66 inches. Silver drawer. List price, $118.00.

Diner. Seat upholstered in Cut Velvet. List price, $19.00

Dining Table. Top, 45x60 inches. 8-foot extension. List price, $102.00. 6-foot extension. List price, $92.00.

Arm Chair. Seat upholstered in cut Velvet. List price $27.00.

No. 857 Suite "THE IVANHOE"

This sturdy Oak Suite is typical of the best Early English traditions. It is a straight, rather heavy lined Suite, somewhat squatty and low in effect. It is simple in structure and intensely practical, as befitted the character of the early Saxons. Under bracing is used to tie the legs together, and this is plain, sturdy and close to the floor. This Suite is fashioned entirely of quarter-sawed Oak with faces of beautiful Pollard Oak. This Suite meets the demand for exclusively distinctive patterns which will appeal to discriminating customers. Finish, Sixteenth Century Oak antiqued. Sides on all pieces are detailed same as fronts. Suite complete as shown $526.00, with 6-foot table, $516.00.

Buffet. Height, 38 inches; Width, 78 inches. List price, $220.00.

Dining Table. Top, 45x66 inches. 8-foot extension. List price, $160.00.

Diner upholstered in Mohair. List price, $53.00.

Arm Chair upholstered in Mohair. List price, $61.00.

China Cabinet, 74 inches high and 46 inches wide. List price, $210.00.

Server. Height, 34 inches; Width, 43 inches. List price, $110.00.

No. 849 Suite "THE COLBERT"

The period from which this Suite derives its inspiration was a great and glorious one. French soldiers carried their standards throughout Europe, and made France a powerful state, feared by all its neighbors. Literature and the arts flourished—it was the age of the Grand Monarch, Louis the Fourteenth. It was an extravagant showy period in every way. The king lived in the midst of ceremony and splendor, dress was exceedingly elaborate. Thus the furniture reflected the times, and was showy and ornate.

The Colbert is a Walnut combination, with beautifully matched diamond veneer Table top, and with half-diamond veneer on Buffet and Server tops. Fronts are of butt Walnut veneer. The doors of China Cabinet and Server are inlaid with marquetry, with Satinwood border and ornamented with Madrone burl. Suite complete as shown $1026.00.

No. 440—Desk. Height, 74 inches; Width, 26 inches. Mahogany veneer and Mahogany. Crotch Mahogany fronts. Early American Mahogany finish. Price, $83.00. With light, $6.00 extra.

No. 442—Desk. Height, 74 inches; Width, 31 inches. Walnut veneer and Gum. Four-way match butt Walnut on falls, crotch Walnut on drawer front and front panels. Antique Walnut H. L. finish. Price $85.00.

No. 441 — Early American open Bookcase. Height, 66 inches; Width, 25 inches. Made of all Maple with Thuya burl overlays. Drawer and writing slide. Price $45.00.

No. 438—Desk. Height, 66 inches; Width, 20 inches. Genuine Walnut Secretary made of Walnut and Walnut veneers with panel door on book compartment with book shelves on either side. Fronts are of highly figured Walnut butts with Thuya burl overlays. Antique Walnut H.L. finish. Price $75.00. With light, $6.00 extra.

(Continued on next page)

No. 436—Desk. Height, 77 inches; Width, 32 inches. Genuine Walnut Desk made of Walnut and Walnut veneers with Maple overlays on stripe Walnut on head piece. Butt Walnut veneer with Rosewood border on fall, top drawer front Satinwood overlays on side and Walnut burl in center. Bottom drawer fronts stripe Walnut cross-veneer. Antique Walnut H. L. finish. Price, $105.00.

No. 422—Genuine Governor Winthrop Secretary. Height, 82 inches; Width, 36 inches. Made of Mahogany veneer and Mahogany. Automatic sliding lid supports. Finished in either light brown or Early American Mahogany finish. Price $149.00.

No. 430 — Genuine Early American Mahogany Secretary. Height, 77 inches; Width, 32 inches. Made of Mahogany and crotch Mahogany veneers. This is an authentic reproduction of the practical furniture used by the founders of this great nation. Finished as desired in early American or brown Mahogany. Price $105.00.

No. 81—Desk. Height, 40 inches; Width, 29 inches. Made of Walnut and Walnut veneers. Thuya burl overlays. Walnut butt on writing fall. Finished Antique Walnut H. L. Price $57.00.

No. 84—Desk. Height, 42 inches; Width, 31 inches. Made of Walnut veneers and Quartered American Gumwood. Fronts of 5-ply construction with beautiful Walnut butts on writing fall and drawer front. Finished Antique Walnut H. L. Price $59.00.

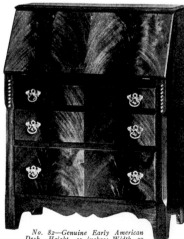

No. 82—Genuine Early American Desk. Height, 41 inches; Width, 30 inches. Made of Mahogany and Mahogany veneers with fronts and writing fall of beautiful feathered crotch Mahogany. Writing fall and fronts 5-ply construction. Finished as desired in Early American or brown Mahogany. Price $85.00.

No. 413—Mahogany combination Adam Secretary. Height, 65 inches; Width, 31 inches. Made in Mahogany veneer and Gum. Front of case being Mahogany and sides of Quartered American Gum. Finished as desired in red or brown Mahogany. Price, $64.00.

No. 67—Genuine Governor Winthrop Desk. Height, 40 inches; Width, 36 inches. Made of Mahogany veneers and Mahogany. Finished as desired in Early American or brown Mahogany. Price $100.00.

No. 101—Table Desk. Height, 30 inches; Width, 48 inches; Depth, 26 inches. Genuine Early American Desk made of Mahogany and Mahogany veneers with front of fine feathered crotch Mahogany and cross-mottle Mahogany tops. Interior construction Mahogany. Drawer sides and 3-ply bottoms. Finished as desired in Early American or brown Mahogany. The back of this Desk is also finished so can be shown anywhere in a room. Price $125.00.

No. 100.—Table Desk. Height, 30 inches; Width, 48 inches; Depth, 26 inches. A genuine reproduction of Early American Desk made of Mahogany and Mahogany veneers with fine feathered crotch fronts and cross-mottle Mahogany tops. Legs turned, fluted, and carved. Interior construction Mahogany, drawer sides and three-ply bottom. Each drawer fitted with drawer slides. Finished as desired in Early American Mahogany or brown Mahogany. The back of this Desk is also finished so can be shown anywhere in a room. Price $107.00.

No. 66—Base of Desk. Height, 39 inches; Width, 30 inches. Made of Mahogany veneer and Quartered American Gumwood, having 5-ply fronts and writing fall. Finished in either red or brown Mahogany. Price $45.00.

No. 102—Table Desk. Height, 30 inches; Width, 48 inches; Depth, 26 inches. Made of Walnut veneers and Quartered American Gumwood, with Mahogany interior construction, 3-ply bottoms. Stripe Walnut top with butt and stripe Walnut drawer fronts. Finished Antique Walnut H. L. The back of this Desk is also finished so it can be shown anywhere in a room. Price $89.00.

No. 80—Ladies' Wall Desk. Height, 42 inches; Width, 23 inches. Made of Mahogany veneer and Gum. 5-ply Mahogany writing fall with Maple overlays. This Desk also has one drawer. Finished in Mahogany or Walnut. Price $27.00.

No. 735—Bookcase. Height, 50 inches; Width, 45 inches. Genuine Mahogany Book case made of Mahogany veneers and Mahogany. Can be finished as desired in Early American or brown Mahogany. Price $69.00.

No. 755—Bookcase. Height, 56 inches; Width, 25 inches. Made in Oak or Gum. Can be finished in either Oak, Mahogany, or Walnut. Price, $23.00.

ROYAL MANTEL & FURNITURE CO.
Manufacturers of Dining Room Furniture
ROCKFORD, ILL.

Dining Room Table. Top,
42x64 inches.

Side Chair.

Arm Chair.

China Cabinet. Height,
67½ inches; Width, 40 inches.

Server. Height, 39¼ inches;
Width, 40 inches.

Buffet. Height, 42
inches; Width, 66 inches.

No. 516 DINING ROOM SUITE

*Suite No. 516 is built of Genuine Mahogany—Mahogany posts and stretchers
with Crotch Mahogany fronts and straight stripe Mahogany tops and ends. The
drawer work in this Suite is also of Mahogany. Chairs of Solid Mahogany.*

Dining Room Table.
Top, 42x64 inches.

Side Chair.

Arm Chair.

China Cabinet. Height, 74
inches; Width, 38 inches.

Server. Height, 41
inches; Width, 38 inches.

Buffet. Height, 45½
inches; Width, 72 inches.

No. 514 DINING ROOM SUITE

*Genuine Mahogany—Mahogany posts and stretchers with Crotch Mahogany
fronts and straight stripe Mahogany tops and ends. The drawer work is also of
Mahogany. Chairs constructed of Solid Mahogany.*

Server. Height, 37½ inches; Width, 40 inches.

Buffet. Height, 42 inches; Width, 66 inches.

China Cabinet. Height, 64½ inches; Width, 40 inches.

Side Chair.

Arm Chair.

Dining Room Table. Top, 42x60 inches.

No. 520 DINING ROOM SUITE

Gum and Walnut veneered combination Suite. Butt Walnut veneers on doors, lower drawer front of Buffet, side panels of China, and doors of Serving Table.

Top drawer of Buffet and middle partition in Server of veneered Lacewood. Genuine hand carvings. Mahogany drawer bottoms.

Server. Height, 38 inches; Width, 40 inches.

Buffet. Height, 40 inches; Width, 42 inches.

China Cabinet. Height, 62½ inches; Width, 40 inches.

Side Chair.

Arm Chair.

Dining Room Table. Top, 42x60 inches.

No. 523 DINING ROOM SUITE

Oak posts and stretchers and ends and mouldings, with Walnut tops and ends, fronts overlaid in Ash Burl. Hand carvings on aprons. Finished in color that blends Oak and Walnut together in a very pleasing manner. Interiors of Mahogany.

PRODUCTS

MANUFACTURERS OF

DINING ROOM SUITES, including the following pieces sold separately:

BUFFETS, CHINA CABINETS, ARM CHAIRS, SIDE CHAIRS, SERVERS, TABLES, Extension

(Continued on next page)

China Cabinet. Height, 70 inches; Width, 44 inches.

Server. Height, 40 inches; Width, 44 inches.

Buffet. Height, 45 inches; Width, 72 inches; also 66 inches wide.

Side Chair.

Dining Room Table. Top, 44x64 inches.

Arm Chair.

No. 510 DINING ROOM SUITE

Solid parts of Gum, with Butt Walnut veneer used on the fronts of drawer and doors. Regular Stripe Walnut on ends and tops. Genuine Wood hand carvings. Interiors of Mahogany. Two sizes of Buffets—66 and 72 inch.

China Cabinet. Height, 62 inches; Width, 42 inches.

Server. Height, 37 inches; Width, 40 inches.

Buffet. Height, 40½ inches; Width, 66 inches.

Side Chair.

Dining Room Table. Top, 42x60 inches.

Arm Chair.

No. 511 DINING ROOM SUITE

Combination Gum and Walnut, with Walnut Butt veneer. Genuine hand carvings. Interior construction of Drawers, Red Mahogany. Simplicity is the keynote of the Suite and it has wide appeal.

SLIGH FURNITURE COMPANY

Nearly One-Half Century of Fine Furniture Building

GRAND RAPIDS, MICHIGAN

OFFICERS

NORMAN McCLAVE, *Pres. and Gen. Mgr.* CHARLES R. SLIGH, JR., *Treasurer*
MILTON C. MILLER, *Vice Pres. and Sec.* LEE W. AVERILL, *Asst. Secretary*
EARL E. DeNEUT, *Sales Manager*

REPRESENTATIVES

HARRY M. STORY HERMAN J. WOHLFERD
IRVING McCLAVE HARRY L. KETTLE
VAN W. KNOX THOMAS WILLIAMS
MILTON McCLAVE CHAS. R. SLIGH, JR.
A. H. MORGENSTERN JAMES C. GREER
THOMAS WELMERS

PRODUCTS

MANUFACTURERS OF

BEDROOM AND DINING ROOM FURNITURE in practically every period design. ALSO Occasional Living Room pieces.

GENERAL INFORMATION

From a line broad and varied "Sligh" offers for those of discriminating taste a choice of fine furniture unmatchable in value in a wide price range.

DINING ROOM FURNITURE

Dining Room Furniture in walnut, mahogany and oak.

BEDROOM FURNITURE

Sligh Furniture Co. is one of the largest manufacturers of Bedroom Furniture in the U. S. Bedroom creations in walnut, mahogany, gumwood, satinwood, rosewood, combinations of rare burls and in enamel. Also specializes in Hotel Contract work.

LIVING ROOM FURNITURE

Smart occasional pieces in beautiful and unusual woods.

DESIGN

Sligh brings to furniture design an understanding born of nearly fifty years of studying and interpreting the requirements of American homes, together with facilities to attract and command the finest designing talent in the world.

It is but natural that Sligh creations embody to an unusual degree the appealing qualities of inspired line and contour, masterful handling of carving and decoration and rich effects in the color values of rare and beautiful woods.

To the best achievements of each famous period of furniture design, Sligh has contributed freshness and originality of conception and charming adaptability to present day needs. And in *art moderne*, that vibrant expression of the new day in artistic expression, Sligh creates with the sure touch granted only to those possessed of a true appreciation of the fundamentals of good design.

The Sligh line is unusually broad and diversified. There are creations for every furnishing need, prices for every purse, types of beauty for every personality and every taste.

SHOWERS BROTHERS COMPANY
Bedroom, Dining Room, Living Room, Kitchen and Radio Furniture
BLOOMINGTON, INDIANA

Factories: BLOOMINGTON, IND., BLOOMFIELD, IND., and BURLINGTON, IOWA

Exhibits: Space 1501, American Furniture Mart, CHICAGO   Space 1607-9-11, New York Furniture Exchange, NEW YORK

PRODUCTS
MANUFACTURERS OF

BEDROOM FURNITURE
—Dressers
—Vanities
—Straight End Beds
—Bow End Beds
—Poster Beds
—Night Stands
—Bedroom Rockers
—Bedroom Chairs
—Chests
—Chifforobes
—Benches

DINING ROOM
   FURNITURE
—Dining Room Tables

DINING ROOM
   FURNITURE
—China Cabinets
—Buffets
—Servers
—Straight Chairs
—Arm Chairs
—Pedestal Extension
   Tables

LIVING ROOM
   FURNITURE
—Occasional Chairs
—Living Room Suites
—Davenports
—Mirrors

The symbol of 60 years of manufacturing furniture of honest value—profitable to handle.

For information on other Showers products see RADIO FURNITURE Catalog page 188, and KITCHEN CABINETS Catalog page 75.

TRADE NAME
All Showers furniture can now be identified by the above trade mark. It is a symbol of sixty years' experience and is your assurance of honest values.

GENERAL INFORMATION
All case goods have five-ply laminated tops; three-ply fronts, backs and ends; dovetail front and rear drawer construction, with three-ply Mahogany bottoms on all but suites Nos. 1950, 1903 and 1940; and all drawers have lip construction, are glue blocked and are finished inside. Frames are well made. Dust-proof construction top and bottom on all but suites Nos. 1950 and 19030, angle brace construction throughout.

Larger pieces equipped with casters, and chairs have metal glides. All furniture is shipped in Speedpak plywood cases which eliminate a big portion of freight damages. All prices shown on these pages are subject to change without notice.

WOODS AND FINISHES
Walnut veneers over selected hardwood cores are used in all bedroom and dining-room furniture. Overlays of matched Butt Walnut, Oriental Walnut, Moire Walnut, Zebrawood, Satinwood and Blistered Maple are used to accentuate the beauty of the various pieces. The woods are finished in the soft, beautiful brown of American Walnut, hand-wiped and rubbed to a velvety surface. Carvings, decorations and overlays are blended and high-lighted to bring out the natural beauty of the wood. Double staining brings out the processing and fluting on a number of the suites.

No. 1906½—Dresser. Top, 22x48 inches. Glass, 26x32 inches. Price, $57.20.

FEATURES OF SUITE No. 1906

Design

This suite is characterized by great elaboration of design with ample but refined decorative features. Top drawers are of Moire Walnut veneer edged by black enamel margins. A Drop Moire Walnut overlay, rectangular in shape, with a crescent cut-out is placed directly beneath. High-lighted branch carvings flank the overlay on either side. Split turnings of the pendant type carry out the arch motif.

Color contrast is provided by two shaded vertical panel designs with routed outlines. Spread carvings on base rails. One-piece old English drawer pulls of delicate pattern.

The suave symmetry of the turned legs is in agreeable harmony with the broad curves of the decorative front.

Construction

Five-ply rotary Walnut tops. Three-ply fronts, backs and ends. Dust-proof top and bottom. Three-ply Mahogany drawer bottoms. Angle brace construction.

Finish

American Walnut Standard as on Plate No. 14 in the Woods and Finishes Section preceding page 9 of this Reference Book.

No. 7906—Straight End Bed. Height, 49 inches. Price, $33.00.

No. 1906—Dresser. Top, 20x42 inches.
Glass, 24x26 inches. Price, $49.20.

No. 2906¼—Vanity. Top, 18x45 inches.
Glass, 20x32 inches. Price, $51.00.

No. 3006—Chest. Top, 20x34 inches.
Height, 48 inches. Price, $37.60.

No. 8906—Night Stand. Top,
14x17 inches. Height, 29 inches.
Price, $15.00.

No. 4906—Chifforobe. Top,
20x40 inches. Height, 64 inches.
Finished inside. Price, $52.00.

(Continued on next page)

FEATURES OF SUITE No. 1940
Design
Top drawers have intricate routed design in striking two-tone shades. Black routed outline decoration on fronts, surmounted by a graceful butterfly overlay of Sap Moire Walnut with contrasting grain. Cluster carving on all base rails and tops of mirror frames.

Construction
Five-ply rotary Walnut tops. Top drawers solid Gum routed. Three-ply ends and backs. Box type drawers with three-ply bottoms. All drawers blocked on under side. Quarter-inch bottoms are used in long drawers of cases over forty-two inches, others of three-sixteenth stock. Angle brace construction.

Finish
American Walnut Standard as on Plate No. 14, Woods and Finishes Section, preceding page 9 of this Reference Book.

No. 2940¼—Vanity. Top, 18x46 inches. Glass 18x32 inches. Price, $43.00.

No. 7940—Bed. Height, 49 inches. Price, $28.00.

No. 3940—Chest. Top, 18x34 inches. Height, 47 inches. Finished inside. Price, $31.20.

No. 1940—Dresser. Top, 18x42 inches. Glass 22x26 inches. Price, $42.30.

FEATURES OF DINING-ROOM SUITE No. 5722

A suite with simple outlines enriched with interesting decorative details. Four-way matched Butt Walnut veneers on Buffet drawers. Buffet doors, Server doors and side panels of China Cabinet are exquisitely embellished by octagonal molded carvings. Heavy contrasting Blistered Maple overlays at the focal point of each add a striking touch of color. The sweeping curves of the generous scroll molding on the Buffet drawers are a distinctive final detail. Attractive routed fret decorations on base rails.

Posts neatly processed and turned in graceful contours. Upright carvings on the stretchers give finish and completeness to the ensemble.

Construction

Five-ply rotary Walnut tops. Three-ply fronts, ends, backs and drawer bottoms.

Box type drawer construction, dovetailed front and blocked on under side. Dust-proof case bottoms. Top Buffet drawer has lined compartment for silverware.

Bottoms of all drawers and back panel of China Cabinet lined with mahogany veneer. Drawers and compartments finished inside. Angle brace construction throughout.

Finish

American Walnut Standard as on Plate No. 14, Woods and Finishes Section, preceding page 9 of this Reference Book.

No. 5722—Table. Top, 45x54 inches.
Height, 30 inches. Price, $43.00.

No. 5722—Buffet. Top, 20x60 inches.
Height, 39 inches. Price, $49.00.

No. 5722—Server. Top, 20x34 inches.
Height, 39 inches. Price, $27.00.

No. 724A—Chair. Price, $10.50.

No. 724D—Chair. Price, $8.10.

No. 5722—China. Top, 15x38 inches.
Height, 65 inches. Price, $36.00.

(Continued on next page)

SHOWERS BROTHERS COMPANY

Main Plants and Offices, Bloomington, Indiana

Kitchen Cabinet Plant, Bloomington, Indiana

Chair Factory, Bloomfield, Indiana

Western Plant, Burlington, Iowa

SHOWERS STRAIGHT LINE PRODUCTION

Showers Brothers Company, in their six huge plants, turn out furniture by the same straight line production methods that form the basis of America's great automobile industry. Today the Showers Brothers Company is the largest manufacturer of wooden furniture in the world.

The Showers production chain starts at the lumber pile and is only completed with the final packing of the finished pieces of furniture in packing cases similar to those which are used for shipping phonographs. Such efficiency in production results in the saving prices at which Showers furniture is sold.

DESIGNING

Skilled designers and craftsmen create Showers designs in a special plant known as the Research Laboratory.

SPINDLE CARVING

Expert operators work on the spindle carving machines, turning out beautifully detailed decorative units.

SHOWERS BROTHERS COMPANY

A ONE-OPERATION TIME SAVING MACHINE

One of the most marvelous machines in the whole Showers system is one invented by Mr. C. A. Sears. This machine takes the rough lumber for drawer ends; molds, planes and sands the four sides; and then grooves the piece for joining, all in one operation.

The final assembling of each piece of Showers furniture resembles very closely the system used in automobile manufacturing. The joined and sanded ends, sides, tops and other units are worked down a line of men, each having his job to do, and each doing it well.

Above is a view of the straight line production—each piece of work is immediately transferred from workman to workman without lost motion or lost time.

AUTOMATIC SANDING
All the operator does is to feed this rapid machine which is almost human in its automatic ability to sand all types of legs.

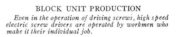

BLOCK UNIT PRODUCTION
Even in the operation of driving screws, high speed electric screw drivers are operated by workmen who make it their individual job.

SHOWERS BROTHERS COMPANY'S NEW SELLING SERVICE

Showers' Plan of Dealer Resale Helps is just as modern and complete as their straight line production methods used in the manufacturing of their merchandise.

Remember, Showers has got more than just merchandise to offer its customers. There are many other important and *new* features that will interest you. A New Selling Service for one, some real high-powered Merchandisers for another (and you will have their personal help in putting on resale plans). Sparkling campaigns to help you sell your merchandise! And they are *tested* campaigns. Each one has been tried out—received the acid test of whether it would pull in the business or not. These twenty-four dollar-producers are ready to be put into action—Profit Action—for each and every Showers' customer. In addition, Showers will advise with you on specific selling campaigns—will

help instruct your salesmen at store meetings—will offer you assistance in merchandising, advertising, operating and management problems. Today Showers offers you the most complete line of merchandise made by one manufacturer; style merchandise at moderate prices. Bedroom and dining-room furniture, living-room suites, kitchen cabinets, occasional chairs, and radio furniture. Showers believe and have made it their policy to build merchandise and develop a dealer co-operative plan that warrants the dealer looking to Showers for this special and unique service—the Key Line of the Furniture Industry—the Key Line for Your Store. You can get quick turnover, quick volume—*immediate profits*—with the New Showers Key Line Merchandise, plus the New Showers Selling Service, plus the Personal Service of the New Showers Merchandisers.

SKANDIA FURNITURE COMPANY
Manufacturers of Dining Room Furniture, Desks, and Bookcases

FACTORY AND GENERAL OFFICES
No. Second Street, ROCKFORD, ILL.

PERMANENT EXHIBITS

NEW YORK, N. Y., New York Furniture Exchange   GRAND RAPIDS, MICH., Klingman Building

---

PRODUCTS
MANUFACTURERS OF

PERIOD DINING ROOM SUITES
—Early American
—Heppelwhite
—Sheraton

Including the pieces listed in the next column also sold separately on order:

Registered Trade Mark

—Buffets
—Chairs
—China Cabinets
—China Closets
—Servers
—Tables

For information on Library Furniture including Desks, Secretaries, Cabinets, High-boys, Bookcases, and "The Viking" Sectional Bookcases see pages 172 to 185.

Buffet No. 129—Height, 40 inches; Width, 72 inches.

Server No. 129—Height, 35 inches; Width, 44 inches.

Host Chair No. 129A. Upholstered in B Grade Tapestry.

Side Chair No. 129D. Upholstered in B Grade Tapestry.

Table, Dining, No. 129. Top, 42 inches by 66 inches.

China Cabinet No. 129—Height, 66 inches; Width, 44 inches.

No. 129 Suite—Sheraton. Walnut Veneer and Walnut. Mahogany Veneer and Mahogany. Tulip Wood Overlay. Top Buffet Drawer Lined and Partitioned for Silver.

Side Chair No. 138—Upholstered in B Grade Tapestry.

Dining Room Table No. 138—Top, 45x66 inches.

Host Chair No. 138—Upholstered in B Grade Tapestry.

Server No. 138—Height, 32½ inches; Width, 40 inches.

China Cabinet No. 138—Height, 80 inches; Width, 40 inches.

Buffet No. 138—Height, 36½ inches; Width, 66 inches.

No. 138 Suite—Heppelwhite. Crotch Mahogany Veneer and Mahogany. Top Drawer in Server Partitioned and Lined for Silver.

No. 129 SHERATON SUITE

The severe, slender, balanced forms with sweeping curves, the tulip wood inlay enrichments, produce the impression of lightness and grace which characterized the creations of Thomas Sheraton.

This style, sometimes called the "English Louis XVI" is classic, simple, and is appropriate for use in any home no matter how modest or pretentious it may be.

The Walnut finish of this suite is the same as illustrated by plate No. 14, American Walnut Standard—see Woods and Finishes Section preceding page 9 of this Reference Book.

PRICE RANGE OF DINING SUITES

$498.00 to $810.00. Subject to change without notice.

No. 138 HEPPELWHITE SUITE

There can be no question of the dainty drawing room grade of the Heppelwhite style. This suite combines much of the simple elegance of this period of furniture design. The table, of Duncan Phyfe inspiration, introduces an unusual yet harmonious note into this dining room ensemble.

We recommend this suite as another Skandia group which will be suitable for the decoration of practically any type of present day dining room.

Its Crotch Mahogany surface susceptible of a high polish gives it a charming touch of lightness and cheer.

See plate No. 19 Sheraton Mahogany in Woods and Finishes Section preceding page 9 of this Reference Book for the finish available with this suite.

(Continued on next page)

SKANDIA FURNITURE COMPANY

Buffet No. 137½—Height, 46 inches; Width, 78 inches.

Buffet No. 137—Height, 46 inches; Width, 72 inches.

Host Chair No. 136½—Upholstered in B Grade Tapestry.

Side Chair No 136½—Upholstered in B Grade Tapestry.

Server No. 127.—Height, 40 inches; Width, 42 inches.

China Cabinet No. 137—Height, 79 inches; Width, 41 inches.

Dining Room Table No. 137—Top, 42x72 inches.

China Cabinet No. 137—Height, 72 inches; Width, 42 inches.

No. 137-137½ Suite—Early American. Crotch Mahogany Veneer and Mahogany. Silver Tray in Right Cupboard of Buffet.

No. 137-137½ and No. 136-136½ EARLY AMERICAN

These two Suites are true "Colonial" designs. Quaint, graceful, and reminiscent of our prim and gentle ancestresses, or the later "American" style evolved by a cabinet maker of genius, Duncan Phyfe.

These Suites will enjoy much popularity, not only in homes of Colonial architecture but in the unpretentious home and the apartment, which gain from them character, charm and individuality.

Early American furniture is particularly easy to sell because of its suitability for use and association with other styles or periods presenting similar characteristics and expressing the same spirit, such as William and Mary, Queen Anne, Early Georgian, Chippendale, Sheraton, Hepplewhite, or post Revolutionary furniture.

There is no furniture period that should interest us as much as our own American Colonial, since it tells a tale of our own past, embodies our own ideals and grew side by side with our architecture, and should, for all these reasons, better than any other style, fit our home requirements.

These two Skandia suites embody the true characteristic details of the furniture made by our Early American Craftsmen, with the added value of better construction and more durable finishes.

Host Chair No. 136½—
Upholstered in B Grade
Tapestry.

Dining Room Table No. 136. Top, 42x66 inches.

Side Chair Upholstered
in B Grade Tapestry.
No. 136½.

Buffet No. 136—Height, 44 inches; Width, 66 inches.

Server No. 136—Height, 35 inches; Width, 40 inches.

China Cabinet No. 136—Height,
80 inches; Width, 40 inches.

Buffet No. 136½—Height, 45 inches; Width, 72
inches.

No. 136-136½ Suite—Early American Crotch Ma-
hogany Veneer and Mahogany. Upper Right Buffet
Drawer Partitioned and Lined for Silver. Cupboard
Server.

CONSTRUCTION OF SKANDIA DINING ROOM FURNITURE

Since the establishment of the Skandia Furniture Company in 1889, the pains-taking care of true craftsmen has been reflected in the furniture which we have produced.

There are workmen in our shops who received their first training from their fathers and grandfathers in the Scandinavian countries, ever known for their excellence in the wood-working arts. Other Skandia workmen are sons and grand-sons of such men.

The fact that Skandia furniture is built by these men who are finished masters of the furniture craft is an important consideration to the dealer who wants assur-ance of the best workmanship in the furniture he recommends to his customers.

STATESVILLE FURNITURE COMPANY
Manufacturers of Bedroom and Dining Room Furniture
STATESVILLE, N. C.

EXHIBITS

CHICAGO, ILL., Space 936, American Furniture Mart—NEW YORK, N. Y., 14th floor, New York Furniture Exchange
HIGH POINT, N. C., 5th floor, Furniture Exposition Building

REPRESENTATIVES

CHICAGO, ILL., Burns-Levee Co., 666 Lake Shore Drive—NEW YORK, N. Y., Louis J. Dorson Co., 206 Lexington Ave.
HIGH POINT, N. C., Charles E. Ragan

PRODUCTS

Manufacturers of

BEDROOM SUITES including full size Bed or Twin Beds, Dresser, Vanity Dresser, and Wardrobe. Also BEDROOM SUITES including the foregoing with the addition of Night Table, Chair, Rocker and Bench.

ALSO the following pieces
    sold separately
BEDS
—Bow End and Straight
    End Types
—Four Poster, and
—Twin Beds
BENCHES
—Bedroom, and
—Dressing Table
CHAIRS, Rockers and
    BENCHES
—Sold separately, or
—Sets of
CHAIRS, Upholstered
    (Boudoir Type)
CHIFFONIERS
CHIFFOROBES
CHIFFORETTES
DRESSEROBES
DRESSERS
DRESSERS, VANITY
DRESSING TABLES
TABLES
—Night
—Toilet, and
—Vanity

Table. Top, 42 by 60 inches.

Buffet measurements: Top, 60 by 22 inches and 66 by 22 inches.

Suite No. 780 of which two pieces are illustrated above has overlays of African Walnut, Walnut fronts and tops. Entire suite consists of 10 pieces and sells for $243.00 in the 60 inch size.

DINING ROOM SUITES COMPLETE, or
    Sold as Separate Pieces, including
—Buffets
—Chairs with Upholstered Seats, Side
    and Arm
—China Cabinets
—Servers, and
—Tables, Drop Leaf or Extension

AUXILIARY FURNITURE including Highboys, Lowboys, and HOTEL and CLUB FURNITURE

THE STATESVILLE LINE
STATESVILLE FURNITURE CO. STATESVILLE, N.C.

This mark is our certificate of honest merchandise ably constructed.

CONSTRUCTION OF BEDROOM FURNITURE

The individualistic feature of Statesville Furniture is of special significance to dealers who realize that their average customers buy on appearance first and last. Tops and fronts five-ply construction; ends of three-ply. Flush end construction; boxed in drawers with three-ply bottoms lined with Oak veneers. Dust-proof construction top and bottom.

EVERY STATESVILLE PRODUCT GUARANTEED

We can not stress too strongly the fact that you can rest your reputation as a dealer on every piece that bears the shop mark of the Statesville Furniture Company. This trade mark illustrated above appears on every Statesville product and we guarantee every piece of furniture to be of good materials, free from defects of any kind. This furniture can be inspected at our show-rooms listed above. Try one or more Statesville suites the next time you order bedroom or dining room furniture.

CONSTRUCTION OF DINING ROOM FURNITURE

The new Statesville Dining Room Suites introduce that "difference" in line, finish and character which means so much to you as a dealer. Tops and fronts, five-ply construction; ends, three-ply. Flush end construction. Boxed-in drawers with three-ply bottoms lined with Oak veneers. Dust-proof construction top and bottom. You need merely to look at these suites "through the eyes of your customers" to realize both the sales and business building possibilities of this line on your floor.

Dresser No. 55. Top, 22 by 50 inches.
Mirror, 28 by 34 inches.

Suite No. 55—Partly illustrated above is constructed with top drawer fronts and overlay of Bubinga from Africa, carved ornaments, and solid pieces of gum. List price for 4 large pieces, $279.00.

Bed No. 55—Supplied in two sizes, 4 ft. 6 in. and 3 ft. 3 in. Four Poster style also available.

WOODS AND FINISHES

Many rare and beautiful woods are used in the construction of Statesville Furniture. Such woods as Bubinga from Africa and African Walnut predominate. Solid pieces are always of a selected grade of gum. Butt Walnut, East Indian Rosewood.

By referring to plates 9 and 24 in the Woods and Finishes Section preceding page 9 of this book, the finishes that we are able to furnish are shown.

PRICE RANGES

Statesville Dining Room Suites range in price from $170.00 to $350.00; while the Bedroom Suites vary from $190.00 to $370.00. All prices shown are subject to change without notice.

STERLING FURNITURE COMPANY
Manufacturers of Bedroom Furniture
SALAMANCA, NEW YORK

No. 85—Vanity. Top 20 by 48 inches. Mirror 22 by 30 inches.

No. 85—Side Chair upholstered with Tapestry.

No. 85—Dresser. Top 23 by 48 inches. Mirror 28 by 30 inches.

PRODUCTS
MANUFACTURERS OF

BEDROOM SUITES COMPLETE, Including Bench, Chair, and Night Table.

DESCRIPTION OF SUITE No. 85

Suite No. 85 is a new and notable addition to the Sterling Line. Made with Crotch Mahogany veneers and Fauxsatine Overlays. The result is a distinctive achievement of real beauty and charm.

The construction is of characteristic Sterling quality. It is dovetailed, with the use of five-ply panels and selected quartered Red Gum. Interiors are neatly finished, with Mahogany drawer bottoms and selected Red Oak sides and ends. Cases are completely dust proof.

Priced very moderately and containing the high degree of workmanship and design that characterizes all Sterling suites. The Number 85 will justify prominence in your windows and on your floors.

RETAIL PRICE RANGE OF FOUR-PIECE SUITES

The Sterling Line at the present time comprises nine distinct suites, each built along the lines of Sterling Quality that makes them real profit makers. The retail prices vary between $200 and $350 in four-piece suite.

WRITE FOR FURTHER INFORMATION TODAY

Sterling Suites are built chiefly of Mahogany, Maple, Satinwood and Walnut veneers with solid pieces of selected Red Gum and White Maple. Photogravures and prices of our entire line showing the many available designs will interest you. Send for them.

No. 85—Chest of Drawers. Top 21 by 36 inches.

No. 85—Night Table. Top, 14 by 16 inches.

No. 85—Bed. Slat 4 feet 6 inches or 3 feet 3 inches.

Henry C. Steul & Sons, Inc.

Manufacturers of Dining Room Furniture

BUFFALO, N. Y.

EXHIBITS

GRAND RAPIDS, MICH., Keeler Bldg.   BUFFALO, N. Y., Factory Showrooms

No. 1494, Silver Cabinet—Measurements: Height, 66 inches; Top, 17 by 45 inches.

No. 1404, Server—Top, 18 by 42 inches; Height, 34 inches.

Host Chair of Suite 1494. Upholstered in Tapestry.

No. 1494, Table—Top, 44 by 72 inches. Furnished with extension leaves to make it 114 inches.

No. 1494, Buffet—Top 22 by 82 inches.

PRODUCTS

Manufacturers of

Dining Room Suites in both the Standard and the apartment (or smaller) sizes. These suites are made up to include combinations of the following pieces which are also sold separately: Benches—Buffets and Colonial Buffets—Chairs—China Cabinets and Closets—Corner Closets—Servers—Tables—Welsh Dressers.

Bedroom Suites in Cherry and Maple.

Breakfast Room Sets including Table and Chairs, and Breakfast Room Suites in several combinations of the following pieces which are also sold separately on order: Benches—Buffets—Cabinets—Chairs—Serving Tables and Cabinets combined—Tables—Extension Tables.

Chairs: Antique Mahogany—Arm—Desk, Home—Ladies'—Living Room and Odd, not upholstered—Rush Seat—Rush Seat Windsors—Windsors, Wood.

Chests of Drawers.

Desks: Bedroom—Ladies'—Library—Highboys—Secretary.

Tables: Butterfly—Drop Leaf—Extension—Gateleg—Gateleg Extension.

GENERAL INFORMATION

The charm of Steul Furniture has and always will be of lasting benefit to the retailer. The durability of Steul furniture is further enhanced by the carvings which are subtly blended with the predominant characteristics of each suite.

FINISHES

Plates Nos. 8, 12, 15, and 27, in the Woods and Finishes Section preceding page 9 of this Reference Book, resemble some of the finishes available in Steul furniture.

DESCRIPTION OF ILLUSTRATED SUITE

Suite No. 1494 after the manner of the Spanish Renaissance Period has real distinction. Constructed of Oak it is the kind of furniture that inculcates pride of ownership. While being imbued with the grandeur of this past period, it retains the comfort so desirable in these modern times. The chairs for this suite are upholstered in Tapestry which harmonizes with the Period presented. Other coverings are available to suit the special requirements of your trade. The finish is a dark somber oak which brings out the grain of the wood to a remarkable degree, and adds to the value of this number. See plate No. 27 in the Woods and Finishes Section preceding page 9 of this Reference Book.

The price of Suite No. 1494 is $996.00, subject to change without notice.

THOMASVILLE CHAIR COMPANY
Manufacturers of Chairs, Stools, Dining Room, Breakfast Room, Dinette and Bedroom Suites
THOMASVILLE, NO. CAR.
PERMANENT SHOWROOMS
CHICAGO, ILL., Space 1636, American Furniture Mart   NEW YORK, N. Y., 2nd Floor, New York Furniture Exchange
HIGH POINT, NO. CAR., 2nd Floor, Furniture Exposition Bldg.

PRODUCTS
MANUFACTURERS OF

MATCHED PERIOD DINERS
OAK DINERS
CHAIRS, BENCH AND ROCK-
ER—BEDROOM SETS
CHILD'S ROCKERS
BATH ROOM STOOLS
KITCHEN STOOLS
KITCHEN CHAIRS
OCCASIONAL CHAIRS

BOUDOIR CHAIRS
ODD ROCKERS
DINING ROOM SUITES
DINETTE SUITES
BREAKFAST ROOM SUITES
—PORCELAIN TOP
BREAKFAST ROOM
SUITES
BEDROOM SUITES

Trade Mark

Buffet for No. 300 Dining Room Suite.

TRADE NAMES

"CHARACTER" is the trade mark and name applied to all Thomasville Chair Company's products.

DINING ROOM SUITES

No. 300 Dining Room.—The No. 300, illustrated by the Buffet shown above, is representative of the best in medium grade, sound construction and saleable design. Many important features found in this suite are characteristic of much higher priced merchandise. Massively constructed with heavy turned posts, double tops and two five-ply veneered panels where deep recessed center matched burl panel appears. Door fronts five-ply Walnut veneered with Satinwood overlays and applied half round turnings. Heavy hardware used throughout and genuine wood carvings on top rails and base rails. Effective stretcher design unusual with turned front pieces. Beautifully finished in rich shaded Walnut.

Chair No. 709.

Chair No. 707.

ODD CHAIRS

Representing the odd chair line we show two popular numbers from our 18 designs in low and high back upholstered chairs and rockers. These designs are the famous odd piece line of "Character Chairs," popular with our dealers for twenty years.

Buffet for No. 200 Dining Room Suite.

No. 89—Dutch Cabinet.   *No. 184—Chairs.*
No. 86—Table

BREAKFAST ROOM LINE

Above illustration indicates a popular number in a line of breakfast room sets offering five table top designs, several styles of chairs and server with and without cupboards. Suites made up from this line can be finished in 12 color combinations and decorative effects. Our breakfast room line constitutes a wonderful sales opportunity for the retailer in the range of style and color. Our enormous production of over 300 suites per day insures a dependable source of supply.

No. 200 Dining Room.—Representative of the Thomasville low priced grade is the No. 200, illustrated by the Buffet above, containing the salient features seldom found at such low prices. Lacewood veneered top drawer fronts, with overlays of same wood in heavy receding panels on doors and center drawer decoration. Selected five-ply Walnut tops and fronts. Genuine carving on top and base rails. Dust-proof cases with three-ply backs. Heavy turnings and posts. Rich finish bringing out contrasting veneers and shading.

GENERAL INFORMATION

Of course, the numbers illustrated are but a few of Thomasville's long line as indicated in the listing of products. A representative showing may be seen at any of our permanent exhibits or full information may be secured by writing direct to Thomasville Chair Company, Thomasville, N. C.

STEWARTSTOWN FURNITURE COMPANY

INCORPORATED 1904

Manufacturers of Bedroom Furniture

STEWARTSTOWN, PENNA.

PERMANENT EXHIBITS AND SALESROOMS
NEW YORK, N. Y., Isse Koch & Co., New York Furniture Exchange Bldg., 206 Lexington Ave.
CHICAGO, ILL., Isse Koch & Co., American Furniture Mart Bldg., 666 Lake Shore Drive

Dresser, No. 172—Top, 22x50 inches; Mirror, 28x36 inches.

Vanity, No. 1172— Top, 18x50 inches. Mirror, 24x34 inches.

Chest of Drawers, No. 272— Top, 20x40 inches. Mirror, 14x16 inches.

Bed, No. 572—Slats, 4 feet 6 inches. Full size or twin bed size.

Wardrobe, No. 1072—Top, 20x40 inches.

No. 172—Bedroom Suite

This Suite is made complete with best Material and Workmanship, having Five-ply Fronts and Tops Quartersawn Striped Walnut Veneers. Dresser three top Drawers of Figured Walnut Bird's-Eye Maple insert Highlighted to harmonize with the Quartered Walnut Veneers, Sunburst Diamond Matched Veneers on Chest and Headboard of Bed Fluted Gum Posts with top Ornament Overlay, Built-up foot, Three-ply Mahogany Drawer Bottoms, Dust-proof throughout all beautifully lined and trimmed dull Satin Rubbed Finish.

*Chest of Drawers, No. 274—Top,
36x20 inches.*

*Bed No. 574—Foot end square returned
corner full size.*

*Wardrobe, No. 1074—Top,
40x20 inches.*

*Dresser, No. 174—Top, 50x22 inches.
Mirror, 28x36 inches.*

*Chest of Drawers, No. 274—
Top, 36x20 inches.*

*Vanity, No. 1174—
Top, 50x18 inches.
Mirror, 24x34 inches.*

No. 174—Bedroom Suite

*Constructed of high class Butt Walnut veneers with Bird's-Eye Maple
trim very carefully finished bringing out a contrast with the Butt Walnut
matched centers. Decalcomania ay making a distinguishing feature between
the Butt Walnut and Bird's-Eye Maple outer trim to the centers of all fronts.*

PRODUCTS

MANUFACTURERS OF

COMPLETE BEDROOM SUITES including Benches, Chairs, Rockers
and Night Tables; and individual bedroom pieces as follows:
BEDROOM BENCH, CHAIR AND ROCKER SETS for Odd Suites.
BEDS, BOW END, STRAIGHT END and TWIN
DRESSING TABLE BENCHES
CHIFFORETTES WITH STANDARD TOILETS and CHIFFOROBES
DRESSERS AND VANITY DRESSERS
Also manufacturers of Lowboys and Lamp Stands.

WOODS AND FINISHES

Stewartstown finishes are in line with the most popular finishes
of the current season. Our Bird's-Eye Maple resembles Plate
No. 13, Chateau Brown and our highlight French Walnut is a close
match for Plate No. 17 as shown in the Woods and Finishes
Section preceding page 9 of this Reference Book.

GENERAL INFORMATION

Stewartstown bedroom furniture enables the dealer to meet the
popular demand for medium priced furniture of good designs, high
quality, dependable construction, and indestructible finishes. The
two suites illustrated on these pages are selections from our stock
which dealers are extensively ordering. We recommend that you
try out these two suites on your floor the next time you order
medium priced bedroom suites. Additional information concerning our products will be promptly forwarded upon request.

L. & J. G. STICKLEY, INC.

Shops at FAYETTEVILLE, N. Y.

AFFILIATED WITH

THE STICKLEY MFG. CO., INC.

Shops at SYRACUSE, N. Y.

Under the personal supervision of Leopold Stickley

Early American Reproductions

SHOWROOM

GRAND RAPIDS, MICH., Third Floor, Klingman Bldg.

No. 1188, Stickley Ridgeless Bed Davenport—Finished in Early American Imitation Walnut or Mahogany.

PRODUCTS

Manufacturers of

BEDS	CANDLE STANDS	CUPBOARDS	HIGHBOYS	SETTEES
BENCHES	CHAIRS	DAY BEDS	LOWBOYS	STOOLS
BUREAUS	CHESTS	DESKS	MIRRORS	TABLES
	WATER BENCHES	WAGON SEATS		

A COMPLETE LINE OF AUTHENTIC DESIGNS IN CHERRY, MAPLE AND PINE

The "Stickley" line, manufactured in Cherry, Maple and Pine, is composed of exact copies of authentic examples designed and built by the carpenters and cabinet makers of primitive American villages of the early 18th Century.

EARLY AMERICAN REPRODUCTIONS

The term Early American has been used to recall to our minds that New England was the center of the first civilization of this country and it is from New England that we get the most artistic and interesting Early American furniture.

The quaint butterfly tables, candle stands, and cupboards furnish the inspiration for some very beautiful medium priced Early American reproductions.

The completeness of the Stickley line—nearly 300 pieces—enables any one to furnish each and every room throughout with one quality, from one authenticated source.

A line suitable not only for the home but for the interior furnishing of Country Clubs, Sanitariums, Hospitals, and so on.

No. 7024, Windsor Chair—Finished in Early American.

No. 5060, Early American Rocker. Exposed surfaces finished in Early American.

No. 4000, Early American Arm Chair—
Rush Seat. Finished in Early American.

No. 4000, Draw Top Table—Early American. Top, 36 by 54 inches
closed; 36 by 96 inches open. Finished in Early American.

No. 4000, Side Chair—Rush Seat.

FURNITURE THAT CREATES AN "ATMOSPHERE"

The pieces illustrated on this page, together with our No. 4000 serving table, comprise one of several artistic and interesting groups to be found in the Stickley line. Groups which always create an atmosphere of culture and refinement in any home.

Early American built today by Stickley has all the quality, style, comfort, utility, and charm of Early American built two centuries ago. In character, in woods, in craftsmanship, in all save age, it is the same.

Every piece bears the Stickley name, like artists' proofs.

This signature is assurance of authenticity and quality in line, material and workmanship.

No. 4012, Cupboard—Finished in Early American. Built of Cherry and Maple.

No. 4017, Corner Cabinet—Finished in Early American. Built of Cherry and Maple.

TATE FURNITURE CO.
Manufacturers of Bedroom Furniture
HIGH POINT, N. C.
EXHIBITS

CHICAGO, ILL., American Furniture Mart   NEW YORK, N. Y., New York Furniture Exchange

HIGH POINT, N. C., High Point Exhibition Building

No. 976—Dresser. Plate, 28x32 inches. Top, 22x50 inches. List price, $77.00.

No. 978—Chifforobe. Top, 20x40 inches. List price, $65.00.

No. 978—Vanity. Center Plate, 18x42 inches. Outside Plates, each 10x26 inches. Top, 18x46 inches. List price, $75.00.

No. 975—Bench. List price, $12.00.

No. 975—Night Table. Top, 14x14 inches. List price, $15.00.

No. 975—Chest Drawers. Top, 20x36 inches. List price, $53.00.

No. 975—Chair. List price, $12.00.

No. 978—Bed. Size, 3 ft. 3 in. List price, $48.00.

No. 975—Rocker. List price, $13.00.

No. 975—Bed. Size, 4 ft. 6 in. List price, $52.00.

PRODUCTS
MANUFACTURERS OF

BEDROOM FURNITURE:
Odd Pieces
BEDROOM SUITES COMPLETE, Including Bench, Chair, Rocker and Night Table
BEDROOM SUITES: Four Pieces Only

BEDS,
—Bow End
—Four Poster
BENCHES, Bedroom
CHAIRS, Bedroom, Sets of
CHESTS OF DRAWERS
CHIFFONIERS
CHIFFORETTES

CHIFFOROBES
DESKS, Bedroom
DRESSERS
DRESSERS, Vanity
ROCKERS, Bedroom
TABLES, Night
VANITIES
VANITIES, Semi

DESCRIPTION OF SUITE No. 975

This suite is made of very selected Butt Walnut in combination with Burl Ash and Burl Walnut. Of course the end panels and non-conspicuous parts are of Rotary Walnut. The carvings and mouldings on this suite are of wood. The hardware is of a distinct type, cast in one piece and in old gold finish. The suite is dust-proof throughout, with center guides in every drawer. Mirror backs are plywood. All cases have the double top effect. The finish is of a rich walnut tone, highlighted where it will show to the best advantage. Chair panel of butt walnut. Mahogany drawer bottoms, boxed in.

No. 897—Chifforobe. Top, 20x40 inches. List price, $58.00.

No. 897—Semi-Vanity. Plate, 18x46 inches. Top, 18x48 inches. List price, $67.00.

No. 896—Dresser. Top, 22x50 inches. Plate, 28x32 inches. List price, $73.00.

No. 895— Bench. List price, $11.50.

No. 895— Rocker. List price, $12.50.

No. 808—Bed. Size, 3 feet 3 inches. List price, $43.00.

No. 895— Night Table. Top, 14x14 inches. List price, $15.00.

No. 895— Chair. List price, $11.50.

No. 895½—Chest. Plate, 12x16 inches. Top, 20x38 inches. List price, $62.00.

No. 896—Bed. Size, 4 feet 6 inches.

DESCRIPTION OF SUITE No. 895

This suite is a worthy addition to the Tate Line that dealers can turn into profits. No choice of woods could be in better keeping with Spanish influence than figured Walnut plywood and pencil-striped Mahogany overlay, enriched by blended tones of Brown Walnut finish and touches of color decoration. Rope molding and rosettes are of wood.

In choice of finish, the popular demand for painted furniture has not been overlooked. This design can also be furnished in Wedgwood Green Enamel Finish, shaded and decorated with restrained use of rose color.

Tops and fronts are five-ply; backs, mirror backs, and sides are three-ply. All cabinet pieces are dust-proof, top and bottom. Drawers, with three-ply Mahogany bottoms, are dove-tailed front and back. All details of finish conform closely to a standard that dealers can take pride in pointing out.

(Continued on next page)

*No. 966½—Dresser. Top, 22x50
inches. Plate, 28x30 inches. List
price, $66.00.*

*No. 965½—Dresser. Plate,
22x26 inches. Top, 20x42 inches.
List price, $52.00.*

*No. 968—Vanity. Center Plate, 22x32
inches. Outside Plates, each 10x26 inches.
Top, 18x46 inches. List price, $67.00.*

*No. 966—Chest of Drawers.
Top, 20x36 inches. List price,
$42.00.*

*No. 965—Chair. List
price, $11.00.*

*No. 965—Bench.
List price, $11.00.*

*No. 965—Night Table. 14x14
inches. List price, $13.00.*

*No. 965—Rocker.
List price $12.00.*

*No. 968—Chifforobe. Top, 18x40
inches. List price, $52.00.*

*No. 966—Bed. 4-ft. 6-in. List
price, $36.00.*

DESCRIPTION OF SUITE No. 965

Walnut veneered five-ply tops and fronts with the best high grade highly figured rotary cut Walnut stock, finished in a delicate shaded rich brown tone. In careful contrast, bird's-eye Maple veneer is used on top drawers, base rails, toilet brackets, and top decorations. Added life and snap are given to the finished pieces by a strip of Zebra wood veneer just above the bird's-eye Maple top drawers, center of foot boards and over doors on chifforobe. A narrow overlay of bird's-eye Maple is mounted on these strips of Zebra wood. Wood moulding applied to the Maple veneered top drawers, finished black, adds the final touch of paneled richness to an already striking suite.

Blocked posts used throughout, with fluting finished black. Heavy cast brass hardware gives an effect of rich quality. Chair panels of bird's-eye Maple.

Dust-proof cases. Three-ply case and mirror backs. Three-ply Mahogany veneered drawer bottoms. Straight-foot bed and square foot design with two styles of dressers, stationery and swing toilets in two sizes, two chests and two vanities of latest mode with desk, chair, bench, rocker and night stand to match. A suite affording many combinations as to size and price.

The Mayfair, No. 965, is good-looking enough for those who buy looks alone—appealing to those who buy for smaller size and looks, and low enough for those who must consider price.

No. 971—Chest. Top, 20x36 inches. List price, $43.00.

No. 972—Chifforobe. Top, 20x40 inches. List price, $45.00.

No. 972½—Dresser. Top, 22x 48 inches. Plate, 26x30 inches. List price, $57.00.

No. 970— Chair. List price, $10.00.

No. 970— Rocker. List price, $11.00.

No. 970 — Bench. List price, $10.00.

No. 970— Night Table. Top, 14x14 inches. List price, $13.00.

No. 973—Bed. Size, 3-ft. 3-in. List price, $36.00.

DESCRIPTION OF SUITE No. 970

All tops and fronts are of five-ply Walnut veneers while ends are of three-ply.

Top drawer fronts are of quartered Oak veneers with the design thrown in sharp relief by routing out and the background finished black. The same treatment, of course, as to design, is carried out on the beds, chifforobe, etc.

All drawer fronts have moulded edges, while the drawer bottoms are of three-ply Mahogany veneers with drawer interiors thoroughly finished.

Cases are dust-proof top and bottom.

The chifforobe has three trays all with three-ply Mahogany drawer bottoms.

Mirror backs are of three-ply veneers.

The suite is finished in a warm brown Walnut tone of the particular shade that has proven so popular.

Hardware is most distinctive in an old gold finish.

All prices shown are subject to change without notice.

No. 971—Bed. Size, 4-ft. 6-in. List price, $34.00.

TILLOTSON FURNITURE CORPORATION

Manufacturers of Sleeping Room Furniture

JAMESTOWN, N. Y.

EXHIBITS

JAMESTOWN, N. Y., 8th Floor, Manufacturers Exposition Building
GRAND RAPIDS, MICH., Klingman Furniture Exposition Building
NEW YORK CITY, N. Y., Mr. Charles P. Sauer, 415 East 47th Street

PRODUCTS

MANUFACTURERS OF

BEDROOM SUITES COMPLETE, Including Bench, Chair, Rocker and Night Table
BEDROOM SUITES, Four Pieces Only

BEDS	DRESSING TABLES
—Four Poster	HIGHBOYS
—Wood	LOWBOYS
BENCHES, Dressing Table	MIRRORS, Bedroom
CABINETS, Radio	ROCKERS, Cane Seat
CHAIRS, Bedroom	STANDS, Shaving
CHIFFONIERS	TABLES
CHIFFOROBES	—Bedside, Invalid
COSTUMERS, Wood	—Cafe
DESKS	—Glass Top
—Bedroom	—Nested
—Library	—Night
DRESSERS	VANITY BUREAUS
DRESSERS	WARDROBES
—Princess	
—Vanity	

DESIGN

Tillotson designs were created for nothing else but the sleeping room. There is a pleasing contour in each suite that gives it a stamp of individuality so desirable in furniture of today. Tillotson has not tried to copy to any marked extent the periods but has striven to perfect a pattern that would be representative of American tendencies.

WOODS AND FINISHES

It is but fitting that designs which are ahead and in keeping with the buying tastes of the people of today should be fashioned in the best woods. Tillotson Sleeping Room Suites are constructed of Mahogany and Walnut. These woods are carefully finished in useable finishes that do much to enhance the beauty and appeal of each number.

CONSTRUCTION

Upon this one predominant feature the success of furniture is entirely dependable—for it decides whether the furniture will give service in the form of durability. Durability means thorough satisfaction and this is what your customer seeks in every purchase she makes.

Point out the salient features of Tillotson Sleeping Room Furniture—they speak graphically why Tillotson enjoys such popularity among retailers throughout the country. In addition to following the accepted principles of construction in furniture, many special features are employed such as special dowel construction, together with glue blocks that are placed at strategic points. Dovetail Drawers—Dust proof—center drawer guides are all sales points that should be stressed in the selling of Tillotson Furniture.

GENERAL INFORMATION

All in all, the Tillotson Line of Sleeping Room Suites are carefully designed to meet the demands of those of your customers who value beauty of contour, good materials, lasting construction, and a useable finish.

In other words, Sleeping Room Furniture built to a high standard of excellence and purchasable at a modest price.

Tillotson invites your inquiries for illustrations, prices and specifications of suites and samples of finish.

Write to Tillotson today.

UNITED FURNITURE COMPANY

Manufacturers of Bedroom Furniture

LEXINGTON, NO. CAROLINA

EXHIBITS

CHICAGO, ILL., Space 520, American Furniture Mart   HIGH POINT, N. C., 10th Floor, Southern Market Bldg.

NEW YORK, N. Y., 7th Floor, New York Furniture Exchange

No. 800—Chest of Drawers. 20 by 38 inches.   No. 801—Vanity. Top, 19 by 48 inches. Mirror, 26 by 36 inches.

Suite No. 800 has five-ply Butt Walnut tops and fronts; three-ply end panels; dust-proof throughout. Oak interior boxed-in drawer bottoms and three-ply mirror backs. All drawers finished and wardrobe is cedar lined. Finished in a rich Brown Walnut resembling plate No. 10 in the Woods and Finishes Section preceding page 9 of this Reference Book.

PRODUCTS

MANUFACTURERS OF

BEDROOM FURNITURE sold as Four Piece Suites (Bed, Dresser, Wardrobe and Vanity) or Complete Suites (Bed, Dresser, Wardrobe, Vanity, Night Table, Chair, Rocker and Bench). Pieces sold separately include Beds, Bow End, Straight End, Four Poster, and other types. Dressers, Chests, Chifforobes, Night Tables, Chairs, Rockers and Benches to match suites.

DESIGNS AND CONSTRUCTION

Designs—Colonial Patterns and Early English including Jacobean and William and Mary Periods.

Tops and Fronts, five-ply construction; ends, three-ply. Flush ends; boxed-in drawers with three-ply bottoms lined with genuine Mahogany veneers. Dust-proof top and bottom.

WOODS AND FINISHES

Matched Butt Walnut, Mahogany and Walnut Woods predominate in United Furniture. Finishes resemble plate No. 10, in the Woods and Finishes Section preceding page 9 of this book.

PRICE RANGES

United Bedroom Suites Complete range from *$228.50* to *$353.00*. Four-Piece Suites vary from *$148.00* to *$295.00*.

Beds from *$36.00* to *$57.00*. Chairs from *$11.00* to *$12.50*. These prices are subject to change without notice.

GENERAL INFORMATION

United's Dealer Policy and Sales Plans will interest you. The accuracy of measurement, correctness of proportion and skilled balance in every detail of United Furniture will satisfy the most exacting requirements of your trade. Write today.

UNION FURNITURE COMPANY
Manufacturers of Dining Room Furniture
18th Avenue, ROCKFORD, ILL.

PERMANENT EXHIBITS

CHICAGO, ILL., Space 1108-1109, American Furniture Mart   GRAND RAPIDS, MICH., 5th Floor, Manufacturers Exhibition Bldg.
SAN FRANCISCO, CALIF., 180 New Montgomery St.   NEW YORK, N. Y., Space 1514, 206 Lexington Ave.

Arm or Host Chair.
List price, $37.00.

Side Chair. List
price, $29.00.

China Closet, Width, 41 inches;
Height, 67 inches. List price, $145.00.

Dining Table. 42x62 inches. 6-foot
extension. List price, $125.00.

Server, Width, 41 inches; Height
37 inches. List price, $80.00.

Buffet, Width, 72 inches; Height, 39
inches. List price, $190.00.

No. 1314 Dining Room Suite
Oak and Walnut

All legs, stretchers, mouldings and carvings in the solid wood. Tops,
ends and drawer fronts in 5-ply veneers. Finish, Walnut Suite in Antique
Walnut slightly hi-lited. Finish of Oak Suite in English Brown.

UNION FURNITURE COMPANY

PRODUCTS
MANUFACTURERS OF
DINING ROOM SUITES and separate pieces for the Dining Room as follows:

BUFFETS   SERVING TABLES
CHAIRS   TABLES
CHINA CLOSETS   EXTENSION TABLES

For information on Secretaries, Bookcases and Desks, see pages 186-187.

UNION
FURNITURE
CO.
ESTABLISHED 1876
QUALITY FURNITURE
ROCKFORD,
ILL.

Trade Mark

WOODS AND FINISHES
Our dining room suites are finished Walnut similar to Plates Nos. 9, 10 and 14 and in Oak similar to Plate No. 7, as shown in the Woods and Finishes Section preceding page 9 of this book. We are equipped to finish our suites in any of the finishes shown in that section.

Side Chair of Suite No. 1314. Red or brown leather chair seats. List price, $17.00.

Arm or Host Chair of Suite No. 1314. Red or brown leather upholstering. List price, $23.00.

China Cabinet, Width, 38 inches; Height, 62 inches. List price, $91.00.

Dining Table, Top, 42x60 inches. 6-foot extension. List price, $88.00.

Buffet, Width, 66 inches; Depth, 21 inches. List price, $94.00.

Server, Width, 38 inches; Depth, 20 inches. List price, $50.00.

No. 1316 Dining Room Suite
Oak only

All exteriors of Solid Plain Oak except table top which is of 5-ply plain Oak veneered. All carvings done in Solid Oak. Drawer bottoms of 3-ply Plain Oak. Finished in English Brown with slight brass green hi-liting in recesses.

VIRGINIA-LINCOLN FACTORIES

Dining Room and Bedroom Furniture

VIRGINIA TABLE CO. AND LINCOLN FURNITURE MFG. CO.

General Offices and Plants at MARION, VA.

BRANCH OFFICES AND DISPLAY ROOMS

NEW YORK, N. Y., 206 Lexington Ave.   CHICAGO, ILL., 666 Lake Shore Drive

Trade Mark

No. 32—Buffet. Top, 22 by 66 inches. $77.00.

No. 32—China. Top, 18 by 40 inches. Height, 72 inches. $59.00.

Trade Mark

PRODUCTS OF THE VIRGINIA TABLE CO.

MANUFACTURERS OF

COMPLETE DINING ROOM AND DINETTE SUITES. Also separate Dining Room pieces as follows:

ARM CHAIRS AND SIDE CHAIRS
BUFFETS
CHINA CABINETS AND CLOSETS
EXTENSION TABLES
GATELEG TABLES
SERVERS

Also manufacturers of Davenport Extension Tables.

Virginia Design No. 32
Burl Walnut, Satinwood and Decorated Avodera

A massive rich design in finely figured woods and rich decoration. The decorative overlay of Avodera wood has a touch of vermillion decoration. The unique carved pulls are polychrome, and give a charming touch of color to the group. The suite has the standard Virginia construction, and thoroughly finished oak interiors.

PRODUCTS OF THE LINCOLN FURNITURE MFG. CO.

MANUFACTURERS OF

COMPLETE BEDROOM SUITES including Benches, Chairs, Rockers, and Night Tables.

Also the following separate pieces for bedrooms.

BEDS   VANITIES   CHIFFOROBES
DRESSERS FRENCH VANITIES CHESTS
CHAIRS, ROCKERS, AND BENCHES with Upholstered Seats.
UPHOLSTERED BEDROOM CHAIRS AND BENCHES.

No. 40DL—Table. Top 20 by 36 inches. $36.00.

No. 40—Buffet. Top, 16 by 48 inches. $63.00.

No. 40—Table. Top, 33 by 48 inches. Seng Automatic Folding Leaf, $44.00.

No. 40—China Cabinet. Top, 16 by 28 inches. Height, 60 inches. $54.00.

Virginia Design No. 40
A Suite of Many Uses—Rare Style and Beauty

Small homes and apartments with one room serving as two have created a demand for a suite of individuality and character that will do double duty. It is an open-stock number, and can be displayed and sold in any desired groups. The group-

ings shown on these pages have proved most successful, and we recommend these for use on your sales floor. Suite, $197.00.

No. 24—Dresser. Top, 50 by 22 inches. Plate, 28 by 36 inches. $78.00.

No. 24—Bed. Return End. 4 feet, 6 inches or 3 feet, 3 inches. $56.00.

No. 24—French Vanity. Top, 50 by 19 inches. Plate 26 by 36 inches, $74.00.

No. 24—Chifforobe. Top, 40 by 22 inches. Height, 62 inches. $62.00.

No. 24—Night Table $30.00.

No. 24—Chest. Top, 38 by 20 inches. Height 54 inches. $62.00.

Lincoln Design No. 24

A suite of unusual character and design at a price to satisfy your most exacting customer. Attractive imported veneers of Avodera and African walnut adorn the top drawers of all pieces. The inlay border in baserail is of zebra wood. The decorations on fronts are genuine imported wood marquetry. All interiors are of genuine oak and cases are thoroughly dust proof. Four Pieces, $270.00.

GENERAL INFORMATION

The Virginia Table Company's factories at Marion, Virginia constitute one of the world's largest organizations devoted exclusively to the manufacture of dining room furniture.

The new Lincoln factory, located in Bristol, was designed and built after many years of experience in furniture manufacturing. It is one of the model furniture factories of America—a spacious, daylight plant, fully equipped and concentrating on the production of bedroom furniture.

The Virginia-Lincoln Factories, located close to the source of raw materials, with abundant native born skilled white labor, are producing bedroom and dining room furniture distinctive in design and moderate in cost.

All prices shown are subject to change without notice.

PRICE RANGES
Dining Room and Dinette Furniture

Ten piece Suites $154.90, $170.00, $189.00, $229.00, and $296.00.
Eight Piece Suites $113.50, $125.00, $134.00, $155.00, and $209.00.
Buffets, $39.00, $41.00, $42.00, $44.00, $49.00, $57.00, $59.00, $63.00, and $76.00.
Chinas, $28.00, $30.00, $31.00, $32.00, $36.00, $48.00, $54.00, and $58.00.
Servers, $14.00, $19.00, $26.00, and $29.00.
Tables, $31.00, $33.00, $35.00, $36.00, $38.00, $40.00, $44.00, $46.00, and $57.00.
Side Chairs, $6.50, $7.50, $8.00, $8.50, $9.50, $12.00, and $13.00.
Arm Chairs, $9.00, $10.00, $10.50, and $16.00.

Bedroom Furniture

Dressers, $42.00, $48.00, $53.00, $54.00, $62.00, and $78.00.
Chifforobes, $40.00, $42.00, $44.00, $50.00, and $62.00.
Chests, $36.00, $40.00, $42.00, $50.00, and $62.00.
French Vanities, $45.00, $47.00, $52.00, $64.00, and $74.00.
Full Vanities, $51.00, $55.00, and $72.00.
Beds, $34.00, $36.00, $40.00, $42.00, $46.00, and $56.00.
Night Tables and Stands, $16.00, and $30.00.
Sets of Chairs, Benches, and Rockers, $29.00, $31.00, $37.00, and $41.00.

No. 6 Dresser—Top, 48 by 20, Plate, 28 by 30, $24.00.

No. 6—Bed. Straight End. 4 feet, 6 inches, $17.00.

Lincoln Design No. 6
Richly Figured Walnut and Maple

A suite which satisfies the demand for a bedroom outfit with real snap at a price. Attractively decorated with molded top drawers and overlays of birdseye maple.

An open stock pattern carrying full quota of various size pieces.

WARD FURNITURE MANUFACTURING CO.
Bedroom and Dining Room Furniture
FORT SMITH, ARKANSAS

No. 1531½—Spanish Walnut Vanity, with hand carved ornaments and molded mirror frame.

No. 1501—Walnut Bed to match. Five-ply Walnut head and foot boards, with turned spindles. All solid carving.

WARD

Trade Mark

PRODUCTS
MANUFACTURERS OF

BEDROOM SUITES COMPLETE, including Bench, Chair, Rocker, and Night Table
BEDROOM SUITES, four pieces only
BEDROOM SUITES, three pieces only
SEPARATE BEDROOM PIECES as follows:
BEDS
—Wood
—Bow End
—Four Poster
—Straight End
BENCHES
BENCHES, CHAIRS, AND ROCKERS FOR ODD SUITES
Also manufacturers of Apartment (Junior Size) Dining Room Suites and Dining Tables.

GENERAL INFORMATION

Here is one of the distinctive new numbers from the Ward Line. For twenty-five years Ward has been striving to produce the best. Years of painstaking effort are represented here—effort proven by quality, style, and fair price. Ward furniture represents a truly American product made according to the American standard of construction.

When you see the Ward line this year, you will realize as never before that the Ward way is the sure way to profits. This is a firm with an outstanding reputation, built upon twenty-five years of quality merchandise, fair price, and good style.

No. 1520—Spanish Walnut Chest. Five-ply Walnut face, veneer drawer bottoms framed in. Dust-proof construction.

THE WINDEMERE
Three-Piece Suite Illustrated

This Spanish Walnut grouping represents the beginning of the new line of Ward Furniture for 1928. No detail has been neglected to make this one of the foremost of its kind. Careful design, honest workmanship, and rich finishes set it apart by itself. This is the type of merchandise your customers want.

PRICE RANGE

Three-piece bedroom suites including Bed, Vanity, and Chest of Drawers range in price from $80 to $160. Four-piece suites consisting of Bed, Vanity, Dresser and a large Chifforobe range in price from $160 to $220. All prices are subject to change without notice.

WOODS AND FINISHES

The Ward line of bedroom suites is made of hardwood in combination with Walnut, Mahogany, and Maple veneers. Our Walnut finish is similar to plate No. 14—American Walnut Standard; our Mahogany finish resembles plate No. 1—Standard American Mahogany; and our Maple finish is illustrated by plate No. 8—Persian Maple. See Woods and Finishes Section preceding page 9 of this Reference Book.

THE WHITE FURNITURE COMPANY

Manufacturers of Bedroom and Dining Room Furniture

MEBANE, NO. CAROLINA

PERMANENT DISPLAY

GRAND RAPIDS, MICH., Sixth Floor, Manufacturers Bldg.   HIGH POINT, N. C., Southern Furniture Exposition Bldg.

No. 20

No. 470

PRODUCTS

MANUFACTURERS OF

COMPLETE BEDROOM AND DINING ROOM SUITES; BEDROOM SUITES, four pieces only. Also separate bedroom pieces as follows:

BENCH, CHAIR, AND ROCKER SETS for odd suites

BOW END BEDS, COLONIAL BEDS, FOUR POSTER BEDS, STRAIGHT END BEDS, AND TWIN BEDS

DESKS AND BENCHES

BENCHES, CHAIRS, AND ROCKERS (Cane or Upholstered)

CHESTS OF DRAWERS

CHESTS, WALNUT OR MAHOGANY (not cedar lined)

CHIFFONIERS, CHIFFORETTES, CHIFFOROBES, AND WARDROBES

DRESSERS, DRESSEROBES, DRESSING TABLES AND BENCHES, AND VANITIES

NIGHT TABLES

Also manufacturers of Highboys, Telephone Benches and Desks, and Chairs, Grip Stands, Costumers and other Hotel and Club furniture.

Trade Mark

WOODS AND FINISHES

The White line of Bedroom and Dining Furniture is available in the latest and most popular finishes. In addition to colored Enamel finishes, the White line is finished as illustrated in plate Nos. 1—Standard American Mahogany; 8—Persian Maple, and 9—American Walnut, Light—see the Woods and Finishes Section preceding page 9 of this book.

MIXED CAR SHIPMENTS

We can make up a car of Bedroom and Dining furniture to suit your needs. This gives you the lowest freight rate and gives you the benefit of the carload discount.

SEND FOR CATALOG

The new White catalog of Dining Room and Bedroom furniture is just off the press. It illustrates many new suites—eight pages are devoted to lifelike reproductions in color. Plans for helping you sell more are outlined in detail.

JOHN WIDDICOMB CO.
Manufacturers of Bedroom Furniture
601 Fifth St., N. W., GRAND RAPIDS, MICH.

PRODUCTS
MANUFACTURERS OF

BEDROOM SUITES COMPLETE including Bench, Chair, Rocker and Night Tables. Also Separate pieces for the bedroom including:

BOW END BEDS
STRAIGHT END BEDS
FOUR POSTER BEDS
TWIN BEDS, and
DAY BEDS
BEDROOM BENCHES, CHAIRS and ROCKERS, Cane or Upholstered.
DRESSING TABLE BENCHES
CHESTS OF DRAWERS, CHIFFONIERS and CHIFFOROBES.
BEDROOM DESKS
DRESSERS, DRESSING TABLES, VANITIES and SEMI-VANITIES.
HIGHBOYS, LOWBOYS, and
SOMNOES

AN EARLY AMERICAN BEDROOM SUITE

No. 1576 Suite is an Early American Collection in mahogany, having mahogany posts, the fronts and tops being fine grain crotch mahogany. The mirrors are mahogany with old gold carvings.

This suite consists of the dresser illustrated, a bed or twin beds, a chiffonier, dressing table, vanity dresser, bedside table, bench and chair.

The finish of this suite is similar to that illustrated by plate No. 18, Colonial Mahogany in the Woods and Finishes Section preceding page 9 of this book.

Send for complete photographs of this suite today.

GENERAL INFORMATION

Furniture made by the John Widdicomb Company is guaranteed as to materials and workmanship to be high grade in every respect. Photographs and prices of our new numbers will be sent to you upon request.

THE WIDDICOMB FURNITURE CO.

Manufacturers of Bedroom Furniture

GRAND RAPIDS, MICHIGAN

This distinguished Heppelwhite group is Suite No. 193.

PRODUCTS

MANUFACTURERS OF

COMPLETE BEDROOM GROUPS and individual pieces, including WOOD BEDS with both Straight and Bow Foot Boards in Full and Twin Sizes

DRESSERS
CHESTS
CHIFFONIERS
CHIFFOROBES
HIGHBOYS
PORTABLE and HANGING MIRRORS
DRESSING TABLES
SEMI-VANITIES and VANITIES
DESKS
NIGHT STANDS
CHAIRS and BENCHES with Cane or Upholstered Seats

BEDROOM FURNITURE OF HEIRLOOM QUALITY

The Widdicomb Line includes furniture in all the popular periods of design. These groups are reproductions and adaptations notable for their art and grace.

Hand carving, marquetry work and rare woods of great beauty all have a part in the enrichment of Widdicomb productions.

The workmanship is of a high order and lasting character.

TRADE MARK REGISTERED IN U.S. PATENT OFFICE

THE WINNEBAGO MANUFACTURING CO.

Bedroom Suites and Plywoods

1109 Seminary Street, ROCKFORD, ILL.

PERMANENT EXHIBITS

CHICAGO, ILL., Space 201, American Furniture Mart   ROCKFORD, ILL., Showroom at Rockford Furniture Co.

PRODUCTS

MANUFACTURERS OF

BEDROOM SUITES COMPLETE, including the following pieces which are sold separately:

BENCHES, Bedroom
BEDS
—Bow End
—Straight End
—Four Poster
—Twin
CHAIRS, Bedroom Sets of
DRESSING TABLES
DRESSING TABLE BENCHES
NIGHT TABLES
VANITIES
SEMI-VANITIES

GENERAL INFORMATION

All Drawers have center guides, are dust proof throughout and are box constructed, the bottoms being set in grooves on all four sides. Dovetail joints are used both front and back. All tops, fronts, ends and bed panels are ¾ inch thick or thicker and are 5 ply.

The Winnebago Manufacturing Company are also manufacturers of plywood.

Illustrations and prices will be sent gladly on request.

No. 278 Chest—Size, 38 by 20 inches; Height, 68 inches; Mirror, 14 by 18 inches.

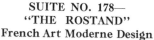

No. 778 Bench.

No. 378 Vanity—Size, 44 by 18 inches; Height, 64 inches; Mirror, 24 by 30 inches.

No. 178 Dresser—Size, 48 by 22 inches; Height, 71 inches; Mirror, 26 by 32 inches.

No. 878 Night Table.   *No. 678 Side Chair.*

No. 478 Bed—4 feet 6 inch slats.

SUITE NO. 178—
"THE ROSTAND"
French Art Moderne Design

Tops, ends, and fronts veneered in Rosewood. Side, mirror brackets veneered in Maple Burl, bracket under mirrors Zebra wood. Overlay is in matched Maple Burl and Zebra Wood. Carvings are finished in Old Ivory. Woods are finished in almost natural color. Trimming is French Gold finish. Legs, stretchers, frames, etc., are quarter sawed gum. Drawer sides and backs are quarter sawed Sycamore.

No. 870 Night Table.

No. 170 Dresser—Size, 50 by 21 inches; Mirror, 26 by 32 inches.

No. 270 Chest—Size, 38 by 20 inches; Height, 50 inches.

No. 370 Vanity—Size, 46 by 18 inches; Mirror, 20 by 30 inches; Height, 67 inches.

SUITE NO. 170 "CANTERBURY"

Tops and Ends Walnut veneered 5-ply. Top drawers of Dresser and Chest Madrone Burl with marquetry border. Center Drawers matched Butt Walnut. Bottom drawers Crotch Mahogany. Head panels of beds Butt Walnut with marquetry border. Bottom of foot board Crotch Mahogany. Panel in footboard Madrone burl with marquetry border. End drawers of vanity Butt Walnut. Center drawer Madrone Burl with marquetry border. All carvings are hand made in wood. Legs, stretchers, frames, etc., in quarter sawed Gum. Drawer sides and backs quarter sawed Sycamore. Suite finished in Roman Walnut, a highlighted finish. Madrone Burl is rich reddish brown.

(Continued on next page)

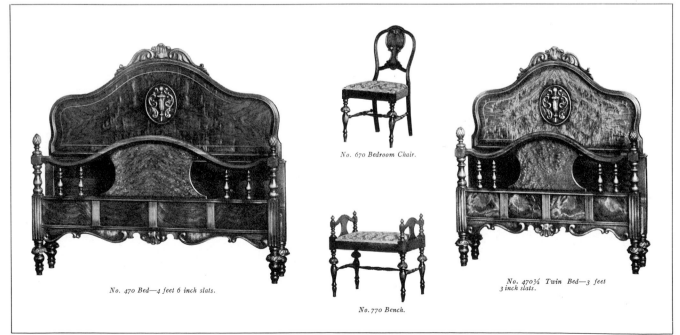

No. 470 Bed—4 feet 6 inch slats.

No. 670 Bedroom Chair.

No. 770 Bench.

No. 470½ Twin Bed—3 feet 3 inch slats.

No. 871 Night Table.

No. 371 Vanity—Size, 52 by 17 inches; Mirror, 30 by 22 inches.

No. 171 Dresser—Size, 54 by 22 inches; Mirror, 32 by 24 inches.

No. 271 Chest—Size, 40 by 20 inches; Height, 56 inches.

SUITE NO. 171
"THE HANOVER"

Heppelwhite design. Legs, stretchers, etc., Solid Walnut. Drawer sides and backs Solid Mahogany. Tops and ends veneered with Walnut. Veneered fronts are combination of butt Walnut and Madrone Burl with Rosewood borders. Floral design is genuine marquetry imported from Germany. Cut mouldings are also German importations. Finish is our highlighted Roman Walnut.

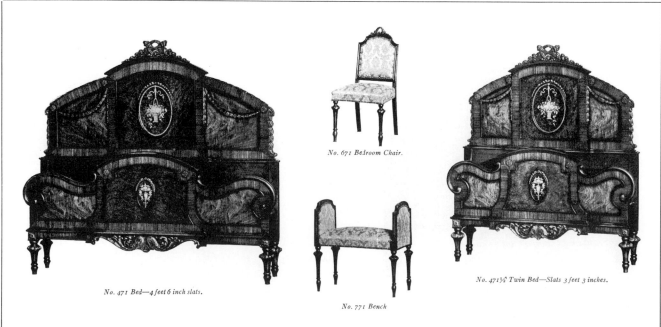

No. 471 Bed—4 feet 6 inch slats.

No. 671 Bedroom Chair.

No. 771 Bench

No. 471½ Twin Bed—Slats 3 feet 3 inches.

No. 375 Full Vanity—Size, 48 by 18 inches; Height, 66 inches; Mirror, 22 by 28 inches.

No. 175 Dresser—Size 48 by 22 inches; Height, 73 inches; Mirror, 24 by 30 inches.

No. 375½ Table Vanity—Size, 44 by 18 inches; Height, 66 inches; Mirror, 22 by 28 inches.

SUITE NO. 175
"THE MADISON"
Duncan Phyfe Design

Tops and ends veneered in Stripe Mahogany. Fronts, bed panels, and mirror standards are veneered in moonshine figure Crotch

No. 675—Side Chair.

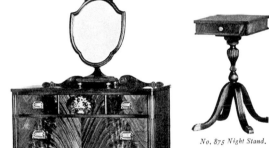

No. 875 Night Stand.

Mahogany. Floral ornament is marquetry imported from Germany. Suite is finished in a warm reddish brown color. Legs, stretchers, etc. are quarter sawed Gum. Drawer sides and backs quarter sawed Sycamore.

No. 275 Chest—Size, 38 by 20 inches; Height, 70 inches; Mirror, 14 by 18 inches.

No. 775 Bench.

No. 475 Bed—4 feet 6 inch slats.

No. 475½ Twin Bed—Slats, 3 feet 3 inches.

KINDEL FURNITURE COMPANY
Bed Specialists
GRAND RAPIDS, MICHIGAN
EXHIBIT
GRAND RAPIDS, MICH., First Floor, Pantlind Exhibition Building

"CHINESE CHIPPENDALE"
No. 555—"The Canton." The inspiration for this pleasing day bed came from originals which Chippendale designed in the Chinese manner.

"FRENCH PROVINCIAL"
No. 558—"The Chalons." A chair found in the Department of Normandy suggested the motif for this day bed.

"COLONIAL"
No. 540—"The Modbury." The design is typical of the furniture produced by the early 18th century craftsmen.

"COTTAGE COLONIAL"
No. 530—"The Chase." Spool turnings came into favor in the 17th century.

"VENETIAN"
No. 551—This design was inspired by the beautiful furniture which had its origin during the third quarter of the 18th century.

"ENGLISH"
No. 556—"The Petherick." The style prevailing between the transition of the 16th and 17th centuries was the source of this design.

"LOUIS XVI"
No. 552—This design is enriched by groovings and fine moldings of the classic order. The design was inspired by the style started during the reign of Louis XV by Madame de Pompadour, though known as the Louis Seize.

"CHARLES II"
No. 553—Oak. "The Brixham." A design with twisted posts suggested by English furniture of the late 17th century.

PRODUCTS

MANUFACTURERS OF
DAY BEDS
—Period Styles
—Modern Styles
DOUBLE DAY BEDS
—With Backs
—Without Backs

For information on Wood Beds, Poster and other types, see Pages 282 and 283.

GENERAL INFORMATION

Kindel Day Beds are made in a Grand Rapids factory by bed specialists. The attractive values are made possible by immense production facilities and concentrated manufacturing effort. The study and attention devoted to the development of the day bed by Kindel designers is in a large measure responsible for the new public appreciation of the desirability of the day bed as a furnishing in the home. Kindel Day Beds take their place with the home's fine furniture. The line consists of 18 distinctive period and modern designs.

The day bed market offers a splendid opportunity to the dealer who is willing to give serious effort to its development. In the first place, the day bed sells for considerably less than a sofa or bed davenport. Like the latter, however, it can be used as a comfortable overnight bed in an emergency. Moreover, it takes up less room, an important feature in these days when homes and apartments are small. The day bed is made in smart, distinctive designs in both period and modern styles to harmonize with the other furniture in the living room, the sun room, the den and the boudoir. We are glad to work closely with dealers who are developing the day bed market. Newspaper mats and other advertising material, also merchandising suggestions, will be furnished on request.

CONSTRUCTION AND SIZES

Kindel Day Beds are made in two sizes, some patterns in the 36-inch width as well as the standard 30-inch width. Length of rails, 76 inches. Thickness of rails,

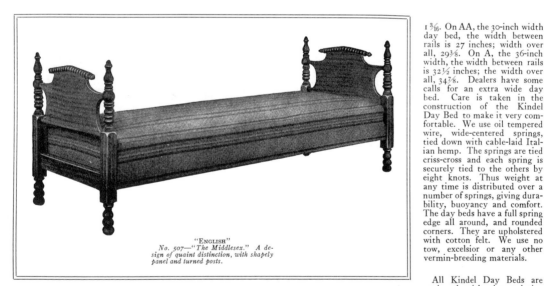

"ENGLISH"
No. 507—"The Middlesex." A design of quaint distinction, with shapely panel and turned posts.

Kindel Grand Rapids **Day Beds**
Trade Mark

1 3/16. On AA, the 30-inch width day bed, the width between rails is 27 inches; width over all, 29⅜. On A, the 36-inch width, the width between rails is 32½ inches; the width over all, 34⅞. Dealers have some calls for an extra wide day bed. Care is taken in the construction of the Kindel Day Bed to make it very comfortable. We use oil tempered wire, wide-centered springs, tied down with cable-laid Italian hemp. The springs are tied criss-cross and each spring is securely tied to the others by eight knots. Thus weight at any time is distributed over a number of springs, giving durability, buoyancy and comfort. The day beds have a full spring edge all around, and rounded corners. They are upholstered with cotton felt. We use no tow, excelsior or any other vermin-breeding materials.

All Kindel Day Beds are equipped with the exclusive patented Kindel wedge shape rail lock, by means of which the ends can easily and quickly be attached or removed, and affording a rigid, solid construction without the use of screws or bolts.

PRICE RANGE

Rails and box springs are supplied as a unit. Kindel Day Beds are priced with ends with rails only, and in three-piece construction, ends with rails and box springs in one, in a range of 12 different prices covering denims, cretonnes, sateens, tapestries, corduroys, velours and damasks. The price range is $24.00 to $135.50, subject to change without notice.

FINISHES

Stock finishes are red, closely resembling plate No. 25, brown and Salem mahogany, resembling plate No. 11 in Woods and Finishes Section preceding page 9 of this Reference Book, walnut, maple on certain patterns. Colored lacquer finishes are available.

"ASHFORD"
No. 4—A quaint design with the popular Cottage Colonial turning on rails and spindles.

"CORNWALL"
No. 19—Made both in maple with amber finish, and gumwood with mahogany finish.

"PRESTON"
No. 39—For those who prefer a day bed with a back, here is a well designed pattern.

"BURNHAM"
No. 25—A low price pattern featured by many stores as a leader. Neatly paneled ends.

"LUFFINCOTT"
No. 29½—A distinctive pattern because of its spool-turned rails and spindles. Can be changed to a comfortable over-night bed at a moment's notice.

"WINCHFIELD"
No. 37—Neat spindles and panels are features of this graceful piece of furniture, appropriate for the well furnished living room.

"STANFORD"
No. 31—The smart ladder back design is always popular and appealing.

NATION-WIDE POPULARITY

The nation-wide popularity of the Kindel Double Day Bed is due to a combination of three qualities, simplicity, comfort and design. It was perfected by Charles J. Kindel, who has spent his life in the bed specialty field and is responsible for many of the basic patents in bed davenports.

Through sheer merit alone, the Kindel double day bed has won the preference of shrewd merchandise buyers in leading stores from coast to coast. Many stores have eliminated every other double day bed line from their stocks and concentrate on the Kindel alone.

SHIPPED K.D.

One man can set up the Kindel double day bed with our simple, rigid long wedge end lock. Space on the truck and time of delivery men is saved. The ends can be quickly removed and carried through any doorway. Shipped K.D. complete in one crate, well protected, compact, easily handled, earning a lower freight rate.

FINISHES AND PRICE RANGE

Stock finishes same as Kindel day beds described on the preceding page. Priced in eleven grades of coverings, denims, cretonnes, sateens, tapestries, corduroys, velours and damasks. Price range, $82.00 to $151.00, subject to change without notice.

Kindel Grand Rapids **Double Day Beds**

Trade Mark

THE KINDEL HAS MANY APPEALING SALES FEATURES

It provides the accommodations of an extra bedroom. It is not so large that it crowds a living room. It is simplicity itself to operate. And it is comparatively inexpensive.

The concealed half of the double day bed glides forward smoothly and quietly with little effort. A child can manage it. A highly perfected, patented equalizer assures positive, even operation, no jamming whatever. Raising the pillow rest raises the springs also—one simple, easy operation to make a full size bed.

The Kindel is trouble-proof. Buyers report no complaints from customers. There is nothing to get out of order. A salesman can make a smooth, convincing demonstration. The amazing comfort and buoyancy is due to special spring construction. The cushions are made by our own upholsterers of high grade aerated Linters cotton, with extra tufting to make a smooth, even spread without bunching. Every bed has a full spring edge seat. The end locks are quick acting, simple and rigid. The metal parts are durable and light, of strong steel construction, electrically welded in our own plant.

C. S. NORTON SALES SERVICE
Conductors of Special Retail Furniture Sales
36 So. State Street, CHICAGO, ILL.
TELEPHONE: STATE 4254

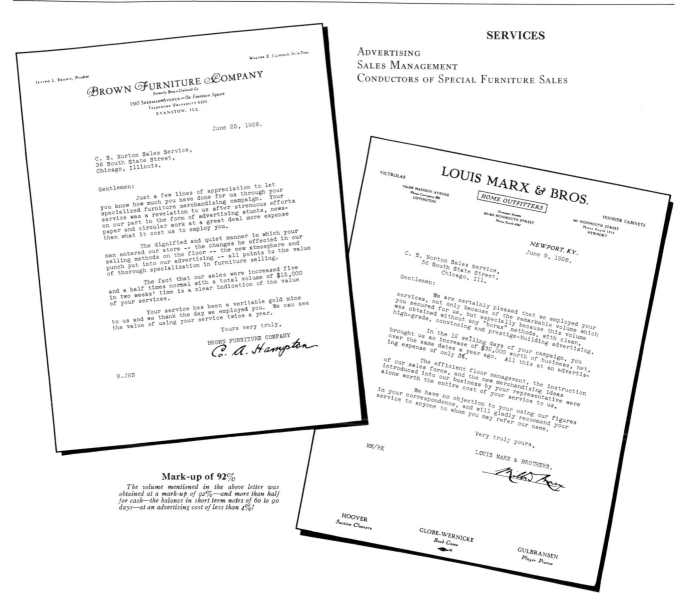

Mark-up of 92%

The volume mentioned in the above letter was obtained at a mark-up of 92%—and more than half for cash—the balance in short term notes of 60 to 90 days—at an advertising cost of less than 4%!

THE ONLY THING
YOU NEED WORRY ABOUT IS DELIVERIES

What will your profits be when your sales are increased from six to eight hundred per cent?

Half and more of these increased sales cash?

The two illustrated letters are among many which prove that our methods get results.

Sales properly engineered are extremely profitable. They sell merchandise quickly with regular mark-ups, build up your cash receipts, and make many new customers.

Our men are trained to conduct successful sales . . . they are trained to prepare advertising to suit your individual store—as each store has its own particular problems. They know how to display furniture, how to write ads that pull, and how to sell furniture and train others to sell in the quickest time.

Investigate our service today and be prepared to call us to handle your next sale. When writing please mention size of your stock, and other information, that will aid us in giving you a complete report—no obligation on your part.

If you are contemplating retiring from business, our Close-out Department can show you a way to obtain 50 to 65% more for your stock than you could obtain through any other method.

Incidentally, the cost of the C. S. Norton Sales Service is within the reach of every retailer. This can be arranged to suit your convenience either on a commission or salary basis.

References: We will furnish you with names and addresses of large and small furniture stores in which we have engineered special furniture sales upon request.

For financial dependability we refer you to the Kenwood National Bank, R. G. Dun & Company, Bradstreet's and Lyon's Mercantile Agency.

Write for complete details—no obligation on your part.

Doetsch & Bauer Company

Manufacturers of Frames for Fine Furniture

1534-44 Altgeldt St., CHICAGO, ILL.

PERMANENT SHOWROOM
CHICAGO, ILL., At Factory, 1534 Altgeldt Street

PRODUCTS
MANUFACTURERS OF
FRAMES FOR UPHOLSTERED FURNITURE

GENERAL INFORMATION
Photographs and prices of other numbers upon request. It will pay you to investigate.

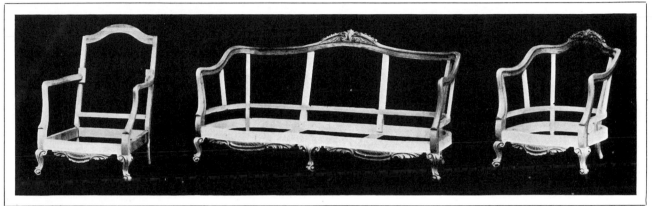

No. 1016½—Width, 27 inches; Height, 38 inches; and Depth, 28 inches.

No. 1016—Davenport Frame. Length, 76 inches; Height, 36 inches and Depth, 25 inches.

PATENT APPLIED FOR

No. 1016—Arm Chair Frame. Width, 27 inches; Height, 35 inches, and Depth, 25 inches.

No. 1007—Frame. Width, 34 inches; Depth, 26 inches and Height, 36 inches.

No. 1007—Davenport Frame. Length, 81 inches; Depth 26 inches; and Height, 37 inches.

PATENT APPLIED FOR

No. 1007½—Width, 32 inches; Depth, 27 inches and Height, 40 inches.

No. 1008½—Frame. Width, 33 inches; Height, 43 inches and Depth, 27 inches.

No. 1008—Davenport Frame. Length, 81 inches; Height, 38 inches and Depth, 27 inches.

PATENT APPLIED FOR

No. 1008—Chair Frame. Width, 33 inches; Height, 38 inches and Depth, 27 inches.

GREEN MANUFACTURING CO.

SINCE 1890

Manufacturers of Parlor Furniture Frames

1500 to 1510 No. Halsted Street, CHICAGO, ILL.

SHOWROOM AT FACTORY

Davenport Frame No. 448—Inside dimensions, 24x66 inches; 37 inches high.

An illustration of a finished frame.

No. 448 Chair—Inside Dimensions, 22x23 inches; 37 inches high.

This pen sketch will give you an excellent idea of the appearance of our frames when finished.

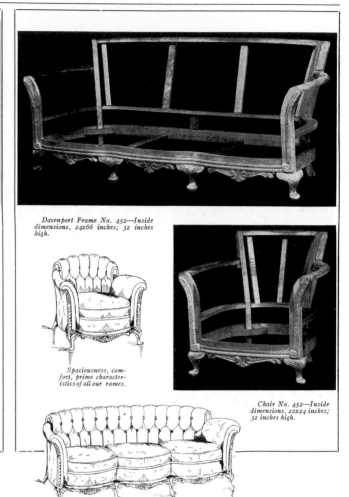

Davenport Frame No. 452—Inside dimensions, 24x66 inches; 32 inches high.

Spaciousness, comfort, prime characteristics of all our frames.

Chair No. 452—Inside dimensions, 22x24 inches; 32 inches high.

The pleasing lines of this finished product speak well for our frames.

PRODUCTS

MANUFACTURERS OF

PARLOR FURNITURE FRAMES designed to fit the special requirements of your customer, or standard patterns that enjoy a lasting popularity.

GENERAL INFORMATION

The frames illustrated on this page are just a few of our new line of "Rapid Sellers." Visit our show-rooms or send for photographs of our complete line.

Davenport Frame No. 444—Inside dimensions, 24x66 inches; 32 inches high.

Chair Frame No. 444—Inside dimensions, 22x24 inches; 32 inches high.

CHITTENDEN & EASTMAN COMPANY

Manufacturers of Upholstered Goods and Mattresses
Distributors of 120 of the World's Best Lines

BURLINGTON, IOWA

EXHIBITS

ST. PAUL, MINN., 2402-2414 University Avenue   BURLINGTON, IOWA, 123 South 3rd St.
CHICAGO, ILL., Space 1507, American Furniture Mart

PRODUCTS

DISTRIBUTORS OF

Square Brand

Trade Mark

BABY CARRIAGES
BARS
—Clothes Drying
BASKETS
—Fancy, Picnic
BASSINETS
—Crib Play Pen
—Wheel, Baby
BEDROOM SUITES COMPLETE, Including Bench, Chair, Rocker and Night Table
BEDS
—Bow End
—Children's
—Couch, Steel
—Day
—Hospital, Institution, etc.
—Metal
—Steel
—Straight End
—Twin
—Wood
BENCHES
—Bedroom
—Cane Seat
—Dressing Table
—Toilet Table
—Upholstered, Living Room
BIRD CAGES
—Fernery Combination
BOARDS
—Bread
—Ironing, Folding
BOOKCASES
—Library Sectional
BOOK ENDS
—Shelves
BOXES
—Matting Covered
BOX SPRINGS
BREAKFAST ROOM CHAIRS AND TABLES in the White for Decorating or Special Finish
BREAKFAST ROOM SUITES COMPLETE
BUFFETS
—Breakfast
CABINET BASES
CABINETS
—Medicine, Bath Room, etc.
—Radio
CARPET SWEEPERS
CEDAR CHESTS
CHAIRS
—Adjustable
—Arm
—Arm, Upholstered
—Assembly
—Baby
—Bedroom
—Bedroom, Sets of
—Bow Backs
—Breakfast Room
—Camp
—Cane, Wing
—Children's
—Coxwell
—Dining Room
—Easy
—Easy, Upholstered
—Fireplace

CHAIRS
—Folding
—Hall, Home
—High
—Invalid
—Kitchen
—Ladies' Desk
—Lawn
—Leather, Upholstered
—Library
—Living Room, Not Uphol.
—Living Room, Upholstered
—Lounging, Odd
—Metal
—Nursery
—Odd, Not Upholstered
—Opera, Hall, Assembly, etc.
—Porch
—Reclining
—Rolling
—Rush Seat
—Rustic
—Slip Seat, Leather
—Splint
—Step Ladder
—Tablet, Arm
—Typewriter
—Upholstered, Odd
—Upholstered Seats
—Windsor, Fibre Rush Seats
—Windsor, Genuine Rush Seats
—Windsor, Upholstered Seats
—Windsor, Wool Only
—Wing, Cane, Living Room
—Wire, Steel, Etc.
—Wood Seat, Bedroom
—Wood Seat, Desk (Home)
CHEST OF DRAWERS
CHIFFONIERS
CHIFFORETTES
CHIFFOROBES
CHINA CABINETS
CHINA CLOSETS
CLUB HOUSE FURNITURE
CONSOLE CHEST
CONSOLE TABLES with Mirrors
CORDS
—Mirror and Picture, etc.
COSTUMERS
—Metal and Wood
COTS
—Camp
—Canvas
—Folding, Metal
COUCHES
—Hammock or Suspension
CRIBS
—Metal and Wood
DAVENETTE BED MATTRESSES

DAVENETTES
DAVENPORT BED MATTRESSES
DAVENPORT BED SUITES
DAVENPORT BEDS
—Cane
—Cane Ends
—Overstuffed
—Wood Ends
DAVENPORTS
—Stationary Upholstered
DESKS
—Bedroom
—Cabinet
—Cashiers' and Bookkeepers
—Cylinder
—Gov. Winthrop
—Kidney-Shaped
—Ladies' for Bedrooms
—Library
—Spinet
—Wall
DINING ROOM SUITES Complete
DRESSEROBES
DRESSERS
—Princess
—Vanity
DRESSING TABLES
FERNERIES
FRAMES
—Picture
GO-CARTS
HALL FURNITURE
HIGHBOYS
HOSPITAL AND INSTITUTION FURNITURE
HOTEL FURNITURE
HUMIDORS
ICE BOXES; CHESTS
KITCHEN CABINETS, CUPBOARDS AND SAFES
LAMPS
—Boudoir

LAMPS
—Bridge
—Desk
—Floor
—Table
—Wrought Iron
LAWN FURNITURE
MATTRESSES
—Bassinet
—Cotton
—Crib
—Excelsior
—Felt
—Floss
—Hair
—Kapok
—Spring
METAL FURNITURE
MIRRORS
—Bath Room
—Bed Room
—Console
—Framed
—Hall
—Mantel
—Venetian
OFFICE CHAIRS
—Swivel
OFFICE DESKS
—Typewriter, Wood
PADS FOR DAVENETTE BEDS
PADS FOR DAY BEDS
PEDESTALS
—Jardiniere
PICTURE FRAME SUPPLIES
PLAY PENS
—Baby
PORCH FURNITURE
—Maple
RACKS
—Books, Magazine
RADIO AND PHONOGRAPH CABINETS
—Interchangeable

RADIO SETS COMPLETE
REFRIGERATORS
—Butchers'
—Cabinet
—Enamel
—Grocers'
—One-Piece Porcelain
—Porcelain
RESTAURANT STOOLS
ROCKERS
—Auto Spring Seat
—Bedroom
—Cane Back
—Cane Back with Loose Cushions
—Cane Seat
—Cane Seat and Back
—Plain, Wooden
—Porch
—Roll Seat
—Rush Seat
—Sewing
—Upholstered
—Windsor
—Wing
—With Loose Cushions
—Wood Seat
RODS
—Curtain
ROLL VENEER SEAT ROCKERS
SEATS
—Chair
—Theatre, Assembly Hall, etc.
SERVERS
SERVING TABLES
SETTEES
—Hall and Office
SEWING CABINETS
SMOKERS' CABINETS; Stands
SPRINGS
—Bed, Upholstered
STANDS
—Grip
—Magazine
—Wash, Metal
STOOLS
—Bath Room
—Camp
—Kitchen
—Office and Store
—Step Ladder
STROLLERS
—Babies'
SULKIES
—Baby
SWINGS
—Baby and Children's
TABLES
—Banquet Folding
—Bedside, Invalid
—Breakfast Room
—Cafe
—Card
—Centre

TABLES
—Coffee
—Coffee, Marble Top
—Console
—Davenport
—Davenport Extension
—Desk
—Dining, Combination Living Room
—Dining Room
—Directors'
—Drop Leaf (Not a Gate-Leg Table)
—End
—Extension, Breakfast Room
—Flip Top
—Gate-Leg
—Gate-Leg, Extension
—Hall
—Hotel
—Kitchen
—Library
—Metal Top (Kitchen)
—Night
—Occasional
—Office
—Pie Crust Top (Usually a Tilt Top Table)
—Porch
—Radio
—Reading, Adjustable
—Sewing
—Tilt Top
—Typewriter
—Wire
TABOURETS
TELEPHONE CABINETS
TELEPHONE SETS
TRAYS
—Tea
UPHOLSTERED BOX SPRINGS
UPHOLSTERERS' SUPPLIES
UPHOLSTERY LEATHER IN HIDES AND CUT TO SIZE
VACUUM CLEANERS
—Electric
VANITIES, SEMI
WALKERS
—Baby
WARDROBE CHIFFONIERS
WARDROBES
—Combination Dresser
WILLOW WARE
—Baskets and Novelties
ARTIFICIAL LEATHER
BROCADE
BROCATELLE
DAMASKS
LINEN VELOUR
MOHAIR
—Figured
—Plain, Flat
—Printed
RAMIE VELVETS
TAPESTRIES
—Artificial Silk
—Cotton
—Miscellaneous
—Wool
VELOUR
—Cotton
RUGS
—Axminster
—Velvet
—Wilton
—Wilton Velvet

If you do not have one we will gladly send it upon request, unless it interferes with previous selling arrangements.

POSSESSION OF THIS CATALOG SIMPLIFIES YOUR BUYING

Because its 748 pages illustrate practically everything a furniture dealer needs, all carried in stock in great warehouses centrally located here in Burlington, Iowa, ready to ship now.

It has been aptly described as a veritable encyclopedia of the furniture industry, for there are few items that a dealer needs which he will not find illustrated in this unusual catalog.

Not only does it show a long and comprehensive line of every kind of medium price furniture—the kind you make your living on—but some of the finest furniture made today. Also low-priced merchandise in all lines from which to select your leaders.

AMERICAN ART BUREAU
An Organization of Manufacturers and Jobbers
of Pictures, Picture Frames, Mouldings and Mirrors
166 W. Jackson Blvd., CHICAGO, ILL.

The daintily framed color prints and the handsome mirror shown in this grouping enhance the saleability of the furniture displayed. These smaller items make quick sales, and should be part of the stock of every furniture store.

A furniture store makes a strong appeal to the homemaker and customer, when it features attractive arrangements of wall decorations with furniture groupings.

Any customer would be attracted to such an arrangement as this in a store—the picture and furniture each enhancing the beauty of the other. Framed pictures, like mirrors, are important items in every furniture store, and make quick sales.

BEAUTIFY WITH PICTURES

PICTURES AND MIRRORS ENJOY QUICK SALES

Fashion today demands that every home of beauty, whether simple or elaborate, shall be adorned with framed pictures and mirrors. Prominent interior decorators throughout the country use these in artistic furnishing.

This endorsement places pictures and mirrors among the most attractive and most desired decorations in the home. Their quick sale is assured when homemakers and decorators alike use them for the walls of well-furnished rooms.

The following comments by decorators show the sure place held by pictures and mirrors:

"Pictures well selected and harmonized add a necessary color note to a room."

"Well chosen pictures and mirrors are necessary to a home. There's nothing so stupid and unimaginative as unadorned walls."

"Good prints are delightful. We cannot live without pictures."

"A paneled room offers a rare opportunity as a background for pictures and mirrors. They must be hung with much study and feeling for harmony."

*Pictures, appropriately grouped with other articles necessary for the home,
help the customer to visualize a corner of her own home effectively furnished
and thus add to the sales value of every item in the grouping.*

PICTURES AND MIRRORS

—increase the beauty and saleability of your stock. They are a great aid in displaying furniture to advantage. They lend color, so much needed as contrast to the dark furniture. They help to make attractive window displays. As part of home-like settings in the store, they show furniture well. Aided by pictures on the walls, customers can visualize furniture as it will look in their homes.

—pictures relieve the bareness of the walls of the store. The day has gone by when a furniture store can look like a warehouse.

—they attract new customers.

—they sell quickly, with the profits coming from quick turn-over.

—increase the prestige of a store, being artistic merchandise. They are the work of artists, and indicate to the public that good taste is part of the service of the store.

—make easy added sales. As the completing touch to an article of furniture, a picture sells itself. Pictures give opportunity to sell harmonizing drapery, an extra rug, or piece of furniture. "They go so well together," thinks the customer—and the sale is made.

—they are shown from the wall, where they take up no valuable floor space. Their sale is stimulated by a national promotional campaign, focused on increasing the demand for pictures.

SEND FOR OUR LIST OF MANUFACTURERS PUBLISHERS AND JOBBERS

The American Art Bureau is the organization of the picture, moulding and mirror trade. It carries on a country-wide promotional campaign to increase the sale of framed pictures and mirrors.

Even if you are already selling pictures in connection with furniture, it is probable that the sales suggestions offered by this Bureau will give you new ideas for "cashing in" on the highly stimulated demand for pictures.

The American Art Bureau does not sell pictures, nor issue a catalogue.

Panelled walls offer specially good background for framed pictures. This homelike grouping is a silent salesman for all the items displayed.

Mirrors, an essential item in the furnishing of every home of good taste, have many sales advantages for the progressive furniture store. They add to the charm of the other articles with which they are shown, and thus make beautiful display material; they are quick sellers to the customer furnishing a home; and they are displayed from the wall, thus taking up none of the valuable floor space.

AMERICAN WALNUT MFRS. ASSOCIATION

American Walnut

616 So. Michigan Blvd., CHICAGO, ILL.

GEORGE N. LAMB, Secretary

Trade Mark

WHY THERE IS PROFIT IN WALNUT FURNITURE

Mrs. Jones has a hundred dollars to spend.

Most business men know it—and most of them are trying to get Mrs. Jones to spend her hundred dollars.

If she buys furniture, it will be because furniture is made more attractive to her than—a fur coat, a vacation, a new Ford.

Mrs. Jones buys with her eyes open. She knows values. She knows materials. She demands more today than she did a decade ago, because she knows she can get more—if she hunts for it.

And Mrs. Jones has learned a good deal about what to expect. She knows that a Ford is not a Rolls-Royce, but she knows that the Ford is genuine, that its materials are of the best.

And she looks for the same excellence of materials in furniture, whether it be in a simple, inexpensive bedroom suite or the finest table that money can buy.

She is far less likely to make mistakes of taste today than she would have a dozen years ago. She has progressed beyond the point where she would put a cumbersome Elizabethan sideboard in a 10x10 dining room. She dislikes the monotony of furniture woods which have no variety. She is done, once and for all, with the furniture which wobbles itself swaybacked in the first year of its life.

The Basis of Walnut's Popularity

In short, Mrs. Jones is the real reason for the popularity of American Walnut today. And she is moulding the tastes of her children in her own ideas and experiences.

Mrs. Jones knows many things about Walnut. She knows the distinction of its figure, she knows the inherent beauty of the grain that wind and weather have built into walnut trees. She knows that though the design of her furniture may be pretty close to that of her next door neighbor's, the infinite variety of the Walnut veneers gives to hers an individuality of its own.

She knows (for at heart she and all women are interior decorators) that the soft color of Walnut blends well with any decorative scheme she may decide upon, and that when she changes colors, Walnut will not "fight" the new tones.

She knows that Walnut is long lived, that to a remarkable degree it conceals the mars and blemishes of use, for its color is in, not on, the wood.

And she knows that her taste is unerring whenever she selects Walnut. She sees it in museums, in the finest creations of the master cabinet makers. She is proud of her Walnut.

Mrs. Jones Has Learned the Value of "All-Walnut"

And Mrs. Jones has begun to learn, during recent years, that all the advantages of Walnut are multiplied when her furniture is of Walnut on all exposed surfaces. She has learned that solid Walnut frame-work means more stable furniture, longer lived furniture, more uniformly beautiful furniture.

She undoubtedly does not know that this is so because Walnut is definitely superior in strength, in shock-resisting ability, in stiffness, and in hardness, to the woods most used as substitutes for Walnut. But she does know the consequences of using these inferior woods.

NAME	Strength as beam or post	Shock resisting ability	Stiffness	Hardness	Specific gravity or weight	Shrinkage from green to dry		
						Volume	Radial	Tangential
Black Walnut..	100	100	100	100	100	100	100	100
White Oak.....	92	98	92	125	114	141	100	127
Red Oak.......	84	99	88	111	108	127	74	117
Red Gum......	76	78	84	67	86	134	98	139
True Mahogany	95	68	87	90	87	70	67	68

THESE FACTS—NOT CLAIMS PROVE THE SUPERIORITY OF WALNUT
Properties of Various Cabinet Woods, Compared With Black Walnut. Black Walnut—100

From Bulletin 909 of the Forest Products Laboratory of the United States Forest Service.

And she is, consequently, looking today for genuine Walnut Furniture. She sees that it is increasingly easier to find, and she has discovered that the making of the exposed solid parts of Walnut does not materially increase the cost.

Advertising to Mrs. Jones

Mrs. Jones has learned a good deal about Walnut from the Advertising of this Association. She and her neighbors will learn more, for the American Walnut Manufacturers' Association are putting their whole strength behind the movement for more genuine Walnut furniture. She and all the other Mrs. Joneses constitute a stable, growing market for genuine Walnut furniture in many price classes.

FURTHER HELPS TO HELP YOU SELL WALNUT

Today no furniture dealer or salesman can afford to be uninformed about Walnut. For estimates show that from 60% to 70% of all furniture sold today is Walnut. Unfortunately it is not all genuine Walnut. Representative groups of visitors at Better Homes Expositions have given Walnut a 93% preference when asked what wood they liked best.

Above is given technical information on Walnut which if studied carefully will help you and your salesmen to cash in to the utmost on the immense popularity of this wood.

Advertising Working for You

Probably no furniture wood has had such consistent advertising

put behind it over a long period of years as has Walnut. This advertising is appearing this year in the leading magazines of the country appealing to the home-furnisher.

The direct benefit from this widespread publicity goes to the retail furniture dealer. Yet this advertising costs you nothing . . . it is entirely paid for by the manufacturers comprising the membership of this association.

When you sell Walnut, this strong, constant force of national advertising is working for you day in and day out. Why waste your time or sacrifice profit by trying to sell products which lack this most important of all merchandising qualifications—aroused public demand?

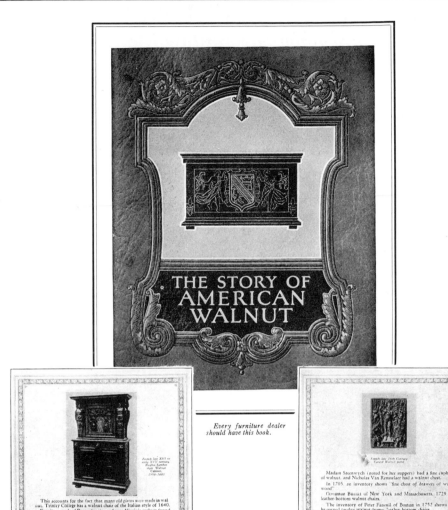

*Every furniture dealer
should have this book.*

*A page from "The Story of American Walnut"
describing the furniture periods.*

*Another page from "The Story of American Walnut." This book is filled with interesting facts about
Walnut and Walnut Furniture.*

EVERY FURNITURE DEALER SHOULD HAVE A COPY OF THIS FREE BOOK

This is "The Story of American Walnut"—a 48-page treatise, interestingly written and beautifully illustrated. It describes the periods in furniture, shows classic examples of the work of the great designers, tells how to identify genuine Walnut and guard against imitation; how to select a piece of furniture, etc., etc.

A careful reading of this book will give you new selling pointers, put new words in your vocabulary, enable you to relate interesting facts about furniture to your customers . . . make you a better furniture salesman in every way.

The Booklet Is Free

We will gladly supply you with a free copy of this book if you will write us for it. Send now and give it to your sales people to read. It will be like a course of study to them in the subject they should be most familiar with—furniture.

FURNITURE MANUFACTURERS' ASSOCIATION
Official Organization of Furniture Manufacturers
of
EVANSVILLE, INDIANA
J. C. Keller, Commissioner

Evansville—a great central source of furniture and stoves!

The variety of furniture and stoves made in Evansville makes it convenient for you to make only one stop from your store to Evansville.

In Evansville you will find furniture and stoves to completely equip any type of home. Save your time and money. *Buy in Evansville.*

Your request to J. C. Keller, Commissioner, will bring you detailed information.

Evansville
Henderson, Ky.

Evansville, a pre-eminent market, a great central source of furniture and stoves.

PURPOSES

Many years ago the Furniture and Stove Manufacturers of Evansville realized the futility of the bickerings and ill feeling that existed in the community in which they lived and built their merchandise. This realization brought about a movement that developed into the present association . . . an association organized to promote the mutual interests of the furniture and stove manufacturers of Evansville.

The success of this association can be easily measured when you consider that within less than a half century Evansville has attained pre eminence as a Furniture and Stove producing center. Its products are sold in every state of the Union, in the countries of the Orient, ancient Greece and the Antipodes.

DISPLAY BUILDINGS

The Furniture Building was Evansville's first permanent display building and is owned by the Furniture and Stove Manufacturers of the city. The Klamer Building is the other permanent display building.

The City of Evansville has thirty-five great Furniture and Stove companies placing about $25,000,000 worth of goods on the market each year. This amount of goods contains all kinds and types of furniture and stoves; high, medium, low priced articles; bedroom, dining room, living room, office and kitchen furnishings, in fact we can furnish any type of home from cellar to garret and also equip the office.

TRANSPORTATION FACILITIES

Evansville has seven railroads, electric lines and the Ohio River, supplying the transportation for its products. Freight rates are competitive and consequently cheaper than in almost any other section of the country. The factories all co-operate in loading mixed cars and this broad-minded service for which no charge is made is a distinct money-saver—a wonderful advantage that you should certainly avail yourself of.

A traffic department is maintained by the Association, and you are assured that correct freight rates will be applied and the most direct routes observed on shipments.

MARKETS INCLUDE OTHERS THAN EVANSVILLE

The key-note of Furniture and Stove Manufacturers in the organizing of this association was and still is to make the purchasing of merchandise by the retailer as simple as possible—to obviate unnecessary travel—loss of time and dissatisfaction.

This attitude has brought about the fact that our markets are not confined only to Evansville Lines. Many numerous outside concerns display their products so that the retailer will have as much of a selection and range as possible to make it profitable for him to buy in Evansville.

Affiliated with the Furniture Manufacturers' Association of Evansville are furniture manufacturers located at Henderson, Kentucky, who produce household furniture of the type and quality produced in Evansville. Henderson is only eleven miles from Evansville.

Thus you can readily see that by buying your needs in Evansville you are obtaining the kind of furniture at prices you want to pay that will satisfy your trade and make your time profitable.

EVANSVILLE AS A FURNITURE AND STOVE MARKET, POSSESSES UNSURPASSED ADVANTAGES

A man's home is his castle and therein are his dearest treasures. It is the ambition of every man to furnish his home with the best that money can buy in order to bring comfort to those who dwell in it. Furniture and stoves are essential to the well-being of modern man and Evansville is recognized as one of the great furniture and stove producing centers of the United States; thirty-six factories produce every article of furniture to enhance the beauty of the home and render it comfortable to the occupants.

For three-quarters of a century furniture of the medium and higher grades has been produced in Evansville factories and sold in every section of the United States and also in many foreign countries to furnish the home completely. Office and school furniture, too, are produced in our factories in large volume, and are used to equip the offices of industrial and mercantile establishments, also school rooms throughout the United States and some foreign countries as well.

Four large stove foundries in Evansville produce stoves and ranges of up-to-date design and equip them with the latest appliances. Housewives in every section of the United States cook their food on Evansville stoves and ranges. Their homes are likewise heated by Evansville stoves, and even in ancestral homes in old England Evansville-made heaters are employed to give warmth.

Evansville-made furniture is distinctive, being conceived by designers of ability and produced by expert craftsmen, and is synonymous with the best furniture made in the United States. Progressive dealers everywhere know that Evansville-made furniture and stoves are pre-eminent in quality and design and give satisfaction to purchasers.

Affiliated with the furniture Manufacturers Association of Evansville, are furniture manufacturers located at Henderson, Ky., who produce household furniture of the type and quality produced in Evansville. Henderson is eleven miles from Evansville.

Evansville has the most central location of the large furniture and stove manufacturing centers of the United States.

The expeditious movement of shipments is guaranteed by excellent transportation facilities afforded by seven steam railroads, boat lines on the Ohio River, and electric lines.

Pool car loading service for furniture dealers without extra charge makes Evansville an ideal place to purchase furniture.

A traffic department is maintained by the Furniture Manufacturers Association of Evansville, and dealers are assured that correct freight rates will be applied and the most direct routes observed on shipments.

Thirty-six factories produce furniture of exceptional design and quality. The annual output is $25,000,000.00.

Four stove foundries produce cook and heating stoves and ranges that will meet every requirement. The annual output is approximately 100,000 stoves and ranges with a valuation of about $2,500,000.00.

It will be profitable to purchase household and office furniture produced in Evansville, Ind., and Henderson, Ky., and stoves and ranges produced in Evansville. Prices are right and will appeal to dealers. Furniture and stoves are displayed in three permanent exhibition buildings.

OAK
The Sovereign Wood

OAK SERVICE BUREAU, Hardwood Manufacturers Institute

Bank of Commerce Building, MEMPHIS, TENN.

Jacobean Suite by Johnson-Handley-Johnson. The soft, rich brown finish, hand-rubbed and highlighted, delineates the inherent beauty of "the sovereign wood." Typical of the standard of "Renaissance Oak."

NEW FINISH TREATMENTS CAUSE A NEW VOGUE FOR OAK

How well Oak adapts itself to any finish treatment is admirably demonstrated in the many new Oak designs now available and the increasing demand for Oak lines.

The beautiful, rich brown or "antique" effects achieved by Berkey & Gay, Johnson, Steul, Baker and many others, have revealed Oak in all its innate beauty and ushered in a new vogue for "the sovereign wood."

Dealers will welcome the revival of Oak, for its practical qualities are a trade tradition. Its hardiness and endurance assure merchandise of trustworthy character. It doesn't scar so easily as other woods and lends itself most satisfactorily to the finest furniture craftsmanship.

"RENAISSANCE OAK"
The First Truly American Period

Character of designs has combined with modish finish treatments to make Oak furniture wanted again. This blending of designs and finish treatments has resulted in a new period of style known as "Renaissance Oak." A period embodying the style smartness of today and the historic, perennial charm of the furniture periods of the Renaissance. "Renaissance Oak" is offered as "the first truly American period of furniture" assuring the heirloom quality, as well as the inherent beauty of Oak, "the sovereign wood."

While it is a practical impossibility to keep informed of the numerous manufacturers who are producing Oak furniture of this desirable character, the partial list on the next page gives the names of manufacturers who have informed us they have Oak lines of this character available. Others will be found in the catalog pages of individual manufacturers herein.

Living-room group by Century Furniture Co., reflecting the distinctive manner of the Early English, faithfully rendered.

With the manifestation of a desire for home-like offices, furniture dealers are giving more thought to office furnishings. Furniture in this private office of a newspaper publisher is by J. L. Strassel Co., Louisville.

PARTIAL LIST OF MANUFACTURERS OF OAK LINES

Dining Room Suites

Baker Furniture Factories,
Allegan, Mich.

Basic Furniture Co.,
Waynesboro, Va.

Berkey & Gay,
Grand Rapids, Mich.

Century Furniture Co.,
Grand Rapids, Mich.

Empire Furniture Co.,
Rockford, Ill.

Grand Rapids Bookcase &
Chair Co.,
Grand Rapids, Mich.

Grand Rapids Chair Co.,
Grand Rapids, Mich.

Grand Rapids Furniture Co.,
Grand Rapids, Mich.

Johnson-Handley-Johnson,
Grand Rapids, Mich.

Wm. A. French Furniture Co.
Minneapolis, Minn.

Kensington Manufacturing Co.
New York, N. Y.

Knetchel Furniture Co.,
Hanover, Ont.

Luce Furniture Co.,
Grand Rapids, Mich.

Chas. P. Limbert Co.,
Holland, Mich.

Ottawa Furniture Co.,
Holland, Mich.

Phoenix Furniture Co.,
Grand Rapids, Mich.

Royal Furniture Co.,
Grand Rapids, Mich.

Saginaw Furniture Shops,
Saginaw, Mich.

Henry C. Steul & Sons,
Buffalo, N. Y.

Steinman & Meyer Furniture
Co.,
Cincinnati, Ohio.

Dinette and Breakfast Room Suites

J. D. Bassett Manufacturing
Co.,
Bassett, Va.

St. Johns Table Co.,
Cadillac, Mich.

Bedroom Suites

Johnson Furniture Co.,
Grand Rapids, Mich.

Allegan Furniture Shops,
Allegan, Mich.

Charlotte Furniture Co.,
Charlotte, Mich.

Jno. Widdicomb Co.,
Grand Rapids, Mich.

Living Room Groups and Occasional Pieces

Batesville Cabinet Co.,
Batesville, Ind.

Century Furniture Co.,
Grand Rapids, Mich.

Erskine-Danforth Co.,
New York, N. Y.

Hastings Table Co.,
Hastings, Mich.

Imperial Table Co.,
Grand Rapids, Mich.

Kindel Bed Co.,
Grand Rapids, Mich.

Kittinger Furniture Co.,
Buffalo, N. Y.

Richter Furniture Co.,
New York, N. Y.

Office Furniture

The Macey Co.,
Grand Rapids, Mich.

Kittinger Furniture Co.,
Buffalo, N. Y.

Erskine-Danforth Co.,
New York, N. Y.

J. L. Strassel Co.,
Louisville, Ky.

AN IDEA BOOK ON INTERIOR DECORATION

"The Charm of the Sovereign Wood, Volume II," is a beautiful 72-page brochure, containing:

1. Illustrated suggestions on interior decoration from hall to bedroom.

2. 3 sets of 4 color plates of room scenes.

3. Illustrated suggestions on making the office livable.

4. Formulae for modern Oak finish treatments, and other helpful information. 50c Postpaid. Address Dept. FDB-2, Oak Service Bureau, Hardwood Manufacturers' Institute, Bank of Commerce Bldg., Memphis, Tenn.

A lovely bedroom suite by John Widdicomb Co., Grand Rapids, of "Renaissance Oak" standard.

AMERICAN GUMWOOD
For Beautiful, Durable Cabinet Work
GUMWOOD SERVICE BUREAU, Hardwood Manufacturers' Institute
Bank of Commerce Building, MEMPHIS, TENN.

Gumwood furniture has a distinctive beauty and structural strength that give it a place of its own as one of America's finest cabinet woods.

ONE OF AMERICA'S FINEST CABINET WOODS

Gumwood has long since proved its merits as a furniture wood. If any wood could be called "*the* American furniture wood," surely this title would go to Gumwood, for it is the most extensively used in the making of furniture. Through years of service both the trade and the public have come to know the intrinsic quality of "Beautiful American Gumwood."

Where once the emphasis was laid on the elegance of veneers, fronts and tops of choice woods, and the use of Gumwood for structural parts passed over, now both manufacturer and dealer appreciate from experience that the mention of Gumwood construction is a warranty of dependable structural material.

Consumers, too, know that in addition to the fullness of sturdy construction assured by Gumwood the use of this comparatively inexpensive wood permits greater value in decorative features, such as choice woods, perfected finish treatments and designs that add character to one's abode, and which formerly were found only in the highest priced furniture. It can be truthfully said that America is a nation of beautifully furnished homes because of the availability of Gumwood.

Another characteristic of Gumwood is the beautiful high-lighting effects it makes possible in carvings and turnings.

USE IN ORNAMENTAL SURFACES INCREASING

Actual experience in the finishing room has shown that Gumwood is entitled to a permanent place and one of increasing importance in the making of fine furniture, because of its beauty as well as structural strength. No wood lends itself so readily to carving, fluting, and turning. None affords the beautiful high-lighting effects so easily as Gumwood.

Even more beautiful, is its fantastic figure which is making it a factor of growing proportions in decorative panels, either alone or in conjunction with other woods.

One of the characteristics of Gumwood, be it remembered, is the facility with which it blends with other woods.

Tho it is largely used for structural parts, as in this table, the fantastic beauty of Gumwood's figure gives it rare interest in ornamental surfaces.

It blends beautifully with the rarest woods—takes any finish.

Gumwood for solid parts permits greater value in decorative features.

"BEAUTIFUL AMERICAN GUMWOOD"

Send for this free booklet, which contains valuable data on this native hardwood and beautiful color plates showing the cordial character of its rich, rare tones. Address Dept. FDB-2, Gumwood Service Bureau, Hardwood Manufacturers' Institute, Bank of Commerce Bldg., Memphis, Tenn.

"Figured Gumwood" end-matched indicating the decorative quality of this wood.

"Plain Gumwood," whose figure rivals the "figured" species of many other woods.

JAMESTOWN FURNITURE MARKET ASS'N
Promoting the Jamestown Furniture Market
102 Hotel Jamestown Bldg., JAMESTOWN, N. Y.

Jamestown Furniture Exposition Building in the background. Markets are held every May and November. Dealers may order l. c. l. through the Jamestown Forwarding Company which pools shipments to large distributing centers.

FURNITURE MAKERS FOR MORE THAN A CENTURY

FIFTEEN YEARS OF SUCCESSFUL MAY AND NOVEMBER MARKETS

The Jamestown Furniture Market Association was organized fifteen years ago for the purpose of promoting a so-called early Market in Jamestown. Prior to this time furniture markets had always been held in January and July, but Jamestown's experience has led several influential manufacturers to conclude that the majority of buyers would prefer a spring and fall date. Hence the Jamestown dates were set for the First of May and November, and the immediate response was so gratifying as to demand the erection of an exposition building which should house all lines under one roof. This building was immediately constructed and the progress of the Jamestown Market from that date to the present is a matter of record with the dealers from coast to coast.

INFORMATION FURNISHED ON JAMESTOWN MANUFACTURERS

The association's work is almost entirely confined to the promotion of the Jamestown Market. Our files, of course, contain a wealth of information on practically all matters pertaining to the industry, and we are always ready to supply this information, not only to members but to anyone who may be legitimately interested. Nevertheless, our chief interest is in the promotion of the "Pioneer Early Market" and our work is mainly confined to this purpose.

Trade Mark

A SHIPPING SERVICE THAT SAVES ON FREIGHT CHARGES

The Jamestown Forwarding Company provides a very definite and beneficial service to retailers by pooling shipments to all large distributing centers. The service is excellent and there are practically no claims arising. By this method of transportation it makes no difference whether the buyer desires one piece or a hundred; he secures the benefit of the carload rate in either case.

JAMESTOWN'S FURNITURE HISTORY

General commercial furniture making began in Jamestown, one hundred and eleven years ago when Royal Keys, whose regular employment was that of a carpenter, began the manufacture of simple articles of furniture. Finding a ready sale for all he could produce he employed an assistant and definitely entered the field as a furniture manufacturer.

It was in 1825 that William Breed and his brother John, whose portrait appears in our trade-mark, built the first furniture factory in Jamestown. This factory, somewhat remodeled, is still standing today. From the time of the erection of the Breed factory the industry flourished and a great many other plants were built in the succeeding decade. Numbers of them are still turning out furniture, although the growth of the industry has brought so many additions to the original structures that few could be recognized today.

Jamestown is justly proud of her furniture heritage and tradition extending considerably over a century, as she is proud of her distinction in pioneering in market dates which have now been officially adopted by the other great furniture centers.

HARD MAPLE FOR FINE FURNITURE
The Northern Hard Maple Manufacturers

319 F. R. A. Bldg.   *Fine Furniture of* **HARD MAPLE** OSHKOSH, WIS.

PRODUCTS

NORTHERN HARD MAPLE LUMBER—cut from the unequalled stands of Sugar Maple (Acer Saccharum) in Michigan and Wisconsin, well manufactured in every detail, scientifically dried and rigidly graded. Some mills can supply kiln-dried stock.

ROTARY-CUT MAPLE VENEERS AND PLYWOOD, Bird's-Eye or Plain—Bird's-Eye Maple Veneer is usually cut $1/28$ of an inch thick and is widely used for decorative overlays, table-tops, drawer-fronts and the like. In Plain Maple Veneers the thicknesses most commonly used for furniture are $1/20$ of an inch for faces and $1/28$ of an inch for linings. Plain Maple Veneers are also produced in thicknesses of $1/8$ inch, $2/16$ inch and $1/4$ inch for piano-cases, etc. Plywood Panels of Maple for case-goods, etc., are made in 3-ply and 5-ply thicknesses and of standard sizes.

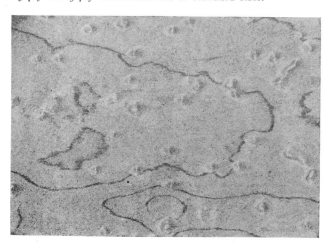

A Fine Specimen of Bird's-Eye Maple Veneer.

HARD MAPLE FACTS OF INTEREST TO FURNITURE DEALERS AND SALESMEN

Characteristic of American furniture alone, Hard Maple has been widely used for cabinet-work since Colonial days. Our first craftsmen often worked in maple and loved it for its golden hued tones and sterling qualities. Today fine furniture of Hard Maple, especially in Early American period designs, is again in high favor —a vogue which is rapidly increasing and bids fair to be of long duration because of the marvelous beauty of the grain figuring under the recently developed transparent stain finishes.

Beside the usual characteristic grain, three distinct markings are to be found in Hard Maple, and to some extent in other species of maples—Bird's-Eye, Curly and Blister. These result from accidental growths, and are found only in occasional trees. When desired, they are sorted out during manufacture but the percentage is exceedingly small to total output. Bird's-Eye Maple, especially, is utilized to make very beautiful veneers and overlays.

Physical Properties—Hard Maple ranks very high in all the physical properties required of a first-class hardwood. Its fibres cleave together with great tenacity, giving rise to its unusual resistance to checking, splitting and shearing forces of any kind.

It leads all woods in screw-holding power, assuring the necessary rigidity and strength in joinery to give the lasting service so essential in good furniture.

Maple Stools and Table of 1650–1700. Reproductions of these in the modern new finishes are quite the vogue.

In hardness, as demonstrated by U. S. Forest Products Laboratory tests, Hard Maple excels all woods commonly used for furniture making. It makes possible the design of intricate patterns in high relief, beautiful carving, is insurance that corners will stay square and the hard, firm surface is protection against mars or dents—all being assurance that Hard Maple furniture will retain its fine appearance indefinitely.

Combined with this quality of hardness, Northern Hard Maple possesses great strength and in this respect is only exceeded by Michigan-Wisconsin Birch. Slender turnings and small graceful proportions are thus made possible in furniture of Hard Maple with the assurance it will stand service. Davenport frames and frames for case-goods, piano cases, etc., are some of the humbler uses to which the lower grades of this wood are used because of its great strength properties.

Maple Gateleg Table of Colonial Days (Metropolitan Museum Exhibit of Early American Furniture). It is typical of the period and of late years has returned to popular favor.

Maple Splat-Back and Bannister-Back chairs, rush seats, common during the period 1650–1700. A curious blending of Dutch and English influence.

HARD MAPLE FOR FINE FURNITURE

Hard Maple is termed a "self-resistant" wood, and merely polishes under friction and abrasion where the fibre of other woods break down. It is, therefore, extensively used for drawer-slides, extension-table-slides, filing case-runners and other uses requiring a hard, smooth, easy-running surface. Wooden caster wheels are invariably of Hard Maple.

The uniform, even growth, straight grain and hard, fine texture of Hard Maple likewise offers supreme resistance to atmospheric changes, making it the wood almost exclusively used for piano keys and actions. Drawers don't stick and doors open easily the year 'round in furniture of Hard Maple.

A truly Colonial setting—Maple desk or secretary of early 18th century. A very characteristic Colonial style is shown in the Slat-back (or Ladder-back) maple chair in front of the desk and the Bannister-back chairs on each side were common after 1700.

MARVELOUS, COLORFUL BEAUTY MAKES EASY SELLING EASIER

The new Maple lines, in both early period and modern designs, are marvels of beauty in the new transparent color finishes developed especially for this northern cabinet wood. Available in a wide range of shades and tones—browns, grays, green, blue, amber, natural or "honey-tone"— these new "in-the-wood" stains bring out and develop the high lights and shadows of a grain figure, almost imperceptible to the naked eye under ordinary finishes, into a revelation of enthralling beauty. Exquisite effects are secured by misting and high-lighting panels, overlays and tops of Bird's-Eye Maple Veneer.

The great strength qualities of Hard Maple permit the fashioning of small, graceful proportions without sacrifice of sturdiness.

Early American Maple furniture owes much of its charm to simplicity of design. In the marvelous new color finishes, modern reproductions are revelations of enthralling beauty.

Furniture dealers and interior decorators, who have viewed the full range of effects to be secured by these new color finishes are one in their enthusiastic prophesy that furniture of hard, durable maple will quickly attain new heights of deserved popularity. A vogue that is destined to be perpetuated by the sterling qualities of this premier northern cabinet-wood. You are invited to "ride with the tide" and cash-in early on this increasing trend to maple.

"Cashing-in" on national advertising of Hard Maple Furniture. This is one of the many fine displays which have recently appeared in the windows of progressive furniture dealers.

LITERATURE AND CO-OPERATION

A complimentary copy of our new brochure, "Maple Furniture of Yesterday and Today," and containing panels and illustrations in the new color finishes will be sent upon request. Our service department will also be glad to furnish you with full information regarding these new developments in Hard Maple furniture and the names of manufacturers making these new maple lines. Address your inquiry to the Northern Hard Maple Manufacturers, 319 F. R. A. Building, Oshkosh, Wisconsin.

SPECIAL NOTE: Existing records show that Northern Hard Maple Floors will outwear stone. Furniture Dealers about to build or remodel their stores will find it a decided economy to put in floors and stair treads of Hard Maple stained in any color to fit in with the decorative scheme.

(Continued on next page)

BEAUTIFUL BIRCH for BEAUTIFUL FURNITURE

The Birch Manufacturers and The Rotary Birch Club

234 F. R. A. Bldg.   *Beautiful* **birch** OSHKOSH, WIS.

PRODUCTS

BIRCH LUMBER AND BIRCH ROTARY-CUT VENEER AND PLYWOOD —made from unequalled stands of Yellow Birch (Betula Lutea) and from Sweet Birch (Betula Lenta), in the great hardwood forests of Michigan and Wisconsin.

No distinction is made between these two species, as a rule. Both produce lumber and veneer sold commercially as unselected or mixed color birch, selected red birch and selected white birch. Red and white birch are produced from the same tree, red birch being the slightly reddish heartwood, and white birch, the sapwood or outer part. Unselected or mixed color birch is the run of the cut from the log containing both the reddish heartwood and the nearly white sapwood in the same board.

Typical Grain of Sawn Birch. About half natural size.

A beautiful variation, especially in veneers, called Curly Birch can be had in either red, white or unselected. It commands a premium as it is only here and there in the forest that there is a tree or part of a tree containing this beautiful wavy grained, pearly or "changeable silk" variety of the wood.

WISCONSIN-MICHIGAN ROTARY-CUT BIRCH VENEER is available in thin veneers and built-up plywood panels. It is cut in long wide sections from around the log—a method that brings out the full richness of the grain. It is adaptable to doors, furniture tops and panel work of all kinds, and for all purposes that require attractively figured wood in larger areas than can be obtained in one piece from solid wood.

Wonderfully beautiful effects are achieved with rotary-cut birch veneers by matching the pattern to secure symmetrically balanced designs while strikingly attractive contrasts are obtained by opposing, reversing or otherwise applying figured veneer of similar pattern.

BIRCH PLYWOOD PANELS—are usually made in 3-ply and 5-ply thicknesses. Built-up of thin layers of veneer with the strength fibres running transversely to each other, these plywood panels resist atmospheric changes to the utmost and are stronger than solid wood of equal thickness. This combination of strength and light weight, plus enticing beauty are the reasons why Wisconsin-Michigan plywood panels of birch are so highly prized by manufacturers of the better grades of furniture.

MAGIC OF COLOR IS CREATING NEW SALES OPPORTUNITIES FOR BIRCH FURNITURE

Color is the most potent selling force today—color in automobiles, color in dress, color in draperies, color in rugs, and now color in furniture of "Beautiful Birch," too. Not coverall lacquers and paint that hide the attractiveness of the figure in the wood but wonderful transparent stain finishes that penetrate, enhance and bring out the intriguing beauty of the birch grain in a brilliancy of coloring that "transcends all by comparison."

A Fine Example of the Beautiful Grain Effects to be had in Rotary-cut Birch Veneers.

The irresistible beauty of these new Birch lines assures quick, easy sales. And, the wide range of colors and tones in which these new finishes are now available—Early American, Spanish brown, autumn brown, silver gray, dove gray, royal blue, pastel green, orchid, seal black, natural or golden and many others—will satisfy any taste, conservative or ultra-modern.

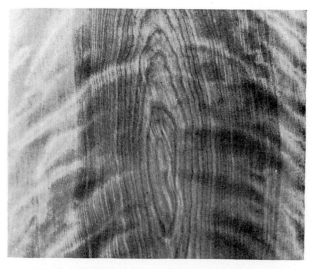

Curly Birch, "Unselected" for color. Note the wavy cast over the graining which characterizes this highly prized variety. Also to be had in "Selected" red or white.

BEAUTIFUL BIRCH FOR BEAUTIFUL FURNITURE

WITH BEAUTY, BIRCH FURNITURE COMBINES STRENGTH AND STABILITY

Beautiful Birch furniture not only has found ready acceptance because of its fine appearance, but is deserving of its growing popularity with the purchasing public on the inherent qualities of the wood itself.

Combining nearly "mar-proof" hardness with great strength (Birch is the strongest of the furniture woods, exceeding Maple, Oak, Mahogany, Walnut in this respect and being nearly twice as strong as Gumwood), furniture of "Beautiful Birch" assures stability of form and a fine appearance permanently.

This Bedroom Suite is of Spanish design. Being Birch it carries assurance of lasting strength and stability.

Because of its great strength, the lower grades of Wisconsin-Michigan birch are frequently used in combination with other cabinet-woods to give the necessary strength and stability to large pieces.

The charm and simplicity of this Dining Room Suite is enhanced by the marvelous beauty of the Birch Graining in the new transparent color finishes.

Beautiful, dependable furnitures, well-made of genuine Wisconsin-Michigan Birch are business builders that offer sales opportunities worthy of your investigation. Many progressive dealers are profitably tying up their selling efforts with our national advertising by strongly featuring their birch lines as "birch" in their local newspapers and windows.

Simple in design, Birch furniture of the character here shown gives that air of quiet dignity which characterized the furnishings in the homes of our forefathers.

AND, IN YOUR STORE, TOO

"Beautiful Birch" can serve you. Used for interior trim, veneer paneling, display window woodwork, its inherent beauty— enhanced by these new stain finishes—provides an impressive setting for the display of your lines that will arrest attention and speed up sales.

Charm, daintiness, colorful beauty and comfort are combined in these pieces of Birch Sun-room Furniture.

CO-OPERATION AND LITERATURE

Our Service Department welcomes your inquiries regarding this de-luxe cabinet wood and is in position to furnish any desired information as to sources of supply for true Wisconsin-Michigan Birch furniture, birch veneer paneling, birch lumber, doors and trim.

There are many selling pointers in our new brochure on "Beautiful Birch." Every furniture dealer and salesman should have a copy. Free with our compliments. Where shall we send yours? The Birch Manufacturers, 234 F. R. A. Building, Oshkosh, Wisconsin.

Where great strength combined with delicacy of line is required, Beautiful Birch has no equal. Hard, as well as strong, and with a close, even grain, Birch holds fine clear-cut edges and guarantees that all joinery will remain tight and rigid.

PECK & HILLS FURNITURE COMPANY

Wholesalers of Furniture, Fabrics and Floor Coverings
Sold Thru Dealers Only

1353 So. Wabash Ave., CHICAGO, ILL.

OFFICES IN PRINCIPAL CITIES

BOSTON   NEW YORK   JERSEY CITY   PHILADELPHIA   BIRMINGHAM   CHICAGO   DALLAS   DENVER
SAN DIEGO   LOS ANGELES   FRESNO   SACRAMENTO   SAN FRANCISCO   OAKLAND   PORTLAND
TACOMA   SPOKANE   SEATTLE

Trade Mark

SERVICES
Nation Wide Displays of Furniture, Fabrics, Draperies, and Floor Coverings for the Use of All Dealers

Large displays consistently improving are maintained for your use in fifteen of America's largest centers. Consider the one nearest you as your supplementary stock—a display building of furniture, floor coverings and draperies from which you may satisfy every taste from the most modest to the most exacting.

Your Peck & Hills' catalog is a complete listing of the "Carried in Stock" merchandise, ready for immediate delivery. Sales can be made from this catalog when your stock is low or when some unusual item is required.

Use our Card of Introduction and when your customer asks for it, provide it willingly. It may mean a sale you could not make otherwise. Whatever may be the need, whether a princely Oriental rug or an inexpensive item of chair or drapery, if you do not have it, send your customer to us with the assurance he will be treated exactly as though he were in your own store. Whatever is selected will be charged and delivered through you.

National Advertising has created a demand for this service.

Keep a supply of Cards of Introduction on hand. Use them. Let our Sales Service work for you.

THE BAY VIEW FURNITURE CO.
A Distinctive Line for the Living Room, Library and Hall
HOLLAND, MICHIGAN
PERMANENT EXHIBIT
GRAND RAPIDS, MICHIGAN, First Floor, Manufacturers Bldg.

Reg. Trade Mark

No. 514 Occasional Table. Top: 26x26 inches; Height, 29 inches. Solid Mahogany or Walnut top; Gum base.

No. 509 Spinet Desk. Top, 21x40 inches; Height, 34 inches. Hinged writing board; three large drawers. Solid Mahogany Top and Front; balance Gum.

No. 498 End Table. Top 26x13 inches; Height, 25 inches. Solid Oak or Walnut. Drawer in front.

PRODUCTS AND PRICE RANGES
MANUFACTURERS OF

SPINET DESKS in all the popular styles and sizes ranging in selling price from $30.00 to $90.00.

SECRETARY DESKS of both Mahogany and Walnut to sell from $50.00 to $125.00

TABLE DESKS in Oak and Walnut, all to sell at retail under $100.00.

PHONE SETS to retail from $20.00 to $45.00.

GATELEG TABLES—a strong line of all shapes and sizes at quantity production prices.

DOUBLE SERVICE TABLES with Seng fixtures, one and two-piece tops—designed and priced for quantity orders.

END TABLES, extensive in variety, most of them retailing at $20.00 and under.

OCCASIONAL TABLES of wide assortment to sell from $20.00 up to $50.00.

BOOKCASES, with and without doors, all sizes, mostly in Solid Mahogany. Retail prices from $32.00 up to $59.00.

All prices are subject to change without notice.

No. 503 Occasional Table. Top 36x36 inches; Height 29 inches. Solid Oak or Walnut top and Gum base. No. 515 is the same with smaller, 30x30-inch, top.

GENERAL INFORMATION

In the designing of Bay View patterns no attempt is made to achieve the ultra stylish. We follow the trend rather than endeavor to create new styles. For that reason the Bay View line is looked upon and accepted by the majority of dealers as a dependable line that enjoys a rapid turnover.

Walnut and Mahogany are the woods mostly used. Quartered Red Gumwood is employed in combination with the above woods. Some Solid Oak patterns have lately been added to the line.

One of the most outstanding qualities of Bay View workmanship is the splendid lacquer finish. Every Bay View piece can be placed directly on the floor after removal from the crate. A dull finish with Antique highlights is chiefly employed.

The prices are in all cases based on large cuttings. Every pattern enjoys quantity orders, and this advantage is passed on to the buyers of individual pieces. The line affords an extensive choice, but is absolutely restricted to only those numbers that have demonstrated their salability in large quantities. There are no slow moving patterns to bring up the price average.

No. 493 Double Service Table with Seng One Motion Top and Folding Leaf. Closed 48x24 inches; Open 48x40 inches. 5-ply Mahogany or Walnut Top; Gum base. Other Double Service Tables with Seng Underfold Leaf.

No. 495 Secretary. Mahogany front; balance Gum. Top 28x17 inches; Height, 71 inches.

No. 501 Table Desk. Top 48x26 inches; Height 30 inches. In Solid Oak with Butt Walnut drawer fronts or in Walnut with Gum.

THE BRANDTS FURNITURE CO.

Manufacturers of Upholstered Furniture

CELINA, OHIO

Club Chair. Width, 35 inches; Depth, 33 inches; Height, 32 inches. List price, $80.00.

SUITE No. 2027

Davenport. Length, 81 inches; Depth, 34 inches; Height, 33 inches. List price, $125.00.

High Back Chair, Width, 35 inches; Depth, 36 inches; Height, 35 inches. List price, $85.00.

PRODUCTS

MANUFACTURERS OF

THREE-PIECE UPHOLSTERED LIVING ROOM SUITES including the following pieces which are sold separately:

CLUB CHAIRS   DAVENPORTS   HIGHBACK CHAIRS

FRAMES

All frames are made of hardwood lumber, the joints bolted, glued and dowelled. All the corner blocks are fitted and glued, and screwed in place. No nails used.

CONSTRUCTION

All springs used are of the best spring wire, finely tempered. We use only the best webbing and all springs are tied with fine Italian spring twine. The more moderately priced suites have the steel slat bottom construction. In this construction similar springs are set into the steel slats instead of webbing, and no doubt gives the best service where furniture is subjected to severe use.

FILLING

All filling used is the best obtainable. We do not use an inferior filling in any of our suites, not even the cheaper models.

COVERINGS

The present day market offers a wide variety of covers. We buy our coverings from the most reputable mills—those who stand behind their products. We buy only new covers and do not offer seconds, which can at all times be purchased at cheaper prices.

DELIVERY

We cater to trade in Ohio, Michigan, Indiana, West Virginia, and Kentucky, and make truck delivery free of charge to any point within a radius of two hundred and fifty miles of Celina, Ohio.

All prices shown are subject to change without notice.

Club Chair. Width, 32 inches; Depth, 31 inches; Height, 32 inches. List price, $57.50.

High Back Chair. Width, 32 inches; Depth, 37 inches; Height, 35 inches. List price, $62.00.

SUITE No. 1927

Davenport. Length, 81 inches; Depth, 34 inches; Height, 32 inches. List price, $120.00.

Club Chair. Length overall, 38 inches; Height, 33 inches; Depth, 33 inches. List price, $56.50.

High Back Chair. Length overall, 38 inches; Height, 37 inches; Depth, 35 inches. List price, $60.00.

SUITE No. 228

Davenport. Length overall, 82 inches. Height, 34 inches; Depth 33 inches. Between arms, 64 inches. List price, $108.00.

THE CHICAGO MIRROR AND ART GLASS CO.

Established 1889

Manufacturers of Silvercraft Mirrors

216-224 North Clinton Street, CHICAGO, ILL.

PERMANENT SALESROOM
CHICAGO, ILL., Space 724, American Furniture Mart

Overall size: Small, 16½ by 45¼; Large, 18¼ by 47⅜.

Glass Sizes: Small, ends, 10 by 12, center, 12 by 24; large, ends, 10 by 14, center, 14 by 26. No. 1701-S—Price small, $20.40. Large, $23.20. This is a beautifully designed, low-priced buffet mirror and a rapid seller.

Overall size: 16½ by 46½.

Glass Sizes: Ends, 10 by 12. Center, 12 by 24. No. 1726-S—Price, $23.20. Another Silvercraft beauty in the popular buffet style, neatly hand engraved and decorated.

Overall sizes: 12½ by 23. Glass sizes: 10 by 20.

Overall sizes: 12½ by 23. Glass sizes: 10 by 20.

No. 1721-S and No. 1722-S—Price each, $7.60. These neat little hand engraved and brilliantly polished and beveled semi-venetians are the trade's choice for special sales.

Overall size: 12 by 16. Glass size: 12 by 16.
No. 1717-S—Price $10.80. A best seller in a high quality mirror of the easel type.

Overall size: 18 by 53. Glass size: 14 by 48.
No. 1716-S—Price $29.60. A Silvercraft favorite and a business-getter.

Overall size: 14 by 18. Glass size: 14 by 18.
No. 3022-S—Price $8.80. This attractively odd shape sells itself at sight.

Overall size: 13½ by 27. Glass size: 12 by 24.

Overall size: 13½ by 27. Glass size: 12 by 24.

No. 1723-S and 1724-S—Price each, $10.40. Here are offered a pair of standard quality neatly engraved Silvercraft mirrors at surprisingly low prices for sale leaders. Get a dozen or two just to try them.

Overall size: 13½ by 31¼. Glass size, 12 by 30.
No. 1209-S—Price $20.48. This lovely shape has taken the eye of the public with unusual favor.

Overall size: 20 by 33. Glass size: 18 by 30.
No. 1214-S—Price $23.20. This is a very attractive mirror for console or dressing table.

Overall size: 37½ by 41½. Glass size: 30 by 40.
No. 1728-S—Price $52.80. For massive beauty and elegance this highly polished and skillfully beveled mirror stands beyond comparison.

Overall size: 19⅞ by 34¾. Glass size: 10 by 28.
No. 1718-S—Price $25.20. Over a console table or desk this delicately engraved mirror lends distinction to the room.

Overall size: 15 by 29. Glass size: 14 by 26.
No. 1705-S—Price $12.40. Another low-priced Silvercraft leader in this popular size and shape.

PRODUCTS

MANUFACTURERS OF

VENETIAN AND SEMI-VENETIAN MIRRORS
—Buffet
—Console
—Dressing Table
—Hall
—Bathroom
FRAMED MIRRORS
MIRROR PLATEAUS
TABLE REFLECTORS
MODERNISTIC MIRRORS
MIRROR PLATES TO ORDER

WINDOW DISPLAY MIRRORS
BATHROOM CABINETS
—Single Compartment
—Three Compartment
MIRROR PICTURE FRAMES
MIRROR NOVELTIES
LIGHTING FIXTURE PARTS
—Mirror
—Plate Glass

Overall sizes: small, 19½ by 45¾; large, 23 by 51¾. Glass sizes: small, ends 10 by 12, center 16 by 24; large, ends 12 by 15, center 20 by 26. No. 1266-S—Prices, Small, $31.60; large, $53.60. This artistically engraved and brilliantly polished buffet mirror is known as the Masterpiece of the Silvercraft line, and highly deserves the title.

Silvercraft mirrors are brilliantly polished, skillfully beveled, and artistically engraved to give each floral design its natural appearance; Silvercraft mirrors are silvered by our own special heavy coating process assuring permanent luster; and Silvercraft mirrors are fitted on our own carefully made sturdy wood backs with harmonizing border ornamentation.

Through our efforts and those of the American Homes Bureau and American Art Bureau, of which we are members, mirrors are being purchased more and more for their decorative value as well as for their utilitarian value.

These are the reasons why Silvercraft mirrors have come to mean *greater dealer profits.*

WHAT SILVERCRAFT MEANS TO YOU

Silvercraft is our trade name. During thirty-nine years of progressive manufacture Silvercraft mirrors have come to be known as of the finest quality that man's ingenuity can produce.

WHAT TO DO

Write for complete catalog. Use these illustrations for interesting customers if you happen not to have all samples in stock. Send us your orders. We make prompt deliveries.

THE GUNN FURNITURE COMPANY
Manufacturers of Lino Desks, Tables and Bookcases
1820 Broadway, GRAND RAPIDS, MICH.
SALES AND SHOWROOMS
NEW YORK, N. Y., 11 E. 36th St.—LOS ANGELES, CALIF., 1027 So. Broadway—SAN FRANCISCO, CALIF., 21 Second St.

PRODUCTS
MANUFACTURERS OF

BOOKCASES
—Sectional, Home and Office
—Open Shelves
DESKS (Composition or Wood Top)
—Flat

DESKS (Composition or Wood Top)
—Roll Top
—Typewriter
TABLES, Composition Top
—Lunch Room and Restaurant

ALSO Library and Other Furniture for Schools. We make Library Tables but not for the home. Our Library tables are used for installations in School Libraries.

GUNN LINO DESKS

Gunn Lino Desks are made in various styles to fit the requirements of any office. They are practically designed in all details. Gunn patented "Lino" Tops are an exclusive feature used only on Gunn Desks.

ELIMINATE GLARE — RELIEVE EYE STRAIN

The soft dull shade of "Lino" is restful to the eyes because irritating light reflections are absorbed. "Lino" wears like iron. Stains are easily removed.

Complete Catalogs and Sample of "Lino" Top Available. Write for them.

"LINO"
Trademark Reg.

"It isn't a Lino unless it's a Gunn."

GUNN SECTIONAL BOOKCASES

For Home and Office. Universally popular for the simplicity of construction and refinement of design.

GUNN LINO TABLES

For Cafeteria and General Utility Use. Made in various styles and sizes. "Lino" saves breakage of tops and dishes.

HEBENSTREIT'S, INC.
Manufacturers of Upholstered Furniture
2122 Vliet Street, MILWAUKEE, WIS.

Suite No. 4194. Davenport length, 84 inches; Depth, 21 inches; Height, 35 inches. Birch. Price, $465.00. Covered with Plain Mohair. (Frieze Reversible cushion.)

Chair of Suite No. 217½. Width, 33 inches; Depth, 21 inches; and Height, 36 inches; covered with Plain Mohair. (Frieze Reversible cushion.) Mahogany. Price, $205.00.

Coxwell No. 613. Seat, 27 by 22 inches; Height of back, 38 inches; Depth, 22 inches. Mahogany. Price, $132.00. Covered with Frieze and Mohair combination.

No. 815—Chair. Seat, 19 by 21 inches; Height of back, 36 inches. Depth, 21 inches. Price, $154.00. Covered with Frieze, and Mohair combination.

PRODUCTS

MANUFACTURERS OF

CHAIRS
—Bedroom, Upholstered
—Coxwell
—Easy, Upholstered
—Living Room, Upholstered
COUCHES, UPHOLSTERED
DAVENPORTS, UPHOLSTERED
DAVENPORT BEDS, OVERSTUFFED
FOOT STOOLS, UPHOLSTERED
LOVE SEATS, UPHOLSTERED
OTTOMANS, UPHOLSTERED
ROCKERS
—Bedroom, Upholstered
—Upholstered
—Wing, Upholstered

Davenport of Suite No. 217½. Length of davenport, 80 inches; Depth, 22 inches. Height, 36 inches. Mahogany. Price, $360.00. Covered with Plain Mohair. (Frieze. Reversible cushion.)

products to meet the standards we have set. We do not sacrifice value for piece work speed production.

CONSTRUCTION

Frames—Selected stock rigidly built.
Fillings—Finest selected all moss or moss and hair, covered, when upholstered, with snowy white cotton felt.
Springs—Made of the best oil tempered steel and hand tied-eight way style.
Coverings—A wide variety of colorful imported and domestic Linen Friezes, Linen Velours, Moquettes, decorative and Period cover creations, are carried by us at all times to make it possible to fill your special coverings orders promptly.
Our product is manufactured by workmen who are paid to turn out quality

"THE ACCEPTED STANDARD IN UPHOLSTERY"

This has been our slogan for the past 35 years. Retailers throughout the central states who have sold Hebenstreit furniture will testify that this furniture lives up to the claims we make for it, that complaints from customers are as few as with any similar line they handle and a great deal less than with many upholstered lines. If you are not displaying any of our numbers we invite you to make a trial selection of a suite or a chair from this page. If you prefer to see our other designs before ordering we shall welcome the opportunity of furnishing photographs and prices.
All prices shown on this page are subject to change without notice.

HEKMAN FURNITURE COMPANY
Living Room, Library and Hall Furniture
GRAND RAPIDS, MICH.

PERMANENT EXHIBIT
GRAND RAPIDS, MICH., Sixth Floor, Fine Arts Building

No. 741—Drop Lid Desk — Mahogany and Gumwood Top, 42 by 19 inches. Height, 33 inches.

Trade Mark

No. 681—Plain Spinet Desk. No. D681—Decorated Walnut and Gumwood; Mahogany and Gumwood. Top, 42 by 20 inches. Height, 33 inches. 4 Drawers.

No. D706—Decorated Martha Washington Sewing Cabinet—Mahogany and Walnut. Top, 27 by 14 inches. Height, 29 inches.

No. 724—Console Table—Walnut and Gumwood. Top, 26 by 12, inches. Height, 24 inches. Fancy Veneer Top.

No. 436—Plain Telephone Set. No. D436—Decorated. Top, 20 by 19 inches. Height, 31 inches. Seat, 14 by 13 inches. Height, 29 inches.

No. 761—Secretary Desk—Mahogany and Gumwood. Base, 42 by 19 inches. Height, 58 inches. With telephone compartment.

PRODUCTS
MANUFACTURERS OF
DESKS
—Console
—Drop-Lid
—Roll-Top
—Spinet
—Tambour
SECRETARIES
—Wall
—Spinetaries
MIRRORS
—Console
SEWING CABINETS
TABLES
—End
—Tilt-Top
—Occasional
—Console
TELEPHONE
—Stands
—Cabinets
—Sets

SUBSTANTIAL VALUE ACCOUNTS FOR THE WIDE POPULARITY OF "HEKMAN" FURNITURE

Hekman furniture gives your customers *all* the qualities they look for and appreciate—beautiful woods—artistic interpretations of the most appealing styles—and sound, enduring construction—qualities that are reflected in fast turnover and lasting customer-satisfaction.

In addition, Hekman prices fit the average pocketbook—an important factor in explaining the constantly increasing popularity of this outstanding line.

Be sure to acquaint yourself fully with the big merchandising possibilities which the true merit and moderate prices of the Hekman line make possible.

LUGER FURNITURE COMPANY
Builders of Quality Furniture Since 1857
173 Glenwood Ave., MINNEAPOLIS, MINN.

EXHIBITS
CHICAGO, ILL., Space 304, American Furniture Mart

Nicollet-Banquet Table No. 1. Closed View (Patented). Ruggedly constructed. Sizes and prices upon request.

Dresser from Suite 1125. Walnut veneers with fiddle back Mahogany and Burl Redwood overlays. Best construction employed throughout. Finish resembles Plat· No. 19 Brown Sheraton in the Woods and Finishes Section. Top of Dresser, 21 by 50 inches. Mirror, 28 by 30 inches.

PRODUCTS

MANUFACTURERS OF

BEDROOM FURNITURE
—Bureaus
—Chairs
—Chests of Drawers
—Chiffoniers
—Chifforettes
—Desks, Ladies'
—Dressers
—Dressing Tables
—Night Tables
—Rockers
—Semi-Vanities
—Toilet Tables
—Vanities
—Vanity-Bureaus
—Suites, Complete, including Bench,
—Chair, Rocker and Night Table
DINING ROOM FURNITURE
—Buffets
—Chairs
—Serving Tables
—Side-Boards
—Tables
—Suites Complete
BREAKFAST ROOM FURNITURE
—Buffets
—Chairs
—Extension Tables
—Serving Tables and Cabinets Combined
—Tables
—Sets

BREAKFAST ROOM
—Suites Complete
TABLES
—Center
—Consoles with Mirrors
—Console
—Davenport
—Davenport Extension
—Dining and Living Room Combination
—Drop Leaf (Not Gateleg Tables)
—Enameled Finished Tops
—Enameled Finished
—End
—End, Radio Cabinet
—Extension
—Gateleg
—Gateleg, Extension
—Library
—Library, Extension
—Occasional
—Pie Crust Top
—Radio
—Tea
—Tilt Top
—Vanity
—Wandering
DESKS
—Ladies'
—Library
—School
—Secretary
—Spinet
—Wall

CABINETS
—Sewing
—Serving, Martha Washington
—Radio
—Radio, End Table
MISCELLANEOUS
—Book Troughs
—Costumers, Wood
—Jardinieres
—Smokers' Novelties
—Telephone Sets
—Telephone Stands
KITCHEN
—Chairs
—Tables
PUBLIC BUILDING FURNITURE
BANQUET TABLES, FOLDING
BANQUET TABLE TOPS
CAFE TABLES
DIRECTORS' TABLES
GRIP STANDS
HOTEL FURNITURE
LUNCH ROOM TABLES
OFFICE TABLES
RESTAURANT TABLES
TRUNK STANDS
FURNITURE - IN - THE WHITE (Unfinished for Decorating or Special Finish Chairs, Breakfast Room Tables, Breakfast Room
FURNITURE LEGS

DINING ROOM SUITE, No. 704

The eight-piece No. 704 Dining Room Suite, "Luger-Made" is built from Walnut veneers, combined with gumwood finished in shaded tones. Buffet is 66 inches wide, with 3-ply Mahogany bottom and removable silver tray. Table, 43 by 58 inches. Massive double top; base absolutely rigid. Chairs have Burl Walnut overlays and are upholstered in Jacquard Velour or Blue Leather.

A BEAUTIFUL SHOWROOM TO SERVE YOUR CUSTOMERS

Luger's spacious showrooms are located at 173 Glenwood Avenue, Minneapolis, and display the products of four factories located in Twin Cities, enable you to sell your special customers and get immediate service on a long and varied line of household furniture. If within convenient distance, bring or send your customers and let them look over the line with leisure.

WE OPERATE FOUR FACTORIES

Four large factories manufacturing Bedroom, Dining and Breakfast Room Suites, Dinettes and Tables of all kinds, offer you an opportunity of obtaining your needs from one source. The furniture we offer you is well constructed and well priced—you can realize profits in money and satisfied customers.

DESIGNS AND FINISHES

Luger Designs and Finishes follow the modernistic trend. Wood finishes for the Walnut resemble plates Nos. 10, 28 and 14 as shown in the Woods and Finishes Section. Mahogany resembles plates Nos. 19 and 24.

PRICE RANGES OF PRODUCTS

The Bedroom Suites range in price from $140.00 to $350.00 for the four pieces; Dining Room Suites from $110.00 to $250.00 for eight pieces; Dinette Sets from $90.00 to $180.00 for 6-piece sets including Table, Buffet and four chairs. These prices are subject to change without notice.

PAALMAN FURNITURE COMPANY
Manufacturers of Tea Wagons and Occasional Tables

250 Ionia Ave., S. W., GRAND RAPIDS, MICH.

PERMANENT EXHIBIT
GRAND RAPIDS, MICH., Keeler Bldg., 6th Floor

No. 486—Tea Wagon. Oak. Height, 29 inches; Top, 26 by 40 inches; Tray, 17 by 27 inches. Border hand carved. Price $82.00.

No. 491—Tea Wagon. Genuine Mahogany. Top and shelf matched Crotch Mahogany. Height, 29 inches; Top, 25 by 35 inches. Tray, 16 by 26 inches. Price, $57.00.

No. 488—Tea Wagon. Genuine Mahogany. Top and Shelf Brazilian Rosewood bordered with striped Mahogany. Height, 29 inches. Top, 26 by 40 inches. Tray, 13 by 25 inches. Price, $80.00.

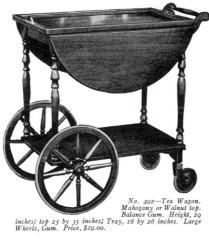

No. 2228—End Table. Genuine Walnut. Top Carpathian Elm Burl bordered with striped Walnut. Height, 24 inches. Top, 14 by 26 inches. Price, $23.00.

No. 492—Tea Wagon. Mahogany or Walnut top. Balance Gum. Height, 29 inches; top 25 by 35 inches; Tray, 16 by 26 inches. Large Wheels, Gum. Price, $29.00.

No. 2229—Book Trough End Table. Genuine Mahogany. Top and End Panels of Redwood Burl bordered with striped Mahogany. Height, 24 inches. Top, 14 by 26 inches. Price, $30.00.

PRODUCTS
MANUFACTURERS OF

TABLES	TEA WAGONS
—End—Nested	MAGAZINE STANDS

TRADE NAME AND SLOGAN

"The Drop Handle" Line—Tea Wagons made by the Paalman Furniture Company as shown

TRADE MARK

by the illustration, is a patented trade-mark feature. Slogan—"Be sure it has a Paalman Drop Handle; Look for the catch" is well known to the trade.

No. 2212—End Table with magazine pocket. Genuine Walnut. Top of Carpathian Elm Burl bordered with East Indian Rosewood. Side and End panels Carpathian Elm Burl bordered with striped Walnut. Height, 24½ inches; Top, 14x26 inches. Price, $48.00.

DETAILS OF MANUFACTURE

All tops and shelves are made of five-ply panels constructed in the most modern approved manner. "Genuine Mahogany" and "Genuine Walnut" indicate that all exposed parts are of the wood mentioned. Concealed rails and other parts that do not show, are of Gumwood, at our option.

Large wheels are Mahogany or Walnut, except as noted. All Pivot Wheels are of Birch, the wood best fitted for the purpose. Decorations are hand applied, not stenciled, nor decalcomania. All decorations are covered with clear maple varnish for their protection.

FINISHES

All Tea Wagons and Novelties, other than decorated pieces are finished with water and heat-proof lacquer, properly rubbed to a satin finish.

All prices are subject to change without notice.

THE B. C. POSTON MANUFACTURING CO.

Overstuffed Suites

465 East Main Street, CHILLICOTHE, OHIO

Poston
"DEPENDABLE"
UPHOLSTERED FURNITURE

Trade Mark

PRODUCTS

MANUFACTURERS OF

OVERSTUFFED	COUCHES
—SUITES	DAVENETTES
—BED SUITES	DAVENETTE SUITES
DAVENPORTS	OTTOMANS
COXWELL CHAIRS	

No. 65—"Rest Easy" Coxwell Chair. Inside width between arms, 22 inches. Height of back, 37 inches. List price, $60.00. Upholstered in Tapestry.

Ottoman for Chair No. 65—List price, $14.00.

No. 62—"Rest Easy" Coxwell. Inside width, between arms, 22 inches. Height of back, 37 inches. Upholstered in Tapestry and cut Velour. List price, $55.00.

No. 63—"Rest Easy" Coxwell. Inside width between arms, 22 inches. Height of back, 37 inches. Upholstered in Tapestry and Cut Velour. List price, $58.00.

"REST EASY" RECLINING COXWELLS

Poston Reclining Coxwells are adjustable to six positions yet the appearance is that of a stationary chair. Reversible spring filled cushions. Finished in Brown Mahogany.

The spacious and comfortable seats, together with the luxurious upholstering, make the "Rest Easy" have definite appeal to home owners. Prices range from $50.00 to $80.00, list.

All prices shown include reversible cushions. Prices are subject to change without notice.

Fireside Chair, No. 552—Outside width, 35 inches; height, 38 inches.

Club Chair, No. 552—Outside width, 35 inches; 35 inches high.

Davenport, No. 552—Length, overall, 87 inches; height of back, 34½ inches.

STATIONARY SUITE NO. 552

Full serpentine front, hardwood frame, brown Mahogany finish. Spring filled cushions. Double cone seat springs anchored to wooden slats with twine tied top. Web back. Spring edge. Pillows filled with Kapok. List price of entire suite, $237.00.

Club Chair, No. 550—Outside width, 36 inches; 35½ inches high.

Fireside Chair, No. 550—Outside width of chairs, 36 inches. 38 inches high.

Davenport, No. 550—Length overall, 81 inches; height of back, 35½ inches.

STATIONARY SUITE NO. 550

Double cone seat springs anchored to wooden slats with twine tied top. Web back. Spring edge. Full serpentine front, hardwood frame, Brown Mahogany finish. Spring filled cushions. List price of entire suite $175.00.

THE TAUBER PARLOR FURNITURE CO.

Manufacturers of Upholstered Living Room Furniture

3633-45 South Racine Avenue, CHICAGO, ILL.

PERMANENT DISPLAY ROOMS

CHICAGO, ILL., Space 841-2, American Furniture Mart, and at Factory, 3633 So. Racine Ave.

Taubilt Quality *Living Room Furniture*

Trade Mark

No. 245 Coxwell Chair and Bench. Solid Mahogany frame; covered in heavy wool tapestry; trimmed with mohair to harmonize; best of construction and filling. Price—Chair, $117.90; Ottoman, $38.20.

No. 215 Chair. Louis XV.—Solid Mahogany hand carved frame; four beautiful carved legs; covered in imported Italian tapestry on inside back and seat, balance plain frieze; trimmed with brass nails. Price, $136.40.

No. 6448, Louis XV Arm Chair. Full length of frame, 36 inches; Between arms, 26 inches; Full depth of frame, 33 inches; Depth of seat, 21 inches; Height of back from seat, 18 inches; Height from floor, 35 inches. Solid Mahogany and Web Bottom.

No. 6448 Davenport of 2-Piece Suite. Louis XV.—Solid Mahogany frame, beautiful cover in a soft Rose colored Frieze with harmonizing Frieze; down filled reversible cushions; trimmings, fillings and construction the very best. Price—Davenport, $477.00; Chair, $212.00.

PRODUCTS

MANUFACTURERS OF

BENCHES
—Bedroom
—Bedroom, Upholstered
—Fireside
—Living Room, Upholstered
CHAIRS
—Arm, Upholstered
—Bedroom, Upholstered
—Bank and Office Chairs, Upholstered
—Coxwell
—Easy, Upholstered
—Fireplace
—Fireside
—Hotel, Club, etc.
—Leather Upholstered
—Living Room, Upholstered
—Odd, Upholstered

CHAISE LOUNGES
DAVENPORT BED CONSTRUC-
  TION
DAVENPORT BED SUITES
DAVENPORT BEDS
DAVENPORTS
—Bank and Office, Upholstered
—Upholstered
FOOT STOOLS, UPHOLSTERED
HOTEL and CLUB FURNITURE,
  UPHOLSTERED
LOVE SEATS, UPHOLSTERED
ROCKERS
—Upholstered
—Wing
—With Loose Cushions

TRADE NAME

"Taubilt Quality" Furniture has been advertised to the trade for a number of years. Although this trade-mark does not appear directly on the furniture itself, it nevertheless is your guarantee that the merchandise is quality clear through.

DESIGNS

Patterns follow Louis XV, Chippendale, Sheraton and Adam Periods. The majority of the designs, however, are of a modernistic character which do not follow any definite period. Modernistic Furniture is a new style of furniture that is representative of the Americas alone.

MANUFACTURING DETAILS

Selected hardwood frames with imperfect parts carefully cut out are rigidly doweled and reinforced in Taubilt Furniture. Please note that each joint is double doweled before reinforcing. Woods used are Birch, Solid Mahogany or Solid Walnut throughout. The woven web bottom with Peerless clips is the most luxurious type and this is the only one used in the construction of Taubilt upholstered furniture.

COVERS

A wide choice of selections of Domestic and Imported cover fabrics is a distinct Tauber feature. Every type of upholstering is procurable: Mohairs, Chintzes, Cretonnes, Needle-Point, Crewell, Cross Stitch, etc.

PRICE RANGES

Taubilt Living Room Suites average from $170.00 to $1200.00, while chairs range from $50.00 to $350.00.

All prices shown are subject to change without notice.

GENERAL INFORMATION

Tauber offers a unique opportunity for the aggressive retailer. Taubilt Furniture is priced right, built right, has a history of achievement in satisfaction, so that any dealer can conscientiously recommend Taubilt knowing that he is offering the best that workmanship, skill and machinery are capable of producing.

TELL CITY CHAIR COMPANY
Manufacturers of Chairs and Rockers
TELL CITY, INDIANA
EXHIBITS
CHICAGO, ILL., Space 1122, American Furniture Mart, 666 Lake Shore Drive

PRODUCTS

MANUFACTURERS OF

BREAKFAST ROOM CHAIRS in the White for Decorating or Special Finish
WOOD ARM CHAIRS
BOW BACK CHAIRS
CANE BACK AND SEAT CHAIRS
CANE SEAT CHAIRS
CHILDREN'S CHAIRS
CHAIRS
—Arm
—Dining Room
—High
—Ladder Back
—Kitchen

CHAIRS
—Lunch Room and Restaurant
—Porch
—Tablet
—Wood Seat
OFFICE CHAIRS
OFFICE CHAIRS, SWIVEL
ROCKERS, CANE SEAT
ROCKERS, CANE SEAT AND BACK
ROCKERS for Porch
SEWING ROCKERS
KITCHEN STOOLS

FOREWORD

Skilled workmen, holding real pride in the sixty-two year reputation founded by their forefathers, do more than merely manufacture chairs. They build into them all the proficiency gained in the years of experience handed down through three generations. To this knowledge, the creative minds of the progressive workmen have added new designs, and improved methods of construction always in keeping with the times, and meeting the demands of economy and progress. Here is a real Chair Line that will mean real business for you.

HERRINGBONE WEAVE

One of the interesting features of Tell City Porch Chairs is the Herringbone Weave which is woven by hand. The uniformity of pattern and number of operations necessary to effect this, speak well for the skill of Tell City workmen.

CONCLUSION

To do business with Tell City Chair Company is to assure yourself of a dependable Chair and Rocker Line. We would like to do business with you.

No. 304—Beech Frame. Brown Mahogany finish. Fibre seat, 17½x15 inches. Height of back, 19½ inches.

No. 305—Beech Frame. Brown Mahogany finish. Fibre seat, 18¾x15½ inches. Height of back, 26½ inches.

No. 265—Hardwood. Seat, 16¼x16 inches.

No. 304—Beech Frame. Unfinished. Fibre seat, 17½x15 inches. Height of back, 19½ inches.

No. 264—Seat, 18x14½ inches.

THE TOLEDO PARLOR FURNITURE CO.

Manufacturers of Upholstered Furniture

City Park Ave. and Dorr Street, TOLEDO, OHIO

No. 902—Davenport (Loose Pillow Arm) finished Walnut. Length, 85 inches; Depth, 34 inches and Height, 33 inches.

No. 902—Scoop Back Chair. Width, 34½ inches; Depth, 32 inches and Height, 36 inches.

No. 902—Chair. Width, 34½ inches; Depth, 31 inches and Height, 33 inches.

PRODUCTS

MANUFACTURERS OF

LIVING ROOM SUITES
LOVE SEATS
COXWELL CHAIRS
BENCHES
DAVENPORT-BEDS
COUCHES
LEATHER UPHOLSTERED CHAIRS
STOOLS

GENERAL INFORMATION

Upholstered furniture made by The Toledo Parlor Furniture Company after years of service retains its beauty and durability, for—

The furniture is made only of high grade materials and constructed by skilled upholsterers.

The frames are kiln-dried hardwoods, 5/4-inch or thicker; firmly doweled, screwed and glued.

The springs are of the best oil-tempered wire, securely tied eight knots by hand. Seat and back foundations—the best woven web bottom or our special slat-construction.

The filling is absolutely guaranteed to be all new clean materials; the filling is always carefully stuffed and anchored in place with stitching and burlap. The edges are double stitched.

The Toledo Parlor unreservedly guarantees the construction; and all fabrics have distinctive beauty.

No. 907—Scoop Back Chair. Width, 34½ inches; Depth, 32 inches and Height, 36 inches.

No. 907—Chair. Width, 34 inches; Depth, 29 inches and Height, 34½ inches.

No. 907—Davenport. Finished Walnut. Length, 78 inches; Depth, 29 inches and Height, 34½ inches.

THE WESTERN SHADE CLOTH COMPANY
Manufacturers of Quality Window Shade Products
CHICAGO

BUFFALO   ATLANTA   INDIANAPOLIS   ST. LOUIS   DETROIT   COLUMBUS

Export Department—NEW YORK CITY

INTERIOR DECORATING SERVICE BUREAU—CHICAGO

THE INTERIOR DECORATING SERVICE BUREAU OF THE WESTERN SHADE CLOTH COMPANY

A special department is maintained in our Chicago offices for the purpose of helping retail dealers sólve problems of interior decoration with which customers confront them daily. Miss Ruth Morton, who is in charge of this bureau, devotes all of her time to developing new uses for shade cloth, new ways of individualizing window shades and bringing them more to the foreground as furnishings of beauty and importance—as well as offering satisfactory solutions to the decorative window shade problems of those who write in requesting information. Miss Morton, who is here pictured in her office from which she directs all the work of the bureau, has developed many decorative ideas which have proved to be immensely popular and profitable to those merchants who have offered them to their trade. Her letters written to customers and dealers have met with great approval and have resulted in many profitable orders.

ARABESK CARVINGS AND DECORATIVE TASSEL PULLS

With their delicate, harmonizing colors infuse a new style note into the decoration of window shades. The *Arabesk* is made in two styles which come in several color combinations that blend with various colors of shade cloth and other window furnishings. The tassel pull has a composition oval between cord and tassel, which is colored with tints to harmonize with the tones of *Arabesks* and window shades. These are exclusive Western Shade Cloth Co. creations.

Window decorations are unified by the shade *Ensemble*, which makes the window shade a more distinct style feature in home decoration. Each *Ensemble* is a creative arrangement, designed to harmonize in color and tone with other furnishings in the room.

The illustrations show how the chintz, cretonne, moire or

other fabric of the draperies is affixed with rubber cement or milliner's paste to the lower edge of the window shade to make the *Ensemble* composition. Originality and distinctiveness are added still more to each arrangement by the use of odd tassel pulls, gold braid bandings and Arabesks.

These window arrangements were designed by our Interior Decorating Service Bureau and are offered merely as suggestions to guide interior decorators and retail salespeople in planning *Ensemble* window shade treatments. Detailed information as to how they are made will be furnished on request.

Realization of the great need of the window shade industry for new ideas and some authority to whom retailers could turn for advice on the practical adaptation of these ideas to their own work prompted us to create our Interior Decorating Service Bureau. Miss Ruth Morton, the director, is a graduate student of art, having studied under several of the leading artists and decorators of the country. Her training for this important position has not only been theoretical but practical as well, as for several years she

was actively engaged in this work in one of the largest retail stores in the country. Miss Morton is anxious to be of service to you in helping to solve the perplexing problems that arise daily in connection with your work of interior decorating and furnishing. If you will write to her giving the full details of the situation, she will be glad to give her individual attention to each of these requests, and write to the customer also if you deem it advisable.

E. WIENER COMPANY
Manufacturers of Living Room Furniture

297 Seventh St., MILWAUKEE, WIS.

EXHIBITS

GRAND RAPIDS, MICH., (January & July) Fine Arts Bldg.   MILWAUKEE, WIS., (All Year Round) Factory, 297 Seventh St.

No. 153—Two-piece suite, covered in Chevron buff hand Blocked mohair.   Price, $354.00.

No. 1752—Chair, covered in linen frieze, down cushion, $61.00.

Super~Upholstered
Wiener
Living Room Furniture
Trade Mark

No. 1714—Chair.   Imported brocade. $139.00.

No. 163—Two-piece suite, plain mohair frieze reverse cushions, $239.50.

PRODUCTS
MANUFACTURERS OF

BEDROOM BENCHES
CHAIRS AND ROCKERS (upholstered)
COXWELL CHAIRS
LIVING ROOM LOUNGING AND EASY CHAIRS
CHAIRS UPHOLSTERED IN LEATHER
ODD CHAIRS (wood only or upholstered)
CHAISE LOUNGES
DAVENPORTS
SETTEES
SOFAS
LOVE SEATS
FOOT STOOLS AND OTTOMANS
HOTEL, CLUB, AND LODGE FURNITURE

GENERAL INFORMATION AND PRICE RANGE

Complete suites of Wiener Living Room Furniture range from $200.00 to $1400.00. Samples of upholstery will be sent upon request, together with quotations on suites covered with fabrics selected.   All prices shown are subject to change without notice.

Frames and fabrics used in Wiener Suites are imported from Europe, insuring your customers the newest and most exclusive designs.

WILSON FURNITURE CO.

INCORPORATED

Manufacturers of Bedroom and Dining Room Furniture

31st and Magazine Sts., LOUISVILLE, KY.

PRODUCTS

MANUFACTURERS OF

BEDROOM FURNITURE sold as complete Suites or as separate pieces including: Beds, Dressers, Vanities, Highboys, Chifforobes, Night Stand, Chairs, Benches.

DINING ROOM FURNITURE sold as complete Suites or as separate pieces including: China Cases, Servers, Arm Chairs, Buffets, Tables, Side Chairs.

No. 1010 China Case. Width, 46 inches; Height, 76 inches; Depth, 18 inches. Inside Bottom and Back, Mahogany Veneers. Shaped Shelves.

No. 110 Dresser. Base, 52 by 23 inches; Height, 76 inches; Plate, 30 by 34 inches.

DESCRIPTION OF SUITE No. 110

Construction—*Fronts*—African Walnut, Butt Walnut, Striped Satinwood and Curly Maple Veneers.

Tops—Butt Walnut and African Walnut Veneers.

Ends—Figured Plain Walnut Veneers.

Tops, Fronts and Ends of heavy 5-ply stock. Full dust-proof construction.

3-ply Mahogany Framed-in Drawer Bottoms. 3-ply Framed-in Backs. Interiors of Mahogany. Drawers dovetailed throughout. Legs of built-up Red Gum. Pin trays in Dresser and Vanity. Center Drawer Guides.

Finish—Two-tone and "Hi-Lite" polished. Waterproof Glue throughout. Mirror Backs—3-ply stock.

Complete Suite......................................*$493.00*

Prices—Individual Pieces

Bed, 4 ft. 6 in.	$ 80.00
Bed, 3 ft. 3 in.	80.00
Dresser	120.00
Vanity	115.00
Chifforobe	100.00
Highboy	105.00
Night Stand	30.00
Chair	21.00
Bench	22.00

DESCRIPTION OF DINING ROOM SUITE No. 1080

Construction—*Fronts*—Figured Stump Walnut Veneers; Overlays of Striped Satinwood.

Tops and Ends of Figured Plain Walnut Veneers; Tops, Fronts and Ends of heavy 5-ply stock. All doors 7-ply stock. 5-ply bottoms and dust-proof partitions; 3-ply Mahogany framed-in drawer bottoms; 3-ply framed-in backs. Drawers dovetailed throughout. Legs of built-up Red Gum. Silver Tray in Buffet.

Finish—Wilson Hi-Lite and resembles plate 17 in the Woods and Finishes Section preceding page 9 of this Reference Book.

Prices—Individual Pieces

No. 1080—Buffet	$150.00
No. 1001—Server	52.00
No. 1010—China	112.00
No. 1060—Extension Table, 6 ft.	84.00
No. 1090—Chair (Panel Back)	16.00
No. 1091—Arm Chair (Panel Back)	22.00
No. 1092—Chair (Upholstered Back)	22.00
No. 1093—Arm Chair (Upholstered Back)	28.00

Prices quoted above include chairs upholstered in Tapestry or Leather. Chairs upholstered in other materials will take the following additions to the list:

1090-1091—Mohair, add $2.50 per chair. Jacquard Velour, add $1.00 per chair. 1092-1093—Mohair, add $9.00 per chair. Jacquard Velour, add $2.00 per chair. Spring Seats on Nos. 1092 and 1093, add $2.00 per chair.

All prices shown on this page are subject to change without notice.

Price Guide

© 1995 Schiffer Publishing Ltd.

The values of the furniture in this price guide will vary tremendously depending on the location and condition of the pieces. The prices which follow were gathered from merchants in the Philadelphia region and are based on furniture in excellent condition (with its original finish, its upholstery in good condition, and free of veneer or structure damage). As furniture deteriorates its value may decrease by as much as 75%.

Some room settings have not been priced, although an approximate value can be set by referring to similar pieces throughout the book. Prices on room settings may vary according to the condition of the set and the number of pieces it has (two or three pieces as compared to a complete set). In the percentages quoted below, the lower figure usually applies to furniture that is veneered and the higher figure to furniture made of solid wood.

A living room set consists of one sofa and two chairs. A complete set may be worth 20-40% more than the pieces priced individually.

A dining room set consists of one table and six chairs, one china closet, one sideboard, and one server. Sets of six or eight chairs increase the dollar value by 10-25%, depending on the type of chair and its quality.

A bedroom set consists of two twin beds or one double, one high chest (with or without mirror), one dresser with mirror, one vanity with mirror, one or two nightstands, and one vanity bench and chair. A complete bedroom set may have an increased value of 30-50% over the price of individual pieces.

Prices in this guide are retail prices. Dealer's margins of approximately 50% must be considered when trying to sell them a piece of furniture.

pg. 68	no. 96X-$290		Prices for cabinets on this page are based on "Golden Oak" wood.		no. 24269-$135		no. 42-AR-$125
	no. 104X-$145				no. 42169-$165		no. 45-AC-$85
	no. 66X-$325				no. 24302-$300		no. 45-ARF-$110
	no. 640X-$325	pg. 73	no. 637-$100		clock-$375		no. 37-AC-$120
	no. 522X-$145		no. 7000V-$500		no. 42169-$165		no. 27-AR-$110
	no. 523X-$225		no. 27A-$145	pg. 91	no. 958-$575		no. 97-CF-$75
pg. 69	no. 1165-$175		no. H637-$175		no. 955-$245		no. 121-CF-$80
	no. 1727-$175		no. 16A-$125	pg. 93	no 45-AR-$140		no. 124-CF-$95
	no. 187-$155	pg. 74	table, top row, $150		no. 122 ACF-$100		no. 124-ACF-$140
	no. 1979-$130		chairs, top row, $65 each		no. 122-CF-$75	pg. 96	no. 1152-$400
pg. 71	no. 3745-$160		Model 15-$260		no. 94-CR-$90	pg. 97	top row, $310, $310
	no. 0415-$280		Model 48-$675		no. 98-C-$60		second row, $145, $125
	no. 5781-$200		Model A-$275	pg. 94	no. 50-AC-$75		third row, $400, $150
pg. 72	no. 2842-$800		Model H-$100		no. 50-ARF-$85		bottom row, $150, $140, $225
	no. 830-$185	pg. 75	no. 9727-$700		no. 50-CRF-$75		
	no. 818-$60		no. 9735-$675		no. 50-C-$60	pg. 98	top row, $175, $145, $120, $145
	no. 2836-$750	pg. 76	nos.471-s & 472 s-$6,500		no. 35-C-$50		second row, $300, $340
	no. 2877-$900	pg. 77	no. 160-f-$400		no. 24-C-$60		third row, $300, $150, $320
	no. 8003-$260		top row, $125, $175, $175, $235		no. 55-CR-$145		
	no. 8004-$340		middle row, $100, $95, $75,$75, $85, $145		no. 34-AR-$170		bottom right, $145
	no. 2855-$800		no. 5200-$425		no. 136-C-$40	pg. 99	top row, $350, $540
	no. 828-$150		no. G6000-$995		no. 79-AR-$190		bottom center. $175
	no. 818-$65	pg. 78	no. 4217-$200		no. 45-CF-$65	pg. 100	top row, $400, $180
	no. 825-$125				no. 48-AR-$85		bottom row, $300,
	no. 818-$60			pg. 95	no. 44-ARF-$135		
	no. 827-$150				no. 44-AC-$95		
	no. 818-$65				no. 42-ACF-$145		

$145
pg. 101 top row, $170, $500
middle row, $100,
$100, $145
bottom row, $100
pg. 102 no. 223-$200
no. 325-$140
no. 1170-$220
pg. 103 top row, $150, $280,
$125
second row, $200,
$400
third row, $140, $270
$120
bottom center, $500
pg. 104 no. 952-$400
no. 152 1/2-$200
no. 931 1/2-$200
no. 931-$375
no. 403 3/4-$220
pg. 105 top, $200
bottom, $350, $165
pg. 106 $675
pg. 107 top left, $475
top right, $145
middle, $175
bottom, $500
pg. 108 no. 745-$135
no. 62-$110
no. 770-$100
no. 287 1/2-$165
no. 283-$175
no. 283-BB-$100
pg. 109 no. 50-$145
no. 51-$275
no. 48-$80
no. 713-$145
no. 780-$110
no. 761-$170
no. 744-$110
no. 740-$120
no. 772-$120
no. 228-$200
pg. 110 top, $160
left, $160; center top
left, $200; center top
right, $160; center bot-
tom, $250; right, $165
bottom left, $275;
bottom right, $275
pg. 111 top row, $425, $145,
$85, $90 middle row,
$175, $190 bottom
row, $275, $300
pg. 113 top row, $375, $300
second row, $200,
$275
third row, $475, $330,
$500bottom row, $650,
$875
pg. 114 top row, $90, $110, $55
second row, $135,
$300, $90
third row, left-$550
right top-$310
right bottom left-$145,
right, $200
bottom row, $500,

$165, $810
pg. 115 top, $165
second row, $225,
$125
third row, $225, $150,
$250
bottom row, $170, $95,
$110
pg. 116 top row, $145, $285,
$200
second row, $325,
$175
third row, $300, $235
bottom row, $125,
$165, $150, $150
pg. 117 no. 180-$245
no. 187-$145
no. 188-$120
no. 186-$145
no. 212-$245
no. 179-$235
no. 178-$295
no. 181-$160
no. 184-$120
no. 177-$140
no. 189-$70
no. 190-$160
pg. 118 top, $195
second row, $135
third row, $110
fourth row, $145, $600
fifth row, $290, $235,
$425
pg. 119 top left, no. 214-$340;
no. 215-$550
top right, $500; second
row, $250, $225
third row, $175, $200
fourth row, $450, $140,
$245, $110
fifth row, $170, $450,
$135, $550
pg. 120 top row, $125, $275,
$175
second row, $125,
$300, $175
pg. 121 no. 3675-$300
no. 3700-$160
no. 3573-$160
no. 3726-$110
no. 3282-$135
no. 3673-$500
no. 3684 3/4-$450
no. 3723-$400
no. 3687-$650
no. 3668-$400
pg. 122 no. 678C-$145
no. 1678-$250
no. 678W-$120
no. 960C-$125
no. 2960-$300
no. 960W-$175
no. 962C-$150
no. 2962-$260
no. 962W-$145
no. 966C-$145
no. 2966-$300
no. 966W-$120

no. 957C-$150
no. 2957-$280
no. 957W-$145
no. 194W-$120
no. 196W-$120
pg. 123 no. 5577-$400
no. 577C-$225
no. 577R-$225
no. 2553-$450
no. 553W-$300
no. 553C-$275
no. 2534-$400
no. 534C-$220
no. 534R-$220
no. 2596-$475
no. 596W-$275
no. 596C-$300
no. 585C-$350
no. 2585-$650
no. 585W-$340
no. R070-$520
no. R099W-$275
no. R5099-$400
no. R099C-$235
no. R096C-$200
no. R060-$165
pg. 124 top row, $175, $225,
$200
middle, $300
bottom row, $300,
$200, $200, $270
pg. 125 top right, $110
second row, $300,
$100, $165
bottom row, $185,
$300
pg. 126 no. 24448-$180
no. 22358-$200
no. 24528-$110
no. 21818-$90
no. 21698-$400
no. 25008-$230
no. 21888-$175
no. 24198-$500
no. 22348-$275
pg. 127 no. 25308-$800
no. 23848-$145
no. 23318-$300
no. 25578-$115
no. 21368-$300
no. 21348-$550
pg. 128 top, $675
bottom center, $125
pg. 130 top, $200
bottom, $175
pg. 131 no. 1528-$200
no. 1532-$210
no. 1525-$210
no. 1519-$270
no. 1533-$250
pg. 132 top row, $170, $525,
$195
center, $600
bottom row, $400,
$235
pg. 135 no. S8788f5-$500
no. S8788D-$275
no. 8788G-$210

no. 8788C-$260
pg.136 top, $210
center, $150
bottom, $170
pg. 137 no. A230-$175
no. A236-$275
no. A234-$200
no. 8882-$185
no. 8872-$55
no. 8880-$170
no. 9030-$245
no. 8866-$145
no. 8861-$65
no. 8869-$170
pg. 138 no. 29-$980
no. 25-$2,700
no. 28-$1,350
pg. 139 no. 103-$750
no. 102-$500
no. 101-$400
no. 107-$1,800
no. 105-$400
no. 119-$500
no. 117-$900
no. 114-$1,050
pg. 140 no. 101 3/4-$225
no. 214-$500
no. 201-$375
no. 116 1/2-$300
no. 208-$700
no. 306-$450
no. 304-$500
no. 308-$650
no. 312-$510
pg. 141 no. 51-$500
no. 69-$500
no. 59-$400
no. 63-$600
pg. 142 no. 1347-$2,100
no. 1439-$3,200
no. 1477-$2,700
pg. 143 no. 1216-$2,200
no. 1453-$3,900
no. 1466-$1,400
pg. 144 top row, $75, $100
second row, $120,
$310, $210
bottom row, $90, $65,
$75, $55
pg. 145 no. 2069-$3,200
pg. 146 top left, $300
top right, $340
center left, $145
center right, $195
bottom, $700
pg. 147 no. 282-$65
no. 234-$50
no. 228-$65
no. 252-$80
no. 263-$80
pg. 148 no. 807-$1,600
no. 1200-$2,000
no. 800-$1,400
no. 705-1,100
pg. 149 no. 315-$850
no. 427-$975
no. 340-$1,100
no. 421-$925

no. 300-$800
pg. 150 pair, $800
pg. 151 no. 281-$325
no. 125C-$175
no. 508-$475
no. 250-$300
no. 375-$300
no. 111-$190
no. 268-$375
no. 125C-$195
pg. 152 no. 1825-$200
no. 1516-$90
no. 140-$750
no. 1204F-$75
no. 1202-$55
no. 1514-$85
no. 1501-$85
no. 1075-$75
no. 1518-$95
pg. 153 no. 48865-$250
no. 44839-$225
no. 48920-$190
no. 44867-$250
no. 48794-$220
pg. 154 no. 802A-$400
no. 606A-$170
no. 705A-$70
no. 151A-$55
no. 150A-$60
no. 716A-$85
no. 718A-$85
no. 708A-$100
no. 709A-$115
pg. 155 no. 21-$600
no. 401-$950
no. 56-$1,400
no. 203-$400
no. 306-$700
no. 55-$950
pg. 156 top center, $700
bottom row, $225, $110, $400
pg. 157 top center, $500
second row, $300, $145, $400
bottom row, $95, $310, $75
pg. 158 top left, $175
second row, $185, $145
bottom row, $75, $115, $100
pg. 159 top pair, $400
bench, $55
center row, $95, $300, $75
bottom row, $175, $320
pg. 160 no. 2449-$500
no. 1828-$170
no. 2305-$280
no. 2137-$170
no. 2407-$150
no. 2006-$300
no. 1972-$200
no. 1993-$400
no. 2404-$110
pg. 161 no. 2400-$200

no. 1784-$500
no. 2422-$135
no. 2049-$150
no. 938-$100
no. 1760-$95
no. 2679-$170
no. 2515-$90
no. 2216-$300
pg. 162 no. D770 1/4-$400
no. K128-$500
no. D770-$250
no. A157 1/4-$250
no. A67-$280
no. A260 1/4-$110
pg. 163 no. L127-$300
no. A228 1/4-$200
no. A232 1/2-$95
no. A250 1/4-$145
no. 223 1/4-$110
no. S455-$400
pg. 164 no. B3179-$320
no.150-$750 (8 pieces)Silver chest, $300
no. S75-$170
no. D379-$475
pg. 165 no. 504-$200
no. 521-$155
no. 501-$250
no. 502-$225
no. 510-$225
no. 506-$210
no. 503-$220
no. 523-$160
no. 505-$200
no. 525-$145
no. 508-$145
no. 527-$130
pg. 166 no. 16648-$300
no. 18646-$250
no. 18448-$200
pg. 167 no. 18848-$325
no. 1954-3-$250
no. 17046-$200
no. 19048-$320
no. 15645-3-$210
pg. 169 no. 1403-$700
no. 1230-$900
no. 1269-$1,300
no. 1404-$800
no. 1268-$800
no. 1284-$1,000
no. 1265-$300
no. 1282-$350
no. 1201-$300
no. 1253-$210
pg. 170 no. 1229-$210
no. 1235-$400
no. 1271-$500 (desk), $95 (chair)
no. 1248-$800
no. 1278-$1,400
no. 1211-$290
no. 1237-$900
no. 1247-$750
pg. 171 no. 1239-$500
no. 1222-$160
no. 712-$300

no. 927-$310
no. 919-$250
no. 903-$325
no. 926-$410
no. 46-47-$170
no. 44-$50
no. 929-$145
no. 1413-$250
no. 1416-$80
no. 1415-$210
no. 1414-$600
pg. 172 no. 1920-$700
no. 1900-$725
no. 1930-$675
pg. 173 top row, $325, $375, $475
middle row, $300, $475
bottom row, $600, $650, $ 710
pg. 174 top row, $200, $200, $235
center row, $300, $325, $325
bottom row, $300, $300
pg. 175 no. 1418-$210
no. 1419-$145
no. 1420-$170
no. 1423-$245
no. 1450-$170
no. 1452-$170
no. 1451-$135
no. 1445-$245
no. 1446-$225
no. 1437G-$300
pg. 176 no. 1200 1/2-$500
no. 1300-$400
no. 1454-$600
no. 1421-$400
no. 1205 1/2-$500
no. 1281 1/2-$550
no. 1218 1/2-$600
no. 1216 1/2-$650
no. 1217 1/2 310
no. 1701-$380
no. 1701 1/2-$140
no. 1700-$200
pg. 177 no. 1298-$700
no. 1299W-$650
no. 1299-$650
no. 1208-$700
no. 1210-$900
no. 1293-$600
no. 1293W-$600
pg. 178 top row, $400, $410, $400, $500
bottom row, $600, $600, $600, $600
pg. 179 no. 1217-$500
no. 1205-$1,100
no. 1207-$950
no. 1200-$900
no. 1216-$900
no. 1281-$1,000
no. 1281 1/4-$1,000
no. 1218-$850
pg. 180 no. 1215-$500

no. 1211-$550
no. 1212-$1,400
no. 1202-$450
no. 1290-$375
no. 1203-$310
no. 1265 1/2-$300
pg. 181 no. 1284-$380
no. 1284 1/4R-$380
no. 1286-$500
no. 1283 1/2-$300
no. 1287-$300
no. 1292-$400
pg. 182 no. 1556 1/2-$335
no. 1557 1/2-$500
no. 1531 1/2-$325
no. 1530 1/2-$220
no. 1553 1/2-$195
no. 1554 1/2-$300
no. 1569 1/2-$275
no. 1570 1/2-$525
no. 1573 1/2-$400
no. 1572 1/2-$275
pg. 183 no. 1566 1/2-$300
no. 1568 1/2-$530
no. 1567 1/2-$450
no. 1561D-$275
no. 1562-$275
no. 1563-$345
no. 1564D-$300
no. 1564I-$275
pg. 184 no. 181 1/4-$650
no. 175 1/2G-$325
no. 175I-$300
no. 175G-$300
no. 175-$345
no. 176D-$400
no. 178-$450
pg. 185 no. 1128-$600
no. 1129-$950
no. 1100-$300
no. 1101-$275
no. 1102-$280
no. 1103-$400
pg. 186 no. 553-$500
no. 553 1/2-$400
no. 540-$325
no. 552-$850
no. 544-$500
no. 541-$525
pg. 187 no. 524 1/2-$450
no. 524-$750
no. 538-$275
no. 607 1/2-$135
no. 607 3/4-$165
no. 607-$110
pg. 188 no. C3-$145
no. J45-$175
no. D100-$175
pg. 190 no. 584-$145
no. 827-$100
no. 669-$125
no. 681-$150
no. 963-$160
no. 250-$300
pg. 191 no. 1665-5-$140
no. 17634-$75
no. 2054-10-$50
no. 199C-$210

no. 1749-4-$85
no. 1743 1/2-$150
no. 2058-5-$120
no. 232-C-$130
no. 212-CS-$110
no. 214-$95
no. 242-B-$175
no. 224-T-$175
no. 199-B-$140

pg. 192 no. 611-$110
no. 21-$160
no. 20-$140
no. 839-$90
no. 935-$95
no. 283-$90
no. 617-$140
no. 263-$100

pg. 193 no. 6003-$250
no. 6418-$200
no. 5186-$145
no. 1077-$325
no. 6008-$135

pg. 194 no. 1117 1/2-$65
no. 1033-$75
no. 1350-$70
no. 1035-$85
no. 1034-$85
no. 1241U-$105
no. 1153-$165
no. 1242-$120
no. 1064-$95
no. 1220U & 520-$145
no. 1108-$135
no. 1222 & 522-$200

pg. 195 top row, $55, $115,
$110, $65, $110, $135
second row, $300,
$145, $95, $85, $200,
$75
third row, $85, $55,
$90, $90, 90, $65
bottom row, $75, $55,
$75, $55, $75, $55

pg. 196 top row, $300, $100,
$95, $220
middle row, $350,
$175, $175, $350
bottom row, $60, $300,
$300, $60

pg. 197 no. 2716-$65
no. 2723-$60
no. 2868-$135
no. 2700-$165
no. 2685-$180
no. 2738-$90
no. 2886-$310
no. 2735-$75

pg. 199 no. 1670-$300
no. 1466-$180
no. 1741-$275

pg. 200 no. 1107-$225
no. 1106-$300
no. 87-C-$60

pg. 201 no. 1687-$175
no. 721-$400
no. 1168-$95
no. 1169-$80

pg. 202 no. 452-$400

no. 91C-$60
no. 450-$300
no. 91A-$85
no. 451-$275

pg. 203 no. 429-$235
no. 88-$275
no. 1345-$275
no. 1484-$245

pg. 204 no. 632-$300
no. 1143-$100
no. 1392-$90
no. 1176-$110
no. 1171-$145

pg. 207 no. 1166-6-$65
no. 6680-6-$110
no. 1178-6-$75

pg. 208 no.4579-$500
pg. 209 no. 7001-$100
no. 4589-$135
no. 7000-$95
no. 4501-$95

pg. 210 no. 4429 1/4-$125
no. 4535 1/4-120
no. 4593-$95
no. 4595-$170
no. 4591-$100

pg. 211 no. 4582-$115
no. 4624-$270

pg. 212 no. 4614-$175
no. 4623-$275
no. 5000-$250
no. 5005-$300

pg. 213 no. 5006-$220
no. 5002-$245
no. 4538-$295
no. 5001-$245

pg. 214 no. 5007-$250
no. 1003-$275
no. 4616-$325
no. 4530-$325

pg. 215 no. 4445-$245
no. 4438-$275
no. 4527-$325
no. 1005-$300

pg. 216 no. 4001-$300
no. 988-$145

pg. 217 no. 995-$300
no. 880 1/2-$200
no. 4002-$250

pg. 218 no. 4004 1/2-$245
no. 970-$295
no. 979-$145
no. 969-$175
no. 965 1/2-$175

pg. 219 no. 16-$100
no. 876-$140
no. 15-$85
no. 989-$110
no. 975-$135
no. 980-$160

pg. 220 no. 906-$170
no. 900-$125
no. 987-$145
no. 978-$170
no. 977-$120

pg. 223 top left, $55, $120
top right, $55, $145

bottom left, $55, $140

pg. 224 no. 776-$275
no. 77614-$60
no. 776TD-$225
no. 776XT-$225
no. 779-38-$90
no. 779C-$300
no. 779XT-$280
no. 779B-$260
no. 779-18-$65
plaque, $70

pg. 225 top row, $55, $130,
$55, $ 125
bottom row, $55, $250,
$275, $150

pg. 226 no. 763-14-$65
no. 763TD-$225
no. 763C-$320
no. 762C-$280
no. 762-17-$75
no. 762TD-$235

pg. 227 no. 777C-$225
no. 777-14-$60
no. 777TD-$175
no. 774C-$220
no. 774XT-$120
no. 774DLT-$130
no. 774-14-$60
no. 774TD-$140

pg. 228 top row, $55, $180
middle row, $55, $135,
$55, $135
bottom row, $55, $275,
$250, $145

pg. 229 top row, $60, $75,
$75, $90
second row, $70, $65,
$60, $75, $70, $75, $85
third row, $70, $55,
$55, $90, $95
bottom row, $65, $55,
$65, $95, $95, $110

pg. 230 top row, $70, $95,
$45, $55
second row, $95, $60,
$85, $50, $55
third row, $75, $85,
$145, $65, $110
fourth row, $190, $115,
$140, $75, $95, $120
bottom row, $160,
$145, $130, $85, $110,
$135

pg. 231 top row, $45, $55,
$45, $55
second row, $50, $60,
$60, $70
third row, $55, $70,
$55, $65
bottom row, $55, $70,
$60, $70

pg. 232 top row, $60, $65,
$60, $70, $75, $85
second row, $50, $60,
$60, $70, $60, $70
third row, $75, $85,
$60, $70
bottom row, $90, $55,

$170, $95, $110

pg. 233 top row, $60, $60
$70, $80, $70
second row, $60, $60,
$80, $65, $70
no. 689-38DD754-
$120
no. 686-38E939-$130
no. 688-38EE1025-
$110
no. 687-38BB403-
$110
no. 849-38CC672-$85
no. 848-38DD839-$70
no. 847-48D752-$70
no. 847-38E930-$70

pg. 234 top left box, top
row, $110, $85; bottom
row, $100, $95, $130
bottom box, top, $85;
bottom row, $135, $80
box on right, left to
right, $85, $135, $70,
$115, $135, $160,
$135, $115

pg. 235 top left box, $160,
$120
top right box, $70, $85
bottom left box, left to
right, $190, $220,
$110, $120; second
row, $145, $120, $170;
bottom row, $70, $70,
$50, $65
bottom right box, left
to right, $220, $170;
second row, $210,
$165; third row, $115;
bottom row, $75, $75

pg. 236 no. 3574-$22
no. 3335-$260
no. 1355-B-$145
no. 1355-T-$125
no. 1355-C-$65

pg. 237 no. 94-$70
no. 94 1/2-$80
no. 56-$55
no. 150-$60
no. 1550-$110

pg. 238 no. 5071-$200
no. 5028-$230
no. 1731 1/2-$160
no. 5049-$115
no. 1455-$70
no. 2216-$80
no. 1850 1/2-$95

pg. 239 center, $65, $50
pg. 240 no. 664-$80
no. 640F-2-$160
no. 59-2-$235
no. 33F-$110
no. 4140-$60
no. 425-$130
no. 608-$130
no. 4131-$85

pg. 241 top row, $250, $60,
$275
bottom row, $250,

$200
pg. 242 top set, $2,000
bottom, $250
pg. 243 center, $275, $250
pg. 245 top, $250
second row, $275, $275, $225
third row, $250, $250, $280 bottom, $275
pg. 246 top row, $250, $275, $225
second row, $215
bottom, bench, $80; mirror, $60; vanity, $220; night stand, $135; chair, $60; chest of drawers, $250; bed, $275; dresser, $225
pg. 247 top, dresser $225; bed $225; vanity, $275; chest of drawers, $275; night stand, $125; bench, $60; chair, $60
bottom, bench, $60; chair, $60; night stand, $120; bed, $225; dresser, $225; vanity, $275; chest of drawers, $275
pg. 252 left, $235; right, mirror, $85; table, $170
pg. 253 center right, $120, $60
bottom, $440
pg. 254 top row, $85, $250, $60
bottom row, $225, $325, $165
pg. 255 top row, $225, $85, $375, $125
bottom row, $275, $275
pg. 256 top row, $300, $325, $175
second row, $300, $60, $85
third row, $275, $275, $160
bottom row, $210, $60, $85
pg. 257 top row, $275, $160, $220
second row, $85, $60, $270
third row, $270, $170, $270
bottom row, $85, $60, $225
pg. 258 no. 61-$175
no. 48-$160
no. 63-$160
no. 57-$420
no. 63 night table, $135
mirrors, $85 each
pg. 259 top row, $60, $220, $85

bottom row, $300, $175
pg. 260 left column, $60, $90, $225
second column, $275, $360
third column, $160, $190, $220
right column, $75, $55, $275
pg. 261 center box, top, $220; bottom, $165 each clockwise, starting at top right, $55, $250, $300, $230, $60, $275, $145, $95
pg. 262 no. 490-$225
no. 509-$375
no. 309-$245
no. 90-$225
pg. 263 top row, $220, $275
bottom, $275
pg. 264 arm chair, $85; buffet, $275; side chair, $60; dining table, $220
bottom, $425, $300
pg. 265 top row, $210, $275, $220, $160, $50
center, $75, $55
pg. 267 no. S61 3/4-$210
no. S62-$275
no. X65-$220
no. 68 3/4-$275
no. 69B-$60
pg. 268 top, $275
center, $260
bottom, $85, $190
pg. 269 no. 525-$235
no. 527 1/2-$275
no. 519-$275
pg. 270 (priced per set)
no. 431-$1,200
no. 430-$1,300
no. 429-$1,300
no. 428-$1,450
no. 426-$1,050
pg. 271 top row, $60, $210, $95
bottom, $300, $225
pg. 272 no. 350-$275
no. 450-$235
no. 45-$225
pg. 273 no. 1599-$85
no. 1598-$60
no. 1595-225
no. 1593-$225
no. 1590-$160
no. 1597-$160
pg. 274 bottom, $250, $250
pg. 275 mirror, $175; commode, $925
pg. 276 top row, $220, $245, $165
pg. 277 left, $300; right, $275
pg. 278 top row, $120, $300, $85

second row, $225, $300, $275
third row, $320, $60, $225, $90
bottom row, $300, $225
pg. 279 (priced per set)
no. 234-$2,700
no. 243-$1,700
no. 241-$2,000
pg. 280 no. 820-$250
no. 860-$275
no. 850-$220
no. 812-$300
pg. 281 suite, $1,200
pg. 282 no. 324-$300
no. 303-$750
no. 129-$150
no. 354-$300 pair
no. 250-$450 pair
pg. 283 no. 285-$350 pair
no. 367-$425 pair
no. 356-$325 pair
no. 244-$260
no. 355-$325
no. 252-$800
no. 319-$500
pg. 284 no. 65-$200
no. 30-$110
no. 70-$300
pg. 285 no. 1007-$95
no. 1031-$300
no. 1030-$150
no. 1035-$275
no. 70-$600
no. 45-$200
no. 60-$300
pg. 286 no. 604-$1,000
pg. 287 no. 600-$1,100
pg. 288 no. 1111-$175
no. 1574-$225
no. 1585-$225
pg. 289 no. 1441-$1,400
no. 1471-$160
no. 441-$200
pg. 290 left, $235
top center, $60
bottom center, $110
right, $190
pg. 291 top left, $225
bottom left, $275
top right, $45, $50
center right, $200
bottom right, $225
pg. 292 top row, $60, $55, $55
middle row, $245, $90, $275
bottom row, $210, $275
pg. 293 top row, $60, $75
second row, $100, $275, $225
bottom left, $220
bottom right, $275
mirror (bottom), $110
pg. 294 top, $240
middle row, $225,

$225
bottom row, $275, $275
pg. 295 left column, $80
mirror, $160, $180
center column, $60, $60, $85
right column, $225, $225
pg. 296 top row, $185, $85, $60
middle row, $60, $185, $260
bottom row, $225, $225
pg. 297 top row, $200, $80, $50, $60
center row, $250, $250
bottom row, $220, $220
pg. 298 top row, $100, $80
middle row, $300, $300
bottom row, $275, $135, $225
pg. 299 top row, $500, $400, $600
center, $300
bottom row, $400, $400, $575
pg. 300 no. 387-$500
no. 367 1/2-$400
no. 387 1/2-$300
no. 367-$600
no. 376 1/2-$350
no. 382 1/2-$425
no. 380 1/2-$400
no. 379 1/2-$375
pg. 301 no. 378 1/2-$400
no. 377 1/2-$300
no. 381 1/2-$325
no. 817-$300
no. 801-$250
no. 816-$350
no. 813-$290
no. 823-$375
no. 821-$425
pg. 302 top row, $275, $180, $235
bottom row, $80, $225, $60
pg. 303 top row, $190, $170
bottom row, $190, $195, $225
pg. 304 no. 2626-$225
no. 2631-$175
no. 2602-$250
no. 2611-$325
pg. 305 top row, $250, $100, $90 (mirror)
second row, $90, $225, $200 (chest)
bottom left, $300
pg. 306 no. 151-$350
no. 315-$310
no. 325-$300
no. 321-$290
no. 320-$210

pg. 308 no. 150-$360
no. 329-$275
no. 340-$310
no. 330-$200
top row, $225, $350, $225
second row, $275, $60, $85
third row, $275, $310, $160
bottom row, $300, $60, $85

pg. 309 no. 231-$500
no. 0193-$600
no. 0150-$700
no. 0188-$750
no. 241-$650
no. 0198-$500
no. 233-$500
no. 0203-$425
no. 0164-$450
no. 232-$400

pg. 310 no. 246-$600
no. 237-$450
no. 0345-$400
no. 0342-$350
no. 0343-$400
no. 0341-$165
no. 341-2-$300
no. 0328-$200
no. 0328-2-$300

pg. 311 top row, $400, $175, $400, $175
second row, $300, $300, $300
third row, $165, $500, $190, $175
bottom row, $210, $275, $375, $300

pg. 312 no. 132-$400
no. 218-$375
no. 256-$450
no. 221-$375
no. 265-$375
no. 250-$450
no. 216-$300
no. 249-$425
no. 0154-$350
no. 251-$410

pg. 313 no. 192-$210
no. 253-$240
no. 252-$200
no. 191-$225
no. 260-$500
no. 254-$375
no. 196-$275
no. 248-$475
no. 240-I-$400

pg. 314 top row, $85, $225, $60
bottom row, $300, $175, $260

pg. 315 top row, $60, $225, $85
second row, $235, $175, $300
third row, $80, $275, $125

bottom row, $475, $375, $225

pg. 316 top row, $60, $225, $85
second row, $300, $175, $240
third row, $60, $250, $85
bottom row, $275, $200, $245

pg. 317 top row, $60, $210, $85
second row, $250, $180, $275
third row, $60, $275, $90
bottom row, $350, $225, $300

pg. 318 top row, $80, $275, $60
second row, $325, $225, $300
third row, $85, $275, $110
bottom row, $450, $235, $400

pg. 319 top row, $80, $300, $110
second row, $475, $275, $450
third row, $60, $225, $90
bottom row, $300, $200, $225

pg. 320 top row, $80, $250, $125
second row, $450, $200, $350
third row, $60, $225, $100
bottom row, $260, $175, $210

pg. 321 no. 111-$350
no. 108-$375
no. 105-$500
no. 110-$425
no. 106 1/2-$320
no. 103-$625
no. 112-$450
no. 112 1/2-$300
no. 100-$600

pg. 322 top row, $100, $250, $100
second row, $620, $340, $500
third row, $300, $550, $175
bottom row, $575, $320, $500

pg. 323 top row, $100, $450, $125
second row, $525, $350, $400
bottom row, $425, $275, $400

pg. 324 top row, $275, $60, $85
middle row, $400,

$250, $300
third row, $400, $125, $175
bottom row, $400, $550, $300

pg. 325 top row, $300, $60, $85
second row, $300, $375, $200
third row, $300, $60, $85
bottom row, $400, $200, $275

pg. 326 no. 17-$300
no. 20-$325
no. 22-$320
no. 507-$475
no. 711-$400
no. 508-$375
no. 500-$450
no. 510-$675
no. 908-$350

pg. 327 top row, $375, $85, $275
bottom row, $250, $200, $60

pg. 328 top row, $400, $300, $500
second row, $85, $300, $125
third row, $310, $165, $245
bottom row, $60, $220, $90

pg. 329 top row, $390, $425
second row, $125, $165, $475, $325
bottom row, $400, $450, $200, $400

pg. 330 no. 436-$475
no. 422-$600
no. 439-$500
no. 810-$300
no. 84-$375
no. 83-$275
no. 413-$360
no. 67-$425

pg. 331 no. 101-$475
no. 100-$350
no. 66-$260
no. 162-$325
no. 80-$275
no. 735-$300
no. 755-$200

pg. 332 top row, $250, $60, $85
second row, $400, $200, $225
third row, $300, $100, $160
bottom row, $500, $250, $400

pg. 333 top row, $300, $200, $225
second row, $60, $85, $225
third row, $390, $200, $300

bottom row, $60, $85, $225

pg. 334 top row, $400, $240, $350
second row, $65, $300, $90
third row, $350, $140, $195
bottom row, $60, $225, $85

pg. 336 top, $250
bottom $250

pg. 337 no. 1906-$250
no. 2906 1/4-$275
no. 3906-$250
no. 8906-$150
no. 4906-$275

pg. 338 no. 7940-$250
no. 2940 1/4-$300
no. 3940-$225
no. 1940-$250

pg. 339 top row $250
middle row, $200, $250
bottom, $75, $50, $300

pg. 342 top row, $350, $250
middle row, $100, $85
bottom row, $300, $400

pg. 343 top row, $60, $250, $85
middle row, $200
bottom $300, $400

pg. 344 top row, $450, $450
middle row, $120, $300, $85
bottom row, $650, $300, $500

pg. 345 top row, $85, $275, $60
middle row, $400, $250
bottom row, $400, $500

pg. 346 top row, $250, $200
bottom row, $225, $225

pg. 347 top row, $200, $60, $225
bottom row, $200, $95, $210

pg. 348 top row, $450, $200, $160
middle, $300
bottom, $400

pg. 349 no. 300-$275
no. 709-$85
no. 707-$75
no. 89-$160
no. 86-$110
no. 184-$60
no. 200-$275

pg. 350 no. 172-$250
no. 1172-$250
n0. 272-$190
no. 572-$220
no. 1072-$250
mirror, $85

pg. 351 no. 274-$200
no. 574-$225
no. 1074-$250
no. 174-$250
no. 274-$200
no. 1174-$275
pg. 352 no. 1188-$500
no. 7024-$275
no. 5069-$200
pg. 353 top row, $225, $300, $150
bottom, $950, $500
pg. 354 dresser, $225;
chifforobe, $250;
vanity, $275;
chest, $200;
chair, $60;
bench, $60;
rocker, $75;
night table, $85;
bed, $175;
bed 975-$225
pg. 355 semi-vanity, $275;
chifforobe, $275;
dresser, $250;
bed, $200;
rocker, $70;
night table, $90;
bench, $60;
chair, $60;
chest, $300;
bed 896-$250
pg. 356 top row, $250, $225, $275
chest, $200;
chair, $60;
bench, $60;
night table, $85;
rocker, $75;
chifforobe, $250;
bed, $250;
pg. 357 chest, $200;
chifforobe, $200;
dresser, $250;
chair, $65;
bench, $65;
rocker, $75;
night table, $85;
bed, $200;
bed 971-$210
pg. 359 no. 800-$425

no. 801-$300
pg. 360 top row, $85, $60
middle row, $400, $250
bottom row, $225, $300
pg. 361 top row, $60, $85
middle row, $245, $375
bottom row, $300, $225
pg. 362 top row, $250, $400
center, $200
bottom row, $200, $225, $350
pg. 363 top row, $225, $225, $275
middle row, $400, $125, $300
bottom row, $225, $225
pg. 364 no. 1531 1/2-$275
no. 1501-$275
no. 1520-$225
pg. 366 mirror, $360;
dresser, $300
pg. 367 no. 193-$2,000
pg. 368 no. 278-$300
no. 378-$250
no. 778-$75
no. 178-$250
no. 878-$85
no. 678-$60
no. 478-$250
pg. 369 no. 170-$275
no. 870-$150
no. 270-$225
no. 370-$350
no. 470-$350
no. 670-$75
no. 770-$85
no. 470 1/2-$300
pg. 370 no. 371-$375
no. 871-$200
no. 271-$500
no. 171-$400
no. 471-$550
no. 671-$125
no. 771-$175
no. 471 1/2-$500
pg. 371 no. 375-$350

no. 175-$325
no. 375 1/2-$300
no. 675-$85
no. 275-$400
no. 875-$125
no. 475-$400
no. 775-$75
no. 475 1/2-$325
pg. 372 top row, $260, $210, $160, $160
second row, $175, $150, $150, $175
bottom, $220
pg. 373 no. 4-$140
no. 39-$285
no. 29 1/2-$260
no. 37-$280
no. 19-$340
no. 25-$175
no. 31-$200
pg. 393 no. 514-$175
no. 509-$300
no. 498-$145
no. 503-$275
no. 493-$125
no. 495-$375
no. 501-$395
pg. 394 top row, $145, $295, $145
bottom left box, top row, $110, $110; bottom, $225
bottom right box, top row, $160, $160; bottom, $360
pg. 395 no. 1701-S-$160
no. 1726-S-$160
no. 1721-S-$85
no. 1722-S-$85
no. 1717-S-$75
no. 1716-S-$230
no. 3022-$140
no. 1723-S-$80
no. 1724-S-$80
no. 1209-S-$80
no. 1214-S-$95
no. 1728-S-$160
no. 1718-S-$95
no. 1705-S-$85
no. 1266-S-$200
pg. 396 top, $400

bottom row, $400, $95
pg. 397 no. 4194-$500 (set)
no. 613-$250
no. 217 1/2-$275
no. 815-$175
no. 217 1/2-$500
pg. 398 top row, $450, $350
middle row, $240, $95, $150
bottom, $600
pg. 399 top left, $250
pg. 400 no. 486-$500
no. 491-$300
no. 488-$400
no. 2228-$80
no. 492-$275
no. 2229-$85
no. 2212-$95
pg. 401 top right, $100, $85
top left, $110, $60
bottom left box, top row, $140, $140; bottom, $350
bottom right box, top row, $125, $140, bottom, $275
pg. 402 top row, $200, $125, $450
bottom row, $250, $650
pg. 403 no. 304-$65
no.305-$90
no. 265-$55
no. 304-$65
no. 264-$45
pg. 404 top row, $300, $150
center left, $150
center, $175
bottom row, $175, $350
pg. 406 top row, $375, $175
middle row, $175, $150
bottom row, $400, $175
pg. 407 no. 110-$300
no. 1080-$350